Hart Crane

For James, Margaret and Alex Sainsbury

Hart Crane
A Life

Clive Fisher

Yale University Press
New Haven and London

For information about this and other Yale University Press publications, please contact:
U.S. Office: sales.press@yale.edu yalebooks.com
Europe Office: sales@yaleup.co.uk www.yaleup.co.uk

Set in Columbus MT by Fakenham Photosetting Limited, Fakenham, Norfolk
Printed in the United States of America

Library of Congress Cataloging-in-Publication Data

Fisher, Clive, 1960–
Hart Crane: a life / Clive Fisher.
p. cm.
Includes bibliographical references and index.
ISBN 0–300–09061–7 (alk. paper)
1. Crane, Hart, 1899–1932. 2. Poets, American—20th century—Biography. I. Title.
PS3505. R272 Z66 2002   811'. 52—dc21   2002000229

A catalogue record for this book is available from the British Library

2   4   6   8   10   9   7   5   3   1

CONTENTS

Contents

ILLUSTRATIONS

PART ONE

Ohio and New York

July 1899–November 1919

And so it was I entered the broken world
To trace the visionary company of love, its voice
An instant in the wind (I know not whither hurled)
But not for long to hold each desperate choice.

'THE BROKEN TOWER'

I
=

Hart Crane's brief life is a story of rented accommodation and receding horizons, of the restlessness inherent in great expectations. For most of his thirty-
two years, convinced as he was of life's possible perfection, he struggled and
travailed – for a habitat hospitable to the muse, for friendships that were colloquial
and true, for an erotic love that was indivisible, for a perfect poetry with cadences
as irresistible as the sea's – and with each new disappointment, while hope held
good at least, he moved on. It was a brave life, for all its recklessness, but one
which could only bewilder its more pragmatic onlookers: even Crane's friends,
aware that they had witnessed a remarkable destiny and half conscious of the
yearnings that impelled it, looked back on the spectacle in confusion and decided
that only a symbolic interpretation could apply – but whether they had known a
pilgrim or a fugitive they went to their ancient graves undecided.

As for Crane himself, while he never tired of explaining his poetry, he resisted
more personal self-scrutiny: it lay outside the urgency of his life and seemed triv-
ial beside membership of the visionary company of great poets to which he
aspired. Why ponder his itinerancy or explain it? He was pledged to the literature
and the myth of America and introspection could scarcely further his attendance
on the colossus. Yet if he had stood back for a moment from his nomadic life he
might have looked to history itself to explain his restlessness, to history both
national and ancestral. After all, to be American was once to be migratory and
Hart Crane's voyaging pedigree was almost as long as his country's: when he came
to speak for America he did so not as the offspring of the great immigrant land-
ings of the late nineteenth century but as the scion of pioneers who had been
involved in the mighty experiment of modern America almost from its inception
and who from that time had tested its mythic possibilities.

The wanderings began from England when in 1646 Hart Crane's paternal
grandmother's Beardsley forebears embarked for America on the *Planter* and settled in Connecticut for a century and more of thrift and industry before moving

again to northern Ohio at the beginning of the nineteenth century. They were part of a wider emigrant English tide which moved west as the interior was claimed and which included in its number Simeon Crane, who in 1801 braved a biblical forty-day passage by ox-team when he departed Saybrook, Connecticut, for the virgin land near Lake Erie, and John and Elizabeth Streator and their children, who established a settlement in what became Windham Township in 1803, the year Ohio was formally admitted to the Union.

Streator, a kinsman of John Adams, second President of the United States, had fought in the Revolutionary War; his wife, no less a patriot, defended the Union by knitting stockings for soldiers during the Revolution, the Anglo-American War of 1812 and indeed the Civil War before dying aged 103. Their son Jason Streator, not content with serving two terms in the Ohio State Legislature, delivered himself of verse orations in the chamber and submitted his legislative reports in carefully tailored stanzas; and his daughter, Sylvina, who taught herself to read with the assistance of the *Warren Chronicle*, proceeded to a career as a schoolmistress whose most promising pupil, Lucretia Rudolph, married President Garfield. Sylvina, Hart Crane's great-grandmother, married the first white child to have been born in Shalersville Township, Edward Manley Crane; and his kinsman Rollin Crane had his hour of greatness when in 1863 he volunteered to General Grant to lead twenty-five men down the Mississippi River under heavy Confederate fire to establish the Union flag at Lower Vicksburg.

Edward and Sylvina Crane had six children, including Hart Crane's grandfather Arthur Edward Crane, who recorded that his mother 'lived to the advanced age of ninety-four years, a dainty little woman with sparkling dark eyes, happily retaining her faculties and the love of all who knew her to the end'.[1] She died in 1914, with a world about to end, and her son, almost as long-lived, died in 1939, in the face of further apocalypse, aged ninety-three. In his waning years Arthur wrote verse and assumed the obligations of family historian: the premature deaths of his stalwart son and impetuous grandson left him as the custodian of Cranean lineage and he diligently recorded what he knew of the achievements of his antecedents. Arthur Crane and his siblings established Crane Brothers, the principal store in Garrettsville, Portage County, Ohio, and Arthur, through his offices as director of First National Bank and proprietorship of a maple syrup factory, became one of the most affluent and prominent citizens of the town and built a substantial house on Freedom Street with tall chimneys, balconies and Doric columns which later became the rectory for the nearby Catholic church. His brother Frederic also had commitments beyond Crane Brothers: he published his own poetry and as 'Enarc' – Crane reversed – he reviewed drama and literature for the *Garrettsville Journal*. In 1870 Arthur married Ella Beardsley, and the couple had four children: Verdi, who died in her tenth year, Alice, Bessie, and Clarence Arthur, the future father of a great poet, who was born in April 1875.

As the heir to commerce and prosperity Clarence was sent to village schools before attending Allegheny College at Meadville, Pennsylvania. There he befriended Byron Madden, later husband to his sister Bessie, later still his executor, but in the winter of 1894 he suddenly tired of the impracticalities of study and returned to Garrettsville unqualified. Madden recorded that his friend 'then went on the road selling crackers for the National Biscuit Company of Akron, Ohio' and while roving for custom he dreamed and schemed for affluence and commercial autonomy.[2] Ambition and impetuosity were a part of him, complements to the more obvious virtues that made him affable to the small town. He was known to be generous and gregarious; an optimist who recited parodies of Shakespeare and played the cornet dutifully and badly. He believed in hard work and easy play, in pretty girls and in the destiny of America. His sister Bessie thought him 'the very best of brothers' and treasured her memories of his impetuosity: of how he gave his sisters his old Packard instead of exchanging it for a new car; and of how, seeing a woman crying on a street corner, he took her to the nearest grocery and bought her lots of vegetables.[3]

But there were more reckless acts than these, not least the dramatic courtship he unleashed on Garrettsville in the spring of 1898 when Grace Hart, a young beauty from Chicago, came to visit her aunt and cousin. Crane and his cousin Orsa Beardsley planned a picnic and proposed to escort Jessie Sykes and Grace Hart respectively. By the time the four friends returned home, however, affections had switched and Crane remained so fascinated by the metropolitan belle that on the day of her departure he boarded her Cleveland-bound train to instigate a courtship of letters, telegrams and flowers which was sustained until her capitulation and the handsome Chicago wedding which occurred on 1 June 1898, with a listing the following day in the *Chicago Daily Tribune*.

Clarence Crane's bride was herself the daughter of old and distinguished families. Her maternal grandfather's family, the Beldens, claimed emigration from England in 1645 and emerge into historical focus with the rise to fortune of Josiah Belden, who was born in 1815 and served an apprenticeship as a jeweller before joining the first migrant wagon train to the Pacific Coast. The caravan convened at Independence, Missouri, in May 1841 and finally settled in northern California in November. Belden was in Monterey the following year but moved again to Santa Cruz where he ran a ranch store for two years for the American consul in California. In 1844 he became a Mexican citizen and was awarded land in the Sacramento Valley. He divided his time between ranching and business ventures in Monterey and San Francisco, survived unscathed the Mexican–American war for California of 1846 and emerged as a merchant in San Jose in 1849. He prospered greatly during the Gold Rush of that year but despite his success he remained popular among the Mexicans of the town, who not only bought his merchandise but entrusted him with quantities of their gold. He married Sarah Jones, another California pioneer,

and moved to San Francisco, where he invested in real estate. He was the first mayor
of San Jose and during the Civil War, in support of the Union, he contributed generously to the Sanitary Fund. He was a delegate to the Republican National
Convention in 1876 and in 1881 he moved to New York City, where he became a
director of the Erie Railroad and the founder of Belden prosperity.

The Harts also asserted English ancestry and traced their descent as far back as
Deacon Stephen Hart, a prominent member of the Reverend Thomas Hooker's
Hartford church. Their Connecticut distinction notwithstanding, the Harts also
felt the pull of the West and Joseph and Rosanna Hart, adventurous enough as the
parents of thirteen children, established themselves and their offspring in
Trumbull County, Ohio, in 1838 or thereabouts. Their ninth child, Clinton Orestes
Hart, Hart Crane's grandfather, was born in 1839 and by the winter of 1860 he
was a schoolmaster in Pennsylvania. It was not his vocation, however, and when,
returning to Ohio through Pittsburgh, he heard of the bombardment of Fort
Sumter which began the Civil War he enlisted in the Nineteenth Ohio Volunteer
Infantry. Although his hearing was impaired in defence of the Union, Hart was not
incapacitated from making a fortune in later years, not least through the operations
of Hart Brothers, a clothing business established in Warren in 1878. In 1890 he
associated with R.G. Sykes to form the Sykes Steel Roofing Company of Chicago
and for twelve years he operated as a manufacturer and contractor with that enterprise before retiring with his family in 1903 to a substantial property at East 115th
Street, Cleveland, Ohio, in the eyes of local esteem 'a first-class business man, a
good citizen, a man who has many friends ... and an enthusiastic Republican'.[4]

In 1865 he had married twenty-five-year-old Elizabeth Belden of Akron, a
schoolmistress whom he had met as a fellow student at Western Reserve Seminary.
She became an abiding, if indistinct, presence in the life of the poet, who adored
his grandmother as the one unfailing figure of love and constancy in his family.
She liked to reminisce about local and family history and was fond of remembering the journey she made on horseback to Cleveland in April 1865 to see the body
of Abraham Lincoln on its 1,700-mile funeral circuit between Washington and the
President's final resting place in Springfield, Illinois. Her life was otherwise without adventure and her surviving correspondence bespeaks a woman content with
her needlework, her domestic routine and the local news.

There was one exotic divergence: in 1898, the year in which they gave away
their daughter to Clarence Crane, the Harts saw their country emerge as an
imperial power following American victory in the Spanish–American War and the
consequent forfeiture by Spain of many of her colonial possessions. Puerto Rico
and the Philippines were ceded to the United States, and Cuba, attaining notional
independence, became an American fiefdom. In the course of this transaction the
fate of Cuba's nearby satellite, the Isle of Pines, considered Cuban by Madrid, was
overlooked, and for some years the territory was without official allegiance.
American interests, confident of American expansionism, assumed it would only

be a matter of time before Washington claimed the island, however, and invested accordingly. Numerous people built second homes or established citrus farms there, the Clinton Harts among them, and Cleveland and Trumbull County soon received report of 'this little plantation ... in plain view of the Caribbean sea' with its 'pleasant and commodious bungalow' which the Harts had built and its 'large grove of orange, grape fruit and lemon trees' where they proposed to 'avoid the long, cold winters of the north'.[5]

But even under southern skies some unhappinesses could not be forgotten and if there were prolepses of tenacity, longevity and distinction among Hart Crane's forefathers, there were also graver intimations. The Harts had three children: Harry, born in 1866, Frank, born in 1869, and Grace, born in 1878. Harry died in 1876, the victim of scarlet fever, and his memory soon dimmed with the age's acceptance of infant mortality. Frank Hart also died young – in January 1893 – but his memory proved an altogether more delicate problem for which suppression appears to have been considered the best solution. Little is known of his career before his death: he had married a young woman named Zell Smith from Warren and in October 1892 the couple had a daughter, Helen. He worked in Chicago as a manager for the Sykes Iron and Steel Roofing Company, a position one assumes his father was involved in securing, and on his death certificate his occupation was given as 'manufacturer'. But his end itself remains mysterious. A first report, in the *Warren Daily Tribune* of 21 January 1893, indicated that Hart had 'died very suddenly' the previous day at his home at 429 West Polk Street, Chicago, 'about noon of heart disease'. On 25 January, however, a fuller report appeared in the *Western Reserve Chronicle*, published to mark the funeral in Warren. Besides extolling the deceased as 'a remarkably bright young business man' whose career to date had been 'unusually good', the newspaper paused to praise him as 'a warm, thoughtful and faithful friend'. As for present distress:

> Mr Hart's death was very sudden and a terrible shock to his wife and parents. He had returned from an eastern trip the earlier part of the week and was apparently as well as usual, although he had been troubled for some time with insomnia. Feeling indisposed on Friday he went home, and to induce sleep took a dose of morphine. His rest was thought to be easy until several hours afterwards when his heavy breathing attracted attention, and by the time a physician had reached him, death had ensued.

On the death certificate the coroner, James McHale, contented himself with the plainest verdict, that Hart had died 'from accidentally taking a[n] overdose of Morphine'. But the newspaper reports are contradictory. The initial assumption, mentioned by the *Warren Daily Tribune*, that heart disease had caused death, was presumably based on the reaction of the doctor called to the scene, who learned of the disturbed breathing prior to decease and applied a plausible, if imprecise, diagnosis. But Hart's parents would surely have known if he had suffered from heart disease, especially since such a condition in one so young is rare and tends to be congenital. If they did know, how could they have considered their son's death the 'terrible shock' recorded in the *Western Reserve Chronicle*? And if he had indeed suffered from such an affliction how could the newspaper or the dead man's family have claimed that in the days immediately prior to his end he was 'apparently as well as usual'?

But then the *Chronicle* announces that Hart suffered from insomnia and that he had done so 'for some time', whatever that means. Had he recently succumbed to depression, acute anxiety or even some form of mental or emotional instability? Or was this condition chronic? The fact that he sought medicinal aid suggests that his infirmity was either acute or protracted, that it was something he was reluctant to trust to time alone to cure. Whatever its degree or duration, however, there is nothing surprising in his taking morphine, which occupied a prominent place in the nineteenth-century pharmacopœia as an analgesic also known for its tendencies to soothe or elate the moods of those with emotional or mental distemper. Just as we shall never know the extent of Hart's insomnia or its causes, so we shall never know exactly how experienced he was in the administration of morphine. Perhaps he was taking the drug for the first time and miscalculated; or perhaps, though an inveterate consumer or even an unacknowledged addict, he misjudged the amount his body could assimilate. Or perhaps his circumstances appeared so distressing that even the easeful death inherent in the opiate seemed preferable to further endurance. It is impossible to say, and family reaction provides few insights. Indeed to judge from the extant correspondence of his close relations it is as though Frank Hart never existed. There is not one reference to him in the letters left by his mother or by his eagerly epistolary nephew Hart Crane, and not one comment in all the various reminiscences put forth by Hart Crane's friends that suggests the poet even knew of the uncle who died so swiftly. On only one occasion was a cause for death supplied, in a newspaper obituary of Frank Hart's widow forty-three years later, where he was said to have been killed by a train. What was there to hide? Perhaps nothing at all. But what is certain is that either accidentally or wilfully Frank Hart ended his life.

Did Clarence Crane ever learn about the brother-in-law he could never meet? Nothing in his surviving correspondence suggests that he did, but there were other, more pressing revelations – inevitably so, in view of the fact that when Hart Crane's parents emerged from church that June day they did so as effective strangers. In an age when bourgeois fortunes were allied in prudently arranged marriages this situation was by no means exceptional but it soon became apparent that the Clarence Cranes conflicted temperamentally as well as holding widely divergent understandings of marriage. Clarence, apparently physically robust, in fact suffered numerous afflictions: hay fever, urethritis, acidosis and high blood pressure were lifelong problems and his letters refer to scruples about the consumption of coffee, meat and alcohol, which he knew from experience disagreed with his system. Byron Madden recalled that he 'was never free in his disclosure of personal matters'.[6] Innate discretion was compounded by a tendency to worry which further undermined his health, not least because that tendency was often suppressed: with a career to pursue and a fortune to build, Clarence Crane had little time for any salutary self-analysis.

It seemed there was little time either for the sort of marriage Grace had in mind. The pretty girl of prosperous and indulgent parents, in effect an only child, Grace had become accustomed to having her interests and her accomplishments indulged. Fair-haired, statuesque, by any measure a beauty, she was gifted with a light soprano voice and as a girl had trained with a vocal teacher who thought that some day she might have an operatic career. Her ladylike refinement extended to a familiarity with, and delight in, all the genteel domestic rites and her extravagant, still-girlish imagination had great expectations of marriage as a sustained courtship of gallantry and masculine adoration, a ritual of dances, romance and finery. The indications are that she read nothing at all, so the inspiration of her thinking remains obscure; but what is certain is that her husband found such ideas of matrimony inconsistent with his own. He wanted companionship and support, a practical curiosity in his business ambitions and a domestic tranquillity that would enable them to thrive. Grace also had ambitions – indeed so great were her longings for admiration that years later she considered pursuing a career in films; in the meantime she featured in the society columns of the Chicago and Cleveland newspapers. Like her husband she was restless, but whereas he avoided uneasy stillness in his commercial travelling and later in the foundation of a company which ramified over several states, she liked country drives and with the advent of the car took to motoring with enthusiasm. Clarence pretended to be healthier than he was; Grace by contrast seems to have had a strong constitution but also a nervous excitability and a psychological suggestibility that exposed her to numerous vague maladies. As for physical relations between them, his temperament has gone unrecorded but hers was controversial. Hart Crane's first biographer met her many years later and suspected that she was 'fascinated by sex' but also sensed that 'she was a somewhat frigid woman sexually'. He knew her in her old age and could look back and speculate: 'Like a lot of women of that type, the sexual relationship became [for her] totally divorced from true emotion and became a kind of intellectual gymnastic. She had the reputation of liking to run around with younger men.'[7] Hart Crane himself never knew his mother in old age but he certainly detected an oddity, confiding to one friend, 'I think my mother has something of the lesbian in her. She's very cold.'[8]

However ill-acquainted and ill-matched they were, the Clarence Cranes seemed to promise their offspring a rich genetic inheritance – combining handsomeness, social accomplishment, enterprise and financial ambition. In the event they had only one child and he was strikingly his parents' psychological legatee. But rather than becoming one of the great American capitalists or a handsome singer or actor Hart Crane was differently disposed. He had his father's frail constitution and his mother's nervous suggestibility and as he grew up he developed her extravagant romanticism and Crane's Midwestern ingenuousness and became the highly strung sensualist who could find no place for himself in frenzied, early twentieth-century America.

To begin with, however, all seemed auspicious. Whatever their differences, Clarence and Grace were besotted with each other and with their matrimonial adventure and Arthur Crane was so pleased with his son's choice of bride that he built the couple a house next door to his own in Freedom Street, Garrettsville, the small Ohio town a mile square with a population of 1,200 to which the young couple returned to begin their life together. Then Grace found she was pregnant, and on 21 July 1899 she gave birth to her only child, Harold Hart Crane. Aunt Alma Crane, assisting at the confinement, was bizarrely prescient when she yielded to the family love of word play and declared the baby's appearance 'a navel engagement'.[9] Grace herself would later assure her son that he was 'born under the star of Luck' but if so it was a star he shared: protagonists of the Twenties as various as Zelda Fitzgerald and Al Capone were born that same year, and on that very same day, in Grace's childhood home of Oak Park, Illinois, Ernest Hemingway was born, also to a woman named Grace.[10] They were the children of an age just dawning, and if Senator Beveridge's ringing prophecy was vindicated, that 'the twentieth century will be American', they would indeed be heirs to change and greatness.

Clarence went back to work and to the realization of his ambitions. He was now employed at Arthur Crane's maple syrup factory, which was situated on the banks of the river above the dam in Garrettsville, and thus part of an enterprise which in a good year produced in excess of 60,000 gallons of syrup and satisfied markets as distant as Denver, Colorado. Arthur Crane, proud of the purity of his product, called it 'Standard of Ohio' but Clarence was restless and soon confided to Byron Madden that 'he was not entirely satisfied with his father's way of doing business'.[11] Madden visited the Cranes in 1900 and remembered accompanying Clarence when the latter took his one-year-old son to the photographer's but there are otherwise few memories of little Harold Hart Crane in Garrettsville. Mrs Scott, a next-door neighbour, recalled him wandering around the gardens of the Crane mansions in admiration of the flowers – and to her he seemed 'sweet and strange'.[12]

In 1901 the Clarence Cranes moved again – to 407 North Park Avenue in the larger nearby town of Warren in north-western Ohio. Confident and quick to learn, and aware that Garrettsville could scarcely sustain two maple syrup producers, Clarence had succumbed to his restlessness and in any case was now convinced that a fortune could be made by combining corn and maple syrups to

produce a commodity cheaper but no less fragrant. He employed an expert confectioner, Erwin Shoot, and signed a lease. Byron Madden visited the premises
once and recalled 'a modest building, one storey and not new', but for a man not
yet thirty the move represented a bold commitment and Crane must have been
reassured when his father-in-law decided in 1902 to sell his steel interests and
hinted that he might consider investing in the syrup business instead.[13] In the
event the new venture succeeded beyond its owner's ambitions and Clarence
Crane – or 'CA', as he now began to call himself – saw his hard work and determination rewarded to such a degree that within five years his production was
unable to satisfy its market. He investigated new ways to market sugar and was one
of the first American businessmen to see the potential of cellophane and to import
it from France for packaging before it was widely available in America. A new factory was envisaged – 'the largest of its kind in the world', the *Warren Tribune* speculated – and CA moved his family yet again, to 249 High Street, Warren, and it
was here that young Harold sustained his earliest impressions of the world.[14]

One of the paramount figures in this world was Frank Hart's widow and Harold's
godmother, Aunt Zell, who had moved back to her native Warren, to 8 South Elm
Street, following the melancholy events of 1893. It was inevitable that she would
see the Clarence Cranes regularly, but with the infant Helen Hart to support and
a busy and adventurous nature to placate besides she was ill-suited to passive widowhood. She took a job with the *Warren Daily Tribune* as a 'society reporter',
which seemed to entail the coverage of everything from funeral notices to advertisements for livery stables, and with her tireless spirit she mastered the business
and management of every department in the newspaper over the next few years.
She became secretary and treasurer of the *Tribune* before 1899 and was besides a
bulwark of local charities, a probation officer for Trumbull County and eventually
a local patroness of the arts. Still indefatigable, Zell found time to support women's
suffrage, local reform, various business ventures and active involvement in
Republican politics. Later, between 1907 and 1918, she lived in Cheyenne,
Wyoming, with her second husband, William C. Deming, publisher of the
Cheyenne Tribune and part owner of the *Warren Daily Tribune*, but following their
divorce she returned to Warren. She became president and general manager of the
Warren Daily Tribune and strengthened the publication to such a degree that in
1924 it was able to take over its local rival, the *Warren Daily Chronicle*, lineal
descendant of the *Trump of Fame*, the first newspaper published in the Western
Reserve. Zell Hart Deming emerged from the consolidation president, general
manager and controlling stockholder of the *Warren Tribune-Chronicle* and for many
years was the only woman member of the Associated Press, the American Society
of Newspaper Editors and the American Newspaper Publishers Association.

With this illustrious destiny to fulfil she was clearly not in a position to place
too practical an interpretation on her role as godmother to the infant Harold – but

other adoring women were on hand, not least Bess Crane, who quickly noted the child's eccentricities. Aged three he was obsessed by Grace's box of haberdashery and sewing scraps (already his intensely sensual nature was developing and here were ribbons and reams soft to the skin and seductive to the eye) and he took to redecorating discarded hats – gardens for the head, in the approved Edwardian manner – in his zeal even reworking some hapless visitor's bonnet. Anxiously wondering what was wrong with lead animals and toy soldiers, Aunt Bess confiscated the box and found the boy noisily inconsolable for days afterwards. As time went by she sensed that he missed his mother when she went on her increasingly frequent visits to Chicago or Cleveland and one day wondered aloud, 'Oh, Harold, what will ever become of you if something happens to your mother?' But he disarmed her – as he was to disarm succouring women throughout his life – with a precocious conviction of love: 'I'll still have my aunt Bess.' He seemed to her to have 'a visionary aspect' and she noted when he was five or six the way he would sit for hours at the piano repeating the same basic melodies or chords. She asked him the name of one refrain he particularly liked to repeat and he replied, 'I call it "The Lamb's First Morning".'[15]

CA, busy as he was, had been similarly delighted on going to his son's room late one night to find him still awake. Why was Harold not asleep? 'Because I haven't yawned yet.'[16] Music as they were to his fond aunts, these comments were evidence of the boy's wider precocity. He walked and talked early. He learned to read quickly and although in later life he would prove vulnerable to all the physical frailties of the Cranes he was at first a strong and healthy child. He easily befriended other children in Warren – Donald Clarke, Catherine Miller, Hall Kirkham, and Courtney Denison who remembered that his playmate in the High Street 'had everything that money could buy' – but despite this apparent popularity Harold seemed equally interested in the society of Mrs Sutcliff, one of the more venerable inhabitants of the town, whose memories and command of local lore extended back to the early days of the Western Reserve and to the struggles of the hardy pioneers whose log cabins were beset by bears and wolves.[17] It was the beginning of an understanding of the rural Midwest and its history and people, all of which lingered in the poet's mind however far he travelled: as late as 1927 he was still visited in his dreams by such redoubtable Warren figures as 'Mrs Potter with her great heart-shaped bosom – and Mrs Gilbert gasping with her goitre'.[18]

In later life Harold Hart Crane was much preoccupied with his past and searched his memory for meaning and for poetry. Yet there is little explicit autobiography in his work: he is no Wordsworth; we are allowed no more than glimpses of a childhood which was abbreviated by the greatest precocity of all in the poet's life – the awareness of adult disappointment and pain. One such glimpse is provided by the mature poet of 'Van Winkle' as he walks along Manhattan's Avenue A and finds himself remembering the morning walk of years before – 'It is the same hour though a later day' – to the Central Grammar School in Warren's Harmon Street. And we can watch him as the legends of the classroom continue to reverberate in his memory: 'Rip Van Winkle bowing by the way'; Hernan Cortés, 'reining tautly in'; Captain John Smith, 'all beard and certainty', who had adopted the term 'New England' and mapped the Chesapeake Bay district only forty-odd years before the Beardsleys had arrived in the New World.[19] The same mature poet can divulge some of the discoveries of the solitary wandering which complemented the rigours of the grammar school, discoveries made when he 'left the village for dogwood' and made for the Mahoning Valley, to experience a tranquillity which exposure to nature was always to give him:

> I took the portage climb, then chose
> A further valley-shed; I could not stop.
> Feet nozzled wat'ry webs of upper flows;
> One white veil gusted from the very top.
>
> O Appalachian Spring! I gained the ledge;
> Steep, inaccessible smile that eastward bends
> And northward reaches in that violet wedge
> Of Adirondacks![20]

On his way home, and passing near his father's factory, he might experience further intimations – of a world beyond the valley and the town, where childhood could stretch limitlessly, like America itself, and where some were destined to wander for ever:

> Behind
> My father's cannery works I used to see
> Rail-squatters ranged in nomad raillery,
> The ancient men – wifeless or runaway
> Hobo-trekkers that forever search
> An empire wilderness of freight and rails.
> Each seemed a child, like me, on a loose perch,
> Holding to childhood like some termless play.[21]

We are allowed even closer, to inspect other Warren incidents and details which, though casual at the time, imprinted themselves indelibly on the mind:

> The cinder pile at the end of the backyard
> Where we stoned the family of young
> Garter snakes under ... And the monoplanes

We launched – with paper wings and twisted
Rubber bands . . .[22]

If the garden at 249 High Street had its mysteries and surprises, so did the sky,
as the Wright brothers demonstrated in 1903, when they taught America the possibilities of flight and turned its boys and men to experiments in backyard avia-
tion. But when the focus of memory narrows to Clarence and Grace Crane and his
relations with them the picture becomes distorted and incoherent. Distress, anxiety and incomprehension are implicit. Maternal behaviour is remembered as
bewildering and suffocating:

'Connais tu le pays . . .?'

Your mother sang that in a stuffy parlour
One summer day in a little town
Where you had started to grow.
And you were outside as soon as you
Could get away from the company
To find the only rose on the bush
In the front yard . . .[23]

But she alone was not to blame; parents generally seemed stern when they were
not distracted:

Is it the whip stripped from the lilac tree
One day in spring my father took to me,
Or is it the Sabbatical, unconscious smile
My mother almost brought me once from church
And once only, as I recall – ?

It flickered through the snow screen, blindly
It forsook her at the doorway, it was gone
Before I had left the window. It
Did not return with the kiss in the hall.[24]

Unsmiling and abstracted kisses aside, there were numerous events and difficulties which never found their way into the passing autobiography of his art. There
is for instance no clear expression of the disturbing incident which occurred when
he was with his mother near Saegertown, Pennsylvania, and she abandoned her
vigilance long enough for him to fall into a river, to be saved from the water – this
time at least – when he was, as she put it later, 'fished out by a Jap'.[25] Some experiences were too painful or too private – as the adult poet declared, 'My memory I

left in a ravine', as though some recollections were better committed to somewhere steep and shadowed and inaccessible.[26] Some experiences were too private – to read many of Hart Crane's mature poems is to apprehend some truth or sense that lies beyond explicit utterance. This reticence is integral to the elusive beauty of his lyrics but it also functions as a reminder of the early world the poet knew, a world where parental actions were unsettling as well as bewildering and where explanations, if supplied, seemed to leave a lot unsaid.

As a child the only way he had of responding to domestic tension lay in sickness, which could also double as a means of attracting parental attention. Indeed preoccupied as they were with growing marital dissatisfaction the Cranes could not help noticing their son's inconsistencies of mood and well-being – 'fits', as they were called – or the fact that they seemed to coincide with periods of embarrassment and distress. Grace dispatched her son in all his finery to convey birthday wishes to her friend Mrs Hall but he misunderstood her directions and went instead to the Misses Hall to declaim birthday greetings in their polished Victorian parlour full of the 'curly leg' furniture which fascinated him. The maiden sisters were too tactful to indicate his mistake but not so Grace, who laughingly chided him and then repeated the story, compounding the humiliation, for CA's benefit that evening – but she never forgot how in bed later that night Harold was overcome by vomiting and hysterical sobbing. A similar scene occurred when CA took his wife and son on a vacation to Mackinac Island, at the confluence of Lakes Huron and Michigan, and Grace, intermittently conducting a gentleman's education, issued her son with a new chapter of manners: that he should stand whenever other guests stopped at the table to talk. When the situation occurred CA rose but Harold – his eyes as usual on his mother – did not. Her reproachful mockery followed and by bedtime, when his parents had forgotten the episode, the boy had a high fever which persisted, doctors and febrifuges notwithstanding, for two days.

That incident probably occurred in 1906 or 1907. Years later the poet dated the beginning of family disintegration to 1908, when he was eight years old, but troubles are recorded almost from the time the Cranes moved to Warren. One of Grace's first decisions on settling in the new town was to agree to appear in a benefit concert, where her beauty and her voice, trained and praised in Chicago for its 'Italian' quality, could be assessed by her new neighbours, even as they admired her philanthropic impulses. CA vainly attempted to dissuade her and when his wife appeared on stage he secured his revenge by noisily and conspicuously leaving the concert hall. Quite how many scenes of highly strung incompatibility, mutual incomprehension and battling will occurred between the couple remains open to speculation in the absence of surviving documentation or precise accounts from friends and family but in later life Harold himself suggested that the discord had been almost incessant for as long as he could remember. Not the least of the difficulties was that there seems to have remained enough affection or attraction between the Cranes to lend a ferocity to arguments and scenes which mutual indifference could never have provided. And whereas CA could and usually did find the opportunity to leave on business soon after any quarrel, Grace, with no close friends or family in Warren and no inclination to suffer in silence, had nowhere to turn for sympathy and support except to her son.

Still a child, Harold found himself standing beside his mother's bed as she catalogued his father's misdemeanours and teetered on the verge of the depressions which began to haunt her. He learned early about resentment, neglect and betrayal, if only from his mother's point of view, while seeing too little of his father to form any close connection with him. He learned he was all she had and a compact inevitably developed between them involving nervous ill health, mutual support and shared distrust of Clarence Crane. It was an unusual education for a small boy and one which helped set him apart from the other children he knew – but then Hart Crane was set apart all his life and photographs of the plump and timid boy register this isolation in the eyes, which were vulnerable, vigilant and full of shy suspicion.

In 1908 CA sold his business to the Corn Products Refining Company of Chicago on advantageous terms: Arthur Crane's operation was also to be bought as part of the deal and CA, whose original investment now yielded a substantial capital gain, was appointed manager of a newly built plant in Warren. The transaction brought the Cranes even greater affluence – CA bought himself a noisy new car and gave his wife a handsome carriage – but to no avail, and later that year, after a decade of marriage, they tentatively separated. CA found he could conduct his job from the local offices of the Corn Products Refining Company and with nothing now to detain him in Warren he moved to Chicago. Grace, supine and facing nervous collapse, entered a sanatorium in the East for prolonged rest. Godmother Zell had moved to Wyoming the previous year and Bess Crane was being wooed by Byron Madden, whom she married in 1909. Suddenly Harold was orphaned by events and his country boyhood was over: Mrs Hart stepped in, and he found himself transplanted to his grandparents' house in Cleveland.

If the severance was distressing it was also not without adventure. His new home, 1709 East 115th Street, was a substantial house situated in what was then one of the most affluent residential quarters of a vital Midwestern metropolis. The adjacent properties were gabled Victorian or imitation Georgian, as favoured by the Protestant bourgeoisie of the day, but Clinton Hart's house was distinguished by the two circular three-storey towers which dominated its 55-foot wide façade and gave the property a turreted romance appealing to its newest inhabitant. Harold was installed in the northern tower and the room remained his until 1925. Its windows faced the golden west and it was here that he would later write his first brave poetic lines, here in what became an ivory tower high above the cherry tree in the back garden, high above nearby Wade Park, Lake Erie and the unlikely city which was his first metropolitan home.

Founded in 1796, Cleveland was a boom town when the Harts chose it as their retirement home: proudly declaring itself the sixth city of the United States, it doubled its size in the first decade of the twentieth century to over half a million inhabitants. The fourth-largest Czech city in the world after Prague, Vienna and Chicago, it also comprised colonies of Poles, Jews, Greeks, Hungarians, Irish, Russians, Germans and Italians, all of whom had come to work in the industries which smoked along the system of natural and man-made waterways connecting Lake Erie to the Ohio River. Yet if the city was immigrant and polyglot it was New England in its social and ethical consciousness and clearly directed by the Protestant oligarchy which built great mansions the length of Euclid Avenue and read about itself in the weekly *Cleveland Town Topics*. John D. Rockefeller's Standard Oil was here, but so also were the executives and proprietors of breweries, Great Lake shipping lines, chemical and pharmaceutical industries, and car, iron, steel and railroad companies. In 1909 this manufacturing might displayed itself in the Cleveland Industrial Exposition and proceeded to finance many of the municipal and cultural monuments which were erected in Hart Crane's adolescence and early twenties. Art followed money, even here – Oscar Wilde had been the pioneer, lecturing the city about Truth and Beauty in his American tour of 1882, but it was not until the new century that major artistic figures came to Cleveland with any frequency: Richard Strauss in 1904; Mahler in 1910; Diaghilev's Ballets Russes in 1916 and 1917; and in 1918 the Cleveland Orchestra offered its first series of concerts, with Ernest Bloch the first director of the Cleveland Institute of Music. But what of writers and poets? The most important in the city's history had just arrived – but he was not as yet aware of his vocation.

At first Harold was aware of little beyond his new surroundings and their inhabitants: servants, a cook, a grandfather who seems to have made little impression and a grandmother he grew to adore now and for ever as the one family figure who loved him unconditionally and refused to burden him with expectations. The new city seemed to bring familial fortune: Bess Crane married Byron Madden and in 1909 Grace returned from her sanatorium to East 115th Street calmer and happier. Relations were resumed with CA, albeit at a distance, and then the latter moved from Chicago to try married life again. He was followed by his parents – with nothing to detain them in Garrettsville, the Arthur Cranes moved to Cleveland in 1910 and eventually bought a house directly opposite Clinton Hart's. Harold's parents were as usual distracted, but for once benignly so: Grace was now absorbed in Mary Baker Eddy's Christian Science, the most popular of the newly fashionable quasi-religious therapeutic creeds, the votaries of which made *Molly Make-Believe* and the *Pollyanna* stories among the most successful American novels of the day. In view of the nervous suggestibility indicated by her recent emotional and physical collapses, she was an obvious candidate for any teaching which asserted the supremacy of the mind over physical suffering, and with her knowledge of her son's tendencies in the same direction and her husband's vulnerability to physical symptoms of stress she soon found a household to convert. And who was to say Mrs Hart would not also benefit? Mother and daughter avidly read the scriptures assembled by Christian Science, and CA, indifferent as a Methodist Episcopalian but now an eager appeaser to his wife, became a temporary proselyte. If he thought such a concession would improve his marital condition he was forced to reconsider with the discovery that the Science imposed an almost complete interdiction on sexual contact. No wonder Grace was a fervent believer. As for Harold, he was sent to the Christian Science Sunday School – which offered a supplement to his weekday lessons at Fairmount Elementary – and encouraged to study the relevant scriptures and whereas his mother's religious convictions, like her depressions, came and went over the coming years, he was to practise Christian Science intermittently but with seeming conviction until early manhood. Later he would insist he had only done so to please Grace and there is no doubt some truth in the claim, but a belief in the power of the will to sustain healing visions was to contribute significantly to the particular iridescence of his poetry.

CA quickly tired of the whole business but then he had other matters on his mind. In the course of one of his business trips for the Corn Products Refining Company he had travelled to Victoria, British Columbia, and had discovered what he considered superlative chocolate. Ever forthright, he negotiated at once with the manufacturers for the purchase of the formula and when they declined to sell he had the product chemically analysed. With an indistinguishable commodity in hand, he was convinced that real riches could now be his and with the encouragement of Arthur Crane and Clinton Hart he decided to venture into chocolate production. By April 1911, $13,000 in capital had been raised, with Grace and her father contributing, and CA found an associate who was connected with the Royal Baking Powder Company. The two men agreed that they would go on the road to sell their product in alternate years and CA volunteered to go first. When his partner proved reluctant to follow him in the second year Crane bought him out for $750. Meanwhile a factory had been acquired in Cleveland at the intersection of High and 2nd Streets and the Crane Chocolate Company began the production of 'Queen Victoria Chocolates'.

With frequent demands on their time and a continuing determination to make their marriage succeed, the Cranes were once again frequently absent and Harold was left with his grandparents, who supervised his attendance at school, his introduction to the public library and his piano lessons. His first extant letter, written to CA in June 1910 when his parents were staying at the Hotel Metropole in Chicago, provides a weather report, a promise that he is brushing his teeth and an announcement that he borrows books from the library. Another letter, from November 1910, mentions that his Crane grandparents took him to a lecture on the art galleries of Europe – an unlikely excursion for a ten-year-old but one which seemed to give him as much pleasure as the other recent outing, to see Eva Tanguay, the vaudeville actress, at the Cleveland Hippodrome. He took piano lessons from his Aunt Alice Crane but frustrated her by claiming that he was 'too nervous' to practise and distressed his mother by indulging his love of insistent rhythm and playing pieces such as the 'Marche Grotesque' with fortissimo enthusiasm. However, she could not complain: his interest in the arts was one she had fostered and by the time he was eleven he drew with enthusiasm and invention and talked incessantly about painting and writing, one day startling Aunt Alice as he stared at the volumes of poetry on her bookshelves by declaring: 'This is going to be my vocation. I'm going to be a poet.'[27]

His cousin Helen Hart, now nineteen, saw a different side to Harold when she visited her grandparents in Cleveland. To her he seemed 'a normal fun-loving little boy' who 'looked like his father' and who in Zell's opinion 'took after' CA.[28] Helen also knew that CA and Zell, alike in their entrepreneurial energy, often exchanged volumes of poetry, so perhaps the strange boy's ambitions were not as bizarre as they seemed at first. Whatever preparations Harold made for his vocation were overshadowed throughout 1912 by the inexorable decline of Clinton Hart, who died in January 1913. The entire family convened in Warren for the funeral, at which CA was a pall bearer, and Zell wrote a long obituary for the *Warren Daily Chronicle*. Mrs Hart inherited 1709 East 115th Street and other legacies which included $5,000 to be held in trust for Harold and payable to him on her death. The Clarence Cranes decided to move in permanently with Mrs Hart and having settled on Cleveland as their residence they chose one of the most prestigious of the city's schools – East High, situated on 82nd Street – to continue their son's education.

Harold first crossed its expansive lawns in January 1914 and was an irregular pupil for the next three years. He was approaching fifteen, the sole inheritor of a restless and eccentric household, and despite his domestic standing as a precocious aesthete he seems to have made very little impression at the school. He fitted in without ever standing out – mediocre, a background pupil, he lacked the competitiveness which impels successful schoolchildren or the scepticism which haunts true scholars. He never joined any of the school's clubs and avoided its sports when possible; neither the school yearbook nor the school newspaper stirred him to achievement. He enrolled in the 'Classical' course, thus committing himself to English, physics, geometry, algebra and three years of Latin and German. One schoolmistress, Ona Kraft, remembered him as 'a very pleasant, quiet sort of boy who got along well with everyone and made no trouble for anyone'; and her colleague Marion Wright, who taught him English, recalled 'his shining brown eyes as he argued with eager interest about everything that came up for discussion'.[29] But schoolchildren are more critical and one pupil, Eleanor Clarage, could find little to excite her even in retrospect:

In appearance, the boy was of medium height and build, with dark hair and rather large features. He wore glasses and had a look of solemnity about him that made him appear much more mature than the rest of us. He was moderately attractive to girls, though I don't remember that he ever showed up at any of our parties or dances ... I do remember that he never said anything either clever or profound, never gave me any hint that he loved good books, good music and good art.[30]

Domestic unrest cannot have made his early months at the school easy. Grace spent six weeks at the beginning of 1914 with her mother on the Isle of Pines and when she returned she and CA started to quarrel again. Travel was an obvious remedy for marital problems and when she decided on another change of scene in the summer of 1914 she took her son with her on a motoring holiday to Boston and Rye Beach.

CA lacked the inclination for such frivolity, and certainly the time. He was devoted to hard work and his endeavours were rewarded in 1914 when Elbert Hubbard visited his factory and wrote about his experiences in 'A Little Journey to Crane's Chocolate Studio'. It was no small honour. Hubbard was a bizarre and controversial figure in American letters – an author, editor, publisher, pamphleteer, lecturer and master-craftsman whose homespun opinions and 1890s appearance were familiar to a wide audience prior to his death in 1915. CA admired Hubbard anyway and found, when the latter published his account, that the feeling was reciprocal. Hubbard had praise for the cleanliness of the factory, the generous terms of employment, the quality of the confectionery, the first-name friendliness everywhere apparent and CA's packaging flair, which had recently led him to acquire the rights to Munch's *The Girl with the Marguerite*, which he proposed to put on the cover of one of his new boxed selections. It was no surprise, Hubbard felt, that CA was the first confectioner to talk Marshall Field into stocking his product and no surprise that his chocolates were also available in Northern-Pacific Railroad dining cars. As for the chocolate-maker himself: '[He] is cosmopolitan. He is bigger than Cleveland. I imagine he would be at home in any sort of society – a working man who has evolved, grown and "arrived" ... Clarence Crane is thirty-nine years of age. He has the heart of youth, and to him all days are Maytime.'[31]

In 1914 also CA concluded a business arrangement with Mary Garden, the celebrated Aberdonian soprano who had come to America in 1883 and for whom Debussy created the role of Mélisande. Garden excelled as Salomé and sang almost all of her thirty-two roles in French. Her following stretched across America but – as Crane well realized – it was particularly loyal in his home market, the Midwest, which knew her for over twenty years as a pillar of the Chicago Civic Opera. 'Music by Mary Garden – Candy by Crane', ran one of the slogans – and their harmony proved commercially persuasive.

Confectionery was clearly an art and CA, like his son an idealist, wanted to raise chocolate to new distinction, to establish it as indispensable to the prosperously discriminating and the promiscuously sweet-toothed alike. The greatest skills were crucial to this campaign and not long after Elbert Hubbard's visit he approached the artist Maxfield Parrish with a view to commissioning packaging which might help sell the more expensive lines of confectionery he envisaged. It was an ambitious overture. Parrish was internationally famous: his illustrations to children's books such as *The Arabian Nights* and Kenneth Grahame's *The Golden Age* were great in their genre and magazines as successful as *Collier's, Scribner's, Life, Century* and the *Ladies' Home Journal* paid dearly for his cover illustrations. He offered America a whimsical world of cobalt skies and silver castles, of fairy medievalism, lush orientalism, Pre-Raphaelite androgyny and erotic innocence – and if the academy found him gaudy and shallow his posters were thought to hang in one out of every four American households.

Despite his popularity, however, and despite the enormous advances in marketing sophistication under way at the time, nobody had thought to enlist Parrish's skills in the commercial promotion of a product. CA, bold, innovative and as eager as Parrish himself to pander to popular yearnings for the nostalgic and escapist, saw his opportunity and commissioned a design for boxes for the 1915 Christmas Selection which the Crane Company was now planning. The artist produced a surprisingly simple illustration – an elegant white crane surmounting a banderole inscribed with the company's name – but when 10,000 of the resulting boxes were sold CA knew his instincts were sure and for the following three years the Christmas Selection of Crane's chocolates appeared in a box emblazoned with a specially commissioned Parrish picture: in 1916, *The Rubaiyat*; in 1917, *Cleopatra*; and in 1918, following a best-selling novel and a theatrical sensation on the same subject, *The Garden of Allah*. The implication was that the confectionery which lay beneath these visions, and which cost an exorbitant $5 a pound, was itself a work of art; and since those who bought the chocolate might also buy the art, CA cannily enclosed order slips for poster reproductions of the paintings inside each box. It was a lucrative partnership – Parrish alone earned royalties of $50,000 on the three later works – and one which CA would happily have perpetuated; but the artist wanted thematic autonomy and more time for other projects and so went his own way. Fisk Tires and Edison Mazda light bulbs later recruited his skills but CA had been the gambler and without his original idea American advertising in the 1920s might have looked very different.

The third of Crane's bright ideas ended less pleasingly. Chocolate was a winter commodity above all, so how could he occupy his factory during the hot Ohio summers? Mints offered a cooling solution but some trick was needed to justify a new product, so he went into business with a pharmaceutical manufacturer who used a pill machine to produce circular mints with a hole in the centre. The shape suggested the name, 'Life Savers', and the name suggested the packaging and the legend: an old sailor throwing a life preserver to a sinking young lady – 'Crane's Peppermint Life Savers … For That Stormy Breath.' They cost five cents and quickly caught on, but then CA's impetuosity got the better of him and he sold the product for $2,900 to Edward J. Noble, who became a millionaire by the acquisition. CA did not live to witness the full extent of his folly and nor did Harold, who rejected the life preservers the sailors were one day to throw him.

2

In January 1915, following weeks of domestic strife, the Cranes left on one of their rare excursions together to join Mrs Hart at her winter retreat on the Isle of Pines, but their long journey, by train to Jacksonville, Florida, thence by steamer to Cuba, with a second boat to take them to their final destination, was prompted as much by desperation as by curiosity. Cleveland, recently the scene of hope and reconciliation, had become a second battleground: a change of environment was imperative if the marriage was to survive, and who knew what the winter sunshine of the Isle might achieve if combined with Mrs Hart's equable arbitration? But as usual there seemed no obvious place for Harold in the arrangement. Conscience dictated that he remain behind in Cleveland, where the Arthur Cranes could supervise his attendance at East High. On the other hand, how happy would he be if left with his grandparents? And surely it was time he saw something of the wider world? So here he was, released after fifteen and a half years from his land-locked boyhood, to gaze at last upon his blue poetic element, the sea. It was the beginning of a lifelong fascination for which Lake Erie, tideless, shallow and earthbound, can scarcely have prepared him: the imagination alone limited these indigo horizons and the majestic Caribbean cloudscapes were all that existed to mark the graves of the many restless men whose lives had been claimed by these warm deceptive waters.

But reverie was one thing, the reality of a family holiday quite another and tension prevailed from the start. CA, by temperament ill equipped for the lazy and claustrophobic life of the island, fretted about Harold's erratic education and a possible business trip to California and counted the days until departure. He struggled to find repose amidst the luxuriant vegetation and sensed release, as he mentioned to his son many years later, only when breezes reminded him of the outer world: 'I will never forget the rustle of the leaves in the late afternoon when the trade winds come up the bay.'[1] Grace, by contrast, was happy and adventurous. The climate delighted her, the island's mountainous interior beckoned and she was all for exploration. When CA suggested premature departure at the end of the third week of January an argument began which escalated into a bitter confrontation culminating in CA's angry departure on the Sunday night ferry. A month later, as he wrote to his wife, their argument still commanded his memory: 'As long as I live I'll never forget your words in your bedroom – "We may never talk again".'[2] Furious as he was, the breach distressed him: however much the departure had been provoked, it constituted a form of desertion, and desertion of the innocent as well the guilty; as he told Grace, 'my heart really broke when I left [Harold]'.[3]

Remorse overtook him as soon as he embarked. On 24 January, abject in Florida, he pleaded with his wife for forgiveness and reassurance: 'If I'm cast off, say the word and I'll drown my feelings the way the weak generally do.' He had 'never been so utterly miserable' and begged for correspondence, enclosing a separate note of reassurance for Harold: 'Life wouldn't be worth but very little [*sic*] without you both and it's worth something to have your father feel that way isn't it?'[4] For the next three weeks he sent Grace as many as three letters a day, in some declaring ardent love, in others resorting to unsubtle negotiation. On 30 January he dispatched detailed instructions on the practicalities of steamer connections in Havana. On 1 February, knowing her passion for motoring, he proposed to buy a Cadillac: 'But I don't want to own a machine to ride around alone so I'm going to wait and hear when you are coming back.'[5] And on 6 February, having 'played solitaire until my brain reels', he told her 'how dependent I am upon you for my sole satisfaction and encouragement to succeed'.[6] It was courtship all over again and with little to occupy her outside the island's narrow social dance Grace had plenty of time in which to calculate her replies and to talk the business over with her mother, not to mention her son: as she had included him since his childhood in all her marital difficulties there was scant hope now that his remaining innocence would be spared. In any case, she had planned to remain on the island until 1 April. If absence made the heart grow fonder, there was no hurry to return to Cleveland; CA's appreciation of her would benefit from her Caribbean stay, just as Harold was benefiting from the fruit juice, the swimming and the sun. In fact Harold was acutely miserable and for the rest of his life would recall the cycles of quarrelling and stormy sexual reconciliation which had recently unsettled the house. He wrote his father a letter which 'busted me all up', in CA's words to Grace, and then some time later, lonely and bewildered, he slashed his wrists in attempted suicide.[7]

Harold later mentioned this desperate act to a friend but Grace herself maintained absolute discretion. She did, however, tell her son's first biographer what happened after all eighteen of her packets of Veronal sleeping powder mysteriously vanished. It may have been on the very night of their disappearance that she lay in bed, anxious and insomniac, only to become aware of a strange noise outside. Mrs Hart had heard it too; and the women went to investigate, only to discover a small herd of cattle cropping the lawns before the Villa Casas. It was a harmless invasion but annoying nevertheless and they decided to wake Harold and ask him to drive the animals away. He never detailed the ensuing events but from what Grace told her son's biographer some twenty years later, it is possible to conjecture that when she and Mrs Hart roused Harold he was in the early stages of drugged torpor. In any event he dressed and went outside with the house dog and raised a clamour which drove the beasts into the nearby grove. Watching from the window, his mother and grandmother were surprised to see him disappear in pursuit into the vegetation and when they went to call him back they heard nothing but the diminishing cries of the dog. Soon they were afraid and when, after an hour, he had still not returned they decided a search party must be organized. Suddenly he came running from the trees and rushed headlong towards the house. His face was white, his eyes bulging and brilliant, his breathing shallow and rapid – and then he was unconscious at their feet, his body rigid and unresponsive.

The women were apparently frantic – was this how Frank Hart had died? – and with the strength of fear they were able to lift the boy into a mule-cart, which they drove as fast as possible to a nearby doctor. He administered an injection, but of what neither mother nor daughter knew, since they spoke no Spanish. Whatever it was, Harold was fully conscious the next day, though still most unwell – and there the matter, or Grace's record of it, ended.[8] If she consulted an American doctor about the matter (and there surely must have been one among the island's large American population) or if she elicited explanations from her son regarding his behaviour, she kept the findings of her research to herself. But the episode was sufficiently disconcerting for her to relay its essence to CA, whose reply of 8 February counselled discretion and oblivion: 'I've just received your two letters and a sad one from Harold. I'm sorry now I spoke of his letter to me. Don't say anything to him about it. I've written him a comforting little note and let it pass.'[9] The surest way of forgetting the drama lay in departure, and on 17 February Grace indicated to her husband that he should come to the island to escort his family home to Cleveland.

At least at home Harold now had firm friends – George Bryan, Kenneth Hurd and William Wright, whose friendship he was to retain for the rest of his life. Short and slight, extrovert and energetic, Wright offered a gregarious foil to his awkward companion at East High, not least as manager of the football team, contributor to the yearbook and subscriber to numerous school societies. His accomplishments naturally included dancing and he and Harold first befriended each other one Saturday at Eleanor T. Flynn's dancing school on Euclid Avenue, where, as Wright recalled, 'an old German lady in a very full brown taffeta skirt rattled her castanets for the class' attention and taught the tango and the Argentine'.[10] There was Harold, 'in the dull leather pumps which he carried to and from dancing school in a silk bag', and the boys discovered their families knew each other through business.[11] Soon, however, stronger affinities emerged. Beyond his energetic school career Wright nurtured more unconventional aspirations – he wanted to write poetry, and was thus amazed by the revelation his new friend made one Saturday on the edge of Wade Park:

> Those were tense days, war days, and even boys of fifteen were talking of their future. I had no idea what mine should be, but I believe I said I expected to become a lawyer. It was then that [Harold] first confided his conviction that he had discovered his bent, and that he would be a poet.[12]

These were not expectations confided to other pupils at Mrs Flynn's. The Brown sisters, Vivian and Hazel, marvelled at Grace's beauty and glamour when she collected her son from the school and Vivian, Harold's first sweetheart, received boxes of Crane confectionery and accompanying tributes of flowers. But the sisters knew nothing of Harold's poetic ambitions; to them he was merely an appealing dancing partner, appealing because he possessed a fastidiousness and gentleness they thought unusual in a boy and because he had about him a vulnerability somehow incongruous with the standing of his beautiful mother and rich successful father. They measured this delicacy differently, however. To Hazel he seemed 'shy, diffident and lonely', but Vivian, who knew him better, could see beneath the winning gaucheness: 'He was bitter even at that age.'[13]

William Wright was less perceptive. Later, when he and Harold became much closer friends and the latter felt able to confess the details of his recent suicide attempts with razors and narcotics, Wright grew to see his companion's inner turmoil. At first, however, the subterranean complexities escaped him, even though the two boys now started to seek each other out at school, at first to 'walk together through the halls talking of this and that', as Wright put it, and later to investigate the serious matter of literature.[14] Before long Harold invited his friend home and so Wright penetrated to what its occupant, mixing East High Latin and French, took to calling his 'Sanctum de la Tour'; it was here in this retreat that Wright saw the cherished library that attested to its owner's literary devotion. For two years now all Harold's money had gone on books. For Christmas 1913 his mother and grandmother had indulged his interest in art by giving him Caffin's three-volume study of Spanish, French and Dutch painting and in 1914 he acquired Voltaire's *History of Charles XII, King of Sweden*, a complete Shelley, and Everyman editions of Plutarch's *Parallel Lives* and Balzac's *About Catherine de Medici*. Then there were recent or impending acquisitions: a collected Lionel Johnson, a volume of Swinburne, of Byron, Edgar Allan Poe's *Tales of Mystery and Imagination*, a volume of Coleridge, a life of Goethe, a history of medieval Europe, Wilde's *Lady Windermere's Fan* and Hawthorne's *Mosses from an Old Manse*. These were the nocturnal companions of the earnest and passionate adolescent that Harold Crane had become; these were the guardians of secrets and the guides for future conduct. Markings in surviving volumes indicate future tendencies as well as revealing the direction of his thoughts as he read in his tower room night after night in a tense and embattled house, with thoughts of the scenes on the Isle of Pines still fresh in his head. Thus, marked in 'Parisina', Byron's tale of a woman's near (?) incestuous love for her handsome stepson:

> Nor are my mother's wrongs forgot,
> Her slighted love and ruined name,
> Her offspring's heritage of shame ...

Literature enabled him to interpret his past but also to plan for his future. Also marked was his Coleridge, where wisdom of another sort was on offer: 'The elder languages were fitter for poetry because they expressed only prominent ideas with clearness, the others but darkly . . .. Poetry gives the most pleasure when only generally and not perfectly understood.'[15]

Harold was developing the literary single-mindedness observed by all his friends in later life. Alternately overlooked and overindulged by his discontented parents, moody, bashful and withdrawn, longing for love and coherence in a world which appeared too shrill and preoccupied to give him hearing, he was forced to find sanctuary elsewhere, and literature seemed to offer the solutions he sought. It was the other world to which he escaped, besides constituting a school of adult passions which helped explain the dramas of manipulation and recrimination he saw ceaselessly enacted by his parents. As he began to sense that he was somehow different from the other adolescent boys he knew, literature offered a world which was unshockable, and as he began to suspect that he was not only alone as an aesthete in commercial Cleveland but also isolated, it introduced him to the idea of metropolitan literary culture, as conducted in London, Paris, New York and the other fabled cities beyond the prairie. He wanted more than just to read, however, more indeed than merely to write – he wanted to be a poet, and he had already announced his ambition. But how could he begin? How could he begin, when writing, if seriously practised, entailed exposure: of himself, of the sordidness and suffering of his family life, of the physical longings he had half begun to concede to himself, which he sensed William Wright, George Bryan and Kenneth Hurd did not, and could not, know? In the spring of 1915 these various thoughts were inchoate, as was the counter-argument that self-exposure, even on a blank sheet of paper before an audience he could never see, might also entail some element of resolution, but inchoate feelings are often the most powerful and Harold knew that somehow he must find a way out of Cleveland and loneliness to literary fellowship and literary achievement.

But where could he begin? He was without literary connection and his parents knew no writers – except his father's improbable admirer, Elbert Hubbard. But it was a start, and CA, still perhaps feeling guilty after recent misadventures, made the necessary overtures. Accordingly in April 1915, avid for the rituals of the literary life, Harold left for Aurora, New York, where Hubbard ran a combined farm, workshop, inn and craft community loosely based on the venture he had seen organized by William Morris in England in 1892. In appearance decidedly artistic – with his flowing hair, wide-brimmed hat and unkempt clothes he challenged opinion wherever he went – Hubbard in fact knew nothing of *fin de siècle* deficiencies of energy or conviction. His community of artistic souls at one stage numbered 500 and was for a while internationally known. It was from here that he issued his monthly Little Journeys pamphlets, to 'Homes of English Authors', 'Great Musicians', 'Eminent Orators', 'Famous Women', 'American Statesmen' and so on; and here that he supervised publication of his idiosyncratic but widely circulated magazines of art, politics and opinion, the *Philistine* and the *Fra*. It was here that the Roycroft Shop, founded in 1895 in honour of the seventeenth-century English printers Thomas and Samuel Roycroft, crafted elaborate editions of the classics and it was here at the Roycroft Inn that visitors congregated for annual conventions geared to the exchange of homespun cultural and political polemic.

Every year from May to September Hubbard took his word to the multitude by lecturing across America and every year he wooed his hard-working capitalist audience with conservative wisdom. Indeed in later life Clarence Crane was fond of quoting Hubbard's notions of practicality and self-dependence to his son: 'Sooner or later in your journey through life your affection will be expressed in beefsteak.'[16] Harold stayed, as was customary with the apprentices, with Hubbard himself, who was now living with his second wife, the writer Alice Moore, and in the morning he worked in the Roycroft book-binding department. Afternoons were spent on the Roycroft farm or in one of the ancillary organizations and in the evening Harold listened to Hubbard's enthusiastic discussions of Poe, Emerson and Whitman. On his departure his host presented him with an inscribed copy of *Little Journeys to the Homes of English Authors*: 'To Harold Crane My valued helper at Roycroft Elbert Hubbard Apr 20th 1915.'[17] The experience was by no means the last exposure Harold was to have to the influence of nineteenth-century English aestheticism but in some ways the visit disappointed his expectations and he returned to Cleveland suspicious that his host had been no more than a pompous self-promoter. In any case he was never to meet him again. Three weeks later Hubbard was dead – drowned on 7 May 1915 on the torpedoed *Lusitania*.

CA's next introduction proved more auspicious. His Mary Garden chocolates were much appreciated in Chicago by a catering business under the command of Harriet Moody, widow of the late poet and professor William Vaughn Moody. During CA's business visits Mrs Moody had often mentioned the numerous artists and writers she knew and now he applied to her for advice. As one of the principal Chicago *salonistes* she was vigilant for new accomplishment that would confirm the Chicago renaissance of the arts and vindicate for ever the standing of poetry in America. She knew many of the most important writers in New York and her circle of friends included Carl Sandburg, Vachel Lindsay, W.B. Yeats and Rabindranath Tagore. But she was no other-worldly artist: she not only understood commerce, she pursued it in order to subsidize her literary enthusiasms. CA felt he could trust her, and after pleasantries about business and about the poets he had admired as a youth – Lowell, Whittier and the New England school – he unburdened himself of his anxieties: about how his introspective and inaccessible son showed no interest in sport or in choosing a practical career or indeed in anything except the arts in general, and wanting to become a poet in particular. What was wrong with a college education, which he would happily fund, followed by a career in the family confectionery business? Mrs Moody listened with interest and sympathy and dispensed even-handed advice: for practicality's sake Harold should be encouraged to go to university; but she advised CA to accommodate his literary aspirations and promised to look at any poetry Harold might send her.

Shy and withdrawn as he was, when Harold learned to trust people he gave himself prodigally. It was the beginning of a philosophy of friendship which set great store by reliability and loyalty and interpreted minor lapses on the part of others as cruel betrayal. The pattern became more pronounced, inevitably, with time; but already Wright, Bryan and Hurd knew they were privileged in being admitted to Harold's confidence and were intrigued by the secrets he revealed. Kenneth Hurd remembered the fascinating asymmetry of his friend's skills – of how he played tennis with gestures 'certainly not graceful or effeminate but rather erratic and awkward with lungings and futile wavings of his racket' yet could improvise 'beautifully' on the piano, over which was hung the original of Maxfield Parrish's *The Rubaiyat*. More marvellous still was the fact that Harold wrote poetry. Hurd was permitted to enter the Sanctum de la Tour, there to be impressed by Harold's 'large library of ultra modern (at least it seemed so to me) verse' and was allowed to watch the mysterious creative mood as it possessed his friend in the interludes between prosaic East High studies.[18]

Following tentative investigation into Socratic and Platonic thought Harold had underlined with red ink expositions dealing with the divine madness of poets and, taking the ancient wisdom to heart, astonished his friends with the elaborate rites by which he conjured the muse – rites in which deep inhalation of scents proved recurrent. Soon he took to smoking cigars for the transports they gave him, but in the meantime Grace's favourite perfumes would do as well; and Hurd never forgot his amazement when Harold buried his nose in a pair of old shoes belonging to the maid, who occupied the other tower bedroom. Having induced the necessary state of reverie he could then proceed to composition, and sometimes even to a reading aloud of his work. Hurd remembered that he was never shy when it came to exposing his compositions to scrutiny but when pressed for an explanation he always demurred. From Plato he learned of the lost continent of Atlantis, which would emerge as a poetic theme years later; and from Swinburne of the myths and gods and goddesses that furnished his earliest compositions. And from his own adolescent yearnings to transcend what seemed his present clumsy, lonely lot he drew the idea of a moth, a blind moth despised among butterflies, which one day flew in the heat of the day the others avoided only to have its wings destroyed by the sun – but not before it had sensed horizons which the cautious and night-dwelling would never behold. 'The Moth That God Made Blind' was the first poem Harold Hart Crane wrote and decided to save, possibly as early as Christmas 1915, and although it reads as derivative and prolix it is nevertheless an interesting testament to belief in the artist as seer ennobled and then destroyed ('These things I have: – a withered hand; – /Dim eyes; – a tongue that cannot tell') by the splendour of his vision.[19] But if it is a work of extreme romanticism it is also one of eerie prediction, which foretells the poet's visionary flight and inevitable fall.

Harriet Moody visited Cleveland in the winter and met its hopeful poet and then on 5 January 1916 CA and Grace left to join Mrs Hart on the Isle of Pines, with CA taking the opportunity to sell his goods on the way south. Following the disasters of the previous winter and in view of Harold's obligations at East High the Cranes had decided to leave their son behind, but the decision distressed him and as he confided to his grandmother in a letter of 7 January he was 'so lonesome now'.[20] If he felt deserted, Harold also had problems at school – examinations loomed and he told Mrs Hart, 'I am not getting along very well [there]'. When he wrote on 26 January, he was alone once more. CA and Grace had returned and gone again – this time on business to New York, where Grace bought a Tiffany lamp – and he was in the thick of exams: English that day and Latin and geometry, 'my hoodooes', the next. His recent sore throat had not been severe enough to merit consultation with Mr Ely, the local Christian Science practitioner, but he urged his grandmother to continue with her own studies, 'and carry the science as far as you can'.[21] In their absence his parents had entrusted him with supervision of the Cleveland store, but when Harold wrote to Mrs Hart again on 10 February it was to report the anxiety caused by this responsibility, exacerbated as it was by dissatisfaction with school. He had suffered from car sickness; and then, 'It is surely lonely for me here, eating alone and seldom seeing any one but in the darkness of morning or night.' East High offered little consolation:

> They are so shallow over there at school I am more moved to disdain than anything else. Popularity is not my aim though it were easy to win it by laughing when they do at nothing and always making a general ass of oneself. There are about two out of the twelve hundred I would care to have as friends.[22]

Like Wilde and Swinburne and the aesthetes before him, he scorned to compromise with philistinism. Poetry would be his solace. Intermittently he was working on a 600-line ballad and neighbouring Kenneth Hurd glimpsed evidence of his late-night labours: 'I'd look out of my window and still see the lights on in his room next door. Harold would be reading or working on one of his poems.'[23] In

Mrs Moody he had a loyal and discriminating audience. He sent another early effort, 'Nocturne', for her appraisal and on 23 March she voiced trepidation that the poem's 'realization in phrase is not quite equal in quality...to the quality of the verse melody and the mood' before going on to declare, 'I have a deep conviction that you are following the real right lead for you, in giving all to poetry.'[24] She sensed the degree to which Harold depended on her and worried when she could not reply to his confidences or his compositions with promptness, admitting on 2 July: 'I am always afraid my long silences after you send me a manuscript may seem discouraging, and that would be a real pain to me.' She liked another poem he had sent despite the obscurity she detected in certain lines. 'The whole', she felt, 'is beautifully felt and delicately written' and reassurance was again in order: 'Love of your words, and work, will give to you your full voice.'[25] She recommended the poetry of Padraic Colum as well as that of Carl Sandburg, chronicler of industrial Chicago, but on the subject of Harold's summer escape from Cleveland, which she had been trying to arrange with her friends the MacKayes in Cornish, New Hampshire, she had to report failure and could only hope that when CA next visited Chicago, Harold would accompany him.

It was a disappointment: he had looked forward to the adventure and even his father, after initial hesitation, had approved of the scheme, going so far as to confide the plan in a business letter to Maxfield Parrish: 'Harold is going to do some things in life that his father wished very much to do. I think the boy has most unusual talent for writing and an appreciation of art which is splendid. Mrs William Vaughn Moody is one of my personal friends ... and on a recent visit here suggested that the atmosphere of Cornish was just what he needed.'[26] But then Harold, along with George Bryan, was invited by Hazel and Vivian Brown to Chautauqua, near Jamestown, New York, where the Browns had a lakeside summer cottage. The visitors stayed in a local hotel but ate with the Browns and spent their more decorous hours escorting Mrs Brown and her daughters in the grounds of the Chautauqua Foundation, home to the famous institute of adult education. Mrs Brown kept a careful eye on the boys and George kept a careful eye on Harold. He knew his alternating moods of gloom and exhilaration and his friend's inability to mask them: 'Harold ... was very impetuous and was in hot water most of the time. And when he was corrected by his mother or Grandmother Hart, he was pouty and sulky to everyone.' Happily all went well, and Bryan was sure he knew why: 'I attributed it to the fact that [Harold] was away from his parents and grandparents who never allowed him much freedom at home.'[27] Not that freedom was always a good thing. Bryan vividly remembered one riotous occasion when he and Harold had decapitated George's sister's dolls under the rocking horse, with Harold gleefully galloping backwards and forwards on the improvised guillotine.

He returned from Jamestown only to catch his breath before a second departure, this time with Grace on a tour of the West. At sixteen and a half he felt himself

too old to share a sleeper with his mother and expressed annoyance at her arrangement by throwing his clothes down from the upper berth each night. He read a
great deal, often in moody solitude, and retreated frequently to the train's observation platform to contemplate the epic of America as it proclaimed itself over the
Great Plains and on towards the Rocky Mountains. They stopped in Wyoming and
admired the geysers, hot springs and petrified forests of Yellowstone Park and
thought of Indians not long vanished from the juniper woods; and in San
Francisco they explored Chinatown and saluted Golden Gate harbour and wandered the steep streets where Grace's Belden forebears had attained wealth and
prominence. They even ventured into Canada and swam, rode and played tennis
near Lake Louise in south-western Alberta – but it was not time yet for the poetry
of America, and back home in Cleveland Harold immersed himself once again in
the London of the decadent Nineties. At least now there were places of study other
than the city library and the solitude of his room. In 1916 Cleveland saw its literary life significantly expanded with the arrival in Taylor Arcade of Richard
Laukhuff's eccentric bookstore. Laukhuff was the son of a German organ builder
who had worked as a journeyman organ repairer in France and Italy. He acquired
two languages and 6,000 books on his travels and on arriving in the United States
he spent time in New York before moving to Cleveland, where he decided his
extensive library should form the nucleus of a bookstore devoted to representation
of the liberal arts to the exclusion of all that was tritely popular in fiction and periodicals. Local artists such as William Sommer, George Henry Keller and Charles
Burchfield held exhibitions at Laukhuff's establishment and here the little magazines were available which published the acts and works of literary Chicago and
exhaled the very talk of Greenwich Village. Laukhuff knew Randolph Bourne and
Sherwood Anderson, both writers concerned with fostering what they saw as
America's forthcoming cultural autonomy, and in his role as semi-tyrannical impresario he encouraged his customers to treat his establishment as an informal educational institution, even providing chairs to welcome relaxed browsing and
impromptu literary debate.

Laukhuff's was the school East High should have been, a place where girls, sports,
yearbooks and examinations were abandoned in favour of literature and the arts;
a place where Harold and William Wright could escape quotidian Cleveland –
indeed America itself – for the greater republic of art. In no time Harold was a
familiar face, eager for literary argument and enlightenment and for the new translations and imported European works Laukhuff saw it as his duty to stock. Here
were *Poetry*, *Soil* and *Seven Arts*, crucial magazines which promulgated the American
renaissance in arts and letters then under way, to say nothing of more obscure publications such as *Pagan* and *Bruno's Weekly*, all arranged for the edification of
Cleveland's intellectual circles, which turned out to be larger than Harold had suspected. *Pagan* had been founded only in May and as a self-proclaimed 'magazine

for Eudaemonists' it invoked Aristotelian notions of happiness as well as sporting a cryptic motto: 'Hang your lantern in your nook/Drink and laugh at Priest and Shah'. Its editor, Joseph Kling, boasted a long list of predictable bohemian aversions, including war and religion, and was notably hostile to Christian Science. To study his eccentric publication was, it seemed, to escape briefly but with a vengeance from provincial morals and family constrictions and Harold was sufficiently enthused to send Kling a brief note which appeared in the October number of the magazine: 'I am interested in your magazine as a new and distinctive chord in the present American Renaissance of literature and art. Let me praise your September cover; it has some suggestion of the exoticism and richness of Wilde's poems. H.H.C. East 115th Street.'[28]

As a devotee of the *Yellow Book* and the English 1890s, Kling was sure to take the Wildean parallel with pleasure, but for Harold the reference spoke the obsession of much of that year. At some stage in mid-adolescence he had his first homosexual experience; years later he could turn it into a coarse and comical anecdote but now it was something to be relived, if at all, in solitude. God forbid that his parents should find out – it was a transgression impossible to imagine committed by other males anywhere, and certainly not by Hurd, Wright or Bryan, who must also be kept in the dark, whatever happened. But then his reading had led him to Oscar Wilde: not only to the figure who dominated literary London in the 1890s until his sudden fall, but also to his writings, which extended from insolence to contrition and seemed to express more than they said – but should one try to understand him *de profundis* or by the dazzling surface of his plays? Why, in any case, the different layers of meaning and significance? What fragment of knowledge was missing from his comprehension of this haunting man? Harold, after all, had not been there to see the aesthete instruct the philistine Clevelanders thirty-four years previously, or to read coverage of his first trial in the *New York Times* in April 1895. Nor did Christian Science offer much opportunity for attendance at the more orthodox Christian assemblies in America at which, it was estimated, at least 900 sermons addressing Wilde's corruption were preached in the last five years of the nineteenth century.

In January and February 1916, however, *Bruno's Weekly* had published a series of articles sympathetically relating Wilde's decline and fall and his time in cell C 33 in Reading Gaol. It was an enterprise which involved various Wildean figures including Lord Alfred Douglas, and when Harold read the essays, either at Laukhuff's or clandestinely in his bedroom, where forbidden texts including an unexpurgated *Decameron* were now secreted, the puzzle resolved itself at last: Wilde had gone to gaol for prolonging the sexual activities with which Harold himself had only just begun to experiment. The effect this example had on him proved so disturbing that some time in the summer of 1916 he was inspired to write what became his first published lyric, 'C 33', which appeared in *Bruno's Weekly* on 23 September 1916, thus stamping him tenuously but publicly as a Wildean.

Before long this status would come to disconcert, but for now he was too delighted with public appearance. In any case, 'C 33' gave little away: it contains no explicit reference to Wilde himself and only other devotees would be able to establish his identity from the otherwise inexplicable title. The poem contains further secrets: by praising Wilde for weaving 'rose-vines/About the empty heart of night', Harold Hart begins his lifelong tendency to punning; and by invoking an unidentified 'Materna' he betrays none of the suffering and humiliation his mother had endured and which, like Wilde, she had borne with Grace and fortitude. At the moment Harold's verse, like Wilde's, is a 'song of minor, broken strain' but one day his muse will be rewarded with greater achievement: 'O Materna! to enrich thy gold head/And wavering shoulders with a new light shed.'[29]

The materna herself already knew all about her son's poetic ambitions and as the two grew closer in trust and friendship Harold continued to delight her with the intensity of the artistic commitment she had first sponsored and to surprise her with his own experiments in sensual gratification. She herself liked to spend money on expensive clothes and scent and black lace underwear; Harold's adolescent gratifications were cruder and less costly. He confided to Kenneth Hurd that he had taken to masturbating with the use of the vacuum cleaner tube – but one day Grace walked in and caught him in the act and the machine, as she later put it in what she found 'an absolutely hilarious story', 'practically tore his private parts off'.[30] No doubt she felt she could afford to be amused: such activities were surely not unnatural in a boy – and whatever Harold wrote about Oscar Wilde and her in his first published poem, was he not healthily interested in girls, especially Vivian Brown? The latter herself never forgot the gentleness of his attentions or the generosity with which he sought to please friends and sweethearts alike.

> He used to take me to shows on the streetcar as all boys did & send me flowers & candy from the beautiful [Crane] store downtown in Cleveland. They carried fresh flowers there & put out gift boxes – big ones with a corsage and matching box of candy. I remember one night after a show he took a bunch of us into the store – with key, as it was after hours & we all fixed up fancy sundaes & ate them. We left everying neat though. He was afraid of his father.[31]

These sweet surprises were crucial to Harold's standing as an eligible young man and a date and now, in a New York magazine, he had been published as a poet. As if that was not accolade enough it became known that he was granted an interview, a very rare interview, by Rabindranath Tagore, who had won the Nobel Prize for Literature in 1915, and who passed through Cleveland the following year. Even CA attached more respect to his precocious son's learning and opinions than the latter suspected, and again mentioned Harold's achievements with pride in a business letter the misspelling of which may have amused its recipient, Maxfield Parrish:

My personal knowledge of art could probably be classed as that of an average American. I certainly am not a critic – I only know what pleases me. Thru the influence of my son, who is making art and literature a study, I am actually arriving at a point where I can approach a picture and being told it is a Rembrandt or Reuben, it will gradually dawn upon me that I should have recognized it as that artist's inimitable style.[32]

On Saturday, 16 September the Cranes, accompanied by Mrs Hart, made one of their last appearances together as a family when they went to Trinity Cathedral in Cleveland for the wedding of Helen Hart to William Griswold Hurlbert. Cousin Helen was now twenty-four, and in its 'Society' column the *Warren Daily Tribune* reported that the bride, given away by Aunt Zell, wore georgette crêpe trimmed with ermine and that 'her only ornament was a beautiful diamond circle pin, the gift of her aunt, Mrs Grace Hart Crane'. Afterwards the families progressed to dinner at the Hotel Statler and the newspaper mentioned that 'Mr Harold Crane of Cleveland' was present at the banquet, along with the officiating minister, the Reverend Archdeacon A.A. Abbott. 'The place cards were blue birds for happiness and the favors were tulle bags of rice tied with ribbon from which hung silver horse shoes for luck.'[33] The horseshoes proved effective the following month when the Hurlberts boarded the British ship *Stefano*. The vessel was torpedoed in the Atlantic by a German submarine but the newly married couple were among those rescued and on 14 October the *Warren Daily Tribune* published a photograph of the Hurlberts smiling with relief at Newport, Rhode Island. The couple escaped in the clothes they were wearing and the newspaper made much of the fact that 'Mrs Hurlbert had on her suit and furs when the Submarine arrived and not being able to go to her stateroom she was not so badly off as many passengers who were at dinner in evening clothes'.[34]

Aunt Zell had made a reappearance in Harold's life on her return visits from Wyoming to Warren. As something of a patron of the arts she kept herself informed about the young artists of her native town, and knowing of her godson's cultural enthusiasm she decided to introduce him to Carl Schmitt, a twenty-seven-year-old painter whose recent year of European travel she had sponsored. She could do little, however, for the Clarence Cranes themselves, as their marriage moved inexorably towards collapse. Temperamentally more in sympathy with enterprising and industrious CA than with her highly strung and romantic sister-in-law, Zell was too often out of Ohio to know whether the rumours of infidelity that stalked CA were accurate or merely vilification of a man who appeared never to have put anything before his wife – except perhaps his work. Ever since Grace's return from California she and her husband had coexisted in a condition of mutual recrimination and intolerance which escalated into ever more frequent quarrels, and Harold – not always able to take shelter in his tower room – showed the extent to which his psychosomatic temperament had developed in his adolescence

by succumbing to asthma and nervous skin rashes with each outbreak of hostilities. At the end of November CA decided enough was enough. Suddenly and
secretly he moved such items as he needed from East 115th Street and took a room
at Cleveland's Athletic Club.

Perhaps he intended the move as nothing more than a truce but Grace took it
as a declaration of formal hostility and instructed the family lawyer, John J.
Sullivan, to instigate divorce proceedings. She charged CA with 'gross neglect of
duty' and informed Sullivan that she wanted 'custody and control' of Harold and
a settlement that would provide comfortably for her for at least five years.[35] As
usual with the Cranes, the arrangement was a bizarre one: John Sullivan was one
of the most prominent divorce lawyers in Cleveland, had indeed been District
Attorney for Northern Ohio under William McKinley and Theodore Roosevelt,
but here he was, officially Clarence Crane's lawyer, now agreeing to act for both
parties in the divorce. Having issued instructions, Grace prepared to leave for
Chicago, even as the severance was reported in the local newspapers. Just before
her departure CA applied to see her, perhaps with a view to attempting reconciliation. She refused him, and he had to content himself with sending her a large
bouquet of roses and violets – love's true emblems – and an adoring valediction:

> Please wear this rose out of Cleveland and if my thoughts and true desires help
> at all – you'll find solace and health. I shall think of you each hour and pray
> for you each night ... you're leaving with my heart and affections tucked away
> where it's been for twenty years.[36]

Convinced by Grace's arguments that CA had abandoned them and sure that
she was doing the right thing in pressing for legal severance, Harold bided his
time. Whether he liked it or not, whether or not his father was as treacherous, cruel
and unfaithful as he had been led to believe, it was clear that his parents' eighteen-
year marriage was failing and that the life he had so far known, perplexing and
incoherent though it had been, was ending. Less clear, however, was his part in
their schemes for the future. With Grace claiming custody, how much of his father
would he see, or desire to see? Equally, did he really want to follow her plans,
which entailed continuing to live in Cleveland, especially when the battle for the
new American literature had been joined elsewhere? Still unsure what to do, he
turned once again to art for security and distraction and continued to read and
write, somehow finding tranquillity away from the dramas around him in his conviction of himself as an emerging poet. Already he was moving away from the
1890s and was now immersed in the Imagism of Ezra Pound, Amy Lowell and the
young T.S. Eliot. Practising its Japanese brevity and conjuring a succession of hard,
clear images, he produced a seasonal vignette in the Imagist manner, 'October–
November', and submitted it to the *Pagan*. It evoked the now distant world of the
late summer – those weeks before his world fell apart – and ended with a lovely

salute to the twilight: 'Then the moon/In a mad orange flare/Floods the grape-hung night.'[37]

Joseph Kling accepted the poem. Putting Harold between covers with D'Annunzio himself he published it in the November–December issue of his magazine – and New York winked at the poet once more. Thanks to Laukhuff's Harold was able to follow the policies of all the new literary magazines and *Others*, founded the year before, particularly impressed him. Already it had published a formidable selection of new poets – Wallace Stevens, William Carlos Williams, T.S. Eliot, Ezra Pound, Marianne Moore, Carl Sandburg and Conrad Aiken – and already its commitment to experimental writing had led to a good deal of outrage in the newspapers. Shy about many things but never shy about his talent, Harold sent the magazine a selection of his lyrics some time in November and was cheered with the reply William Carlos Williams, an associate editor, wrote him on 16 November: 'Damn good stuff. "Others" is in a state of transition – to say the least, so – We'll keep your things in the hope that someday – someday – when we get some money – we may print them.'[38]

Little magazines might have futures indefinite, but suddenly Harold did not. With his parents divided and embattled there was no one remaining force strong enough to tell him what to do and he seized his opportunity. Whether or not *Others* ever published his latest poems its felicitations were another endorsement from America's literary capital and he knew now that he wanted to leave Cleveland to join his peers and to test his aspirations in New York. East High, for some time a dull distraction, seemed irrelevant to the needs of a published metropolitan poet and with his father's impetuousness and his mother's blind disregard of the financial future he walked out of the school never to return. Manhattan beckoned, his precocious poems were applauded – and everything else would fall into place.

He took a job selling prints and mezzotints at Korner and Woods and bent his will to saving money and moving to New York, possibly as soon as the summer of 1917. Carl Schmitt, already living in Manhattan, was alerted to recent developments and to the fact that despite 'this disturbing age of adolescence which I am now undergoing' Harold felt calmly certain of the course he had chosen:

I have had tremendous struggles, but out of the travail, I think must come advancement ... I feel a great peace; my inner life has balanced, as I expected, the other side of the scale. Thank God, I am young. I have the confidence and the will to make fate.[39]

However, events moved with unforeseen swiftness. On 11 December John Sullivan filed an annuity agreement subscribed by both the Cranes which entailed generous capitulation to all of Grace's demands. Over five years she was to receive a total of $20,400 in cash and an additional sum of $210 forthwith for miscellaneous needs. CA resigned his claim to the furniture at East 115th Street, met all the legal costs of the settlement, including the attorney's fee of $1,000, and agreed to repay with interest the $5,000 he had borrowed from his wife when he incorporated the Crane Company. Furthermore he undertook to clothe and feed Harold for the remainder of his minority and promised to pay for his college education.

Such concessions were all very well, but talk of the completion of Harold's education was as much formulaic as realistic. He had already left school unqualified: without the necessary diplomas, which college would accept him, and what would he study? Again Harold had a solution and one his parents were too preoccupied to challenge: once in New York he would find a temporary job which would pay for the private tuition necessary for the entrance examinations to Columbia University. Grace liked the glamour and excitement of New York and went along with the plan and CA had alimony to pay and had never gone to university himself so what did he know? Perhaps his son understood what he was doing, unconventional though it all seemed. As for Harold himself, he suddenly wondered why he had contemplated moving next summer. Grace was in Chicago and CA was living at the Athletic Club; he might as well begin his great future in New York as remain alone with Mrs Hart. Accordingly, Carl Schmitt was nominated an informal guardian and just after Christmas 1916, having packed copies of the Bible and Mary Baker Eddy's *Science and Health with Key to the Scriptures*, Harold departed Cleveland for the crystal city of New York.

3

The twelve-hour journey from Cleveland translated Harold to a new city and to what was in effect another life in a different country. When he emerged four days after Christmas from the recently perfected splendours of Grand Central Station he did so as an apprentice New Yorker and as a poet who would henceforth acknowledge no other calling. Yet if he had wilfully travelled to the cultural capital of America he set foot in a beflagged frontier town: however distant the European conflict had appeared in Ohio, in New York involvement in the Great War seemed both illustrious and imminent. The city's newspapers fed the crowds fresh details of each crisis; its streets were brave with bands and parades which fêted the Entente Powers; and as the principal port of embarkation for Europe it cleared more munitions, supplies and volunteers bound for the hostilities than any other American city. Furthermore, each departure was heroic, when German submarines threatened not only American shipping in the Atlantic but the very harbour of New York. Woodrow Wilson, resolutely neutral in his first term of office, had just been returned to the White House but his impartiality appeared increasingly unsustainable and within four months of Harold's arrival the United States was at war.

But if Europe was internecine, in America there was a mood of expansiveness and buoyant expectation. It was no coincidence that in 1912 in the last presidential election prior to the outbreak of European war all three candidates had promoted themselves as progressive politicians – a confident gesture appropriate to a confident society recently come to intellectual maturity. And it was in New York that this new assurance was most established. Here the world's finances were soon to be regulated and here, by inevitable succession, the arts assembled. Here an apprehension of America's imminent sovereignty was growing, and here a self-sustaining urban culture was developing which was more secular and sophisticated, more experimental yet more confident, than any other in America. When Mabel Dodge, heiress, literary muse, cultural midwife and friend of the famous returned to live in Manhattan in 1912 she sensed this optimistic inquisitiveness: 'Barriers went down and people reached each other who had never been in touch before; there were all sorts of ways to communicate as well as new communications'.[1] She was one of the organizing spirits behind the celebrated International Exhibition of Modern Art which in 1913 exposed astonished crowds to the work of the French Impressionists and led the *New York Globe* to declare that 'America will never be the same again'.[2] Without resting on her laurels, she also convened the most influential and celebrated salon in American letters: the brightest and the most eccentric spirits of New York regularly gathered at 23 Fifth Avenue and it was later claimed that there, under her aegis, the idea of Greenwich Village as a state of mind first came into being.

In fact the Village had been a bohemian enclave since the turn of the century but as New York challenged, and then assumed, Boston's status as the seat of American culture, and as artistic misfits fled there in increasing numbers to escape what they saw as the provincialism and puritanism of a country dedicated to big business, the enclave became something of a recognized colony. If the latest European ideas, of Shaw and Wells, Ibsen and Dostoevsky, Sorel and Freud, Expressionism and Futurism, were first evaluated beneath the white porcelain chandeliers of Mrs Dodge's famous white drawing-room, these assessments were eagerly prolonged on the other side of Washington Square, where the Village's unassuming terraces proved hospitable to artists, writers, anarchists, communists, free lovers and free-thinkers. Here youth and paganism were advocated. Here, in the interests of fashionable self-expression, Cubism and *vers libre* were indulged. And here New Women agitated for the suffrage they finally gained in 1920. Although the aestheticism of the English 1890s lingered to perpetuate the reputations of George Moore and Oscar Wilde, many bachelor girls already wore batik sandals and smoked defiantly, urging as they did so the wisdom of birth control. Indeed once cartoonists discovered Greenwich Village it became axiomatic among them that only its women wore their hair short, and in the long term this easy parish of new life and new thought was doomed, not merely by improved transportation, which would make it costlier, but also by the stealthier encroachments of self-consciousness – it was only a matter of time before the colony found itself satirized in fiction. By then, however, a revolution in manners and morals had overtaken urban life across America and it is no exaggeration to say that many of its liberal characteristics were first the tenets and truisms of Greenwich Village.

Even as Harold discovered it, however, this colony was about to change: with American entry into the war, many freedoms were curtailed by emergency powers and that essential Village publication, the *Masses*, was banned by the United States Mail and brought to trial in a federal court for its socialist and anti-bellicose tone. But although many Villagers fled to Mexico or were incarcerated as conscientious objectors enough remained at liberty to continue one of the greatest cultural campaigns of Harold's youth: the vindication of an American literature. This noble ideal had enjoyed intellectual currency for many years, with Emerson himself presenting the arguments for America's literary entitlement in *The Poet*, published as long ago as 1844:

> Time and nature yield us many gifts, but not yet the timely man, the new religion, the reconciler, whom all things await ... Banks and tariffs, the newspaper and caucus, Methodism and Unitarianism, are flat and dull to dull people, but rest on the same foundations of wonder as the town of Troy and the temple of Delphi, and are as swiftly passing away. Our log-rolling, our stumps and their politics, our fisheries, our Negroes and Indians, our boasts and our repudiations, the wrath of rogues and the pusillanimity of honest men, the northern trade, the southern planting, the western clearing, Oregon and Texas, are yet unsung. Yet America is a poem in our eyes; its ample geography dazzles the imagination, and it will not long wait for metres.[3]

Only eleven years before Harold's birth Walt Whitman had gone further, insisting in 'A Backward Glance O'er Travel'd Roads' that since America was the world's engine of democratic and material change, it had no choice but to create a fresh and appropriate literature: 'For all these new and evolutionary facts, meanings, purposes, new poetic messages, new forms and expressions, are inevitable.'[4] Yet by the beginning of the twentieth century, beset by what came to be scorned as the Genteel Tradition of writing, American literature appeared to have betrayed the visions of these founding fathers. It seemed to take no stock of all that had happened to the country since the Civil War – the immigrant inundations, the robber barons, the forging cities, the technical inventiveness, the unexampled plurality – and offered instead a vision of American life which, while promoting the Bostonian virtues of morality, humanitarianism and didacticism, appeared also to be nostalgic, evasive and dishonest.

Even at Harvard this schism between American culture and American reality was apparent and was most famously codified by the philosopher George Santayana in his celebrated lecture of 1911, 'The Genteel Tradition in American Philosophy', which suggested that the American Will inhabited the skyscraper, and the American Intellect the colonial mansion. 'The one is the sphere of the American man; the other, at least predominantly, of the American woman. The one is all aggressive enterprise; the other is all genteel tradition.'[5] It was a situation which could not survive the quickening pace of change in American life at the beginning of the twentieth century, and before the first decade was over malcontents had gone overseas to work for change: like other revolutions in history, this one would be begun abroad.

Gertrude Stein, sure that American arts would flourish but only with initial European confirmation, left for Paris. She befriended Picasso and Matisse, mourned 'all the little magazines which have died to make verse free' and established a salon which introduced American pilgrims to Parisian cultural experimentation.[6] Ezra Pound, for whom the United States was 'a half-savage country, out of date', left for London and then Paris, and worked for what he termed a 'risorgimento' of American literature. In Chicago, meanwhile, a new generation of poets emerged which was convinced of the poetic validity of the stockyards and skyscrapers of their lakeside city and in 1912 Harriet Monroe, poet and champion of the new, founded *Poetry: A Magazine of Free Verse*, initially to accommodate these new writers but eventually to extend publication to some of the most important American literary innovators of the forthcoming decade. In 1914 the *New Republic* was established and Herbert Croly, one of its founders, insisted that 'American intelligence has still to issue its Declaration of Independence' and that same year saw the advent of the *Little Review*, another of the magazines integral to the cultural stirring then afoot.[7] Influential journalists such as H.L. Mencken maintained the campaign against the Genteel Tradition in his essays and in 1918 the critic Van Wyck Brooks issued his celebrated clarion call for a 'Usable Past', for the rediscovery of a literary history which might nourish the endeavours of the present and the future. In 1919 T.S. Eliot, like Brooks the product of a Harvard education which had concentrated exclusively on European literature, refined the nature of the quest by countering that this past, this tradition, could not simply be discovered – 'if you want it you must obtain it by great labour'.[8]

Thus the excavations began – to continue throughout Crane's literary career – among the forgotten monuments of nineteenth-century American fiction and poetry. The idols of Gentility – Longfellow, James Fenimore Cooper, Washington Irving and others too Anglophile for their own good – were cast out and a new pantheon constructed: the achievements of Poe, Melville, Hawthorne, Thoreau and Emily Dickinson were reassessed and over a quarter-century interval American literature acquired an altogether darker lineage. But if this re-creation of the past was a significant literary enterprise, and one which had profound implications for Crane's later career, it occurred in and was championed by publications which were also eager to promote fresh writing in the United States and to detect an American culture in the trappings of daily life. Hence *Soil*, a literary and art magazine that saw poetry in the factories and machinery of the United States as well as in the shabbier quarters of New York and insisted that Indian beadwork was as much a function of an American art as the skyscraper. Hence *Others*, to which Hart had already applied for publication, or *Seven Arts*, a magazine which in 1916 declared its belief in 'a renascent period, a time which means for America the coming of that national self-consciousness which is the beginning of greatness' and which exerted an immense influence in its brief year of publication.[9] Hence the *Little Review*, which moved from Chicago to New York in 1917, and hence *Modern School*, *S4N*, *Plowshare*, *Quill*, *Contact* and others. Here hopeful young poets would prove themselves and earn the later accolade of slim volumes and anthology inclusion, here in these publications which had the wayward courses and the brief lives of butterflies.

Before he could prove himself at all, Harold had to find affordable accommodation and a circle of friends. CA had told him to make himself known to Hazel Hasham and Miss Bohn, who ran the Crane Company offices at 18 West 33rd Street, but his only other acquaintance in New York was Carl Schmitt and it was to his studio at 308 East 15th Street that Harold proceeded on arrival in the city. Busily committed to a career in poetic landscapes and portraiture that had already led to representation at the Corcoran Gallery in Washington and the National Academy in New York, Schmitt rose without hesitation to the responsibilities of unofficial guardianship and with his help the newcomer quickly found somewhere to live. The idea of a first address in New York, at 139 East 15th Street, was exciting but the reality was less glamorous: Harold's uncertain finances were hardly ample in Cleveland but in Manhattan they bought even less: one cold, dark, dirty room infested with bedbugs, with communal bathrooms so squalid he had to go to Schmitt's to satisfy the demands of nature and cleanliness. Yet this was the reality of the literary life; this was where the struggle for greatness was to begin; and there was certainly neither time nor excuse to repine when either one of his parents might recall him to the Midwest if he betrayed the slightest hesitation or unhappiness. He explored eagerly, despite the bitter cold – Little Italy one day, an omnibus ride down Fifth Avenue another – and dispatched reports to his divided parents. The mansions of the rich were astonishing but he was more intrigued by the teeming crowds of the tenemented Lower East Side, which seemed to offer an anonymity at once frightening and desirable. As he remarked to CA, 'It seems sometimes almost as though you had lost yourself, and were trying vainly to find somewhere in this sea of humanity, your lost identity.'[10] New York was a brave new world and he fell in love with it, as he had done with the sea: both could overwhelm and both could liberate and after the constrictions of Cleveland he began, slowly at first, to develop a taste for the dangerous embrace, unquestioning and unmanning, which is the exhilaration of his mature poetry.

Letters arrived from the Midwest: preoccupied and remote as his parents were, they were not entirely sanguine about Harold's limbo status. Although Grace now began to sign herself 'dearest Grace' or, in more skittish mode, 'your Gracie', she continued to stress the importance of university education, telling him on 3 January 1917 that he should keep his 'body & mind clean' and prepare himself for study and examinations. 'It will be time well spent & you will never regret it.'[11] Two weeks later, though bound for Florida, she reiterated her conviction that he must never abandon the hope of university and declared, 'You know I shall never give in on that for I firmly believe you will regret having passed it up, if you do'. Furthermore she demanded a daily letter – he was, after all, the centre of her existence: 'You in my trouble have been able to pay me for all the care & anxiety I have had for you since you came to me nearly eighteen years ago – I am expecting great things of you.'[12] Harold expected great things of himself. He was in earnest about his life and was the first to tell his father so when he struggled to reassure him about the steps he had taken. Preparing for what he was convinced would be 'a fine life' he told CA 'that I have powers, which, if correctly balanced, will enable me to mount to extraordinary latitudes'.[13] Less effusive than his wife and less confident than his son, the elder Crane waited and wondered, distracted as he was by impending business trips to Kansas City and Denver.

On 17 January he admitted to disappointment that Harold had not written him more often and the following day he demanded a summary of his son's plans and ambitions and an idea of the budget needed to pay for them. If he was forthright, he was also affectionate and dependable and promised, 'I want you to have good food, and a good room, and if you will set your mark on what it will cost you to do this, and follow for a little while your inclinations, I will try and do the needful.'[14] He wrote again on 20 January, enclosing $25. He was still determined to resolve the matter of Harold's future, even though he knew his son was 'supersensitive' and could often misconstrue advice and opinions. Despite Harold's promises that he was about to embark on studies of Latin, German and French, CA remained uneasy. He had 'no other interest in life than to see you map out your career along good and consistent lines' but surely Harold did not need to be in New York to continue private study? He had left Cleveland promising he would secure a temporary magazine job but now it appeared that that ambition had been jettisoned. 'As long as I am living and fairly prosperous, you can have an allowance which will be adequate for your needs', he wrote: but Harold must endeavour to live within it. Again he requested an account of his son's activities and a projection of his ambitions. In the meantime, would he like to continue college preparation by going to summer camp at Culver Military Academy in Indiana?[15] Harold wrote to CA that same day, 20 January, admitting that he was 'abnormally sensitive' and aware of his father's 'disappointment' at his behaviour so far. It was 'a difficult time' for him now, but although he had overspent he hoped henceforth to live frugally and to avoid frivolous expense: 'My hopes are and always have been that you would not distrust me; that you would feel ... I am sincere, and am far too ambitious to be much tempted by frivolous things.' As for his daily regime, he got up at seven, breakfasted at Child's in Union Square and after a two-hour walk settled to his books. His writing was subordinate, he promised, to his studies and to the organization of his future autonomy, because 'after I am twenty I shall never ask you for a cent, because I shouldn't respect myself at that age, to be dependent'. And however matters resolved themselves, 'In the end I won't disgrace you.'[16]

Zell saw her godson in New York in January and shared CA's concern about his future. On her return to the Midwest she told him she would find a job for Harold at the *Tribune* at any time and CA duly relayed the offer to New York on 2 February. Having promised his father that 'smoking is my *only* dissipation' Harold also wrote on 2 February with further promises of good intent: he was moving to better accommodation, in West 10th Street, this time with running water in his room, and he detailed his principal expenses – board and lodging came to $12 a week and laundry was an additional dollar.[17] The likely cost of his clothing remained uncertain but 'I always want to look neat'. He was still searching for work, 'somewhere in the writing line', and signed off with advice of his own to his father: 'I hope you are following Science all the time. It is the great thing for you, and for all of us, for all that.'[18] CA sent $25 the next day. He was worried about Grace as the divorce drew near and asked Harold to write frequently to his mother. He was also working hard and on 11 February he left via Chicago for a vacation on the Pacific Coast. To cover expenses for two weeks he sent $50 and promised a similar sum in a fortnight. However, if Harold was 'in trouble, ill, or need[ed] any advice', he was to apply to Hazel Hasham.[19] Grace meanwhile was coming to terms of a sort with semi-divorced life among the expensive distractions of Palm Beach and each letter to her son contained details of her activities at the Hotel Royal Poinciana – *thés dansants* in the Coconut Grove; expeditions to the oyster beds at Lake Worth; participation in the hotel cakewalk; with every contingency requiring costly new clothes. She thought the terms of the divorce settlement parsimonious and sometimes felt very depressed. In general, however, she assured her son that 'I am optimistic about my future because it lies with you I *hope*', and she now proposed to join him in New York for an indefinite period at the end of the year.[20]

With her son as a companion, she would find much to occupy her in a city that offered numerous diversions from the European war: Efrem Zimbalist at the Metropolitan Opera House, Damrosch at the Aeolian Hall, Alma Gluck with the New York Symphony, Anna Pavlova in *The Big Show*, Geraldine Farrar in Cecil B. DeMille's *Joan the Woman* and, of course, the annual poultry show at the old Madison Square Garden, then the second-tallest structure in Manhattan. Harold himself attended concerts and plays in his first weeks in the city and saw something of two acquaintances from Ohio, David Page and Harold Thomas, who earned $9 a week in Wall Street and can only have envied a friend whose father extended an allowance nearly three times greater than their salaries and apparently on the loosest of terms. For companionship and enlightenment, Harold turned increasingly to Carl Schmitt, and the two friends ate together regularly at Strunsky's Stuyvesant Restaurant and spent hours smoking their pipes and discussing the harmonies of art and nature. The painter was a tireless mentor and insisted that Harold wrote a certain number of poems each week for him to analyse. He determined to break the poet's bad habits of prosody – his insistent end-stopping and crude metre – and compelled him to write nonsense poems, parodies of famous lyrics and alliterative exercises to test his literary strengths and reflexes. He was an enthusiastic theoretician and held that balance was cardinal to all artistic endeavour: under his influence the literary novice came to see art as something that resulted from the tensions existing between life's opposites, whether good and evil or beauty and ugliness. Schmitt admired Dante and Gerard Manley Hopkins and seems to have believed that too much education formalized and deadened the poetic spirit. Hart was only too happy to agree; he placed poetry and study on an equal footing and reassured his grandmother, 'At this stage there is no necessity to drudge, when so much awaits me in the future.'[21]

Schmitt was a Roman Catholic and introduced his protégé to the rites of an exotic church but Harold was far more interested in gaining admission to the sodality of artists and here the painter could bring about numerous introductions. He knew the poets Conrad Aiken and Ridgely Torrence, Earl Derr Biggers, another fugitive from Ohio and author of the *Charlie Chan* detective stories, Alfred Kreymborg, one of the poet-editors of *Others*, and Padraic and Mary Colum, prominent members of the expatriate Irish literary circle. The Colums knew Frank Harris, whose inventive autobiography *My Life and Loves* would presently be banned in England and America and who in the meantime exercised a claim to fame as libertine raconteur, editor of *Pearson's Magazine* and surviving witness to the lives of Oscar Wilde and his circle. Padraic Colum was convinced that Harold's débutante volume would be published within two years and undertook to write an introduction and when Harriet Moody visited New York she naturally included her young protégé in the party she gave. There were poetry readings by Vachel Lindsay and meetings to be attended at the Poetry Society of America. 'Really, as I expected, I am right in the swing,' Harold promised his mother.[22] Exalted as this circle seemed, it was not without surprises, and Earl Derr Biggers seemed particularly incongruous, as Harold relayed to Cleveland: 'I was shocked nearly off my feet by the quietness and unworldliness of his behaviour.'[23]

Perhaps he thought himself sophisticated by comparison, but to others Harold seemed painfully gauche and vulnerable. He became especially attached to Mary Colum, 'a dear, red-haired, cultured Irishwoman', and willingly helped her with housework or with the preparation of tea and scones.[24] She recalled that he appeared once late at night specially to discuss Yeats's friend Arthur Symons and discovered that he had subsequently immersed himself in Symons's book in the 42nd Street library. His combined literary earnestness and shyness led her to conclude that 'he seemed to have no sense of humour' and she thought that 'he was psychologically, though perhaps not emotionally, so involved with his mother that he doubted if he could ever pull himself free of her'. Harold marvelled at the extent of the Colums' literary knowledge and they marvelled at the limitations of his sophistication: even as they dazzled him by reciting French poetry, they wondered at his alien speech – ' "Have you ever read Bodderlaire or Rimbodd?" he would ask with his queer pronunciation.' Harold may have been awkward, but he certainly had no shyness when it came to reading his latest compositions aloud to his new friends. Mrs Colum heard nothing of genius in his callow lines but liked him nevertheless. She had always been attracted to those 'who regarded writing as an art and who took no interest in the fabulously paid magazine writers of the period' and the 'gangling, semiliterate youth' before her was an extreme case of this literary fastidiousness: 'That such a one could have a subtle sense of the art of poetry and be so determined to become a poet, to be willing to sacrifice so much and with such little encouragement to write poetry, was very surprising.'[25]

Welcoming as they were, the Colums could scarcely entertain Harold all the time and often he was acutely lonely. He had taken to visiting Joseph Kling at the offices of the *Pagan*, not least in the hope of persuading the editor to accept more of his poems, and although Kling never objected to the visits he had work to do and sensed the adolescent's isolation, recalling later: 'I felt sorry for him. He'd come in and hang around the office half the day. He never had anything to do.'[26] Even the loyal Schmitt had other claims on his time and because Harold – never suspecting those commitments – had gradually lengthened the duration of his visits until they now occupied much of the day, the painter had taken to locking his door. At first Harold assumed his friend was out when he called but one day, bearing a potted Easter lily in thanks for Schmitt's support and counsel, he heard a footfall behind the locked door and realized his exclusion. Deeply wounded and embarrassed he deposited the lily and left; the friendship was never the same again. When Schmitt finally opened his door he was profoundly unsettled: 'There sat the lonely plant,' he remembered. 'It troubled me for years.'[27]

Thrown back on his own resources Harold attended concerts and exhibitions alone, read in the 42nd Street library and explored New York. One Sunday he went by omnibus to the Bronx and returned home via Fifth Avenue, reporting to Grace: '[New York] is the most gorgeous city imaginable, besides being at present the richest and most active place in the world. The swarms of humanity of all classes inspire the most diverse of feelings ; envy, hate, admiration and repulsion.'[28] He was working on a new poem, 'The Hive', which addressed the pain of solitude in a metropolis, where 'Humanity pecks, claws, sobs, and climbs' up the walls 'of my bleeding heart'. In art, this isolation matured into 'Mercy, white milk, and honey, gold love'.[29] In life, however, Harold was grateful for his mother. Though demanding, capricious and impossible, she was also constant; and if she could not recite French poetry she needed him more than anyone else appeared to do. As he confessed to her on 22 February, he became 'terribly lonesome' in the evenings and if they were no longer under one roof their emotional contract remained paramount:

> Mother, you do not appreciate how much I love you. I can tell by your letters that there exists a slight undercurrent of doubt, and I do not want it there. If you could know how I long to see you perhaps that might make some difference.[30]

Bored, lonely and slightly depressed herself, Grace took him at his word and announced that she would arrive in New York on 4 March. She had grown very thin and looked 'like a girl until you get a good look at my face' and needed somewhere comfortable in which she could recuperate during her stay.[31] Harold was accordingly instructed to book a quiet room at the Waldorf-Astoria.

With the divorce hearing approaching, she arrived at her favourite hotel in a state of high anxiety, convinced that CA was having her watched by private detectives. Whatever happened, Harold was on no account to divulge details of her actions or whereabouts, especially to Hazel Hasham and other employees at the Crane New York offices. Dutifully discreet, her son organized a full programme of metropolitan distraction which included shopping and cultural diversion as well as evenings with the Colums, Schmitt and Charles Brooks, a writer who had known Grace slightly before his move from Ohio to New York. Both Grace and CA repeatedly held before Harold the example of artists and writers who had made their aptitude pay and in Brooks Grace found another useful case of profitable artistry. Although born in Cleveland, he sparkled with a Yale education and supported himself as a playwright and essayist who did much of his travelling on a bicycle. *Journeys to Bagdad* had been published in 1915; further volumes of travel writing about England and Italy would appear before his death in 1934. Brooks was instrumental in the establishment in 1916 of the Cleveland Playhouse and – of particular fascination to Grace – he claimed kinship, as did she, with the founding Harts of Hartford, Connecticut. With this full social round, and a new interest in eurhythmics, Grace was happy until her departure, although it was ominous that on the eve of her divorce she did nothing to trim her expenditure in accordance with her less expansive means. Worse still, she involved Harold in extravagance he could hardly sustain and because he could think of no other way of paying for her pleasures, especially when he was under oath not to mention her whereabouts to his father, he took to borrowing money from the Crane offices and succeeded in extracting $168 before his scheme was discovered. CA furiously demanded that his son return to Cleveland forthwith but as soon as Grace had left Harold replied to his father on 23 March to explain that his return to Ohio was impossible: he had begun tuition for the summer course at Columbia and continued residence in New York was essential. There was no time to waste – 'I shall have to cram day and night to attain the examinations.'[32]

In Ohio Grace consulted John Sullivan about Harold's position and the lawyer conveniently endorsed the feelings of mother and son, that Harold would do better to pursue his education in New York. She herself was now determined to move to the city as soon as possible and was increasingly dissatisfied with Cleveland, where 'people look too fat & slow & sleepy'.[33] The nearer the divorce approached, and the more she saw her destiny as fused with Harold's, the happier she felt about his Manhattan life: 'I was impressed very strongly with the thought that you are a child of fortune after all, to be thrown so easily into the society of the people that you wish to know ... You are a brave soul my boy & that fact will carry you to success.'[34] More surprisingly, CA relented yet again and on 29 March sent Harold a sweet and reasonable letter explaining why not even the chairman's son could take cash from an incorporated company. Again he appealed to Harold for frankness in financial matters: 'My dear boy, if I am to be in every sense a father to you, as I want to be, I want you to take me into your confidences.' He continued to feel sceptical about Harold's chosen course of preparation for Columbia among the distractions of New York, but 'I am willing to be surprised'.[35] That month, a further good omen blossomed for the appeasement of his parents. The *Pagan* published 'The Hive' and in East 115th Street Grace and Mrs Hart executed a few eurythmic steps in celebration. Grace had only one criticism. 'In signing your name to your contributions & later to your books do you intend to ignore your mother's side of the house entirely[?]' She felt his matronymic should appear somewhere in his signature, unless he subscribed to the Cranes' claim that all his literary gifts were inherited from them. 'If you feel that way leave "Hart" out – but if not, now is the time to fix it right. How would "Hart Crane" be[?] No partiality there. You see I am already jealous, which is a sure sign I believe in your success.'[36]

Thus, his irreconcilable parents, soon to be divided, found themselves fused eternally in the name their son now adopted. CA was not particularly pleased by the decision, but when he wrote to Hart on 4 April it was with reassuring news. The previous evening Grace had summoned him by telephone to a discussion at East 115th Street and although at first he had been reluctant to see her, bearing in mind their awkward legal limbo, he had in the end been reassured. 'We talked only of you, and I have gotten . . . a much better idea of what you are trying to accomplish.' Although he and Grace were about to be legally parted, 'Our ownership in you is the strong rope that will always bind us together.' Both parents were prepared to make any sacrifice to enable Hart to fulfil his ambitions and 'both of us have felt that you will come up to our expectations'. Regarding the divorce, CA's position was less clear. He was sure Grace was right to continue with the severance – 'if she goes ahead it will be the best thing that has ever happened to us' – but seemed to imply that once it was completed he wanted to go on seeing his former wife: 'Conditions have made the past few months very cruel for both of us, but there is only one way to get the dross out of our lives, and that is to stand facing each other, bound by no ties, and only the inclination to make life a success and perhaps a desire to do it together.'[37]

Hart sent CA another budget on 7 April that set weekly expenses at approximately $25: 'The tutoring comes to 6 dollars; the board 6 dollars; food that is decent amounts to nearly eleven dollars ; laundry comes to about 1.50, and then there is carfare, paper, stamps and a hundred lesser things. Of course clothes vary.' He was working six hours a day, though whether at his books or at his poems he failed to specify, and was hopeful that 'within a year' he would be published in *Scribner's, Harper's* or the *Century*. He was determined to accomplish 'what I am sure is my life-work' and his destiny shone clearly before him: 'I shall really without doubt be one of the foremost poets in America if I am enabled to devote enough time to my art.'[38] He sent more recent poems to *Others,* only to learn by reply from William Carlos Williams that the magazine was suspended owing to insolvency. However, Williams promised he would one day appear in an edition dedicated to the writing of newcomers and assured him, 'I like your things very much'.[39] Hart made a quick trip to Cleveland to assist his mother and grandmother in preparing for the move to New York and to collect some of his books. An employee at the Crane factory glimpsed the owner's son and was struck by the likeness between the two Crane men:

> CA was a bull of a man. He was big, heavy set, and he knew what he was after. Harold always thought he and his father were worlds apart, but you had only to see the two of them together to know they were father and son. And they both had the same sort of intensity, the same sort of drive; and they were both passionate men. With CA it was business and women. With Harold it was poetry and men. But it came to the same thing.[40]

In fact Hart and his father did not get on particularly well during the visit but the latter pleaded after Hart had gone back to New York, 'I am sure that our interests will be found to be mutual if we properly diagnose the case.'[41]

On 6 April 1917 the United States declared war on the Central Powers and on the 14th the Cranes' divorce was made final. Hart could have been talking about the latter when he confided to his father that 'the war has set such a turmoil in my head, that I am not sure just where I am standing, or am going in the future to stand'.[42] CA sent a suit and some new ties to his son and on 16 April dispatched words of comfort: Hart should not worry about the war and if their country needed them they would go together. The younger Crane continued to feel wretched, however, despite attempting to find comfort and reassurance over dinner with Hazel Hasham, and when he wrote to his father again on 17 April he was grandiose in disillusion:

> I've seen far too much of the world to ever go back to my old delusions and ideals, but I shall try and be contented with a sort of grotesqueness which is after all the world's true demeanor. I think it is really a good thing to have arrived at this outlook for afterwards you are more able to face reality, and nothing affects one much. I suppose C[hristian] S[cience] does this, only in a much more saintly fashion.[43]

In the immediate aftermath of the divorce Hart's gloom appeared ill-founded: CA was convinced that he and his former wife were henceforth going to be the best of friends and was delighted that Grace now telephoned him daily. But on 27 April Hart told CA he was anxious because his mother had fallen completely silent and on 28 April CA wrote with an explanation. A few evenings previously she had asked him to visit her and when he refused 'she became provoked and declared that it was the last time she would ever make a request of me'. CA was now of the opinion that continued contact between his former wife and himself was inadvisable; furthermore, Grace 'has to get her mental house in order'.[44]

This ominous pronouncement boded ill for the latter's stay in New York, where she arrived with Mrs Hart at the beginning of May. To make matters worse, accommodation still had to be arranged and it was only in the second week of May, after a dispiriting search in wet weather, that Hart and his mother found an apartment to their liking, at 44 Gramercy Park. Situated in what was then one of Manhattan's most exclusive enclaves, the accommodation was expensive and Grace and her mother had to share the bedroom while Hart slept on the couch. There was one bathroom and what Hart called a 'kitchenette'.[45] Nevertheless the new occupants had a telephone – Gramercy 2887 – and the tenancy gave them access to the garden square, no inconsiderable luxury in New York's torrid summer.

For a while Grace rallied and it was CA's turn to feel gloomy. On 5 May Hart warned his father that the New York confectioners had repackaged their commodities in an effort to sustain sales: boxes of chocolates now sported pictures of Washington and Lincoln and red, white and blue ribbon. 'If the candymakers are to live at all now, they have GOT to be patriotic,' he counselled his father.[46] But the onset of war, coupled with the melancholy – and the expense – of divorce, had filled CA with gloom and he could see no hope of profit in a belligerent economy. Production at his factory had already decreased, in Chicago recently he had never seen Marshall Field's so empty, and 'if it was not for the luncheons that I buy at my own store, I think there would be no use to keep it open'. Nevertheless the Crane Company was introducing more patriotic packaging and although for the duration of the war everyone would find it more difficult to survive, 'what would this life be if there wasn't some striving in it [?]' As for their new domestic circumstances, 'We can all forget the past, so far as the unpleasantness is concerned, and strive to keep our thoughts for each other in the right channels.'[47] But what were those channels? On 15 May, without consulting Hart, Grace cabled CA in Cleveland: 'Must see you this week either here or in Cleveland wire me immediately.'[48] CA felt he could not comply and Sullivan agreed: there was nothing to be gained by contact and as he explained to Hart he could not come to New York in the near future either. As for the financial difficulties Hart and his mother had already brought upon themselves by their extravagance, CA could not be reproached: he had indicated that he would pay half the rent on any accommodation Grace and Hart shared and they would have to try and budget accordingly. He was now allowing his son $1,680 annually, 'much more than anyone in my employ outside of Ervin [Shoot, his principal chocolate maker] and Miss Hasham, and it is yours for the development of your education and under such conditions as I have never known before'. Taking into account the alimony he owed Grace, and interest on debts incurred in recent company expansion, he was over-extended and had had to borrow more in order to pay the New York bills. His two years at Allegheny College had cost less than Hart spent in a year. He did not begrudge the cost, 'only I want you to know that your father is doing it because of his affection for you and not because any Court would grant you such an allowance under such conditions as exist'.[49]

Aware that Grace was confused about their finances, Hart showed her CA's letter and, as he informed the latter, 'its tone wounded Mother a good deal, [but] that was probably planned anyway'. Pointing out that it was already very warm in New York he admitted to having taken $10 that morning from the Crane office in order to buy a straw hat, a cap and some low shoes. He and Grace were happy together and he would be glad to see his father, but he wanted him to know the extent of his resentment as their pawn and victim:

> [I] do ask you to be a little considerate of me, and realize that I have suffered a good deal – more than anyone of my age whom I know, and I think that I deserve to have a little consideration and allowance in the measurement, estimation and treatment, which perhaps would be rightfully denied to others who have had a little happiness during their younger years. You know, poverty and obligations thrust on the shoulders of a child are not the only hardships which may warp and deform and sadden. I do not want you to do for me anymore than you have planned, but I do want you to remember that I have suffered terribly, and am an old man before twenty. So please do not regard everything that you do for me as unprecedented, and 'unheard-of'. If it is 'unheard-of', it has been caused by things almost as rarely heard of.[50]

The *Pagan* took two more poems, 'Annunciations' and 'Fear', which betrayed a familiarity with the early poetry of T.S. Eliot, and Hart continued his studies under his mother's distracted supervision. Columbia required proficiency in algebra and American history, but since languages were his weakest field Hart chose his French tutor with care. Ever eager to present himself as frugal to his money-minded father, he announced that he had engaged Monsieur Tardy at an additional $2 a week – 'I went to Brentanoes and got a clerk there to do it twice as cheap as anyone at Columbia would.'[51] All his life he would remain incurably monolingual – but algebra was the immediate worry, since he faced a preliminary examination in the middle of June. Yet in some ways university entrance seemed superfluous to the times and he told CA that he had heard large contingents of undergraduates from Dartmouth, Yale and Harvard had abandoned their studies to enlist. Union Square was now dominated by an astonishing recruitment device – a battleship complete with crew which washed down decks and practised signalling, all at a cost, Hart understood, in excess of $15,000 – and there had been protests and street brawls against conscription. The young aesthete knew where his loyalties lay, however: 'I claim it treason to talk anti-conscription now, and time to take things seriously. The war is bound to be hard and long, and if we are slow in our response, we may have to fight single-handed, for if the truth were published, we would find that France and England are fearfully low, and are nearly finished.'[52]

CA meanwhile was bracing himself for wartime taxes and rationing and dreaded the effect they would have on his business. Fortunately, the Crane 'Patriotic Package' had been well received and the company was about to introduce two new selections, 'The Egypt' and 'The Patrician'. Furthermore Maxfield Parrish had recently paid a surprise visit and the two men had gone together to Akron, Ohio, to inspect the house of the rubber king, Mr Seiberling. The prosperity apparent in the town had inspired CA and by the middle of the summer he was convinced it was the next place to open a store. Hart agreed: 'Akron people have money, owing to the main business there, even in war-times, and perhaps more then, for the auto-tires are now so much in demand abroad.'[53]

Feeling that Grace was satisfactorily settled, Mrs Hart returned to Cleveland. Zell was in New York for part of the summer but Grace preferred the companionship of Charles Brooks and his wife Minerva and their friend Mrs Spencer, also formerly from Cleveland and a fervent Christian Scientist. Hart's dealings with Brooks and his wife were amicable, although the Ivy League belletrist remained suave in the face of the young poet's defences of new verse, and he was on good terms with Mrs Spencer. Much more significant, however, was the friendship he now forged with her daughter, Claire, his first close adult female friend. While Grace, Mrs Spencer and Mrs Brook reviewed the lessons of their church, Hart and Claire took long walks in the hot summer nights and discovered a shared aversion to Cleveland and a shared interest in literature. She later became a novelist and already had the makings of a devotee of psychoanalysis and in Hart – with his soaring ambition, his awkward public manner, his endless minor illnesses, his half-orphaned condition and his oscillations of mood – she found much food for thought. The evening walks would frequently end at Churchill's, a Village restaurant they both liked, and here she was able to pursue her investigations into his inner workings. Afterwards they often went dancing and she remembered: 'He always wore sailor trousers then as he liked the way they flared out at the bottom as he danced.'[54] She took a quick dislike to Grace, who seemed to her 'a silly vain woman', forever 'either weeping or flirting' and playing 'on his affection all the time'. She was indeed 'a vampire as far as he was concerned', yet 'no matter how upset he used to get about her, he always seemed to have a curious admiration for her'. He was 'starved for confidence' and both his parents seemed culpable: 'I always felt that all faith in himself as a poet or a person had been so shaken by his Mother ... and then by his Father's treatment of him, that it almost paralyzed him at times.' Above all, however, 'he was definitely in love with his Mother'.[55]

Claire was able to observe Grace's behaviour at first hand but she drew her conclusions about Clarence Crane from his son, and it appears from her assessment that Hart had already begun the broadcasting of hostile opinion about his father which most of his friends were sooner or later to hear. Yet even as she listened to these accounts of paternal tyranny, Hart and his father were happily exchanging letters about the numerous sicknesses they shared in the summer months: coughing, sneezing, rose fever, hay fever and problems with eyes, head and neck. CA had taken his medical problems to orthodox practitioners as well as to Christian Scientists, and as the summer progressed he decided to contravene his lawyer's advice and renew correspondence with his former wife. Grace had written a friendly letter to CA on 7 July and three days later he replied, informing her of his health problems and his determination to extend the Crane business into Akron and Kansas City. He was delighted to have heard from her because more than anything he wanted them to become good friends – although his definition of good friendship was ardent and bizarre: 'If out of all this curtain fire of trouble we can emerge, seeing the best in each other and blinded to the mistakes and hasty utterances, I shall have much satisfaction and confidence that perhaps life is really worth living.'[56]

Grace and Hart had their picture taken by a Broadway photographer and sent a copy to CA and with the imminence of Hart's eighteenth birthday his mother found herself with a perfect pretext for writing her former husband a long letter which addressed not only Hart's virtues but also, more indirectly, the yoked careers of his parents. She reminded CA of 'what a fine son you have' and predicted the success of his ambitions. 'Of course he has his faults, but in most instances I recognize that they are only reproductions of yours and mine.' She had stayed in New York to study Hart, to rectify such wrong ideas as she encountered and to atone 'for my share of the unhappiness which has come into his young life'. A happy bond between father and son 'will be one of the most satisfying forces that can come into your lives' and whether they liked it or not she and CA were involved for ever, not least through their son: 'For after all, one's greatest and surest claim to posterity is through one's children, and I feel that whatever mistakes you and I may have made, Harold was not one of them.'[57] CA sent his son birthday greetings on 20 July and enclosed 'the price of two good dinners, and I hope that you and mother will find some quiet retreat and celebrate the occasion'.[58] He was benign and apparently more satisfied with the New York venture than before, not least because he suspected that distance suited his dealings with Grace: matters had not been so amicable between them since their impetuous courtship and now that they were divorced she might as well live in New York as anywhere else, especially if by so doing she was able to superintend the education which would so crucially strengthen his son's future. For reasons that remain obscure, however, Grace appears to have misinterpreted CA's responses and to have decided that his well-intentioned remarks implied a longing for new proximity. So towards the end of July, ostensibly to visit Mrs Hart, she returned to Cleveland with her son and to what she appears to have seen as the unfinished business of her marriage.

4

The details of the crucial ten days that followed Grace's return to Cleveland are irrecoverable. The Cranes' marriage, like every other, remains mysterious to outsiders and the eavesdropping facilitated by surviving correspondence is no longer possible when, as happened at the end of July, the members of the family were once more together. However happily the three were reunited, it seems that relations soon deteriorated, that CA and Grace quarrelled badly and that Hart was back in New York alone by 1 August, having told his parents, as he later indicated, that he 'was through' with them both.[1] The catalyst to the disagreement remains unclear – though Hart's future and its attendant costs could have been involved – but the larger Crane family in Cleveland felt convinced that the real difficulty lay with Grace's pressing hopes of remarriage to her former husband. CA never described the drama in any later correspondence so his position is hard to establish but there is no suggestion in any of his extant letters that he either desired or foresaw this remarriage. Throughout, his hopes seem to have been for friendly, indeed warm, relations with his former wife but nothing more. No letters from Hart survive either to indicate a belief that his parents could or should remarry. Grace, by contrast, was sufficiently sure of events to catalogue them in a letter she drafted to CA some weeks later. Whether or not the letter was ever sent, it expressed her hope that it would be 'my last communication to you for quite some time'. And the reasons for her animosity remained vivid in her mind:

When I was last [in Cleveland] you made a spectacle of me and yourself before the neighborhood, my family, our son, and our mutual friends, and after forcing your attention and devotion upon me until I forgave you every confession of wrong you voluntarily made me and all past wrongs, at your own repeated requests I consented to once more become your wife. As you well know, we painted a beautiful picture of our future together, in which all mistakes of the past were to be avoided, Harold made happy and successful through our united efforts, and love of the highest order for you and me. All of this would have been possible and just as it should have been, but just at this point you chose to change your mind, leaving me with nothing but a cruel, hard note telling me of your departure and a request to forget you.[2]

Perhaps Grace's account was accurate, but no documentation surviving from Harts or Cranes or miscellaneous extras to the drama endorses her story. In any case, whether or not CA led her on or whether she merely imagined that he did, what is certain is that a few days later Grace attempted suicide by swallowing a near-fatal quantity of bichloride of mercury.[3] CA's aunt Alma Crane, who had assisted eighteen turbulent years before at Grace's confinement, now stepped in to tend the patient and to be counted on not only as a woman with nursing experience but also as a family member inclined to discretion. Having been spared a death, the families were certainly eager to be spared a scandal and garrulous nurses were to be avoided where possible. Mrs Hart's reactions to the episode, like her reactions to Frank Hart's untimely decease can only be surmised while CA, in successive bulletins to his son, made only oblique references to the drama. Thus, writing to Hart on 1 August and promising that 'you are the only treasure I have on God's green earth', CA informed his son that 'your mother called me up this morning, and seems to have spent a very comfortable night, and is in a good frame of mind'.[4] On 4 August he reported again: 'Your mother had a very bad spell the other night, and Dr Lytle and myself were out at the house until four o'clock in the morning.' Imprecise as he was, Crane keenly registered the anxiety of the situation: 'I think before very long you will hear of your father as residing in a cave, secure from the approach of all human kind. There doesn't seem to be any way out of my multitudinous troubles.'[5]

Hart too was extremely unsettled and told his father on 8 August that he had been 'diabolically nervous ever since that shock out at the house' – the shock, one assumes, of discovering that his mother's extremity equalled his own at the time he attempted suicide on the Isle of Pines. He was 'very, very sorry that things are going so badly' with Grace, had heard nothing from her regarding her condition and hoped that his parents were avoiding 'any meetings as much as possible ... she is not yet established well enough to endure the strain which you know any contact causes'.[6] In his letter to Hart written the same day CA stressed that Grace knew nothing of the correspondence that passed between them regarding her convalescence but was at least able to report that she appeared to be improving and that 'we have been out nearly every evening for a little ride'.[7] On 10 August she was 'a little bit downcast' but CA still hoped she would soon be able to return to New York and knew that he could depend on Hart's ministrations when she did: 'It is a great thing to have a boy, and I can never tell you how much I appreciate your devotion and interest in her.'[8] The following day he reported another 'sick spell' but gave assurance that Grace was 'now nicely on the mend'.[9]

By then, however, the weight of stress had overwhelmed Hart, distant though he was in New York, and on 15 August he cabled his father: SICK IN BED LAST FOUR DAYS WHY NO EXPLANATION OR WORD FROM ANY OF YOU.[10] CA cabled by return that Grace's continuing crisis and his own work claimed all his time, and it was only on 20 August that he found the opportunity to send his highly strung son a little timely reassurance: 'You have got a dad who thinks the world of you, and my determination to never again awaken the past only intensifies my interest and my devotion to you.'[11] And the following day, feeling that matters had stabilized sufficiently for him to take a vacation, CA sent Grace a brief letter acknowledging her plans to return to New York and indicating that he was avoiding seeing her only because he wanted to avoid upsetting her. Possibly written in the haste of imminent departure, his letter was perhaps a little brief but was far from being unkind. 'Pluck wins,' he reminded her, 'wins everything', and her best hope lay with forgetting that 'C.A. Crane does or ever did *live*'. Every street had its sunny side and 'You're due to cross *over*'.[12]

Grace returned to New York under the supervision of the stalwart Mrs Hart and CA went on vacation and then business to Denver, Kansas City and Chicago. He suffered from hay fever in the course of his travels and later remarked that he was in general 'just as nervous as ever' but life was little easier at Gramercy Square.[13] Grace's mood on emergence from her prostration was one of determined forgiveness, possibly inspired by Mrs Hart's reminders of Christian Science, but there was no saying how long such a tendency would last and for Hart the strain of the uncertainty, and of shouldering 'the curse of sundered parentage', as he later put it, was immense.[14] But if Grace's tranquil condition was to be prolonged and his own emotional welfare considered, it was vital, as Hart explained to his father on 18 September, that in all future communications CA should try and keep to himself all thoughts of Grace except those which were amicable. Although their son had 'seen more tears than I ever expected in this world', his heart was 'still as responsive to both your loves, and more so, than ever'. So all he could do was to entreat CA 'not [to] make the present too hard – too painful for one whose fatal weakness is to love two unfortunate people, by writing barbed words'.[15] The next day CA replied, conceding that his exhausted state might have led him to ambiguous expression of his feelings but nevertheless promising warm thoughts towards his former wife and his son. But the past could not be reinvented and his course was clear: 'We must both of us tread our separate paths.'[16] Once again Hart foolishly showed his mother a letter better kept private and at a stroke destroyed her hard-won equanimity. It was then that she drafted her grand remonstrance, in which she catalogued CA's transgressions as she saw them and assured him: 'The door between your life and mine is closed, locked and the key thrown away.' If only matters had been that simple: the connection between their two lives was with her under the same roof: eighteen, financially dependent, vulnerable, sensitive, idealistic, sexually bewildered and entirely without rocks of purchase in any world except the literary.

The protracted war between the Cranes is profoundly tedious but its effect on the volatile optimist who struggled to reach the sun between them cannot be overestimated and for the rest of his life Hart Crane would refer to his parents' difficulties as one of the principal blighting forces in his life. Yet if he had been able to share these difficulties with siblings there would have been a reduction in the pressure that produced the poetry – or at least his particular kind of poetry, with its distinctive yearnings for erotic and emotional resolution and its charged tone of wonder, so revealing of the awed child Hart Crane in some ways never left behind. Grace returned to Cleveland where she apparently found the town alive with rumours – and whatever their details they were sufficiently annoying for her, and for Hart when she described them, for him to tell his mother on 28 September that he found it 'hard to express my rage and disgust at what you say concerning C.A. Crane'. He was 'too low for consideration' and Hart now knew suddenly but definitely where his loyalties lay: 'You have all my love.'[17] Grace attempted to find some distraction from her woes in swimming lessons, facial treatments and redecoration of her house, but as she confessed to her son, the moment she was idle the familiar longings overcame her: 'My love for [CA] is not the kind to leave when bidden, but unless he can feel different and treat me as I feel I should be treated I never wish to see him again.'[18]

The tenancy at Gramercy Park expired; the actress Eva Le Gallienne moved into Hart's old apartment and he took a room in a lodging house at 25 East 11th Street run by Mrs Frances Walton and continued his studies, albeit in increasingly unconvincing fashion. His French tutor, Monsieur Tardy, had been dismissed because he had only been able to offer lessons at what Hart told Grace was 'the inconvenient hour of seven P.M.'[19] It was a strange objection from a pupil with a diary officially unencumbered but finding a replacement at least proved easy: Mme Eugénie Lebègue was a fellow tenant at the lodging, and Hart was delighted to discover that she could teach French literature as well as language. Mrs Walton took a motherly interest in her young tenant and suggested, on learning of his literary aspirations, that he try his hand at writing stories for films. She had friends in the film world in New York, then the largest in America, and knew that a prolific industry suffered from a chronic shortage of new stories. Sadly he had no aptitude for this potentially lucrative work but that discovery came slowly. In the meantime he mentioned the idea to Grace, who assured him that if Mrs Walton could get work in films for her – obviously in front of the cameras rather than behind – she would travel to New York overnight. He continued to attempt other fiction: short stories for *Smart Set*, a magazine of self-conscious cosmopolitan sophistication edited by H.L. Mencken and George Jean Nathan, and a novel, set on the Isle of Pines and involving a New York society maiden and a hero based on Walter Wilcox, the handsome manager of Mrs Hart's plantation.

Although all these ventures were stillborn, Hart was beginning to make a name for himself as a poet. Shortly after Grace's departure he had met Maxwell

Bodenheim, a slightly older poet and critic already prominent in the Village, and had been delighted when Bodenheim praised his work and reassured him that editors were only difficult because they were themselves failed writers. He had survived years of neglect himself before receiving any recognition and undertook to spare Hart that frustration by taking some of his most recent lyrics to his friend James Oppenheim at *Seven Arts*. Joseph Kling continued his patronage by accepting 'Echoes' for the October number of the *Pagan*, 'The Bathers' for December and 'Modern Craft' for the following January. 'Echoes' was another exercise in Imagism and 'Modern Craft' in particular displayed a cool and ironic descriptiveness far removed from Hart's endeavours of only two years previously. Yet both were works of convention rather than conviction, since the longings they involved concerned women and it would be many years before Hart Crane could truthfully declare, 'I have touched her flesh of moons.'[20] 'The Bathers' was the most beautiful work of the three and besides indicating a growing descriptive confidence – 'The dawn, a shell's pale lining restlessly/Shimmering over a black mountain-spear' – it represents the first appearance in his work of the sea – not the cold Atlantic off New York but the tropical waters he had seen from Cuba. And already there is a fascination with its treacherous beauty, which sparkles and devours: 'Only simple ripples flaunt, and stroke, and float, – Flat lily petals to the sea's white throat.'[21] Kling had given Hart the crucial encouragement of early publication and continued to hold his young troubadour in the highest esteem, going so far as to inform the Village that he considered him the equal of any living American lyricist. But Hart knew it was time to move on and indicated as much to Carl Schmitt: 'I don't trust Kling's criticism very far judging by the "tone" generally prevalent in the magazine. But I *am* improving and would just as soon be deceived a little as not.'[22] More importantly, he knew now where he next wanted to be published.

He was, he told CA, 'quite well acquainted' with Margaret Anderson. They had first met not long after his arrival in New York and she had asked, 'Why, you are connected in some way with "Crane's Mary Garden Candy" aren't you?'[23] A flattering reference to his poetry would have been more pleasing but any recognition was welcome from a young woman already seen in the Village as a significant contributor to American literary life. Born to a prosperous but unsuspecting family in Indiana, Anderson had drifted to Chicago, as she later related, blissfully unfettered by domestic aspirations: 'I am no man's wife, no man's delightful mistress, and I will never, never be a mother.' She worked in a minor editorial capacity for *Dial* magazine as well as writing book reviews under Floyd Dell for the *Chicago Evening Post*, and through Dell's wife, who maintained a modest salon, she met many of the luminaries of the Chicago renaissance. In her insouciant autobiography, *My Thirty Years' War*, Anderson declared that all her life she was financially incapable. She was shrewd and determined, however, and when in Mrs Dell's salon inspiration called and she resolved to found a little magazine, she decided not to let economic considerations impede her. The result was the *Little Review*, established in 1914 and for much of its life one of the most important vehicles of American modernist writing. A great admirer of Nietzsche and a partisan of the avant-garde, Anderson was also by her own admission an incurable editor: 'I can't make things. I can only revise what has been made. And it is this eternal revising that has given me my nervous face.'[24]

As her magazine became established it published many of Chicago's most prominent writers – Carl Sandburg, Amy Lowell and Edgar Lee Masters – as well as sponsoring others still unknown such as H.D., Witter Bynner and Sherwood Anderson. Money was inevitably problematic and even among other little magazines – where solvency, like artistic perfection, seemed a goal as desirable as it was unobtainable – the *Little Review* became notorious for not paying its contributors. Yet it survived, defiantly impecunious and defiantly uncommercial, and when Anderson decided she must move her publication to New York early in 1917 it appeared with a newly boastful cover which proclaimed that the *Little Review* was 'Making No Compromise With The Public Taste'. Not long before the magazine moved it had seen its prestige fortified by Ezra Pound, who defected from Harriet Monroe's magazine *Poetry* to search for new European writing for Anderson instead, and it was thanks to his transatlantic vigil that the *Little Review* was able to publish important new work by T.S. Eliot, W.B. Yeats, Wyndham Lewis and Ford Madox Ford, as well as making literary history with serial publication of James Joyce's *Ulysses*. Not all the magazine's triumphs were Pound's work, however. Anderson was pretty and persuasive and men found it hard to turn her down. So did women: for a while she was very thick with the celebrated anarchist Emma Goldman and for much of the *Little Review*'s life she was in partnership in more ways than one with her fellow editor Jane Heap. Heap, the 'jh' of editorials, favoured tailored clothes and severely bobbed hair while Anderson preferred a feminine stylishness which led the young writer Malcolm Cowley to assume she was 'the woman of the couple'.[25] Whatever its inner workings the partnership between the two women eventually dissolved: at the end of the 1920s Anderson moved to France and later in life, for more than twenty years, she lived with the former wife of the Belgian Symbolist poet and dramatist Count Maeterlinck.

The *Little Review*'s first New York office was at 31 West 14th Street but the publication finally settled at 24 West 16th Street in a brownstone formerly inhabited by the poet William Cullen Bryant and here the women contrived one of the most famous salons in Village lore, where writers were succoured and provoked amidst Chinese wallpaper, cream woodwork, purple floors, Victorian mahogany and a large divan depending by heavy chains from the ceiling. Owing to their straitened circumstances Heap and Anderson were obliged to involve themselves with many of the mundane aspects of their magazine's production and were known to spend days with their printer, Mr Popovitch, the cheapest at his trade in all New York and son of a poetess laureate of Serbia. Nevertheless the *Little Review* enjoyed a reputation unmatched by any other literary magazine in New York, and Hart was naturally elated to meet Anderson and fascinated to learn that she and Heap knew all about his Mary Garden connection because they had published an essay on the singer in the March 1917 issue and had applied, unsuccessfully, to CA in the hope that he would replenish their funds with a little timely advertising. Eager not only to assist the cause of literature but also to appear in one of its most prestigious publications, Hart pondered and schemed, and wondered if Anderson's famous appetite for chocolate could be turned to the advantage of his new poem, 'North Labrador', which was so far homeless. He took to calling on the women as part of his campaign but found them marvellously inaccessible and reported to Joseph Kling: 'I go up there day after day. But the door is always locked. What do those women *do* in there?'[26]

It was a matter for some Village speculation, but besides decorating and eating such confectionery as they could afford the two editresses did contemplate their newest supplicant and the three quatrains of 'North Labrador', which addressed a continent as unknown to the poet as the female anatomy, a land 'of leaning ice' where there was 'No birth, no death, no time nor sun', a land of deathly immutability which chilled the poet to comtemplate, for without change there could be no life, and without life there could be no poetry. The women deliberated, only to reject: Anderson, with a cavalier disregard for geography, found the poem to contain 'a vague reference to the immaculate white ice of Norway' while Heap faulted the word 'immaculate' itself, which she felt made the ice 'so white it looks black.'[27] Capricious as these verdicts seemed there was no appeal and Hart confided to his father that following the rejection he was 'inconsolable for three days'.[28] He had after all been convinced that Anderson 'likes my work and thinks there is much promise in it'.[29] CA offered such sympathy as he could. He had been following his son's poetic endeavours in the *Pagan*, but though eager to praise and encourage he doubted his own judgement, to say nothing of modern literary thinking. He disliked Kling's magazine for a start – 'there are certain things in it that one would hesitate to say in polite society to say nothing about putting in black and white' – and was bewildered by Hart's work: 'You must excuse your father if he does not always get the drift of your poetical productions. My reading has always been of a very light nature and while I would not be willing to say that it was only "trash" that interested me, I presume that is really the case.' As for his son's designs on the *Little Review*, it was certainly better than the *Pagan*, but 'I would fail to classify it exactly as you do – "the finest in the world" '.[30]

In fact Anderson was not the enthusiast Hart had supposed and later recalled: 'I was never a great fan of his poetry, and ... our discussions were mostly on this prejudice of mine.'[31] There were many heated exchanges and Hart would 'sometimes leave us in fury'.[32] But he was determined to penetrate this particular ivory tower, determined to be seen among its illustrious company of contributors, and further offerings of Crane Chocolate, combined with a poetic aptitude in strong and daily evolution, soon proved irresistible. He submitted a new lyric, 'In Shadow', yet another oblique meditation about an involvement with a woman which had left its speaker regretful and dissatisfied, but now written with more controlled harmonies than anything he had previously attempted, and this time the *Little Review* capitulated. The poem was 'the best you've sent yet: I'll tell you details of just why when you come,' Anderson promised, announcing that the work would appear in the December issue of the magazine.[33] In September, convinced that 'North Labrador' was about to appear in the *Little Review*, he had told Grace that 'success seems imminent now more than ever', which was why Anderson's eventual rejection had been so disappointing.[34] Now, however, he was exalted to membership of a distinguished group of writers and intellectuals; now he was one step nearer to being seen as a great poet. In London Ezra Pound read 'In Shadow' in the *Little Review* and disapproved, perhaps annoyed that any literary magazine appeared to be capable of making discoveries of its own. In February 1918 he dispatched succinct advice to Anderson regarding Crane: 'Don't publish him.'[35] And to the young poet himself he sent what he termed an 'Easter Sonnet' advising him in future to send his work to 'that consummate milk pudding *milieu* Contemporary Verse'. The fact was that 'beauty is a good enough egg, but so far as I can see, you haven't the ghost of a setting hen or an incubator'.[36] But Hart was delighted: a man may be judged by the stature of his detractors and as far as he was concerned Pound's damnation outweighed the approbation of lesser men and poetasters.

As though it was a destiny one could simply select, Hart had determined, like Milton or Keats before him, to become a great poet and as the autumn of 1917 progressed his ambitions and his convictions tended increasingly in that direction. He was eighteen years old and forthright even with his mother about his rejection of mundane aspirations:

> Believe me when I tell you that I am fearless that I am determined on a valorous future and something of a realization of life. The smallness of hitherto large things, and the largeness of hitherto small things is dawning. I am beginning to see the hope of standing entirely alone.[37]

Heroic words – but so far premature: the valorous future included rent bills; and if Hart instinctively knew he needed to free himself from certain aspects of his parents' lives – their personal struggles, their fighting and their small-town talk – he also knew he was far from resolving the problem of financial dependence. To further complicate the difficulties of entanglement, CA and Grace varied in their respective positions regarding his future. His mother could for instance demand absolute adoration and loyalty one day and then remind him that he also owed these intangibles to his father – but only on certain terms:

> You can and should write [CA] a courteous letter giving him your address and some idea of what you are doing. As long as you receive his support, you must

do that at least and I beg of you not to be foolish and cut off your nose to spite your face. I appreciate more than I can say your loyalty to me and it comforts me in many a lonely hour ... [but] you know now what he is capable of being with one whom he proposed before every one, to love better than life. It is horrible to think such natures exist.[38]

Assured that CA was hypocritical, Hart could easily see him as such. Following Grace's advice, he wrote his father another account of daily life and money matters on 8 October, since those were subjects apparently important to paternal thinking, only to prompt a reply which seemed both critical and unsympathetic. Promising that in the course of his next visit to New York they would review the big questions of money and career CA in the meantime wanted to know what his son was doing with his time and his allowance, when he was spending only $2 a week on tuition. And why was he allocating so little, when his education was the pretext for his apparently unavoidable presence in New York? He was happy to maintain the allowance of $25 a week for the time being, 'but I do not believe in letting you go on in this way indefinitely without some thought as to where the money is coming from and whether or not it is the right course to pursue'. What about a part-time job, which would augment his income and give Hart some independence? 'This is your youth; it is the time in which you are laying the foundation for your life; and life is work and nothing but work.' How did Hart propose to earn his living? How was he ever to understand the value of money unless he started to earn some of his own now? 'Your thought and purpose must be earnestly along the lines of good useful citizenship.' His own father had insisted that he learn the value of money at an early age and the responsibilities he had quickly assumed had entailed hard work for him 'at every sunrise'. 'I have now reached an age when I think more seriously than ever before. I have gone through experiences which tell me every day that "life is earnest".'[39]

Entirely reasonable as CA's misgivings appear, one wonders at his inability to exercise paternal authority. It lay within his power to revoke his son or to impose more stringent conditions on his generosity but he seemed incapable of doing so – though whether because of the distractions of hard work or the guilt and anxiety of divorce it is impossible to say. Hart of course saw matters differently. He was indeed working very hard – there was no labour harder than the balancing of a perfect poetic line – and what were money matters in comparison to these? The problem was that whereas Grace now appeared to understand his determination to become a great poet, only CA, who seemed to think that writing was something done between other commitments, had the money to sustain him during his literary apprenticeship. Hart's ambition was grandiose and precocious; and his experience of life and emotion was in some ways ahead of that of other young men of his age. Where he fell short of his age, however, was in subtlety, tact and humility and many fathers would have found his reply of 14 October provocative and annoying in the extreme. He could not see why CA should find his living in New York impractical or unusual; as for Cleveland, 'I don't intend to live there again if I can help, and I am sure I can help it.' He had had enough of Midwestern values and asked CA not to assume 'the attitude of your Father, that is, the outlook on all questions of money that he seems to have held all his life'. He had no desire to hear about CA's finances but was certain (without explaining how) that he cost his father less now than a year previously. He felt no qualms about accepting an allowance, since he was confident that in a year or two he would no longer need it, and on the subject of money, 'Very soon you will probably be able to feel entirely free from any obligations even in the mercenary way, – to the woman who gave you the best of her life during the twenty years of her youth and womanhood.' He resented accusations of distracted self-indulgence – 'of all people to accuse of superficiality, I think I am the least deserving' – and thought it was time his father should know, if not what great poets were, exactly, or why society needed them, at least what he himself intended to do to attain that status in the next five years: 'During this time I must master a technique of writing; – read a tremendous amount, – for these are the years when I must have time for that, and must survey a great deal of the work of the masters; – and thirdly must I be in a fair way to establish a market for my own wares.'[40]

Whatever the rights and wrongs of these bargainings the financial talk between the Cranes had a deeper, almost a symbolic, significance, as it commonly does in divorced families, where money can double as a tool or a weapon or be substituted for the more time-consuming abstractions of loyalty and love. CA, the distractions of work permitting, was generous and well-intentioned but if his impulses were sound they were also undermined by ambivalence towards his former wife and by self-reproach when it came to his son, and although he had the means and the strength to ensure that Hart had a university education he was too feeble and pre-occupied to insist on it. Grace was still not reconciled to her newly single status and there seems to have been an element of vindictiveness in her behaviour, which encouraged Hart to ask his father for money while failing to remind him of CA's other financial obligations. As for Hart, divorced from financial reality as he was and convinced of the rightness of his cause, he never allowed his father to forget the sufferings he had undergone or the authorship of those wrongs. No doubt he had his frustrations and anxieties but it has to be said that he was unfair to CA who, for all his imperfections, was generous, loyal and well-meaning and far from the impatient and philistine ogre repeatedly described by the son who continued to take his money. Mary Colum remembered a story typical of those Hart used to tell, about Clarence Crane's reaction when Hart suggested he support him until he could make a living as a writer:

To [Hart's] mind, fed on literature, being a poet was a distinction to any family. To his father, poetry writing was a sissy game, and he lectured the boy in contemptuous words. 'Do you see that girl out there?' – pointing through the glass partition to a secretary in an outside office. 'She has more manliness and independence than you have.'[41]

Yet this story seriously misrepresented CA's position: he simply believed in good chocolate and the inestimable virtues of financial prudence and could not understand how his son was ever going to support himself or live within any paternally appointed stipend when he appeared so financially irresponsible. On 3 November his fears were vindicated yet again when Hart – with holes in his shoes and only a light suit against the New York winter – applied for further assistance. CA sent money and reminded him that he had 150 people to employ. To add to his worries Washington had recently announced the likelihood of wartime sugar rationing. A few days later he learned from the New York office that Hart had been drawing his allowance in advance and on 5 November he strictly forbade him to do so again and told him that $25 was his budget and that was that. He made no apologies for not sending more: most of his secretarial employees in Cleveland made only $16 a week and many of his factory boys made even less yet still managed to live and to invest in Liberty Bonds. Why could Hart not get some kind of job? With manpower in short supply, Hazel was desperate to find a delivery boy for the New York office – why would Hart not work there? Or why not take the place of a conscript at Brentano's, where his knowledge of literature would serve him well?

> These are not ordinary times, Harold; manpower is needed and it is needed in a thousand ways ... I want you to wake up to the fact that we should all be doing something, making a living, taking the place of brains and muscle that have had to go across the water to fight for liberty. Poetry is alright; your chosen vocation is alright, but when you are living in New York and spending $2 a week for tutoring, out of an allowance of $25, it is not alright; it isn't as things should be.[42]

In the course of this wrangling all talk of a career at Columbia was forgotten and although Hart's clear lack of interest was the principal reason for the change, CA as usual got the blame. As Hart explained to Schmitt, 'I must explain to you that on twenty-five dollars a week, Columbia is out of the question. That is all I am to get, – clothing and everything. While it will do for a decent living, it really is too meager for any college.'[43] What he proposed now was a year of personally directed reading – and the further wooing of the muse that would lead to greatness. But these ambitions were threatened in their turn by Grace, who indicated with increasing frequency how much she missed him and how much her existence now revolved around his. She had decided to join him in New York, and although at first Hart was inclined to deter her he began to suspect that such a course might prove dangerous and that she might succumb to further despair or self-destructiveness if opposed. It was therefore agreed that she should come to New York for Thanksgiving, stay in another room at Mrs Walton's for three weeks or so and return to Cleveland with Hart for Christmas.

In the days prior to her departure Grace's condition had been equable and continued so in New York but her overwhelming proximity was too much for her son, and he suffered what seems to have been a complete nervous collapse within days of her arrival. Although doctors could find no symptoms he was apparently extremely unwell, so unwell that Grace telephoned CA in the hope that he would come to New York to redress what she thought had the makings of an ungovernable crisis. Neither Grace nor Hart knew much about good timing and it was not an opportune moment of appeal. CA had severe laryngitis and in any case he had had no dealings with his former wife since she had taken him to court to settle certain debts; he now declared, or so she later claimed, that 'he would not come to New York even if his son were dying'. Whatever CA's true response it was too much or too little for Grace and she herself collapsed and was in bed for two days. Somehow Hart cabled his godmother Zell, who arrived to restore order, and that same day he found the strength to write a brief account of his condition to Carl Schmitt, the only confidant he could find. He was, he said, 'holding on to health and sanity with both hands'. Grace was 'in a worse state than I have ever had to cope with' and 'the hardest thing for me to bear is the blame [she] puts on me for being in a major way responsible for her present condition'. He was resigned to any course events took on Zell's arrival but the worst of the drama was its apparently chronic nature: 'This trouble will never, never end, I'm afraid, or if it does, it will be in insanity. I no longer anticipate, there is enough, it seems in the present.'[44]

Mother and son were sufficiently recovered to travel to Ohio for Christmas and Grace's hopes of reunion with CA were rekindled once again when she and Hart were invited to his New Year's Eve party and regaled as the guests of honour. They returned to New York at the beginning of 1918 but Hart began to suspect that remarriage to CA took precedence in his mother's mind over all his own hopes and welfare, and his fears appeared to be confirmed in February, when his father threatened to suspend his allowance unless he got a job, and Grace, blithely disregarding all her recent demands for loyalty, urged him to work for the Crane Company. Outraged by this apparent betrayal he turned for sympathy to Mrs Walton, who learned too late that warring families will draw all onlookers into their feuds. Grace in turn was scandalized and once again prostrate. In Cleveland Mrs Hart appealed to Mr Ely for the guidance of Christian Science and in windy letters lauded the virtues of strength and tranquillity. In New York meanwhile Mrs Spencer applied Scientific doctrine on the spot: Grace regained her composure sufficiently to be reconciled with her son and it was agreed that she should return to Cleveland and that Hart should find cheaper accommodation in New York.

Installed at 78 Washington Place he got a job in order to perpetuate his allowance, and for a while worked at Brentano's, selling books, he claimed, 'on wet nursing, care of mothers during pregnancy, the Montessori method and how to know the wild flowers'.[45] The *Pagan* published 'Modern Craft' in its January issue, and in March in confirmation of his admiration Joseph Kling made Hart an associate editor of the magazine. That month also *Bruno's Bohemia* published 'Carmen de Boheme', seven quatrains of polychrome atmospherics written two years earlier which attest to the distance Hart had travelled since his admiration for the 1890s. He had become friendly with Stanislaw Portapovitch, a member of Diaghilev's Ballet Russe who supported himself and his wife Anna by dancing from six until two every night for $100 a week at Healy's Restaurant. The Russian taught Hart the 'gotzotsky', a squatting, kicking Cossack dance with which he was later to enliven many Greenwich Village gatherings, and in so doing inspired a poem of thanks, 'To Portapovitch', an eight-line invocation to the artist to observe the duty of his brotherhood by wresting from oblivion some aspect of human existence:

Release, – dismiss the passion from your arms.
More real than life, the gestures you have spun
Haunt the blank stage with lingering alarms,
Though silent as your sandals, danced undone.[46]

The April–May issue of the *Pagan* appeared and contained an essay, 'The Case against Nietzsche', by its new associate editor, as well as two recent poems, 'Carrier Letter' (later retitled 'Exile') and 'Postscript', and a column of theatre criticism also by Hart and subscribed 'A. Pagan Knight'. One of the poet's rare excursions into politics and philosophy, the essay undertook to defend Nietzsche against the anti-Germanism then gaining momentum to such a degree that even Richard Laukhuff in distant Cleveland felt vulnerable. This new propaganda condemned Nietzsche as the herald of modern Prussianism, but Hart sought to establish Nietzsche's hostility to the centralized and ubiquitous power of the German state, to stress his Francophile literary taste and to remind his readers that the philosopher was 'a Pole in all his views and sympathies'. 'Nietzsche, Zeppelins, and poisoned-gas go ill together'; by extension it was foolish and wrong to confound an artist and his native culture. Yet perhaps there was an inevitability to the ambivalence that Nietzsche provoked – as a thinker he was allied to artists, and artists were a race apart, incomprehensible to others and inviolably enigmatic: 'One may envy Nietzsche a little; think of being so elusive, – so mercurial, as to be first swallowed whole, then coughed up, and still remain a mystery!'[47] His theatre review contained appraisals of a batch of one-act plays performed by the Other Players which included *Two Slatterns and a King* by Edna St Vincent Millay and *Manikin and Minikin* and *Jack's House* by Alfred Kreymborg, as well as Eugene

O'Neill's *Ile*, 'a picture of the silence, solitude, and desolation of northern waters', which was appearing at the Greenwich Village Theatre.[48] But it was his two newest lyrics which offered the surest index to his progress and his priorities – and both 'Carrier Letter' and 'Postscript' concern the aftermath of trysts or love affairs. The former contained one of his prettiest sea-inspired couplets to date – 'And with the day, distance again expands/Voiceless between us, as an uncoiled shell' – and the latter dwelt explicitly on the theme of emotional and amorous desolation which was one of the preoccupations of Crane's apprenticeship:

> Mine is a world foregone though not yet ended, –
> An imagined garden grey with sundered boughs
> And broken branches, wistful and unmended,
> And mist that is more constant than all vows.[49]

In one sense this was literary posturing, the sort of precocious disillusion one would expect from a poet not yet nineteen who was well versed in the Romantic tradition of forlorn love. But that was not the only school of emotions Hart had attended, nor the most arduous. From his parents, those ancient victims of passion, he knew much about love, its betrayals and its regrets: emotionally, he was old before his time while simultaneously being amorously inexperienced. Hence the irregular poetic course he pursued, in which love is mourned even before it is encountered, and in which songs of experience precede those of innocence.

In the third week of April Hart's Cleveland friend George Bryan came to stay, his brief visit offering a welcome interlude in a lonely life. After his departure Hart wrote to say that 'I haven't had as much pleasure and happiness in two years as was crammed into those few hours' and to admit that he had been 'practically starved for any happiness whatever' for many months. Loneliness was not his only problem: Bryan's visit was a relief from domestic problems: only the day before Hart had received a letter from Grace, as a result of which, he told his friend, he had 'had "the blues" nearly all day'.[50] Meanwhile he had invested $1 in a Liberty Bond and divided his time between his programme of reading and his commitments at the *Pagan*. By the end of April, however, he had begun to tire of Kling's unscheduled wanderings from the office and to indicate to Bryan his suspicions that 'the old Hebrew' was taking advantage of him. But before he could decide his future with the publication, events in Cleveland again intervened, this time with CA's dramatic announcement that he was engaged to marry Frances Kelley, a young Irish beauty who worked in the Kansas City branch of the Crane Company. Since that branch had been running for less than a year, CA's acquaintance with his future wife had been relatively short-lived. Nevertheless he appeared resolute in his plans and Hart knew when he learned of them that Grace's uncertain stability would once again be threatened.

Early in May she wrote suggesting that he return to Cleveland, if only for the summer, and offered various blandishments including free food and the use of the car she was thinking of buying. In any case, the government had ordained that in view of the war all men over the age of eighteen must find themselves useful occupations and she could not help feeling Hart was more likely to achieve that end in Cleveland than in New York. Above all, however, she needed his support. 'I am not going to say I am glad that [CA] is to be married so soon – because I had thought that someday with the necessary separation and time to view things more broadly we might all three again be happily reunited.'[51] Cleveland was not an easy prospect and he played for time, sending a copy of the recent *Pagan* by way of indication that he was busy and productive in Manhattan. Mrs Hart replied on 16 May with word that Grace was involved with riding lessons, driving lessons, lunches and participation in a play. Perhaps with so many activities she would be less demanding than he feared – and on reflection Hart concluded that there was much to be said for living for a while without money worries, especially when, in the absence of metropolitan distraction, he was sure to advance with his reading and writing. Hard work at the *Pagan* was all very well, but he could hardly persuade himself that he was indispensable to the publication, any more than the publication was indispensable to New York.

So he returned at the end of May and got a job tightening bolts on to machine components on a conveyor belt at Warner's, an ammunition factory. Dull as the labour was, there was some satisfaction to be had in contributing to the war effort and even working in a factory proved less exacting than evenings at home, which grew increasingly fraught as CA's wedding approached. When Grace, by way of distraction, conceived the scheme of a driving tour of New England Hart urged her to go and it must have been with a sense of relief that he watched his mother, his grandmother and Charles the chauffeur settle into 'Diana', as the new car had been named, on the morning of Independence Day. They would be gone for a month and Grace promised that in the course of their adventures she would investigate the Eastern colleges on her son's behalf. Hart resigned from his job at Warner's in mid-July and a few days later he wrote to William Wright, now working at a boys' camp outside Cleveland, and invited him to stay for the weekend of his approaching nineteenth birthday. Knowing that it would be easy to find further work in an industrial city geared to wartime production he made light of his unemployment to his old schoolfriend, even going so far as to suggest that his favourite ambition of the moment was to marry, particularly for money. There were certain declarations which were inadmissible, even in this old friendship, and Hart was to continue to tell Wright that he had marital ambitions for some years to come. In other respects, however, their relations continued with ease and pleasure, despite the fact that they had been out of touch for some time. Wright came to believe that their closeness transcended the requirements of regular contact and later claimed that however little he and Hart wrote to each other, 'he was always present as a unique and personal phenomenon, something that belonged to me and to only a few others'.[52] As far as Hart was concerned a profound kinship existed between them, as he one day indicated to his friend: 'I can understand you, I think, because in many ways we are alike. We demand so much from life, and so seldom are we satisfied.'[53] Despite being destined for Yale, Wright had continued to write poetry and Hart was happy to arrange the publication in the July issue of the *Pagan* of one of his more recent lyrics, 'Mood'.

Meanwhile he was working on a new poem of his own, a poem about fantasy and the importance of imaginative reverie, which eventually appeared in the August number of the *Pagan* as 'Forgetfulness'. The title was misleading, but the opening lines of the lyric, in their confident marriage of form and sense, offered a more sustained flight than anything else he had yet written. He was also in print in July in the *Little Review*, which in March had begun the serialization of James Joyce's *Ulysses*. All that year the magazine had continued the wayward education of its readers and it seems likely that Hart had first been exposed to the crucially influential work of Arthur Rimbaud in February, when Ezra Pound had decided in the *Little Review* that 'the time when the intellectual affairs of America could be conducted on a monolingual basis' must end.[54]

It was one thing, however, to introduce Americans to Corbière, Laforgue and Rimbaud, but quite another to sponsor Joyce, and the heroic venture almost finished the magazine. The *New York Times* was hostile to Joyce in general and *Ulysses* in particular and Burton Rascoe, literary editor of the *Herald-Tribune*, took a view no less partisan, which was why Jane Heap later insisted he would fail to recognize the Sphinx outside Egypt. But the most dangerous opposition came from the United States Post Office, which in its self-appointed defence of public morality burnt no fewer than four instalments of the publication, thus inflicting grave damage on the finances and the morale of the *Little Review*. Joyce and literary modernism clearly needed every ally, and Hart Crane would not shrink from the call. In a long letter to the magazine, published as 'Joyce and Ethics', he sought to vindicate not only the embattled novelist but the right of the artist generally to a self-expression beyond prevailing notions of morality. Stressing that 'the most nauseating complaint against [Joyce's] work is that of immorality and obscenity' he declared that 'sterility is the only decadence I recognize'. *A Portrait of the Artist as a Young Man* was 'spiritually the most inspiring book' he had ever read and its author was a supreme modern artist, a peer even of Baudelaire, since the 'principal eccentricity evinced by both is a penetration into life common to only the greatest'. It was a generous gesture, if one which Hart as an ambitious young modernist had to make, and the only sour note of the apology concerned its treatment of his former idols Swinburne and Wilde. All artists turn for a while on their makers but there was something small in his references to the 'meaningless mouthings' of Swinburne and a positive lack of honesty and grace in his dismissal of Wilde. To insist that once the dramatist's 'bundle of paradoxes' had been investigated 'very little evidence of intellect remains' was unfair to the man whose suffering and example he had once venerated and treacherous to the first-rate intellect that spent itself in epigrams.[55]

Grace and Mrs Hart returned on 8 August and Molly the cook, who had taken care of the boy in their absence, now went away herself. Hart saw CA and had a tooth crowned and once again began to chafe under his mother's possessive restrictions. Liberty from parental intervention, once secured, cannot be forgotten and an annoying situation was aggravated by the fact that because he was unemployed he was once again dependent on Grace for money. Four days of this awkward arrangement proved too much and on 12 August, hoping to combine the noble causes of patriotic duty, gainful employment and freedom from meddling women, he went to the enlistment office determined on immediate military service overseas. Grace was not so easily escaped, however, as he learned from the guard on duty at the office, who reminded him that all minors were excluded from volunteering and that if there were any conscription his future would probably lie with some industrial apprenticeship. Reporting to Wright later that day he detailed the fiasco and insisted that his attempts to get into uniform were not motivated by the desire to achieve 'certain effects with the ladies'. It was all academic anyway: although 'some would call me a demon of the Huns' for suggesting as much, he was sure the war was soon to end.[56]

CA married Frances Kelley in Kansas City on 14 August and in another attempt to get out of the house and away from family drama Hart took a job as a riveter in a shipyard on Lake Erie. What he learned about ships and the company of the unlettered men who worked with him he left unrecorded but in the course of this brief career he was introduced to certain aspects of industrial technology the knowledge of which he would later deploy, as the Georgian poets used memories of their country boyhoods in evocation of nature: 'Down Wall, from girder into street noon leaks,/A rip-tooth of the sky's acetylene.'[57] With summer in full bloom, however, Hart was vulnerable to his usual seasonal afflictions and within three weeks acute symptoms of hay fever had left him jobless. Then in early September his draft papers arrived and he wrote jubilantly to Schmitt, confident that his rise in the army would be swift: 'They say that all grouches stand excellent opportunities for promotion, so my ambition is becoming dreamily tickled at the prospect.'[58] But an influenza epidemic swept the country, closing recruitment camps and halting further mobilization, and then on 11 November the Armistice was declared and all draft calls were cancelled.

5

Hundreds of miles away in New York the end of the war was marked by frenzied celebration – on the wrong day. On 7 November United Press issued an announcement that an armistice between the belligerents had been signed and because everyone knew the end of hostilities was imminent the declaration was believed. Despite the denials of the State Department, Manhattan came to a standstill, overwhelmed by an urge for celebration that closed schools and businesses, prompted spontaneous parades and the illegal dispensation of liquor to soldiers and saw an unprecedented precipitation of 155 tons of ticker tape in Fifth Avenue. It was a portent of things to come: the New York that Hart Crane would know, evoke and finally reject was the capital of the impending Jazz Age and there was no delaying the festivities.

Armistice celebrations in Cleveland were tame by comparison and Hart pursued his literary aims without the slightest change in mood or tempo, despite the frustrations of his recent failure to get into the army. Possibly on the strength of an 'Armistice Sonnet', now lost, which he submitted to the newspaper, he secured a job as a junior reporter at $20 a week with the Cleveland *Plain Dealer*, but if he hoped his lofty lyric calling would bring him easy renown he was wrong, and before long he discovered that all poetry not written by Walt Mason, Edgar Guest or Robert Service was regarded 'rather superstitiously' by the newspaper.[1] Among the many young journalists who appeared at the *Plain Dealer* with the onset of peace, however, Hart found friends in Albert Clark, and Thomas Lempertz, who worked hard to become a bohemian and was proud to include the poet in his circle of acquaintances.

Confined by duty to the office Hart found himself with ample time to concentrate on external schemes, paramount among which was his overture of 13 November to the Reverend Charles C. Bubb, a Cleveland minister who combined parochial obligations with management of the Church Head Press. Aware that only the previous year this small imprint had published Richard Aldington's collection of war poems, *Reverie*, Hart wrote to the clergyman hopeful that his press would release some of his own lyrics, ' "gleanings" as it were, from my work of the last two years'. He proposed the title 'Six Lyrics' for the pamphlet he envisaged and trusted that the clergyman would not consider him 'guilty of an officious presumption' in making the suggestion. Since Bubb's critical acumen was of 'the highest standard' he knew he courted rejection with his application – but assured the clergyman that all would not be lost if he disliked the proffered lyrics: 'There is still hope, as I am yet under twenty.' The elaborate modesty of the letter disguised a sustaining conviction: indeed so confident was Hart of his vocation that he sent Bubb works which he could now half-classify as juvenilia – 'To Earth', 'Exile', already published as 'Carrier Letter', 'Naiad of Memory', 'Love and a Lamp', 'Echoes', 'Medusa' and 'Meditation' – as though these largely outgrown efforts, conservative in form and diction, were good enough for the provincial tastes he had to please while still in Cleveland. Rather than intrude on Bubb at home at 2077 East 36th Street he proposed to leave the poems at Laukhuff's for his inspection, 'and while I am certain that you will be the first to detect any flaws and aberrations in these lyrics, I know that you will also be alive to whatever beauty they may contain'.[2] Perhaps Bubb never went to Laukhuff's or perhaps he was unimpressed, because the plan came to nothing and 'Love and a Lamp' and 'Naiad of Memory' were reworked as 'Interior' and 'Legende'.

With the approach of Christmas, drunken driving and suicide, those rituals of the season, began to call him from the office and on 12 December Hart assisted with coverage of a serious car accident in which twelve Clevelanders died. The job entailed witnessing the washing and identification of the corpses at the local morgue, where he returned at the end of the month to report on an unfortunate young woman who had ended the year by throwing herself into Lake Erie. George Bryan, now living with his family in Pennsylvania, was due in Cleveland at Christmas and Hart looked forward to his friend's visit, writing to assure him of his constancy on 14 December: 'You know, or ought to know, that I am always with you in whatever troubles or "blues" you may be having.'[3] The reunion was much enjoyed by them both: Hart was as always grateful for a confidant, and when work at the *Plain Dealer* began to pall, it was to his friend that he wrote to intimate his dissatisfaction. He envisaged returning to New York in April or May but promised Bryan, 'when I go this time, it will probably be permanently, and when we meet it will be upon Broadway'.[4] Not for the first time, however, he underestimated his own impetuosity and without warning resigned from his journalistic post almost immediately after writing the letter. Again it was characteristic that he left one job without having found another first, and with the return of thousands of men from the European front there was suddenly a surplus of labour and Hart found himself unqualified and unwanted.

He settled down to writing at home again, even though recent experience of cohabitation with his mother should have deterred him, and saw publication in the

January *Pagan* of his review of Lola Ridge's *The Ghetto and Other Poems.* Her description of a sparkling traffic-burdened bridge at night would haunt him when he came to evoke a similar scene of his own and despite anxieties that Ridge's metaphoric technique occasionally succumbed to 'a barren cleverness' he was largely enthusiastic about her imagery and technique. He insisted that sincerity was 'the essential to all real poetry' and admired Ridge's work because it seemed 'so widely and minutely reflective of its time'. And what a time it was: already the pre-war age seemed remote and already there was a quickening pace, an intimidating incoherence to this new, and heavily industrialized, time:

> Extremities in the modern world clash in a close proximity, so that there is a finer, harder line than usual to divide them ... Science, grown uncontrollable, has assumed a grin that has more than threatened the supposed civilization that fed it; science has brought light, – but it threatens to destroy the idea of reverence, the source of all light. Its despotism recognizes no limits. In one sense it has become a gargoyle.[5]

CA would almost certainly have questioned the statement that scientific advance was a mixed blessing but for Hart this was an important expression of opinion, and an aspect of an intellectual dilemma that would become increasingly significant as the 1920s progressed. There was no doubt that industrialization was gaining ground everywhere, but to what effect on America and its people? With machines replacing men in so many aspects of life how could bridges of understanding be constructed between the many diverse races of a disjunct and culturally uncertain country? Since cultures arose through human understanding and endeavour, would industrialization threaten or even submerge artistic and creative ambition? Or could industry supply the inspiration for new kinds of art, and new futures for its artists? At the moment these were unanswerable questions, but soon they were to divide literary and intellectual opinion in the United States and Hart, like the other writers he knew, was compelled to take sides in the controversy.

By the first week of February the inmates of East 115th Street were once again besieged by nervous crisis and the impossibility of proximity. Grace took to her bed with acute, if asymptomatic, distress and Hart took up smoking again, unable to visit William Wright in Pennsylvania for fear of what his mother might do in his absence. At least he had a film scenario up for sale, and if that found any takers he would have some money, but there was little other comfort on the horizon. As he confided to Bryan on 15 February Grace had had 'one of the spells you know about' and as for himself he had recently felt 'discouraged enough to kick the bucket'.[6] Help came from unimagined quarters: CA once again offered to support his son – for an indeterminate period, admittedly, and on dangerously imprecise terms – and Hart booked the overnight train for New York. He emerged into the

Manhattan morning on 21 February and made at once for Mrs Walton's, having first sent a postcard of the 42nd Street library to George Bryan with the needless admission, 'It sure seems good to be back in the old town.'[7] Unfortunately Mrs Walton's other lodgers complained of being disturbed by late-night typing so before long he was tramping the streets in search of new accommodation. Once again the return of veterans from Europe complicated his situation, this time by greatly inflating the cost of rented accommodation. With a budget of only $1 a day for lodging Hart faced daunting competition but he finally reported to his mother on 23 February that he had found a new premises, a large front room with running water at 119 West 76th Street, for $7 a week. In later life Hart Crane would find there was no landlady eccentric enough to tolerate his particular ideas of tenancy but in these still tender years he was discouraged by the excesses of his newest housekeeper, who appeared in his room unannounced, regularly saw invisible objects and failed to report telephone messages. Three weeks of this behaviour was enough and Hart had just decided to take to the streets again when another tenant in the same house suggested that they share accommodation and by the middle of March he was more acceptably situated: at 307 West 70th Street in an apartment of three rooms overlooking the street, which cost its two inhabitants only $3.50 a week each.

Grace was at first unhappy that Hart had moved to an unfamiliar neighbourhood and anxious that he was sharing with a man she had never met. But the modesty of the rent, which she was paying, combined with Alexander Baltzly's credentials as an officer and a gentleman, soon reassured her: Hart's new friend was, after all, a champion tennis player, a Harvard graduate and a lieutenant just out of the army – he would be bound to exercise a wholesome influence, and his ambition to make a career in insurance could set her son no harmful example either. With little spare cash between them the two young men were forced to rely on inexpensive entertainments in the time they spent together: they went frequently to the cinema and to the 57th Street gallery run by 'Putzi' Hanfstaengl, who later serenaded Hitler, and they enjoyed long walks along Riverside Drive, where views of the Hudson River competed with the spectacle of the male prostitutes for which the area was then notorious.

As cohabitation grew into friendship they spent increasing amounts of time in mutual education and after being instructed in the strengths and achievements of the Romantic poets Hart was happy to advise his mentor to study Cézanne and the Post-Impressionists. Literature inevitably featured prominently in their conversations. Baltzly was struck by the poet's response to language and recalled: 'He wasn't much concerned with the meaning of words at all ... but he did love the sound of them.'[8] An intense, almost romantic, element was incipient in many of the friendships Hart developed with other men in the course of his brief maturity and this pattern, already present in his closeness to Wright and Bryan, could easily have come to include Baltzly. It was a tendency only natural in a lonely young man of confused sexuality who felt instinctively that confession was the only way of unburdening himself of the inescapable weight of domestic anxiety and in no time he was confiding details of his family problems to Baltzly, who was not only slightly older and obviously a sympathetic listener but also, as Hart explained to Grace, 'someone completely outside of any knowledge of me or my family'.[9] He lost this disinterested listener when Baltzly left New York, and Hart's life, for a career in insurance in Boston but before his departure he did introduce his young friend to a woman he thought would like him. Baltzly knew Charmion von Wiegand because he had been at school with her husband, Hermann Habicht, who coincidentally worked for Habicht-Braun, an import–export business which supplied the Crane Company. It was not these connections, however, which forged the friendship that developed immediately, and abidingly, between Hart and her. She wrote poetry, and 'I instinctively felt he was a poet from the beginning'. Hart always showed her his latest work and she was fascinated by his methods of composition: 'he spent a great deal of time with the thesaurus' and would 'sit and read columns of words'; in all his work, she felt, 'he'd go for the sound as well as the meaning'. But more than his literary travails endeared him. 'I thought he was a beautiful boy, a very typical American boy, very strong and very vivacious and lively.' She noted 'the brown eyes and a very warm and sweet personality': 'I took a fancy to him immediately.'[10]

Despite initial difficulties with accommodation Hart had been delighted to return to New York, which now seemed more enchanted than ever after an interval in the Midwest. Later he would find that all that glitters is not gold and that there was a duplicity to Manhattan's moneyed aspect but for now the animation of the metropolis mirrored and vindicated his own optimism about the future. As he related to Grace: 'The city is ablaze with life ... the avenues sparkle and money seems to just roll in the gutters. I am looking on it all with different, keener eyes than ever before.'[11] He was helped in his happiness by the feeling that now he had a circle of friends in the city, and upon his return Kling, the Kreymborgs, the Colums, Mme Lebègue, Charles and Minerva Brooks and Claire Spencer, now married to Harrison Smith, a publisher and editor, extended support and hospitality. Mrs Spencer, Claire's mother, took a particular interest in his welfare, not least because she was eager to further his knowledge of Christian Science, and throughout March and April Hart was subjected to her preaching. One evening, he told Grace, she regaled him with 'astounding stories about the numerous demonstrations she has made' and on another, after he had escorted her to a performance at the Greenwich Village Theatre of Sinclair Lewis's *Hobohemia*, he discovered 'how very deep' her convictions ran. As for his own belief, he assured Grace: 'In Science, too close a sense of limitation must not be admitted. I am trying to keep all channels open for the entry of everything good that there is, and fear must not close them.'[12] When it looked as though Minerva Brooks might be consumptive Hart took comfort from the thought that 'she is doubtless putting up a strenuous Scientific fight', while Charles Brooks found him greatly improved in character, a development Hart told Grace 'I should blush to tell ... were it not such an interesting testimony to the influence of Science'.[13] Grace was eager for news of her son's progress, spiritual and otherwise, but when Hart learned that she had entrusted Mr Ely in Cleveland with the task of applying Scientific thought to the resolution of his problems he began to feel that a coercive circle was closing around him. He told Grace that he no longer wanted her spiritual intercession or Mr Ely's and a few days later, clearly feeling that matters had got out of hand, he told his mother once and for all that she should not expect daily Scientific observance from him:

I think you are holding the wrong and un-Scientific thought concerning me and my attitude toward Science. The fact that I do not talk and write about it continually is no sort of testimony that I am not as much interested as ever in it. You know that I am not and probably never will be one of those who make the matter a complete obsession, reducing every subject and thought and description to the technical language of the textbooks. ... Perhaps it may serve as sufficient testimony to the efficacy of right thought, etc. that I am finding far less problems and fears that demand denial. I certainly have not felt quite so well or quite so clear-headed for several years.[14]

However, when William Wright dispatched inquiries about the extent of Hart's faith, the latter chose to qualify his loyalty. He had 'unbounded faith' in the effectiveness of Christian Science to address certain mental and nervous problems, 'but as a religion, that is where I balk', since 'the total denial of the animal and organic world' seemed quite untenable.[15]

And there the matter rested: Hart never again devoted time or specific thought to Christian Science, although the suggestibility his early involvement implied never left him, nor did its concomitant urge to overleap obstacles and disappointments on the wings of volition. Born a few years later, and in New York rather than the Midwest, Hart Crane might instead have become a devout disciple of Sigmund Freud – but then he would have been a very different poet, if a poet at all.

In these early weeks in New York Hart wrote little poetry and his literary projects were minor and sporadic, as though he was biding his time or unwittingly consolidating his poetic gains even as he appeared to be fretting about money and the difficulties of metropolitan life. In the February *Pagan* he reviewed Maxwell Bodenheim's *Minna and Myself* and contested Bodenheim's conviction – 'inordinately precious' – that 'true poetry is the entering of delicately imaginative plateaus, unconnected with human beliefs or fundamental human feelings'.[16] Since December he had been in correspondence with Carl Zigrosser, editor of the

Modern School, with a view to persuading the publication to take some of his lyrics and at the end of February his persistence was rewarded when Zigrosser took 'To Portapovitch' for his belated February issue. At the beginning of March he reported to George Bryan that he was thinking of trying to find work in advertising, but in the meantime he was still awaiting news of the two film scenarios he had written. One of the stories involved a plot which culminated in a shipyard strike – fruit of his recent experiences in Cleveland – but neither one sold and it added insult to injury to learn that another writer he knew had been offered $2,000 for a scenario it would take only a day to write. Padraic Colum sent him to the publisher Boni and Liveright to apply for a job as a proof-reader but by the middle of March Hart had found no work at all and his finances were parlous. Letter after letter to Cleveland reported that unskilled jobs and inexpensive accommodation were repeatedly seized by the soldiers and sailors now back from Europe and by 17 March, when Hart wrote again to Bryan, his predicament seemed hopeless. Prospects for employment in New York were 'critical' for everybody and he was having 'a devil of a time' trying to find any work. 'Why you cannot even get a job as a waiter or a street-cleaner.' At such times the emotional intensity of his male friendships became even more precious to him, and now he reminded Bryan: 'Whenever you chance to remember a confession I told you one night last summer when we were together, remember that it still holds good, and will, – for a long, long time.'[17]

Important as these Cleveland friendships were to Hart they remained insufficient: more even than money he needed an intellectually sophisticated contemporary of parallel ambition who could challenge his respect and stimulate him to real achievement and in March he finally met him. He had continued to spend much of his day with Joseph Kling, who had recently added to his responsibilities by opening the *Pagan* Book Shop on West 8th Street. The shop was hung with works by artists dear to its proprietor – John Sloan, Stuart Davis, George Bellows, Auerbach-Levy, Paul Signac, Gaudier-Brzeska and William Gropper – and Hart spent much time noisily assessing the merits of their achievement with Kling, who recalled somewhat airily that 'he fancied himself as an art critic, and a music critic, and a literary critic'.[18] In fact the various *Pagan* enterprises were dependent on such youthful artistic enthusiasm for their survival and it was fortunate for Kling that the Village was alive with young men prepared to work for nothing in the service of literature: Hart had been one valuable volunteer and now he had found another, whose job as unpaid clerk Kling rewarded with another associate editorship of the *Pagan* magazine. His name was Gorham Munson, and he was to become one of the crucial influences in Hart Crane's ascent to artistic maturity, not least because he had an unquestioning faith in his powers, a faith which had been kindled the previous autumn when he had read 'October–November' in the *Pagan Anthology* . The poem's closing lines had enchanted him and thereafter he never forgot 'the thrill of my first reading that made me note the poet's name'.[19]

Munson was born at Amityville, Long Island, in 1896 and graduated from Wesleyan University in 1917, after which he moved to New York to become a man of letters, a vocation which was to involve him in much of the European avant-garde writing of the 1920s and bring him eventual distinction as an academic. In later life he wrote numerous books and taught at Hartford and Wesleyan universities besides conducting a prestigious writing course at the New School for Social Research where his pupils included Jack Kerouac and William Styron. In 1919, however, he was simply an impecunious young man with a passionate belief in literature and it was this conviction which underlay his friendship with Crane and which informed the important correspondence they were to exchange. Munson was then living in a room in one of the old Rhinelander houses in West 11ᵗʰ Street and he was on duty at the *Pagan* Book Shop one morning when 'a young man came briskly in'. As he later recalled, the visitor and Kling immediately began to shout at each other in friendly fashion until the latter paused, 'to introduce me to an obvious midwesterner'. The shouting resumed and Munson observed the newcomer:

Hart Crane did not look like a poet. A slim, brown-haired, brown-eyed fellow, he could have been an energetic businessman. His voice was midwestern, vigorous, almost harsh. The general effect of his personality was masculine.[20]

Once the banter had subsided Hart turned to Munson and suggested that they should have dinner one evening, which is why that very night Munson found himself discussing literature with the poet in a cafeteria at Broadway and 72nd Street and discovering that 'the world of artists for him then was a wonderland, as it was for me'.[21] He established that Hart shared his admiration for the *Little Review*, and since that magazine had just begun serialization of *Ulysses* talk turned to James Joyce, a writer they both venerated. Munson, slightly older and certainly better educated, should have exercised the deciding opinion in their conversations but in fact 'from the start I looked up to Crane'. He merely admired the poetry of William Vaughn Moody, whereas Hart knew Harriet Moody herself and his poetry had been sponsored by her. Although they both zealously read the *Little Review*, Hart had also been published in it, and before he was twenty, an achievement by which Munson felt 'especially impressed', and although Munson's fable 'The King of the Strange Marshes' had appeared in the February *Pagan*, Hart was there also, with his review of Maxwell Bodenheim. On every front the older man found himself outflanked:

It did not occur to me to size him up as incompletely educated. ... I was dazzled by the literary education he was giving himself. His private 'college' was the *Little Review*, which he read from cover to cover, advertisements included. The head teacher in the *Little Review* was Ezra Pound, and Hart was quick to take the courses of reading that Pound recommended.[22]

In the ensuing weeks a firm friendship developed based on reciprocal esteem, shared ambitions and a mutual need for trenchant yet sympathetic literary criticism. By then, however, the admiration for the *Little Review* which Munson had noted had been transformed into something approaching a business arrangement: at the end of March Heap and Anderson, learning of Hart's financial plight, suggested that he work as advertising manager for their magazine. They were obviously not in a position to pay him a salary but proposed instead that he take a commission on every advertisement he secured – and since both literature and practicality appeared to be served by the arrangement, and since he had made scant effort to find more profitable work, Hart quickly accepted their offer. Divulging the scheme to Grace on 2 April he expressed his hope that once smoothly running the job 'would prove to be reasonably remunerative for me'. He would have 'unrestricted initiative [and] freedom' to manage 'my department systematically' and was sure the only reason the publication had had no advertising revenue before lay with its lack of an advertising manager.[23] He began the new job on 11 April and six days later he had sold his first advertisement, admittedly to a friend – 'Stanislaw Portapovitch: MAITRE DE DANSE', with a telephone number and an address on West 42nd Street, occupied half a page in the May and June issues of the magazine. By Easter Hart was able to inform his mother that he had an assistant, and although the young man had just turned up in search of a job rather than having applied to a fast-expanding business, Hart continued to be optimistic and assured Grace they expected to secure contracts the following year 'of no less than $480 each'. 'We are after about all the great establishments on Fifth Ave., and I am learning a few things in going about.'[24] Ominously, the assistant absconded, but when Hart wrote to his mother on 3 May, he still believed that if he could sell all the advertising space available in the *Little Review* he would be able to earn $4,000 a year in commissions. But by 30 May all hope had died. Fifth Avenue had proved less eager to advertise in a slender and eccentric literary magazine of uncertain circulation than Hart had imagined and forlornly he told Grace he was looking for other work again, 'anything that comes along – with the intention of one way or another establishing my independence from all outside assistance'.[25] The only other advertisement Hart succeeded in placing came from CA, and even here his success was qualified, since Clarence Crane only agreed to pay for advertising in what he considered an unsuitable magazine when Heap and Anderson followed Hart's initial plea with what Anderson called 'a magical letter' of their own.[26] There was something decidedly anachronistic in Mary Garden's appearing in the *Little Review* to endorse Crane's Chocolates but she did so nevertheless, in every issue excepting one between May 1919 and the September–December issue of 1920. For some reason, however, CA was slow to pay, even though Hart had already announced he intended to use the commission to enrol in a Columbia summer course in business advertising. The course began on 8 July but CA had still not paid on 10 July and Hart once again voiced his bitterness and bewilderment to his mother: 'All my friends think his treatment of me is disgraceful and unaccountable ... It is only when hunger and humiliation are upon me that suddenly I feel outraged.'[27]

Long before then, however, friends had interceded, as they were to do again and again in Hart's life, to remedy the crisis that broke in May when the poet was rendered homeless by Alexander Baltzly's move to Boston. Unable to pay the rent outright on West 70th Street he faced destitution or another humiliating return to Ohio until Claire and Harrison Smith, who had anyway been keeping him fed, came to the rescue. Hal had rented two rooms directly above the offices of the *Little Review* in West 16th Street and he proposed to sublet the apartment to Hart for $10 a month, the cheapness of the deal being based on the understanding that he would sometimes use one of the rooms as a secondary office. Gratefully accepting the offer, Hart repaid in kind when he could, proffering 'very shop-soiled boxes of chocolates that his father had made'. As Claire remembered, 'They had usually been in some shop window, so that the chocolates inside of the sun-faded boxes were always pale grey in colour.'[28]

The Smiths' gesture placed Hart one floor above the centre of American literary modernism, an underfunded business which shared a roof with unlikely cohabitants, as the poet soon discovered: a visitor descending from his top floor would encounter Heap, Anderson and their magazine, then an embalmer and undertaker who made toothpaste as an avocation, and in the basement one of the brightest of the bizarre fauna of bohemian Manhattan, the Baroness Elsa von Freytag von Loringhoven, a living art-work whose husband had shot himself rather than join the German army and whose significance as a Dadaist poet was much championed by Anderson and Heap. The Baroness put her genius into her life and her talent into her work to the extent that whereas she is now a minor literary footnote, to those who knew her she was an unforgettable apparition who commonly wore spoons as earrings and decorated her face with postage stamps or painted its profiles two different colours; who wore coal scuttles for hats; and whose ever-changing hair colour was a matter for daily speculation from Houston Street to Washington Square. Even Margaret Anderson, whose contempt for bourgeois propriety equalled her conviction of the Baroness's brilliance, was startled one day when she opened the door to find von Loringhoven clad in nothing but mourning crêpe, her shaved and lacquered head an audacious vermilion. For the vigilant Charles Brooks 24 West 16th Street proved an irresistible target and the eccentric household eventually found itself immortalized in 'A Visit to a Poet', one of the essays in Brooks's *Hints to Pilgrims*. The latter noted the fading splendour of the house, its 'heavy stairways with black walnut rails', its 'large drawing rooms with tarnished glass chandeliers and frescoed ceilings and gaunt windows with inside blinds' and thought it all evocative of 'more aristocratic days'. Hart, the poet of the title, whose 'verses are of the newer sort', 'came down to meet me, with slippers slapping at the heels' but thereafter, sure his readers wanted to know about the ways of the literary life but not its works, Brooks avoided the subject of poetry. He noted the existence of the magazine 'The Shriek', however, and introduced his audience to 'the Countess Sillivitch', thus perpetuating the reputation of the Baroness, whose Dadaist days were numbered: in 1927, six years after the appearance of *Hints to Pilgrims*, she died in Paris, gassed by a lover in her tenement.[29]

Hart's dealings with the Baroness were cordial if guarded: when she needed a typewriter he deprived himself and lent her the machine borrowed from Hal Smith but otherwise he was content to imitate her guttural accent and Germanic insistence and to hide behind doors when he saw her in the street. His relations with Matthew Josephson, begun on the same black walnut stairwell, were to prove more significant. Already an aspiring writer and a committed Francophile, Josephson had ventured to the *Little Review* offices in the hope that Heap and Anderson would buy some of his poems, although it was not as a poet but as a biographer of Zola, Rousseau, Hugo and Stendhal, and as a historian of the robber barons, that he would achieve renown in later life. He spent much of the Twenties in Paris, where he befriended Aragon, Ernst, Breton and Eluard and, in impassioned debate at the Dôme and the Rotonde, explored the very vertex of French Surrealism. Always known for his pronounced opinions and blunt delivery, he had already developed strong literary prejudices but Anderson and Heap were not at home to hear them when he came to the *Little Review* in pilgrimage. He was about to leave when a young man in a grey suit appeared over the balustrade at the top of the stairwell and invited him up. Dressed for the sale of advertisements, Hart was as usual happy to talk about writing and he and Josephson at once commenced a lengthy discussion of poetry. They met again a while later and the latter inspected Hart's poems. He liked the poet himself, 'a stocky young man with a big round head', but his work seemed 'weak in sentiment and formal traditionally' and he urged destruction and a fresh start.[30] It was sobering counsel: who was Hart to question a student from Columbia? And presently he informed Munson that he had met 'a real poet ... a deep student of modern French verse' who was 'a very strict judge'.[31] It was a deference he was never entirely to outgrow.

He asked Josephson his opinion of Columbia and the summer advertising course he was hoping to attend once CA paid for the advertisements in the *Little Review* but his new friend was disillusioned with university life and told him so. William Wright, now destined for Columbia instead of Yale, was also consulted about the course, at the same time learning why his friend now aspired to membership of the businessman's world: 'The commercial aspect is the most prominent characteristic of America and we all must bow to it sooner or later. I do not think, though, that this of necessity involves our complete surrender of everything else nobler and better in our aspirations.'[32] Between bracing himself for this world and not selling advertising space for Heap and Anderson Hart read and read: D.H. Lawrence, Plato, Mark Twain, Cervantes, Chaucer and Henry James. He continued to go to the theatre when he could afford it and on one such occasion he met the daughter of Robert Frost and escorted her back to Columbia at the end of the evening. Mentioning the incident to Wright he reported that he hoped to see her again, 'as she is worth looking at'.[33] When Wright himself ventured similar remarks in letters to Hart, however, and with rather more sincerity, he was rebuked: 'Your remarks "about the ladies" really hurt me with a kind of ragtime vulgarity.' Although free from 'Puritanical preoccupations' Hart strongly resented 'that gross attitude of the crowd that is really degrading and which is so easily forced upon us before we know it'.

Whatever Wright thought of these conflicting positions he should have been able to detect a growing ambivalence in his friend's views about New York, only recently a wonderland but now apparently a place of trial, fascinating still but exacting: 'To one in my situation N.Y. is a series of exposures intense and rather savage. ... New York handles one roughly but presents also more remedial recess, – more entrancing vistas than any other American location I know of.'[34] The exposures seemed increasingly savage as his finances went from bad to worse. Had it not been for the Smiths he would have been in extreme need and when Grace complained some time at the end of May that she only received two letters a week his temper snapped and he wrote back angrily pointing out that without more money he was not in a position to generate ample news for her entertainment. He knew she was annoyed by his moving to the Smiths' without prior consultation, but what did she expect in his financial straits? He had discovered she was paying his allowance out of her income and not reclaiming it, as the divorce settlement entitled her to, from CA. That was all very well, but he was certain her generosity would soon return to haunt him. He hated his financial dependence, but how conducive had life around him ever been to settled study and smooth progress through the customary stages of growing up? He bore grudges from the previous summer and grudges from his earliest memory and suddenly it was time for plain speech:

> You know, Mother, I have not yet forgotten your twitting me last summer at my not paying my board expenses when I was at home, and I don't welcome your generosity quite so much now on the possibility of a recurrence of such words at some future time. I don't want to fling accusations etc. at anybody, but I think it's time you realized that for the last eight years my youth has been a rather bloody battle-ground for your's and father's sex life and troubles.[35]

Claire's mother had a cottage in West Englewood, New Jersey, and she and Hal offered further respite from the anxieties of New York and the annoyance of Cleveland by inviting Hart for weekends. The regime was easy: canoeing, swimming and sunbathing, but for the country boy it was agreeable, as Hart told Wright, just to 'see the moon and stars and hear the frogs croak'.[36] By the end of

June the Smiths had decided they wanted to leave New York for the summer but decided they would have to take Hart along because, as Hal remarked, 'He'll starve if we don't.'[37] Instead of returning to New Jersey, however, they had rented a house at Brookhaven, Long Island, and conceived the notion of sparing their guest's notorious pride by coaxing him into acting as gardener and chauffeur in return for their hospitality. Hart accepted the arrangement sunnily, perhaps counting on the presence of the Japanese cook to save him from too much work. In any case the property the Smiths had taken could only guarantee a happy summer: the eight-bedroom house had been converted from an ancient barn and if he tired of reading in its well-stocked library he could always resort to its peach orchards and rose gardens. The sea was accessible and he told Grace he anticipated 'idyllic days of sailing, bathing, romping and reading'.[38]

At first everyone was happy, and Claire and Hart danced by moonlight to a Victrola dragged nightly on to the lawn. Soon, however, this exercise had to stop: she was pregnant and disinclined to continue such exertions in the heat and Hart, accepting generosity he could not requite, began to detect imagined signs of resentment at his presence. As usual the obverse of his high-spirited nature, always so eager to participate and to be loved, was an insensitivity to moods not in accord with his own and a childish readiness to take offence. Often in a state of what she termed 'nasty irritation' with her condition, Claire felt unable to give her demanding guest all the attention he needed, although she did remember later how much he laughed at CA's annoyance when the latter saw the *Little Review* and realized the nature of the magazine in which he had advertised.[39] And she listened as he described his last stay in Cleveland, and how vastly annoyed he had been to discover that Grace, in bed and distressing him by consistently refusing to eat, had in fact been getting food behind his back – so annoyed, indeed, that the only conceivable response on discovering her manipulative behaviour had been to get wildly drunk. Hal was less familiar with Hart's family dramas but soon discovered that there was no escape from them, even for his friends: 'He used to recite over and over again his difficulties with his father, his father's new wife, his mother and grandmother. In his mind it had become a dramatic subject that only Eugene O'Neill could have handled.' The repetitiveness was bad enough, but there was also Hart's deep insecurity, which Hal began to find wearing: 'He was a difficult guest to put up with ... that loud, boisterous, rough manner of his – which I think he used to cover his inner doubts'.[40] Once Hart began to suspect, half accurately, that he had become a tedious presence paranoia alerted him to every indication, and every suspected indication, of boredom and annoyance. Arguments began and he took to maintaining a diary of the dramas, which he left open and lying around for inspection, before expressing new threats that he would pack his bags and return to New York, if only to starve. Later Claire would remember one particularly distressing scene, precipitated when Hart revealed his conviction that Hal disliked his guest because he was jealous of him.

I was truly astonished – and said so – then Hart told me everything about himself – about his having been a Homo. The gist of it was that he blamed me entirely: 'It's your fault. We should have got married. You are the only woman I could have anything to do with. You betrayed us both when you married Hal.' I remember saying, 'I never was in love with you and you never were in love with me either', but he insisted, saying, 'Yes, you are, you simply won't be honest about it.' Then he went on to say that if I had not made such a mess of things he would not have become a Homo. I asked him, 'I don't see why you should become a Fairy for any other reason except that you are one.' He answered, and I remember that he was on the point of crying: 'No one has ever told me I was beautiful before.'[41]

Then one night the Smiths were woken by dramatic sound effects: Hart was staging a departure he was to re-enact many times over the ensuing years – banging a trunk down the stairs to alert unsuspecting (and sleeping) hosts to the enormity of their indifference and incomprehension.

Tearful recriminations and forgiveness were the usual resolution of such scenes, but this time CA himself interceded at the end of Hart's second week at Brookhaven by telling his son to present himself for a job interview at the New York offices of Rheinthal and Newman, the company which supplied Crane with its Maxfield Parrish reproductions. The interview with Mr Rheinthal occurred on 29 July: Hart felt that it proceeded in 'very satisfactory' fashion and it was agreed that he should start work in the company's order department early in September.[42] He dispatched the news to Grace, in so doing indicating how glad he was to be back on good terms with his father: now all seemed set for harmonious relations and Hart attributed the change in paternal disposition to the workings of his allies at the Crane office in New York, whom he suspected of alerting CA to his lonely and insolvent struggle for artistic laurels. Grace reacted mercurially to this new shift in relations, one day counselling Hart to treat CA with sympathy and co-operation, another, with vigilance and cunning – but a fierce argument with the Smiths in early August eclipsed all other matters and Hart left Brookhaven for good. Clarence Crane had finally paid for the Mary Garden advertisements and Hart sent the money, along with complimentary chocolates, to Margaret Anderson, at the same time complaining about the way the Smiths had treated him. Anderson replied on 24 August with thanks for 'the beautiful Mary Gardens and the check' and looked forward to hearing the details of Hart's 'Brookhaven abdication', since the tone of his last letter had 'suggested vast irritations'.[43] Back in New York earlier than he had planned, Hart started work at Rheinthal and Newman in the second week of August, as usual full of eager expectation and blithe conviction that a few weeks of apprenticeship would quickly lead to power, affluence and plenty of spare time in which to write poetry.

Disillusion would soon follow, but at least for the time being he was in funds and his mood was further elated with the publication of more of his work. 'North

Labrador', 'Legende' and 'Interior' were accepted for publication by the one and only edition of the *Modernist* and in September the *Pagan* published his review of *Winesburg, Ohio*, a collection of stories by Sherwood Anderson which had already appeared separately in the *Little Review*. Anderson's tales are set in agricultural Ohio in a period of unspecified, turn-of-the-century tranquillity and besides being relics of the pre-industrial age which was dying when Hart was born his characters are all burdened by sexual guilt and repression; to a man they have become introverts, secretive, lonely and too strange for the public exposure of small-town life. It was a literary achievement which had profound appeal to Hart Crane's personal experience and later he insisted that he could 'understand [the book] perfectly myself, having lived for a while in a small town of similar location and colour'. But there was more to his admiration than that: *Winesburg* 'represented a work of distinct aesthetic achievement, an example of synthetic form' and its author was 'beginning to be recognized as among the first few recorders of the life of a people coming to some state of self-consciousness'.[44] These opinions were formulated two years later; for now he contented himself with assuring the *Pagan's* readers that Anderson's work was of a 'flawless' style, that its author equalled Balzac in his sympathetic drawing of character and Maupassant in narrative deftness and that 'America should read this book on her knees' since it constituted 'an important chapter in the Bible of her consciousness'.[45]

Anderson was naturally delighted by such high-flown encomium and sent Hart a note of thanks, adding to the usual amenities a cryptic remark: 'Surely it is to the minds of men such as yourself the American workmen in the arts must look for new fuel when his own fires burn low.'[46] A correspondence was instigated between the two writers and although Anderson, born in 1876, was considerably older there was enough in his career to hold promise and instruction for the poet. His education had also been unfinished and he had meandered from one routine occupation to another before ending up as the manager of a paint factory, a job from which he had simply walked away one day in frustration. This defection marked the turning point of his life; thereafter he drifted to Chicago and became involved with that city's cultural resurgence and through an epistolary friendship with the critic Waldo Frank he developed an association with *Seven Arts* magazine. Frank admired his fiction and he and Anderson sent each other mutually sustaining letters about the problems of national puritanism and the literary promise of the Midwest. Although in some respects Anderson was more successful than Hart Crane in reconciling his artistic vision with the demands of commercial life he admitted a similar yearning to belong to what he termed 'an America alive, an America that was no longer a despised cultural foster-child of Europe, with unpleasant questions always being asked about its parentage'.[47] He was the great laureate of small-town American life and although he saw Cuba during the Spanish-American War and Gertrude Stein in Paris in the 1920s, like Hart Crane after him he proved incapable of expatriation.

Such affinities as the two men shared became apparent later. For now it was enough for Hart to see himself in print again and to have won the esteem of another man of letters. He was in confident mood at the end of September when William Wright and another friend, Roger Zucker, were in New York and took it upon himself to show his friends the town, an ambition which entailed attending Oscar Asche's oriental fantasy *Chu Chin Chow* before adjourning to Churchill's for beer, sandwiches and cabaret. Wright had just suffered the first of several nervous breakdowns and Hart found him much changed, although he hoped that a new life at Columbia would restore him. Zucker seemed appealing enough, but Hart told Grace he could have liked him more had he not insisted on 'talking "naughtily" about ladies'.[48] But then it was back to work, and by the beginning of October, following the now familiar cycle, Hart's enthusiasm at joining Rheinthal and Newman had turned to boredom, then despair, and by the end of the month he had resigned, determined, he explained to his mother, to find 'a job where I can have a chance to use my brains a little'.[49] He was still on happy terms with CA, however, and drew some comfort from the thought, as confided to Grace, that 'his business is now well beyond the million mark'.[50]

Clarence Crane was indeed working extremely hard and rushing from Kansas City to Chicago to San Francisco besides wondering whether his next venture should involve some sort of publishing association with Maxfield Parrish or else diversification into the soft drinks business. With Hart's decision to leave Rheinthal and Newman, however, the elder Crane had more pressing matters to resolve. Hart's hopes of finding work through Charmion with Habicht-Braun came to nothing and he was again desperately short of money. Following their summer quarrels his relations with Hal and Claire Smith had never been quite as easy and dependable and with the onset of cold weather it became apparent that even if money permitted he would not long be able to remain in the unheated rooms in West 16th Street. He took up temporary residence at the Hotel Albert in East 10th Street but when CA, perhaps sensing that at last his time had come, suggested that his son return to work in Ohio, either for the Crane Company or for uncle Fred Crane at the Burroughs Adding Machine Company, Hart was hard put to find excuses. So he bought a ticket for 6 November, his departure for the cornfields alleviated, as he told Charmion, by the letter of thanks from Sherwood Anderson and by a new project of his own: 'I am beginning something in an entirely new vein with the luscious title: "My Grandmother's Love Letters". I don't want to make the dear old lady too sweet or too naughty, and balancing on the fine line between these two qualities is going to be fun. I hope that living close to her in the same house won't spoil it all.'[51]

PART TWO

Akron, Washington and Cleveland

November 1919–March 1923

You ought, really, to try to sleep,
Even though, in this town, poetry's a
Bedroom occupation.

'PORPHYRO IN AKRON'

6
=

Akron, as its Greek name implies, commands what is almost the highest point in Ohio and here at this prominence, and long before the city came into being, a restless nation paused briefly in its westward expansion. At this elevated terrain, where the great river systems of the St Lawrence and the Mississippi lie only eight miles apart, the Erie Indians had marked a trail which linked the two waterways and which came to be known as the Portage Path, and it was this immemorial track which by treaty of 1785 with the Six Indian Nations was recognized as the western boundary of the United States. History quickly overtook it, and the frontier continued its inexorable westward encroachment, defining as it did so American nineteenth-century domestic history, and vanishing into myth and into the Pacific only a decade before Hart Crane was born.

By then the city of Akron, born in 1825 and, like Cleveland, a beneficiary of the connection by canal of Lake Erie and the Ohio River, had grown into an industrial centre where clans of New England and Pennsylvania Dutch manufacturers produced huge volumes of oatmeal along with a variety of honest hardware including sewage pipes and farm implements and machinery. It was in 1870, however, with the foundation in the city of a rubber company by Doctor B.F. Goodrich that Akron awoke to its destiny as a centre of rubber manufacture: Lake Erie supplied the volume of water crucial to a thirsty industry and only 150 miles away the car industries of Detroit would soon constitute an insatiable market for rubber tyres. The Goodyear Company was founded in Akron in 1898, Firestone in 1900, and the General Tyre and Rubber Company in 1916, the year which also saw the development in the city of the pneumatic rubber tyre. By then, with over half a million Model T Fords being sold annually, Detroit's demand for tyres was so great that Akron processed three-quarters of the world's production of rubber. In the decade beginning in 1910 its population almost trebled and just before the depression in rubber prices in 1921 the city boasted 122 millionaires, pre-eminent among whom was Frank Seiberling, founder of the Goodyear Company, who only four years previously had completed construction of Stan Hywet, a sixty-five room Tudor manor complete with lodge and stables and a mural depicting the *Canterbury Tales.*

Such legends were music to the money-minded but it was only after Maxfield Parrish took him to Akron and he saw Stan Hywet that Clarence Crane decided his company should have a presence in the rubber capital, a decision the Chamber of Commerce seemed to vindicate when it announced in 1919 that in the previous year alone the value of manufactured goods produced in Akron had increased by $100 million. Then there was Hart, at last showing signs of understanding that art must take second place to practicality, at last indicating that he might perhaps be talked into returning to the Midwest to work for the family business. Why not let him prove himself in Akron? Situated thirty-odd miles from Cleveland he would have some sense of autonomy, and there were enough challenges in the fledgling operation to keep him busy and to make him realize that money was more easily spent than acquired.

On 12 November, five days after his return to Cleveland, Hart accordingly found himself in Akron with his father, and there the scheme was broached and agreed, although the shift which CA ordained for his son, from six in the morning until eleven at night, suggested not so much paternal wisdom as the worst excesses of the Industrial Revolution. When Hart reported to Munson on 13 November, however, his mood was buoyant: still a week away from his new responsibilities, and with no idea what such a long day would be like, he had been greatly encouraged by a letter that morning from Sherwood Anderson in which the latter had described the business life he had endured before his own ascent to literary fame. CA had proved 'much pleasanter than I expected him to be', Hart declared, and the scale of his ventures, now grossing about three-quarters of a million dollars annually, astonished even his son: 'Things are whizzing, and I don't know how many millions he will be worth before he gets through growing. If I work hard enough I suppose I am due to get a goodly share of it, and as I told you, it seems to me the wisest thing to do just now to join him.' Once he had proved himself he would surely be transferred – to Kansas City, San Francisco or even New York – but in the meantime Akron was 'a hell of a place', a raw town that could have existed in Bret Harte's fiction, with demolition and construction on every corner and 'as many Slavs and jews on the streets as on Sixth ave.'[1]

Towards the end of November Hart installed himself in the Hotel Akron prior to taking up his new job, knowing as he did so that CA was wooing the town's confidence and prosperity with exuberant promotion in the *Akron Beacon Journal.* 'Akron Must Go Forward!' trumpeted one advertisement which announced the Crane luncheon service and displayed a picture of the opulently mirrored soda fountain and its enticing selection of confectionery – all aspects of a venture of unprecedented luxury which foretold the town's moneyed prospects. 'One store that is representative of the future Akron is Crane's – A store that would be distinguished on

Fifth Avenue.'[2] In the event, however, it was not in this establishment that Hart found himself engaged but behind a specially contrived counter in the Portage Drug Store which CA had forgotten to advertise, with the result that the commercial apprentice was isolated for many long hours behind his stand of the inevitable Mary Garden Chocolates hoping to sell merchandise no one knew about. There were consolations, however. His working day was shorter than originally planned and he was able to take long lunch breaks to explore his new home, to watch the Ohio Canal as it struggled through locks and under bridges on its uphill journey to join the Ohio River, and to investigate those areas of Akron which were still without telephones, paved streets or sewers, so rapid had the city's expansion been and so inadequate its planning for the immigrant hordes who came to work in rubber. In a sense the frontier still stopped here: like the early pioneer towns of California and Alaska, Akron was a city of strangers and because there were disproportionately few women among the population of 200,000 who struggled daily to satisfy the demands of Ford and General Motors, it was also a town of unattached and restless males.

Hart was the newest stranger: he knew absolutely no one in Akron and nothing survives to suggest that he was drawn to the saloons and stews in which the town might have compensated its lonely workforce. Happily, there was a bookshop near to the Portage Drug Store and soon Hart had befriended its proprietor, Herbert Fletcher, and through him, Harold Churchill Candee, another incongruous figure in the city, and one who was to prove something of a liberating force in his life. To Hart, Candee appeared 'a very sophisticated and erudite fellow', and there was no escaping the conclusion that he was 'another soul, like myself, in Akron exile from N.Y.'[3] But the few remaining facts of his life suggest that the exile was more far-reaching. To his older friend Wilbur Underwood, Candee was 'an attractive brilliant young man' and 'most worldly in point of view' but there is a sense that this social accomplishment brought him no ease.[4] He was a heavy drinker, and if he instigated Hart's alcoholic apprenticeship, and there is some evidence to suggest that he did, the poet noticed that there was a joyless side to his debauchery, that life was in fact 'a frightful torture to him'.[5] He was born in 1887, the son of Helen Churchill Candee of 1049 Park Avenue, New York, who survived the *Titanic* disaster to become an art historian and travel writer. Jacobean furniture was one of her specialisms but she was also associated with the tapestry department of the Metropolitan Museum in New York and in 1912 she published a history, *The Tapestry Book*. She ventured briefly into fiction with *The Oklahoma Romance* but exotic investigation pleased her more and she travelled extensively in Indo-China, impressions of which she recorded in *New Journeys in Old Asia* and *Angkor the Magnificent: The Wonder City of Ancient Cambodia*, for which achievement she was decorated by the French government and by the King of Cambodia.

Harry's restlessness took another form: he moved from one job to another in quick succession, forever pursued by what Herbert Fletcher described as 'boy trouble', and when Hart befriended him he was living in rented rooms at 1043

West Market Street and working as the private secretary to Edwin Coupland Shaw, an Akron philanthropist who had made a fortune with the Goodrich Company.[6] For such an urbane being the job had about it the aspect of an antipodean posting and if at least it kept Candee safely remote from the possibility of New York scandal, whatever the sexual temptations available in Akron, it also left him bored and lonely. To Underwood the job seemed like 'a sublimation' but to Candee himself it must have appeared as a penance, and certainly not one he could endure for long. Hart's correspondence indicates that by summer 1922 he was once again in his beloved England, infatuated with some youth he had met there and dividing his time between the Eton and Harrow cricket match and the treacherous wharves of Limehouse, and the following year he was in Cambodia with his mother. At some stage, and for reasons presumably philanthropic, he secured the position of president of the Working Boys' Home in Birmingham, England, and there, suddenly and unglamorously, his wandering ended when he died of pneumonia in July 1925, aged thirty-nine.

He maintained contact with Hart throughout his later travels, as the latter's correspondence reveals, but none of the letters Candee wrote has survived: they were too explicit for Grace Crane's liking and after Hart's death she destroyed them. How soon the Akron exiles found themselves on terms of sexual frankness, and whether this frankness led to any greater intimacies, it is impossible to know. What is certain, however, is that within a few weeks of meeting they were in the habit, as Munson was told, 'of talking until two and three in the morning'. The erotic opportunities of Akron may have been discussed in the course of these exchanges, with Candee, one assumes, the presiding authority and cicerone, but Hart was soon astonished by the range of his friend's experience and acquaintance. For a start, he knew the Baroness. As if that was not remarkable enough, Munson was informed, 'He goes on for hours telling of exotic friends of his and strange experiences. He knows Europe well, English country house parties, and Washington society, – prizefighters, cardinals, poets and sculptors.' How remarkable to find him among the rubber factories, 'forced to earn his living as secretary for some wheezing philanthropist'.[7] Candee knew his way around the intellectual, as well as the social, world and he lent Hart a copy of a book he had himself recently borrowed from Fletcher, P.D. Ouspensky's *Tertium Organum*, published in 1920 but already available to Fletcher through the offices of its translator Nicholas Bessaraboff, a customer in his bookshop and an employee of one of the rubber companies. This book was presently to have a significant influence on Hart, but in the meantime Candee had other forms of education to conduct, notably with alcohol, and soon Fletcher, who sometimes went out with them in the evening, was unable to keep up with their excesses, as he later remembered: 'They fell in with a bunch of Roumanians and really started their serious drinking about the time I was ready to go home.'[8] Soon Munson was informed of another 'purple evening' in Hart's education where Candee was also involved: 'I got dreadfully drunk on dreadful raisin brew, smoked one of the cigars made especially for the Czar, defunct, of Russia, and puked all over a boarding house. You will believe me an ox when I tell you that I was on the job again next morning.'⁹ Unedifying as the incident was, Hart almost evoked it in the one poem he wrote about the rubber town, 'Porphyro in Akron', an Eliotic venture in autobiography and disillusion written months later:

> I remember one Sunday noon,
> Harry and I, 'the gentlemen', – seated around
> A table of raisin-jack and wine, our host
> Setting down a glass and saying, –
>
> 'One month, – I go back rich.
> I ride black horse ... Have many sheep.'
> And his wife, like a mountain, coming in
> With four tiny black-eyed girls around her
> Twinkling like little Christmas trees.
>
> And some Sunday fiddlers,
> Roumanian business men,
> Played ragtime and dances before the door,
> And we overpayed them because we felt like it.¹⁰

It may also have been through Herbert Fletcher that Hart met another Akron eccentric, Hervey Minns, an ageing photographer who lived in artistic mess and dereliction and whose work, friends were soon informed, had been garlanded in Dresden and Munich. In Akron, however, where he had lived and worked for twenty years, the photographer avowed anarchist sympathies and only photographed faces he found engaging or sympathetic. Mr Seiberling himself had petitioned in vain for a sitting but Hart was more successful, although the resulting portrait, with the poet in black tie and tuxedo, evoked the fiction of F. Scott Fitzgerald more immediately than the canons of modernism and anarchism or the realities of hard work in a confectionery company. As he was to do throughout his life, Hart determined to redress what he saw as unjust artistic neglect and campaigned by letter for Minns's recognition in New York. Margaret Anderson eventually yielded and some of the photographer's work appeared in the *Little Review* in September 1920, with Hart's accompanying 'Note on Minns' assuring the magazine's readers that the portraits revealed 'the urge of an ethical curiosity and sympathy as strongly evident as in the novels of Henry James'.¹¹ Minns must have been delighted by such praise, not least because the implications of formalist perfection behind Hart's words did indeed reflect a belief on the photographer's part that art concerned harmony and control. Some months later, when his

own poetic theories had matured and found themselves at variance with the fashionable lawlessness of Dadaism, it was tellingly to Minns that Hart went for reassurance. He found that the photographer despised Man Ray and doubted 'the
theory of interesting "accidents"'. It was a conversation that had to be reported to
Munson, who now learned Hart's new position on the nature of creation: 'There
is little to be gained in any art, so far as I can see, except with much *conscious*
effort.'[12]

Hart changed and developed rapidly in Akron and books were as crucially cat-
alytic to his growth as people. Whatever the boredom of his hours at the Portage
Drug Store he could at least read undisturbed: Maupassant and the *Little Review*
were kept near at hand and in the last weeks of 1919 he marvelled at Pound's
Pavannes & Divisions and T.S. Eliot's *Prufrock and Other Observations*. Literature had
been the sustenance and salvation of his troubled adolescence and now he turned
to it again with catholic enthusiasm, reading the *Smart Set* and exploring Mark
Twain's suppressed *1601*, Edgar Lee Masters, Walter Savage Landor, Stendhal's *The
Charterhouse of Parma*, Dostoevsky, Somerset Maugham's rendition of the life of
Gauguin, *The Moon and Sixpence*, and as a corollary, Gauguin's own account of life
in the South Seas, *Noa Noa*, and Samuel Butler's dramatization of filial revolt, *The
Way of All Flesh*. Furthermore, though he felt himself to be banished from New
York he did not lack for mentors: American writers instinctively worked long-
distance, aware that the cultural cross-pollination taken for granted in the
European capitals was impossible in the immensities of the continent beyond
Boston and New York. Matthew Josephson proved himself a useful correspondent,
not only by keeping Hart abreast of New York's literary fashions but also by sug-
gesting that he investigate the Elizabethans and the Metaphysicals – Marlowe,
Webster and Donne were all to prove vital influences in the formation of Crane's
mature poetry and now he immersed himself in their greatness. Sherwood
Anderson endorsed a different school, and on 3 December he recommended that
Hart read the cultural criticism of Van Wyck Brooks and also Waldo Frank's newly
published *Our America*, which he suggested the poet pass on to CA afterwards.
Frank was later to become not only a close friend to Hart but also one of his most
significant mentors and this discipleship began now with the discovery of Frank's
best-selling study of American cultural possibility.

Our America went through three editions in its first six months of sale and made
its author famous in intellectual circles across the nation, where an anxiety was
emerging that the utopian ideals of the Republic were becoming increasingly sub-
ordinated to vulgar materialism and mechanical advance. Frank's study appeared
at exactly the time when this concern had begun to supersede the spirit of national
unity of 1917 and 1918 and his conviction – that 'America is a promise and a
dream' – revived the myriad idealists of a continent. Frank assessed American
literature, still dishonoured by oblivion, and commended the visionary tradition of

Twain, Thoreau and Whitman. In the recent achievements of Sherwood Anderson, Robert Frost, Paul Rosenfeld, Carl Sandburg and Amy Lowell he detected a restoration of this national spirit. He attacked the historic forces of puritanism and plutocracy which he found inimical to visionary Americanism and championed modern cultural figures such as Charlie Chaplin, whose clownish persona appeared to undermine a philistine and unjust capitalist society. In short he offered a prospectus for a new cultural America and he was explicit in appointing its creators: 'The leaders of a to-morrow forced to spiritual discovery are men of letters.'[13] His work was a clarion call and Gorham Munson remembered that his generation, with no knowledge whatever of an American literary tradition and little sense that their country could be rediscovered by its artists, was overwhelmed by *Our America*'s peroration:

> We must begin to generate within ourselves the energy which is love of life. For that energy, to whatever form the mind consign it, is religious. Its act is creation. And in a dying world, creation is revolution.[14]

Ten days after Anderson dispatched his advice Hart had read Frank's book. Many of its tenets, and in particular its anti-puritanism, were already familiar to him from parallel assaults by Van Wyck Brooks, Randolph Bourne and H.L. Mencken, but Frank's study was the first to present a visionary apology within such a long context of literary culture and to assert so resonantly that America remained a land of myth and mythic self-expression. These ideas were later to have a profound effect on Hart Crane's thought, but at first, immersed as he was in the wide learning of Pound and Eliot and the distant glamour of Elizabethan London and Symbolist Paris, he was unconvinced, as he explained to Munson on 13 December. There was no doubt that *Our America* would 'never be allowed to get dusty on the library shelves', and Frank had worked wonders 'to limn the characters of Lincoln and Mark Twain as he has, – the first satisfactory words I have heard about either of them'. And he was glad to see Sherwood Anderson receive just recognition. However, 'this extreme national consciousness troubles me', and he found it hard to imagine that writers such as Dreiser, Anderson and Frost could have achieved what they had done if they had read Frank's study as younger men. 'After all, has not their success been achieved more through natural unconsciousness combined with great sensitiveness than with a mind so thoroughly logical or propagandistic (is [that] the right word?) as Frank's?'[15]

Yet the place of American writers beleaguered by American commercialism and industry was very much in his mind when Hart granted an interview to Alice Chamberlain, a journalist with the *Akron Sunday Times* introduced to him by Herbert Fletcher. She clearly found Hart's very presence in the rubber capital bizarre, and the title of her article, 'Millionaire's Son Is Clerk In An Akron Drug Store', published on 21 December, indicated as much. Hart, however, had other preoccupations behind the 'nice smile and brown eyes' Chamberlain noticed and he did not hesitate to share them. Convinced that 'I don't think you'd care about my poetry, or care to publish any of it', he warned her cryptically that 'I am not in sympathy with this jazz stuff, and I simply won't jazz for your public'. There were bigger concerns at hand, not least America's new culture, and after praising the work of Sandburg, Dreiser, Anderson and Edgar Lee Masters he insisted: 'These men have recognized realities that are close to us and our present day life, and we cannot afford to ignore them.' The realities in question were stark: unless they embraced the culture of business and industry which dominated America those writers and artists who hoped from now on to depict her were doomed to frustration: 'Living as we do in an age of the most violent commercialism the world has ever known, the artist cannot remain aloof from the welters without losing the essential, imminent vitality of his vision.' Frank's thinking was clearly behind much of this deliberation but CA, unaware of the broader polemic, took exception to the interview and was particularly annoyed by what he saw as the veiled complaint of Hart's assertion, quoted directly by Chamberlain: 'The modern American artist must generally go into business life. He is often forced in anyway by necessity.'[16] Writing to Munson six days after the interview's publication Hart confided that CA was 'furious, at the headlines in particular, and I spent a nervous day yesterday with him in explanations'.[17]

One of the writers Hart did not mention to the readers of the *Akron Sunday Times* was Wallace Stevens, whose development he had followed since the poet's first appearance in *Poetry* magazine in 1914: his work, Hart assured Munson, 'makes most of the rest of us quail' and his 'technical subtleties alone provide a great amount of interest'.[18] It was these subtleties that he attempted to imitate in 'My Grandmother's Love Letters', the poem he had begun before leaving New York and which he had continued to rework in his short hours away from the Crane Company. Most of the poems of Hart Crane's apprenticeship had addressed the lonely suffering of a sensitive adolescent bewildered by a cruel world but this new poem rejected such juvenile solipsism in favour of larger inquiries into the emotional travails of others and the destruction by time of love and all love's declarations. Yet if the mature ambition of 'Love Letters' marks a departure, the poem still reads as somehow reticent, unresolved, even incomplete, despite the assurance of its twenty-six lines of free verse and the subtlety of its half-rhymes and internal cadences. Hart's generation was haunted by T.S. Eliot's dictum that no *vers* is *libre* to the man who does a good job, but it was not for technical reasons alone that Crane struggled with this poem. The real difficulty was personal: was he to imagine or to remember? Should he draw on, and transform, his own experience or should he attempt the projection of someone else's? Later, schooled by the Elizabethans in brocaded language and by the Symbolists in poetic representation and indirection, he learned to write about his most personal feelings and experiences in a manner which was both cryptic and evocative, illuminating and opaque

– but now, struggling to speak in a borrowed poetic diction which was clear and simple there was nowhere to hide if he chose to examine personal experience in a document his parents would be certain to read. The opening pleased him at least:

> There are no stars tonight
> But those of memory.
> Yet how much room for memory there is
> In the loose girdle of soft rain.

There was something pleasing in the idea of memory as a series of points of light in the encircling darkness of lost experience; but memory is melancholy as well as comforting because it is all that ever remains of life's great intangibles of happiness and love. At twenty, the poet is old enough to know something of both these conditions at first hand – but not old enough for the confidence of self-exposure or the skill of self-concealment, so he determines instead to confront the subject indirectly. But having decided to write about the evanescence of love with his grandmother as an example, what can he say about Mrs Hart's distant romantic life, concerning which he had nothing whatever to say in prose? He had stalled, and Munson was the first to know:

> Grandma and her love letters, are too steep climbing for hurried moments, so I don't know when I shall work on that again. As it is, I have a good beginning and I don't want any anti-climax effect. If I cannot carry it out any further, I may simply add a few finishing lines and leave it simply as a mood touched upon.[19]

Munson sent back encouragement and Crane tackled the ascent again. Not choosing to divulge his own emotional experience and not knowing about his grandmother's, he resolved to turn imprecision to a virtue: whatever the identities of the protagonists in love's games all that eventually remains is misty memory or its analogue, fading love letters,

> That have been pressed so long
> Into a corner of the roof
> That they are brown and soft,
> And liable to melt as snow.

Having turned the poem into a meditation on the frailty of memory and the distancing power of time, Crane continues in generalities and adopts impersonal syntax to acknowledge that all emotional archaeology is a delicate business even for the poet:

Over the greatness of such space
Steps must be gentle.
It is all hung by an invisible white hair.
It trembles as birch limbs webbing the air.

Doubting his skill to trace memory back through time he asks himself: 'Are your fingers long enough to play/Old keys that are but echoes ...?' At this stage it is an unanswerable question and the poem ends with a change of gear and an implicit admission that the poet has retreated in the face of his self-appointed task. He declares that he would like to introduce his grandmother to new experience even though that exploration would lead her 'Through much of what she would not understand'. It is not the right time for Hart to exchange amorous confidences with this 'grandmother', indeed may never be the time, 'And so I stumble'. The rain which fell at the poem's opening is heard once more: it is still soft, but now it strikes the rooftop differently and seems to convey to the poet 'a sound of gently pitying laughter', as though aware that Crane kept his secret, even as he lost his courage.[20] As Valéry was prone to remark, all poems are in the end abandoned rather than completed and Hart feared 'My Grandmother's Love Letters' confirmed the observation. Thanking Munson for his encouragement he conceded the poem's final imperfection:

> ['Grandma'] would get very fretful and peevish at times, and at other times, hysterical and sentimental, and I have been obliged to handle her in the rather discouraging way my words attest. However, I think that something has been said, after all, although the poem hasn't turned out as long as I had expected.[21]

Munson liked the poem, as did Matthew Josephson, and Hart decided to submit it to the *Dial*, the prestigious Chicago magazine which two wealthy Harvard aesthetes, Scofield Thayer and James Sibley Watson, moved to New York in 1920 and turned into an important vehicle of international cultural range and sophistication. It was an inspired destination: the magazine accepted the poem and on 28 January 1920 he exultantly informed Munson that he had that morning received an acceptance fee of $10, his very first earnings as a poet.

Hart felt proud of 'My Grandmother's Love Letters', its inconclusiveness notwithstanding, and remained sufficiently happy with it to include it in his first volume of poems. For a while he was anxious that it marked a point of excellence unreachable ever again but friends hastened to reassure him. The one dissenting voice was that of Sherwood Anderson, who felt the poem failed to 'give me anything of yourself, the bone and flesh quality of you as a man'.[22] It was an imperceptive remark, if understandable: all poems are personal testaments and if 'My Grandmother's Love Letters' is hesitant, even, it might be argued, evasive, those aspects in themselves were telling. There were new reasons why Hart felt reluctant to begin an explicit disquisition into the nature of love in his own name and why instead he constructed such an inquiry around his grandmother. Whatever Harry Candee knew, the first person to learn by letter was as usual Gorham Munson. On 13 December Hart told him that he was involved in a love affair; he supplied no other details, beyond adding that the involvement had him 'broken in pieces most of the time'.[23] About then also Hart must have confided the development to Anderson, because the latter wrote on 17 December and noted 'how the fact of your being in a love affair vivifies you'. He promised to give the predicament some thought, but he knew none of the details beyond the 'hungering and being defeated and arising all the time to new days' which he gathered Hart experienced.[24] Hart was in correspondence with William Wright in mid-December, but there are certain transformations one cannot easily unleash on old friends and he made no mention of his passion. Finally he unburdened himself of the full truth to Munson, knowing as he did so that CA had decided to transfer him to Cleveland, and that with a clear term set on his time in Akron his affair might soon end:

> This 'affair' that I have been having, has been the most intense and satisfactory one of my whole life, and I am all broken up at the thought of leaving him. Yes, the last word will jolt you. I have never had devotion returned before like this, nor ever found a soul, mind, and body so worthy of devotion. Probably I never shall again ... You, of course, will consider my mention of this as unmentionable to any one else.[25]

The admission is striking: whether or not its terms came as a revelation to Munson, or merely as confirmation of existing suspicions, it is as though Hart were at last making a declaration to himself. Whatever his earlier experiments, and they are lost to biography, and whatever his previous assumptions about his eventual sexual choices, it must have become apparent to him in the improbable surroundings of Akron that any earlier fumblings and any precedent longings involving other men were more than passing fancies, that they were instead the prologue to the intensities of feeling which preoccupied the love poets themselves. And now, experiencing such intensities, he judged them in poetic terms: always supposing that this was his first serious affair, how could he assume that it would prove impermanent, or that it gave him pleasures no other liaison in future years could ever confer? Even allowing for the dispiriting emotional example set him by his parents, these were unsustainable assertions in life, however axiomatic they were to the romantic canon.

At first it seemed that events would confound his pessimism: CA recalled Hart to work in Cleveland and he left Akron on 11 January 1920, fearful no doubt that distance would expand 'voiceless between us, as an uncoiled shell', as he had described the lovers' dilemma in 'Exile'. But a month later, as Munson was informed, Hart was still rhapsodically happy: the affair brought him 'new treasures all the time' and 'new satisfactions at each occasion' and he lived 'from Saturday to Saturday':

> Gold and purple. Antinous at Yale. So the wind blows, and whatever might happen, I am sure of a wonderful pool of memories. Perhaps this is the romance of my life, – it is wonderful to find the realization of one's dreams in flesh, form, laughter and intelligence – all in one person.[26]

But by the first week of March the paragon had begun to prove elusive, in confirmation of romantic forebodings, and by the end of April it was all over. Hart reported to the faithful Munson that he had 'seen love go down through lust to indifference'.[27]

To begin with, however, the liaison was a deliverance, not only from years of sexual uncertainty but also from the cheerless realities of daily life in Cleveland and as he made arrangements to move back to the larger city he anxiously wondered how he would explain his repeated weekends in Akron to Grace. He learned on returning, however, that she and Mrs Hart were about to leave for the Isle of Pines, there to spend the remainder of the winter, and as there was no question that the big house in East 115th Street could be kept open for his solitary occupancy he found himself able to continue his long-distance liaison from a satisfactorily incurious boarding house in Euclid Avenue. His life assumed the dislocated aspect of infatuation: every Saturday marked a voyage into a world of heightened existence and lyrical possibility among the improbable Akron smoke-stacks, with the intervening days a marking of time punctuated by intermittent poetic endeavour and by fluctuating hopes of accommodation with CA, his business and his beliefs. At first these hopes were high, and Hart confided to William Wright on 5 February that 'I dream of becoming a business man! And I suppose someday I shall even meditate marriage!' But even as he divulged them he knew there was something surreal in these expectations and he laid them to rest accordingly: 'My epitaph shall be: – "Il fumait sa pipe."'[28] Less than three weeks later, again to Wright, Hart was less optimistic. His ten-hour day at the Crane factory began at 5.30 every morning and he returned home 'with a head like a wet muffin'. His diet was insufficient; his lodging was cold and uncomfortable, 'to say nothing of trying to exist on starvation wages'. His unmentionable affair aside, life's consolations were few and intangible: he was looking forward to Grace's return at the beginning of March and to the renewed comforts of East 115th Street; and although the *Dial* had only paid him $10 for 'My Grandmother's Love Letters' the psychological coin accruing from the publication was much greater, as he implied to his friend: 'It is quite a feather in my cap to appear in the assemblage that "The Dial" claims now, and I am quite encouraged about myself. All I need is time for a small amount of leisure, and time when I am not all tired out from previous exertion, mental or physical, it makes no difference, and I would turn out better stuff than even this opus.' He was beginning to suspect that such liberty was an improbable luxury, however, and told Wright that his father's guiding policy for his future invoked 'the old bunko stuff about "working from the bottom up" and "earning an honest dollar" '.[29] CA's senior employees, charged with executing this policy whenever he was away on business, soon found that the proprietor's son, at this stage working as a shipping clerk, was not an easy responsibility. Alan Howard was an assistant to the superintendent of the Cleveland chocolate factory and as his wife recalled he was issued with explicit instructions whenever CA left the city:

> When Mr Clarence Crane was out of town on business he always asked Alan 'to see that Harold gets down to work'. This was an impossibility as they knew nothing of each other personally and Harold came in to work only when out of funds. One day when he *was* at work, my husband remembers Harold reading from a manuscript while they were eating their lunches in the shipping room.[30]

Perhaps Hart's involvement at the Crane Company was unenthusiastic but the conditions under which he lived and worked, and in the context of his father's undoubted prosperity, would have tried anyone's resolve. To make his dilemma more complicated, although he had never had any serious interest in the confectionery industry he continued to set great store by paternal approval, and the opportunities for catching his distracted father and mentioning his hopes and frustrations were infrequent. They did at least have a discussion on 6 March, when Hart recited his grievances, to be rewarded by CA with a pay increase of $5 a week, and a few weeks later he reported to Munson that his father appeared 'to be very much satisfied with my present devotion to office hours' and even began to speculate that soon he would be moved to the New York office. As usual, however, when one of his parents appeared reasonable and tolerable the other seemed unbearable. Grace's return from the Caribbean had proved less pleasurable than he had expected and now, as he told Munson, she struck him as 'satisfied, shallow, unemotional', and obsessed with the dullest of domestic details. To make matters worse, her moods remained worryingly unstable, since if he failed to 'beam out the dinner and evening in proper style', however exhausting his day had been, 'there are exclamations culminating in excruciating tears'. The worst of it all was her complacent acceptance of Christian Science, the weight of which 'I feel growing heavier and heavier on my neck'.[31]

It was a life of constriction and loneliness in need of expansion and companionship and Cleveland seemed to offer little of either in the few hours of freedom available to him. At some stage he took to roaming Euclid Beach in search of other men and in the company of a journalist who had lived in the same lodging house he attended several boxing matches where, he told Munson, 'I get very heated, and shout loudly'. Beyond the mere excitement of the contest, it was the erotic stimulus of the evenings that most gratified him: whoever the victor and however heroic his triumph, there was something thrilling and fascinating in the brutality of the scene and in the crowd's cruel and atavistic thirst for blood: 'Of course, many matches are boresome, but provide two sublime machines of human muscle-play in the vivid light of a "ring," – stark darkness all around with yells from all sides and countless eyes gleaming ... and I get a real satisfaction and stimulant.' Perhaps this same arena might also yield poetic inspiration – as he told Munson, he longed to distil the essence of these lurid evenings in a poem, but he sensed that a new tone and diction were necessary to the enterprise: 'A kind of patent leather gloss, an extreme freshness that has nothing to do with the traditional "dew-on-the-grass" variety conveys something suggestive of my aim.' And again he found that T.S. Eliot had been there before him, 'once merely with the name "Sweeney"'. But he never wrote a poem about pugilists and the next day it was back to work as usual. He felt 'utterly alone' but knew that the aspect of solitude would win him no friends at the factory. Greenwich Village might judge its artists according to the quality of their despair but blue-collar Cleveland had other expectations and Munson was told of the newest refinement in a complex personal camouflage: he had determined to be 'very flexible' in order to survive and accordingly tried to practise 'much camaraderie with the other employees'.[32]

The need for such a performance no doubt added to the exhaustion of the day but it rendered at least one surprising dividend when a factory employee was injured by a machine and Hart found himself coming forward to apply first aid. The episode occurred in March or early April and despite the stultifying boredom of factory routine which, he told Munson, left him with 'an infantile awe before any attempt whatever, critical or creative', he found that first moment of contact between himself and the injured man revolving in his mind and its consequent sensations arranging themselves on paper:

The unexpected interest made him flush.
Suddenly he seemed to forget the pain, –
Consented, – and held out
One finger from the others.

The resulting poem, 'Episode of Hands', was merely, he informed Munson, 'a mood', and although its twenty-four lines contain some vivid images the work retains a provisional aspect attesting to its author's dissatisfaction. He told Munson that he felt 'much at sea about [its] qualities and faults' and the poem remained unpublished in his lifetime.[33] Yet if it lacked the surface hardness he admired in Eliot's work, 'Episode of Hands' had a documentary interest which compensated for its technical deficiencies. As 'the fingers of the factory owner's son,/That knew a grip for books and tennis' continued their ministrations his hands seemed 'Like wings of butterflies/Flickering in sunlight over summer fields' and he glimpsed a lyricism in the 'knots and notches' of the worker's coarsened palm: 'They were like the marks of wild ponies' play, – /Bunches of new green breaking a hard turf.' The din of the factory fell away and with the knotting of the bandage, 'The two men smiled into each other's eyes.'³⁴ These were the uses of adversity: liberal New York could never teach the emerging, actively homosexual poet the lessons of Cleveland – that the freemasonry of males potentially alive to homoerotic *frisson* and experiment extended beyond the rites of pugilism and the lingering glances of Euclid Beach to the unlikeliest bastions of industry and respectability.

It was a relief at Easter to share these lessons with a kindred spirit and Hart departed for Akron and Harry Candee armed with 'two bottles of dago red', as he told Munson. Whether or not he hoped to see his lover in Akron there was little time left for anything apart from drinking once he and Candee were reunited. Hart's two bottles of bootleg Italian wine were quickly consumed and they proceeded to drink a quart of raisin jack, with the result that the next day 'was spent very quietly, watered and Bromo-Seltzered, with amusing anecdotes occasionally sprouting from towelled head to towelled head'.

Back in Cleveland he felt that 'the bath in the unconscious did me good', but the interlude had been all too brief and served to throw into tedious relief the social opportunities available to him at home: CA's parents' golden wedding anniversary and a collegiate ball which saw Hart saddled with 'two hysterical, extremely young and innocent females'.³⁵ There was also the challenging prospect of acting as his restless mother's escort and in the course of one evening of chaperonage he found himself attending a dinner for the Warren Society at the Union Club in Cleveland. The only other guest of his own age was his parents' attorney John Sullivan's daughter and the two young people found themselves thrown together. It was not the prelude to firm friendship, however: she found Hart 'utterly boring' and remembered that as they watched the other guests 'he made most uncomplimentary remarks about them – as I recollect they were not even amusing – just cynically superior. I felt sort of sorry for him.'³⁶ Matthew Josephson would have understood this boredom with provincial life and so would Margaret Anderson – but where were they now? Morale was further depressed when he developed inflamed abdominal muscles as a result of repeatedly lifting barrels of sugar and cases of chocolate and in late April he had to take a week off work. The arduous literary self-schooling continued whenever he could find the time and letters of the period mention Apuleius, Rabelais, Villon, Vildrac, Saltus, Henry James, Aldous Huxley, Joseph Conrad and the Noh plays of Fenolosa and Pound. But these masters were intimidating as well as inspiring: how was he ever to fulfil his own literary destiny, let alone attain their greatness, when shackled to a shipping clerk's desk?

As usual, with nowhere else to turn, it was to Gorham Munson, now reviewing books for the *New Republic*, that he looked for solace and advice. The commerce between the two writers was by no means one-way: as a firm believer in the fraternity of artists Hart was always happy to help and advise with the literary enterprises of his friends and Munson sent his poems and plays to Cleveland for appraisal even as he monitored Hart's growing literary adventurousness and technical accomplishment. But Hart's was the greater talent, and his the longer journey within a shorter life, and it was inevitable that the correspondence which passed between them would see him expanding more rapidly and more unpredictably than his friend. Munson's role was nevertheless crucial: he admired and credited and accepted the poet without attempting to shape him; and in allowing Hart to take the intellectual initiative in their discourse he permitted him to test himself and his evolving literary theories before the time came to execute them. Thus it was to Munson that Hart confided the literary suspicion growing in his mind in the early months of 1920:

> The modern artist has got to harden himself, and the walls of an ivory tower are too delicate and brittle a coat of mail for substitute. The keen and most sensitive edges will result from this 'hardening' process ... forget all about aesthetics, and apply yourself closely to a conscious observation of the details of existence, plain psychology, etc. If you ARE an artist then, you will create spontaneously. But I pray for both of us, – let us be keen and humorous scientists anyway.[37]

It was Munson who was told that 'humour is the artist's only weapon against the proletariat' and Munson who was shown an early draft of a new poem 'Garden Abstract', which Hart began during the course of his affair and continued to rewrite for months. Again the problem was personal as much as technical – to what extent could he speak freely about eroticism? – and the fear that he could not involved him in endless verbal tangles which saw the poem evolve from an exercise in free verse with echoes of Imagism and Symbolism to a more formal arrangement comprising two sestets of blank verse. The more he tried oblique and symbolic description, the more complicated the lines became, as he suggested when he submitted the work to Matthew Josephson in March: 'My poem, the phallic theme, was a highly concentrated piece of symbolism, image wound within image.'[38]

He was still working on it and still convinced that the venture could be redeemed at the beginning of April, but it was no easy business to write about a subject such as sexual desire, when all he knew of it took him into realms beyond parental, let alone legal, sanction. Yet the happiness of his Akron affair, and the sexual hunger it had awakened, were not so easily banished as he went through the motions of shipping clerkage or read the visionary artists whose ranks he envied. The goal was hardness, he had said, but might it not also include the catharsis of confession and the act of revelation conducted in disguise? 'The apple on its bough is her desire', he declared in the opening line, apparently invoking Eve in the Garden of Eden, but by line three Genesis is completely forgotten in an evocation of sexual passion involving the myth of Daphne and Apollo: dumb inarticulacy, blurred eyes and breathlessness, until 'She is prisoner of the tree and its green fingers.' This was the strength of erotic longing and abandonment, which haunted Daphne and haunted Hart, who now knew the oblivion of the final lines: 'She has no memory, nor fear, nor hope/Beyond the grass and shadows at her feet.'[39] Editors were not convinced by the poem and 'Garden Abstract' was rejected by the *Freeman*, the *New Republic* and the *Dial* before finally being accepted by the *Little Review*.

And now that affair was over what did he feel about Akron? He had grown and changed in his time there but in ways he could not divulge; in any case it was not only with confessional and personal poetry that he would win his place in contemporary American literary discourse. What of the crusade to which Sherwood Anderson had alerted him, what of the literary army Waldo Frank hoped to raise to reclaim America for the visionaries? Surely his time in the rubber capital, a city truly American in the way that New York could never be, offered raw materials for the cause? Surely Akron settled as decisively and depressingly as any place in the United States the status the country afforded its artists? This was no subject for the elusive music he found in Wallace Stevens, however, nor did any of his previous poetic allegiances offer much guidance as to the realization of this idea that would see his experiences in Akron turned into an indictment of modern America. There was only one poet whose example offered inspiration: and in the late spring, when he began his next poem, the manner of writing he hoped to match, full of learned elegance and studied disillusion, was that of the emerging master poet, T.S. Eliot.

By 8 June he was able to announce the project to Munson as 'a set of sketches connected with Akron life now' and enclosed the thirty-four lines in three sections he had so far written.[40] Already the mood and the stage set were established, and as Crane described a shift of rubber-workers making its way down South Main Street, and then the interval with Candee and the Romanian fiddlers, he began to formulate his picture of desolation, in which weary and displaced workers were set beside bored afternoons of pointless intoxication. There is only one strong impulse in this desolate immigrant wasteland, hence only one preoccupation which fuses the disparate elements of modern America:

The dark-skinned Greeks grin at each other
In the streets and alleys.
The Greek grins and fights with the Swede, –
And the Fjords and the Aegean are remembered.

Above their jokes and contraband
Niggers dream of Kentucky melons,

> Yellow as gold, – golden as money.
> And they all dream of money.

He paused and thought again and was dissatisfied; the last four lines were excised and he continued to rework his idea: America, though hard-working and acquis-itive, was also miserable and lethargic – but what place did writers hold in this gloomy scene? Were they as demoralized as America herself? Presently he sent Munson a further thirty-seven lines and by now Eliot's influence was clearer: modern society, exemplified after all by America, was an urban hell, its populace no better than automata, and the surest poetic way to expose that banality was by the juxtaposition of descriptive passages with trite comments of overheard con-versation and the incorporation of mythological, religious or literary references from nobler ages. By now he knew his title: like Keats, dead a century before, Hart Crane chose poetry over the security of a profession and felt himself to be the victim of a cruel urban society, and like Keats's Porphyro in 'The Eve of St Agnes' he inhabited a frigid and imprisoning world where sexual encounters were the only solace: he would call his poem 'Porphyro in Akron'. The new lines he sent to Munson contained quotations from Keats's poem and had shifted the scene to the poet's bedroom, where he is lying at night and trying to read 'The Eve of St Agnes'. He is disturbed, however, by the noises emerging from a tawdry nightclub nearby:

> Tumult of weariness from a basement cabaret
> splashes up into my room.
> Bucket of blood. Peggy dancing her guts out.
> Sweat and powder and rubber-dust on her sash.
> Whoops, my dear!
>
> Her usual morning remonstrance over the soda-bar
> Will again be muffled by what her
> fellow's teeth are letting out, –
>
> 'You're the clev'rest girl I know ...
> How do you do it?'
> For, sure, her father preaches up at Norton,
> and sends her money every week.

Distracted by the music, he thinks back to his childhood and to the songs his mother used to sing and now Crane writes the passages about Grace singing in the stuffy parlour and about his infantile escape into the yard where he picks the rose. Painful as the memories were of those remote and crucial years, they were also inextinguishable and must be committed to paper. As he told Munson when he sent revisions in August, 'I don't much care whether anyone will care for ["Porphyro"] or not. What I seem to want to do more and more as time goes on, is to preserve a record of a few thoughts and reactions that I've had in as accurate colors as possible for at least private satisfaction.'[41] After all, it was those distant years that had begun his formation as a poet and it was as a poet that he felt despised by a philistine and mechanical society. It was not as matters should be in Frank's picture of a new visionary America – and it was not as matters should be in the poem either. He revised again, this time deleting the description of the cabaret, which would reappear in a greater vision two years distant, and tightening the remaining lines. As a final homage to Eliot he inserted a five-line epitaph on the modern American poet:

O City, your axles need not the oil of song.
I will whisper words to myself
And put them in my pockets.
I will go and pitch quoits with old men
In the dust of a road.

And he closed the poem with three wonderful new lines which evoked not only the subaltern status of poetry in middle America but also the bitter fact that now his Akron affair was over there was nothing else for him to do once he climbed the stairs. Watching his poetic *alter ego* in bed and trying to read Keats, Crane advises:

You ought, really, to try to sleep,
Even though, in this town, poetry's a
Bedroom occupation.[42]

At last he set the poem aside and thanked Munson for his advice: 'There was nothing, good or bad, that you seem to have missed, and such criticism does me no end of good as surgery and instigation.'[43] For all Munson's help, 'Porphyro in Akron' bears the scars of its long evolution and remains an imperfect work – and as such was rejected by the *Dial* and the *Little Review* before finally appearing in the New Orleans magazine the *Double Dealer* in August 1921. Despite its imperfections, however, it marks another significant development: the cycle of time it describes, from morning until night, prefigures the structure of Crane's great work *The Bridge* and the themes it ponders mark his awareness of the influence and example of Eliot. 'Porphyro' also stands as his first attempt to support Frank's visionary company of evangelists – but by negative, Eliotic, means he would soon discard. It was one thing to produce yet more evidence that artists were ignored in a mercantile society and thus made supine and nostalgic with gloom but such findings would scarcely further the visionary cause. America was an inspiration, not a defeat, and her artists must will themselves into celebration and song or accept the certainty of irrelevance and retreat, as Eliot had done, to distant shores and cultures older, but more enfeebled, than the Republic. But for now, uncertain of the way, Crane bided his time.

His progress on the poem and the thoughts that governed it were interrupted twice during the course of the summer. In June, in view of their harmonious relations and his son's apparent determination to adhere to the exhausting realities of the agreement they had reached, CA rewarded Hart with a generous gift ahead of his twenty-first birthday: two weeks of paid vacation with a further cash supplement. Hart decided easily on a visit to New York and many happy letters of announcement were dispatched, principally to Gorham Munson, who was charged with meeting the exile at the cigar and magazine stand in Grand Central Station when his sleeper arrived on the morning of the Fourth of July. Two weeks flew by in a whirlwind of socializing and cultural activity: he saw Charmion and Joseph Kling; he attended plays and concerts; he ate Sunday breakfasts with Munson at the Brevoort Hotel; he swam and sunbathed on Long Island; he found Greenwich Village still standing – and returned to Cleveland just before his birthday. He had a short time in which to catch his breath, however. Now that Hart had attained his majority a discussion about his future was clearly necessary but when he and CA met to explore the subject Hart discovered that his father already had a plan. With the continuing success of his company Clarence Crane felt expansive: the time had come to develop wider sales territories and in view of the strong presence he already maintained in the Midwest he inclined to the view that surer rewards on investment were to be had on the East Coast. With New York already covered he looked further south and decided to create a market in Washington DC: it would be Hart's job to open this new sales territory and while he was there he could try and tempt the Virginians – issuing his brief, CA made it clear that he wanted his son to explore commercial opportunities in Richmond and as far south as Norfolk.

Like Akron before it, the federal capital would constitute a considerable challenge but there was much that was flattering about CA's offer, not least the logic of his choice, made, as Hart informed Munson, 'on account of the better sort of business type that is in Washington and also on account of Washington's "literary and journalistic associations" '.[44] CA was not a man for half-measures and as Hart contemplated his new assignment he did so in the knowledge that his father proposed to entrust him with a drawing account at a bank and with a commission on any sales made. But compliments engender anxiety because they imply expectation of future achievement and as his time for departure neared Hart indicated to Munson that he was 'full of a lot of doubts about my capacities for "salesmanship" '.[45]

By the time he left Cleveland on 8 September, however, his confidence had returned once again and he settled into a hotel in Woodrow Wilson's Washington as a prelude to finding cheaper accommodation. By 13 September Munson learned that he was established at 1310 L Street 'in an unexceptional maison in a row of other rooming houses' and that initial sightseeing had proved reassuring: 'There is a certain easiness about it, and geographically it is, I should judge, the nearest like Paris of any American city.' Although large areas of federal, monumental Washington were still under construction, Hart was nevertheless sure that it was 'more elegant than any other American city and with a very different psychology than N.Y., Cleveland or Akron'. But like all American cities Washington was also a lonely place, a neighbourhood of strangers, and after three days there he was once again dreading attempts at selling Crane's confectionery and felt 'a terrible vacuity about me and within me and a nostalgia for Cleveland'.[46] In the event his forebodings were vindicated. Hart made a poor salesman because there was nothing glib in his nature: when it came to promoting commodities in which he believed, such as modernist poetry, he was impassioned and persuasive, but confectionery, even his father's, aroused no such zeal, and the few potential buyers he found were discouraged to find that the unseasonable heat had mottled his chocolates with grey. On 27 October he returned to Cleveland.

But another brief interlude in another strange metropolis did confer rewards, though none envisaged by CA. By now, transplanted across four cities since the threshold of his adolescence, Hart should have been accustomed to the solitude of the wanderer but the hot twilights of the capital struck him as unusually forlorn. Washington offered little in the way of café, commercial or factory life since it revolved around the federal bureaucracy and there was something both poignant and unnerving in the commuter migrations, in the way that 'thousands of clerks pour out of government offices at night and eat and go to the movies'. But he was not alone in his estrangement from this life and his fellow misfits adorned the city's streets and parks quite as beautifully as its majestic magnolia trees: whatever the architectural and historical significance of Washington, Hart confided to Munson that he was 'really more interested in the soldiers and sailors that one meets than in anything else'. Even as he stalked his quarry he discovered that he was by no means unique in his curiosity: indeed Washington confirmed the recent lessons of Akron and Cleveland, that those who shared his sexual interest, in his adolescence a guilty and isolating secret, constituted a clandestine brotherhood apparently represented in every city he visited.

In Washington rumours circulated suggesting that membership extended to the highest reaches of politics and diplomacy, since the city was then enthralled by the emerging revelations of the Newport Scandal, details of which had begun to filter from the naval training station in Rhode Island the previous year. A group of naval personnel, calling themselves the Ladies of Newport, were suspected of recruiting other sailors at the station for sex; once the stories became sufficiently insistent the Assistant Secretary of the Navy in Washington was called upon to act. He convened and supervised an agency known as Section A which was charged with amassing enough evidence to convict the ringleaders – but he apparently overlooked the Section's liberal methods, which saw enlisted men used to entice and sexually entrap the offenders. Details of the operations inevitably reached the press and when the public learned that youthful and innocent sailors were being asked to perform actions which lay well beyond the widest definition of patriotism there was an outcry. The Assistant Secretary responsible for Section A, publicly chastised the following year by senatorial investigation into the scandal, was the young Franklin Delano Roosevelt, and by the time Hart heard the rumours they had tainted the ascendant statesman's reputation. His example, Hart informed Munson, was now 'scenting the air', and if what he had heard was true, 'about every other person in the government service and diplomatic service are enlarged editions of Lord Alfred Douglas'.[47]

Hart was better placed than Munson knew to receive such intelligence. He had gone to Washington armed with a letter of introduction from Harry Candee and the subsequent meeting filled another long-standing void. In Gorham Munson he had found a correspondent capable of challenging and stimulating his literary mettle while at the same time preferring to remain incurious about his private life. Yet here too the poet needed sympathy and guidance and Wilbur Underwood now emerged, a veteran in the lists of forbidden love, to lend encouragement in the difficult amorous quest which characterized the remainder of Hart's life. Wilbur Walter St John Underwood was born in Washington in 1876 and lived all his life in the city. He was of the same generation as Grace and Clarence Crane and his career in government service spanned the poet's life. In the year that Hart was born he had graduated from Columbian – later George Washington – University and entered the State Department, in the Division of Communications and Records, at a salary of $900 per annum and by the time of his retirement in 1933, two years before his death, he had risen to become Chief of the Bureau of Index and Archives. This dutiful career notwithstanding, Underwood's real loyalties lay elsewhere: he was a member of Washington's Cosmos Club and he sustained his inquisitive mind with New York weekends and European vacations. He assembled a fastidious library of rare books and he wrote and published poetry. His work appeared occasionally in the American magazine *Commonweal* but he had much greater success in London: Oscar Wilde's publisher Elkin Matthews had released Underwood's *A Book of Masks* in 1907 and in 1909 *Damien of Molokai,* which told the story of a Catholic priest who had sacrificed his life to work in a leper colony. Underwood's last book, *The Way*, was published in 1927.

His writings were modest in quantity but by no means in accomplishment: there was a confidence and ease to his poetic sensibility and talent as well as a restless and questing aspect; and if he was preoccupied with the familiar lyric agonies of youth, truth, death and beauty he at least sought new solutions to the impasse. Hart turned to him for romantic counsel but an element of literary sympathy also fortified their friendship: Underwood was particularly well versed in the work of the English Romantics, Swinburne, the Pre-Raphaelites, the 1890s and the early

Yeats, but in the library of his house at 1331 Park Road Hart also found Rabelais, Petronius, Apuleius and various American writers then considered minor, most notably Herman Melville.

With nowhere else to turn for friendship in Washington, Hart soon became a regular visitor at the older man's house and was happy to accompany him to see theatrical productions bound for Broadway, even as he complained to Munson about the way Underwood's literary hopes had been withered by practical observance: 'A better critic and more interesting person one seldom meets, yet the routine of uninteresting work has probably killed forever his creative predisposition.'[48] Their absent friend Harry Candee was a frequent subject of conversation and Underwood was touched to learn that Hart 'looked up to him and adored him', even though Candee 'high-hatted' him and 'regarded Hart and the Candy Maker as high comedy' and 'ridiculed Hart's poetry and snubbed him'. Hart could have no complaints about Underwood's loyalty, however: the latter remembered that only a few days after they had first met 'I found him sitting on my door step when I came home from [the] office. He begged my help in a difficulty he was having with a black-mailing sailor'.[49] Underwood himself knew all about such entanglements and his interest in soldiers and sailors had reached a more exacting connoisseurship than Hart's. Later in their friendship the poet asked to hear all about some 'brass-buttoned-tattooed vision'[50] Underwood had met in New York and even Gorham Munson, an unlikely recipient of such confidences, was told that 'the episodes of the Satyricon are mild as compared to [Underwood's] usual exploits in N.Y. during the vacations'.[51] Appearances were deceptive, however. When Hart's friend Samuel Loveman met Underwood the last thing he suspected was a libidinous nature; instead he appeared 'a fantastic chalk-faced man of middle-age, with an extremely deliberate and artificial manner of speech'.[52] Sadly none of this manner of speech survives in his correspondence with Hart: although twenty-seven letters written by the poet to Underwood are extant, all the latter's replies have disappeared, almost certainly destroyed by Grace Crane as being unfit for posterity's eyes. An impression emerges, however, that the older man liked an ordered existence, that he resisted importing a perilous love life into a neat and bibliophile house, that dangerous pleasures were best pursued either in New York or on the other side of Capitol Hill: there was indeed another aspect to life in Washington and it was one he felt the young visitor should see.

His acquaintance in this underworld was a fantastic figure calling himself Madame Cooke, a self-styled androgyne whose appearance much intrigued the writer Allen Tate; they were introduced some months later and Tate marvelled at the 'scurrilous old devil that continually reminded me of the catamite at the Temple of Priapus in Petronius – his bullet head, thick knife-edged lips'. He was struck that Madame Cooke 'professed much affection' for Hart; and Hart himself was certainly fascinated.[53] Madame Cooke's evenings were a joy for all the government clerks who longed to meet sailors and for Hart it was the beginning of an enduring and famous infatuation. In later years he liked to quote Melville's 'The Temeraire' to Underwood – 'O, the navies old and oaken,/O, the Temeraire no more!' – and looking around at the orgies Madame Cooke hosted he began to see how erotic longing and escapist yearning could be fused in the bodies of the men who worked the seas, began to see also, as he admitted to Gorham Munson, that 'my satisfactions are far more remote and dangerous than yours, and my temptations frequent, alas!'[54] Whether he attended these evenings as a participant or whether he drank deeply merely of the bootleg liquor Madame Cooke dispensed it is impossible to know but when he came to look back fondly on his Petronian nights in Washington he could playfully suggest to Underwood that he had brought more than the appetite of curiosity to the feasts Madame Cooke contrived:

> Something terrible must in time happen in those 'parlors,' – you must guard the aged enchantress ... Her tender flesh, nourished from the flesh of a thousand lovers, and her over-refined sensibilities (think of the degradation of those maritime breakfasts!) must not be allowed to fall into unsympathetic hands! The roving eyes and suffering hands ... gobs may come and gobs may go, but *Smith* comes on forever![55]

7

Now that Hart was back in Cleveland, prosaic with work and parents by comparison, Washington's diplomats and drunken soldiery – indeed Madame
Cooke herself – assumed the aspect of a dream; and sexual encounters were once
again adventitious – part of the greater quest for love rather than the conveniently
arranged parlour games of a cynical imperial city. Perhaps he preferred it that way:
it was not that Hart Crane was too virtuous for the debaucheries he had seen, he
was too romantic, and no amount of intellectual or emotional inventiveness could
turn freely available flesh into a lyrical embodiment, a living mystery, a human revelation of the sublime, that he could love and adore in the grand tradition of the
poets. And what point did life have if it held no hope of love? His priority, to be
sure, was the creation of great art, but all the artists he admired taught him that
passion was as much a part of the creative process as cerebration – without it he
was therefore neither man nor artist; and for all the tattooed and easy sailors who
gave themselves at Madame Cooke's, for all the coarse attractive men whose eye
he sometimes caught as he rode the Cleveland tram lines, there would be one who
was invulnerable and unavailable except through love and that man must be the
object of his necessary search. As he explained to Munson a few weeks after
returning to Ohio,

> I don't believe in the 'sublimation' theory at all so far as it applies to my own
> experience ... Lately my continence has brought me nothing in the creative
> way, – it has only tended to create a confidence in me along lines of action, –
> business, execution, etc. There is not love enough in me at present to do a thing.
> This sounds romantic and silly, – you will understand that I mean and refer to
> the strongest incentive to the imagination, or, at least, the strongest in my par-
> ticular case.[1]

Washington had given him Underwood's friendship and a taste of easy hedonism he was not to encounter again for several years but the city itself now seemed, Munson was informed, 'the most elegantly restricted and bigoted community I ever ventured into', and although CA talked vaguely of sending him back there in January when cooler weather made confectionery a more appealing commodity, Hart never returned.[2] As it was he was glad to be back at home – at least at first. Books he had ordered from Paris – Rimbaud, Vildrac and Laforgue – had arrived and he had discovered Suetonius' *Lives of the Caesars*. Underwood had recommended his rare book dealer in England, Edward Baker of 14 John Bright Street, Birmingham, and Hart had written to order a copy of the *Satyricon*. At Munson's suggestion he was reading, and greatly enjoying, Dostoevsky, and because he never forgot the dues of friendship he set aside *The Possessed* in mid-November in order to read Sherwood Anderson's new novel, *Poor White*. By the same token he wanted to read Waldo Frank's latest publication, *Dark Mother*, but a review had convinced him that the book would prove 'too exclamatory, Semitic'.[3]

As usual, reading and the leisure it required were luxuries. After the fiasco in Washington, and with no idea how to keep his son busy, CA had decided for the time being to put him back in the factory at 208 St Clair Avenue, now struggling to satisfy Christmas demand, and soon Hart found himself, as he explained to Munson, 'elbow and knee-deep in shipping and packing'.[4] Grateful for his father's approbation, he was at first contented, if tired. By the end of November, however, Munson learned of boredom, exhaustion and disgust and by 5 December Hart had nothing but a sense of futility to share with his friend: 'Literature and art be hanged! – even ordinary existence isn't worth the candle in these States now.' Christmas with Grace and Mrs Hart loomed ahead as a potentially fraught occasion and thereafter, with their annual winter departure for the Caribbean, he would be consigned to another depressing lodging house. He was short of money, he was lonely, he had written nothing of significance for months and without knowing what exactly his next move should be he longed to escape his father's employment. In short, as he told Munson, he was 'very much at sea about everything that personally concerns me'.[5]

And then it happened again: by way of complication or deliverance, at the beginning of the third week of December he fell in love. Underwood had superseded Munson as a sexual confidant, and he received the dramatic news about a week into the affair. Hart's letter of announcement was typed – how could he expect his friend to struggle with his handwriting? – but its greater clarity would make it more immediately incriminating in the wrong hands, so he ensured discretion by expressing himself in oblique terms: 'The "golden halo" has widened, – descended upon me (or "us") and I've been blind with happiness and beauty for the last full week.' He was convinced he had 'found God again' and had become 'reconciled, strangely reconciled, to many aggravations'. There was as usual an unreality to the ecstasy – how could life appear so dispiriting and jejune one moment, and so coded with beautiful enigma the next? 'I have so much now to reverence, discovering more and more beauty every day, – beauty of character, manner, and body, that I am for the time, completely changed.' If only there were a way of perpetuating this heightened existence, this keener vision that came with being more alive, what challenges as man and poet might he not meet? 'How my life might be changed could this continue, but I scarcely dare to hope.'[6] The affair sustained him over Christmas and on 28 December, with mother and grandmother bound for the tropics, he moved into the Del Prado, a residential hotel at Euclid Avenue and 40th Street. More than ever convinced that he wanted to leave his father's employment he nevertheless found any decisions beyond the manoeuvres of love impossible.

A month into the affair he was so consumed that there was no possibility of writing to Munson and not mentioning his condition, which saw him 'caught dead tight' in passion. Of course he could write no poetry in such a situation – not only was he without ideas, he was almost without personality, so complete had his surrender been: 'I don't know how much blood I pay for these predicaments, – but I seem to live more during them than otherwise. They give the ego a rest.'[7] If Munson had not known before the extent of his friend's emotional and romantic idealism he could certainly not overlook it now: love was to be a repudiation of equable feeling, a certainty of extremes, an immersion of the self – it was to be love in the grand tradition, because there was no other way in which Hart could hope to mature as a love poet. And whatever happened he did not want to develop in the same manner as Matthew Josephson, who seemed increasingly reluctant, Munson was informed, 'to use any emotion in his poetry, – merely observation and sensation [and] I call such work apt to become thin'.[8] By 11 February the affair was still in progress and Hart continued to send accounts to Underwood and to Munson, coded for the former and rhapsodic but undetailed to the latter. Sometimes he wondered if Munson should be told at all; how much, after all, could he understand of these illicit passions? So Hart apologized if he had embarrassed his friend by being too frank: 'I have perhaps been a little too personal, – perhaps vulgar. But if anything's to blame it's the Subconscious rioting out through gates that only alcohol has the power to open.'[9]

One friend who could observe Hart at first hand rather than having to depend on letters was Bert Ginther, who had met the poet through Hervey Minns. Ginther at that stage worked in a bank in Cleveland; later he would serve time in prison for embezzlement. Although he and the poet never became close friends Ginther was granted a privilege accorded to very few in Hart's life at this time, as he himself recalled:

One Sunday morning when Hart came impromptu to my apartment, he brought with him his friend Bren – whose name in full was not given in my introduction to him. No matter that Bren was tall enough and handsome enough to make anybody – including myself – like him at first sight ... Hart laughed off fools who make over much great fuss about sex by saying from the way they talk you would think sex is a new discovery never known before our time.[10]

Ginther recalled weekend breakfasts of bootleg liquor, with readings from the newly arrived edition of Petronius. Harley McHugh, a Crane employee who had befriended Hart and who knew of his growing enthusiasm for drinking, occasionally accompanied him on expeditions to buy 'dago red' wine in the Little Italy around Cleveland's Mayfield Road and noted the poet's fluctuations of mood: 'He was never the same from one day to the next. One day he'd have the highest enthusiasm and the next day the deepest depression.'[11] However, the acquaintance who got to know Hart well at this time and whose friendship continued when the two men were living in New York met the poet one day at Laukhuff's book emporium. Hart was preparing to leave as the newcomer arrived, but Laukhuff detained him: 'Mr Loveman, here is Cleveland's great poet. You must meet him.' Hart was at ease and smilingly replied to the stranger, 'You know, most people want to meet me because I'm the son of a millionaire candy manufacturer.'[12]

Samuel Loveman was thirteen years older than Hart, had recently been discharged from the army and was now embarked on a career of writing, bookselling and general bibliophilia begun when he had been adopted as a protégé by the writer Ambrose Bierce. When Hart met him Loveman was working on a biography of the novelist Edgar Saltus and in later years he edited two magazines, *Trend* and the *Saturnian*, as well as publishing translations of Heine, Rilke, Rimbaud, Verlaine and Baudelaire. In 1926 he issued his most renowned achievement, a long poem called *The Hermaphrodite*, and once established in New York he became a well-known book dealer and publisher through his company, The Bodley Press. He was a man of considerable erudition and although by no means liked or trusted by all of Hart's Manhattan friends he certainly proved himself a stalwart in Grace Crane's declining years, even though she struck him as 'a spoiled child' who could be 'cold', 'a very commanding person, tall [and] imperious' with 'social ambitions which were never realized'.[13] But first he had to get to know her son.

A few nights after the meeting at Laukhuff's Loveman went by invitation to the Del Prado, no doubt in expectation of a discussion of the glories of prosody. He was both disappointed and astonished. Hart's welcome was 'assured and unhesitating' but it quickly progressed to revelation: '[His] practically instantaneous divulgence of himself as an active homosexual was as surprising as the fact that he could actually be one.' The confession was no doubt made on the presumption that Loveman shared the same sexual interests. What he lacked, however, was a sceptical eye or an inclination to question the construction of appearances, which is why Hart had to explain his evolving persona: 'He confided to me ... that he had so practised the art of camouflaging and hiding anything that might possibly be construed as feminine in his makeup – [hence] the long and somewhat ponderous, swaggering stride, his inveterate cigar-smoking, the Whitmanesque habit of wearing expensive but extremely comfortable and easy "crash" clothes – what had once been assumed actually became a part of him.' Later on in their friendship Loveman would notice that 'a subject that never seemed to evade Hart for very long was his inborn predilection – homosexuality'. Now he learned about the observances of the cult, including the details of Hart's nocturnal life at Madame Cooke's, 'where he had become extensively involved in the progressive activities of a well-defined circle of inverts', and in support of his claims Hart read aloud letters he had received from Underwood and Candee, letters 'of an outrageously suggestive nature in a jargon that bore largely on the enormous sexual activities in their lives'. The next exhibit, the snubbing letter from Ezra Pound, was literary, however, and thus the conversation veered towards poetry, and by the time Loveman 'staggered dizzily out at two in the morning' he had had readings from T.S. Eliot, Edward Thomas, Robert Frost and Hart's own work.[14]

Declaring himself sexually to Loveman was one thing but at this stage Hart could see little point in divulging his artistic uncertainties, which remained anxieties reserved for more seasoned literary correspondents. Yet as his spell of poetic silence persisted he considered the prevailing literary sectarianism and wondered where his loyalties should lie. Waldo Frank and the new Americanists aside, wherever he looked he found disillusion with contemporary life tending to despair. It was one thing to evoke the modern discontent with Eliot's sophistication and technical assurance, but there were so many practitioners of inanition now and how many of them merited serious attention? He admired Aldous Huxley, for instance, but his 'Leda' poems, 'dry and very clever', had been a disappointment. 'Is real poetry so obviously clever?' he asked Munson. 'Modern life and its vacuity seems to me to be responsible for such work. There is only a lime or a lemon to squeeze or a pepperpot left to shake.'[15] At least Huxley had formal elegance and polymathic brilliance – but what was one to make of the latest gossip from Greenwich Village, now enthralled by the nihilistic charades of Dadaism? How could one react to the antics of Man Ray and Marcel Duchamp, with their exhibitions of bicycle wheels and urinals and their strident determination to make the public herd reconsider its aesthetic complacency, but in the most futile, sterile way? The Baroness had now been proclaimed, he understood, a Dadaist avatar, and friends intelligent enough to know better credited the nonsense. Matthew Josephson became a conspicuous convert, but Hart's conscience was clear where that apostasy was concerned. After all, he indicated his doubts to Josephson early in 1921: 'I cannot figure out just what Dadaism is beyond an insane jumble of the four winds, the six senses, and plum pudding. But if the Baroness is to be a keystone for it, – then I think I can possibly know when it is coming and avoid it.'[16]

But if he stepped aside from this literary vogue that appeared to be sweeping all before it where did he belong? Art was not random or meaningless and the more he read of the European canon the more convinced he was of that fact. Yet there was Eliot, not only more assured as a poet than he but with all the scholarship of the Renaissance apparently at his fingertips – but for all that a timid renunciant of modern life whose fear of humanity seemed equalled only by his impatience with the limitations of its learning. Joyce and Pound – similarly indifferent to the multitude – were no better: although he admired them greatly, did he want to belong to their impenetrable ranks? Hart already knew enough of Shakespeare and Marlowe and Webster to admire not only their verbal richness and allusiveness but also their determination to woo the crowds with spectacle and sensation. Did his own age allow for nothing similar, a literary art which appealed to broad humanity while at the same time honouring the lyric flame? Was there even a theoretical hope any longer of democratic high art? The consensus seemed to be that there was not, and his own sense of isolation and relegation as a poet in Akron and Cleveland seemed to corroborate that conviction.

But did he see the dilemma clearly? What if his sense of lonely incongruity stemmed instead from his illegal sexuality, which gave him no choice but to write about erotic love in oblique – and possibly coded – terms he was still struggling to master? In any case, whether he was set apart by his artistic, or by his sexual, ambitions, the thought of proceeding as a poet on the basis of estrangement, and hence of writing only for a knowing coterie, dismayed the American within him. Audiences should be wide, as wide as poetic ambition: looking within himself he saw the artist, eternal and striving, the lover, here illicit, and the American, yearning forever for the vindication of a myth, and as a poet he must speak for these varying optimists. But how be prolocutor for all three at once? Perhaps more than one manner, more than one literary idiom, was required for the tasks that lay ahead? It was a daunting thought, especially when he still felt himself to be writing in imitation of others – in so far as he was writing at all.

But inspiration was like love – it came when least expected – and suddenly in February 1921 he ascended to a loftier plateau of accomplishment when the weeks of literary silence ended as mysteriously as they had begun. One day perhaps he would be able to agree with Frank and the visionaries who insisted that the pristine possibilities of American expectation still existed, that the country continued to enshrine restless humanity's mythic and perfectionist yearnings – but not yet. When he began his first new poem in months he wrote once again in disillusion. But he was no longer a Porphyro in Akron diligently reworking the supine regrets of Eliot and Pound in order to be considered for membership of a fashionable group of literary malcontents: with 'Black Tambourine' Hart Crane emerged as a mature poet who had his own tale to tell about the pariahs of the modern age. His poetic taciturnity had enabled him to absorb and reconcile the lessons of his various mentors and now he found himself able to speak in accents almost all his own and to project personal observation in terms which were symbolic but none the less powerful. Now he could fault the divisiveness and materialism of modern America not in abject and miserable terms but with a lapidary elegance that gave 'Black Tambourine' the concision and finality of an epitaph.

In the weeks since Christmas CA had moved Hart from the factory to the warehouse which processed bulk orders for the Crane stores in Cleveland and then to the basement of the Crane restaurant at 13th Street and Euclid Avenue – all in the hope of finding some occupation which would keep his son both busy and absorbed. The job in the restaurant storeroom, where Hart replaced a discharged black handyman, left him with ample hours for reading and writing and, when he was in the mood, for joking with the workers in the kitchens opposite, all of whom were also black and thus excluded as patrons from the establishment upstairs. Sherwood Anderson, travelling in the South, had written from Alabama that 'the Negroes are the living wonder of this place'. What an achievement it would be, he thought, for a writer to 'penetrate into the home and life of the Southern Negro and not taint it in the ordinary superficial way'.[17] The challenge echoed in Hart's mind as he sat in the basement waiting for the working day to end; no doubt his neighbours across the corridor were equally impatient, although unlike him they could not ascend to parity with the white and affluent world above when they went home. Theirs was a relegation more absolute than that faced by any artist – they were indeed supreme symbols of American exclusion. Rather than attempt the penetration of their lives that Anderson had recommended – and that Hart knew to be impossible – he would evoke the blacks he knew symbolically. 'Black Tambourine' would not be a contribution to racial polemic – as Hart later told Munson, 'A propagandist for either side of the Negro question could find anything he wanted to in it' – but rather an indictment of a society which demanded mercantile conformity and relegated its dissidents to basements of day-dreaming and despair.[18]

Having found his appropriate symbol Crane wrote protestingly, but in terms which were neither petulant nor self-pitying. Eliot and Baudelaire may have contributed to the compression and polished assurance which only weeks ago would have been beyond him but the style and authority are the author's. The first of the poem's three stanzas is particularly fine – Imagism's clarity and succinctness have been remembered, and combine with a symbolic ease and strong visual imagination to evoke a state of lethargic torment:

The interests of a black man in a cellar
Mark tardy judgment on the world's closed door.
Gnats toss in the shadow of a bottle,
And a roach spans a crevice in the floor.

The central stanza invokes Aesop, the fabulist thought to have been a slave of Samos about 600 BC. Whether or not he ever existed, his legend survives in 'mingling incantations on the air' and his appearance in Crane's poem indicates that there is, as it were, a moral to this elegant poem, a 'tardy judgment' on those who close society's doors. Businessmen aside, America is a society of the displaced which consigns its misfits to limbo. For artists that no man's land lies between the inspiration of a cultural past and the possibilities for its future expression. But artists are not alone in their neglected hinterland:

> The black man, forlorn in the cellar,
> Wanders in some mid-kingdom, dark, that lies,
> Between his tambourine, stuck on the wall,
> And, in Africa, a carcass quick with flies.[19]

Blacks are also stranded, but their state of 'mid-kingdom' dispossession is even more poignant. The 'world's closed door' of white sovereignty relegates them to crass minstrelsy: however passionately they strike their token tambourines, the Africa of their past is lost for ever and can never be anything more than a decaying inheritance of racial memories.

Hart sent a copy of his new poem to Munson on 24 February and more in hope than expectation he dispatched a duplicate to the *Dial*, which promptly rejected the offering. That disappointment notwithstanding, he knew self-congratulation was in order and as he undertook revisions he told Munson that 'Black Tambourine' was 'something definitely my own ... I am getting nearer to what core I have, right along, I think'.[20] Not the least of the satisfactions came with the confidence that he could now use words with a new liberty of nuance. As he put it to Sherwood Anderson some months later when describing his general poetic policy, 'What I want to get ... is an "interior" form, a form that is so thorough and intense as to dye the words themselves with a peculiarity of meaning, slightly different maybe from the ordinary definition of them separate from the poem. If you remember my "Black Tambourine" you will perhaps agree with me that I have at least accomplished this idea once.'[21] Anderson, in no sense a Symbolist, missed the point of the poem altogether and even the more incisive Munson applied for an explanation, only to be informed by Hart that the poem was 'a description and bundle of insinuations' the value of which lay 'in what a painter would call its "tactile" quality, – an entirely aesthetic feature'.[22] Happily the *Double Dealer* liked 'Black Tambourine' unequivocally and accepted it for publication in June: when Allen Tate, a great critic in the making and soon one of Hart's most important friends, read the poem he thought he had seen 'nothing like it previously in Anglo-American poetry'.[23]

It was the last poem Hart wrote in his father's employment. Ever since his return from Washington his responsibilities in the Crane Company had been provisional and unsatisfactory and his job in the storeroom, for all its easy hours, could never constitute a permanent solution to the problem father and son faced of what Hart was to do. As far as the poet himself was concerned the situation was straightforward in an abstract sort of way – without knowing how he was going to pay the bills he at least knew he wanted no part in his father's enterprises. Since CA was more practical, the situation struck him as more complicated, although it was now clear to him that unless he wanted to see his son maintained in a succession of menial jobs there was no room for him at his company: quite simply, he lacked the initiative or commitment necessary to an heir apparent. Again the two men met to discuss the future, but this time they could agree only on the vaguest principle: that Hart must be allowed to go his own way if he was so determined. This conclusion, such as it was, occurred early in 1921 and Munson was the first to hear not only of Hart's strategy but also of its victorious outcome: 'You see I have not said anything to him about my personal interests for almost two years, leaving him only what details of indifference to business as naturally revealed themselves throughout my association with him, to judge from.'[24] It was agreed that Hart should find some more literary occupation, whereupon he and CA would part professional company. There was talk of journalism, but talk it remained and weeks drifted by. Hart wrote 'Black Tambourine' and began another work, a poem, he told Munson, 'on adolescence, – which, very adolescently, I have never finished'. He polished four lines before dismissing them as being too derivative of Eliot and Huxley but they were sent to his friend anyway as representing 'somewhat my mood':

'The mind shall burst its aquarium vagueness,
Its melon opacity of graduate dawn'; –
Wise-youthful prophecy to the tired pillows
Resentful of the room and shades, – still drawn. –[25]

Though inconclusive, the words spoke volumes about boredom and accidie: Hart was indeed directionless and dissatisfied and as such in no frame of mind to find a satisfactory job. CA's prevailing thoughts and feelings are now unknown but one assumes that with the best will in the world he sometimes felt beside himself with frustration that his son could be so lovable and yet so difficult, so extreme in mood and reaction and so reckless in youthful idealism and financial understanding. Every time he went downstairs it was to find Hart reading or writing in the storeroom; he was hardly likely to find another job that way, whatever his declared ambitions on the subject, and such obvious disaffection scarcely set an example to the other employees. He must stop – so CA indicated that he would like his son to leave his literary projects behind in the morning. Hart was always ready to find onslaughts and insults where none had been intended and Clarence Crane's words were still rankling when Grace and Mrs Hart returned from the Isle of Pines in

April. Grace was appalled to learn that her son was working in a basement in a job, moreover, formerly held by a black man: the very idea was an outrage and an attempt on her former husband's part to humiliate her; and now that Hart was back in his third-floor tower at East 115th Street he was an easy prey to his mother's righteous indignation. All his life he was defenceless against her verbal assaults, whether of anger or sarcasm, and now her articulate displeasure reawakened grievances accumulated at the Crane Company in the last eighteen months.

It had not, after all, been an easy time. Irrespective of the hard work his father had imposed upon him there had been other psychological strains: in theory he had been an integrated member of the company – equal to some and subordinate to others – but all along of course he was the boss's son, the bearer of a symbolic name and conspicuous in all his failings. CA's dealings with Hart had doubtless been well intentioned but as a man he was not always nimble when manoeuvring to assist. In any case, what preparation had he ever received for negotiating with his exotic offspring? In a more diplomatic and equable family this difficult situation would have resolved itself peacefully but among the Cranes it had the makings of grand recrimination and on 19 April the drama unfolded. Its details survive in only one account: we shall never know how Clarence Crane viewed the fight which estranged him from his son for two years but in the narrative put forth by Grace Crane the collision seems both petty and theatrical. CA descended to the restaurant basement that morning but this time Hart was not reading or writing on company time: he was in the kitchens eating a late breakfast and joking with the employees. It was one thing that his son should do nothing, but quite another that he should cause others to be idle, and CA rebuked Hart publicly and told him to return at once to the storeroom. As Hart turned in compliance he heard his father add that since he was now living with his mother he could eat with her as well. Accusations of dependence and disloyalty, of immaturity and ingratitude, were implicit in this ill-judged coda and perhaps before knowing what he did Hart turned and threw the storeroom keys at his father's feet and announced he was finished with the Crane Company. CA threatened disinheritance unless his son apologized at once but there was no going back now, given the audience, and Hart hurled imprecations on his father and his father's fortune and exited stage left. By the time he reached East 115th Street, at least according to Grace, his face was disfigured with the red hives that always plagued him in times of intense stress. He went to bed, emerging the next day to inform Munson of the stand Art had taken against Commerce:

I've been treated like a dog now for two years, – and only am sorry it took me so long to find out the simple impossibility of ever doing anything with [CA] or for him. It will take me many months, I fear, to erase from memory the image of his overbearing head leaning over me like a gargoyle. ... Whatever comes now is surely better than the past. I shall learn to be somewhere near free again, – at least free from the hatred that has corroded me into illness.[26]

Of course his rebellion could not prove domestically liberating: at a stroke he become more reliant on his mother, and she on him, and without knowing it he eliminated the counterbalance to her emotionally demanding presence. As for Grace, if she did spur the confrontation, however unwittingly, she brought upon herself a dependant and one she could no longer easily support. The consequences of the fight lay some years distant but for now, once dust and silence had settled over the opposing encampments, the question was simple. What was Hart to do?

Writing was out of the question – he felt far too unsettled – and it could only be hoped that he would find a job with the new Cleveland newspaper he had heard was about to be established, or with the advertising company a friend had told him would be looking for copy-writers in the summer. In the meantime, he informed Munson on 3 May, he was seriously considering getting a job 'running automobiles around a garage'.[27] On 16 May he was still unoccupied and increasingly convinced, he told his friend, that jobs and friendly job offers were no more than 'slippery fish'. Relations with Grace were harmonious for the time being, but he knew that situation would not last: 'I am practically on my mother's hands here at home, – and you can believe me that such a situation is far from a pleasant one for me who have been used to paying my own way now for some time.'[28] He read books about advertising and brochures about business, hoping to prepare himself for the wide world, and he showed willing around the house, thus putting himself, he told Munson, 'at the mercy of every domestic want that comes up, and [I] am in turn chauffeur, parlour maid, dish washer and errand chaser'.[29] Physically he felt well, at least, but poverty was so depressing, and he longed to have the money to buy some cigars and a new suit. He considered working as a postal clerk, but despite the $135 monthly salary he contented himself instead with seeing the odd film and being alternately entertained and irritated by the *Dial*, the *Freeman*, the *Little Review* and the *New Republic*.

There was rejoicing when he secured the job as an advertising copy-writer but bitter disappointment a few days later when he found that his responsibilities were those of an office boy. In October, as 'foreman' of a small group of men responsible for distributing advertising material around Cleveland, he earned $2.50 and in November his one week as a commission salesman with the S.H. Kleinman Realty Company yielded precisely nothing. If he stayed at home he faced the increasingly reproachful glances of his mother and if he set out in search of a job he ran the risk of encountering his father; in either event it was hard to know whether it was his fault that he could find no work or Cleveland's. His birthday should have been a brief respite from self-doubt and dejection but that date coincided with Cleveland's 125th anniversary and as Hart watched the festivities he felt an angry isolation he was sure Munson would understand. Held up in traffic, 'I spent two hours of painful rumination ending with such disgust at America and everything in it'. There amidst the crowd, 'decked out in Colonial rags as the founder of the city', was Cleveland's richest citizen, and as Hart pondered the spectacle he found himself concurring with the Baroness: 'Our people have no *atom* of a conception of beauty – and don't want it.' Some stray Chinese, 'in antique vestments & liveries' passed by 'the (inevitable) Soldier's Monument' and lent such dignity as they could to the scene, but overall it was a distressing spectacle and one which made him yearn for flag-free Greenwich Village: 'If ever I felt alone it has been today.'[30]

He was not the only Clevelander to remain aloof from the patriotism and the pageantry. In March Sam Loveman had shown him some drawings and watercolours executed by a local artist named William Sommer and Hart's excitement was such that he insisted on being introduced to the painter. The meeting occurred about two weeks prior to the confrontation with CA and within days, assuring Munson that Sommer's work exhibited 'the most astonishing marks of genius that have passed before my eyes in original form', Hart was dispatching letters to New York aimed at rescuing this ageing genius from Midwestern neglect.[31] As he later discovered, however, Sommer's priorities were not his: the painter's life was one of cheerful obscurity and his worldly ambitions extended no further than the Ohio hills which loomed in his landscapes and portraits. Sommer, born in Detroit in 1867 of German ancestry, received a basic education and a Sunday morning schooling in art before being apprenticed for seven years to the Calvert Lithography Company, where he acquired the technical skills which enabled him to support himself as a journeyman lithographer in Boston and a poster artist in New York. In 1890 he went to London and through the generosity of a friend was able to attend an art school in Munich before returning to America, married life, and a job with the Otis Lithography Company of Cleveland. In 1914, with savings of $1,200 amassed after years of frugal living, he bought a house and a nearby abandoned schoolroom at Brandywine Falls in Northfield Township twenty miles from Cleveland and it was between these two properties that he divided his time when the newly fatherless Hart Crane befriended him in May.

To the young romantic Sommer's life was a paradigm of artistic passion far removed from the mercenary ordinances of Clarence Crane. In fact his existence rested on ordered practicality and an understanding that art, however zealously practised, was likely to be an avocation in need of disciplined subsidy. Painting was a weekend pastime – for the remainder of the week Sommer struggled daily to his lithographer's desk in Cleveland and then home again each evening, a journey which began and ended every day with a five-mile walk, undertaken by lantern light in winter, between Brandywine Falls and the nearest stop on the inter-urban trolley line. Between 1933 and 1941, engaged by the Public Works of Art Project under the aegis of the Works Progress Administration, Sommer was to complete several important municipal commissions: the Board of Education Building in Akron, the post office in Geneva, and the periodical reading room in Cleveland Public Library were all enlivened by his murals and until his death in

1949 the 'Sage of Brandywine' was recognized as an important figure in Ohio's cultural life. He was fond of saying that 'no man can find greatness on a road which has led to greatness for another – he must find his own road', and for the painter that route was commanded by German literature and by the speculations of Hegel, Kant and Nietzsche.[32] He had made a pilgrimage to New York in 1913 to see the Armory Show of European Impressionists and the effect of the exposure was lifelong: he followed the meanderings of European modernism thereafter and when Hart befriended him he was emerging from his apprenticeship to Gauguin and Matisse to embrace instead the influence of Klee, Kandinsky and the English Vorticists before finally submitting to the greatness of Cézanne. He drew tirelessly, in every spare moment in the week and on every scrap of paper, but it was at weekends that he applied the style and chromatic sense of his mentors to renditions of the life around him – his wife working in the kitchen, local children, cows in Gauguin's mauves and glimpses of the Brandywine Creek reinterpreted in the geometrical harmonies of Cézanne.

With characteristic generosity and zeal Hart determined to rescue Sommer from obscurity: his work was beyond doubt superior to that of Henri Gaudier-Brzeska and Boardman Robinson and sketches and minor fragments were hastily sent to whet the curiosity of Joseph Kling. If he was unimpressed then other overtures could be made, to the *Dial*, the *Liberator* and the *Little Review*, as well as to Marius de Zayas, director of the Modern Gallery in Manhattan. With New York's acclaim, mercantile Cleveland would understand the extent of its dereliction and what marvels of renaissance might not then ensue? As he wrote to Munson, recruiting his assistance in persuading the Manhattan art world to buy the painter's work, 'If we could realize enough to give Sommer a year's freedom from the drudgery of the lithograph factory, – he would then have a real opportunity to realize his tremendous reach.'[33]

The artist had absolutely no interest in metropolitan patronage but it was impossible not to be disarmed by Hart's enthusiasm and conviction and a friendship rapidly developed between the two men, with Sommer no doubt flattered to find a young and impassioned disciple more alive to art and ideas than his own three stolid sons. For his part, disappointed and embittered by paternal incomprehension, Hart thought he had found the father he should have had: Sommer understood the travails of creation in a way that CA did not and he had a capacity for fun that equalled his intellectual and philosophical curiosity. Hart was determined, he explained to Munson, 'to regain a mental and spiritual status that has been lost to me for over a year' and here was providential guidance. Soon he and the artist were meeting weekly in Cleveland and retreating to the Sanctum de la Tour to spar with an old set of boxing gloves Hart had discovered, to declaim Heine, to listen to records of Chopin and Debussy, or even to draw together. Ever since childhood Hart had been interested in drawing and painting and as an adult he befriended many artists and acquainted himself with their ideas of form and technique. Sommer now revived that interest and under his guidance Hart began to draw and paint once more. He found the activity 'a tremendous stimulation', he informed Munson, and on the basis of the older artist's approbation was convinced that 'my drawings are original'.[34]

It was in the course of weekends at the schoolhouse at Brandywine Falls, however, that Sommer really came into his own and on returning from his first visit at the end of June Hart sat down drunk at 'Saturday Midnight' to share with Munson an excitement he could not contain overnight: 'Forgive my enthusiasm – I have been so dazzled for the last 8 hours that I may seem somewhat incoherent in my expression.' He had brought back numerous watercolours and drawings soon to be forwarded to Munson for potential sale in New York but the treasure trove he had discovered was still rich with wonder: he had found the white walls of Sommer's schoolhouse densely hung 'with such an array of things as you have never seen', and it took little imagination to picture this hermitage overrun with Manhattan art dealers 'all tearing each other's hair for the first chance of exhibiting such stuff'. Art was not the only distraction: Sommer's house and studio were littered with scraps of paper bearing quotations transcribed from treatises on art, philosophy and aesthetics, and his conversation was no less various. Both he and Hart liked to declaim and then analyse favourite passages of poetry but the artist was also well versed in the aesthetic speculations of Roger Fry, Clive Bell, Blake and Cézanne, and it was this learning that lent him the renown of a sage and attracted younger artists and writers to the informal, cider-merry salons he held each weekend. Although Hart visited Sommer numerous times over the next two years and was without doubt a special protégé he often had to share the painter's companionship with other admirers. And so it was on this first occasion, when Hart gauged the tempo of the conviviality – depending on mood Sommer might hold court at the large studio table or turn ham actor and recite his favourite soliloquies or pontificate about prevailing cultural endeavour. '"Dynamism" is the splendid & fitting word for Sommer', Munson was assured, and no doubt many of the other guests concurred. What the visitors did not see was the incessant and anguished self-assessment that underlay the painter's artistry and which exposed him in his last years to alcoholism. For much of his adult life, however, he looked to his wife Martha to alleviate these anxious tendencies, which Hart Crane certainly shared, even if he never knew about them.[35]

Indeed the artist and the poet were brought together because similar aesthetic convictions proved soothing to similar anxieties. Sommer had a holistic comprehension of existence, as Hart and the other guests would discover in the course of the long symposiums that often ended with guests drunkenly proceeding along the dirt track in the darkness to catch the last trolley back to Cleveland, hoping along the way that their torches of lighted newspapers would persuade the driver to stop. Sommer believed that since all life was unified there could be no such thing as a discrete art – how else could one explain the phenomenon of synæsthesia, the 'seeing' of music as colour and the possible interpretation of poetry in like fashion? For Hart, avid always for epiphany, and newly reminded by the rift with CA of the fractured aspect of his own life, such a conviction of universal wholeness was both alluring and compelling. It was the artist's duty to penetrate beneath life's shimmering surface in search of that inner coherence. Art was not just about seeing and believing – it entailed an experience of personal transformation almost akin to possession, as Sommer insisted in a cherished theory: 'For most a work of art means imitating the object, the reproduction of what is before us, but to the real artist it all goes through a process of recreating under the spell of driving powers, that he partly controls but has no power to unfetter, unchain or free from bonds.'[36] There was a glory to this notion of creativity, and as the poet absorbed the implications he discovered that Sommer was much impressed by the thinking of P.D. Ouspensky's *Tertium Organum*, lent to Hart by Harry Candee in Akron, which asserted that there was a higher reality beyond that apprehended by the senses and that the higher consciousness which understood this fact transformed the emotional and physical awareness of quotidian life. Although it was to be at least a year before Hart read Ouspensky the origins of the enormous influence he was to have on the poet's thinking began now.

As Hart and the painter grew closer together in friendship and spiritual communing, as they scanned the Ohio hills for their subterranean poetry, Sommer decided to execute an ink and matchstick portrait of his friend – and rendered him as a severe and intense visionary, his eyes focused on invisible horizons. Meanwhile, at considerable cost to himself, Hart had the painter's best pictures photographed for New York appraisal and suggested to Munson, still acting as his Manhattan agent, that it should be easy to tempt potential buyers to pay $20 for life drawings and $30 for watercolours. Youthful enthusiasm was soon confounded, however: Munson bought one picture himself and sold a couple to James Sibley Watson of the *Dial* and another to William Carlos Williams, incidentally another believer in the artist's need to transcend sensory impression for invisible revelation, but the remaining works went unclaimed. Sommer was unmoved by the failure but Hart had a great capacity for disappointment and swore in future to avoid the turbid waters of the New York art world, with their 'scurvy picture dealers that suck their sustenance by putting themselves between the artist and the public and bleeding them both'.[37]

It was a sentiment that might well have been appreciated by a new social circle that claimed him as 1921 proceeded. Either through Sommer or Laukhuff he met a young French-Swiss painter named William Lescaze who had moved to Cleveland from Switzerland the previous year because his 'Cleveland' bicycle had carried him so faithfully around the streets of Geneva. A recent exhibition of his art had 'caused a terrible furor', Munson was informed, and when Hart visited the gallery he noted 'a peculiar sharp diabolism' to the painter's work which set it as far apart from Sommer's vision as Rabelais was from Baudelaire.[38] Knowing how uncertain the artist's lot could be, Lescaze had come to Ohio in the hope of find-ing work as an architectural draughtsman. Although he was a pragmatist, however, he had not renounced his passionate conviction in the importance of the arts: his illustrated monographs and his violin had accompanied him into emigration and within months of arriving in Cleveland he had declared his European seriousness about art and ideas by convening a salon for the city's painters, writers and musi-cians. Since Hart had already demonstrated his loyalty to creative endeavour by sending some of Lescaze's work to the *Little Review* he was a natural candidate for membership of this coterie, which began by meeting opposite the Cleveland YMCA on the top floor of the hotel where Lescaze lived. Gradually, Truth and Beauty also found themselves discussed in the ballroom of the New Amsterdam Hotel, Klein's Hungarian Restaurant on Prospect Avenue, and of course Hart's Sanctum de la Tour. Loveman, Laukhuff and Sommer were among the group's familiar faces, but Hart now met Charles Harris, an engineer who also wrote poetry; Charles Baldwin, a writer and journalist; Dudley Carroll, a Nashville lawyer; Jean Binet, who taught eurhythmics at the Cleveland Institute of Music and was studying composition under Ernest Bloch, composer-conductor at the Cleveland Orchestra; and Richard Rychtarik, a twenty-seven-year-old set designer for the Cleveland and Metropolitan Operas who had emigrated from Prague the previous year.

All his life Hart instinctively sought membership of a group or school, even as he remained somehow alone, and this sort of weekly conviviality was a delight to him: a reassurance of the significance of his self-appointed calling and, albeit ten-uously, a connection to European sophistication and the historic citadels of its expression. Loveman remembered how in the course of these evenings Hart's 'boisterous and unmorbid streak of humour would free itself from the restraints [of] home'; thereafter he would deliver 'himself with an incessant, roaming and ever-widening variation over the literary field'.[39] Richard Rychtarik, along with his wife Charlotte, proved loyal if long-distance friends to Hart for the rest of his life and the Czech's fascination with the poet began now. Sensing that Hart 'didn't want to be alone too much', he found him 'more smiling than anybody I know'. 'He did everything with the greatest enthusiasm ... and every person on the street was either funny to him or remarkable.' He was charming, pipe-smoking and gre-garious; he drew with accomplishment and he revered Stravinsky.[40]

Lescaze also noted the exhilaration, but thought it the obverse of a coin: Hart could be 'very out-going when he was not depressed, because he could be extremely depressed'. This oscillating energy was responsible for his conver-sational fluency, and often he and Lescaze dominated the cultural discourse, the poet with monologues ranging from his current poetic passion to the pleasures of driving his mother's car or the glories of red wine. These were men's evenings as far as Hart was concerned – the bibulousness was a part of the male *bonhomie* that went with smoking and cologne and he resented the intrusion of women:

they distracted the other participants from higher matters and insisted, he informed Munson, 'upon being the center of attention irrespective of their ability to take part in any argument'.[41] But then he and Lescaze took to meeting alone at East 115th Street, particularly on Sundays, and the latter explained his admiration for Matisse, Picasso and Braque, for Gide and for Proust, or they exchanged theories and admiration about shared deities – Pound, Joyce, Donne and Eliot. Grace struck the visitor as a 'quite elegant, quite handsome woman [who] dressed very well' and sometimes she would allow her son and his guest to drive into the country in her electric car. 'It never went awfully fast but it was quite a thrill,' Lescaze remembered, and he and Hart would spend a morning in poetry-quoting matches. The poet's Victrola was another much-cherished toy and Lescaze was struck by the way he would play records very loudly while declaiming poetry. It was during one of these happy interludes that he drew Hart in his book-lined chamber with its floral wallpaper. Like Sommer before him he saw his model as a sort of visionary, but this time there was an angular urgency to the face, tilted as it was on a dramatic axis, and whereas one eye was hollow, the other gazed upward with unblinking intensity on some elevated enigma. Hart had the picture framed and carried it with him for the remainder of his peripatetic life.[42]

After the brilliance of 'Black Tambourine' the vision had once again receded from reach, however, and for all the leisure of his unemployed summer Hart achieved little significant writing. Ambitions to produce articles on Ezra Pound for *Shadowland* and on James Joyce for the *Double Dealer* came to nothing and plans to write a play about the abolitionist John Brown, recently the subject of a new biography, proved equally forlorn. He did succeed in completing an essay on Sherwood Anderson for the *Double Dealer* for which the magazine paid him $20 but Munson and Lescaze were unimpressed by the tribute and there was something about Hart's admiration for this writer which already belonged to a past phase of a short but rapid life. Even the two lyrics of the summer, 'A Persuasion', published in October by the *Measure*, and 'Pastorale', appearing concurrently in the *Dial*, where Hart shared covers with Santayana, D.H. Lawrence and Anatole France, seemed slight and a poetic biding of time. Inspiration eluded him – so with encouragement from Lescaze and indispensable assistance from a dictionary he translated De Gourmont's *Marginalia* on Poe and Baudelaire, as well as some poems by Vildrac and the three 'Locutions des Pierrots' by Laforgue. These renditions were truly labours of love, since Hart had difficulties with even simple French, but he relied on his emotional sympathies with the poets as his linguistic mediator and eventually sold the translations of Laforgue to the *Double Dealer* and bought a pair of shoes with the proceeds. He needed more than footwear, however, and for the time being he had no new work to sell: in any case, even if he had, what good would it do financially? What money would he ever make from his art? After a summer of dependence on Grace he knew he needed some kind of job more urgently than ever and if he had at least resisted the temptation to appeal to CA for forgiveness and help, his father's parallel refusal to volunteer assistance showed him where he inherited his principled steadfastness.

To compound his sense of gloom and isolation, one New York correspondent after another confirmed that a great migration from Greenwich Village was under way: a discontented argosy of writers, painters and mavericks was preparing to embark for the capitals of bankrupt Europe, there to escape 'Babbitry', Prohibition, memories of the xenophobic Palmer Raids instigated by former Attorney-General Mitchell Palmer and numerous other manifestations of American intolerance and to enjoy instead a favourable rate of exchange and a social lustre they considered themselves denied at home. Alfred Kreymborg, Matthew Josephson, Sherwood Anderson and, loneliest thought of all, Gorham Munson all booked passage in 1921, along with a host of figures still only known to Hart by name or reputation; friendship, or acquaintance, would come later with e.e. cummings, Djuna Barnes, William Slater Brown, Malcolm Cowley and Paul Rosenfeld. The majority settled in Paris, where Gertrude Stein maintained her expatriate court at 27 rue de Fleurus, but colonies of American malcontents also established themselves in Vienna, Rome, Florence and Berlin. Hart would happily have joined the exodus, but as matters stood he was stranded in sultry Cleveland with his mother, his grandmother, his estranged father and an adopted stray cat, penniless and lonely, in need of the stimulus provided by letters but jealous of the adventures his correspondents related.

To compound the gloom, he was once again without a love life. The liaison with which he had begun the year, and which had promised such intensities of feeling and such possibilities of transcendence, had ebbed away, like the affair before it. Was this the preordained pattern of life, that it should be a succession of hopes and disappointments and passions and desires which washed and flowed with the inscrutable predictability of the tides, only to end in remorse and regret? There was nobody at hand to advise, as usual, but whatever the expectations with which Hart had pursued his last two affairs he now knew that loss of innocence did not mean loss of virginity but loss of faith: lovers always absconded and promises, it seemed, were always broken. His parents had taught him this lesson but now he suspected it was something each generation had to learn for itself. By the beginning of September this wisdom, conceived as the great divide between adolescence and maturity, was working itself poetically in his mind. Once again, a symbolic instinct interceded: rather than picture the loss of innocence as occurring on some mundane threshold he transferred it to the great sea-shore of life. How long ago his own innocence seemed – when he looked back on his earlier self he appeared as remote as the group of children he now envisaged at play by the sea in the opening lines of the new poem: 'Above the fresh ruffles of the surf/Bright striped urchins flay each other with sand.' Disembodied and disillusioned the poet watched them at play, with the scene around so beguiling and beautiful: 'The sun beats lightning on the waves,/The waves fold thunder on the sand.' The children were right to enjoy themselves, but they should know the imminence of the danger: the sea of life which they are certain to explore contains many treacherous depths, none more dangerous than those of emotional disappointment, and it is this knowledge that charges the happiness of life with such poignancy:

> O brilliant kids, frisk with your dog,
> Fondle your shells and sticks, bleached
> By time and the elements; but there is a line
> You must not cross nor ever trust beyond it
> Spry cordage of your bodies to caresses
> Too lichen-faithful from too wide a breast.
> The bottom of the sea is cruel.[43]

And there he left it, not quite knowing how to conclude. Experience was cruel, and at this stage Crane was still too philosophically immature to recognize that disappointment and betrayal lent heroism to the quest for love and formed a crucial contrast to its ecstasies. On 1 October, convinced that it had 'a certain crispness to recommend it', he sent the poem to Munson, but thereafter it was set aside and a year later he still felt unsure about its merits.[44] Now, he told Munson, it was a slight experiment, 'a kind of poster, – in fact, you might name it "Poster" if the idea hits you. There is nothing more profound in it than a "stop, look and listen" sign'. Only the last line continued to please, since it was 'bold and unambitious like a skull & cross-bones insignia'.[45]

In September Hart enrolled in an advertising course taught under the aegis of Western Reserve University at the headquarters of the Cleveland Advertising Club, situated in the basement of the Hotel Statler at Euclid Avenue and East 12th Street. The programme extended over sixty evenings and its instructors – Charles W. Mears, president of Mears, Richardson and Briggs Company; L.E. Honeywell, advertising manager of the National Acme Company; and S.A. Weisenberger, advertising manager of the Halle Brothers Company – offered a diploma at the end of the course to all class members deemed worthy and any who had attended 80 per cent of the lessons. The programme was divided into three terms – 'The Consumer', 'The Tools of Advertising' and 'The Common Carriers of Advertising' – and when he sent his usual report to Munson on 1 October Hart was already convinced that the mysterious arts of persuasion which regulated his father's ledgers of success could be turned to his advantage: 'I am now pretty sure of making advertising my real route to bread and butter, and have a strong notion that as a copy writer I will eventually make a "whiz".'[46]

In some ways the evening classes were almost a diversion; an alternative to Grace's demanding company and the short-lived and tedious jobs he managed to find. Occasionally he went to the cinema: he enjoyed *Deception*, Ernst Lubitsch's account, filmed in Germany the previous year, of Henry VIII's marriage to Anne

Boleyn, and particularly applauded the mob scenes, 'that only the screen can produce', but entertainment of an altogether different order was available with Charlie
Chaplin's new offering *The Kid*, which Hart saw at the end of September.[47] He was
enraptured by the film, and assured Munson that cinematic comedy had 'never
reached a higher level in this country before'. Chaplin himself was 'a dramatic
genius that truly approaches the fabulous sort', not least because his comic flair
outwitted the excisions of the state board of censors, whose misgivings had
delayed the film's American release by a year. 'I could write pages on the overtones
and brilliant subtleties of this picture,' he assured Munson, but resolved instead to
distil his admiration into a poem. There was something about Chaplin's clownish
persona, with its expressive gestures and physiognomical eloquence, that extended
the very history of the pierrot, besides lending reassurance that individuality, when
combined with love of laughter, intuitive sadness and reflexes faster than authority's, could survive or even triumph in a puritanical world. His poem, he assured
Munson, would be 'a sympathetic attempt to put [into] words some of the Chaplin
pantomime, so beautiful, and so full of eloquence, and so modern'.[48] On 6
October 'Chaplinesque', which Hart initially dedicated to the actor, was dispatched to Munson in almost perfect form: he was sure that the work had 'a real
appeal' and insisted that 'from my standpoint, the pantomime of Charlie represents
fairly well the futile gesture of the poet in U.S.A. today'.[49]

'We make our meek adustments', the poem began, with Crane, very much in
autobiographical mood, allocating roles to his stray kitten and to his father, and
indicating the personal application of the poem with a pun on his own name:

> For we can still love the world, who find
> A famished kitten on the step, and know
> Recesses for it from the fury of the street,
> Or warm torn elbow coverts.
>
> We will sidestep, and to the final smirk
> Dally the doom of that inevitable thumb
> That slowly chafes its puckered index toward us,
> Facing the dull squint with what innocence
> And what surprise!

Free verse nodded occasionally towards iambic pentameter and subtle half-rhymes
and synaesthetic imagery combined with discreet alliteration as the poem made its
case against CA and the dull squint of every other businessman in the great counting house of American conformity. The creative and sensitive spirit was powerless
and unwanted in such a society; there was no point in pleading for accommodation and the only hope of survival lay in the clownish and Chaplinesque antics
of outright rejection:

And yet these fine collapses are not lies
More than the pirouettes of any pliant cane;
Our obsequies are, in a way, no enterprise.
We can evade you, and all else but the heart:
What blame to us if the heart live on.

Life was a fight against the relentless pressures of money-minded orthodoxy and Chaplin's clown showed the way, as Crane explained to William Wright:

> I am moved to put Chaplin with the poets (of today); hence the 'we'. In other words, he, especially in *The Kid*, made me feel myself, as a poet, as being 'in the same boat' with him. Poetry, the human feelings, 'the kitten', is so crowded out of the humdrum, rushing, mechanical scramble of today that the man who would preserve them must duck and camouflage for dear life to keep them or himself from annihilation.[50]

'The game enforces smirks,' the poem concluded,

　　but we have seen
The moon in lonely alleys make
A grail of laughter of an empty ash can,
And through all sound of gaiety and quest
Have heard a kitten in the wilderness.[51]

When Munson saw *The Kid* in Europe he found it sentimental and told his friend so, but Hart countered on 3 November that although Chaplin himself might well be a sentimentalist 'he carries the theme with such power and universal portent that sentimentality is made to transcend itself into a new kind of tragedy, eccentric, homely and brilliant'.[52] The *Dial*, the *Post Literary Review*, the *Double Dealer* and the *Little Review* had misgivings about the poem if not about the comedian himself, and 'Chaplinesque' had to wait until December for publication, when it appeared, thanks to Gorham Munson's intercession, in *Gargoyle*, earliest of the magazines founded in Europe by American expatriates. Hart had written the poem because, he told Munson, he felt 'so particularly futile just now', but with 'Chaplinesque' he refutes his own accusations of pointlessness.[53] Let others escape to Paris: far from being displaced in modern America he was so much at home there despite himself that he could turn its new medium, its new obsession, the cinema, to great poetic account. His own chance for expatriation would come, but later than for others of his generation; and when Hart Crane left America he did so more finally than any of them.

He was pleased with the poem but the remaining weeks of 1921 were otherwise short of consolation. Letter after letter to Munson and Wright complained – of being too poor to buy books, of feeling lonely, of having no money and no love life, of feeling nothing but 'gall and disgust'.[54] 'Wonder if this sitting on the wall will ever end for me?' he asked Munson, only to beg him to 'keep on writing me your bright and kindly letters ... I sometimes wonder if, without you, I should have kept writing so long.'[55] Often Munson's replies amused – by startling coincidence he had encountered one of Hart's old loves on his travels and the poet was tickled by the confrontation: 'So – little fat "Dougie" is with you! ... He will probably not have the slightest memory of me unless reminded by such "bare" facts as are hardly permissible above a whisper in even the society of the boulevards.'[56] At other times, however, Munson's dispatches annoyed their recipient with the latest details of the tiresome quest for artistic novelty under way in Europe. Did the Dadaists think they faced the problem alone? Hart knew all about the struggle for freshness of expression, as he explained to Wright:

> I am only interested in adding what seems to me something really *new* to what *has* been written. Unless one has some new, intensely personal viewpoint to record, say on the eternal feelings of love, and the suitable personal idiom to employ in the act ... why write about it? Nine chances out of ten, if you know where in the past to look, you will find words already written in the more-or-less exact tongue of your soul.[57]

Dadaism, he told Munson on 26 November, seemed to him 'nothing more than the dying agonies of this movement, maladie moderne' and as he sat, 'biting and munching my nails with envy' at the latter's travels, he felt increasingly in sympathy with Eliot's adoration of the Elizabethans, especially after his own recent discovery of Ben Jonson. 'The fact is, I can find nothing in modern work to come up to the verbal richness, irony and emotion of these folks, and I would like to let them influence me as much as they can in the interpretation of modern moods.'

These Elizabethan longings were appropriate: there was something almost Marlovian in Hart Crane's ambitiousness and he looked in vain in recent literature for the marriage of grandiloquence and emotional exactitude that increasingly defined his notions of poetic worth. Already beginning to be recognized as one of the most interesting new American poets, he remained frustrated: 'I am not at all satisfied with anything I have thus far done, mere winnowings, and too slight to satisfy me. I have never, so far, been able to present a vital, living and tangible, – a positive emotion to my satisfaction. For as soon as I attempt such an act I either grow obvious or ordinary, and abandon the thing at the second line.' There was no point in imitating Eliot, so what direction could one take but perseverance and a continued faith in one's destiny? When the right words came they did so of their own accord, and 'no amount of will or emotion can help'. He must continue to immerse himself in great poetry and to hope: 'Oh! it is hard! One must be drenched in words, literally soaked with them to have the right ones form themselves into the proper pattern at the right moment.'⁵⁸

With the Christmas season imminent he was able to get a job selling books at Burrows Brothers from 30 November until 24 December and with his usual recklessness he decided, rather than saving money, to make the most of the company discount and stock up on reading material – Wyndham Lewis's *Tarr*, Ben Hecht's *Erik Dorn*, Sherwood Anderson's *The Triumph of the Egg*, James Branch Cabell's *Jurgen* and Rémy de Gourmont's *Un Coeur virginal*, recently translated by Aldous Huxley. More than anything, however, he yearned to read *Ulysses*, and although he had already ordered a copy at the beginning of the year when publication of the first edition was announced he now charged Munson with buying him another edition in Europe, just in case Joyce's puritanical American enemies should succeed in having the work proscribed. Then G.W. Freeman, a classmate from the advertising course who remembered Hart as being 'above the average' in the programme, contacted him: there was an opening at his firm, Corday and Gross, and if the poet was interested he would be interviewed on Christmas Day.⁵⁹ Life looked even brighter when Hart picked up an improbable Frenchman in Cleveland – 'I was quite nicely entertained in *my* usual way,' he told Munson – but this diversion was completely overshadowed by news received on 15 December.⁶⁰ Ernest Nelson, an acquaintance he had made through William Sommer, was killed when hit by a passing car and Hart was invited, along with Sommer, to be a pall bearer at the funeral. So even as he attended the interview at Corday and Gross, to be offered a job early in the New Year, his mind was preoccupied with resolving the death of someone he had scarcely known into what would become one of the finest elegies in American poetry. Once the poem was completed, Munson would naturally be the first to read it. As Hart wrote to his friend on Christmas Day, 'You are always my final and satisfactory "court of appeal", and it is useless to attempt to tell you how much this means to me. So believe me when I tell you that I love you, and plan and plan for that glorious day when we shall get knees together under the table and talk, and talk, and talk.'⁶¹

8
=

Corday and Gross, where Hart started work on 3 January 1922, offered a variety of printing, publishing and copy-writing services to numerous industrial clients in Ohio and contiguous New York and Pennsylvania. Pittsburgh Water Heater, Pittsburgh Plate Glass, Pennsylvania Rubber Company, Westinghouse Batteries, Frigidaire, Chandler Motor Company, Firestone and Seiberling rubber, Jap-a-lac, Art Metal Construction Company and Griswold Cooking Ware placed the orders for the art-work, product catalogues and instruction manuals which had sustained the company for twenty-five years and helped it maintain an office in New York as well as its headquarters in Cleveland at 1771 East 24th Street. Hart was engaged at a salary of $100 a month and given an office on the second floor of the company next door to Freeman's. The latter considered Corday and Gross a 'busy, hard-driving firm' but Hart had no doubt he would prosper there.[1] Indeed the day before his job began he was already writing exultantly to Munson, 'One year of this and I shall probably be trained in a profitable vocation that can be practised anywhere.' It was the sort of work he had been seeking for years and 'with the burden of continual fear and depression lifted, I *may* now begin to write a little'.[2]

Hart's new day began with a streetcar journey to work: the Euclid Avenue line stopped near East 115th Street and proceeded, along Cleveland's principal thoroughfare, to the light industrial area of the city in which Corday and Gross was situated, passing as it did so those recent staging posts of the poet's life, the Crane Company shop and restaurant and the Hotel Statler, scene of his night classes in advertising. He was put to work on a product catalogue for the Art Metal Construction Company of Jamestown, New York, and on more than one occasion he visited his clients while their brochure of office partitions, elevator enclosures and steel cabinets was in preparation. His other principal assignment involved developing humorous copy for the Pittsburgh Water Heater Company – Freeman would instigate the treatment, which usually sought to promote the water heaters using famous stories from the Bible or antiquity, and then send it to Hart for embellishment and expansion. Sadly, attempts to apportion the glories of authorship to final copy are doomed to frustration. With nothing to go on but Freeman's account – 'Crane ... did not often originate a theme, but once the idea was set could play variations ad lib'[3] – we shall never know if one of the greatest of American lyricists was responsible for 'Bathing by the Kalender', which considers how Pliny the Younger's life would have been simplified by the newer legend of American plumbing:

> Just consider how trying it must have been for a Roman aristocrat like Pliny to wait for days while a flock of slaves lugged water enough from near-by brooks and wells to fill one of his pools. ... The baths of Ancient Rome were famous and enormous but complicated to cleanse and fill. The American home of today is equipped with a porcelain bath whose size is ample and whose service is always immediate and available. The bath or shower is served with water, instantly at the turn of a faucet, in the homes where the Pittsburgh Water Heaters conscientious service is appreciated.[4]

Freeman noted that the new recruit 'had a craftsman's attitude toward what must have been pretty prosaic writing in his mind'. He was 'a strange combination of shy and friendly ... yet one instinctively liked Hart'.[5] Hart himself was equally enthusiastic and reported to Munson on 23 January that he enjoyed his job and was 'treated wonderfully at the office' where, incredibly, praise was spontaneously awarded to work well done: 'Never guessed a commercial institution could be organized on such a decent basis.'[6] Employees at the Crane Company might well have voiced similar praise for CA, but Hart could find nothing enlightened or generous in Clarence Crane's commercial or domestic life, a fact he was quite happy to impress upon a relative stranger like Freeman: 'He said his father ... would have nothing to do with him because he wouldn't go into the business with him. Crane had no use for the old Turk.'[7]

With work, purpose and new prosperity, however, Hart told Munson he could pass 'my goggle-eyed father on the street ... without a tremor!'[8] It was also a relief to be able to supplement Grace's dwindling resources and to have the cash to spend on luxuries long desired – in these optimistic weeks he bought a complete *Webster*, records for his beloved Victrola and prints to adorn the Sanctum de la Tour of works by Vlaminck, Toulouse-Lautrec and Gauguin. With the return of solvency even Cleveland became a *faubourg* of cultural and sensory delight: in one restaurant he could eat pigs' trotters and sauerkraut with William Sommer while in another he was delighted to see the *patronne* reading *La Nouvelle Revue Française* at the cashier's desk. When he and Sommer tired of listening to Debussy, the Institute of Music under Ernest Bloch offered an ambitious musical programme which included performances of the composer-conductor's own work: the previous winter Hart had heard Bloch conduct his Symphony in C# Minor, an experience that had left him 'shaken with such effects as I had never heard before',[9] and in March 1922 he saw the composer conduct his *Trois Poèmes juifs* which, he assured Munson, 'were magnificent enough for Solomon to have marched & sung to. I occasionally pass [Bloch] on the streets or in the aisles of the auditorium and realize that genius, after all, may walk in Cleveland.'[10] To complete his contentment, William Wright came to visit in February and the two old friends were happy to renew confidences that had lapsed over a period of some months. Wright had his own discontents – with girls – and would not learn for some years why his friend could extend only the most generalized emotional counsel. Hart had told him nothing about his own erotic adventures and the letter he sent a few days after Wright's departure continued the discretion. Urging his friend 'not to let the caprices of any unmellow ladies result in your unbalance or extreme discomfiture', he stressed that the Roman Catholic Church had given women a significance wisely denied them by Greeks, Romans and Egyptians. Emotional suffering was futile, Hart insisted, and he should know: 'I have been through two or three of these cataclysms myself, harder than yours because of their unusual and unsympathetic situations'.[11]

On 13 February, a few days after Wright's departure and still mindful of his flagging morale, Hart wrote to his friend again. He was at Corday and Gross and about to meet Sommer for lunch 'at the joint around the corner' and wanted to send greetings. He had spent the previous Sunday immersed in his new *Webster* and had greatly enjoyed reading *Appius and Virginia*. And did Wright know Hippolyte Taine's *History of English Literature*, which contained sage assessments of such literary heroes as Jonson and Massinger? What a continued inspiration the Elizabethans and Jacobeans were: 'I kept getting up out of bed to add words and phrases to a thing I hope may turn into a poem.'[12] It duly did – and its subject was no doubt part of the conversation exchanged with William Sommer that February lunchtime. Ever since December Hart had been preoccupied with the untimely death of Ernest Nelson, not so much because of the cruelly random nature of his decease as because of the way it seemed to confirm his worst forebodings about the artistic struggle for survival. The Norwegian had come to America to escape religious restrictions and had thrived at school, only to discover on graduation that the aunt who had provided his education was disinclined to continue her sponsorship. Despite a poetic gift apparent in lyrics published in *Scribner's* and *Century* he had been forced into lithography to survive, hence his friendship with Sommer, and then his life and its promise had been brutally extinguished that cold December day. The funeral, Hart had told Munson at the time, 'was tremendous, especially the finale at the crematorium', but he had felt 'emotionally bankrupt' afterwards.[13] The shock and sadness wore off, but left in their wake a growing romantic bewilderment. Assuring Wilbur Underwood that there had been nothing more to his relations with Nelson than affection and admiration, he stressed the virtues of the deceased, who had been well-read, kind, tolerant 'and a true

Nietzschean'. 'He was one of the many broken against the stupidity of American life in such places as here. I think he has had a lasting influence on me.'[14]

That influence is now difficult to assess, but in view of the fact that Crane and Nelson knew each other only for a period of months, and given Nelson's absence from the poet's later recollections and correspondence, it seems reasonable to speculate that his importance was as much symbolic as emotional. Certainly 'Praise for an Urn', the poem which Crane wrote as his epitaph, is not so much a psychological portrait or an elegy for lost promise as an assertion of the futility of all poetry:

> It was a kind and northern face
> That mingled in such exile guise
> The everlasting eyes of Pierrot
> And, of Gargantua, the laughter.

Artists, the poem begins by romantically insisting, must be wanderers and exiles. Restlessness seems to have marked Nelson's life, as it marked Crane's, and the parallel between the two men is emphasized by the third and fourth lines: Hart had written this couplet about Pierrot and Gargantua over a year before and submitted it to Munson as his own potential epitaph. Now he applies it as a broader requiem for those whose wide emotional range marks them out as artists. Thinking back to the funeral, Crane remembers the pallid face in the open coffin prior to its immolation and imagines that the dead man had surrendered his wisdom, his 'delicate riders of the storm', to the young poet who mourned him. But what of it? The antechamber of the crematorium was no place to search for comfort or to hope that even the thoughts of men would be granted a reprieve from oblivion:

> The slant moon on the slanting hill
> Once moved us toward presentiments
> Of what the dead keep, living still,
> And such assessments of the soul
>
> As, perched in the crematory lobby,
> The insistent clock commented on ...

In the end, the poet understands, all will be destroyed. Nelson was transformed from a golden-headed youth to a disillusioned man with broken brow and he will himself follow a similar path of decay. Indeed even his hard-won words, his funeral panegyric and his lyrics of love and longing will be turned to evanescent smoke:

> Scatter these well-meant idioms
> Into the smoky spring that fills

The suburbs, where they will be lost.
They are no trophies of the sun.[15]

For a poet not yet twenty-three, 'Praise for an Urn', poised, succinct and discreet in its verbal beauties, constitutes a very fine achievement – and one that is in no way undermined by Crane's later equivocations. At this stage he could accept, though reluctantly, that in principle all poetry was fugitive but when he later came to suspect that his own was particularly transient the idea would prove psychologically intolerable.

The poem was sold to the *Dial*, for June publication, but its acceptance could scarcely redeem deteriorating family finances. By the terms of the divorce settlement CA's alimony was about to cease, and with nothing whatever saved from the generous provision he had made her, Grace was now compelled, at forty-five, to earn a living. Hart could do nothing beyond paying his own way but his father's apparent reluctance to help, at a time when his businesses seemed to be prospering mightily, was an added affront he was quick to share with Munson: 'My pater is too much of a cad to really do anything for his former wife except what the agreement between them says. The fact that this was made when she was partially out of mind and very ill, makes no difference to him.'[16]

Munson had money worries of his own: roaming across Europe – Paris, Dijon, Pisa, Rome, Florence, Venice and Vienna – he had become distressed by what he saw as a poverty of artistic patronage in America as compared to Europe. In Paris, through the photographer Man Ray, whose first sitter he had been, he encountered Tristan Tzara and the other Dadaists and was seduced by the impassioned cultural experimentation which the City of Light seemed to foster. At Hart's suggestion he sought out Matthew Josephson, also in Paris at the time, and although the two writers eventually became great enemies the initial interview, with Josephson persuasively besotted by Parisian culture and counter-culture, fortified an ambition Munson knew had been stirring within him since he left America: he would found his own literary magazine, however daunting the financial obstacles might prove, and thus offer hospitality, not only to Dadaism and other new writing emerging in Europe, but also to a rising generation of American authors. If new material was not in short supply, money, as usual, was and Munson remained defeated by practicalities until he moved to Vienna, where he discovered that a war-ravaged and inflationary economy would permit him to publish a twenty-four-page magazine for only $20 an issue. What did Hart think of the idea?

He was unenthusiastic and told his friend so. There were so many periodicals already that the promotion of another could do nothing but cost Munson untold time and trouble, and all for no glory. There were numerous happier courses of extravagance, not least because so much of the new French writing was vapid and pretentious. 'By all this you must not think that I have joined the Right Wing to such an extent that I am rollicking in F. Scott Fitzgerald.' Instead he was more and more the disciple of Chaucer and the Elizabethans. As for Josephson's obsession with all things French, 'I suppose it is up to one in Paris to do as the Romans do, but it all looks too easy to me from Cleveland, Cuyahoga County, God's Country.'[17] Enough of chic Parisian formlessness – art depended on discipline and harmony; writers should address personal experience and forget about schools and herds of opinion. On 25 February, already aware that Munson was determined to disregard his advice not to publish, Hart confided that he was 'hopelessly tired of Art and theories about Art'.[18]

A month later, however, with the first issue of Munson's magazine, which was to be called 'Secession', almost ready for publication, Hart promised he would spread the word. But Munson should be warned that America was no place to expect concerted literary curiosity: 'The indifference you will encounter when you return to these States you must be prepared to face. Everyone is suddenly and enormously *busy* – making money, attending teas, motoring, starving – God knows what all.'[19] By 19 April the first copies of *Secession* had arrived in Ohio, and although Hart liked an article by Louis Aragon and quite liked a poem by Malcolm Cowley the number as a whole disappointed. Munson's attack on the *Dial* portended sordid literary squabbling and Josephson's defence of Dadaism, in which he argued that American writers should be as familiar with modern technology as their French avant-garde counterparts, perplexed him and he admitted as much to Munson. 'Will radios, flying machines, and cinemas have such a great effect on poetry in the end? All this talk of Matty's is quite stimulating, but it's like coffee – twenty-four hours afterwards not much remains to work with.'[20] His American common sense had clearly been suborned by giddy Gallic theory and Hart wondered if 'one ought to consider the semitic element' in Josephson which made him so amenable to fluctuating enthusiasm. After all, 'Jews are so damned adaptable'. As for Munson himself, he belonged in America, Hart felt: 'Something is happening. Some kind of aristocracy of taste is being established – there is more of it evidenced every year. People like you, Matty and I belong here.'[21] And when Munson did return his priority, Hart insisted, must be to visit the poet, 'here in my tower-study, rimmed with Sommer paintings and grey cracked paper'. After all, he had never seen any of the Midwest and 'it ought to be part of your education'.[22]

Two years previously Hart would never so brazenly have challenged Ivy League opinion but his recent literary achievements had given him a degree of confidence which threw Josephson's literary modishness into relief – a confidence fortified when at the beginning of May Charlie Chaplin himself wrote 'a most delightful acknowledgement' of 'Chaplinesque'.[23] Whatever the orthodoxies of Montmartre, Hart was increasingly certain where his own devotions should lie: greatness, and inspiration, were to be found with the Elizabethans and the Metaphysicals and with Yeats, Pound and Eliot, although for variety he also turned in these months to Gogol's *Taras Bulba*, Huxley's *Crome Yellow*, Louis Hémon's *Maria Chapdelaine* and, most enriching of all, *Moby Dick*. Melville's novel was a revelation to him and he hastened to mention it, with its 'memorable and half-exciting erotic suggestions of dear Queequeg', to Underwood. 'Melville is probably an old story to you, – but until the recent craze about him, I never had heard of him.'[24] Here was an intimation of the literary greatness – mythic, symbolic and visionary – with which America was still instinct. Here was the tradition that must be revered and nurtured. What was Matthew Josephson doing, he asked Munson, disregarding this native school in favour of ultramontane literary ambitions he could never hope fully to understand? 'All this talk from Matty about Apollinaire ... about the telegraph, the locomotive, the automat, the wireless, the street cars and electric lamp post, annoy me. There is no reason for *not* using them – but why is it so important to stick them in. I am interested in possibilities. Apollinaire lived in Paris, I live in Cleveland, Ohio.' Instinctively Hart distrusted 'this mad struggle for advance in the arts'. Now at last he had the confidence 'to write something the way I like to (for my own pleasure) without considering what school it harmonizes with'.[25] Some time in May he had begun just such a venture, a 'metaphysical' endeavour of his own, he told Munson, which sought to emulate distinctively American rhythms. The poem in question was called 'For the Marriage of Faustus and Helen', and when he sent his friend what would become the second section of his great tripartite poem at the beginning of June he revealed that 'the jazz rhythms in that first verse are something I have been impotently wishing to "do" for many a day':

> Brazen hypnotics glitter here;
> Glee shifts from foot to foot,
> Magnetic to their tremulo.
> This crashing opéra bouffe,
> Blest excursion! this ricochet
> From roof to roof –
> Know, Olympians, that we are breathless
> While nigger cupids scour the stars!

No doubt what he had so far written would require modification but he knew nevertheless that it was 'something entirely new in English poetry' and he contemplated his endeavour with fond wonder: 'As I see it now in the red light of the womb it seems to me like a work of youth and magic.'[26]

Munson later remarked that Hart Crane's friends instinctively kept all his letters, as though somehow aware not only of their wider significance to American literature but also of their explanatory importance to a life too short and disordered for the complacent summations of middle age. They are the autobiography of a man it is impossible to imagine in serene retrospection: Crane looms before us youthful, struggling and self-destructive, happy or anguished in the fleeting moment but a stranger to nostalgia and regret because there was time for neither in his brief terrestrial term. Again and again – after allowing for his gloom and unaffected melancholy – those who knew him noted his exuberance and laughter, his pleasure-loving enthusiasm, his spontaneity and generosity, and in so doing evoked a being who gave himself to his friends and to the passing hour itself with the same trust and prodigality. He apprehended his vivid and fast-revolving world as a sensualist rather than a sceptic, which is why his pleasures were so quick and intense and why, even as a mature poet, he could bring something of the child's capacity for awe to his contemplation of existence. As a correspondent he betrayed the same sense of exhilaration and discovery: as though short of time to experience and to record, he dispatched his news, his secrets and his opinions with fervent candour and largesse and expected a like response. But it was not for this reason alone that friends valued his correspondence. Hart Crane became a great letter-writer paradoxically by virtue of his refusal merely to entertain: his letters constitute the education and self-discovery of a poet and their ingenuous self-portraiture and aesthetic insights, their frank ambition and agonizing dread of failure, are relayed with a passion and an earnestness that put cynicism to shame. Immortal achievement mattered more than anything to Hart Crane. It was what set him apart from everyone around him and gave his friends the sense that they were witnesses to poetic history and honour-bound to treasure its letters of intent.

He made an important addition to his epistolary circle in the spring. Looking through the *Double Dealer* for his translations of Laforgue, Hart noticed a poem called 'Euthanasia', contributed by a writer named Allen Tate and, as he told Munson, the lyric interested him to such a degree that he wrote to its author, whose response arrived on 16 May. John Orley Allen Tate, then still an undergraduate at Vanderbilt University, was born in Kentucky in November 1899 and inherited from his mother a reverence for his Virginian antebellum forebears that was to influence one of the most distinguished careers in twentieth-century American letters. By the time of his death in 1979 Tate had written a significant corpus of poetry, a novel, *The Fathers*, biographies of the Confederate leaders Stonewall Jackson and Jefferson Davis and much important criticism, besides teaching at various universities and contributing editorial advice to the *Kenyon Review*, the *Sewanee Review* and *Hound and Horn*. He was at different stages in his life a Guggenheim fellow, a consumptive, a convert to Roman Catholicism, a champion of the incarcerated Ezra Pound and a Southerner who spent much of his life in the northern United States. Like the New Criticism of close textual scrutiny with which he was associated and which commanded American university literature courses in the 1940s and 1950s, his reputation was at its apogee in the mid-century: his own poetry was lucid rather than lyrical, his criticism astringent in its defence of classical virtues and his protruberant brow, most prominent feature in his fair, scholarly and ascetic face, the manifestation of his incisive intellection.

His professional life was devoted to a vindication of Southern history and culture: increasingly he came to feel that the scientific technology which had established the Yankee hegemony in America was inimical to the intellectual life of the Republic and this conviction would later estrange him from poets such as Walt Whitman who appeared to celebrate such triumphant industrialism. The belief was more than latent as early as the autumn of 1921 when the Vanderbilt undergraduate was first welcomed by the Fugitives, a distinguished university alliance which convened each Saturday for the discussion of philosophy and aesthetics. Since three of its most important members, professors John Crowe Ransom, Robert Penn Warren and Walter Clyde Curry, were also poets, however, the circle's preoccupations inevitably shifted towards literature, and in particular poetry. The participants saw themselves as a *salon des réfusés*: as Southerners they felt rejected by the mercantile North and excluded from the press and publishing trade it dominated, and it was this sense of relegation that led to the foundation of the *Fugitive* magazine, which first appeared in April 1922 as the organ of Southern intellectual secessionism.

The publication was much admired by T.S. Eliot, who was from the outset integral to relations between Tate and Crane. When the latter read 'Euthanasia' he immediately detected Eliot's influence and in his first letter to Tate, now lost, he referred not only to the older poet's importance but to a tacit allegiance the younger men owed him. Hart's words, as Tate remembered them, were cryptic: 'I admire Eliot very much too. I've had to work through him, but he's the prime ram of our flock.'[27] Romantically convinced that poets were set apart, not least by their sexuality, Hart was sure his erotic tastes were shared not only by Tate but by the mighty and mysterious Eliot, inscrutable in his London bank. There, he and Tate diverged – but the fact remained that both young poets admired not only the same Elizabethan writers but the same moderns and did so, moreover, under similar provincial restrictions, with Tate even more restless in Nashville, Tennessee, than Hart was in Cleveland, Ohio. Writing on 16 May Hart stressed the theme of shared aims: 'Euthanasia' was 'so much in line with the kind of thing I am wanting to do' that he looked forward to seeing more of Tate's poetry soon and wondered if he would consider submitting material to *Secession*. He signed himself 'fraternally', and was sure the Tennessean would understand the dilemma he faced in his own writing: 'The poetry of negation is beautiful – alas, too dangerously so for one of my mind. But I am trying to break away from it. Perhaps this is useless, perhaps it is silly – but one *does* have joys.' A new verbal music was called for and now he was sure, he told Tate, what form it should take: 'Let us invent an idiom for the proper transposition of jazz into words! Something clean, sparkling, elusive!'[28]

When Tate wrote back praising *The Duchess of Malfi* Hart was more than ever convinced he had found a spiritual ally: how well the great tragedians of revenge understood the price of love, 'the old betrayals of life', as he called them in his reply. 'And yet they are worth something – from a distance, afterward.' Going back to Eliot, however, Tate was not the only writer who felt dumbstruck with admiration: Hart had also wondered what could be added to a technical accomplishment and an Elizabethan vocabulary now made to speak in such modern accents of despair. 'I have been facing him for *four* years,' he wrote, and still the flaw in Eliot's genius eluded him. He found the temptation to imitation so great that 'at times I have been almost distracted', and the problem for admirers and imitators alike was that 'in his own realm Eliot presents us with an absolute *impasse*'. Yet having read 'Prufrock' and the 'Preludes' dozens of times Hart was convinced that the master could be transcended. 'He can be utilized to lead us to, intelligently point to, other positions and "pastures new". Having absorbed him enough we can trust ourselves as never before, in the air or on the sea.' The trick was to adopt Eliotic techniques for separate ends, to go *'through* him toward a *different* goal'. As he had already said, one did have joys, and to exclude those emotions from poetry simply for the sake of literary fashion seemed doctrinaire in the extreme. He wanted to write a form of verse that could embrace the wide spectrum of human mood, that had an Elizabethan richness of diction but a modern syncopation of happiness and melancholy – hence his determination to reproduce the rhythms of jazz as he began 'For the Marriage of Faustus and Helen'. Now he felt he had mastered the musical transposition and assured Tate that he wanted to leave behind Eliot's negations and 'risk the realm of the obvious more, in quest of new sensations, *humeurs*'.[29]

When Tate finally met Hart he noted that he 'more or less identified himself with Rimbaud' without being able to establish when exactly the obsession had begun.[30] Hart had owned a Paris edition of the poet's works since 1920 but in view of his slowness with foreign tongues and the intractability of Rimbaldian French it is hard to imagine he found his apprenticeship easy. At some stage, however, he became familiar with Rimbaud's 'Lettre du Voyant' and its celebrated prescription, written in 1871 when the prodigy was seventeen, for the visionary writing of excess, made possible when the poet turns seer through 'a long, immense and systematic derangement of all the senses' in which 'all forms of love, of suffering, of madness' are undergone. By June 1922, as he struggled to rewrite in jazzy rhythms the cabaret scene long ago excised from 'Porphyro in Akron' and to incorporate it as an evocation of the times in the still inchoate 'Faustus and Helen', Hart was becoming quite adept at systematic derangement, which he knew was easily achieved in Cleveland's Little Italy. Here, he told Munson one well-fuelled Sunday evening, there was a ready supply of 'good three-year Chianti' and hosts sufficiently easygoing to overlook the eccentricities of the customers – 'Tristram Shandy read to a friend with a Spanish "Bolero" going on the Victrola sounds good in such a milieu! I never should live without wine!'

When Munson finally visited Cleveland they would explore its Italian quarter regularly but until that time Hart's life would follow its ordered routine: each evening he rushed home from Corday and Gross, isolated himself in his ivory tower, had a drink, turned on the Victrola at high volume, had another drink, played the same record again, louder than ever, and struggled with his jazz rhythms. History does not relate how Grace and Mrs Hart survived this nightly torment on the floors below but Hart had no doubts now about what he was doing. Intoxicated by music and alcohol he felt at last that he could conjure lines – beautiful, expressive, innovative and heroic – as the bootleg liquor kindled the accumulated impressions of literature and life and the disembodied voice from the Victrola endlessly wailed the same enticements – as he put it in 'Faustus and Helen': 'The siren of the springs of guilty song – /Let us take her on the incandescent wax/Striated with nuances, nervosities/That we are heir to.'

But despite this exhilaration, poetry did not come easily and Hart assured Munson that he would write finer, swifter lines if he could afford to drink wine every evening. Happily, alcohol was not the only key to the mysterious portal. Had he told his friend about his winter visit to the dentist? Drugged with ether for the filling of a cavity he felt his mind ascend 'to a kind of seventh heaven of consciousness and egoistic dance among the seven spheres'. As if that was not remarkable enough, a voice repeatedly assured him that he possessed 'the higher consciousness' and as the drill penetrated his tooth and he followed 'its long revolution as detached as a spectator at a funeral' he felt 'a happiness, ecstatic such as I have known only twice in "inspirations"' envelop him. Young as he was, he had known moments in eternity, he was sure. And now, ambitious for 'Faustus and Helen' and for the acclamations of greatness he hoped it would bring, he was convinced a great arc of achievement extended before him: 'At times, dear Gorham, I feel an enormous power in me – that seems almost supernatural. If this power is not to be dissipated in aggravation and discouragement I may amount to something sometime.' He lived for his poetry, and well before the new century was half expired he would astound it: 'I shall do my best work later on when I am about 35 or 40.'[31]

On 15 June he reported to Underwood that the first component of 'Faustus and Helen', 'a jazz roof garden description in amazing language', was complete.[32] The new muses – or were they bottled genies? – had done their job and Hart halted for a moment, satisfied yet apprehensive. Facing his twenty-third birthday he was about to make a bid for greatness. Rimbaud had achieved it at seventeen, but there was no point in denying his own attainment, as he told Munson. 'Faustus and Helen' was emerging as 'the most ambitious thing' he had yet contemplated, 'and in it I am attempting to evolve a conscious pseudo-symphonic construction toward an abstract beauty that has not been done before in English'.[33] If he could only realize his scheme he might be considered for the *Dial* prize for literature – $2,000-worth of prestige for which T.S. Eliot was the obvious contender. After all, he was now convinced that he could match Eliot in music if not in erudition, and who was to say his own song of affirmation might not prove as persuasive to the age as the dissonances of the older expatriate? Although still only published sporadically in insolvent periodicals Hart felt expansive and, like his Marlovian heroes, sure of conquest and oratory: he knew he was good and would get better; and he knew, whatever the *Dial* thought, that it had published nothing quite like the first completed section, eventually Part II, of 'For the Marriage of Faustus and Helen'. Drawing, one assumes, on memories of nightclubs in Harlem, Crane combined Eliotic bathos with wit, visionary slapstick, a sophisticated banality and his own extraordinary rhythms to evoke the bankruptcy of culture and imagination he needed to establish before proceeding to the later affirmations of the larger poem:

> O, I have known metallic paradises
> Where cuckoos clucked to finches
> Above the deft catastrophes of drums.
> ....
> This music has a reassuring way.

Here were 'nigger cupids', the black musicians whose band plays the sexual and suggestive music so liberating to the white patrons of the nightclub – 'slim skaters of the gardened skies' who disport themselves until dawn: 'Rhythmic ellipses lead into canters/Until somewhere a rooster banters.' Glamorous and enchanting as the scene appears, it is also tawdry and almost primeval. Not for nothing does the poet detect beneath the 'gyrating awnings' of the rooftop nightclub 'the incunabula of the divine grotesque'. Not for nothing is seduction so easy here as to seem more an act of easy clowning than a translation to disgrace: 'And you may fall downstairs with me/With perfect grace and equanimity.'[34]

He began writing what would become Part I of 'Faustus and Helen' on 18 June but the theme of transcendence – where palpability yielded to abstraction and where carnality surrendered before absolute beauty – was no easy matter. Such revelations were akin to alchemy and for the moment he lacked the skill of the magus. Bored after work and frustrated with his words, he at least knew that having made a good start on his long poem he deserved a respite: the fragrant parks beckoned across the summer dusk and by the beginning of July he was haunting the municipal glades and stalking the shades that vanished behind crepuscular trees. Fired perhaps by alcohol, he may still have been afraid: who knew when the police might appear, or when the thickets might disclose a blackmailer – or worse – or when his adventures might be observed and reported to his vigilant mother? But fear was integral to the *frisson* of these excursions. In any case every quest entailed rewards as well as perils. If he was lucky he might meet an attractive and compliant man; luckier still, he might encounter an embodiment of beauty and love. Poetry was littered with such incarnations, why not the parks? In the event, he struck gold at once, but the encounter furnished nothing of poetic ecstasy, only an anecdote for Underwood: 'The first night brought me a most strenuous wooing and the largest instrument I have handled. Europa and the Bull are now entirely passé.' It was hard to imagine he could soon do better, Hart told his friend, and if sex was all that counted he feared 'for all the anti-climaxes that are surely now in store for me'. But he wanted more than this quick release, and a sincere confession lay behind the flippant claim he sent to Washington: 'I yearn for new worlds to conquer, and I fear that there are only a few insignificant peninsulas and archipelagoes left.'[35]

In the second week of July Gorham Munson paid his long-promised visit to Cleveland and for two weeks slept in Hart's bed while his host decamped to a nearby guest room. Hart met his friend at Cleveland station and that night Munson was introduced to the mother and grandmother he knew so well from filial anecdote. He particularly liked Mrs Hart but contemplated Grace more equivocally, perhaps because of misgivings about the dominance she seemed to enjoy in her son's life. He sensed that she was 'baffled' by Hart's poetry and 'wanted some kind of confirmation of Crane's own high opinion of his work'. In short, 'it was plain she didn't believe in him.'[36] He met Lescaze, Laukhuff and Loveman and was taken on a pilgrimage to Brandywine, where he found Sommer to be 'a hearty fellow' and noted, from the way his friend and the painter laughed and shouted together, that 'Hart liked hearty people'.[37] Before long the writers made their way to Little Italy, where Munson met Simoni and Dominick, the father and son who concocted Lake Erie Chianti, and on one occasion he was part of the appreciative and bibulous audience that heard Hart compose and then declaim obscene limericks about Ezra Pound, Edna St Vincent Millay and Maxwell Bodenheim. For all this conviviality, however, Munson concluded that his friend was lonely in Cleveland and discovered, as their conversations became franker with drink, that the poet's attempts to widen his friendship were not without their dangers. Hart was being blackmailed by a former boyfriend and the nocturnal meetings in which each month he handed over $10 taxed his nerves as well as his financial resources. He also confided that he was involved with a young Italian man, identity undisclosed, and that he had recently attended a sex party involving four other debauchees where nervousness had undermined valiant intentions.[38] Unsurprisingly, Munson concluded that his host was 'definitely over-sexed' – an impression no doubt vindicated when he learned that Hart was obsessed by Allen Tate's sexuality and looked upon him as a potential lover. Tate himself can only have fuelled these fires when on 13 July he asked Hart for accounts of his 'fabulae pornographiae',[39] and when Hart replied it was to advise his correspondent against marriage – with the question, 'Are you easily satisfied?'[40]

Indeed excess appeared to have become an element of Hart's mercurial personality since Munson had last seen him almost three years ago: he had of course been passionate about literature then, but had not been the same wild practitioner, whose extravagant determination to capture great visions on paper was somehow analagous to his nocturnal pursuit of visions in bottles. Sam Loveman had a young guest named Alfred Galpin staying with him at the same time and when all the writers congregated in the evening Galpin, enthusiastic for French poetry and in particular for Rimbaud, contributed eloquently to the literary discourse and helped Munson see the way Hart's excesses were tending. 'Crane aspired to play the role of poet,' he later decided, and in the lives of the great Symbolists he found models of bohemian excess which accommodated his increasing thirst for alcohol, his romantic conception of the poet as pariah and his rejection of Clarence Crane's sober virtues. It was at this stage, Munson felt, that he formed 'his conception of the artist in twentieth-century Western society': Joyce's *Portrait of the Artist as a Young Man* was influential, but more significant still were the lives of Verlaine, Baudelaire, Laforgue, Corbière, Mallarmé and Rimbaud above all, with their chronicles of poverty, riot, sexual unorthodoxy and self-destruction.[41] At first this identification offered possibilities of altered states and ways of escaping Grace, Corday and Gross and quotidian Cleveland. Later, when in advanced states of intoxication Hart would declare, 'I am Rimbaud', the dangers of wholesale acceptance by one volatile being of the life patterns of another would become apparent. In the meantime Munson had another example of the literary life to offer. He had brought with him the contraband copy of *Ulysses* which his host had expected for so long and more excitingly still he told tales of his several meetings with Joyce in Paris. The book itself was a marvel, Hart assured Underwood – comparable to Goethe's *Faust*, full of 'matchless details' and 'sharp beauty and sensitivity' which made it seem 'the epic of the age'.[42] But the author offered inspiration besides. Munson reported that he was neat and quiet in dress and manner, reluctant to relegate the Elizabethans, or his favourite Latin and Greek texts, in favour of contemporary writing, and often to be found returning home drunk. Hart yearned to meet the Irishman but in the interim he would look upon his novel as a modern marvel, an evocation of a disjointed contemporary world which was verbally rich, affirmative in its view of existence, and as grandiose in conception as the heroic texts of the Renaissance.

These were the qualities of greatness, Hart decided, and now was the time to strive for them in his own poetry: whatever the way forward with 'Faustus and Helen', once the work was completed he would never be overlooked again. But how could he affirm the present when writing in the language of the past? This and similar problems preoccupied the two friends night after night as they discussed the future of literature in Europe and America. Knowing that Hart would be busy at Corday and Gross during the day Munson had brought with him the project on which he was currently engaged, a study of Waldo Frank, veneration for whom had superseded his recent loyalties to Dadaism. *Secession* continued, edited in Vienna under the temporary direction of Matthew Josephson, but Munson was now absorbed with Frank's search for the spirituality, the religiousness, inherent in a modern, mechanical age. This quest had begun before *Our*

America, but even since the book's appearance three years previously the pace of change in America, the technical inventiveness, the speed of communication and the collapse of continental distances had been so relentless as to make Frank's pre-occupation more urgent. America, he had argued, was a land of myth and mythic self-expression. But as the country outpaced the globe in technical resourcefulness, as skyscrapers ethereal yet indomitable watched over New York's portals to the New World, it seemed impossible that its mythic nature could any longer be considered without due reverence being accorded to its mechanical prodigies. Munson, as his study took shape, extended the argument: the machine was now so important that it stood beside man and nature as one of the pillars of existence and must henceforth be granted the same stature as nature in human appraisals of the world. Hart paused. Only months ago he had been contemptuous of the Dadaist determination to see the machine in rapturous aesthetic terms. Now, however, with alcohol-induced capacity for new comprehension and the rhapsodies of Frank and Munson as inspiration, he thought again: with the higher consciousness as his guide he could look beyond the machine's aesthetic status and see it instead as something almost symbolic of human aim and achievement, and as such a crucial element of the poet's vision.

The new trinity of nature, man and machine would constitute an order of life distinct from anything that had gone before in American or human history – and it followed that a new human understanding or consciousness would be required to comprehend it. Because America was more technologically advanced than any other country it seemed likely that this consciousness would emerge within her shores and of all the classes contending for such spiritual vision, artists were surely the likeliest to possess it. As he and Munson deliberated, Hart turned for confirmation to the book he had finally read at Harry Candee's insistence, Petyr Demianovich Ouspensky's *Tertium Organum*, the transcendent omniscience of which was proclaimed in the subtitle of the first American edition of 1920: 'The Third Canon of Thought: A Key to the Enigmas of the World'.

Ouspensky's mystic philosophy, which embraced the riddles of time and space and asserted the existence of a cosmic consciousness, insisted on the privilege of the artist and declared that he alone had an understanding of a reality beyond daily sight and apprehension, a reality of reconciliation in which love united previously contradictory forces. Ouspensky's book was not merely a call for unity, but a pledge of its certainty: 'The founders of the religions of the world have all been bridge-builders,' he asserted, thus opening for Hart a prospect of fusion and harmony which contrasted with the divided world he had known since his parents' divorce. 'The aim of art is the search for beauty' – and in the Russian's conviction Hart heard an almost religious importance conferred on his poetic calling. Above all, Ouspensky maintained, 'The artist must be a clairvoyant: he must see that which others do not see: he must be a magician: must possess the power to make others see that which they do not themselves see, but which he does see.'

The anaesthetic intimation in the dentist's chair had proved to Hart that he had the higher consciousness, and when ether was not available to him he now knew that intoxication through alcohol could induce similar revelations. The distant inheritance of Christian Science inclined him to a belief that the mind could work its own wonders; and if he could not mend the fractured world inhabited by his parents he could at least project bridges of mutual comprehension and enlightenment through the beauty and spiritual penetration of his poetry.

The world suddenly fell into place in the course of these discussions and the new section of 'Faustus and Helen', recently intractable, received fresh impetus. Munson recalled Hart working in the evenings 'by fits and starts' at the poem, to the incessant accompaniment of the Victrola. One night he showed his friend the drawing Lescaze had made, with its arresting angularity and its enigmatic eyes, the left blind, the right ardent and all-seeing, and remembered being struck by the claim of the German philosopher Jakob Boehme that the right eye of a mystic was the 'eye of eternity'.[43] It was one thing to feel one had far-seeing powers, but quite another to have that impression confirmed by an artist and that evening, at last resuming the challenge of his poem, Hart produced four lines for Munson's inspection:

Accept a lone eye riveted to your plane,
Bent axle of devotion along companion ways
That beat, continuous, to hourless days –
One inconspicuous, glowing orb of praise.

In the third week of July Sherwood Anderson unexpectedly arrived in Cleveland: at last Hart would meet the correspondent whose soothing words had meant so much when he began his Midwestern exile. Since 1919 and his enthusiasm for *Winesburg, Ohio*, however, the poet's admiration for Anderson's fiction – then at the zenith of its popularity – had begun to wane and as Hart made his way one Wednesday after work to the rendezvous at Laukhuff's he may have felt forebodings that certain friendships are best conducted at epistolary distance. He and Anderson went to what the latter remembered as 'a cheap little Italian restaurant' and the visitor was surprised that Hart 'talked constantly of his poverty'. He had 'a warm, tantalising personality' but the older man suspected 'that he lived pretty much in a dream world'. After dinner they adjourned to East 115th Street. Following presentations to Grace and Mrs Hart, Anderson was taken upstairs, but 'was very sharply disappointed that a third man came in'.[44] Conversation had begun to flag by the end of dinner, but with Munson's advent it revived with unwelcome animation. Anderson inspected the assembled works by Sommer and Lescaze but Munson, already sceptical about his fiction, found his rapturous comments self-conscious and insincere. His disapproval, either suggested or expressed, led Anderson to self-defensive mention of his friend Paul Rosenfeld, the New York art critic who had publicly attacked Waldo Frank's novel, *Dark Mother*, and before the evening was over the Sanctum de la Tour had become the battleground of Manhattan's intellectual rivalries. For the remainder of his stay in Cleveland Anderson avoided Hart and sent a disingenuous note of apology, along with an offer to promote Sommer's work with Rosenfeld, prior to his departure. On returning to New York, however, he spread word of Munson's truculent disposition and Munson in turn denounced Anderson and Rosenfeld in the pages of *Secession*. At the beginning of August Hart nevertheless dispatched twenty-seven works by Sommer, in the hope that Anderson's offer of promotion might lead to the painter's recognition, but Anderson finally reported that Rosenfeld considered Sommer 'unable to paint a head of anything, animal, man or woman'.[45] Hart, a child of desertion, set great store by loyalty; he blamed Anderson for the disappointment and confided to Munson his ambition to create 'our own little vicious circle', to be erected on 'the remains of such as Paul Rosenfeld'.[46]

Munson returned to New York on 26 July and the following day, released from the obligations of hospitality, Hart promised Underwood he would 'break out into fresh violences'.[47] Happily, he was on vacation between 27 July and 7 August, so whatever the extent of his alcoholic and sexual excesses he was free of the early-morning streetcar to work – except in his imagination. The evening heat in the Sanctum de la Tour was almost unbearable but with new convictions of artistic purpose and affirmative possibility he knew that whatever his conquests in the parks he must return to 'Faustus and Helen', the new section of which was now developing in his mind as an Ouspenskian quest for beauty. And what after all were his twilight predations under the trees? They may have been prompted by a desire for carnal gratification but there was always a hope, however faint, of something more. Everywhere the artist sought beauty, Ouspensky had said, but the search for beauty was really the search for love: love was the ideal of a lonely life and the power that could transform a plain face into a vision; but it was also the great fusing force which promoted the transcendent coalescence of hearts and minds and offered a healing power for the discordant aspects of all life. To reunite what had once been whole, to repair what was unhappily broken – these were the yearnings of the higher consciousness, the longings of a poet who believed in absolutes and the hopes of a lonely young man doubtful of human couplings ever since his parents had made him so.

But now that he was ready to write about his search for Love and Beauty and his conviction of their transforming powers he could scarcely do so in terms of his pursuit of male perfection – which must remain under cover of darkness, in more ways than one. More than prevailing morality drove him to symbolism, however. He wanted to couch his search in accessible terms because, as he explained a few years later in his essay 'General Aims and Theories', '[The poet] must . . . have a sufficiently universal basis of experience to make his imagination selective and valuable.'[48] He would invoke a symbol, and in so doing declare a literary allegiance: Helen of Troy, universal cipher of beauty and unwitting agent of the world war of her day, was available to so much poetic interpretation precisely because nothing was known of her. Indeed she had served Christopher Marlowe himself, favourite among Hart's Elizabethans and his fellow devotee of male beauty and excess. But although he was resolved to write about his quest for beauty in language almost as sonorous as Marlowe's, Hart wanted to shift the scene to a setting as familiar as possible in his own age and in so doing incorporate the machine, which was the foundation of modern life. 'So,' as 'General Aims and Theories' has it, 'I found "Helen" sitting in a street car.' Everybody knew about the morning commute to work, but as Hart later declared to Waldo Frank, 'The street car device is the most concrete symbol I could find for the transition of the imagination from quotidian details to the universal consideration of beauty, – the body still "centered in traffic", the imagination eluding its daily nets and self-consciousness.' But what device could indicate the human presence? Again Marlowe guided him: the 'action' of the poem would be reported by Faustus himself who, although unmentioned in the work, constitutes, Hart revealed, 'the symbol of myself, the poetic or imaginative man of all times'.[49]

Part I opened, not with further Marlovian references, but with an epigraph from Ben Jonson's *The Alchemist* to indicate the element of magic Ouspensky had said was indispensable to the revelation of eternity in daily routine. And then, two stanzas on, Crane identified the reasons for transcendence: '*There is the world dimensional for those untwisted by the love of things irreconcilable.*' His own world was thus sundered, had been so since his parents were divorced, but as the poet sits on the streetcar bound for work he reflects that all of modern life is a succession of divided days:

Across the stacked partitions of the day –
Across the memoranda, baseball scores,
The stenographic smiles and stock quotations
Smutty wings flash out equivocations.

Every morning multitudes of workers are transported from the place in which they eat and sleep to the office or factory in which they earn their living, only to retrace their path each evening to the 'less fragmentary' residential neighbourhoods relegated by contemporary life to the peripheries of cities:

Numbers, rebuffed by asphalt, crowd
The margins of the day, accent the curbs,
Convoying divers dawns on every corner
To druggist, barber and tobacconist,
Until the graduate opacities of evening
Take them away as suddenly to somewhere
Virginal perhaps, less fragmentary, cool.

Returning to his own home in the 'graduate opacities' of the same evening, the commuting Faustus finds himself dreaming, 'lost yet poised in traffic'. Across the aisle of the streetcar he sees a beautiful girl, 'Prodigal, yet uncontested now,/Half-riant before the jerky window frame.' Impatient for journey's end, and in homage to Marlowe's description of the first meeting between Man and Beauty, he indulges the familiar erotic day-dreams of the office rush hour, rapt in amazement and longing before his paragon:

> There is some way, I think, to touch
> Those hands of yours that count the nights
> Stippled with pink and green advertisements.
> And now, before its arteries turn dark
> I would have you meet this bartered blood.

It is easy – and poignant in the context of the poem – to imagine Crane himself riding such a streetcar of desire as the Euclid Avenue line passed the coloured neon of commercial Cleveland and the poet forgot the exhaustions of a day at Corday and Gross, with another soon to follow, in appreciative contemplation of a nearby fellow passenger. However tantalizing such proximities could be in life, in the magical moment of the poem Faustus is able to imagine a consummation which will unite man with absolute beauty:

> Reflective conversion of all things
> At your deep blush, when ecstasies thread
> The limbs and belly, when rainbows spread
> Impinging on the throat and sides ...

But divine beauty, symbol of the universal force of reconciling love, cannot be attained by physical overtures: 'Inevitable, the body of the world/Weeps in inventive dust for the hiatus/That winks above it.' Only the magic intercession of the imagination, of that higher consciousness that transcends dimensional reality, will enable Faustus and Helen to meet and join, and then their union will occur beyond the squalid disorder of modern life, 'in that eventual flame/You found in final chains, no captive then'. The invocation of the imagination, both liberating and enriching, is also purging – once it is exercised the fractured dross of the dimensional world falls away to reveal realms which are transcendent and pure and accessible through solitary and individual willpower:

> White, through white cities passed on to assume
> That world which comes to each of us alone.[50]

Although Hart's vacation passed quickly it was happy and productive. He read:

Ulysses, of course, but also e.e. cummings's *The Enormous Room* and Clive Bell's *Since Cézanne*, and besides completing the second section of 'Faustus and Helen' he tentatively began the sequence's concluding poem. He sold $60-worth of second-hand books, settled dentist and hay fever bills and, on 6 August, after a blissful day at Brandywine, he wrote what he told Munson was 'a homely and gay thing', a poem prompted by 'sheer joy': 'Sunday Morning Apples', twenty complex but jubilant lines in honour of his friendship with William Sommer.[51] This delightful lyric was more than a tribute to the Sage of Brandywine, however: intellectual exchange, the glories of intoxication both spiritual and physical, the transforming powers of art and the imagination, and the courage to adhere to personal vision despite prevailing fashions are the stuff of its exuberant lines, which locate Sommer's inspiration firmly in the traditional soil of seasonal change:

> The leaves will fall again sometime and fill
> The fleece of nature with those purposes
> That are your rich and faithful strength of line.

Hart had always considered his friend 'dynamic' above all and it was this quality that lent his artistic vision its inventive strength:

> But now there are challenges to spring
> In that ripe nude with head
> > reared
> Into a realm of swords . . .

Hart and Sommer well understood, however, that just as there was more to writing than literal description, so painting could not content itself with rendition of the visual. Art was a function of the imagination and its purpose was illumination, and enduring monuments of human enlightenment could result only when the faculties of this higher consciousness were engaged – as Hart himself had learned at the painter's studio:

> A boy runs with a dog before the sun, straddling
> Spontaneities that form their independent orbits,
> Their own perennials of light
> In the valley where you live
> > (called Brandywine).

The intense contemplation which could discern eternity in running limbs could also find in apples an inspiration as intoxicating as the cider which had enlivened so many Brandywine discussions and had proved the mead of an enriching friendship:

> I have seen the apples there that toss you secrets, –
> Beloved apples of seasonable madness
> That feed your inquiries with aerial wine.
> Put them again beside a pitcher with a knife,
> And poise them full and ready for explosion –
> The apples, Bill, the apples![52]

By the time he began his vacation Hart had been at Corday and Gross for six months and if enthusiasm for the work was beginning to wane it was nothing a pay rise could not put right. When he applied for an increase, however, he was turned down; a long-planned visit to New York would have to wait for months more. Salvation arrived in the guise of Stanley Patno, who met Hart for an informal discussion in mid-August, having heard from Drew Martin, who was responsible for the Pittsburgh Water Heater account at Corday and Gross, that the poet might be looking for a new job. In partnership with Nelson Amsden, whose initials were also incorporated in the enterprise, Patno had established NASP, a company which described itself in its letterhead as a 'PERSUASIVE direct ADVERTISING service' offering the usual expertise – 'Plans & Layout & Copy & Art & Mailing' – with only 'Engraving & Printing' being entrusted to the Roger Williams Press, the Cleveland company which would eventually acquire the smaller enterprise.[53]

The interview went well, not least because talk shifted quickly from advertising copy to the type of writing the job applicant really took seriously: Patno was impressed to learn that Hart knew Sherwood Anderson, a writer he admired, and was sufficiently swayed by his passion for Joyce to order a $25 copy of *Ulysses* from Laukhuff's. No amount of articulacy could muster similar enthusiasm for copywriting but Patno was convinced anyway, although as he later conceded, 'I really hired [Hart] on the basis of conversational ability.'[54] It was agreed that he should start at NASP on 1 September at an initial salary of $35 a week and Hart was able to announce the news at Corday and Gross just as his boss, he told Munson, was beginning 'a series of gentle reprimands'.[55] In the event Corday and Gross allowed him to leave the company early: the hay fever season that year was overwhelming and Freeman remembered Hart 'simply *dripped*; eyes running, face scarlet'.[56] He was in fact more tired than he knew and confided to Munson that he had been brought 'very near the ground' with exhaustion, inability to retain food, and the unnerving suspicion that 'at any moment something would snap and I would go into a million pieces'.[57] He lived on his nerves more completely than he admitted to himself or his friends and the week of freedom between jobs gave him a much-needed respite. He finished *Ulysses* and Waldo Frank's new novel, *Rahab*, and continued to ponder 'Faustus and Helen'. He told William Wright on 25 August that his long poem had 'taken the kick out of everything else for me', that he had never had 'as steady an interest in my writing as lately' and that escape from his father had clearly benefited the poetry to which he had proved himself 'so antipathetic'.[58] Munson was also kept abreast of progress: he delighted Hart with his approval of Part I of 'Faustus and Helen' and was rewarded at the end of August with a fore-taste of Part III, which the poet had decided should include 'a comment on the world war – and be Promethean in mood'.[59]

The new job turned out to have several familiar aspects. Since NASP was situated at 2307 Prospect Avenue, Hart once again found himself boarding the Euclid Avenue streetcar each morning, only to discover on arrival that his new employ-ers also did business with such clients as the Pittsburgh Water Heater company. Patno put him to work on copy-writing for Pittsburgh Plate Glass, the Seiberling Rubber Company and the Fox Furnace Company of Elyria, but had ambivalent views about his advertising expertise. He liked Hart enormously: he was 'a nice conscientious lad' and it was hard to deal strictly with him even when he was detected infringing office regulations. Patno remembered being particularly anx-ious about some copy that had to be in Pittsburgh the next day: it had been entrusted to Hart and he seemed incapable of finishing it, although from his desk the typewriter clicked tirelessly. 'Becoming a bit impatient I dropped in his office after he had gone to lunch to take a look at what he had written. There in the typewriter was a dithyramb about some gal with "arms like coal ivory".'[60] Whereas Freeman had found Hart happy to divorce poetry from advertising Patno remem-bered that 'he'd spend half a day brooding, groping for the right word, sitting there in front of his typewriter trying to get a poetic delicacy into ads that didn't require it'.[61] He himself would work out the basic plan for any copy and then pass it to Hart, but it eventually became apparent that the new recruit 'just didn't pos-sess the hard sell instincts of a good all-round advertising man'. His work often needed to be rewritten and 'he lacked the kind of personality that could be toler-ant of unliterary clients'.[62]

For all that, Hart was an attractive and enlivening presence at NASP and Patno enjoyed his company. Since they both lived on the eastern side of Cleveland he would often drive his employee home in the evenings and came to enjoy their journeys together and the literary discussions that would occupy them. He liked hearing the gossip from Greenwich Village and was touched whenever Hart proudly showed him a payment for a poem sent by one of the periodicals. Occasionally there were office parties at NASP. Hart drank his fill, but it was only when they went out together in the evening that Patno saw the effect alcohol could have on his employee: 'He was quite a wild man when the drinks came too fast. The kind that jumped on chairs, threw things around and really let off steam.'[63] He also sensed the kind of steam Hart had to release – 'I rather suspected he was a homo' – and this suspicion was confirmed when Patno heard about preparations for the forthcoming masked ball to be given by Cleveland's society of artists, the Kokoon Club. A poster was called for to advertise the event and Hart was happy to contribute his description of dancers from 'Faustus and Helen' as a text: 'White shadows slip across the floor/Splayed like cards from a loose hand.' It was envisaged that the poster should be 'wild, colorful and pretty abstract', Patno remembered, and one of the figures involved with the design was Joseph Jicha, a commercial artist known to Patno through the work he did for NASP. Jicha knew and liked Hart but his enthusiasm diminished, he confided to Patno, when in the course of discussion about the poster Hart 'made a pass at him in an intimate manner'.[64]

Underwood knew all about the desperation that prompted such overtures. At the beginning of September Hart identified life's imperatives more forthrightly than in any other letter yet sent to Washington:

> But how I am stalked by lust these dog days! And how many 'shadowy' temptations beset me at every turn! Were I free from my family responsibilities I would give myself to passion to the final cinder. After all – that and poetry are the only things that life holds for me.[65]

There was some relief two weeks later: Underwood learned he had been 'taken into the arms of love again' by 'an athlete – very strong – 20 only'; and, Hart wrote, since it was not often that 'I had such affection offered me' he hoped the liaison would last for a while.[66] It may have been this affair that he mentioned to Munson, who heard that he was 'almost' in love, and with 'an object more than usually responsive this time'– but if so the man in question was an inadequate compensation for all of life's worries and by early October Hart was consuming a gallon of rabbinical sherry a week.[67] He told Charmion von Wiegand that 'the muse has been taught to slip a few things over on the guardians of the faith'[68] but to Munson he was laconic in his pragmatism: 'Rabbi Crane! What strange conversions there are.'[69] Allen Tate sent word that T.S. Eliot and Hart himself were his poetic idols; pleasing as the words were they failed to kindle a flagging poetic spirit further debilitated by long hours at NASP, and besides contemplating the completion of 'Faustus and Helen' Hart managed no new poetry other than the minor lyric 'The Great Western Plains', a quizzical look at contemporary excesses which nevertheless foreshadowed his interest in Indian America: 'and yet they know the tomahawk./Indeed, old memories come back to life'.[70] 'Frankly,' he told Munson, 'I'm tired to death.'[71] Whatever Patno thought of Hart's commitment to his copywriting the fact remained that the poet found himself imaginatively and physically drained by the work and unable to foresee a time when he would be free to write well and to gain the acclaim for which he hungered. By the end of 1922 he had had twenty-seven poems published in eleven different periodicals and enjoyed a growing reputation as a poet – but it was not enough. He was still seen as minor and he knew it. The only solution was to write and publish more – but these easy solutions were dashed when the *Dial* rejected Part I of 'Faustus and Helen' at the beginning of November, thus irritating him to such an extent that he told Munson he was inclined to send the magazine nothing new for two years. 'But, of course, I am merely cutting off my own nose with such tactics.'[72] Then once again Eliot interceded, and just as he was struggling to establish himself as the great poet of affirmation. With the appearance of 'The Waste Land' in November's *Dial,* modern poetry was changed for ever, but Hart was at first too disappointed, with the poem and with the *Dial* itself, to understand the greatness of the event. 'It was good, of course,' he conceded to Munson, 'but so damned dead. Neither does it, in my opinion, add anything important to Eliot's achievement.'[73]

In the same letter he undertook to contribute words of praise to the jacket of Munson's forthcoming study of Frank. On 30 November he introduced himself by letter to Waldo Frank and praised the latter's story in the current edition of *Secession.* Perhaps it was an overture inviting praise, but he was delighted when Frank replied on 6 December to say how much he had heard about the poet from Munson. He had read Hart's poems as they appeared and now reported 'an organic impression confident of growth as it is nourished by the reading of more of your work'.[74] That same day the *New Republic* published 'The New Patricians', an essay by Louis Untermeyer which examined the work of the writers loosely associated with *Secession* – John Dos Passos, Edmund Wilson, Malcolm Cowley, e.e. cummings, Kenneth Burke and Hart himself – and found a commitment to form, style and complexity in their disparate achievements that distinguished them from the naturalists of the preceding generation. In more buoyant mood Hart would have been elated by the inclusion, since Untermeyer's word carried considerable metropolitan weight, but he could only manage lethargic comment to Underwood: 'I shall probably never amount to anything – but the others ... will do things of considerable importance.'[75]

Letter after letter suddenly complained of boredom and futility; he was desperately stale in Cleveland and shackled by a demanding mother and a dull job in a dull city. All that made life sweet – drink, sex, solvency and public acclaim – proved either elusive or unsustainable and he was left crying to his friends about an endless catalogue of little grievances that interceded between present reality and golden aspirations. Despite living in one of the giddiest and fastest decades in American history he dreamed, he complained to William Wright, of water heaters, and saw stagnancy and futility as the attributes of the age. They inhabited 'a period that is loose at all ends, without apparent direction of any sort. In some ways the most amazing age that ever was. Appalling and dull at the same time.'[76] Underwood's correspondence was full of 'exquisite delights' of erotic adventure but by return Hart could only complain that a projected liaison with a black man had failed to develop, as a result of which 'the dark and warm embrace is yet to come!' The final irritation came, inevitably, from Grace, who knew about the heavy drinking, either by observation or report, and decided, two weeks before Christmas, to ban wine from the house.

Hart retaliated by moving into a hotel, and when he wrote to Underwood on 10 December it was to say that he was thinking of finding rooms to inhabit in order to avoid being 'questioned about every detail of life'. Although it was a Sunday, he was writing from NASP, where in a moment of Christmas carelessness somebody had left behind a bottle of sherry. He had already had two glasses and would no doubt drink more before the evening. He hoped Grace would relent, and he hated the scenes that went with confrontation: 'Family affairs and "fusses" have been my destruction since I was eight years old when my father and mother began to quarrel. That phase only ended recently, and the slightest disturbance now tends to recall with consummate force all the past and its horrid memories on pretext of the slightest derangement of equilibrium.'[77] That night he went with Sam Loveman to see Isadora Duncan dance to the same programme of Tchaikovsky she had interpreted for the Soviet celebrations in Moscow but in Cleveland her performance evoked nothing but incredulous silence and catcalls – except from Hart, who claimed to Munson that his was the only applause in an audience otherwise unimpressed by the dancer's revelation that 'the truth was not pretty'.[78]

Grace capitulated over alcohol, Hart spent Christmas at East 115th Street and his mother gave him a walking stick and a pair of puce-coloured gloves to complement the brown and orange striped coat she had bought him earlier in New York. He went out carousing on New Year's Eve and sat down later that night determined to resolve Part III of 'Faustus and Helen' within the next few weeks. As far back as August he knew his original ambitions for the third section were insufficient: greater substance was needed than the original theme of speed could provide and as he reminded Munson, poetry could not be rushed. What had made the earlier section of 'Faustus and Helen' 'so good was the extreme amount of time, work and thought put on it [sic]'.[79] At least now, with the publication of 'The Waste Land', the task ahead became somehow easier: the enemy had identified himself more fully than before and convinced Hart that his desire for literary affirmation was the way ahead. As he explained to Munson on 5 January, 'After this perfection of death – nothing is possible in motion but a resurrection of some kind.' His own experience made him certain, 'through very much suffering and dullness', that he longed 'still [to] affirm certain things. That will be the persisting theme of the last part of my "F and H" as it has been all along.' Not, he reminded his friend, that he wanted to denigrate Eliot's achievement. After all, over the last two years his own poetry had been 'more influenced by Eliot than any other modern', and no doubt the great émigré had compelling reasons for personal pessimism. But what pitch of distemper had Western literary culture reached if all writing was expected to be concerted in mood – and bad mood at that? Cry and the world cries with you seemed now to be the orthodoxy, but Hart was dissident in his happiness and reminded Munson that 'a kind of rhythm and ecstasy' remained, however infrequently, 'a very real thing to me'. Again he went back to his earlier goal: he would muster Eliotic 'erudition and technique' but apply it differently, 'toward a more positive, or (if [I] must put it so in a sceptical age) ecstatic goal'. Ever since the end of the world war it had been intellectually fashionable to insist that civilization was moribund if not self-destructive, but the fact was that life went on: Helen's war, between the Greeks and the Trojans, may have marked the end of the Heroic Age but other ages and other cultures had succeeded it – and so it would be as the twentieth century unfolded. Eliot ignored 'certain spiritual events and possibilities' which remained as compelling now as they had been to William Blake. But Part III of 'Faustus and Helen' would not commit the same oversight.[80]

Though fought over a woman, the Trojan war, like numberless subsequent conflicts, was very much a man's affair and the brotherhood of the Greek heroes found its recent counterpart in the trenches of Belgium. These wastelands were inseparable from Eliot's vision of a bankrupt world but they would also form the background to Crane's declaration of faith in the human spirit and imagination. At first sight, however, as Part III begins, this declaration is made in suggestive, almost homoerotic, terms. The poem opens, not with the marriage promised by the suite's title but with the union of two men in the first light, and although Crane proceeds to talk about battles of the air he does so in terms evocative of other struggles for dominance:

> We know, eternal gunman, our flesh remembers
> The tensile boughs, the nimble blue plateaus,
> The mounted, yielding cities of the air!
>
> That saddled sky that shook down vertical
> Repeated play of fire ...

The dark moments preceding the dawn are not only associated with lovers' meetings and farewells but with the apparition of spirits and the glimmering of hope and the man standing beside the poet is the ghost of war:

> Capped arbiter of beauty in this street
> That narrows darkly into motor dawn, –
> You, here beside me, delicate ambassador
> Of intricate slain numbers that arise
> In whispers, naked of steel ...

There was no denying the suffering and the carnage that had occurred in the recent war and not the least of the engines of destruction was the aeroplane, so fascinating to the poet since those distant boyhood experiments with rubber bands and twisted paper. Mankind, it had to be faced, had become more ingenious in its methods of destruction – 'corymbulous formations of mechanics' now flew over towns and countryside and 'spouting malice/plangent over meadows' could reduce human settlements to 'rifts of torn and empty houses'. Yet these new engines of destruction were also testaments to human ingenuity and audacity and, as such, portents of further Promethean achievement in future years. Man had yearned, immemorially, for wings and one day he would put them to beneficent use. Life was opulent and various and the prodigal spirit was always eager to rejoice, despite the ultimate certainty of death:

> A goose, tobacco and cologne –
> Three winged and gold-shod prophecies of heaven,
> The lavish heart shall always have to leaven
> And spread with bells and voices, and atone
> The abating shadows of our conscript dust.

Remembering Anchises, whose son had established the Roman Empire, and Erasmus, whose hands, 'dipped in gleaming tides', did so much to interpret the learning of the Italian Renaissance for the new humanists of northern Europe, the poem asserts the profligate continuity of history and the certainty that when one culture dies, it is to make way for another. 'Laugh out the meager penance of their days,' Crane insists, of those 'Who dare not share with us the breath released'. The timid and defeatist missed life's opportunities and treasures, elusive as they might be, but the empyrean could be gained by those who had the courage to trust to the imagination:

> Distinctly praise the years, whose volatile
> Blamed bleeding hands extend and thresh the height
> The imagination spans beyond despair,
> Outpacing bargain, vocable and prayer.[81]

At last the labour of almost seven months was finished and on 14 January Hart sent Part III to Munson, declaring that it contained 'a bit of Dionysian splendor' as well as 'an overtone of some of our evenings together last summer'. Ouspensky himself had said: 'That which can be expressed, cannot be true.' But as he looked at his concluding lines he wondered if they did not contain too many 'tangential slants, interwoven symbolisms' – his work was not becoming any more transparent, and he regretted the tendency. Nevertheless he was satisfied that Part III 'consorts with the other two parts of the poem as I intend them'. His only misgiving was that it seemed too short. That reservation apart, the last three evenings of work on the poem had been sublimely fulfilling, 'a kind of ecstasy and power for WORK'.[82] There would perhaps be modifications but he felt sufficiently sure of the perfection of the suite to send a copy on 19 January to Louis Untermeyer, partly in recognition of his inclusion in the 'New Patricians' article and partly in response to what Untermeyer had to say in the current issue of the *Freeman* regarding 'The Waste Land'. Perhaps he was acting with the impetuosity traditionally accorded to poets in sending manuscripts to complete strangers but he was sure the conviction he and Untermeyer shared regarding Eliot's pessimism justified his overture. The critic would notice his poem's insistence on parallels between the modern and the ancient worlds and their affinities of beauty and spirituality but he dared to hope that he had succeeded in fusing these two worlds coherently. 'This mystical fusion of beauty is my religion,' Hart declared, and his poem was, he assured Untermeyer, 'a kind of bridge that is, to my way of thinking, a more creative and stimulating thing than the settled formula of Mr Eliot, superior technician that he is!'[83]

Hart turned critic himself when he reviewed *Eight More Harvard Poets*, an anthology edited by Foster Damon and Robert Hillyer which contained work by John Brooks Wheelwright, Norman Cabot, Grant Code, Jack Merten, Royall Snow and Malcolm Cowley, among others. In his review – which finally appeared in the March issue, released in May, of the cryptically named magazine *S4N* – Hart declared that 'there are as many incipient "Georgians" in America as in England'. Among the 'familiar nostalgias and worn allusions' of Ivy League prosody, however, there was one conspicuous exception: Malcolm Cowley's lyrics indicated 'the possibility of a 20th century "pastoral" form', not least because of their 'fresh record, city and road panorama, and ironic nuance'. Indeed, he concluded bizarrely, 'Cowley seems to be civilized in the same sense as the older Chinaman.'[84] At the end of January he began a new poem, a 'strange psychoanalytic thing', he informed Munson, with the equally strange title of 'Stark Major'.[85] Its theme was 'the lover's death' which, with his parents' example never far from his mind, he associated with unhappy marriage. Every morning the man leaves his pregnant wife behind to walk to work, 'only to look/At doors and stones with broken eyes' and to suspect that 'Henceforth her memory is more/Than yours, in cries, in ecstasies/You cannot ever reach to share.'[86] Hart was himself the subject of a poem begun at the same time – he had sent his disciple in Nashville a copy of Lescaze's drawing and on 30 January Tate replied with 'Sonnet: To a Photograph of Hart Crane'. Hart wrote back with the news that *S4N* was to publish 'America's Plutonic Ecstasies', his comic tribute to e.e. cummings and the American obsession with laxatives, but he was already looking to the future. He had started a new poem, 'The Bridge, which continues the tendencies that are evident in "Faustus and Helen", but it's too vague and nebulous yet to talk about'.[87]

Promising as the traffic of photographs and sonnets was between them, Hart could expect nothing more romantic from Tate for the time being. But the heart was ever hopeful and in the first week of February he looked across the aisle during a concert and 'some glances of such a very stirring response and beauty threw me into such an hour of agony as I supposed I was beyond feeling ever again', he reported to Munson. This was the poetic aptitude for love at first sight and for Hart it was a curse: he had not been so smitten for two or three years but now suddenly he was defenceless and the worst of it was that such infatuations brought all creative work to a halt. 'O God that I should have to live within these American restrictions forever, where one cannot whisper a word, not at least exchange a few words!'[88] Ten days later, on the same subject and, one assumes, the same young man, he was more drunk and more garrulous with Underwood. 'Those who have wept in the darkness sometimes are rewarded with stray leaves blown inadvertently'; one of the random consolations for life's emotional frustrations turned out to be his cousin Joseph Frease, who was then studying engineering at Case Institute of Technology in Cleveland. Since Joe was usually accompanied by his brother Hurxthal there had never before been any opportunity for intimations of more than familial affection. But on 19 February he and Hart attended a vaudeville show and as the latter told Underwood there appeared to be indications enough of the possibilities of passion, even though 'it was only a matter of light affectionate stray touches – and half-hinted speech'. What were the attributes of beauty that moved the twenty-three-year-old poet?

> A face not too thin, but with faun precision of line and feature. Crisp ears, a little pointed, fine and docile hair almost golden, yet darker, – eyes that are a little heavy – but wide apart and usually a little narrowed, – aristocratic (English) jaws, and a mouth that [is] just mobile enough to suggest voluptuousness. A strong rather slender figure, negligently carried, that is perfect from flanks that hold an easy persistence to shoulders that are soft yet full and hard. A smooth and rather olive skin that is cool – at first.[89]

Frease himself could only ever remember one evening spent with his cousin but there was nothing of the epiphany about it, as he later recollected: 'Hart made one attempt one weekend to be pleasant to me – taking me to dinner and imbibing in port wine – somewhat scarce at the time (Prohibition times). It turned out somewhat unpleasant for me.'[90] Hart's tastes in men would change. Meanwhile, as he told Underwood, he had a sense of the extraordinary compression of his own existence – already he felt old, as though he could know he had consumed more than two-thirds of his life's span. A sense of creative urgency went with the intimation: having reached his poetic maturity he would not delay with his ambitions and schemes. 'I'm bringing much into contemporary verse that is new,' he told his friend in Washington, enclosing some thirteen lines from *The Bridge*, 'a synthesis of America and its structural identity now'.[91]

Intimations of mortality aside, his new ambition, still inchoate, filled him with confidence, as though attaching a new intensity of purpose to his life. Waldo Frank, one of the most famous writers in America at the time, bolstered his self-esteem with unsolicited praise in February, assuring Hart that 'a passionate abstraction takes the place in your work of the rhetoric, the clay-tricks, the ancient associations, so usually found in even verse of the best sort'. He had just read Part II of 'Faustus and Helen' and could not remember 'when I have seen the raw and sophistical qualities of jazz and dancing and repressed debauch so amazingly made into an aesthetic form'.[92] Louis Untermeyer, due to lecture in Cleveland on 11 March, indicated that he hoped to meet Hart in the course of his visit and Allen Tate, assiduous in discipleship, told him he was the greatest living poet. *The Bridge* was Hart's paramount interest but numerous other projects also diverted him: 'Euclid Avenue', a lyric of modern urban evocation, was begun and abandoned; he planned a review of Munson's study of Frank for the *Double Dealer*; and he executed a caricature of Paul Rosenfeld entitled 'Anointment of our Well Dressed Critic or Why Waste the Eggs?' which he sent to the *Little Review*. The drawing was, he told the magazine, borrowing Clive Bell's formation, 'a bit of real "significant form"' and when it appeared, in the belatedly published Winter 1922 issue, it did so as a 'Three-dimensional Vista, by Hart Crane'.[93]

His confidence was suddenly so great that he advertised his designs for *The Bridge* among all his correspondents. The work was from its inception public property, as befitted a poem of national destiny, and in these early weeks of conviction the idea that the scheme might one day prove difficult to complete never crossed his mind, nor did it occur to him as peculiar that his great vision was begun largely at the end, so that he would be working backwards from the outset, in defiance of common, and visionary, sense. These may have seemed defeatist reflections, however, when he sent some closing lines to Underwood, or what he thought would be the opening quatrain, later repositioned in the work, to Allen Tate:

Macadam, gun grey as the tunny's pelt,
Leaps from Far Rockaway to Golden Gate,
For first it was the road, the road only
We heeded in joint piracy and pushed.[94]

On 18 February he at least indicated to Munson an awareness of the difficulties that lay ahead if he was to realize his ambition. All he could think about, to the detriment of letters, advertising or any other writing, was *The Bridge* but the more he contemplated it 'the more its final difficulties appal me'. He envisaged throwing himself 'at white heat' into the mould of ideas he hoped his initial thinking would form but the idea so far was that the poem would constitute 'a mystical synthesis of "America"'. Already he knew that the poem would take many months to complete; after all, there was nothing modest in his self-appointed task: 'The initial impulses of "our people" will have to be gathered up toward the climax of the bridge, symbol of our constructive future, our unique identity, in which is included also our scientific hopes and achievements of the future.' He apologized in advance for any future failings as a correspondent but he rather sensed where his

spare hours would go. If he could only succeed, he told his friend, 'such a waving
of banners, such ascent of towers, such dancing etc. will never before have been
put down on paper!' And Munson should not forget how influential he had been
in the conception of *The Bridge* – his suggestion that 'mechanical manifestations'
might form the subject 'for lyrical, dramatic, and even epic poetry' was now ger-
mane to Hart's thinking and as the poet pondered the arc of myth he would build
he told his friend that 'the field of possibilities literally glitters all around one with
the perception and vocabulary to pick out significant details and digest them into
something emotional'.[95] Frank sent further praise for 'Faustus and Helen' on 21
February and the substance of his praise – that there was a 'luminosity' to the
poem that was 'lyric', 'but it is lyric only as an overtone: you have builded more
dimensionally than mere song' – prompted an elated reply from Cleveland.[96] In
view of Frank's evident understanding of his poetic aims Hart now felt 'a calm-
ness on the sidewalk – where before I felt a defiance only'. What pleased him
greatly was the extent to which his hard-won poetic idiom seemed to have conveyed to Frank 'so completely the very blood and bone of me'. There was, after
all, 'only one way of saying what comes to one in ecstasy', and having spoken the
rhapsodic truth he found that a man he had never met could discern his awareness
of Ouspenskian dimensions from his ecstatic lyrics. Here surely was proof of a profound communion of understanding which Hart hoped would yield 'a consciousness of something more vital than stylistic questions and "taste"'. What he hoped
he and Frank and other spiritually sympathetic writers would establish was 'a
vision, and a vision alone that not only America needs, but the whole world'.[97]

The elation continued with the new month and on 2 March he told Munson
that the more he considered *The Bridge,* and the more he thought about the belief
both Munson and Frank held in the possibility of mystic union of men and
machines, the more he felt himself 'quite fit to become a suitable *Pindar* for the
dawn of the machine age'. In recent months he had discarded 'the last shreds of
philosophical pessimism' and now felt within himself 'currents that are positively
awesome in their extent and possibilities'. The contemporary artist, he asserted,
required 'gigantic assimilative capacities, emotion, – and the greatest of *all* – *vision*'
but now Hart was sure of his spiritual credentials. Only the preceding night, listening to d'Indy's Second Symphony, he had quivered with its revelations and was
now determined to absorb the intimations of Ravel, Strauss, Bloch and Scriabin
and fuse them with the language of the Elizabethans and the scientific and
demotic talk of the modern age in order to justify the poetic capacities of his
epoch. 'I claim that such things can be done!' he exulted and so great was his confidence in his ability to sing of America that he now felt himself 'directly connected with Whitman'. Only one problem remained: how could he render the great
fusion of hope, myth and distance that constituted America in the heroic tongues
he invoked when all day he was committed to writing about water heaters?[98]

Once again Patno came to the rescue – by firing him. Some time in the middle of March he decided there was not enough work at NASP to justify Hart's continuing presence, increasingly half-hearted as it was, and what Patno remembered as 'an amiable parting of the ways' was agreed.[99] Relief was qualified by embarrassment: Hart had long outgrown Cleveland and long needed to be in New York and now at last events had conspired to free him for a necessary life change – but in a manner he suspected the outside world, and in particular Clarence Crane, might consider humiliating. So in order to avoid gratifying his father with satisfactory bad news he determined on secrecy: the tale would be put about that he was being sent by NASP to New York where, after a plausible interlude, he would find better employment which would compel him to move permanently. Grace, Mrs Hart, his friends, even Stanley Patno, were signatories to this pact; his Crane grandparents, on the other hand, were the audience to elaborate rituals of deception which involved courtesy calls to relate the official story and strategic packing to ensure that Hart would be seen to be travelling on business with only a small suitcase of essentials. He spent his last night in Cleveland, Saturday, 24 March – implicitly the eve of his final departure from the city – with his mother and grandmother and the Rychtariks, who all accompanied him to the station. As he boarded the sleeper bound for New York he glimpsed the endorsement of myth by machine: the train was called 'The High Bridge'.

PART THREE

Greenwich Village, Woodstock and Brooklyn

March 1923–May 1926

And this thy harbor, O my City, I have driven under,
Tossed from the coil of ticking towers . . .

'THE TUNNEL'

9

New York was as much a part of Hart's poetry as the sea and no less indiffer-ent a muse. Although cumulatively only a small amount of his short life was spent in the city it pervades his poetry because it commanded his memory and imagination, however wide the oceans he later crossed to escape it. It too was an immensity, a place of inspiration to those it did not destroy, and for a while, until he grew to fear and loathe it, Hart Crane found a lyricism in the streets that Melville and Whitman had walked and saw in the brownstone terraces of a recently provincial Victorian city the white buildings of enchantment where firm friendship, true love, great poetry and great myth, his country's myth, would be lived and written.

At first aspiration equalled inspiration and he wrote well and was happy here. But Crane was a romantic precisely because his expectations were beyond realiza-tion: ultimately everything was sure to fail him, even New York, and when disen-chantment with the city came it was predictably acute. He finally abandoned hope, and poetry, far south of this overloaded island but it was here that they really died, the casualties of a despair that matched his initial exhilaration. Having been a would-be New Yorker for more than six years he stepped back into its sunless canyons on 25 March 1923 with all the happiness of the spiritually repatriated. The metropolis was more than a city, it was a prospect of new beginnings and great expectations, and as he emerged once more from Grand Central Station Hart might well have echoed the contemporary belief of F. Scott Fitzgerald, another Midwesterner no less dazzled by the mirage, that 'New York had all the irides-cence of the beginning of the world.'[1]

There was more to the claim than the astonishment of provincial fugitives: New York did indeed shine as the capital of the new world of American sovereignty which had come into being after the Great War and was fast recreating itself not just as an international cultural and financial centre or as a polyglot metropolis the population of which doubled in the two decades after 1910 but as an art deco future world entirely without parallel. The city was coming into its own when Hart moved here and it was a mark of New York's cultural largeness that the circle of writers the poet from Cleveland came to know seems never to have included the Fitzgeralds as they rode on the top of taxis down Fifth Avenue or plunged into the fountains of the Plaza, or Carl Van Vechten as he galvanized the black writers of the newly black citadel of Harlem, or the Algonquin Wits at their Round Table. Hart Crane's circle lived and worked in Greenwich Village, which they left for the country or the coast but seldom for other parts of a metropolis which was suddenly in the grip of dramatic change. When Hart returned, Grace's favourite hotel, the Waldorf-Astoria, was soon to move northwards to make way for the tallest building in the world. Grandiose cinemas were starting to appear among the shabby theatres around Times Square and the Roaring Forties, and Madison Square itself was transformed by new development. Along Fifth Avenue the last palaces of the Gilded Age fell to the tide of commerce and even millionaires were beginning to inhabit the opulent apartment buildings which became a feature of New York life. Skyscrapers, at first restricted to the commercial tip of Manhattan, marched northward, growing taller as they clustered around Pennsylvania Station and 42nd Street, sheltering in their shadow the city's numberless immigrant dreamers and creating its profile of stupendous unreality – by day an Oz, rising from the plain, and by night an illuminated affirmation.

Like Yeats's Byzantium it was no country for old men: by the end of the 1920s there were more cars here than in all of Europe and the jazz rhythms that gave the decade its name filtered down from Harlem and through the countless speakeasies that came and went across the city after 16 January 1920 – that dark day when drinking was made illegal, when the oldest bartender at the Waldorf wept and his crowd sang 'Auld Lang Syne'. For a young poet with a growing taste for liquor, New York was at once the best and worst of places: the city was the most lawless and inebriated area of the United States and in Hart's day it was thought to sustain between thirty thousand and one hundred thousand illicit drinking establishments. Among writers in particular the parlance of intoxication was so widespread that Edmund Wilson compiled a 'Lexicon of Prohibition' and Scott Fitzgerald observed that 'the hangover became a part of the day as well allowed-for as the Spanish siesta'.[2] Once Hart took to self-destructive drinking he placated his demons in solitude but that tendency came later: arriving in New York he discovered that intoxication was implicit in gregariousness and a necessary part of the literary life.

A Clevelander no more, he made his way south from Grand Central Station to resume that life. Gorham Munson, newly married, had just taken a small apartment at 4 Grove Street in Greenwich Village and it was agreed that Hart should stay for two weeks while he organized his own accommodation and a job that would pay for it. The Munsons had been installed for only four days and their house was still in disarray: bookshelves were under construction but otherwise there was little furniture apart from the couch in the sitting room, which also doubled as the guest bedroom. Hart was happy, however, and Munson remembered that 'he participated in our life and in a very nice way'. He 'managed very well' on the couch, challenged the din of carpentry by 'reciting poetry, very excited', and reciprocated hospitality with his customary sweetness: 'We had no facilities [for eating] and so Hart went ... to the five and ten cent store, brought back forks and spoons and knives, cheese and ham, and we had a lovely luncheon.'³ Distracted as he was, Munson did not neglect his guest's literary and social needs. It was high time Hart met his own mentor, so on Monday, 26 March Hart finally had lunch with Waldo Frank, who was to prove one of his most enduring and influential friends. As the poet wrote in a note of acknowledgement sent to the older writer the next day, 'I have not wavered in an enthusiastic conviction that yours is the most vital consciousness in America, and that potentially I have responses which might prove interesting, even valuable to us both.'⁴ Frank's impressions were equally keen, but divergent – to him Hart seemed like 'a man of the provinces, almost like a farmer dressed in his best suit'. There was 'an inner vibrance' and 'a boyish quality' about him that made him appear 'spring-like'. Nevertheless, 'in his tastes, in his selections, his predilections, already there was something tragic. He reached beyond himself. He probably always would.'⁵

From the outset there was a paternal element to this friendship: however much Hart later distressed his contemporaries with the honesty of his excesses, with Frank he remained discreet, reticent and respectful, as though hesitant to shame a relationship built on lofty aspirations. It was a deference determined as much by Frank's ten-year seniority as by his seriousness: born in 1889, he was the grandson of a German-Jewish immigrant and the son of a successful Wall Street lawyer who rejected orthodoxy to become a Jeffersonian Democrat and an avenger of Tammany Hall corruption. Lawyer Frank spoke German and French and was widely read and the woman he married was no less passionate about music, so that the house on West 78th Street where young Waldo grew up was liberal, intellectual and philharmonic. He was sent to school in Switzerland and there dreamed of studying philosophy at Heidelberg, but his elder brother disapproved: 'You're queer enough as it is. You're going to be not only an American, but as human an American as I can make you.' So Waldo Frank went to Yale. It was already clear, however, that he was not destined for convention. In 1905 he had completed his first novel, *Builders in the Sand,* and in 1906 he took to visiting the slums as part of a growing anxiety about social injustice. He carried his literary ambitions to France in 1912 but despite coinciding in Paris with Pound, Stein and Eliot he was reluctant to ape their modernist expatriatism. His background notwithstanding, he never felt himself to be an exile: America would provide him with his literary material – so he went home and took a room on Washington Place. He started to produce fiction and journalism for *Smart Set* and *Onlooker* and when H.L. Mencken began the *American Mercury* Frank was among the first writers invited to contribute. In 1925, as 'Searchlight', he began a column in the newly established *New Yorker*.

He was no mere belletrist, however: aged ten, confronted by a black cat on snowbound steps, he had had a mystical experience which taught him the paradox of unity in diversity and he developed a conviction, misty, German and pantheistic, that nobody has an existence outside the collective consciousness, and that consciousness he called God. He was sympathetic to Emerson's ideal of the Whole Man and to Whitman's sense of the 'I' who was both the poet and mankind. At Yale he investigated mystic philosophy and the religions of the East. In 1913, through Bernard Hart's *The Psychology of Insanity*, he discovered a fresh field of speculation and soon he had read all of Havelock Ellis, Freud and Jung. His interest in psychology was fortified by his friendship with Margaret Naumburg, who founded the Walden School, the first to adopt the learning of psychoanalysts, in 1914, and in 1916 the couple were married. That same year Frank was appointed associate editor of the hugely influential *Seven Arts* and in the first issue of the magazine he published his study of Sherwood Anderson, 'Emerging Greatness', which led to a friendship between the two writers and the appearance in the periodical of many of the stories that would eventually constitute *Winesburg, Ohio*. Anderson appeared to Frank to be the embodiment of a new American cultural consciousness and for a while the two writers exchanged a mutually sustaining correspondence, in which Anderson declared his literary struggles and his oneness with what he called Mid-America and Frank dilated on a new American culture which was at once whole and uninhibited by puritan tradition. Frank visited Chicago in 1919 and for a while thought of moving to the Midwest, such was his expectation of greatness from the American heartlands. But when Van Wyck Brooks, his colleague at *Seven Arts*, learned of the ambition he was severe: 'All our will-to-live as writers comes to us, or rather stays with us, through our intercourse with Europe. Never believe people who talk to you about the West, Waldo; never forget that it is we New Yorkers and New Englanders who have the monopoly of whatever oxygen there is in the American continent.'[6]

Frank therefore stayed in the East, worked as an editor for the *New Masses* and the *New Republic*, and charting a hard course of 2,000 words a day produced a steady flow of articles, novels and books of cultural and literary criticism, as well as two plays. *Our America* made him very famous and assured a readership for the works of fiction which followed – *Dark Mother, Rahab, City Block* and *Holiday* – but his intellectual investigations were still incomplete. He read the medieval Jewish mystics and venerated Spinoza, and even as he was lionized in Europe as a major modern writer he dwelt on the ideal of an America made culturally whole by the union of its subcontinents. His interest in South America led him to explore Spain and his determination to know Spain introduced him to North Africa. He established a reputation as an important Hispanist and an authority on Latin America and further works of cultural criticism followed – *Virgin Spain* in 1925; *The*

Rediscovery of America in 1929; and *America Hispana* in 1931. He took a keen interest in Soviet Russia, which he visited in 1931, and in contemporary labour unrest in the United States, and in later life he wrote studies of Simón Bolívar and Fidel Castro. By the time of his death in 1967 his reputation, always greater abroad than at home, was in eclipse and when Malcolm Cowley, who neither liked nor admired Frank, delivered his epitaph – 'What enormous talent and dreams and ambition, what consecutive growth over the years, have gone into the construction of a huge monument that nobody visits'– there was more than mere satisfaction in his words.[7]

Frank's great fame added lustre to a friendship which had a profound influence on the young poet, and an influence that was not only intellectual. Hart brought several provincialisms with him to New York, among them a disbelief that accomplished writers could be heterosexual, and a cheerful aversion to Jews. Writing to Munson about *Our America* only three years previously he had declared: 'I am as anti-semitic as they make 'em'.[8] Now, in view of Frank's clear ethnic and sexual loyalties, such opinions would have to be reconsidered. Other prejudices could not be discarded, however. The Munsons had returned from Paris as eager Francophiles but when they proposed to feed snails and sweet chestnuts to Margaret Naumburg and their resident poet the latter balked and American food had to be ordered in. Normally it was Hart's enthusiasms rather than his aversions that were impressive: Munson's wife, Eliza Delza, remembered his love of Italian food and a poetic conviction so great that he thought nothing of waking his hosts in the middle of the night to read them newly written lines. During the day, with pleas that he read *Tertium Organum*, he was equally ready to interrupt Munson's book reviewing and the latter soon concluded that 'Hart was a difficult man to have in a small space'. The problem was simple: 'Hart's feelings, he always considered, were the feelings of everybody around him', so that whether elated or gloomy, 'the environment always had to correspond to [his] psychological states'. It must have been a relief when he went out to visit other friends or to explore New York, which seemed to have changed enormously since his departure for Ohio. 'It is the center of the world today,' he informed William Sommer, 'as Alexandria became the nucleus of another older civilization.' He admired the opulent Upper East Side but preferred the vivid and vibrant quarters of the poor, with their street markets and faces spectating from upper storeys. 'Life is possible here at greater intensity than probably any other place in the world today.'[9] One afternoon he returned late from such an expedition and Munson recalled that 'his eyes were popping about a walk he'd taken over Brooklyn Bridge. He kept ejaculating about the beauty of the bridge and how marvellous this walk had been and how he was going to do it again'.[10]

On one such excursion he made up for lost time with William Wright and greatly impressed his old friend by a declaration made on Fifth Avenue: 'I believe I have it in me to become the greatest singer of our generation.'[11] With nowhere

of his own to write, however, such aspirations would have to wait. As he wrote to
Richard Rychtarik on 4 April, 'What I want in the end is a decent room with plenty
of quiet to work. I never before felt TIME as I do now. It is the most precious thing
in the world.'[12] He longed, he said, to resume *The Bridge* but for the moment he
had to resume old friendships instead and duly sought out Claire and Harrison
Smith, Padraic Colum and Matthew Josephson, now editing *Broom* in West 12th
Street. The ever-restless Harry Candee appeared in New York, in transit from the
Far East, and presented his Akron friend with a brown jade Buddha from the Han
Mountain as well as selling him a Chinese smock which he duly gave to the
Rychtariks. Reassuring as these acquaintances were, Hart also longed for acceptance in new artistic circles, but as he told Rychtarik on 13 April such recognition
was more elusive in New York: 'Meeting some of the older poets and writers down
here is an odd experience. Most of them are very disagreeable, and don't talk the
same language as we do.' He had read 'Faustus and Helen' to a group of writers
the previous evening 'and very few of them understood anything that I was talking about'. Had it not been for the praise of Frank, Munson and Tate, 'I would
begin to feel that I might be to blame', but the fact was that 'this "new consciousness" is something that takes a long while to "put across" '.[13] The following
day, however, and again through Gorham Munson, he met a man who seemed to
understand everything that he was trying to achieve – Alfred Stieglitz, sometimes
acclaimed, not least by himself, as the greatest photographer in the world.

Stieglitz was nearing sixty when he and Hart met but he had been taking photographs ever since his student days in Berlin, when the sight of a camera in a shop
window had begun a career which was to bring the prestige of art to a despised
and still experimental activity. With a camera at his disposal Stieglitz found himself to be 'a master of the elements' – and when he returned to America it was with
the radical conviction that photography was an end in itself. He was the earliest
photographer to take pictures at night or in snow and rain: he saw in cars and skyscrapers a beauty the academicians had overlooked: his lens could transform a
cloud into a nimbus: and his pictures of lost Victorian Manhattan transcend documentation and reveal the city as a work-in-progress of the Machine Age. Stieglitz
was the first to promulgate his own greatness but he also found time to promote
the work of painters and sculptors as well as of other innovative photographers.
He helped establish the careers of John Marin and Charles Demuth, Max Weber
and Arthur Dove, but he was above all associated with the artist Georgia O'Keeffe,
who became his wife in 1924. She was also one of his favourite models and the
exhibition which Hart attended on 14 April, at the Anderson Galleries on East
59th Street, promised photographs of O'Keeffe, Sherwood Anderson and Paul
Rosenfeld among the '116 Prints, 115 of which have never been publicly shown'.[14]

Hart went determined to admire. Here, after all, was a man who, in Frank's
appraisal, was 'an unconscious mystic, because without knowing it he was expecting a revelation in his America', and when poet and photographer were introduced

Frank noted that it was 'like putting a firecracker to a match'.[15] Hart was particularly taken by *Apples and Gable*, and as he dilated on the stillness and poetic expectancy of the images before him and listened to the aims of their author he felt, as he subsequently explained to Stieglitz, that he had been able 'to share all the truth toward which I am working in my own medium ... with another man who had manifestly taken many steps in that same direction'.[16] No wonder Stieglitz felt that 'there was never surer way of seeing' than the poet's;[17] and no wonder that O'Keeffe marvelled at the young man's enthusiastic face – 'young, and clear and fresh and very alive as if always in a hurry'.[18] Writing to his new friends the next day Hart declared his ambition to write 'a fairly comprehensive essay' on the photographer's work, so great was his admiration and his sense of creative empathy, and he enclosed some preliminary ideas to indicate the direction his assessment would take: 'The eerie speed of the shutter is more adequate than the human eye to remember, catching even the transition of the mist-mote into the cloud. ... Speed is at the bottom of it all – the hundredth of a second caught so precisely that the motion is continued from the picture indefinitely: the moment made eternal.'[19] This was the glimpse of all time in an instant that he and Sommer had pondered – and it was this encapsulation that he would attempt in *The Bridge*, which he now knew would have to fuse successive moments of American history into the eternal present of myth. Three years later, saluting Brooklyn Bridge, great portal to his poetic continent, he would reiterate the possibility of this compression of time:

Again the traffic lights that skim thy swift
Unfractioned idiom, immaculate sigh of stars,
Beading thy path – condense eternity:
And we have seen night lifted in thine arms.[20]

Exciting as these friendships with the great and famous were, Hart was without money or work and the Munsons were without a vacant couch, which they had promised as temporary shelter to the writer Jean Toomer. With Zell's arrival in the city to address the Associated Press Convention, Grace suggested that Hart apply to his godmother for contacts among New York's journalists, and Allen Tate, with similar convictions about where Hart's future lay, sent word from Nashville that his friend Ridley Wills could easily help the poet find employment with the *World* or the *Herald*. But Hart was not eager to repeat his experiences as a reporter in Cleveland, especially when Waldo Frank proposed the much more attractive idea of writing to a friend at J. Walter Thompson. An initial interview with the company required the completion of a solemn questionnaire – but with great poetry awaiting financial subsidy, and hunger and humiliation biting at his heels this was no time for literal truth, and when the advertising agency looked at Hart's application they received the impression that he had graduated from Western

Reserve University in June 1921, that he read German and French 'moderately well' and that at school he had excelled at history, psychology and literature. He described his work at Corday and Gross as 'mostly apprenticeship' and his obligations at NASP as the writing of 'good copy, which was all that was required'.[21] He cited Munson, Harry Candee and Harrison Smith as referees and attended numerous interviews in which he was invited to appraise recent advertisements in the *Saturday Evening Post* – for Barreled Sunlight paint, Cyclone fencing and American Radiator.

His interviewers at J. Walter Thompson might have moved with greater speed had they known the extent of the disarray and concern their deliberations were causing among Hart's friends. By the beginning of May Munson was in arrears with all his literary commitments and the strain of having a large guest presence in a small apartment was beginning to tell. Hart informed his mother that his hosts 'don't know anything about housekeeping in a tiny apartment', a charge which speaks volumes about invaded territory and privacy sadly missed, and after an initial assumption that his boisterous presence was always welcome he too was becoming aware that the cramped conditions at 4 Grove Street were not ideal. As usual his anxiety took physical form and he told Grace, 'I nearly died for a while with haemorrhoids and extreme constipation'.[22] She meanwhile continued to agitate for assistance from Zell and by the middle of May was convinced that Hart should advertise for a job in the *New York Times* and the *Christian Science Monitor* rather than wait indefinitely on advertising. Allen Tate wrote phlegmatically from Tennessee: 'Write me very soon, Hart, and tell me more about how you manage to live without a job. Or is the formula esoteric?'[23] But it was not – he had to borrow to stay alive and by the time his luck turned, Hart's first pay cheque was already spent in debt. At last, however, fortune did smile. On the same day he received two offers of employment: with *Machinery*, a trade journal, and in the statistical department at J. Walter Thompson, a job secured through the offices of Frank's friend Alyse Gregory, formerly of Thompson's editorial department, and Evelyn Dewey, a senior copy-writer. The latter company offered him $35 a week and would require him to start work on 22 May. The salary was equivalent to his emolument at NASP but would have to stretch very much further – for all that, there was no denying Thompson's prestige and so, to universal relief, Hart accepted the job.

Well before he resumed his career in advertising, he had begun to penetrate a writing world of another order, and in these early weeks in New York he encountered John Dos Passos, Kenneth Burke, e.e. cummings, Marianne Moore, Louis Untermeyer and, most significantly, William Slater Brown, a minor writer but an adored friend who met Hart at Munson's and from the outset 'liked him very much – you couldn't help liking him at once when you saw him, because he was so outgoing and naturally very friendly'.[24] Three years older than Hart, Slater Brown was the son of a physician and the great-great-grandson of Samuel Slater, an

Englishman who had founded the cotton-milling town of Webster in Massachusetts where the future writer was born. Brown escaped Webster for Tufts and then Columbia, where he read English and French literature, and by the time he left university he had embraced pacifism and the friendship of the famous anarchist Emma Goldman. He demonstrated in Washington against American involvement in the European war and then volunteered for ambulance service in France.

Embarking on the *Touraine* in New York he met and befriended e.e. cummings and the two writers served in the Norton-Harjes Ambulance Corps, a division of the American Red Cross. Posted to a quiet section of the front near St Quentin, cummings and Brown annoyed their superior officers by fraternizing with French mechanics and busied themselves by cleaning the mud from ambulances. Their letters home were voluminous and detailed – and when censors read their accounts of low morale among the French troops and saw the notorious name of Emma Goldman the two writers were judged seditious and imprisoned at the dépôt de triage in the Norman town of La Ferté Macé. While behind bars Brown celebrated his twenty-first birthday and cummings heard of the publication of some of his earliest poetry in *Eight Harvard Poets* but by the time the combined influence of their prosperous New England families had secured their return to America in April 1918 Brown had developed scurvy.

The veterans shared an apartment in Greenwich Village soon infamous for its squalor and they spent the summer of 1920 in New Hampshire, where cummings began *The Enormous Room*, his account of their time in the French military prison, in which Brown appeared as 'B'. Meanwhile in New York the latter was drawn into the circle cummings had known at Harvard and was soon friendly with the painter Edward Nagle, whom he judged to have 'very little talent but plenty of temperament', Nagle's stepfather, the sculptor Gaston Lachaise, and the new proprietors of the *Dial*, Sibley Watson and James Scofield Thayer.[25] He worked for a while as Thayer's private secretary, contributed to *Secession*, involved himself with *Broom*, helped inspire the character of Jimmy Herf in John Dos Passos's novel *Manhattan Transfer* and eventually emerged as a freelance translator of various works by Henri de Régnier, Henri Beraud and André Salmon. He wrote one novel, *The Burning Wheel*, and in later life, embracing religion and Republicanism, he produced books which were either pious or patriotic. His second wife was a great-niece of Henry James and his sustained enthusiasm for alcohol did nothing to compromise a constitution that served him until his death, at the age of one hundred, in 1997.

Brown's long career produced few books but his lazy, affable and easygoing nature were lifelong credentials of friendship and he and Hart found each other congenial from the start. Brown liked Hart's open and generous nature and in no time proved his loyalty to friendship and to letters by lending the poet money, buying him drinks and offering him hospitality when the Munson household succumbed to grippe. They walked for miles in the discussion of literature; they went to Italian restaurants in the Village; and, at Brown's instigation, they attended burlesque shows in the Lower East Side where, Hart informed Sommer, 'they do everything but the ACT itself right on the stage'.[26] At this juncture he was discreet about his sexuality – but whether or not he pretended for Brown's benefit to enjoy looking at naked girls, his friend's evident enthusiasm for the spectacle must have given Hart some indication as to his erotic tendencies. But to no avail: Brown's obvious heterosexuality could do nothing to dissuade Hart's too eager affections and in no time his new friend's affability, his stocky frame and dark-featured handsomeness had found a devoted admirer. As Hart related to Underwood on 9 May, 'You must have guessed by now that I'm in love'. Relations between him and Brown remained 'quite unsensual' and Hart had to content himself with 'a real reciprocation' of mere affection. Nevertheless, 'the man's beauty of manner, face, body and attitude has made me a most willing slave'.[27]

Of course Brown knew: but as he later remarked there was never anything overwhelming or menacing in Hart's interest: 'His long crushes on me he consistently treated with reticence and a high degree of delicacy.'[28] One day the poet was sure he would meet a man who combined literary sensitivity with handsomeness and availability; in the meantime Hart enjoyed his last moments of freedom before the morning commute to work recommenced. He wrote nothing besides a six-line fragment about children dancing in the street but the prose coda he attached when he sent the poem to Charlotte Rychtarik – 'The children in springtime come out and dance on the streets of the crowded city. Why in hell can't we older people have the same freedom, to join the rhythm of life?' – betrayed a restlessness ill suited to the office discipline that lay ahead.[29] Indeed the letter he wrote on 11 May to his Cleveland friend Charles Harris indicated the pleasure Hart took in clowning and the extent to which it was facilitated by New York and its abundant alcohol. 'Policemen here don't mind if you step up and occasionally use their tummys as tom-toms, neither do neighbours mind your "early" shouts from windows hailing far from gently all the dawn.' He had danced the gotzotsky to such a degree that his calves would hardly enable him to walk and 'if you haven't enough to buy a bottle there is always someone near at hand to help you'. He was quickly learning 'what a rich place this village is, I mean the whole town, of course, from Battery to Bronx' and if his letter was suggestive of a hangover, 'I'm not the one to cry surprise'. All he asked of his friend in return for these revelations was discretion in Cleveland: 'I have enough trouble keeping my family reassured', he wrote, without further details of his escapades reaching their ears.[30]

When Hart set out for J. Walter Thompson on 22 May he was following a path taken by numerous writers of the 1920s: Alyse Gregory, Frank's ally at the agency, was a novelist and critic ; F. Scott Fitzgerald and Dorothy Parker wrote advertising copy in their apprentice days, and the suasions of the art were a source of fascination to e.e. cummings and Marianne Moore. Hart himself was less interested in the slick world into which necessity had propelled him, but when he made his

way to Thompson's he was at least happily convinced of the prestige of the establishment. Indeed J. Walter Thompson, situated at 244 Madison Avenue, emerged
during the decade as the largest and most prominent agency in a business which
was integral to the transformation of America from a nineteenth-century society of
conspicuous accumulation to a twentieth-century society of conspicuous consumption. National revenue from advertising surged between 1914 and 1929 and
Thompson, which famously placed emphasis on market research, had doubled its
staff by the time the Depression began. All considerations of practicality aside, it
was a bizarre choice of occupation for an idealistic poet: there is something about
Hart Crane's life that suggests an instability of identity, which is why he clung
with such bravura to his self-appointed destiny, and an occupation which notoriously prostituted words to sales would surely prove unsatisfactory before long. At
first, however, all was happy certainty and Hart assured Grace that 'I never would
have got [the job] if my samples and conversation had not convinced them'.[31]
Three days after starting work he sent an enthusiastic report to Cleveland: the
views from the office were wonderful and Thompson's 'provides a maximum of
opportunities'. Although his earnings were so far modest, many of the company's
copywriters were paid between $75 and $100 a week and Hart had no doubt of
advancement: 'They liked my copy from the first, and so much so that they have
practically made a place for me in the dept. of statistics and investigation until they
need me in my real field.' Life had improved dramatically and the move from
Cleveland was vindicated: 'I think I have, all things considered, made a big jump
in the last 2 months, though it would astonish you to know the many sleepless
nights and dreary days it has cost me.'[32] Five weeks later, optimism continued.
Florence Clark, the personnel secretary, had invited him out to tea and if he so far
knew few people in the company the reason was simple: 'It's too immense and I'm
confined to a highly specializing dept.' Many other writers were employed there
and the agency's attitude towards artists was refreshingly serious. 'In fact it's a
feather in your cap if you know a little more than you're "supposed to" here.'[33]
Within two months his boss in the statistical department, Paul Cherington, had
sufficient confidence in Hart to send him to Chicago, Buffalo and Rochester to
interview paint-sellers prior to a new advertising campaign for Barreled Sunlight,
a paint manufactured by Thompson's client the US Gutta Percha Company, and
on his return to New York he was told that he was to be transferred at once to the
editorial department under Albert Leffingwell. His salary would stay the same but
at least he had a new office and from the fourteenth floor could survey Murray
Hill and the East River, perennial reminder of the nearby Atlantic.

Hart's first decision on hearing of his acceptance by J. Walter Thompson was to
find somewhere else to live. After nine weeks he finally left the Munsons in peace
and moved in temporarily with Bill Brown, who lived nearby at 6 Minetta Lane.
A loan from Richard Rychtarik, secured to keep him solvent until his first pay
cheque, enabled him to move from Brown's to a room at the Hotel Albert in East

10th street and by 1 June he had installed himself a few doors down from the Munsons at 45 Grove Street, which was reputed to have been the former town house of the Ogden Reid family and was now owned by the most prominent land-lady in the Village, Signora Bellardi. His fellow tenants here included Eleanor Fitzgerald, business manager of the Provincetown Players, and Stark Young, the drama critic. Again Brown had come to the rescue: Hart's new accommodation was sublet through his friend's recommendation from a journalist named Louis Kantor, now on assignment in Europe, and Hart considered himself lucky to have a large second-floor room for only $30 a month. It had just been repainted in grey and white, Grace and Mrs Hart were informed, it was adjacent to the bathroom and had its own running water, and with Kantor's furniture at his disposal there was no need to send for anything from Cleveland. Presently he would embellish its walls with works by Lescaze, Sommer, Rychtarik and Nagle. With his rent less than half what Munson paid each month, Hart soon talked himself into affording an extra 50 cents a week for a cleaner. At last he had somewhere in which, by entertaining, he could begin to defray the many debts of kindness he had incurred during his first difficult weeks in New York, weeks in which, as he remarked to Grace, 'My friends have been everything to me.'[34]

Hart was very happy, and so too were the Munsons, whose next guest now arrived to join the growing ranks of the Village circle. Jean Toomer had graduated from New York University to teach in a rural black school in Georgia and later in 1923 he would release *Cane*, a collection of stories, songs and poems based on his experiences in the South which was to become one of the most significant publi-cations of the Harlem renaissance of black writing. Toomer had grown up in Washington, DC, and the previous summer he and Waldo Frank had travelled to South Carolina to research rural black culture for their current books. Toomer would incorporate his findings in *Cane* while Frank's impressions furnished material for *Holiday*, his fictional protest against lynching. Preoccupied as they were by the very arbitrariness of racial inequality the two men posed as blood brothers: Toomer was a light-skinned black man and Frank a swarthy white and they were gratified by the success of their imposture. This close alliance continued in New York, where Frank decided that Toomer was a harbinger of the new national literature he prophesied and as such an appropriate comrade for Hart, so he introduced his two friends shortly after Toomer's arrival in the Village. For a little over a year the young writers corresponded when they could not meet to explore their evolving ideas about literature and life. Their relations were always harmonious and affectionate but there seems to have been an immovable ambi-guity in Toomer's view of Hart, as an entry in one of his unpublished notebooks reveals:

Hart Crane says, People are willing to admit their ignorance on everything but life. . . . He seeks unification in literature or, rather, in literary tradition. *Through* literature? does the tradition exist? He will make a tradition which does not exist. He placed his hopes on a horse he could not bet on. A black man comes before him and he sees black. He has a strain of cruelty which, if fired by anger, would make a demon of him. ... Habit makes him pay more attention to the question of prejudice than the problem of love.[35]

Surveying his collection of paintings, fastidiously keeping his sanctuary clean and dusted and watching the coalescence of a friendly group around him, Hart was, he told Grace, 'about as happy "as they make 'em",' as New York's brief spring blossomed before the blazing summer.[36] On 30 May, reassuring the Rychtariks that all was well, he indicated the extent to which he found the promptings of prose-poetry down every Manhattan vista: 'The streets are full of life, color and sunlight and everybody is out. They have lemon-yellow shades on all the lamps on Fifth Ave. and it gives the street and everybody the color of champagne in the evening. How fine it is that I am here and settled for good!'[37] There was more to New York than exhilarating sparkle, however, and Hart knew exactly what he meant when he praised the city's incurious liberalism to Grace. Here there was no worry about forgetting any carefully structured camouflage, here where one had 'the perfect freedom of wearing what you want to, walking the gait you like ... and nobody bothering you.'[38]

Infatuated as he was with Bill Brown, it was wonderful to have his inebriated company night after night as they deliberated on the future of *The Bridge* – and no less wonderful to watch him take on all rivals in contests Hart eagerly related to Charles Harris in Cleveland: '[Brown] also has the champion bladder, winning all the endurance tests and in altitude rivalling C[leveland] F[ire] D[epartment]'s ladder towers. [The writer] Gilbert Seldes and [Scofield] Thayer once tried to outdo him, but no fires were put out.'[39] Any hopes Hart might have entertained regarding Brown were checked when the latter became involved with Susan Jenkins, the young woman he would shortly marry, but Hart was delighted to discover that he liked her as much as she liked him, and soon Grace was informed of expeditions the three friends undertook to the markets of Little Italy, where they bought spinach and asparagus and pots and pans: 'I've never been with young people I enjoyed so much, and they, of course, have had real lives.' Sue had been the secretary to the Provincetown Players, the theatrical troupe largely responsible for introducing the Village to the dramas of Eugene O'Neill, and she took Bill and Hart to the first-night parties held above the tiny theatre in MacDougal Street, parties famous for their eclectic bohemianism where one might encounter Edmund Wilson, Albert Barnes, the art collector of Philadelphia, Eugene and Agnes O'Neill, Scott and Zelda Fitzgerald, Alexander Berkman, would-be assassin of Henry Clay Frick, Abraham Cahan, editor of the socialist Jewish *Forward,* Hart's old acquaintance 'Putzi' Hanfstaengl, and painters such as Marsden Hartley and Charles Demuth.

Meanwhile, like love sonnets at the Elizabethan court, the three parts of 'Faustus and Helen', still unpublished, were circulating loose-leaf around Greenwich Village and establishing for their author a reputation for latent greatness. At the beginning of June Frank invited Hart to lunch and told him, as he later related to Grace, that he was 'the greatest contemporary American poet with that piece alone' and suggested an introduction to his publisher, Horace Liveright. As a token of expectation as well as affection his friends pooled their scant resources and bought Hart a new Victrola and some records and Grace was assured that now, equipped with his portable sirens, he was 'all ready to start again' on his great undertaking.[40] With work on *The Bridge* set to recommence Hart advertised his ambitions and recruited opinions far and wide, explaining to Charles Harris that the work was often at the centre of 'sharp arguments with Burke, Brown, Munson, Frank, Toomer and Josephson'.[41] William Lescaze suddenly appeared in New York from Paris, bringing his architectural wisdom to the discussion, and Allen Tate involved himself from Tennessee, promising Hart on 14 June that he was 'looking for the first parts of The Bridge any time ... I'm betting on you in the coming year, and I'm not going to lose.'[42] Two weeks later he wrote again: he was glad to hear that work had recommenced and assured Hart that if *The Bridge* 'surpasses "Faustus and Helen" it will have to be almost unbelievably good'.[43]

Inspired by New York and adored by his friends, Hart felt elated and confident and as he began the orchestration of the ecstatic lines which would later form 'Atlantis', the concluding section of *The Bridge*, he assured Grace that he was 'doing things of universal consequence and better work than I have ever done before'. He warned her also that in future, owing to the exactions of advertising and poetry, his correspondence might fall into arrears, 'for it is very hard, extremely painful to tie your mind down to anything as personal as a letter when you have the drive of a hundred horse power steed propelling your brain in other directions'.[44] He could scarcely expect his mother to comprehend the rigours of his toil or the glory of his goal, but as he pondered the advice of Frank, Toomer and Munson he envisaged himself as the member of a visionary sodality, a new philadelphia of writers committed to the spiritual understanding of America. Stieglitz, though a photographer, was an obvious candidate for membership and when Hart wrote to him on the Fourth of July it was to address him as an enlightened brother and fellow quester. He explained that he had not written recently because work on the last section of *The Bridge* had often kept him occupied until two in the morning 'for several days during which I was extremely happy'. Almost every day saw him in argument with 'those really sincere people, but limited, who deny the superior logic of metaphor in favor of their perfect sums, divisions and subtractions. They cannot go a foot unless to merely catch up with some predetermined and set boundaries'. But he knew Stieglitz was not so benighted – rather, he seemed 'the purest living indice of a new order of consciousness' and Hart insisted on their shared horizons: 'I am always seeing your life and experience very solidly as part of my own because I feel our identities so much alike in spiritual direction. When it comes to action we diverge in several ways, – but I'm sure we center in common devotions, in a kind of timeless vision'.[45] And in support of his visionary claims he enclosed a salutation, to his bridge of dreams, his visionary fellowship, and the ecstatic conviction that could span the divides of doubt:

> To be, Great Bridge, in vision bound of thee,
> So widely straight and turning, ribbon-wound,
> Multi-colored, river-harboured and upborne
> Through the bright drench and fabric of our veins, –
> With white escarpments swinging into light . . .[46]

Ecstasy was a dangerous inspiration, however: the emotional exaltation that enabled him to write was inevitably unsustainable and with the descent into other moods which were necessarily equally extreme would come poetic silence and thus self-reproach. The summer set in, unmitigated by air-conditioning, and oppressed the cramped tenements where poets lived. Independence Day receded and New York changed from a wind-blown Atlantic citadel to an inferno his friends hastened to desert. By the middle of July Hart was unable to sleep, owing to the heat and the noisy proximity of neighbours brought home to him through gaping windows, and his insomnia was aggravated, not by fresh inspiration for *The Bridge*, but by worries about Barreled Sunlight and Naugahyde suitcases, and in no time rose fever and hay fever descended to compound the irritations of the airless journey to work. He escaped twice – to stay with Lescaze's friends the Simeon Fords at Rye, New York, and with Frank at Darien, Connecticut – and each time found refreshment in nearby woods and water. But then he quarrelled with Lescaze, whom he believed to have stolen his copy of *Ulysses*, and the stress of the disagreement induced an attack of hives. Those who might have consoled him, or questioned what looked like an unreasonable accusation, were preparing for departure – the Munsons for the Catskills, Slater Brown for Woodstock, Kenneth Burke for New Jersey – and letters from Harry Candee, who was enjoying an English summer near Windsor Castle before leaving once more for China, only emphasized his sense of desolation. Suddenly his birthday arrived – and with nowhere to go and nobody to see he made his way to a restaurant in Prince Street and remembered the happy dinner he had enjoyed there with Richard Rychtarik as he consumed a solitary dinner and a lonely bottle of wine. He turned twenty-four that miserable day – and one pauses to marvel again at the compression of precocious lives: only recently arrived at legal manhood he was already the author of major lyric poetry, already the dreamer of an epic America, already a nomad. To make the evening more distressing, the only birthday wishes came from the Cleveland he had forsaken: 'One's birthday ought to be celebrated,' he wrote to Grace in thanks for the gifts she had sent.[47] It was to Charlotte Rychtarik, however, that he sent his fullest and saddest acknowledgement: her birthday wishes had arrived punctually, to be read on the way to J. Walter Thompson, and on returning drunk from Prince Street Hart confided a loneliness he knew he must keep from Grace. His birthday had fallen on 'a frightful day, torrid and frying' and although as he wrote his letter, with Ravel playing on his Victrola, he felt fairly contented, the music brought back to him his Sanctum de la Tour and 'when I think of that room, it is almost to give way to tears, because I shall never find my way back to it':

> It is not necessary, of course, that I should, but just the same it was the center and beginning of all that I am and ever will be, the center of such pain as would tear me to pieces to tell you about, and equally the center of great joys! The Bridge seems to me so beautiful, – and it was there that I first thought about it, and it was there that I wrote 'Faustus and Helen' ... and all this is, of course, connected very intimately with my Mother, my beautiful mother.

He enclosed what he had written of *The Bridge* and told her he was sure the work would be finished within a year. What he had so far completed had been written 'verse by verse in the most tremendous emotional exaltations I have ever felt' and he had no doubt that Waldo Frank would persuade his publisher to release the work. He thanked Charlotte and her husband for keeping an eye on Grace – he knew more and more the value of friendship and loyalty and under-stood more and more the elusiveness of contentment: 'Do not think I am happy here, – or ever will be, for that matter, except for a few moments at a time when I am perhaps writing or receiving a return of love. The true idea of God is the only thing that can give happiness, – and that is the identification of yourself with *all of life*.'[48]

'The city is a place of "broken-ness"', Hart told Stieglitz, now that the friends who were integral to its enchantment had disappeared.[49] But there were arrivals also, among them Malcolm and Peggy Cowley, who departed Paris on 2 August, the day President Harding died, to reach New York ten days later. Two months previously, sending thanks for Hart's flattering comments in his review of *Eight More Harvard Poets*, Cowley had taken the opportunity to say how much he admired the critic's own poems: 'For several months I have been telling people how good they are. ... You write with a bombast which is not Elizabethan but contemporary and you are one of the two or three people who can write a twentieth century blank verse, about other subjects than love death and nightingales.'[50] He hoped they would meet on his return to America – and in the third week of August Hart made his way to the Cowleys' two-room apartment in Dominick Street for an inconclusive meeting that gave no indication of the friendship that was later to blossom between the two men.

Cowley found him 'a solidly framed and apple-cheeked young man dressed in a brown suit to match his prominent eyes'. The evening was very hot and Hart was in no mood to discuss poetry with his hosts: 'Gesturing with a dead cigar, he tramped up and down the living room announcing that he was sick of being a copywriter, that advertising appealed to nothing but the acquisitive instinct.' Too exact to be a romantic, Cowley demurred, but his reasoning failed to impress. 'Hart flushed and his mouth turned down at the corners. "You don't know what you're talking about," he growled in a Midwestern voice.' He shook Cowley's hand when he left, with his dead cigar between his teeth, but it seemed to Cowley that 'he stamped out of the house almost as if he were shaking the dust of it from his feet'.[51] A few nights later, however, and in company with Kenneth Burke, Hart saw the Cowleys again and an evening of heavy drinking concluded when the friends 'came roistering in' to 45 Grove Street. A note from Toomer awaited him and Hart replied on 19 August to say how dull the evening had really been. 'I'd much better have talked it out with you.' He knew he should husband his resources, if not for his writing then at least for exalting discussion with the visionary brothers, and he had to confess that there were other distractions besides drink. Sex seemed to be available everywhere in New York and without saying as much Hart now assured Toomer that 'for a while I want to keep immune from beckonings and all that draws you into doorways, subways, sympathies, rapports and the City's complicated devastations'.[52]

It was not a resolution he held for long, but then the temptations New York provided were so various and enticing. Nine hundred thousand unmarried men lived in the vice capital of the Eastern Seaboard during Hart's time there, and as the *New York Times Magazine* suggested, 'they are not all in a [Madison Square] Garden line-up waiting for admission to the next fight, neither are they all concentrated in speakeasies and along the docks. . . . The city has something for every kind of bachelor.'[53] These facilities were generous and comprehensive beyond anything Hart had known in Ohio and included seven YMCAs notorious for homosexual activity, bath houses on Coney Island and in Manhattan, many restaurants in the Village and Times Square which smiled on an all-male clientele, numerous hotels around Union Square, Times Square, Battery Park and to the west of Central Park where male couples could rent rooms by the hour, and a small cluster of speakeasies on Third Avenue in the 50s where the love that dared not speak its name could be audaciously articulate.

Sex between men was, of course, legally proscribed, but at a time when Prohibition was critically undermining the sanctity and authority of the law and bringing a permanent refinement to the activities of organized crime in America, the police had challenges enough without worrying too much about the sexual activities of New York's countless immigrant bachelors. Yet although Hart could have found safe and immediate gratification almost anywhere in New York, the surviving evidence suggests that he chose not to do so. Perhaps Cleveland had simply accustomed him to hunt for what could not easily be found; perhaps the hazardous stalking of men not certain to be compliant or even civil was part of the larger romanticism of a life and a poetry that both avoided ready solutions. But as though believing that only the prosaic are attracted to the easily available, Hart seems to have shunned the safe resorts New York offered in favour of shadowed streets and the unspoken contract eyes could exchange in the time it took to give a stranger a light. Perhaps Ernest Hemingway meant well with his famous remark – 'Poor Hart Crane, always trying to pick up the wrong sailor' – but there was something both easy and uncomprehending in his sympathy.[54]

The middle of August, when Hart wrote to Toomer, was a difficult time, as he indicated when he told Grace that owing to the heat and a variety of personal anxieties he 'came near a collapse near the middle of the week'.[55] Cruising for sex may have been a solution to these stresses but it entailed worries of its own – infection, perhaps, or violence – and it was certainly not something he could discuss with his mother. Indeed as he came to cast in poetic form the late summer search for gratification he found himself unable to write in anything other than the most ingrown and cryptic terms. 'Possessions', probably begun in early September and all but completed at the end of the month, remains a challenging lyric, even to the initiated, its dense metaphorical texture giving an indication not only of the secrecy with which he felt obliged to shroud his nocturnal activities but also of the lack of poetic precedent which confronted him – whose literary example could he follow when it came to writing about the search for casual sex? And to what extent did he understand the powerful stirrings that led him, 'In Bleecker Street, still trenchant in a void', or anywhere else in the midnight city, to roam and search for fleeting fulfilment at a time when his friends and contemporaries were pairing off for life? How could he explain these nightly quests to Brown or Munson or Cowley? Candee would have understood, but he was forever travelling, Loveman was in Cleveland and Underwood was another age altogether: there was no coeval impelled by the same dangerous urges – so Hart was driven to confess 'Upon the page whose blind sum finally burns/Record of rage and partial appetites' and to submit these confessions to a heterosexual man set apart by his colour. 'Habit', Toomer had thought of his friend, 'makes him pay more attention to the question of prejudice than the problem of love' – but as he read the first of the four irregular stanzas of 'Possessions' he will have seen that the problems of love, or at least its simulations, were also recurrent. Under the dark unseeing sky of an indifferent city, burdened by 'this fixed stone of lust', the speaker describes the moment of 'trust', and preliminary incursion, in which he admits a complete stranger to his house:

And the key, ready to hand – sifting
One moment in sacrifice (the direst)
Through a thousand nights the flesh

Assaults outright for bolts that linger
Hidden ...

How many times the poet had imagined this moment as he sat bored at work or
momentarily distracted by the sight of a handsome man as he walked with the
Munsons or listened to Brown's domestic plans. And how many times he had
experienced it – but 'the thousand nights' of imagination and enactment, so
unreal, so surreal, all resolved themselves in the familiar scene of fearful and 'trembling' surrender:

Accumulate such moments to an hour:
Account the total of this trembling tabulation.
I know the screen, the distant flying taps
And stabbing medley that sways –
Rounding behind to press and grind,
And the mercy, feminine, that stays
As though prepared.

Crane eventually excised the fifth line – it was really too suggestive – but the
'stabbing medley' of assorted lovers, and the surprisingly 'feminine' gentleness
they could show when implored, remained. Even for the poet the memories of
the different men became indistinguishable and blurred into a cityscape against
which he pictured himself as eternally consumed: 'I, turning, turning on smoked
forking spires,/The city's stubborn lives, desires'. Every sexual encounter was a
little death, as the poet – 'Tossed on these horns, who bleeding dies' – had
learned from the Metaphysicals. Yet as he walked once more down Bleecker
Street, now 'As quiet as you can make a man', he suspected that each such death
also entailed enrichment and the possibility, to quote another line later edited, of
'dabbling sure possessions in new reach'. One day, surely, his quest would lead
to more than just another entry in the 'Record of rage and partial appetites'. One
day, surely, 'The pure possession, the inclusive cloud/Whose heart is fire shall
come' and then the 'fixed stone of lust' would be crumbled by a force stronger
than anything except the adamant gems of mutual love and comprehension.
Then would 'the white wind rase/All but bright stones wherein our smiling
plays'.[56]

Toomer chose, understandably, to read the lyric as much for its beautiful disso-
nances and poetic associations as for any strict meaning and told Hart that he
found it 'a deep, thrusting, dense, organized, strong, passionate, luminous, and
ecstatic poem'.[57] Allen Tate later declared himself 'hit squarely' by the work, perhaps finding in its strangely vivid evocations a poignant cry of urban dislocation
and distress.[58] But Crane himself knew he could expect only limited applause:
writing a few years later about the problems of addressing what he termed 'the

more imponderable phenomena of psychic motives' he admitted that he had had to 'rely even more on these dynamics of inferential mention' to convey his intention. Perhaps to some people he wrote 'nothing but obscurities' and, he conceded, 'A poem like "Possessions" really cannot be technically explained. It must rely (even to a large extent with myself) on its organic impact on the imagination to successfully imply its meaning.'[59]

'By the end of a summer in New York,' Hart informed Grace, 'everybody is at the limit of endurance; there is no place to rest, get away from the constant noise and vibrations of trucks, etc., and there's a kind of insidious impurity in the air that seems to seep from sweaty walls and subways. Next year I shall have at least a month in the open country or by the sea.'[60] His correspondence is full of these promises against the future, still envisaged as a bright blue horizon, but for now he would have to content himself with the realities of J. Walter Thompson and tenement life. Waldo Frank's marriage collapsed when Margaret Naumburg fell in love with Jean Toomer and the remainder of the year stretched ahead as an endless succession of days devoted to paint and suitcases and nights consumed by financial worry, with illicit liquor and illicit sex as intermittent consolation and *The Bridge* an elusive rainbow. Writing to beg a loan from Charlotte Rychtarik on 23 September Hart admitted that the seemingly interminable heat did nothing for his moods but the fact remained that his life suddenly seemed disappointing again after the earliest happiness of moving back to New York. Although he was 'getting along very well at the office' he resented the fact that Thompson's paid some of their art directors $30,000 a year when they were so miserly with junior copy-writers. He was 'learning quite a good deal' and 'accepting new responsibilities' but at the same time he sensed that 'it is quite a stylish and almost snobbish set of educated people at J. Walter Thompson's – they are very lofty and certainly seem to think that the social superiority of the place is enough to make up for low salaries'. All in all he felt that the lot of the artist in America was becoming harder, rather than easier, to bear, and whatever the iridescence of one's poetic vision, money mattered:

> Most of my friends are worn out with the struggle here in New York. If you make enough to live decently on, you have no time left for your real work, – and otherwise you are constantly liable to starve. New York offers nothing to anyone but a circle of friendly and understanding brothers, – beyond that it is one of the most stupid places in the world to live in.

The worst of it was, he was not by nature pessimistic: temperament and destiny required a different response: 'I want to keep saying "YES" to everything and never be beaten a moment, and I shall, of course, never be really beaten.'[61]

A few nights later, on 4 October, he was already in his pyjamas and preparing to face another day at Thompson's when there was a knock at the door and

Waldo Frank walked in with Charlie Chaplin. The two men had eaten together in the Village – continuation of a friendship begun when Frank praised Chaplin in *Our America* – and because the writer admired the actor as 'our most significant and authentic dramatic figure' and an important participant in the country's mythic renewal, it followed that he was eager to introduce him to his poetic disciple.[62] They had hoped to recruit Munson for after-dinner talk as well, but he had just moved to new accommodation in West 11th Street and was exhausted. Despite having to get up the next morning, Hart was intrepid and as soon as he had changed the three men walked to 77 Irving Place, to the apartment Frank had borrowed from Paul Rosenfeld pending his divorce. Not everyone had inspired a lyric by the young Hart Crane, but then not everybody was visited by the most famous actor in the world and Hart was radiant with excitement. Writing to Grace the next day he mentioned that Chaplin's was 'one of the most beautiful faces I ever expect to see' and to Munson he insisted that he himself had acted naturally out of astonishment.[63] Idealist as he was, Frank realized the introduction was unlikely to prove significant but was pleased to see that his two friends got on: 'They had nothing to say to each other, and were a little like two animals, sort of licking each other's necks.'[64] Nevertheless it was five o'clock in the morning when Chaplin dropped Hart at Grove Street before proceeding to his bed at the Ritz. The actor was then at the pinnacle of his fame – with *The Kid* behind him and *The Gold Rush* still two years away – and Hart noted on the way to Irving Place, as the three men were followed by an admiring crowd, that 'people seem to spot Chaplin in the darkness'. He was in New York to promote *A Woman of Darkness*, the film he had recently written, directed and produced, and besides discussing that and other forthcoming ventures he described his notorious extra-marital liaison with the Polish screen vamp Pola Negri. Greying at thirty-five, Chaplin declared himself lonely in Hollywood but seemed to Hart 'a perfect and natural gentleman'. There was talk that the poet and the actor would have dinner together some time soon and when Hart closed his letter to his mother he was confident of the beginning of a significant new friendship: 'I am very happy in the intense clarity of spirit that a man like Chaplin gives one if he is honest enough to receive it. I have that spiritual honesty, Grace, and it's what makes me dear to the only people I care about.'[65]

Toomer was very much a member of that valued circle, and Hart was touched to receive a copy of *Cane*, lovingly, if cryptically, inscribed by its author: 'For Hart, instrument of the highest beauty, whose art, four-conscinal, rich in symbols and ecstasy, is great – whose touch, deep and warm, is a sheer illuminant – with love, Jean.'[66] The dinner with Chaplin never occurred, however: the actor was overwhelmed by parties and a bad cold and soon Hart found himself distracted by other events that compounded his growing disillusion with literary New York. For nine months now he had been eagerly hoping to see 'Faustus and Helen' published in its entirety: until *The Bridge* was complete, whenever that might be, his tripartite poem remained his proudest achievement and he was tired of his stature as a poet being taken on trust by those who had not been able to see the work as it circulated in typescript. Frustration was compounded by the fact that although he numbered several editors among his friends none of them had been able to agree on publication of the poem in its final form. Part II, the first to be completed, had been submitted to *Broom* in June 1922 as 'The Springs of Guilty Song', to languish unpublished, and was joined there in November by Part I, after its rejection by the *Dial*. By that time, however, *Broom* was beset by financial problems and rumours circulated of its imminent demise – and Hart concluded, despite editor Matthew Josephson's protestations of enthusiasm for the poems, that wherever they appeared it would not be in *Broom*. Against all odds, however, the magazine rallied and in January 1923, not knowing that the two poems were intended as part of a greater whole, Josephson published Part II alone, presumably intending to use the other poem on a later occasion.

That month saw the completion of Part III, and with it Hart's resolution to see the work published whole, but he had to wait until the summer of 1923, when Munson promised it would finally appear in its full integrity in *Secession*. That magazine was now being published in Florence under the supervision of John Brooks Wheelwright, who decided to revise and edit the poem without consultation with Munson or its author. When news of Wheelwright's intentions reached New York in September Hart attempted to withdraw the poem from publication and Munson cabled frantic vetoes to Florence, but there was already a sense that it was too late and when Hart wrote to Munson in mid-October it was with resignation that the work that meant so much to him would appear in mutilated form: 'I can only gnash my teeth about my "F&H" – at last completely slain! People now will never get the correct impression – that it wasn't written like a patched blanket.'[67] At the end of October the new number of *Secession* finally arrived from Italy and Munson opened the magazine to find that the worst had indeed happened: true to his declared intentions Wheelwright had published 'Faustus and Helen', but with Part II omitted and Parts I and III riddled with elisions and errors. Consulting the honours of art and friendship, he decided the only possible course lay with literally excising the poem from the magazine prior to its distribution in America. Wearily, on 28 October, Hart agreed, by now too bored and dispirited for any response beyond the suggestion that Munson contact the consulate in Florence to prevent Wheelwright from attempting any more unauthorized editing.

So much for the new philadelphia he had envisaged only six months before: writers, even in their guise as editors, were, it began to seem, disorganized, self-promoting and jealously competitive. How could a spiritual brotherhood emerge from such disarray? His disillusion was intensified that October when the battle of the scribes that had been looming all summer was finally joined in the name of American literature, the future of which both *Secession* and its rival magazine *Broom* had determined to promote. From its inception *Secession* had been provocative and embattled – happily critical of the complacency and mediocrity it ascribed to the *Dial* and the *Little Review* and fiercely protective of the claims of modernism – and there was something inevitable in its eventual collision with *Broom*, which gradually challenged *Secession*'s modernist and Francophile loyalties as Munson and his allies began to see themselves as a brotherhood of Ouspenskian idealists. The writers who slowly coalesced around *Broom*, including Kenneth Burke, Malcolm Cowley, Harold Loeb and William Slater Brown, were hostile to mysticism and found much that was amusing in its claims – but the difficulty was that both magazines were dependent on many of the same writers and readers as the *Dial* and the *Little Review* and there were too few of either to go round. By the middle of 1923 this paucity was beginning to tell: *Secession* had always had financial problems and even *Broom* was foundering. Matthew Josephson, who had defected from the former magazine to the latter, complained that it was impossible to find sufficient material and Malcolm Cowley, recently returned from France and its climate of intellectual seriousness, complained to Harold Loeb that the literary people he encountered in New York 'seem to have lost all capacity for indignation and are content to accept the unimportance of their lot or to solace themselves with piddling drinks'.[68] In the event both magazines were shortly to die – *Broom* in January and *Secession* in April 1924, casualties of public apathy and literary faction – but Cowley, literature's earnest servant, was determined to do all he could to ensure that *Broom* in particular was either revived or at least killed off in spectacular manner and to this end he convoked a meeting of the squabbling writers on 19 October.

About thirty people convened at the Italian speakeasy in Prince Street that Cowley had selected and in the noisy shadow of the elevated railroad set about addressing their grievances. Such an amiably unfocused meeting was scarcely likely to achieve much, not least because several of the important players were absent. Munson, convalescing from tuberculosis, was in Woodstock, New York; Toomer was in Washington and Waldo Frank was otherwise engaged, 'so I seem,' Hart told Munson, 'to be the only delegate from the higher spaces at the Broom enclave'. He was annoyed to discover that wives had also been invited – 'I don't approve of making it so feministic' – and was in any case 'unconcerned with [the meeting's] issues'. Cowley, however, had begged him to attend, so he went prepared to listen to 'the lecture on reasonable affabilities' while expecting to play 'the most contrary role' in the proceedings.[69] At Cowley's request Munson had sent a statement of intent to be read on his behalf, but much of it was an attack on Matthew Josephson, and within a few minutes Cowley, entrusted with reading the letter to the meeting, took to declaiming it, as he later recalled, 'like a blue-jawed actor reciting Hamlet's soliloquy'. Within fifteen minutes pandemonium prevailed and Cowley, surveying the proceedings, saw James Light, one of the founders of the Provincetown Players, muttering drunkenly yet passionately while

Hannah Josephson called vainly for order. Kenneth Burke remained aloof and the writer and poet Glenway Westcott swept from the room. At one stage Cowley saw Hart 'shaking his finger like an angry lawyer' and 'exploding into argument with Josephson on the subject of Munson's letter' while a little later the poet, 'with red face and bristling hair, stamped up and down the room, repeating, "Parlor, hell, parlor"'. Cowley wondered grimly why businessmen could unite to sell a product, why politicians could form alliances when it suited them, when writers were unable to 'come together for ten minutes in the cause of literature.[70] Even apprentice gangsters from the neighbourhood complained about the noise, and the meeting ended in near violence.

Out of loyalty, Hart had contradicted Munson's detractors in his friend's absence and once outside he and Josephson almost came to blows. Cowley was calmer but also disappointed by Hart's allegiance, as he indicated to Harold Loeb a few days later: 'Crane elected to stand by Munson, which disappointed me, for although Munson would be no asset to Broom if he did cooperate Crane can write.'[71] Hart had found Josephson personally antipathetic for some time and after the fracas in Prince Street the two writers were never close friends again. Ten days later, in another confrontation subsequently enshrined in literary lore, Josephson and Munson opted to settle their differences in a field brawl in Woodstock and by the end of November, unaware that his magazine had only four months of life left, Munson had determined to assume total editorial control of *Secession* and publish it in America. As he explained to Alfred Stieglitz, his aim would be to further the visionary work produced by Frank, Toomer and Hart himself. 'The thing I feel is this: that in your photography, in Crane's poetry, in Toomer's work and in Frank's work there is a FORCE that is pure and of the utmost significance. I think that this FORCE will dominate the future and that those who manifest it should stand back to back.'[72]

Since the end of September Hart had been feeling increasingly disillusioned about J. Walter Thompson and in letters home had begun to make ominous complaints about low pay. In view of the fact that he had been at the company for less than four months, and had been accepted in the first place on the basis of modest experience, his expectations of a salary increase were unreasonable. However, by the third week in October, owing to the disastrous history of 'Faustus and Helen' and the farce in Prince Street, Hart's morale had plunged and he told his mother and grandmother that 'my state of nerves and insomnia here due to the mad rush of things and the noisy nights around the place I am obliged to live, makes it imperative that I get away before I have a real breakdown'. Anxiety about the future was not assuaged by the thought that he had no time for his poetry and that both Waldo Frank and Slater Brown, increasingly valued pillars of support, were planning temporary departures from New York. His scheme now was to go to the Isle of Pines and devote his winter to writing and to inspecting the state of the citrus orchards at the Villa Casas. 'Compared to this metropolitan living with its fret and fever' the island was a paradise and the family was foolish ever to have considered selling the property, particularly when he was convinced, as he assured Grace, that 'that grove is going to pay, and *pay well* sometime'.[73]

His application for a salary increase was inevitably rejected but when Hart submitted his resignation on 24 October Thompson's responded generously by granting him an eight-week leave of absence and the offer of his old job when he returned. Then Grace dashed his hopes: without even consulting him she had put the Villa Casas up for sale and the only comfort she could extend was a ticket to Cleveland. Hart's recent letters home had done much to stress not only how much she would hate living in New York (which he would have hated even more) but also his conviction that he would never again live in Cleveland. Quite simply, even with a ticket in his hands, there was no going back and when he wrote to his mother it was to say that although he was 'very, very sorry' about her plans for the Caribbean property he had decided, rather than returning to the Midwest, to accept the offer of spartan hospitality extended from Woodstock by Slater Brown and Edward Nagle: he would go upstate for a month or so the following week. Having hoped that Grace would lend him $200 to cover debts and his fare to the Caribbean he now proposed instead that she send him $15 a week, promising by way of repayment that he would get 'some other kind of literary work' when he returned to New York.[74] Frank supported the plan to go to Woodstock, as did Margaret Naumburg and Jean Toomer, but Munson looked askance at the vagueness of it all and later reflected that Hart 'wanted to be with the rest of us who didn't have jobs. He wanted to bum around the Village. He wanted to write and read and he couldn't discipline himself to take the job.'[75]

On the day that Hart wrote to Grace with his plan to visit the Villa Casas he also wrote his father a letter which CA, in his reply, termed 'a six line challenge after a silence of years'. The poet's overture is not extant, but Clarence Crane's dignified, modest and moving reply survives as another testament in the long story of intense and misdirected emotions which binds father, mother and poet together. It was almost three years since they had spoken, CA reckoned, and now he was sure Hart felt himself 'humbled if you suggest a warm affection for your father'. He declared 'a pride in your accomplishments' but still could not understand why his son had turned against him. But then many of his ancient certainties were now reversed: 'My vision has always been dwarfed by my poor conception of the opportunities in the outside world at a time when I should have struck out for bigger and better things. So I count that I have poorly played the game and wasted many of my inherent talents.'[76] Perhaps Hart would never know the depth of paternal feelings until he had children of his own. In the meantime CA promised that when he was next in New York they would meet. Fumbling as the reconciliation was, it constituted another cause for celebration in addition to the recent liberation from Thompson's and a farewell party was arranged for 1 November, Hart's last night in New York. That day he wrote to Grace assuring her he knew 'damned well' what he was doing and asking her for $15: 'Even if you have to pinch a little bit, I think that the things I am trying to do deserve a few sacrifices.'[77]

In the evening he got drunk, surrounded by his married friends, and on leaving the party he made his way to the water, to bid it and the city it encircled farewell. In March, before his last return to New York, Munson had asked Hart what the situation was about his sexuality – was it classified information or not? – to learn that secrecy was now the guiding principle. Hart felt he had been 'all-too easy' in his declarations so far but told Munson that 'a more discreet behavior' would henceforth be the rule.[78] His friends, if they speculated where he went when the night claimed him, were similarly tacit, so for a while still there would be no talk of his dockside adventures, such as the one that occurred before he left New York when he met a sailor named Jerry bound for Antwerp. Underwood was kept informed, but even he was told on 3 November that the details of the encounter could only be disclosed 'vive voce' since Hart was still 'overwhelmed by the appalling tragedy' of the encounter. He 'never even undressed, and it will be weeks before I can get the thing out of my mind'.[79] He confided the event to Toomer prior to departure and referred to it again when he wrote on 4 November: the rendezvous now haunted him with 'a kind of terrific rawness' but he knew that 'it does cry for words ... and I'm wondering if I am equal to such an occasion, such beauty and anguish, all in one'.[80] Nearly three weeks later Toomer received 'This Way Where November Takes the Leaf', a beautiful fragment Hart initially called 'White Buildings', which was as far as he ever got with the transcription of that troubling midnight. Even as the piece stood it was 'one of the most consciously written things' he had attempted but Hart knew that it would remain unpublished whether or not he managed to perfect it.[81] In the event it remained inchoate, a moving distillation of November mist, the heightened reality of bliss, a parting by sunrise, and the poet's nagging sense that he had failed to capture the embrace, 'in words which no wings can engender now':

And, margined so, the sun may rise aware
(I must have waited for so devised a day)
of the old woman whistling in her tubs,
and a labyrinth of laundry in the courted sky;
while inside, downward passing steps
anon not to white buildings I have seen,
leave me to whispering an answer here
to nothing but this beam that crops my hair.[82]

Having sublet his room, Hart left New York on 2 November and travelled with Malcolm Cowley to Ridgefield, Connecticut, to spend the weekend with Eugene

O'Neill and his second wife, Agnes. He had met the playwright only the previous week through Susan Jenkins but the introduction had gone so well that when O'Neill issued his invitation he promised Hart that if need be he would himself drive him on to Woodstock on Sunday. The playwright was then in the first days of his fame: although he had been writing plays for several years his work had only recently starting drawing the Broadway crowds and the great dramatizations of incest, murder, alcoholism and Oedipal longing which were to dominate American theatre for the rest of Hart's lifetime still lay in the future. He liked Hart from the outset without ever getting to know him well – he seemed 'a super-sensitive tortured personality [who] was at the same time a simple, likeable human being' and the two men found shared interests in drinking and the mystery of the sea, since O'Neill had once been a sailor and like Hart he knew the dives that lined the strand.[83] Peggy Cowley, veteran drinking companion to half the Village, had come to the country earlier with Agnes O'Neill and once the dramatist and Malcolm Cowley had observed the proprieties by discussing German Expressionist playwrights and O'Neill's work in progress, *Desire under the Elms*, the party abandoned itself to what Hart told Toomer was 'a roisterous time', with cakewalks, belly dances and all-night capering.[84] Hart found Agnes O'Neill charming and flirtatious but the latter might well have cursed when Cowley showed his host how to tap one of the barrels of hard cider stored in the cellar: Hart later told the Rychtariks he was 'drunk on cider most of the time' but O'Neill himself easily outdrank his guests and some time after the weekend he disappeared on a drunk's progress, to be found by his long-suffering wife several days later, comatose in his favourite Village haunt, the Hell Hole.[85]

Hart and the Cowleys reached Woodstock in time for dinner with Slater Brown and Edward Nagle on Sunday, 3 November and the next day was devoted to walks in the woods, hide-and-seek and wrestling on the lawn. The Cowleys returned to New York on Tuesday but for Hart there was no such obligation and the ensuing weeks of freedom from office and city were among the happiest of his life. Nagle was the friend of a painter named Anne Rector and the house he and Brown had rented belonged to her family and was situated half a mile from the Saugerties highway. There were four bedrooms, one bathroom, a dining room, a kitchen with an oil stove and a studio with north light and large fireplace attached to the house where the friends gathered in the evening to discuss the eternal verities and, of course, to drink. As Brown remembered, the chores were routinely divided: he and Hart gathered and sawed wood; he cooked; he and Hart washed up; and Nagle, who frequently accused them of being untidy, spent many hours sweeping the floor of his room or sleeping or 'yawning in a desolate way'.[86] Hart was happy, he told Toomer, 'to hear the wind in the boughs, use the axe and saw and even enjoy the bit of cooking which I share in doing' and the mood of the entire household was exhilarated by the discovery in the cellar of a barrel of elderberry wine left by

Mr Rector himself, an eccentric inventor then perfecting his designs for a kerosene-burning automobile. Hart eventually developed an allergy to the drink and suffered head to foot from what Brown thought one of the worst cases of hives he had ever seen – but not before there had been numerous nights of wine-fired debate. On 23 November Hart told Toomer about the previous evening's session, which had seen a 'great defense of the MACHINE by Brown opposed by Crane and Nagle. Went furious to bed. The night before it was Marinetti, John Brown, KKK and Jesus Christ'.[87]

Hart decided to grow a moustache to complement the heavy shirts, woollen socks and corduroy trousers bought at an army and navy store in New York prior to departure and in letter after letter he spoke of glowing cheeks, stiffening muscles and long walks in the fields and woods, now orange, pink and incarnadine in the crispening winter air. Brown sensed that he was 'very much worried about finances' but was nevertheless 'very good company'. He 'loved' being in the country and had 'a very deep feeling for nature', so that even the walk into Woodstock to collect mail and provisions was a lyrical exercise rather than an obligation. When it rained he stayed inside, played with the cats, read Lucretius and Sir James George Frazer's *The Golden Bough* and, as Brown put it, played 'the same record, over and over and over again, so that you'd almost go mad in the house, because the record would get worn and cracked, but still it would go on and on and on'; it was as though the same music, endlessly repeated, 'had some sort of hypnotic effect'.[88] Brown's very presence and beauty offered entrancing reveries of another kind and not the least of Hart's happiness in these weeks came with the proximity and that faint hope, faint but never dying, that Sue's absence in New York might lead to intensities of affection, or even contact, which had so far eluded him. But it was not to be; and soon Hart was pining and then complaining to Toomer that for all his happiness in the country and his trust in its restorative powers he had 'been through enough passions and frustrations ... out here to have slowed up this reinstatement of myself' that he had left New York to enjoy.[89]

Primitive as conditions were, the friends were not isolated. Woodstock, in the foothills of the Catskill Mountains, had been an artists' colony ever since 1902, when Ralph Whitehead, a disciple of William Morris, had established a hamlet of co-operative workshops for sculptors, weavers, potters and painters, and by the early Twenties, during the busy summer months, the colony had grown large enough to publish two magazines. The poet Richard Le Gallienne lived here, and poets Edna St Vincent Millay, Will Durant, Clemence Randolph and Lawrence Langner came and went, associating with numerous painters who included Henry McFee, Andrew Dasburg, Ernest Fiene and Eugene Speicher. Relations between the two groups were fostered by Munson's friend and host at this time, the art critic William Murrell Fisher, described by Brown as 'a tall, bearded, scholarly Englishman, crippled in early youth by polio', and Miss Rixcon, a young Finnish woman of means, enlivened the locality with the affairs she conducted with husbands and bachelors.[90]

Hart got to know Fisher and spent a lot of time in the studios of Ernest and Paul Fiene but the most important addition to the Woodstock circle came with the advent of the sculptor Gaston Lachaise, who arrived in November for the duration of the winter. Born in Paris in 1882, Lachaise had attended the Académie Nationale des Beaux-Arts and emigrated to the United States in 1906 in pursuit of an American woman who was to become his model, muse and wife – Isabel Nagle, Edward Nagle's mother. He landed in America without a word of English but his mind was filled with quotations from Rimbaud, Baudelaire and Verlaine and his passionate and romantic nature soon found inspiration in the mistress, then wife, thirteen years his senior. The eroticism and monumentality of his mature sculpture – evocative of the heroic ambitions of Rodin and devoted to a celebration of the female body – convinced the painter Marsden Hartley that Lachaise was 'a lyric architect of the human form'. He became a favourite sculptor of the *Dial*, which commissioned busts of Marianne Moore and e.e. cummings, and the stature he enjoyed in his adopted country was formally recognized when he was commissioned to execute works for the AT&T Building and the RCA Building at the Rockefeller Center in New York. He was a large man, with dark eyes and dark flowing hair whose ardours and idealisms were clear in every gesture. Hartley detected 'an elemental animalistic burning in him like flames on the hilltop of a burning city',[91] and Gorham Munson soon noted that Hart had become his 'worshipful friend'.[92]

Gaston and Madame Lachaise were naturally prominent on the guest list when the Brown household decided to give a Thanksgiving dinner which also included John Dos Passos, who travelled from New York, Elaine Orr, recently divorced from *Dial* publisher Scofield Thayer and later the wife of e.e. cummings, Marjorie Spencer, sister of the artist Miles Spencer and a source of some interest to Edward Nagle, and Stewart Mitchell, a contributor to *Eight Harvard Poets* and eventually director of the New England Historical Society in Boston. As always in bohemian hospitality the feast was a collective venture: apples had been sent from Maine for Madame Lachaise; Grace dispatched a fruit cake from Cleveland; Brown and Nagle bought a barrel of hard cider to complement the locally brewed red wine; and Hart, although never a noted cook, produced the apple sauce and stuffed the turkey. The company sat down at five and consumed potato and onion soup; turkey and traditional trimmings ; salad; pumpkin pie; fruit pie, mince pies, nuts and raisins. At eight the Victrola was turned on and the friends danced to jazz records, with Hart partnering Isabel Lachaise until both were exhausted. The evening was deemed a great success, and when Hart reported to Stieglitz on 5 December he declared himself still rather 'buzzy' with the aftermath. He felt resilient, nevertheless: 'My first taste of the country for years – and a month of it has put me in a steadier mood than I remember since childhood.' The only disquieting thought was that his imagination was now 'sunk in a kind of agreeable vegetable existence' – even writing letters had become something of a chore and of more serious literary activity there was so far little indication.[93] Susan Jenkins, then working in New York as an editor on a love-story magazine called *Telling Tales*, attempted to get him to write some love poems for the publication, if only for the sake of the $10 payment, but to no avail, but he did at least apply to Gilbert Seldes at the *Dial* for reviewing work: 'I need these occasional bucks badly, the woods aren't full of them'.[94]

Despite country distractions, Hart did find the determination to resume a poem begun before he left New York and already sent to Munson in provisional form. It was called 'Recitative', and in its earliest shape Crane saw it as being a kind of 'confession', an effusion of the 'somewhat flamboyant' weeks prior to his departure which had also seen the completion of 'Possessions'.[95] Indeed the two poems were in many ways linked in his mind and when he eventually sent them to Allen Tate for appraisal it was with the suggestion that they were almost complementary. Still presuming him to be a member of the same sexual brotherhood, and a perspicacious one at that, Crane was convinced Tate would not only see that the poems were thematically linked but would also interpret them correctly – 'Possessions' as an encrypted confession, an account of the nights in which its author was 'possessed' after he waved his friends goodbye; and 'Recitative' as a meditation on this double life and by extension on the ambiguities of many-faceted existence. But Tate stumbled. For all his enthusiasm about 'Possessions', he found 'Recitative' virtually impenetrable and his bemusement prompted a concession from the poet. The poem was 'complex, exceedingly, – and I worked for weeks ... trying to simplify the presentation of the ideas in it'. He always hated 'to be taken as wilfully obscure or esoteric' and the fact remained that he was striving 'for a more perfect lucidity' but until the two writers finally met both would have to content themselves with Hart's admission that 'there are, as too often in my poems, other reflexes and symbolisms in the poem ... which it would be silly to write here'.[96] When he was finally able to gauge Tate face to face he would be able to see if he shared the same sexual reflexes: until then symbolism could cover a multitude of sins. In the meantime Crane explained to Munson that he was making 'Recitative' 'more metaphysical and restrained' – and it was in this new guise that the work would appear in the *Little Review* in 1924, only to be expanded from four to seven quatrains before its final completion in 1926.[97]

If 'Recitative' proved problematic for its author, readers have found it no less challenging, despite an unusual offer of assistance from its author:

Imagine the poet, say, on a platform speaking it. The audience is one half of Humanity, Man (in the sense of Blake) and the poet is the other. ALSO, the poet sees himself in the audience as in a mirror. ALSO, the audience sees itself, in part, in the poet. Against this paradoxical DUALITY is posed the UNITY, or the conception of it ... in the last verse.[98]

The first two stanzas of the poem reveal the poet contemplating himself in the mirror, and there he sees not only himself, and Everyman, riven by contradictions, but also his double – that proverbial other half, the lover, without whom he is incomplete, a mere 'shadowed half':

Regard the capture here, O Janus-faced,
As double as the hands that twist this glass.
Such eyes at search or rest you cannot see;
Reciting pain or glee, how can you bear!

Twin shadowed halves: the breaking second holds
In each the skin alone, and so it is
I crust a plate of vibrant mercury
Borne cleft to you, and brother in the half.

In the third and fourth stanzas Crane recognizes the nocturnal, lustful animal which lurks within himself, his lover and every other human being – but with the ebbing of the darkness this presence retreats and the 'white buildings' of hope, of the mythic city, of a society held together by bonds nobler and more enduring than the merely physical, come into view:

Inquire this much-exacting fragment smile,
Its drums and darkest blowing leaves ignore, –
Defer though, revocation of the tears
That yield attendance to one crucial sign.

Look steadily – how the wind feasts and spins
The brain's disk shivered against lust. Then watch
While darkness, like an ape's face, falls away,
And gradually white buildings answer day.

Not for the first time with Crane's poetry one has the feeling of being in a dream. Image yields to image with a vividness which is not always clarifying; his poems, especially the shorter lyrics, evoke a state of reverie and one emerges from the trance, as from the haunting yet elusive visitations of the night, bewildered by the multiple possibilities of meaning. The 'fragment smile', the 'darkest blowing leaves' of lust are integral to the poet, to mankind, to the double who may be the poet's lover, but they are no more significant than any 'crucial sign' of spiritual possibility. The body and the soul – both impenetrable in their impulses – contend for supremacy in every human being. But now Crane appears to narrow his focus and to consider himself, like Absalom, a rebellious son, and his double-lover, and to ask what course in life they should pursue:

> Let the same nameless gulf beleaguer us –
> Alike suspend us from atrocious sums
> Built floor by floor on shafts of steel that grant
> The plummet heart, like Absalom, no stream.

The solution seems to lie in self-assertion – for the fractious son imprisoned in the tower of paternal incomprehension – and in self-understanding for the man and his lover, who must realize that the body bridges flesh and soul. Only with this realization will they be free to walk clear of life's chaos and thus reach the eternal present of happiness; and only in happiness is the divided self made whole once more:

> The highest tower, – let her ribs palisade
> Wrenched gold of Nineveh; – yet leave the tower.
> The bridge swings over salvage, beyond wharves;
> A wind abides the ensign of your will ...
>
> In alternating bells have you not heard
> All hours clapped dense into a single stride?
> Forgive me for an echo of these things,
> And let us walk through time with equal pride.[99]

In one sense 'Recitative', like much of Crane's work, is a plea for the restoration of a fractured world and as such it might appear needlessly difficult. But no poet so committed to the sincerity of his art would have written verses so abstruse, with meanings so protean, without good reason: the narcissistic twinship of male love; the dark ape of desire; the fractious son suspended above chasms of lust and longing; and the lonely idealist yearning for direction are all here, like the mysterious figures in an elaborate carpet – and if Tate was unable to understand the poem, at least its author could console himself with the thought that his parents would never grasp it either.

Just before Thanksgiving Hart had written to Grace to break the news that he would not be returning to Cleveland for Christmas – 'You will be jolly enough at Zell's without me this time', he insisted, knowing she would not be but determined nevertheless to establish a new precedent of independence.[100] The plan now was that he should remain at Woodstock until the beginning of the new year and then return to New York to get another job – but the metropolis was not an enticing prospect and he spoke with feeling when he told his mother, 'I think city life is a fake and a delusion.'[101] He felt increasingly drawn to the idea of a country existence and it was this rural yearning that had recently led him to climb Mount Overlook, the 2,500-foot mountain which overshadowed the artists' colony. He reached the summit at about noon one day and marvelled as the winter radiance revealed the distant meanderings of the Hudson River. It was an exhilarating and poetic prospect – and one enjoyed only by a caretaker all alone in his cottage. Nearby stood the ruins of a house and a hotel, recently consumed by fire, but besides the guardian hermit the only other inhabitants of the summit were his cow, two horses and some poultry. And now even the caretaker was preparing to leave: after seven months, he told Hart, he was eager to descend to human companionship again, despite the nebulous responsibilities of his post and its salary of $40 a month. For a happy hour, at last envisaging the resolution of his financial problems, Hart contemplated taking over the job himself and assured Toomer that 'I could milk a cow, feed chickens and two horses and keep myself from freezing with enough time left over for some uninterrupted reading and writing, provided hurricanes didn't blow us all off the cliff some night.'[102] He applied to the Brooklyn owner of the cottage but despite his enthusiasm for the scheme and his determination to escape what he told Munson were the 'scattered prostitutions' of city life, nothing came of the idea and Hart would learn by other means how ill suited he was to solitude.[103] First snows fell. He read Pater's *Plato and Platonism*, composed a nonsense poem called 'What Nots?' and wrote letters to Malcolm Cowley and to CA. He bought a hunter's coat and this time received letters, from Waldo Frank, who was in Paris enjoying 'the whole extraordinary kaleidoscope of intellectual life in a city which is indeed drooping and fading under a somber sky';[104] from Stieglitz, who had just completed his sequence of cloud pictures – 'Some people feel I have photographed God';[105] and from CA, who purported to marvel at the way his son had addressed the challenges of existence: 'If you live in the woods and still carry on your work, you have solved the problem much better than most of us.'[106]

'There is someone here for tea almost every day,' Hart told Grace, and one of the more frequent visitors was William Murrell Fisher, the critic, poet and director of the Woodstock Art Gallery who had taken care of Munson during his convalescence from consumption.[107] With the latter's departure Fisher sought companionship further afield and after several visits to Brown's bachelor household Hart reported to Munson: 'He has a great fondness for Brown and myself, too, I think. I certainly enjoy him most alone, as the other day when I came over to his place in the afternoon and stayed until nearly midnight.'[108] In fact Fisher viewed Hart more equivocally, indeed experienced 'a feeling of being uncomfortable' when alone with him, so much so that on one occasion, when the two men were left together in the critic's library following Brown's departure, Fisher was at such a loss for words that he could do no more than thrust a folio of manuscripts at the poet in a bid to keep him entertained. It proved an inspiring decision, however, and the older man watched as Hart 'opened the package very dubiously; when his eye lighted on some of the poems, he became very excited. He flared up in a corner with it.'[109]

The lyrics in question were the work of a poet named Samuel Greenberg whom the critic had befriended in 1913 while he was working at the Metropolitan Museum of Art and whose posthumous reputation he was determined to establish with the assistance of seventeen extant notebooks containing over 600 poems. Greenberg was an Austrian-Jewish immigrant who had died in 1917, overwhelmed at twenty-four by poverty, hard work, the premature death of both his parents and the agonies of consumption, traditional nemesis of precocious artists. Uneducated and determined to write in an alien tongue, he read Emerson, Carlyle and Pater, the English Romantics and Edgar Allan Poe, and harnessed his gift for arresting images, his transcendent spirit and the heightened perceptions of the consumptive to create a corpus of luxuriant work which was charged with a passion for solitude and the sea, and tense with imminent death and the urgency of utterance. After his decease his brothers had entrusted the poems and their future reputation to Fisher for custody and he had published an essay about the poet, and one of his lyrics, in the *Plowshare*, a Woodstock magazine of which he was associate editor. By the time Hart saw the manuscripts, however, Greenberg's reputation had hardly advanced at all and the discovery of his rhapsodic work had a profound effect on the poet, who wrote to Munson on 20 December that Greenberg was 'a Rimbaud in embryo' and wondered if his friend had ever seen any of the 'hobbling yet really gorgeous attempts that boy made without any education or time except when he became confined to a cot'.[110] The dead poet offered a paradigm of frustrated genius which had predictable appeal for Hart, although Brown, in the course of the discussions that ensued, was less convinced by Greenberg's genius and found his poems 'fugitive and incomplete'.[111] For Hart, however, they betrayed 'a quality that is unspeakably eerie'.[112]

To Brown's surprise Hart persuaded Fisher to lend him the notebooks and as December came to a close he busied himself with transcribing the stronger poems – prodigal in their imagery of rainbows, waves, fountains and flowers – before deciding to arrange a selection of favourite lines in a collage he entitled 'Emblems of Conduct' in homage to the dead poet's similar but much flatter poem, 'Conduct'. Hart's composition evoked a still and dreamlike landscape animated only by a wanderer and an apostle who admire spiritual curiosity and dogmatic learning respectively. Radio evangelists, incurious scholars and other spurious authorities proclaim false wisdom to the people and 'The apostle conveys thought through discipline'. The wanderer, however – an artist by another name – maintains a spiritual freedom which comprehends the significance of ecstasy and chooses to end his life's journey by the ocean. Perhaps his visionary spirit will only be posthumously honoured but dolphins will sport at his grave and the 'spiritual gates' his artistry opened will be venerated, 'Where marble clouds support the sea'. Though not one of his most successful endeavours, 'Emblems of Conduct' bears witness to the strong artistic judgement of its author, which forged a characteristic, and somewhat prophetic, document from borrowed materials. Hart's chosen title was clearly an acknowledgement of indebtedness for a poem he seems not to have considered important. Later, Allen Tate and Malcolm Cowley took a different view and persuaded him to include the piece in his first volume of poems, not knowing of its Greenbergian inspiration. If Hart had appended a note to indicate his source a scholarly controversy about plagiarism would have been avoided – but much critical ink was subsequently spilt over the full extent of Crane's debt to Greenberg, to the detriment of the reputation of both poets. All artists are plagiarists until they become transcenders but the fact remains that although we can never know what Greenberg might have achieved in a fairer world there is nothing in the corpus of his work to equal even the secondary achievements of his famous admirer.

Christmas loomed and with it guilt that he was not returning to Cleveland. He wrote to Grace on 21 December, strenuously making light of his decision and at the same time preparing the ground for future disappointments his behaviour might inflict on her. He was not a conventional son to enjoy conventional family Christmases, but at this stage there was no point in dropping anything other than the vaguest hints that he might yet betray some of his mother's other domestic expectations: 'I don't know whether it is possible for all people to understand certain ardours that I have, and perhaps there is no special reason why you, as my mother, should understand that side of me any better than most people.' But what he did want her to understand now was that although he returned to the prospect of menial work in New York he was resolved not to subjugate his poetry to conventional notions of prosperity:

> I expect I'll always have to drudge for my living, and I'm quite willing to always do it, but I am no more fooling myself that the mental bondage and spiritual bondage of the more remunerative sorts of work is worth the sacrifices involved. If I can't continue to create the sort of poetry that is my intensest and deepest component in life – then it all means very little to me.[113]

She sent him some collars and money for Christmas and with festivity imminent he joined Brown and Nagle in felling a tree which was then hung with baubles and candles provided by Gaston and Mme Lachaise, who joined the bachelors for roast chicken on Christmas Eve. The following day the hospitality was returned and gifts were dispensed: Hart received a pipe from Nagle, a harmonica from Isabel Lachaise, a horn and an embroidery set from Brown, and Zell and the Rychtariks sent him money. Miss Rixcon gave a party, there were dinners organized until New Year's Day – and to end 1923 he posed nude for a drawing by Lachaise.

He left behind a landscape blanketed with snow when he returned to New York on 2 January to install himself once more at 45 Grove Street prior to resuming the dispiriting search for work. He inspected Stieglitz's new cloudscapes and saw Kenneth Burke and the Cowleys, Lisa Munson, Jean Toomer, Margaret Naumburg, Paul Rosenfeld, Glenway Westcott, Eugene O'Neill and even Matthew Josephson, but nevertheless he confided to Munson that he was 'about as solitary as I ever felt in my life'.[114] Then CA, having heard from Grace that Hart was without employment, wrote to his son on 7 January with the news that the continued expansion of the Crane Chocolate Company had forced him to move to new premises in Cleveland and that he was looking for a travelling representative who would visit trade customers in various states. Would Hart like the job? Although to begin it would pay only 'a small living salary' it offered promise for the future, that is, if Hart wanted to return to confectionery manufacture rather than make himself 'a real advertising success'.[115] It was a benevolent and modest overture, but despite CA's insistence that he did not want to make his son into something he was not Hart rejected the offer at once, assuring Grace that he saw through his father's schemes to reduce him to 'a mere tool'.[116] In the meantime, he needed a further $15 to cover the rent.

When it came to replying to CA, however, discretion was the better part of outrage and if Hart still had a lot to learn about his father one of the lessons so far acquired had been that it seldom pays to alienate the prosperous, however questionable their motives might be, and his response of 12 January showed the poet to be every bit the son of his mutually manipulative parents. Summoning all his eloquence, Hart appealed to CA's compassion in one sentence, his paternal pride in the next, and insisted that he only desired 'to talk to you as a son ought to be able to talk to his father'. Politely declining the offered job, he pointed out that he could not accept it for the same reasons that he had been unable to continue at J. Walter Thompson, 'the largest agency in the world': he had to have time 'to do some real thinking and writing, the most important things to me in my life'. Surely his father could see that he would long since have jettisoned his poetic aspirations if they been no more than youthful fantasy? He was down to his last $2, but until he found 'something humble and very temporary' to pay the bills he knew he could count on the loyalty of his friends – and what friends they were, 'not the kind of "Greenwich Villagers" that you may have been thinking they were' but people of fame and distinction – O'Neill, Lachaise, Stieglitz and Chaplin – who happened to believe that their young poet was making 'a real contribution to American literature'. Indeed Hart himself was now sure that if he sustained his poetic growth CA would 'live to see the name "Crane" stand for something where literature is talked about, not only in New York but in London and abroad'. Lastly, appealing to an altruism he privately felt his father lacked, he asked CA to ponder the idea of a labour which overlooked profit and practicality and sought its justification only in the creation of beauty. Poetry was such a discipline and Hart was sure his father would understand his decision to follow 'what seems sometimes only a faint star' if he could recognize the poet's aim, which was to engineer 'a communication between man and man, a bond of understanding and human enlightenment'.[117] CA was moved – and on 15 January, enclosing some money and the promise of future assistance, he conceded that 'there is much more in this world than money'.

A week later there were two promising opportunities for work. Hart had lunch and an interview with the publisher Ben Huebsch – 'one of the smartest men in New York', Grace was told, and certainly superior to Munson's publisher Horace Liveright, who was 'pretty commercial and pettifogging' by comparison – but in the event it was to the small advertising agency of Pratt and Lindsey, at 461 Eighth Avenue, that he directed himself on 28 January to start work once more.[118] The company's president, Verneur Edmund Pratt, had enjoyed a successful career in mail order at Sears, Roebuck before establishing his own enterprise and in 1924 he published a book devoted to his calling, *Selling by Mail: Principles and Practice*. Hart was installed in an office on the fifteenth floor and put to work – at $50 a week – on writing a promotional booklet on the virtues of cheese commissioned by a large importing house. His deadline was tight but with the services of what appeared to be an efficient company he was sure he would prosper – and optimism appeared vindicated when the finished booklet was accepted for publication without any modifications. More good news came on 2 February: CA was in New York to inspect business at the Crane Company office at 6 East 39th Street and to attend meetings which would lead to the opening of further Crane stores in Boston and Philadelphia the following year and he invited his son to the Waldorf for what turned out to be two hours of happy talk. The conversation began badly when the elder Crane asked the wrong sort of questions about his son's professional ambitions but Hart 'quietly kept on doing my best to explain myself in terms he would understand', Grace was informed, and CA 'ended by accepting me quite docilely as I am'. He even asked his son's advice on how best to advertise a new product and told him that his determination to live his life on his own terms marked him out as the proud scion of both sides of his strong-willed ancestry. At parting he gave his son 'a greenback' and promised future meetings whenever he was in New York and the next day Hart was happy to inform his mother that CA 'really respects me'.[119]

But fortune changed as suddenly. On 11 February he arrived at the office to be told that his job was to be terminated forthwith: Pratt and Lindsey had overestimated its business and could find him no more work. After only two weeks he was back on the streets, and with suspicions of malpractice souring his departure. As he told Grace, in strident defence of his credentials, Pratt 'couldn't say a thing against my work or copy as an excuse, but he had to invent some fantastic pretenses that I saw through right away ... it was a dirty deal.'[120] The blow fell hard on self-esteem, and problems were compounded when on 13 February he learned

he would have to move because the principal lessee of his apartment was returning to New York and wanted possession on 1 March.

In the midst of these dramas Hart and his fellow Villagers were galvanized by
the arrival in New York of the mystic Georgei Ivanovitch Gurdjieff, whose forty
attendant pupils were to perform dances at the Neighborhood Playhouse in
Grand Street. Gurdjieff was a native of the Caucasus and claimed to be the survivor of a group of archaeologists and explorers who had imbibed the secrets of
man's inner life from montane lore acquired in Tibet in the 1880s. As interpreted
by Gurdjieff, the learning held that man comprised three different personalities
bound in a trinity of mutual incomprehension and in Constantinople a decade
previously the mystic had begun to attract attention as the high priest of a new
religion whose votaries learned tranquillity and self-control through a system of
exercises performed to music. Ouspensky himself was among the credulous, and
Munson remembered that 'Hart was in a state of high excitement one morning
... when he rang my doorbell: "Gurdjieff is coming!" he burst out. "He is the
master Ouspensky found." '[121] The Village turned out in force to witness the rites,
and Hart and Susan Jenkins were intrigued to note that Margaret Anderson and
her companion Georgette LeBlanc stood throughout with their backs to the
stage. Jenkins recalled that she and Hart were 'irreverent but well-behaved, even
at the sight of Mr Gurdjieff visible from our sixth-row seats standing in the
wings dressed in a costume resembling that of a lion-tamer',[122] but when Hart
reported to Grace the next day it was to proclaim the dances 'very, very interesting – and things were done by amateurs which would stump the Russian
ballet'.[123]

The evening proved decisive in several lives – but not in Hart's. Munson and his
wife 'were sleepless for hours afterwards, such was [the meeting's] awakening
effect upon us' and Munson himself was surprised by the poet's tepid response to
the demonstration he had so eagerly announced, concluding merely that 'Hart, for
all the intensity of his poetry, was highly affectible by the attitudes and opinions
of his friends, and I suspected that he had been scoffed into a scoffing mood'. A
few days later Heap and Anderson hosted an evening where twenty writers and
artists gathered to hear Gurdjieff's prolocutor A.R. Orage, editor of the *New Age*,
dilate on the mission of the Institute for the Harmonious Development of Man,
the mystic's headquarters at Fontainebleau outside Paris, but again Munson was
surprised to note that 'Hart was silent throughout the meeting and expressed no
views afterwards'. With increasing conviction the Munsons read Orage's journalism and essays and joined Jean Toomer and Margaret Naumburg in hailing the significance of Gurdjieff's cult – but once more Munson noted that 'Hart stayed away
and seemed to be waiting for our infatuation to run its course'. It never did, and
the advent of the mystic and his disciples marked a turning point in Hart's
relations with Munson, a believer thereafter, and with Toomer, who shortly afterwards abandoned his career as a writer in order to study at the institute at

Fontainebleau. The mystic brotherhood, such as it was, broke ranks that spring, although Munson made a final attempt to help Hart see the light by taking him to another meeting held by Orage, but although the latter's utterances were 'unresentfully endured' by Hart it was clear that no apostasy would occur.[124] Munson went to his grave mystified by the poet's indifference to Gurdjieff but for Slater Brown – who considered the mystic dances an outrageous charade – the matter was simple: 'Hart never took Gurdjieff seriously because Waldo Frank did not.'[125]

There were other, more pressing reasons for his indifference, however. The untimely departure from Pratt and Lindsey instigated one of the most difficult times in Hart's life so far, when food and accommodation proved even more elusive than philosophical certainty. On leaving Grove Street he went to stay with the O'Neills in Connecticut before moving on his return to Manhattan into a furnished room at 15 Van Nest Place: the bed was comfortable and there was a maid but at $10 a week it was more than he could afford and the traumatic upheaval of his few possessions had taken 'more time and consternation than seems believable', he informed Tate.[126] Dire insolvency compelled him to ask Grace to pay his $9.32 life insurance premium: 'I can't spare a cent now. If I should ever be killed by accident, on the other hand, it means $4,000 to you.'[127] The job with Huebsch came to nothing and the personnel director at J. Walter Thompson, whence he had so blithely resigned only weeks before, missed several appointments for interviews that Hart had made. There was nothing for it but to approach CA for the loan of $100 but the tone of his application was so suspicious and embattled that he offended his father, who replied with weary reason – and presumably a subvention – that he was unable to see how Hart could survive without taking 'a real interest' in his advertising career. 'If your writing could only be a side line, a sort of pleasure to be taken up in the evening ... if you would only think of it just as men play golf, then I would see things differently.'[128] By the end of February stress had again assumed physical form: a cold turned into chronic coughing and bronchitis, and homesickness began to plague him. When funds did run out he took to bribing his landlady with Mary Garden Chocolates, and accepted every single invitation to dinner – from the Habichts, the Munsons, the Smiths – in order to stay alive. Plans to approach O'Neill for a loan were abandoned only at the last minute when Stewart Mitchell from the *Dial* gave him a little money but by the end of March Hart told Grace he had only the sparrows to feed him and by the beginning of April, once his landlady had had her fill of chocolate, he was sleeping on a sofa at Susan Jenkins's apartment at 30 Jones Street. CA had fallen silent once again and Hart took the cessation of letters to be part of a scheme to pull him back to Cleveland. For the time being, however, he remained determined to live in New York, sustained if not by food then by the conviction of his literary destiny. He began to think that he would never find another advertising job and was now reconciled to becoming a stevedore or a truck driver – but whatever happened he urged Grace not to worry about him: 'My work is in advance of the times, and I'll probably have to wait for a good while before getting my dues. At present – only writers, themselves, and a few advanced intelligences understand me. That has been true of many others in the past. But I am proud of my admirers.'[129]

The advanced intelligences would soon be put to the test when Crane started another poem in the early months of 1924. 'Lachrymae Christi', begun in February, occupied its author intermittently for almost a year and like the other poems from this period it ranks among the most challenging in modern literature. 'Experience', he told Toomer some weeks after beginning the lyric, he took to be 'the effort to describe God', but since God was unknowable except through personal conviction it followed that a poem about His son's redeeming tears, begun when the seasons of Lent and of earthly renewal coincided, would involve intensely personal notions of redemption and description.[130] Indeed 'Lachrymae Christi', one of Crane's densest metaphorical endeavours, appears on close inspection to subvert all traditional notions of Christian devotion and to prescribe celebration rather than penitence as the necessary obeisance to divinity. At the time of early composition and in the midst of grave financial anxiety he assured his mother: 'I have a revived confidence in humanity lately, and things are going to come very beautifully for me – and after not so very long, I think. The great thing is to Live and NOT hate.'[131] For Crane this prescription entailed the rediscovery of a pristine vision, crucial to the poet who sees and names the universe, and his new poem hoped to

> recall
> To music and retrieve what perjuries
> Had galvanized the eyes.

This cleansed – and cleansing – vision, pure like the light of the moon, evokes the two opening stanzas of the poem, which transform the season of earthly renewal into a bloody and cannibalistic rite. The mill which cruel nature surrounds is meanwhile seen both as the factory which weaves the wool of the Paschal Lamb and as a crude mechanistic construction which poetic vision can transform into a face, where windows become eyes and the light of understanding can provoke a smile:

> Whitely, while benzine
> Rinsings from the moon
> Dissolve all but the windows of the mills
> (Inside the sure machinery
> Is still
> And curdled only where a sill
> Sluices its one unyielding smile)

Immaculate venom binds
The fox's teeth, and swart
Thorns freshen on the year's
First blood. From flanks unfended,
Twanged red perfidies of spring
Are trillion on the hill.

Crane was acutely, physically, responsive to the seasons and knew that the blossoms of spring portended the annual torment of the summer. In 'Lachrymae Christi' this ambiguity is suggested by the implied transformation of Christ's tears into drops of blood which fertilize the yearly breaking forth of nature. Though the spring is a period of pain and anguish it is also the most appropriate time for the poet to hope for forgiveness for his transgressions and inspiration for his future expectations. But if the lowliest creatures of nature whisper the virtues of forgiveness, the poet insists that joy and song are more propitious than penitence and superimposes the figure of Dionysus on that of Christ, just as the early Christians usurped the temples of antiquity:

> While chime
> Beneath and all around
> Distilled clemencies, – worms'
> Inaudible whisper, tunneling
> Not penitence
> But song, as these
> Perpetual fountains, vines, –
>
> Thy Nazarene and tinder eyes.
>
> (Let sphinxes from the ripe
> Borage of death have cleared my tongue
> Once and again; vermin and rod
> No longer bind ...

The poet, it seems, is granted clear speech and inspired sight by the 'perpetual fountains' yielded by the vine; borage cordial cleanses his palate and the scourges of traditional Christian observance are made redundant. This is a poem in which poetic speech is authorized by alcohol but it is also a Lenten offering: the natural compulsion of seasonal renewal is marked by the eternal truth of Christ's Passion on the sable arms of the cross:

> Names peeling from Thine eyes
> And their undimming lattices of flame,

Spell out in palm and pain
Compulsion of the year, O Nazarene.

Lean long from the sable, slender boughs,
Unstanched and luminous.

Yet if each Easter witnesses the release of spring's 'lilac-emerald' breath,
'Lachrymae Christi' ends with a homoerotic glimpse of a sacrificed and dismem-
bered god: whatever the pieties of spring and Christianity, Crane could not be
their votary and looked instead for vision and sustenance to the impaled male
body and the pleasures of the vine:

             Thy face
From charred and riven stakes, O
Dionysus, Thy
Unmangled target smile.[132]

Some mitigation of his low morale and financial plight came when the *Little Review*
accepted 'Possessions' and 'Recitative' for publication in its spring issue. No matter
that after reading the poems Margaret Anderson wrote from France: 'Hart Crane
should be killed, perhaps, but certainly not printed.'[133] Then Frank wrote from
Madrid on 24 February to prove that distance had done nothing to diminish his
belief in the significance of spiritual unity – and, by extension, Hart's power to
invoke it in poetry:

> Isaiah and Saint Francis are far more truly our contemporaries than Henry James
> or Mark Twain or Van Wyck Brooks. ... We are in a state of starving in our
> rational continent. For nourishment, we must have a Bridge to the mysterious
> sources of our hunger. This Bridge is denied to Picasso: who says with marvel-
> lous success, 'we are self-sufficient'. Well, the only trouble with that is, that his
> sense both of 'we' and of 'self-sufficiency' is too delineated, and eventually
> sterile.[134]

A month later he wrote again. He had seen Valéry Larbaud, 'who knows ten times
more about Am[erican] letters than Gide', but regretted having nothing of Hart's
to show him. He had heard about his protégé's problems of unemployment and
now wanted to send reassurance: 'You are a man of genius. Of this I have not the
slightest doubt.' But he had heard other rumours besides and delicately reminded
his young friend that he could only fulfil himself by husbanding his resources.
Extravagances at midnight sponsored few epic visions: 'Our human existence is
essential in the sense of a tool: we cannot articulate God, as we are called to, without a well-functioning human body, any more than we could write a poem with a

punk pen or a typewriter . . . . That is why, my friend, you will study more as time goes on, the problem of conserving your physical and emotional forces.'[135]

Another figure who felt anxious about the excesses of Hart's life was Malcolm Cowley, who had already divulged his misgivings to Kenneth Burke early in 1924: 'Hart Crane – lost job – losing room – disgusted with New York and thinks of returning to Cleveland, Ohio. It is disquieting to find a man more episodic than myself.'[136] Since meeting the previous August Cowley and Crane had slowly found themselves spending increasing amounts of time together but the friendship which eventually developed between them, as significant as any in Hart's life, was by no means the result of immediate attraction. Shortly after the initial meeting Cowley had confided to Burke: 'I like Crane but every time I see him we fight on another subject.'[137] And Hart was no less guarded, declaring to Munson: 'I wouldn't make any compromises with C[owley]. I like many things about him, but he is still in his adolescence when it comes to certain reactions.'[138] That spring, however, with Frank in Europe and Munson and Toomer falling inexorably under Gurdjieff's sway, Hart found himself looking for new friends and through Slater Brown and Susan Jenkins he began socializing more often with Burke and the Cowleys despite their open mockery of the spiritual brotherhood. Hart's mystical loyalties were no doubt part of the reason for Cowley's initial assessment of the poet's mental faculties, as divulged to his wife:

'Hart isn't very bright,' I told Peggy one evening at dinner. I meant that he hadn't the quick competence I had come to expect of my friends, most of whom had been scholarship boys in college ... although he read intensely, rather than widely, there were immense gaps in his knowledge of things we took for granted.[139]

Cowley himself was famously quicker than he appeared. He had about him an aspect of method, almost of ponderousness, which belied his intellectual acuity and provoked impatience among the worldlier figures of the Eastern literary establishment, many of whom might have smiled when the poet and novelist John Peale Bishop dismissed him as 'the plowboy of the western world who has been to Paris'.[140] Gorham Munson also disliked him but knew that only the obtuse underestimated him: as far as he was concerned, Cowley was 'pen-clever but not speech-clever ... slow in speech, a little countrified, apparently phlegmatic; a plodder, one would wrongly guess'.[141] This provincial aspect was at once genuine and a camouflage, the vestige of a country boyhood begun in 1898 when Cowley was born, the only child of an unsuccessful homoeopathic doctor, in the Allegheny Mountains seventy miles east of Pittsburgh. Cowley senior was a Presbyterian of Scots-Irish descent who every day read to his son from the works of the Swedish mystic and visionary Swedenborg; his wife was the strong and capable daughter of German immigrants. The Cowleys sent their son to Pittsburgh High School, where he befriended Kenneth Burke and Susan Jenkins: there he read the school library's restricted texts – Shaw, Ibsen, Wilde and Dostoevsky – and there his literary ambition took shape. Concurrently, he learned the lessons of another school: every summer the family returned to its holiday home in the Alleghenies and the growing boy spent idyllic hours wandering woods and climbing trees, discovering the secret places and boyish epiphanies which instilled in him a lifelong love of nature and inspired much of the poetry he wrote in later life, when that boyhood paradise had been lost to industry, lumbering and modern farming.

In a sense he already had the credentials of an exile when in 1915 he won a scholarship to Harvard, where the sceptical humanism and aesthetic pluralism of William James, George Santayana and Josiah Royce still lingered and where the undergraduates surrendered themselves to the affectations of a belated Oxonian aestheticism. Modesty was not among the university disciplines – 'You can always tell a Harvard man but you can't tell him much,' Cowley assured Burke – but when America entered the war in 1917 he left Cambridge without hesitation to drive supply vehicles in France.[142] On leave he fell in love with Paris and embraced Francophilia. On duty, in the face of history at its most immediate and dangerous, he kept a diary of his activities and thus developed a spectatorial habit and a sense of historical discrimination which informed his later writing. He knew that participation in the European war represented 'the great common experience of the young manhood of today'. It was 'an experience that will mould the thought of the next generation, and without which one will be somewhat of a stranger to the world of the present and the future'.[143] He failed to predict that those soldiers who returned would experience estrangement of another kind, marked as they were by memories of physical suffering which civilian society never could, or would, understand. Cowley settled in New York in 1919, convinced that the city was 'the homeland of the uprooted', and that same year he married Peggy Baird, a Village drinker and artist who was to introduce him to the writers and editors who helped Cowley establish himself as a literary journalist.[144] He began writing for the *New Republic* and the *Dial* before deciding to return to France in 1921 on an American Field Service scholarship, and in the two years the Cowleys spent there the young critic consolidated his enthusiasm for French literature. He interviewed numerous Paris writers for *Bookman*; he found a prescription for literary virtue in the terse lucidity of Racinian tragedy; he frequented Gertrude Stein's salon and discussed Shakespeare with Ezra Pound in the Hotel Jacob; he met Valéry; and through Louis Aragon and Tristan Tzara he encountered Dadaism and its veneration for 'significant gestures' – in service of which he earned himself a place in literary folklore by immolating a pile of books and, on Bastille Day 1923, by punching the disagreeable proprietor of the Rotonde.

The Parisian intellectuals taught other and more important lessons, however: Cowley began to see America through French eyes, which admired jazz and skyscrapers, and to find an exhilaration in a society he had previously dismissed as culturally barren. The religion of art to which France had exposed him was all very well but Cowley began to worry about the excesses to which it inevitably led – whether Proust's cork-lined asylum or Valéry's self-imposed poetic silence. So he returned to America 'excited by the adventure of living in the present' and took a job as proof-reader and copy-writer with Sweet's Catalogue Service in order to subsidize his literary activities.[145]

Sweet's was situated at 119 West 40th Street and here Cowley earned $65 a week as one of a team of seven copy-writers who produced *Sweet's Engineering Catalogue* and an annual *Sweet's Architectural Catalogue*, which offered a comprehensive inventory of building materials, equipment and supplies. At the end of March, on learning of a copy-writing vacancy, Cowley urged Hart to apply for the job and the latter was employed from 7 April at a salary of $40 a week. He was put to work at once on what would become the *Twentieth Annual Edition, 1925–1926* of the *Architectural Catalogue* and although the work was pedestrian to say the least, Hart got on well with Edward Hanley, the chief of copy, and enlivened the office by raucously relishing any verbal or pictorial suggestiveness in material submitted by the building manufacturers and by smoking five-cent Philly cigars.

10

Shortly before leaving for Woodstock Hart had gone for one of his regular dinners at 30 Jones Street and there Susan Jenkins had introduced him to Emil Opffer, the second of four blond-haired, blue-eyed Danish brothers, who had adopted her as an unofficial sibling. She and Emil were both born in 1896 and it was this near twinship that lent a particular closeness to their relations: whenever he had disagreements with his family it was to her house that he went for sympathy and support, and in the winter of 1923 those disagreements revolved around his occupation as a steward in the merchant marine, an occupation his mother and stepfather, Johanne and Henrik Boving, considered menial and unpromising.

The Bovings lived at 285 West 12th Street and Susan remembered that their small house seemed like 'a corner of old Denmark' – 'there one always found good cheer, good wine, good akvavit, good food, good conversation and many "skøling" Danes.'[1] Boving, a senior research scientist at the Bell Telephone Laboratories, felt his stepson should aspire to accountancy – a vicarious ambition which took no account of temperamental disinclination or lack of appropriate training. Opffer had enlisted in the US Army before he was seventeen and in the course of artillery service on the Western Front during the Great War had sustained permanent damage to his hearing. The impairment had only become apparent, however, when, after seven years in the army, he became a naval cadet and attempted to qualify as a radio operator. Happily, whatever his stepfather's misgivings, the job he eventually found in the merchant marine accommodated his restless nature while its periods of shore leave allowed him sufficient opportunity to satisfy the promptings of a generous and gregarious disposition: Susan remembered that 'he would appear unexpectedly at one's door loaded down with large bags containing Scandinavian delicacies, bottles of wine protruding, and proceed to lay out a Danish smørgasbord for all present'.[2]

Opffer returned to sea when Hart went to Woodstock but in March 1924 he was once again on leave – and once again at variance with his mother and stepfather.

His visits to Jones Street increased and, as Susan remembered, 'on several of these occasions he found Hart at my place, and the two got along well'.[3] Emil was indeed a charming figure: beyond his Nordic handsomeness there was an exuberance which, in Susan's estimation, 'excited high spirits in others', and for those who cared to listen his family history was both vivid and romantic.[4] His father, Emil Opffer Senior, had been the prosperous editor and publisher of several newspapers in Denmark, and his flamboyant disposition, proclaimed by the opera capes and wide-brimmed hats he affected, seemed well matched with his prominence and popularity. He married into a distinguished family, the Schønheydrs, and he and his wife enjoyed extensive travels across Europe in the course of which he regularly wired dispatches to his newspapers: indeed so adventurous were the couple that their eldest and youngest sons, Elbano and Romolo, were born on Elba and in Rome. Opffer was no wandering hedonist, however, and finding something rotten in the state – treasonable corruption in a government ministry – he determined that his newspapers would expose it. An ensuing legal action, with the possibility of gaol in the event of defeat, caused him to panic and he fled to Mexico, entrusting Elbano and Romolo to the Schønheydrs and taking Emil and Ivan into exile. By the time he was vindicated he had decided to settle in America – and although it was as a minor hero that he made frequent visits to Copenhagen the remainder of his life was spent as the editor and part-owner of *Nordlyset*, 'Northern Light', a Brooklyn newspaper established in 1891 and read by the 200,000 Danes then living in New York.

Apart from three years spent in a Catholic boarding school in Denmark, Emil had lived in America since 1906 and by the time Hart got to know him he was twenty-eight: a likeable latter-day Viking whose charms were at once alien and appealing to a Midwesterner. F. Scott Fitzgerald spoke longingly of 'the lovely Scandinavian blondes who sat on porches in St Paul' and as his compatriot Hart might have endorsed the spirit, if not the letter, of this admiration for the Nordic.[5] At any rate, confronted by this handsome seafarer – in Sam Loveman's words Emil was 'yellow and stocky, nice [and] very wholesome-looking' – Hart soon found more than his curiosity aroused.[6] Susan Jenkins was a witness to the earliest sympathy and curiosity, remembering an evening when Emil arrived at her house 'in a most depressed state' after 'an especially gruelling session with Mr Boving'. 'Hart was with me again, and, as I had to go out, he applied himself to cheering up Emil. They made a night of it, and Emil was soon overwhelmed by the devotion of that tornado.'[7]

The exact nature of that devotion is now hard to determine: neither party kept a written record of the ensuing relationship, or if they did those records have disappeared. One assumes extensive correspondence passed between them – since by virtue of Emil's calling they were inevitably more apart than together – but nothing has survived, although Emil recalled that Hart's frequent letters to him at sea were 'long and full of intense statements and large-scale poetic visions'.[8] Long before then, however, in April 1924, there was the longing that each suddenly and overwhelmingly felt for the other. Emil remembered:

> Walking the streets, remembering Hart Crane, calling Susie and finding out his address: 'he said he had some pictures he wanted me to see.' Find the house, knock on the door, Hart writing with the radio going, and stayed all night with him on the narrow bed.[9]

It was one thing for a reasonably sober Emil to arrive unannounced at 15 Van Nest Place but quite another for Hart then to turn up in West 12th Street at 3 a.m. to deliver plangent and bibulous declarations of love outside the front door of the Bovings' house. Johanne Boving in particular was enraged by the scene and Emil was forced to threaten his new lover, 'If you don't go away I'll never see you again.'[10] Henrik Boving told Emil that he was 'bringing disgrace on his mother' with these intrusions but in the argument that followed Opffer stood his ground:

> I told Boving that if my presence in their house brought disgrace on him and my mother I wouldn't go there any more. I told Boving that I have to lead my own life as best I can. I don't want to give up Hart's friendship. I like him very much and I like to hear him recite his poetry. In a way, he and I are both waifs. After my dreary life at sea, I need some fun.[11]

For different reasons both men needed new accommodation: but if it was tiresome for Opffer to have to accept the bourgeois constraints of the Boving household it was positively impossible for insolvent Hart to continue his occupancy of Van Nest Place – something had to be done, and Emil thought he had the perfect solution. His father lived at 110 Columbia Heights in Brooklyn in a brick terrace which overlooked the Brooklyn waterfront and commanded the skyline of lower Manhattan. The house was one of three, 106–110, which had been turned into a kind of artists' colony by their owner, the painter and art teacher Hamilton Easter Field, and although the property passed to Field's adopted son, a sculptor named Robert Laurent, in 1924 the disposition of the colony remained unchanged. The houses were connected on the basement and parlour floors, with an art school situated in the basement; the upper storeys were residential – John Dos Passos lived here for a while – with a variety of single rooms and apartments available for rent. The genius of the inhabitants adorned the walls and common parts of the houses and the tone of the establishment, as remembered by Susan Jenkins, 'was that of the "arty" middle-class, those who wished to lead a quiet life in non-garish, non-modern, but also non-Greenwich Village surroundings'.[12] This was the ideal establishment for Emil's quixotic father, whose commitments at *Nordlyset* were still interrupted by wanderings of the most extravagant nature – only recently he had gone gold-prospecting on donkey-back in Guatemala – but for Hart too Columbia

Heights seemed admirably appropriate. So when Emil learned that on his father's floor there was a room at the front of Number 110 for immediate occupancy at only $6 a week the decision was made and by the third week of April Hart was a Manhattanite no more.

Knowing that her son was anxious to move Grace had urged the virtues – tennis courts and better air – of the neighbourhood around Columbia University but Hart knew that the attractions of his next address far eclipsed these prosaic amenities. Columbia Heights formed the westernmost street of Brooklyn Heights, a Victorian settlement set apart from the rest of Brooklyn on a promontory overlooking the East River: the wharves and warehouses below were still aromatic with the spice trade and all around were the monuments of the clipper princes – mansions in Victorian Gothic, Greek Revival, Classical Revival, Italianate and Second Empire – who had once made the Heights their home. The merchants fled when the construction of the subway in 1908 made their citadel accessible to the commuting hordes and their villas became boarding houses and lodgings. Yet if the neighbourhood had changed character, it remained tranquil, although the nearby waterfront, including Sands Street, was lined with sailor saloons and the roads which descended steeply from the Heights to the strand were infamous for vice and violence. To the poetic imagination the prototypes of Melvillian fiction still peopled these riverine quarters – but modern Manhattan was only an exhilarating walk the other side of Brooklyn Bridge. It was as though Hart had strayed into nineteenth-century New York: then Opffer Senior indicated that he was considering relinquishing his room at the back of the house and Hart discovered that for only $8 a week he might be able to rent a room which would give him a prospect not of history but of myth. As he explained to Grace, he would have 'the finest view in all America':

> Just imagine looking out your window on the East River with nothing intervening between your view of the statue of Liberty, way down the harbour, and the marvelous beauty of Brooklyn Bridge close above you on your right! All of the great new skyscrapers of lower Manhattan are marshalled directly across from you, and there is a constant stream of tugs, liners, sail boats, etc in procession before you on the river![13]

Later, when he inhabited this room, Hart learned that Washington Roebling, son of bridge architect John Augustus Roebling, had supervised the construction of Brooklyn Bridge by telescope from the very same set of windows after being crippled by caisson disease. The symbol of union and national transcendence which Hart proposed to adopt in his poem about mythic America had come to completion from this very apartment – and the omen seemed doubly propitious when he reflected that his introduction to the neighbourhood, the house and its vista had been made by the man he now loved.

Soon Emil was christened 'Goldilocks' in recognition of the yellow forelock that tumbled perpetually over his brow and Hart confided to Sam Loveman that he was 'very much in love' with him.[14] Grace could obviously not be told, but when he wrote to her in the third week of April his excuse for not attending the Easter service at St Patrick's came as close to an admission as anything she was to get for some years. He had been out late the night before, he explained, with Emil Opffer, 'an old man but very distinguished as an editor and anarchist, and whose two sons, Ivan and Emil, jr. I am very fond of' and they had enjoyed 'a drinking bout' at an Italian restaurant on West Houston Street.[15] A day or two later, however, he sent a very different letter to Waldo Frank. Now he was 'quite dumb with something for which "happiness" must be too mild a term' and could imagine nothing 'more profound and lovely than this love'. He had seen 'the Word made Flesh' and knew that 'there is such a thing as indestructibility. In the deepest sense, where flesh became transformed through intensity of response to counter-response, where sex was beaten out, where a purity of joy was reached that included tears.' Whatever the future held, his past humiliations and disappointments were redeemed 'in this reality and promise'. Life was now a chapter of ecstasy, 'of walking hand in hand across the most beautiful bridge of the world, the cables enclosing us and pulling us upward in such a dance as I have never walked and never can walk with another'. Nor could he wait for Frank to see his new home, because he sensed that his spiritual mentor would grasp immediately the eerie coincidence whereby 'the moment of the communion with the "religious gunman"' in Part III of 'Faustus and Helen', with the street narrowing darkly against the bridges of the city, foreshadowed the actual geography of Columbia Heights. 'Imagine my surprise when Emil brought me to this street where, at the very end of it, I saw a scene that was more familiar than a hundred factual previsions could have rendered it!' Those lines from the conclusion of his first important poetic suite had mysteriously portended his present good fortune, and his present good fortune vindicated the great poetic ambition that would make his name eternal.

In more ways than one his life was now lived in the shadow of Brooklyn Bridge, which commanded the prospect of his imagination as surely as it spanned sea waters to dominate the vista at his window. 'That window', he told Frank, 'is where I would be most remembered of all: the ships, the harbor, and the skyline of Manhattan, midnight, morning or evening, – rain, snow or sun, it is everything from mountains to the walls of Jerusalem and Nineveh, and all related in actual contact with the changelessness of the many waters that surround it.' Having spent most of his life in America's tideless midlands he suddenly found himself living on the edge of the Atlantic, ocean of migration and Old World yearnings, inscrutable vehicle of his nation's birth, while at the same time loving a man whose work lay on those waters. As he surveyed the new order and coherence of his life it seemed as though symbol led to symbol even as myth endorsed coincidence and he told

Frank: 'I think the sea has thrown itself upon me and been answered, at least in part, and I believe I am a little changed – not essentially, but changed and transubstantiated as anyone is who has asked a question and been answered.'[16]

When on leave Emil now divided his time between West 12th Street and Columbia Heights, although at the latter address he usually stayed in the apartment of John Dos Passos, who was frequently away. He liked the opera and when too poor to buy cinema tickets he and Hart would often listen to Lauritz Melchior from the wings at the Metropolitan Opera. Sometimes Emil would join Hart in his lunch break from Sweet's, when the poet and Malcolm Cowley often went to the Brazilian Coffee House in West 43rd Street for coffee and cinnamon toast; Matthew Josephson, Slater Brown and Waldo Frank were also regulars here and Emil remembered that Frank often exhorted his lover, 'You must write'. Soon he discovered that Hart disliked solitude and that his moods, and his opinions about people, fluctuated wildly between gloom and great expectation. He often wondered if these irregularities were caused by the fluctuating toxicity of prohibition liquor: but he knew categorically that Hart was 'impossible when drunk'. There were often scenes late at night when they were returning on the subway to Brooklyn after an evening of carousing yet when they walked into Manhattan over Brooklyn Bridge Hart would expand poetically on the benign coherence he found in existence and assure Emil, 'All of life is a bridge'. Emil listened when Hart read his poems but 'never understood any of [them] ... and merely reacted to the sounds of various words without really understanding what it was all about'. By contrast the poet was fascinated by tales of ocean life and when Emil mentioned that there was a legend, credited among sailors, of a submarine city off the coast of Jamaica the bells of which sometimes sounded to passing ships Hart 'went wild' with excitement.[17]

Even at this early stage there were quarrels, especially at times of financial stress; on one such occasion Hart shouted, 'Long after you're dead and gone I'll be known', to provoke Emil's reply, 'What good will that do, Hart?'[18] The former sometimes failed to understand the causes of his lover's fury and never forgot a scene in the Russian Tearoom when he sat waiting for Hart to keep a rendezvous. The poet finally arrived, 'came marching in across the hushed floor like a madman, stood glowering and masculine, pointing his finger, & cried – "You whore!" and marched out'.[19] The roles were reversed when Emil found Hart drinking at O'Connor's in the Village with a friend called Peggy Robson and said archly, 'Here's to your change of life.'[20] For all its turbulence, however, the liaison between the two men appears to have been one of the most significant, as well as one of the most poetically productive, of Hart's life, whether or not it was predominantly emotional or sexual or indeed a brief love made large by a great lyric imagination. As for Emil's later views on this strange affair, the writer Philip Horton found that 'he was very proud of it' and said that 'he bragged about their relationship'.[21]

James Broughton, a novelist who became Opffer's lover a decade later, sketched the Dane's character for possible incorporation in a novel: he was 'lovable, laughable, stubborn, and of no use to himself whatsoever … [with] shining white teeth – intensively, carefully cleaned'.[22] Hart's friends liked him, feckless or not, and he was accepted as part of the group, but one forms the impression that none of them could be quite certain what construction to put on the involvement. Slater Brown, as close to the poet as anyone at this time, spoke very much as a spectator rather than a confidant when he remembered that 'Hart did not do so much talking about his sailors during [the relationship with Emil] although he continued to pick [them] up and take them to his room when Emil was busy elsewhere. There were constant "betrayals" on both sides.'[23] He knew no more; nor, it seems, did the others. Perhaps delicacy made them reticent to question, and perhaps Hart felt reluctant to divulge – what is definite is that many of the group who now settled around him in an enduring circle of friendship subsequently went into print with theories about the extent of the poet's sexual ambivalence. 'He did not look or talk like a homosexual,' Malcolm Cowley insisted.[24] 'Hart's real comrades were not homosexual – his real friends. He was unlike any homosexual I've ever known,' remembered Allen Tate.[25] 'He seemed to be a normal male' with 'an unusual capacity for friendship', Susan Jenkins claimed.[26]

It is a recurrent theme of their reminiscences about the great figure who overshadowed their lives and by extension there was no shortage of speculation about the poet's true nature: he was a tortured, would-be family man; his intense friendships with women suggested struggles for greater intimacy; he befriended heterosexuals because he wanted to be one of them; his growing interest in sailors was a form of retaliation against his parents; his increasingly salacious talk was mere bravado, the wilful talk of an uneasy child. It was the early age of Freud and there was a premium on elaborate constructions, but the fact was that however little the friends liked or understood it, and however difficult it is to categorize something as fluid and mysterious as sexuality, Hart's interest, if his actions can speak for him, was directed almost entirely towards men. The writer Nathan Asch, who suspected that Hart was in love with Malcolm Cowley, met the poet at the end of the 1920s, and because he was less proprietorial of his genius he was also less eager to redeem the libidinous sailor-chaser he encountered. If he knew Hart less well than the others, he knew himself better, or could at least be more frank about the values by which he judged: '[Hart] had none of the outward characteristics of a homosexual, nothing of either the wolf or the bugger boy about him; so that I who ordinarily resent homosexuals could not resent him for that reason.'[27] To say that Asch was honest is not to condemn the other friends for being mendacious: they were merely less liberal than they thought. Hart was ambivalent about most of the shaping forces of his life – most obviously his parents – and if this uncertainty extended to his sexual appetites it was both specious and tendentious of his friends to insist on interpreting it as revulsion when the likelihood is that he was simply anxious about breaking the law or exposing himself to blackmail or violence. It seems never to have occurred to them either that Hart might have attempted a degree of disguise, in part to protect himself against legally enshrined hostility, in part to placate heterosexual friends whose affection he craved and whose real views on unorthodox eroticism are betrayed not only by their persistent attempts to reclaim him as one of themselves but also by the request Malcolm Cowley sent to the poet's first biographer, which smacked of more than mere respect for historical truth: 'It would be a good thing, and very much appreciated ... if you could stick into the proof of your book at some place the absolutely bald and definite statement that Hart's friends were not homosexuals.'[28]

Emil spent his periods of leave in New York – and Munson was told that in these first weeks of romance each precious furlough seemed to Hart 'an indefinite brevity'.[29] Meanwhile in the springtime stuffiness of the Sweet's office the poet found his mind drawn again and again to the sea, so that visions of its argosies shimmered beyond the dull small print of office life – '*As apparitional as sails that cross/Some page of figures to be filed away;/ – Till elevators drop us from our day*', as he would later put it.[30] Again and again, alone or with Emil, he marvelled at the marriage of city and sea, of dream and machine, which the variable elements disclosed from the windows of Columbia Heights. 'Everytime one looks at the harbor and the NY skyline across the river it is quite different, and the range of atmospheric effects is endless,' he told Grace.

> But at twilight on a foggy evening ... it is beyond description. Gradually the lights in the enormously tall buildings begin to flicker through the mist. There was a great cloud enveloping the top of the Woolworth tower, while below, in the river, were streaming reflections of the myriad lights, continually being crossed by the twinkling mast and deck lights of little tugs scudding along, freight rafts, and occasional liners starting outward. Look far to your left toward Staten Island and there is the statue of Liberty.... And up at the right Brooklyn Bridge, the most superb piece of construction in the modern world, I'm sure, with strings of light crossing it like glowing worms as the Ls and surface cars pass each other ...[31]

CA arrived unannounced in New York on 26 April – travelling as usual without Frances – and he and Hart had lunch at the Commodore before going to the theatre. Clarence Crane made no attempt to explain his long period of silence and Hart made no inquiries: the encounter was amicable enough, however, and CA revealed that he was now eager to sell his chocolate business because there was no money to be made from confectionery in the Midwest, where people expected superlative merchandise at bargain prices. Hart doubted his declared aim and was blithe in his incomprehension of the reasoning advanced, later mentioning to Grace that 'I'm sure I don't know what he means by all this talk about his continual loss of money'. CA had always complained financially, whatever his margins, 'and whether he makes or loses, I like to think, is much the same to me'.[32] Hart's social life diminished because of Emil, but he went to dinner at Jones Street on 10 May and there met Paul Robeson and his wife. Robeson was currently appearing in O'Neill's controversial drama *All God's Chillun Got Wings* and struck the poet as having 'a very fine mind and nature' besides being 'very black, [with] a deep resonance to his voice and actor eyes'.[33] His correspondence decreased also, and if Hart was conscientious about writing to his mother he let several letters from Jean Toomer go unanswered, with the result that the latter finally complained. Hart duly replied, albeit briefly, on 28 May: he apologized for his silence but said that 'Heaven and Hell has transpired' since they were last in correspondence and now he felt that 'life is running over me and destroying me'.[34] He wrote again on 16 June, apologizing for his last letter, which had been written 'in a state of almost hysterical despair', and once again alluded to the taciturnity that had offended many other friends. He would expand on its causes at some stage but simply wanted to state now that over the last three months he had been engulfed by 'a maelstrom' of 'unbelievable promises' and 'beautiful realizations'. When he looked back on this education of his emotions it was to conclude 'that such a love would forever be impossible again – that it would never be met with again, if only because one knew that one would never have the intensity to respond to a repetition of such'. He hoped his friend would understand that he would 'never be able to be very personal about it' – the fact was, however, that he was delinquent in correspondence because he had 'never been given the opportunity for as much joy and agony before'. 'The extreme edges of these emotions were sharpened on me in swift alternation until I am almost a shadow.'[35]

Not the least of Hart's problems besides his turbulent love affair was a possible case of venereal disease which was presently disproved; the symptoms which had given him so much anxiety turned out to be nothing more than urethritis and excessive uric acid brought on by heavy drinking. He put himself on a diet of buttermilk and water and kept mother and grandmother informed, busy as they were with the Republican Party convention. Grace in turn told CA, a chronic victim of such problems, and he sent his own rules of advice: Hart should avoid meat, coffee and smoking. The greatest vice for sufferers from the tendency was drinking, however, 'but I do not believe you are foolish enough to indulge in that'.[36]

That June saw the extension of Hart's circle of friends with the return to New York of a twenty-nine-year-old woman originally from Wisconsin named Lorna Dietz. She had been the previous occupant of Susan's house in Jones Street before moving to Philadelphia with her husband, Baron Alexander Boije of Gennas, whom Susan described as 'a penniless but pleasing Swedish-Finnish aristocrat'.[37] The Baron was unable to please Lorna, however, and she left him for another, only to discover in the spring of 1924 that he too was involved with another man – Emil Opffer. She returned to New York with a view to reclaiming a disordered life, and when Hart met her she was staying at Jones Street prior to moving into a new apartment at 49 East 10th Street. She observed him as he stood 'next to the fireplace in the middle room smoking a pipe'. He appeared 'ill at ease and chunky, and his laugh was rather cackly'. She decided 'he was shy' and then that 'he was feeling sorry for himself'. If initial impressions were tepid their friendship blossomed into one of the most important of Hart's life. They left behind almost no correspondence but the impression one forms is that she was a sane and stalwart being whose Midwestern common sense did much to protect the poet from the consequences of his own excesses a few years later. There was nothing literary to their friendship – as she recalled, 'We were always paired off because we were the odd ones in a "couple" crowd' – but there was nothing merely convenient to it either, and at the end of his life, when he had alienated so many, Hart was still eager to explain himself to Lorna.[38]

That month also saw the long-overdue meeting between the poet and Allen Tate, who had come to New York via Washington, having recently been fired for over-educated ineptitude from his brother's coal business in Kentucky. Tate had few acquaintances in New York but his loyal correspondent Hart would not fail him now and the visitor later reported to fellow Fugitives in Tennessee that the poet had treated him 'royally'.[39] A party was convened at the apartment of James Light, one of the directors of the Provincetown Playhouse, and there Hart introduced Tate to most of his friends. The Southerner arrived wearing a dark suit and a Phi Beta Kappa key and carrying a walking stick – only to be told that 'we no longer wear our Phi Beta Kappa keys' by Malcolm Cowley, who found an old stick somewhere and carried it around in mocking imitation for the duration of the party.[40] Far from being offended by New York manners, however, Tate dispatched further praise to Tennessee: the city's writers were less obsessed with literary theory, less 'conscious of themselves as poets', than the Fugitives.[41] In fact Cowley had been favourably impressed by Tate: he seemed to have 'the best manners of any young man' he had ever known and to deploy politeness 'not only as a defence but sometimes as an aggressive weapon against strangers'.[42] A few days later, on 24 June, the two writers set out to visit their mutual friend in Brooklyn and although the Southerner, on his first visit to New York, was anxious about the inexorable conquest of human culture by technology he was nevertheless astonished by the mechanics of modern urban life, as he informed fellow Fugitive Donald Davidson: 'I'm greatly thrilled by the mere *physique* of this great city! The subway is simply marvellous. Fancy going under a huge river at 40 miles an hour!'[43] Having arrived in one piece, Tate and Cowley proceeded to 110 Columbia Heights, where they admired the spectacular view before settling to a discussion of poetry. As Cowley noticed, 'Hart gestured, as always, with a dead five-cent cigar while he declaimed against the vulgarity of Edgar Poe.' His friends demurred, and chancing upon a volume of Poe Cowley read aloud 'The City in the Sea': 'While from a proud tower in the town/Death looks gigantically down.' The discussion continued as they left the house and wandered 'through the streets lined with red-brick warehouses until we came to the end of a scow at the end of a pier at the Brooklyn end of the bridge'. Across the East River a huge electric sign proclaimed WATERMAN'S FOUNTAIN PENS, 'and all those proud towers beyond it with the early lights flashing on' lent the moment the quality of an epiphany. 'Suddenly,' Cowley recalled, 'we felt ... that we were secretly comrades in the same endeavour: to present this new scene in poems that would reveal not only its astonishing face but the lasting realities behind it.'[44]

Reporting to Munson, Hart extolled Tate's newly apparent virtues. Although he had had little opportunity for serious conversation with the Tennessean he had nevertheless discerned 'a very good mind and a kind of scepticism which I respect'. Furthermore he felt that they had 'established an idiom or code for future understandings' and he looked forward to hearing what Tate thought about 'this bronco-busting city' that he now inhabited.[45] Tate himself was unsure and he returned to Washington in hopeless pursuit of work, assuring Hart two weeks after his departure that he was now 'a complete opportunist' when it came to jobs. So far, his efforts had gone unrewarded and he kept thinking of how courageous in penury Hart had been when he moved to New York: 'I suppose I am not so firm as you.... It isn't, my dear Hart, that I lack a kind of endurance, but only that my case of mystical conviction may not be so tough and persistently inviolable as yours.' He remembered that in the course of his New York visit Hart had 'alluded to a centrifugal character of your own mood' and now he felt that his own disposition was similar.[46] Hart tried to think how he could help Tate find work and in the meantime – with suspicions continuing to attend the Tennessean's sexuality – he put him in touch with Wilbur Underwood, who promptly took him to visit Madame Cooke. Eventually Hart talked Susan Jenkins into finding work for Tate on *Telling Tales* but before these negotiations were concluded Tate wrote with gratitude for the poet's endeavours:

My dear Hart, if I do get something then it will be due to you.... My concept of poetry is at once widening and defining itself; but it will take time, and the transition must be necessarily gradual.... It isn't that I don't object to not writing; it is that the fact of not being able to, in the external sense, heads me directly to my 'disapproval' of the present civilization. If I had had sense enough to realize the indictment of Baudelaire against the growing mechanization of life, five years ago, instead of holding to a priggish rationalism, I'd probably be better off today. I suspect I'm very late in discovering I've always been a mystic.[47]

The Rychtariks arrived in New York from a European holiday at the beginning of July and Hart took them to see *All God's Chillun*, knowing that with Sweet's annual *Catalogue* about to go to press he would soon have no time for anything but work. It was as well that Emil was on a voyage in the West Indies: Hart was able to devote his evenings to overtime, although he did manage to send a long letter to Mrs Hart on her eighty-fifth birthday and availed himself of the new air-mail service to ensure prompt delivery. Then Emil returned and he and Hart spent a blissful Sunday afternoon escaping the heat on the roof of 110 Columbia Heights and taking pictures of each other. Hart wanted his mother to see what Emil looked like and so sent a photograph in which the latter was wearing a sweater 'which I liked so much that I had to have myself taken in it', he told Grace. Emil was 'a very lovely person, and I know you would like him very much'. All too soon he would embark on the *Leviathan* for England but at least he had been in New York for Hart's twenty-fifth birthday and had organized a dinner which included Susan Jenkins, Slater Brown and James Light. Susan gave him a tie and Grace and Mrs Hart dispatched a dressing gown, socks, a tie and hand-kerchiefs from Cleveland.[48]

What Hart termed 'anvil weather' prevailed throughout July and as usual he suffered badly from hay fever – and as if catalogue publication did not entail stress enough, Sweet's decided to move its office at the end of the month in order to be nearer to its parent company, Dodge Publishing.[49] Hart helped with the operation one Saturday afternoon, 'although I was ready to keel over any moment', he told Grace, but once installed in the new office, at 119 West 40th Street, he enjoyed the view, twenty-one storeys above Times Square and the Astor Hotel, and hoped that the higher altitude would bring cleaner air to relieve his eyes and nose.[50] Cowley worked in the same office and quickly discovered, once the catalogue had gone to press and normal routine had returned, that Hart appeared to be devoting much of his working day to a project of his own: 'I remember his frantic searches through Webster's *Unabridged* and the big *Standard*, his trips to the library – on office time – and his reports of consultations with old sailors in South Street speakeasies.'[51]

In April, when declaring his love for Emil to Waldo, Hart had said he felt the flood tide of inspiration rising once more within him and now – after weeks of exposure to that same passion, enacted on that high promontory above the sea, the same sea that took Emil away for weeks at a time, only to return him safe again for the intenser continuance of their affair – Hart felt ready to distil his passion in poetry. Three years earlier, still landlocked in the Midwest but already mysteriously summoned by the sea, he had likened the dangers of love and sexual discovery to the perils of ocean bathing: once initiated one was changed for ever; once out of one's depth, there was no hope of salvation. But since then he had met Emil and had trusted himself to deeper emotional waters than ever before – and was richer and happier for the danger. Hart now knew something still undiscovered in Cleveland: to love men of the sea is to love men who go away, yet for all the inevitability and pain of love's ending, it was better to love than not. Since then, also, he had been exposed to the poetry of Samuel Greenberg, and when he chose to return to the subject of the sea, memories of the dead poet's opulent tapestries of flowers, fountains and waves returned to him. He began to write; and in the first eight lines of the poem he provisionally incorporated Greenberg's 'Silhouette Set the Sceptres Roving':

> Take this Sea then; enlisted by what sceptres
> roving wide from isle to isle have churned
> already the crocus lustres of the stars to breath.[52]

The lyric took shape over several weeks, with Greenbergian borrowings being transformed out of recognition: numerous extant modifications attest to the problems Crane surmounted in the execution of what became one of the most beautiful love lyrics in modern poetry – many of these modifications surviving on scraps of paper subsequently used for mundane household business. Thus, the obverse of one version, rich if still imperfect in its sonorousness, bore this honest reminder in the poet's unmistakable script to some now forgotten housekeeper at Columbia Heights: 'Mrs Keene, Whenever I leave milk on the table it's for you if you can use it, Hart Crane.'[53]

Three years earlier, earthbound in Ohio, he had declared, in what would now become the first of his six 'Voyages' poems, 'The bottom of the sea is cruel'. Now, a resident of the littoral and a recipient of love, he no longer saw the immersion of the self as inevitable annihilation. In 'Voyages' II, resuming that claim of cruelty, he knew he must qualify it with a mitigating 'And yet':

> – And yet this great wink of eternity,
> Of rimless floods, unfettered leewardings,
> Samite sheeted and processioned where
> Her undinal vast belly moonward bends,
> Laughing the wrapt inflexions of our love ...

The sea is many things, we discover, besides being a voracious destroyer: if it is a proverb for the infinite and the eternal, and if it is also regularly associated with the sheetings of death and the processions of marriage, Crane now insists that it is an agent of birth, regulated by the moon, and quick with the force of love. There is a quality of music to the beautiful poetry, which moves by evocation and association far more than by close description, with its second stanza insisting that love and lovers, although vulnerable to the sea's destructive powers, are also honoured by the sea alone, since she is contemptuous of 'all but the pieties of lovers' hands'. Emil's tale of the sunken city emerges in the third stanza: the sea is now evoked as a patroness of lovers and all her attributes are beautiful and benign as the poet calls on his lover to join him in the submersion that will lead to death and then rebirth:

And onward, as bells off San Salvador
Salute the crocus lustres of the stars,
In these poinsettia meadows of her tides, –
Adagios of islands, O my Prodigal,
Complete the dark confessions her veins spell.

It had taken Crane years to attain the harmonious authority and evocative strength that now enabled him, through what he termed the 'logic of metaphor', to suggest such complexities of thought, emotion and sensation. The arduous self-education, the single-minded subscription to literature, borne at such penurious cost, the belief in art as a noble force of speculation, the earnest commitment to poetry – all at last yielded dividends when he found himself able to conjure such sumptuous imagery and to marshal it in blank verse that seems as irrefutable as a symphony. He knew he had emerged as a master, and when he came to explain his poetic technique with reference to this poem he did so in accents both undoubting and unapologetic:

When in 'Voyages' (II) I speak of 'adagios of islands,' the reference is to the motion of a boat through islands clustered thickly, the rhythm of the motion, etc. And it seems a much more direct and creative statement than any more logical employment of words such as 'coasting slowly through the islands,' besides ushering in a whole world of music.[54]

The fourth stanza of the poem reminds the lover that the sea's 'turning shoulders wind the hours': in the realm of time, love is transient and unless the lovers make haste to unite their love may 'close round one instant in one floating flower' – may become no more than a wreath of remembrance for what has withered and died. In the final stanza the poet invokes the seasons which guard the destiny of sailors and prays for a union within the realm of time: once united the lovers can transcend temporal existence but they know that only death in the quotidian world will enable them to behold the paradise of eternal love which lies beyond the waves:

Bind us in time, O Seasons clear, and awe.
O minstrel galleons of Carib fire,
Bequeath us to no earthly shore until
Is answered in the vortex of our grave
The seal's wide spindrift gaze toward paradise.[55]

These lines alone entitle Crane to consideration as one of his century's greatest poetic exponents of love besides making him one of the major literary celebrants of the sea – yet there is nothing in his extant correspondence to suggest that he ever sought to explain to himself the fascination he found in the oceans. The surviving drafts of 'Voyages' II do, however, enable us to understand the way in which he constructed his poetry. Numerous friends testified that he liked to read dictionaries in quest of words of splendour and obscurity and notebooks survive containing bejewelled phrases jotted down as they came to him for possible use in future lyrics. This verbal connoisseurship never infects his correspondence which, if incorrigibly misspelt, uses language which is fluent and serviceable but seldom lyrical, except in letters to Waldo Frank. In poetry, however, Crane abandoned linguistic utilitarianism for the construction of blocks of beautiful sound; and as composition proceeded these seductive clauses would be rearranged repeatedly, usually to gramophone accompaniment in order to test for musical and metrical truth, and then expanded and arranged again, as the associations he wished to convey emerged.

One association he could not convey was, of course, his personal idea of eroticism – that quality had to remain mystical and imprecise, partly because great love poetry transcends particular sexual constituencies, and partly because great love poets have prying parents. He moved on to write the next lyric – aware by now that his undertaking was shaping itself as 'a series of six sea poems', as he described them to Grace – and confronted at once the problem of describing a union between the poet and his sailor lover, a union which was inevitably partly sexual.[56] Again early drafts of 'Voyages' III betray the laboriousness of composition, besides revealing how the new poem began as a more erotic celebration in which,

> Serene, I know your flesh shall rest prostrate
> as kissing all that deck, the stars
> call back your words ... and with some other there
>
> Chants there an octave and it brims
> more than confession ... in which your tongue
> slips mine ...[57]

The completed poem proclaims the 'infinite consanguinity' that now prevails between the two lovers, and by extension between all those who find eternity in love's ecstasy. The poem's nineteen lines evoke calm and peace as the benign sea accommodates the lovers, 'through wave on wave unto/Your body rocking!' True love is a submersion of the self in another; it is an oblivion transcending time, a dangerous deliverance but not a destruction, as the lovers find out when they reach those deep calms

> where death, if shed,
> Presumes no carnage, but this single change, –
> Upon the steep floor flung from dawn to dawn
> The silken skilled transmemberment of song;

Permit me voyage, love, into your hands . . .[58]

The last line of the poem forms the subject of the first line of 'Voyages' IV:

Whose counted smile of hours and days, suppose
I know as spectrum of the sea . . .

Crane sent a provisional version of this poem to Frank in early September and told him that the lyric was to be seen as 'an "even so" and "All hail!" to a love that I have known'.[59] Now, following the 'transmemberment' of union, the poet is beyond the power of time and can envisage a world where the love which binds him and his lover, even in separation, is all-encompassing and transcendent, like the rainbow which forms a spectrum of the sea's breeze or like the wings 'whose circles bridge, I know'. The poet is certain of this new coherence of existence and writes rapturously of 'this mortality alone/Through clay aflow immortally to you'. The conviction is 'irrefragable' but it is also elusive like a 'fragrance' – how then put it into words? The poet can only trust to 'madly meeting logically' in a disarray of syntax, can only trust to 'bright insinuations' to convey the certainty that he had reached 'islands' hitherto 'secret' where 'all love' prevailed:

In signature of the incarnate word
The harbor shoulders to resign in mingling
Mutual blood, transpiring as foreknown
And widening noon within your breast for gathering
All bright insinuations that my years have caught
For islands where must lead inviolably
Blue latitudes and levels of your eyes . . .[60]

From his adjacent desk at Sweet's Cowley looked on, wondering at his friend's creative labours and at the difficulties he struggled to overcome:

There were many poets of the 1920s who worked hard to be obscure, veiling a simple idea in phrases that grew more labored and opaque with each version of a poem. With Crane it was the original meaning that was complicated and difficult; his revisions brought it out more clearly. He said, making fun of himself, 'I practice invention to the brink of intelligibility.'[61]

Great as his love was, and great as the labours of its transcription appeared to be, external events sometimes reminded him that the blue latitudes of love's 'indefinite brevity' might prevail in poetry but in life there were constant interruptions. Early in September Emil's father died suddenly after an operation – his room, with its ravishing views, would now definitely be Hart's but Emil was away when old

Opffer died and as the poet told Grace he dreaded the moment of revelation: 'My happiest times have been with Emil, and I am looking forward to his return again from another South American trip next week. He is so much more to me than anyone I have ever met that I miss him terribly during these eight week trips he takes for bread and butter. He doesn't know his father has died during his absence, so it will be a considerable shock to him on landing.'[62] In the event, hopeful of softening that shock, he accompanied Ivan Opffer to meet Emil with the news when his vessel returned. Revelation of another order was in store for Zell's daughter Helen when she and her husband Griswold Hurlbert arrived in New York. Helen naturally hastened to see her cousin, but something in his manner was new to her and she confided her suspicions to Grace, who promptly wrote Hart that Helen 'says you are in love'.

> You haven't been very confidential with me in that respect. I do not care how much you are in love, just so you do not *marry*. You know that would end your writing career and other ambitions. *So keep your head.* Love is a *sickness*.[63]

Maternal jealousy aside, other tempests menaced those who set sail for love's timeless island and as he began 'Voyages' V Crane contemplated the cruel intrusion of forces by which 'we/Are overtaken'. Emil would always have to return to sea, however intense the ecstasies they shared together – and who was to say in any case that the sentiments were equally felt? Perhaps the poet's lover had indicated an impatience with the idea of a love between them that was transcendent and all-embracing? At any rate, in the world where Mrs Keene collected the milk and Emil went away to sea, no love remained the same:

>   Now no cry, no sword
> Can fasten or deflect this tidal wedge,
> Slow tyranny of moonlight, moonlight loved
> And changed ... 'There's
>
> Nothing like this in the world,' you say,
> Knowing I cannot touch your hand and look
> Too, into that godless cleft of sky
> Where nothing turns but dead sands flashing.

The more beautiful the vision, the crueller the disillusion. 'In all the argosy of your bright hair I dreamed/Nothing so flagless as this piracy.' Returning from his dream of love the poet finds 'The cables of our sleep so swiftly filed'. Suddenly nothing remains of that promised vision but 'remembered stars'. In the end he is alone – deserted by another inevitably enigmatic human being, one who must leave him to go to sea and one with a past history of love which he himself could never exorcize:

But now
Draw in your head, alone and too tall here.
Your eyes already in the slant of drifting foam;
Your breath sealed by the ghosts I do not know:
Draw in your head and sleep the long way home.[64]

Yet this melancholy knowledge cannot eclipse the splendour of the dream of love and 'Voyages' VI, written in measured quatrains which set it apart from the preceding sections of the poem, asserts that for those willing to drift, as the poet has drifted, on the wayward oceans of emotional experience, and for those willing to believe, as Hart Crane the affirmer always believed, there is an unmapped island where Love remains sacred and undiminished by the failings of its human votaries.

Beyond siroccos harvesting
The solstice thunders, crept away,
Like a cliff swinging or a sail
Flung into April's inmost day –

Creation's blithe and petalled word
To the lounged goddess when she rose
Conceding dialogue with eyes
That smile unsearchable repose –

Still fervid covenant, Belle Isle . . .

It is this isle which all lovers hope to find, and nothing can undermine the glory of their quest, however doomed it may be. Somewhere beyond the tides of life there is a promise waiting to be redeemed; somewhere beyond flux there is permanence; and somewhere beyond disappointment and departure there is a great affirmation which informed all existence:

The imaged Word, it is, that holds
Hushed willows anchored in its glow.
It is the unbetrayable reply
Whose accent no farewell can know.[65]

As usual the return of autumnal weather came as a great relief and once Hart had been assured that his job would continue at Sweet's despite the completion of the *Catalogue* he was able to contemplate the last weeks of the year with happiness and optimism. There seemed no limit to his poetic fertility now: besides the completion of 'Voyages' he found himself inundated with ideas for *The Bridge* and told Grace that 'there are days when I simply have to "sit on myself" at my desk to shut out rhythms and melodies that belong to that poem and have never been written because I have succeeded only too well during the course of the day's work in excluding and stifling such a train of thoughts'.[66] He now occupied the room at the back of 110 Columbia Heights; it was just large enough to allow for pacing during the parturition of a lyric and its prospect offered seemingly unfailing inspiration and vindication – so much so that he even found himself sleeping well again. Following the death of his father Emil lapsed into gloom and for once his presence seemed onerous – but even this adversity Hart turned to profit with the controlled and unflinching lyric 'Paraphrase', which devoted its four terse stanzas to regretting the poet's inability to do anything but 'paraphrase' the enigmatic processes of life and death. The writer might find himself dutifully 'rushing from the bed at night' to record a word or an idea, but what was the point – it all ended in death, which was often terrifying in its suddenness and unpredictability. For everyone there would come that dawn 'When systematic morn shall sometime flood/The pillow' yet fail to eclipse 'that antarctic blaze' of death which now commanded 'Your head, unrocking to a pulse, already/Hollowed by air'.[67]

CA passed through New York in September and mysteriously failed to contact his son, but Hart took some consolation from the thought that soon he would see Zell, who was expected at the Waldorf *en route* for a holiday in Europe, an expedition her godson commemorated with an elegant three-stanza *jeu d'esprit*, 'To Zell, Now Bound For Spain'. With expectations of a pay increase Hart took a week's vacation on 14 October and saw Sam Loveman, now living in New York, and Harry Candee, just back from a holiday with his mother in England and Italy. In some ways, however, there was sufficient entertainment to be had by simply looking from the window of his room, as he found himself doing on 21 October, when he wrote to his mother on the last day of his vacation. The imminent Atlantic lent an exquisite acuity to 'this glorious light' that irradiated the harbour view – 'the water so very blue, the foam and steam from the tugs so dazzlingly white!' He loved to watch the plumes of steam that rose above the skyscrapers and to contemplate the commercial shipping that rested in the waters before them – 'I like the liners best that are painted white – with red and black funnels like those United Fruit boats across the river'. It was already very cold but there was an electric stove in his room and as he looked from his prospect of Manhattan back to his books and writing table he felt 'a kind of keen sensual bliss, that is in itself something like action'.[68] All of life lay beyond the wide channel before him – and as he contemplated it from his Brooklyn remoteness his mind wandered speculatively. At any time he could walk across Brooklyn Bridge into Manhattan but the world he would find there could never be the same as the one he saw from his window, any more than he could enter the parallel and enticing world he glimpsed through the looking-glass. We are all lifelong spectators of existence, but because we watch it from different perspectives we can never share what we take to be its truths with another – 'reality' is elusive, a mirage as personal and undependable as one's mirrored reflection:

As silent as a mirror is believed
Realities plunge in silence by ...

The idea grew, and in the course of his week at home he worked it into 'Legend',
the lyric with which he would eventually open his first published volume of
poems. If the poet could not define reality after contemplating it perhaps he would
have better luck assessing himself, or at least his mirrored reflection – but such
self-scrutiny was also fraught with hard questions. What was Hart Crane? Why did
he punish himself and his body, as his friends had begun to complain, with his
frequent excesses? Why did he live hand-to-mouth, when men with half his intelligence drew large bureaucratic salaries? Why was he set apart, not only from his
married friends, but from the commuting world of compromise and middle-aged
expectations? Why and how was he a poet? His reflection retained many of its
secrets, but there were certain truths he did know about himself:

I am not ready for repentance;
Nor to match regrets. For the moth
Bends no more than the still
Imploring flame. And tremorous
In the white falling flakes
Kisses are, –
The only worth all granting.

At twenty-five he was not ready for the golden mean: years before, beginning
his poetic career, he had seen himself as a moth made blind, a man set apart from
those who flew lower and saw less, and now, many bottles and countless kisses
later, the analogy still seemed apt – and the flame of intense experience, which was
the only kind that was valid or educative, was still as dangerously enticing. To give
oneself again and again to intense intoxication, carnal passion, impossible love, to
stalk potentially dangerous men for that possibility of feral ecstasy, 'This cleaving
and this burning', was worth it, even though such extremes reduced one to a
'smoking souvenir' or 'Bleeding eidolon'. Eventually by such trials 'the bright
logic is won' – there was no other way of trying to live life, no other way of trying
to comprehend its facsimile, reality, and certainly no other route open to a poet.
For how else could he win the authority to speak in the rhymed harmonies of his
calling – and what other authority did he covet, conspicuous as he was in the early
blaze of notoriety, with the long sunset of existence looming ahead of him?

Then, drop by caustic drop, a perfect cry
Shall string some constant harmony, –
Relentless caper for all those who step
The legend of their youth into the noon.[69]

Early in November Hart found himself staying with the Munsons as guests of Kenneth Burke at his farm in New Jersey: six quarts of home-made blackberry wine did much to enliven the interlude and may have gone some way towards explaining the painfulness of Hart's clowning, as divulged to Grace: 'I sat down in the wrong place once, and in the darkness whacked my head against a tree'.[70] Back in New York the poet saw Waldo and Jean Toomer, both returned from European travels, and Wilbur Underwood, about to return to Washington after one of his Petronian holidays. Allen Tate had now begun his job working for Susan Jenkins at *Telling Tales* and Harry Candee came and went, departing for England before Hart had time to see him. The Provincetown Players presented a quartet of one-act plays about the sea by Eugene O'Neill and not long after watching them Hart saw the playwright himself, along with his wife, when they arrived in New York for the opening of the tragedian's new drama, *Desire under the Elms*, at the Greenwich Village Theatre. O'Neill enjoyed more renown in Europe than he did at home, an injustice also borne by Waldo Frank: as Hart explained to Grace, 'The American public is still strangely unprepared for its men of higher talents, while Europe looks more and more to America for the renascence of its creative spirit.' As for his own work, with 'Voyages' nearing completion and other lyrics in circulation, it was 'becoming known for its formal perfection and hard glowing polish'. As usual he was writing on a Sunday evening, with the winds and waters outside providing what had become a regular backdrop to the events of his life. 'It darkened before five today,' he wrote, 'and the wind's onslaught across the bay turns up white-caps in the river's mouth.' How fascinating the gulls were – endlessly wheeling and circling for food in the harbour and far out at sea – and how magical the fog that had endured eighteen hours earlier in the week:

One couldn't even see the garden close behind the house – to say nothing of the piers. All night long there were distant tinklings, buoy bells and siren warnings from river craft. It was like wakening into a dreamland in the early dawn – one wondered where one was with only a milky light in the window and that vague music from a hidden world.[71]

Yet when the mist cleared what immense Manhattan structures it disclosed – just as poetry might emerge from the raw but beautiful stuff of prose. Later Hart reworked that epistolary vision for incorporation in 'The Harbor Dawn' section of *The Bridge*:

Insistently through sleep – a tide of voices –
They meet you listening midway in your dream,
The long, tired sounds, fog-insulated noises:
Gongs in white surplices, beshrouded wails,
Far strum of fog horns ... signals dispersed in veils.
....

The window goes blond slowly. Frostily clears.
From Cyclopean towers across Manhattan waters
– Two – three bright window-eyes aglitter, disk
The sun, released – aloft with cold gulls hither.

The fog leans one last moment on the sill.
Under the mistletoe of dreams, a star –
As though to join us at some distant hill –
Turns in the waking west and goes to sleep.[72]

Further recognition of Hart's growing poetic mastery came when Paul Rosenfeld invited him to a reception he was giving on Saturday, 29 November to welcome to New York the French critic Jean Catel. Ever since Gorham Munson and Sherwood Anderson had quarrelled about Sommer's art in Cleveland – and then drawn various allies, including Rosenfeld, into the hostility that persisted in New York – Hart had maintained an aversion to the critic who now solicited his company. He knew, however, as he told Grace, that 'everybody (spelled with a capital E) in modern American painting, letters and art generally' would be at the party and that it would be foolish of him to reject the overture, especially in view of Rosenfeld's suggestion that he join Alfred Kreymborg and Marianne Moore in reading some of his work aloud to the assembled guests. Rosenfeld had been one of the founders of *Seven Arts* magazine and during the 1920s, as the music critic for the *New Republic* and the *Dial*, he championed the work of Schoenberg, Ernest Bloch, Leo Ornstein and Stravinsky. He wrote essays and one novel and took a particular interest in the arts in New York. As an heir to the Rhinegold brewing fortune he could afford his famous generosity, which he dispensed with largesse among artists, the class he venerated above all others. He was shy and aesthetically sophisticated and his close friends included e.e. cummings, Edmund Wilson, Malcolm Cowley and the poet Louise Bogan: his invitation was a compliment and Hart knew it. A severe case of food poisoning almost prevented him from attending, however, and when he did arrive the prospect of reading aloud daunted him, even though, as he told Grace, 'I lack almost no assurance on the value of my poems'.[73] Rosenfeld had assembled an illustrious party: Jean Toomer, Stieglitz and O'Keeffe, Paul Strand and his wife, Marianne Moore, Van Wyck Brooks, Lewis Mumford, Alfred Kreymborg, Edmund Wilson and his then wife, Mary Blair, and Jacques Seligman, a prominent art dealer, were among those who had assembled to bid Catel welcome – and, of course, to enjoy the poetry readings. Hart dosed himself with whiskey and soda 'and everyone thought I was the picture of health', Grace was informed. Aaron Copland performed one of his compositions and then the poets took the floor. Hart read 'Chaplinesque', 'Sunday Morning Apples', 'Paraphrase' and, by popular request, 'Faustus and Helen', and told his mother afterwards that he had 'been recognized with the applause of the most discriminating'.[74]

One of the writers conspicuously absent from Rosenfeld's elysium was Gorham Munson, whose subscription to Gurdjieffian metaphysics had done much to lessen the contact he and Hart had once enjoyed. The poet's growing friendship with Malcolm Cowley had implied further social realignments and then at the end of the year Hart found himself involved with preparations for a publication to be called *Aesthete 1925*, which Cowley and his allies were planning in retaliation against a journalist named Ernest Boyd, who had attacked the group a year previously in an article published in the first issue of the *American Mercury* and entitled 'Aesthete: Model 1924'. Even among the younger generation of writers the catalogue of unforgotten skirmishes awaiting vengeance was so extensive that once the principle of reprisals was invoked hostilities rapidly broadened and in no time it looked as though Hart would be drawn into Cowley's long-standing feud with Munson.

A preliminary meeting to discuss *Aesthete 1925* occurred at the end of November and once Hart – by nature disinclined to partisanship – saw the way plans were tending he tried to extricate himself rather than hurt Munson, or indeed Frank, who also looked likely to be attacked. Inevitably the former heard rumours of conspiracy and when he and Hart met for lunch on 4 December *Aesthete 1925* was discussed: Munson wanted to know where his old friend now stood. Hart attempted to placate a man seldom slow to umbrage – but sensing the insufficiency of his efforts he wrote to Munson the next day and appealed to him to consult Allen Tate, who had witnessed the council of war and would testify that Hart had 'consistently defended [Munson] and Waldo' when in the company of his other literary friends. He stressed that he was 'growing more and more sick of factions, gossip, jealousies, recriminations, excoriations and the whole literary shee-bang' and consequently yearned for independence and neutrality – but 'I have not been so situated that I could possibly maintain the complete isolation which it has been your desired good fortune to maintain'. In any case, now the matter had been broached, although he had great admiration for Munson as a critic and enormous gratitude for his faith and literary guidance, Hart also thought his friend too ready to dismiss causes and beliefs out of hostility for their proponents. Hart saluted the 'rigorous program' Munson had espoused with his Gurdjieffian loyalties but nevertheless suspected there were aspects to his friend's thinking that were increasingly 'unwieldy, limited and stolid'. Dogma and churchly certainty worried him: life resisted rigid interpretations and if life did, so should honest men and artists. He cited Wyndham Lewis: 'one must be broken up to live', which he took to mean that 'the artist must have a certain amount of "confusion" to bring into form'.[75] But Munson was in no mood for pragmatism and when the two men met for lunch again on 8 December Hart found that his remonstrances had been too little, too late. Again Munson demanded assurances of his loyalty and when the poet insisted that he was unable to give them if it meant severing his friendship with Cowley and his circle Munson accused him of being an opportunist and suggested that he would have to 'excommunicate' him from his own literary group. Whatever the tone in which this threat was made it was enough to annoy the poet for the rest of the day and that night he sent his earliest literary mentor a brief note. He was 'not prepared to welcome threats from any quarters' and on reflection was convinced Munson should take 'whatever decisions or formalities' he thought necessary to bring about the ostracism he had mentioned.[76] The drama precipitated a closure which increasingly conflicting opinions perhaps made inevitable. Thereafter the two writers were friendly but never significantly friends.

In accordance with pledges long since exacted by Grace, Hart returned to
Cleveland for Christmas, armed, as promised, with 'two quarts of something
good from the metropolis'.[1] Whatever fire-water he selected would be useful, not
only in honouring the conviviality of the season but in mitigating the strains and
revelations inevitably entailed by his visit, the first since his departure for New
York almost two years before. In that time Grace's life had diminished considerably, largely as a result of financial constraints – the easy means of her youth and
married life were now no more than taunting memories and all that remained of
CA's generous alimony were the fading accoutrements of vanity: Hart liked to tell
his friends his mother was so extravagant that on one occasion she bought two
identical fur coats to alternate between trips to the cleaner's. Newly impecunious,
she had found a job in Cleveland selling bric-à-brac in the Josephine Shop at 7218
Euclid Avenue but the necessity of work did not come easily after a lifetime of
leisure – and if Mrs Hart gave her daughter what moral support she could she also
represented an ageing burden whose medical bills eroded dwindling resources and
whose needs curtailed what remained of Grace's freedom.

To make matters worse, the two women could no longer afford to retain the full
complement of domestics needed to run a substantial house and Grace's spare time
was often spent in helping Margaret, the only maid she still retained. At one stage
the Villa Casas might have represented some insurance against these difficulties
but the value of the Caribbean property was linked directly to American control
of the Isle of Pines, precariously maintained by a consortium of powerful interests
since the Spanish-American War despite the Isle of Pines Treaty, subsequently
endorsed by the Supreme Court, and the campaigns of certain sections of the
press, all of which insisted that the territory was Cuban. With restitution looking
increasingly certain, it was already too late to sell the plantation, the worth of
which would sharply decrease with the island's change of status. Money would
have to come from other sources and so far Grace had thought of only two sol-

utions: she decided to move to a smaller, cheaper house, and resolved, if possible, to find a prosperous second husband.

She may well have assumed that Hart would prove indifferent to the sale of the old house but apprehensive about the advent of other male claimants on her love and attention – after all, had she and her son not supported, adored and admired each other through thick and thin? He had never even implied that he had found any young woman he considered her equal, so how now could she prefer another man over him? There was more than mere flippancy to the remark she made to Mrs Hart, which was subsequently transmitted to the poet himself: 'It gives me more of a thrill to get a letter from "*my* boy" than from any lover I ever had'.[2] For all his accomplishments, however, Hart could never be her husband: nor, by the pragmatic calculations which so often inform second marriages, could he do anything to remedy her financial plight. So when Grace began tentatively to socialize with bachelors, with Mrs Hart a party to the dalliance, her son was not kept informed, and it fell to Sam Loveman to relay news of the emergence of Charles Curtis as a determined suitor. At once Hart wrote to his mother, eager to know why she had been so 'sweetly shy' about her changed circumstances. If he was disingenuous in insisting that 'I certainly would never be timorous about writing you any news about myself, however intimate', the possibility that someone else might at last share the burden of his mother's exacting love no doubt came as a relief and he spoke with conviction when he assured her that 'nothing would make me happier than your marriage'. Whatever happened, however, he begged her not to marry 'a mere moneybag' – 'it has always hurt me to hear you jest about such matters'. He knew, because Mrs Hart had confided in him, that Grace felt 'no alliance was worth anything that "broke" our relationship' but now he wanted to insist that, 'whoever you chose and no matter what the circumstances might be', nothing could sever the bonds that existed between them. All enduring relations had to take account of future changes and Grace had to be prepared for the fact that she was not always going to be the priority or paramount being in his life: 'As the years go by I am quite apt to be away for long periods, for I admit that the freedom of my imagination is the most precious thing that life holds for me, – and the only reason I can see for living. That you should be lonely anywhere during those times is a pain to me everytime I contemplate the future.'[3] One day he would have to brave greater explicitness but for the time being a hint would do. In any case it seemed to work because when Grace replied she was at last candid: 'Yes I think I am in love or something, & I do not want to be – it is slavery ... I just feel myself slipping, slipping, slipping.'[4]

It was agreed that Hart would meet Grace's new beau at Christmas and only the whereabouts remained to be decided, since 1709 East 115th Street was put up for sale, Hart's grave misgivings notwithstanding, in September 1924. Knowing his mother's extravagance and financial naïvety, which was blind to the perils of living on capital, he was sure the plan to sell was misguided and opposed it from the outset, arguing instead that Grace and Mrs Hart should put tenants in the big house while themselves renting somewhere more modest. But his reasoning went beyond prudence: houses were more than their constituent bricks and mortar and part of himself, his poetry and his America resided immovably in this clapboard home, the only true sanctuary he was ever to have. Such thinking was sentimental, he realized, but none the less persuasive for that, as he told his mother when the house was put on the market: 'I have gotten so used to never being sure of next week's rent ... that I feel like never accumulating an extra sheet of paper because it's painful for me to think of giving up things that have become a sort of part of me. I should rise above such feelings, I know, but haven't been able to thus far.' Indeed the more he thought about the loss of the Hart mansion, the more distressing it became: 'I can scarcely imagine the old house as a foreign property, perhaps no more standing. It's so deep in my consciousness and so much the frame of the past.'[5] In the event the house was still in Mrs Hart's ownership at Christmas and there Hart met Charles Curtis, 'a thoroughbred', Grace promised, who enjoyed dancing, swimming and poker besides loving 'life & beauty, music & art – & all of the best things life has to offer', so much so that even at sixty-four he still retained 'the figure of youth'.[6] By day he was an insurance adjuster with children by a previous marriage – a daughter in Cleveland and a son who was also a writer in New York: Kent Curtis was eight years older than Hart and became a popular novelist in the late Twenties with works such as *The Blushing Camel* and *The Tired Captains*. Hart seems never to have encountered him and for all the record that survives of Charles Curtis, presently his stepfather, he might as well never have met him either.

Hart was back in New York by New Year's Eve and celebrated with the rest of the gang at Squarcialupi's Restaurant in Perry Street. Festivities continued until 3 January and it was not until the next day, the first Sunday of 1925, that he found himself with sufficient leisure to write to Grace. Later in the afternoon Susan Jenkins, Allen Tate and Slater Brown were expected for tea but in the meantime his room, still festooned for Christmas, was aromatic with intimations of the spring – a whole quarter's worth of marigolds and narcissi, bought from the local florist, sparkled in the strange radiance of the snow-light reflected from the rooftops of the piers below. Over the ensuing cold but happy weeks these were the friends Hart would see repeatedly in the periods of time not claimed by Sweet's or Emil, or by the coexistent impulses towards high self-expression and less exalted self-gratification.

Preparations for *Aesthete 1925* were well under way by early January and the vengeful conspirators – Malcolm and Peggy Cowley, Kenneth Burke, Slater Brown and Matthew Josephson – regularly congregated after five o'clock at the *Telling Tales* office on East 11th Street near University Place, which Susan had talked her boss, Bill Clayton, into making available. Hart often dropped in after leaving Sweet's and besides following the progress of the publication, which went to press in mid-January for February distribution, he was glad to see Susan, Allen Tate, her deputy, and Bina Flynn, Susan's friend at *Ranch Romances*, the sister magazine to *Telling Tales*. The evenings would often progress to a speakeasy on West 4th Street which the group knew as 'Punchino Palace', 'a grim six-by-eight hole', in Susan's words, 'where for fifteen or twenty cents we drank lethal speakeasy "rum" in hot water'.[7] Sometimes the friends all found themselves working on Saturday and on one such occasion, after lunch in MacDougal Street, they decided on a frivolous expedition to Times Square. Walking along the northern side of Washington Square to catch the bus they stopped, at Hart's suggestion, in front of Number 3, home to Edmund Wilson, whose study, scene of the intellectual endeavour that was to make him a commanding figure in New York's literary world by the end of the decade, was clearly visible from the street. Only five years later the young Lionel Trilling, inspired by the sight of the critic labouring at his desk in the window, thought his lucubrations proof 'that what the Village stood for in American life was not wholly a matter of history'.[8] The intoxicated poet could muster no such reverence, however, and performed an Irish jig outside Wilson's house before the others dragged him away to Times Square and to an afternoon of silliness in photograph booths. The surviving images are poignant with the carefree transience of youth: Susan and Bina as cowgirls, in chaps and sombreros, against the background of a Wild West saloon; Crane, Tate and Slater Brown, incongruous in the same setting as private detectives and looking for all the world like foreshadowings of *film noir*.

In nostalgic retrospection Malcolm Cowley remembered this period as 'the good winter' when all the friends, still in their twenties, seemed happy with the present and enthusiastic about the future – although Hart's exhilaration was intenser than anybody else's and alternated with more menacing periods of gloom. Once or twice a week the group would gather at Squarcialupi's for what Susan called 'a gay, impromptu, Dutch-treat dinner party', with their number sometimes reinforced by irregulars such as Eleanor Fitzgerald, e.e. cummings and his wife, Emil, and the writer and editor Harold Loeb, then arranging the publication of his first novel, *Doodab*. Dinner cost 75 cents a head and the wine, Susan said, was 'Prohibition *vino rosso* ... cheap and not *too* bad'. There was an upright piano in the room and Hart often played 'his versions-by-ear of his favorite popular songs – a foot on the loud pedal, accentuating the pronounced rhythms, shaking his head with its bristly, brush-cut stand of hair in time to the music'.[9] After dinner the group would adjourn to a back room for gossip and literary talk; Loeb remembered one occasion when Hart recited a fragment from *The Bridge* and then declared he was 'through with poetry for life'.[10] Cowley's impression was that Hart 'always made more than his share of the jokes, laughed louder, if possible, than anyone else, and drank more of John Squarcialupi's red wine', but the end of the evening might nevertheless find him 'as morose as a chained bear in a Russian tavern'. When, one night, he stormed out after upsetting a bottle of wine and Cowley wondered where he was going, one knowing girl replied: 'He's going to Brooklyn to pick up a sailor.'[11]

If the poet's nocturnal adventures were still only half acknowledged the drinking was now becoming an item of Village lore. When Howard Lovecraft came to New York to visit Sam Loveman the two friends naturally saw something of Hart, now described by Lovecraft as 'an egotistical young aesthete who has attained some real recognition in the Dial and other modernist organs, and who has an unfortunate predilection for the wine when it is red'. Since their initial meeting in Cleveland Lovecraft noted that Hart's appearance had changed – he was now 'a little ruddier, a little puffier, and slightly more moustached'. A subsequent visit to Hart's apartment explained the reddening skin: 'We found Crane in and sober – but boasting over the two-day spree he had just slept off, during which he had been picked up dead drunk from the street in Greenwich Village by the eminent modernist poet e.e. cummings – whom he knows well and put in a homeward taxi.'[12] Grace was kept ignorant of these excesses but Hart was nevertheless increasingly open with his mother about the amount of alcohol he consumed and when he told her about parties he had attended it was not to give details of the occasion commemorated or the other guests invited but the recipes for distraction the Jazz Age concocted: 'Imagine making anything fit to put in one's stomach out of two quarts of heavy cream, a dozen eggs and a bottle of Johnny Walker whisky!' he complained of one winter party. The potion had tasted 'just like ivory [soap] melted down in a wash tub' – not that that had deterred him. Three days later he complained: 'I haven't been the same since.'[13]

If the proprietors of Sweet's had known of Hart's indulgences they might have been doubly impressed that he showed up for work at all – but somehow he did, though with growing reluctance as the weeks went by. It was from a fire escape at the office, twenty-one flights above Bryant Park and the 42nd Street Library, that he witnessed the solar eclipse of 24 January, when 'the total darkness and stars at the moment of totality – the mad crowds in the subways on the way to see it' all made a strong impression.[14] A few days later the light was again veiled, but this time by an unprecedented fog which unleashed such a cacophony of sirens on the East River that Hart was denied sound sleep for three nights. A few weeks later New York was shaken by an earth tremor which was detectable, Hart gathered, in Cleveland. He was writing to the Rychtariks at the time it occurred and 'when the room began swaying frightfully' he had 'the most sickening and helpless feeling' he ever hoped to experience.[15] To compound the series of portents, heavy fog returned to New York at the end of February and newspapers reported that numerous liners, fearful of collision in New York waters, had congregated beyond the bay. More mundanely, CA moved the Crane Company offices from East 39th Street to smaller premises on Madison Avenue which had absolutely no storage room but, beyond complaining to Grace that the transfer 'puts me a little out on free candy',

Hart gave the move no thought, distracted as he was by the possibility of accompanying Emil on a Scandinavian cruise which would be made practicable by the $2,000 inheritance Opffer expected from his father's estate.[16]

With the arrival of March, his enthusiasm tended elsewhere: after years of being embarrassed to call himself a poet with no published collection to his name Hart now decided he had enough strong poems to form a first volume. *The Bridge*, whenever it was completed, could have a book to itself; but it was time the best of his work so far appeared in a carefully arranged sequence before the public. He decided to call his first volume 'White Buildings' (neat evocation of the skyline of pale stalagmites he saw across the river), in part because the title evoked an early enthusiasm for the paintings of Di Chirico, in part because white buildings had been a component of the waking dream enacted in a sailor's arms that misty night 'where November takes the leaf', and since so often repeated, much to the benefit of his lyric imagination. Once he had made the decision to assemble work for a first volume he committed himself to revising the lyrics involved and to arranging them in a careful order, before learning of a printer named Samuel Jacobs who ran the Polytype Press at 39 West 8th Street. Having typeset e.e. cummings's *Tulips and Chimneys*, Jacobs knew about the punctiliousness of poets and the insolvency of their calling and he now undertook to waive his charges as a compositor in the production of a privately printed edition of 500 copies of *White Buildings*, which he was sure could be managed for as little as $200. There was one caveat: the production might take a long time, since Jacobs could devote himself to it only when there were no paying commitments on his presses. In the event nothing came of the scheme: Jacobs backed out owing to pressure of work but offered in mitigation to set the book free of charge for any publisher eager to release the volume. Hart duly approached Thomas Seltzer, and Waldo once again promised to raise the matter with his publishers, Boni and Liveright. But for once the poet did not expect miracles and did his best to dampen Grace's expectations: 'The radio and cross-word puzzles and other such baby-rattles for the great American public have so badly cut into book sales this last year that most publishers have felt it seriously – and shy at such philanthropic interests as good poetry.'[17]

That spring, after the United States Senate finally ratified the Isle of Pines Treaty, the Caribbean island formally passed to Cuban sovereignty: Grace was disappointed but not surprised: at least now the uncertainty was over. She and Charles Curtis agreed to marry but decided to wait for the ripening of several financial schemes instigated by the latter before they did so. After all, as Grace said, 'we can't live on bird seed'.[18] The strain and uncertainty of the situation took its toll – she suffered three severe colds and lost twenty pounds before the end of the spring. The Cleveland house was still unsold but for the last time the cherry tree in the yard put forth its blossoms for Grace and her mother. They took photographs of each other standing beneath it and sent them to Hart, who was at once pleased and saddened to see them, since 'the tree and the entire yard, for all that, have a great place in my memories'.[19] The blossoms foretold the summer and Hart thought of it with dread: the hay fever, the hives brought on by sweating, the insomnia of hot nights, open windows and noisy neighbours, the daily journey beneath the East River with hundreds of other underpaid commuters – and all for $40 a month. With no news so far of Emil's inheritance, escape to Scandinavia looked unlikely and although Hart had been thinking since early March of taking a job for the summer on a boat sailing to South America he had come no nearer to realizing his scheme than admitting to himself the degree of his boredom at Sweet's. Cowley was among the first to hear that Hart felt 'like a rat caught in a trap' and was sympathetic but not encouraging.[20] He was planning to leave the catalogue service to support himself as a freelance writer but knew his friend had no facility for writing prose for publication and felt he should settle for work in an undemanding job that left him solvent for prosody. As part of this transition Cowley had also decided to leave New York and he and Peggy were now installed in a five-room house on Staten Island, with ocean views beyond the cherry and plum orchards, for $30 a month. Kenneth Burke had been the pioneer but suddenly it seemed that all Hart's closest friends had rural longings: the Tates and Slater Brown were thinking of leaving Manhattan, Matthew Josephson had already departed to Katonah, New York, Waldo planned to spend the summer in Massachusetts and presently Gaston and Isabel Lachaise would leave for Maine. They had pressed Hart to join them whenever he could, convinced that he would benefit from the change and the coastal proximity, and he was very tempted. As he confessed to Grace when comparing the merits of that invitation against his plan to sail to South America, 'I am still considering a trial of ocean.'[21]

The dispersal made the prospect of the summer doubly upsetting. If he remained in New York in those torrid months where would he go for food, love and sustaining conviction? As he thought longingly of escape, however, he realized it was not just his job that compelled him to remain: *White Buildings* awaited publication and he would have nobody but himself to blame if a publisher came forward when he was in New England and accessible only by letter or out on the blue yonder with nothing at his disposal but ship's radio to confirm the details crucial to publication of his gossamer lyrics. If he had to remain in New York, let it at least be with more money – so at the beginning of May he applied for a pay rise and indicated that if Sweet's could not accommodate him he had other prospects. Cowley was astonished when he learned that Hart had asked to be paid $100 a month – the salary commanded by the top copy-writer – and took the move to be a ploy. Sweet's made no immediate response but Hart's confidence in the omens of change was reinforced when he had lunch a few days later with Bill Freeman, who had employed him at Corday and Gross and who assured him on the basis of his copy-writing skills that his company would always give him another job if he ever decided to return to Cleveland.

Grace was informed of this propitious news on 7 May and the same letter told her that Hart had once again brought up the subject of his pay increase and that he was determined, if denied, to leave: 'It's me for the sea during these summer months, and a change from office routine for awhile.'[22] Sweet's turned down the application and Hart resigned at a fortnight's notice, 'without money saved or much prospect of earning it', Cowley grimly noted.[23] A week or so later CA arrived and offered his son a job 'which I was all ready to take', Hart assured Grace, until his father became 'pettily dictatorial' and told him that if he accepted the work he would have to shave off his moustache, whereupon the reluctant businessman walked out of the restaurant.[24] It was a defiant gesture: he had no obvious destination to walk towards – but then something like providence interceded and planned his summer for him.

On the strength of a small legacy Slater Brown had bought a dilapidated farmhouse complete with rope beds and other old furniture near the village of Pawling, in Dutchess County, New York: he and Susan were planning to marry and assumed that the house would provide a home for at least part of the year but it needed urgent modernization and restoration. Would Hart like to help? Work would begin at once and there was plenty of room for him to stay. The location was less exotic than he had planned – but the sea would wait and in the meantime Brown's house was only seventy-five miles north of Greenwich Village, so if *White Buildings* did suddenly find a publisher Hart could return to New York to sign contracts at a day's notice. He accepted the offer, handed over his room in Columbia Heights to Emil until the end of October and planned to leave New York on 6 June. It was not a moment too soon: intense heat engulfed the city at the beginning of the month and compounded problems brought on by nerves – headaches, bladder trouble and urethritis – and aggravated by his favourite palliative, alcohol. To make matters worse, he had to make three visits to the dentist to resolve a suspected dental abscess: by the time he boarded the Albany-bound train he was depleted by sleeplessness and a diet of milk and crackers.

Slater Brown had first seen his house while staying for weekends with Eleanor Fitzgerald, who had a home nearby: it had been built before 1776 and was surrounded by ancient apple orchards and almost a hundred acres of land. To Malcolm Cowley it was 'an eighteenth-century cottage' but there was nothing pretty about its circumambient legends – the house was situated on South Quaker Hill and in the nearby woods, behind a rocky ledge and precipice, there was a brief maze of small, deep caves that had been used as a refuge during the Revolutionary War by the bandits who preyed on Washington's army and on the supply carts which travelled the nearby Coldspring Turnpike to furnish it.[25] It was this opportunistic thievery, rather than any specific loyalist affiliation, that led to the brigands' being stigmatized as 'Tories'; by extension their subterranean retreat, scene of several bloody incidents during the hostilities, became known as 'Tory Rocks' or sometimes 'Robber Rocks', and this latter name, once Hart took a fancy to its vivid associations, was applied to Slater Brown's property.

Brown and his future wife, discovering that outlaws and hermits still populated the folds of the hills that marked the border between New York and Connecticut, termed their new locality 'Tory Hill': there were several bootleggers nearby, among them a Wall Street bankrupt and cashiered army officer named Wiley Varian, as well as a predator infamous as the 'Russian Woolf', who always brewed himself tea while robbing a deserted house. Without a functioning home to call their own, however, the fugitive New Yorkers had little time to dread these local miscreants and set to work at once on the decayed fabric of the house. Aware that Robber Rocks was in need of repainting, Hart had brought from Sweet's a catalogue for a paint named 'Dutch Boy White Lead' and following its instructions he and Brown mixed the paint with turpentine and linseed oil and gleefully rendered the exterior of the house white, all the while so astonished by the quantities of paint the wood absorbed that Susan threatened that if she heard one more time the refrain 'this old wood certainly drinks it up' she would leave for New York never to return.[26] The achievement proved satisfying but short-lived: with the onset of winter Brown discovered that the siding was rotten and removed it. Hart also helped with the exposure of the original beams in the ceilings and followed deliberations about the installation of a bathroom, which eventually went ahead despite the counsel of their old neighbour Charlie Jennings, who remarked, to much subsequent mirth, 'I'm glad to see you an't putting in one of those bathrooms. I always said they was a passing fad.'[27]

Jennings himself presently sold his own home to a man named Henry Allen Moe, who was to enter Hart's life a few years later, but in the meantime his cellar, though not open to women, soon became a popular place of sanctuary for Bill and Hart, who developed an enthusiasm for the farmer's home-made hard cider. Malcolm Cowley later noted that Hart was 'at home in the country without belonging in the country' and now he developed an affectionate interest in the activities of the neighbouring farmers.[28] Susan remembered that one of his favourite destinations aside from the Jennings cellar was the nearby Aiken farm, where he went to buy milk; on the way home 'he would carry it, swinging the milk pail with him, sometimes spilling it on the way back'.[29] Robber Rocks was situated outside the village of Pawling but its postal address was Patterson and the nearest town for provisions, accessible in the Model-T Ford Brown had bought for $35, was New Milford. It was here that the friends bought Dutch Boy paint and timber for shelves, bookcases and tables as well as the groceries they needed before the garden began to repay their labours. There was rubbish to be cleared, plaster to be stripped, woodwork to be scrubbed, with only oil lamps and an oil stove that cost 10 cents a day to sustain their endeavours – yet if these were hard-working days they were also, for Hart, extremely happy and when he wrote to his grand-mother on 17 June it was to enthuse about the 'great quantities of fine Guernsey milk' and 'the finest butter and eggs and fresh vegetables' that he was now eating and to inform her that he was sleeping 'like a top', that his uric acid complaint had gone and that he was 'brown as a nut already with the sun and all greased up at the joints'. Although the day began early, at 5.30, 'the air is so fresh and the birds so sweet that you simply can't stay in bed a moment longer. And how good break- fast tastes!'[30] His first letter to Grace from Robber Rocks continued the idyll: he and Brown had built mosquito screens; the vegetable garden had been planted with peas and beans; there were abundant blueberries, gooseberries, blackberries and raspberries as well as stands of sap maples and walnut trees; as for huckle- berries, 'there will be simply bushels of them'. His enthusiasm for country – or, more precisely, non-urban – life was such that he was already thinking of moving nearby and Slater Brown, no doubt eager for rural companionship, had offered Hart a strip of land and the timber with which to build his own cabin.

All things considered, there was much to celebrate – and the Browns decided to hold the first of the Fourth of July parties that would become one of the annual rites for the group and for the locality many of them came to inhabit. Grace was informed that 'about an omnibus-full of people' arrived from New York on Friday the 3rd, to be plied with a case of gin and Jennings's hard cider over the course of what became a three-day saturnalia.[31] Malcolm and Peggy Cowley, soon to move to nearby Sherman, Connecticut, were among the guests, with the former assess- ing for the first time the slightly disturbing combination of bleakness and plenty that characterized the region:

> Most of the houses on the back roads were inhabited by childless couples or old bachelors or widows living alone. The second-growth woods crept over the stone fences and crowded into the dooryards. Tory Hill was a decaying, even desolate neighborhood, but it had dirt roads for walking, blueberries in the unpastured fields, deer in the woods, trout in the brooks that tumbled through secret glens, and never a game warden or No Trespass sign.[32]

The other guests were too busy celebrating to conduct such observations – and Hart in any case offered his own vivid spectacle. 'You should have seen the dances I did,' he told Grace; 'one all painted up like an African cannibal. My make-up was lurid enough. A small keg on my head and a pair of cerise drawers on my legs!'[33] Cowley noted Hart's 'pagan ecstasy as he capered on a stone fence built by God- fearing Yankee farmers'[34] and the others joined the poet in revelries catalogued for Grace: tree-climbing, midnight swimming, blind man's buff, riding in wheel- barrows – the gratification of 'every caprice for three days' until everyone was exhausted and ready for recovery in New York.[35] Allen Tate wanted to ask Hart about his current work and plans for a published volume but 'the whirlwind' of distractions, which also included 'Peggy and orange-peel throwing incapacited my wits so utterly that I could never get to the question'.[36] Caroline Tate, Allen Tate's heavily pregnant wife, endured it all sober, so she knew she was not suffering some bootleg hallucination when she saw Hart, still clad as his idea of a cannibal on Saturday afternoon, sitting by the lilacs near the house and pensively empty-ing a box of salt into the phonograph. Every so often he would consult the radi-ant sky, repeating again and again: 'Where the cedar leaf divides the sky ... where the cedar leaf divides the sky ... I was promised an improved infancy.'

On Sunday, 5 July the weather changed: drizzling rain put an end to croquet on the comically irregular lawn and Hart went to his room, which was next door to the big kitchen where the others had settled for drink and gossip. For the next hour, Cowley recalled, their chatter meandered to a bizarre accompaniment audi-ble from next door: fierce typing clattered in counterpoint to music being played at full volume on a phonograph now cleaned of salt. Over the years the records would vary and the friends became familiar with them all: one month Hart might find a Cuban rumba an inspiration to composition but the next would see him loyal to Marlene Dietrich, Ravel's *Bolero* or the songs from *Hit the Deck*. What never varied was the process: the record would be played again and again as the type-writer hammered and then recast the lines in composition. The loud music, fol-lowed by readings of what sounded like lines of verse, proclaimed the activity within, brought on by the state of ecstatic literary inspiration towards which the poet had been working for the last twenty-four hours, so no one was surprised when his door finally opened: 'Hart came stamping out,' Cowley recalled, 'his eyes blazing, with a dead cigar in one hand and two or three sheets of heavily corrected typescript in the other. "R-read that," he growled exultantly, like a jungle cat standing over its kill. "Isn't that the greatest poem ever written?"'[37]

The result was 'Passage', a beautiful, if esoteric, poem which Crane wrote and rewrote between July and December and saw rejected by T.S. Eliot at the *Criterion* and Marianne Moore at the *Dial*. The latter praised 'the rich imagination and the sensibility' Crane's authorship revealed but insisted the poem's 'multiform content accounts, I suppose, for what seems to us a lack of simplicity and cumulative force'.[38] For Hart 'Passage' was 'the most interesting and conjectural thing I have written': thirty-seven metrically and stanzaically irregular lines, exquisite but often intractable, about the inexorable aspect of time, which burdened one with cum-bersome memories before extinguishing hope, achievement and life itself.[39] The escape from New York to carefree country life had rekindled memories long dead of innocent boyhood: the blue sky the poet saw above, the blue sea he yearned for – both offered existences of freedom, both commended the child's way of living, which lay in a present uncomplicated by nostalgia or anticipation:

> Where the cedar leaf divides the sky
> I heard the sea.
> In sapphire arenas of the hills
> I was promised an improved infancy.

Eager to live in this immediate present, and thus 'sanctioning the sun', the poet makes a bold determination: 'My memory I left in a ravine'. It was nothing but useless baggage, a 'Casual louse' that at best 'tissues the buckwheat' of life, at worst 'wakens alleys with a hidden cough', and could lead one at any time down byways of past experience that echoed with the cough or tears of an unhappy boyhood. 'Dangerously' the poet pursues his dream of living in the moment even as 'the summer burned'. The sun is time, however, as well as the illuminator of present happiness, and soon the would-be innocent feels 'the shadows of boulders' lengthening down his back. At the moment when he glimpses the paradise of 'Vine-stanchioned valleys' which awaits those innocent of memory or anticipation, the shadows of the evening of life begin to gather. There is no escape from one's temporal destiny. It is impossible to step outside time – the lone voyage has been futile; the outcome of every life is predictable: 'So was I turned about and back, much as your smoke/Compiles a too well known biography.' But even if he must walk 'the dozen particular decimals of time', the poet can still take consolation in the 'opening laurel' of his lyric fame, or so he thinks until he encounters a thief – time's vassal, death, holding his book and mocking the futility of his endeavours. But the poet insists that even if he and his work are doomed to oblivion he must still be 'justified in transience' with some achievement. Supine acquiescence, abjection in the face of inescapable extinction, is not an acceptable policy for life. But death will always close the book of poems and of existence: everyone, from the kings of Egypt downwards, is sooner or later buried in the deserts of decease. Death extinguishes all, even memory, and revenges itself on the glory of sunbound human aspiration:

> He closed the book. And from the Ptolemies
> Sand troughed us in a glittering abyss.
> A serpent swam a vertex to the sun
> – On unpaced beaches leaned its tongue and drummed.
> What fountains did I hear? what icy speeches?
> Memory, committed to the page, had broke.[40]

'It is really the most perplexing kind of poetry,' Hal Smith wrote on 10 July, rejecting *White Buildings* on behalf of Harcourt Brace. It had not been an easy decision to take: 'I feel certain that you are a genuine poet – and there are not many genuine poets lying around these days. But I should not want to publish you, nor could I probably persuade the others around here, unless by some blinding revelation we suddenly became aware of just what you were driving at.'[41] It was a great disappointment, but when he relayed the news to Waldo, who continued to hope for a more sympathetic response from Boni and Liveright, there was incomprehension in Hart's tone: 'My "obscurity" is a mystery to me'; he wondered at times if publishers and book buyers had ever really attempted to understand Donne, Baudelaire or even Emily Dickinson.[42] As he pondered his next assault on fame, and reworked his notion of its ephemerality in 'Passage', the furnishings of time and memory were suddenly shifted and regrouped. On 10 July, the day Hart wrote to Grace about the Fourth of July festivities and Hal Smith wrote with rejection, Harry Candee died in England, a victim of pneumonia at thirty-nine. The death occurred in St Chad's Hospital at Edgbaston outside Birmingham, where Candee was presumably discharging commitments related to the Working Boys' Home. His death certificate described him as 'of independent means a citizen of the United States', and announcements appeared in the *Birmingham Post*, *The Times* in London and the *New York Times*, from which, one imagines, Wilbur Underwood and perhaps Hart learned the news.

Even though almost no posthumous reference to Candee survives among Hart's papers one can assume that the ending came as a great shock to him. After all, he had had almost no exposure to death so far and it was doubly distressing to think that this decease had come to one so terribly young and temperamentally vital; almost two years later he could still tell Underwood, 'It seems hard to realize that he's gone.'[43] A day or two after this sombre announcement news came of another ending: at last the event he had been dreading for months had occurred – the old house in Cleveland was on the verge of sale and Grace asked him to return to help with the dispersal. Hart wrote on 19 July to say that his present funds – $5 and some silver – would not get him to Cleveland; he needed the fare but definitely wanted to come if the house was indeed about to be relinquished: 'I would like to say "goodbye" to the property (wherein have occurred so many intense experiences of my life) and I would like to sort out a few articles for preservation that have especial personal associations for me.'[44] Grace supplied the means and Hart travelled via New York where he stayed in his old room and saw a little of Emil, now temporarily in charge of publication of *Nordlyset*. The city heat horrified him and seemed symptomatic of a malaise he found prevalent among friends: Dos Passos had had severe flu and e.e. cummings looked terrible. Only two weeks previously Hart had promised Grace that the Fourth of July had marked his only 'blowout' since leaving New York: 'The desire for booze in the city comes from frayed nerves and repressions of the office,' he had assured her.[45] Now, once more in the cauldron, there was nothing for it but drink – his twenty-sixth birthday offering a good enough pretext – and his excesses were such that when he wrote to the Browns a month later from Cleveland he admitted that he was 'just getting over it'. Since then, implicitly conceding his slide into alcoholism, he had vowed to stay sober for a year. 'What is life without a bladder!'[46]

He arrived in Cleveland on 27 July and that day the sale of the house was made final. The new owner, Sabina O'Brien, proposed to rent the property to a fraternity in September but before she could do so what was in effect the combined contents of two households, the mahogany and the detritus of more than twenty years, had to be moved and tempers soon collided in the ensuing chaos and trauma. Grace was already talking of investing the proceeds of the sale in real estate in Florida – 'that dry and tourist-ridden place', in her son's estimation – but Hart aggravated her volatile condition by attempting to persuade her that the money would be better spent on repairing the property she owned in the Caribbean if all she wanted was tropical winters.[47] She and Mrs Hart were to move to Wade Park Manor, a fashionable residential hotel in Cleveland, but before the transfer could be achieved Mrs Hart fell ill and had to be nursed and it was in an atmosphere of nervous exhaustion and recrimination that Hart wrote to the Browns on 3 August. Somehow he had survived 'the turmoil' of his first week back but decisions about which possessions were to be sold and which salvaged had not proved easy and he was now almost beyond caring: 'Minds are changed each day about what I am to have preserved for myself – so much so that I at times feel enough indifference to make any surrenders.'[48] Nevertheless he proposed to send several cases of books, his *Everyman's Encyclopedia*, pillows and bedding and his old desk to Robber Rocks. It was a relief to visit William Sommer in the middle of August and at last Hart learned that it was the artist's reluctance to part with any of his works that had made him so laggard in co-operating with schemes for his fame. Writing to Waldo on 19 August Hart wondered if the painter was wiser than he seemed in overcoming any aspirations towards recognition: 'I admit that I haven't, at least not entirely. I still feel the need of some kind of audience.'[49] At about the same time he dispatched another bulletin to the Browns to thank them for writing to him; their letters were 'a brace to the nerves'. He hoped to be back in the East in the third week of September but warned that he was proposing to send 'Crane antiquities, portraits, libraries and knick-knacks' before then. He also had his eye on an Indian rug the future ownership of which had not yet been decided. 'But there is so much hysteria around here that I doubt it would be noticed much if the house slid en masse for fifty feet.'[50] On 27 August he wrote again, this time from Wade Park Manor, to notify the Browns of impending chattels: the day before he had sent five cases of books, a trunk of china, bedding and pictures, and a desk and chair.

Among the treasures which eventually found their way to Robber Rocks were the coveted Navajo rug – red, brown and white until Hart's obsession with cleanliness led him to wash it – and numerous items from Grace's wardrobe, including black and white riding breeches, a brown hound's-tooth overcoat, a lace dress and a blue négligé, which were subsequently distributed among Hart's surrogate mothers. What he could he removed by stealth – so eager was he to shore these memories against his ruins – but there was only so much he could salvage, and many of the accessories of his early years were blithely given away by his mother and grandmother or else consigned for sale. And although he could not know it, numerous items that were retained and put into storage Hart would never see again. Standing in front of the apartment building where his grandfather Crane's house had once been he took numerous pictures of the Hart mansion –

compressing in the flatness of film its complexities of memory and association – copies of which were later sent to various friends, including Munson and Slater Brown. As he told the latter, 'Believe me, I'm in a strange state.'[51] In some indefinable manner his life had narrowed with surrender of the old house and Hart Crane was never the same again. Just as one grieves with the death of parents whose authority one grows up longing to escape, so Hart fretted now that his early Midwestern constrictions were no longer there to flee. He had evaded Cleveland for New York but that in turn he now sought to escape: it was as though as a wanderer he had come full circle, only to find the original point of departure receding implacably before him and forever pulling just out of reach the certainties of place and past without which all voyagers become mere castaways.[52]

Traumatic as the dissolution was, it prompted Hart to press ahead with a scheme contemplated since June and the subject of hints, subtle and broad, dropped since then to mother, father and grandmother. The moment Slater Brown had made the suggestion it crystallized in Hart's mind as an ambition: more than anything he wanted to own a plot of land, complete with cabin, near to this potentially adoptive couple, whose companionship would provide him with emotional support as well as diversion whenever he wanted a respite from his labours on *The Bridge*. The plan seemed entirely reasonable – and only the cost of the acreage involved withheld him from immediate action. Then on 4 September Susan wrote with news that 80 acres near Robber Rocks looked likely to be sold: the tract would cost $400 but she had established that Charlie Jennings would accommodate Hart with a three-year mortgage for half that amount. 'Bill is very anxious to have you get this place. Jennings has taken a great shine to you, apparently. He told us that this year he would press cider only for himself, us and you.'[53] She assured him that the land contained several sites well suited for the construction of a cabin as well as all the loose stone and timber he would ever need for its completion. But where could he apply for the outstanding $200? CA's recent erratic behaviour was unpromising, Grace insisted that all her and Mrs Hart's surplus funds were required for investment in Florida, and Zell, when she acknowledged her godson's request for help on 12 September, took the opportunity to deliver a homily of refusal. 'It is a poor plan to borrow from any place except a bank,' she admonished:

> You can't live there and work in New York and you should be getting yourself established in something permanent . . . . Of course I understand how you hate the regular hours and the grind of business. But do you think any one likes it? I certainly don't. It's nicer to loaf in the country but for every one who is doing that, some one else is working and providing the 'wherewith' to keep that person in leisure.[54]

Hart was outraged: the letter, he told the Rychtariks, was 'a perfect document of typical American conduct' and merited museum preservation.[55] He broke with Zell for some time, but not before his dignified reply insisted that he had always given her credit for possessing an imagination unknown to other members of his family. In any case, 'One doesn't often have the assurance beforehand in patronising art that one will accrue six percent interest.'[56] He approached the Rychtariks, proposing to borrow the money at 6 per cent over five years, adding, 'I know you trust me.'[57] Indeed they did and despite their own straitened circumstances they generously lent him $225. No sooner had the money arrived than Bina Flynn bought an eighteenth-century Dutch farmhouse in Tory Hill and offered, in order to subsidize the purchase, to sell Hart a slice of the land she had acquired – 20 acres of his choice for $200. He selected a hilltop site commanding valley views with open and wooded stretches and when he told the Rychtariks of the news in early October he did so with assurances that he would 'roll in the grass with prayers and pleasure when I really get this tract of land for my very own'.[58] The deal was concluded on 13 October, and for a brief spell Hart was a shareholder in the New World.

He had returned to Robber Rocks via New York but his stay there was unsatisfactory: the city was becoming a place of transition for him, a port to be passed through, and self-imposed sobriety did little to improve it in his eyes. At least he adhered to his resolve and not even a temptation proposed by Emil, who had secured an invitation to dinner on board a Danish ship then in the harbour, could corrupt him. He continued sober at Robber Rocks and when he wrote to the Rychtariks enclosing an acknowledgement of debt for $225 he told them he was 'getting back to enough poise' to read again and although he was without any money at all he knew he could return to New York to search for work 'with a much better feeling of independence than before'. He had no particular kind of job in mind and was still considering working 'on the sea' but he would cross that bridge nearer the time. Here at Robber Rocks the weather had been blissful: he and the Browns took long walks by day and sat before huge fires at night; the garden yielded an abundance of vegetables; Susan was tireless in the confection of jams and preserves; the quinces were producing their 'kid glove golden fruit'; and Slater Brown was making applejack. 'But this is forbidden drink for me these days!'[59] To add to his contentment the items salvaged from Cleveland had now arrived and the Browns hospitably ordained that their largest downstairs room should henceforth be Hart's room. Here the desk and chair were installed, rude bookcases were made for the *Everyman's Encyclopedia*, and the Navajo rug and other beloved items were augmented by the loan of a picture Brown had acquired with the house: a coloured lithograph from 'Barnum's Gallery of Wonders' of 'Miss Jane Campbell, the Great Connecticut Giantess, 18 years old, weighs 628 pounds'.[60]

When not contemplating this prodigy Hart could take advantage of the golden autumnal weather to acquaint himself with nearby residents no less fascinating: he was particularly taken by the idea of Mrs Porwitski, the wife of a local Polishman,

who weighed 250 pounds and had given birth to sixteen children without medical aid. The old Quaker meeting house invited veneration of a different sort but
most compelling of all was Mizzentop, a deserted nineteenth-century hotel on the
peak of Quaker Hill which was awaiting demolition. The carriage trade which had
once sustained it was now no more than a ghostly procession up Quaker Hill Road
but Hart heard the poetry of time in its echoing corridors and loved its sweeping
views of the Harlem Valley and the white church spires of Pawling. All around
there was a usable past, a sense of the present instinct with history, and numerous
details from Tory Hill would later be evoked in 'Quaker Hill', *The Bridge*'s elegy
for America the Promised Land, and for the lost homes and lost love of poets.

He was back in New York for good by the second week of October and his tranquillity, and the sobriety it had made possible, died in Manhattan's mauve twilights.
When Hart wrote to Brown several days after returning to the city to find work it
was with the news that a recent night out with some friends from Woodstock had
'nearly killed me' owing to excesses of applejack.[61] Once again Sam Loveman was
entertaining Howard Lovecraft and when Hart turned up the latter was distressed
by the newest symptoms of self-destruction. Although the visitor was 'only about
¼ "lit up" by his beloved booze' he still presented a melancholy spectacle: 'A real
poet and a man of taste, descendant of an ancient Connecticut family and a gentleman to his fingertips, but the slave of dissipated habits which will soon ruin both
his constitution and his still striking handsomeness!'[62] Perhaps the writer of horror
stories would have been appeased if he had known that at least Hart was using
intoxication as a subject for his poetry. By 21 October he had finished 'The Wine
Menagerie', a poem – like 'Passage' – inspired by the excesses of the Fourth of July
weekend, and one which Hart had struggled to perfect during the interceding
weeks in Ohio and Tory Hill. Bert Ginther, his friend in Cleveland, remembered
that when Hart visited him in August the painted corridor of his apartment building, plaster disguised as marble, rang with Hart's derisive diagnosis of the simu-
lation: 'Painted emulsion of snow, eggs, yarn, coal, SHIT.'[63] When the poet
incorporated the line in 'The Wine Menagerie', the last word was changed to
'manure' in Crane's evocation of the counterfeit wall of the speakeasy in which
eternally predatory woman is seen practising her counterfeit reflexes of entrapment:

> Against the imitation onyx wainscoting
> (Painted emulsion of snow, eggs, yarn, coal, manure)
> Regard the forceps of the smile that takes her.
> Percussive sweat is spreading to his hair. Mallets,
> Her eyes, unmake an instant of the world ...

'The Wine Menagerie' is a paradoxical poem, in some ways one of Crane's frank-
est, yet also one of his most intractable. Its dense and defiant involution of

metaphors has provoked much scholarly exegesis as well as critical frustration with the poet's apparent contempt for his readers' powers of comprehension – even though it might be argued that its intensely personal range of reference and the angry remoteness of its thinking mimed well the isolation into which alcoholism was gradually but ineluctably drawing him.

If this is the one major poem in which he addresses the subject of drink as his liberating force it is also the only work in which he suggests his distate for women as physical beings. Nobody who knew Hart Crane well thought of him as a misogynist: some of his closest friends, by the old token, were women – but the thought of women as sexual flesh and blood was apparently intensely distressing to him. This distress is inherent in the manifold implications of the 'forceps' which not only evoke the horrors of childbirth and the potential castration that awaits the engaged (and ensnared) male but suggest also the animal force, for predation and procreation, by which women are gripped. A couple are sitting in a speakeasy on a winter's day while a few tables away the poet spectates. 'When wine redeems the sight', as it is doing now, he finds 'A leopard ranging always in the brow' – Bacchus's pard, great feline of vitality, which enables him to assert his vision 'in the slumbering gaze'. But if at first drink spurs animation and curiosity it also distorts the sight, just as the 'glozening decanters', the treacherous bottles behind the bar, throw back the poet's twisted reflection. 'Conscripted to their shadows' glow', he surveys the scene and watches as the woman's flirtatious eyes 'unmake an instant of the world', thus transporting her admirer to reveries of imagined happiness. In no time one can almost hear the 'whispered carillon' of the wedding, final scene of his entrapment, and then picture the 'arrow into feathered skies' that will eventually produce some 'urchin' not perhaps dissimilar to the one who now enters the bar with 'a cannister' to have filled.

Everywhere the poet looks – 'Each chamber, transept, coins some squint' where the same ritual of seduction is enacted – the same entrapment, the same spurious romance conceals the same bestial needs: 'Between black tusks the roses shine!' But then intoxication sways the spectating cynic and he begins to feel himself drawn to 'New thresholds, new anatomies!' Perhaps he too will respond to some woman's 'receptive smile/Wherein new purities are snared'. But he is brought to his senses with the realization that the painful bite of reality – 'Ruddy, the tooth implicit of the world' – entails 'dominoes of love and bile', games of chance and deception which end in bitterness and betrayal: 'Though in the end you know/And count some dim inheritance of sand,/How much yet meets the treason of the snow.' The poem ends with mention of those trapped and undone by women – Holofernes, slain by Judith, and John the Baptist, executed at Salomé's insistence, with only Petrushka, the 'exile', surviving. There seems to be no hope or resolution available in the closing lines – and significantly although the poet talks of rising 'from the dates and crumbs' he never actually gets up and leaves the bar.[64]

On 20 October Hart accompanied Emil to see George Bernard Shaw's *Arms and the Man*, which Opffer was going to review for *Nordlyset*, and presumably at greater length than Hart, who found the play 'very amusing, if ancient'. Despite Slater Brown's enthusiasm, he had not so far been tempted to see Chaplin's new film, *The Gold Rush*: 'Broadway', he informed his 'Tories' at Robber Rocks, 'is, to me, a depressing promenade, and unless someone urges me thither I don't seem to trickle up there.'[65] The Tates had invited him to stand as a godfather to their daughter Nancy but when he saw the couple in New York he may still perhaps have been anxious that family dramas would make him 'but an insane godfather for any child to be doomed by'.[66] Whatever Tate's expectations of Hart as a godparent he continued to admire his work and informed Fugitive Donald Davidson that he was one of two major new poets then emerging: 'Laura [Riding] ... is destined to great fame before two years are out. She'll be the most famous of us all, and she deserves to be; she's the best of us all. There are two poets I'm betting on – Laura and Hart Crane; if I'm wrong about them I'm wrong about everything.'[67]

Tate's fellow Fugitive, Laura Riding Gottschalk, as she then was, had recently transferred her literary ambitions to New York following a divorce, and from the moment they were introduced she and Hart appeared to be well matched in exuberance and poetic conviction. She was, he informed the Browns, an 'engrossing female' and not long after they met Hart took 'Rideshalk-Godding', as he termed her, to Robber Rocks for the weekend.[68] As Susan recalled, they 'cascaded into and out of most of the households in our small literary community, Hart carrying with him a jug of hard cider, playing jazz records, dancing, shouting their literary opinions, picking up a driver here and there to chauffeur them to the next stop, leaving each household somewhat the worse for wear but with echoes of merriment in the air'.[69] There was a romantic idealism to the literary opinions they shared and promulgated. Hart, after all, was almost an incarnation of Riding's prescription for the new poets she felt her age needed: 'They will be egoists and romanticists all, but romantics with the courage of realism: they will put their hands upon the mysterious contour of life not to force meaning out of it ... but press meaning upon it, outstare the stony countenance of it, make it flush with their own contours.'[70] For a while the two poets shared enthusiasms, antipathies, money, even, it was briefly suspected, a romance – but if it was indeed true that Riding had undertaken to 'cure' her friend of his proclivities, or if the inseparable poets for a while encouraged speculations of an entanglement, Hart himself finally put an end to conjecture when he turned up drunk in a speakeasy after he and Riding had been noticeably absent from their usual Village haunts. Another regular, curious on behalf of the crowd, asked him, 'Well, did she succeed?' And Hart, with arms raised in benediction, replied: 'Boys, she failed.'[71]

Riding's friendship came as a lively consolation at a time of great circumstantial difficulty. As usual Hart was critically short of money and it was a keen disappointment to learn that he had missed getting a job as a deck yeoman with a South

American steamer, which would not only have solved his financial crisis but would have entitled him to a white uniform, brass buttons, the freedom of the ship, 'mess with officers or any first class passengers that seemed colloquial', he told Brown, and all for $75 a month.[72] He was thinking of trying to get some reviewing work at the *Dial* out of Marianne Moore, the 'Rt. Rev. Miss Mountjoy', as he now termed her, and Waldo had once again promised to approach Boni and Liveright about publishing *White Buildings*. At least now he would do so with a stronger hand: in August Eugene O'Neill had undertaken to write a tribute, as preface or endorsement, to accompany the volume and however shy of unknown poets the public might be the accolade of the mightiest dramatist on Broadway could only further sales. The O'Neills invited Hart to Brook Farm for the weekend early in November but when he indicated that he was unable to go Agnes O'Neill wrote back with assurances that 'Gene ... wishes to talk things over with you when he gets in town'. In the meantime, she added, unaware that Hart and Opffer were gradually surrendering romance for friendship, 'best wishes and send my regards to Emil'.[73]

Once Boni and Liveright heard of the dramatist's offer they 'practically agreed', Hart told William Sommer, to the publication of his first volume; now all that remained was to coax the diffident O'Neill into execution of his promise.[74] Hart wrote some notes to guide his friend, notes he headed his 'General Aims and Theories', and although the piece remained unpolished it encapsulated his poetics to date. He described, with regard to 'Faustus and Helen', his belief that correspondences between past and present could be illuminating and gave an account of his metaphorical usage in 'Voyages' II. These poems, clearly, he regarded as his principal achievements so far but he foreshadowed his next endeavour with observations about his Americanism: he was concerned, he said, with the future of his country,

> but not because I think that America has any so-called par value as a state or as a group of people. . . . It is only because I feel persuaded that here are destined to be discovered certain as yet undefined spiritual quantities, perhaps a new hierarchy of faith not to be developed so completely elsewhere. And in this process I like to feel myself as a potential factor.

But all poems, not just those which hoped to broker the myth of America, constituted a sort of covenant: 'It is as though a poem gave the reader as he left it a single, new *word*, never before spoken and impossible to actually enunciate, but self-evident as an active principle in the reader's consciousness henceforward.' Above all he sought to vindicate his poetry as the practice of the 'logic of metaphor' by which the contents of each line of verse were chosen 'less for their logical (literal) significance than for their associational meanings'. This linkage of ideas antedated 'our so-called pure logic' and was the foundation of all speech and consciousness. No doubt he exposed himself to criticism in defending his theories, particularly when they underlay poetry which he knew was often censured for obscurity, 'but as it is a part of a poet's business to risk not only criticism – but folly – in the conquest of consciousness I can only say that I attach no intrinsic value to what means I use beyond their practical service in giving form to the living stuff of the imagination.'[75]

Meanwhile Crane worked on another poem which he sent to Waldo Frank in pro-visional form on 26 October and continued to perfect until December: 'At Melville's Tomb', which explores the far boundaries of associative thought Crane's metaphoric technique entailed while at the same time conscripting a lyric gift at the height of its persuasiveness in the service of literary epitaph. One wonders, however, whose requiem one reads as the opening stanza's beautiful rhythms and anfractuous syntax evoke the rise and recession of the sea:

> Often beneath the wave, wide from this ledge
> The dice of drowned men's bones he saw bequeath
> An embassy. Their numbers as he watched,
> Beat on the dusty shore and were obscured.

'At Melville's Tomb' would be Crane's contribution to a literary endeavour then in full progress: the restoration of Herman Melville, who had died embittered and obscure, a customs inspector on the piers at Gansevoort Street, only eight years before Crane's birth, his heroism signalled by his determination to produce books the public no longer wanted, his humiliating neglect proclaimed by the second-hand book sellers who, as late as 1919, centenary of the writer's birth, were sell-ing first editions of *Moby Dick* for 50 cents. Even at the time of his death Melville's fall from fame as the popular romancer of South Sea adventures, to unconsulted status as a writer of baroque and symbolic fictions, was an accepted morality tale in the ways of fickle literary fortune and it was only when the first assaults on the Genteel Tradition of American literature were made that critical pioneers began to question his relegation. Among the earliest reassessors were Waldo Frank in *Our America* and D.H. Lawrence in *Classic American Literature*, with Lewis Mumford endorsing their enthusiasm a few years later in *The Golden Day*. A first biography, *Herman Melville: Mariner and Mystic*, by Raymond Weaver, appeared in 1921 and *Billy Budd*, the writer's last work, unfinished at his death, was rediscovered in 1924.

Hart read *Moby Dick* a total of four times but he also knew *Typee, Omoo, Mardi* – 'Better to sink in boundless deeps than float in vulgar shoals' – *Israel Potter, Piazza Tales* and Melville's poems. He knew Weaver's book, the subtitle of which he must surely have found appealing, and would have absorbed in the course of reading it the parallels between the novelist's life and his own: Melville too was displaced and nomadic, obsessed by his mother, an autodidact incapable of accommodating himself to the American financial system, an inveterate symbolist, a poet of the sea. Determined to serve the reclamation of a forgotten literary past Hart could equally well have written a poem about Edgar Allan Poe or Nathaniel Hawthorne – but neither writer offered the same scope for self-reflection. Yet the enigmatic 'he' who appears in the opening stanza of Crane's poem is not standing beside the novelist's tomb, situated, as recent history had established, in Woodlawn Cemetery in the Bronx; instead he looks seaward from the nameless strand in contemplation of the oceans from which Melville had returned to face a long life of earthbound failure. This then is not a literal homage; indeed only the lyric's title suggests the forgotten novelist's connection with a poem which appears, according to its second line, to be preoccupied with 'drowned men' – those tragic beings Eliot, rival poet and nay-sayer, had also invoked in the fourth section of *The Waste Land*. His elegy for Phlebas the Phoenician was clearly influenced by Ariel's song from *The Tempest*, Hart's favourite among Shakespeare's plays, and that song is audible now as Crane contemplates his Melville, who lies, it transpires, at the bottom of the sea, among the diced bones of other drowned men which are either buried for ever in the sea bed or cast ashore to be ground to sandy obscurity. Visible from the bottom of the sea are the phantom argosies of the second stanza, the wrecks of countless ships which now sail silently by, releasing as they do so scattered flotsam and livid jetsam:

And wrecks passed without sound of bells,
The calyx of death's bounty giving back
A scattered chapter, livid hieroglyph,
The portent wound in corridors of shells.

Death is bounteous in the release of this information – the vortex of each sinking ship's destruction becoming a cornucopia of suggestive remains – but it is information which nevertheless remains hieroglyphic, as unrevealing of the fate and purpose of the sea's victims, or indeed of oceanic nature itself, as are the shells which impart the sea's voice to the ear but not its words. But if the living are mystified, the shipwrecked of the third stanza, though they cannot pass us their wisdom, are not:

Then in the circuit calm of one vast coil,
Its lashings charmed and malice reconciled,
Frosted eyes there were that lifted altars;
And silent answers crept across the stars.

In a clear evocation of the closing lines of *Moby Dick*, where the *Pequod* sinks into the sea, Crane envisages the immediate aftermath of shipwreck, a moment of 'lashings charmed and malice reconciled', as the hour of revelation in which the solutions to life's eternal mysteries are finally conceded. The second stanza had insisted that no significance can ever be salvaged from the mysterious deaths that occur at sea but the third presents a qualification: death at sea is now held to entail not just epiphany but redemption. Blind though the dead sailors are, they understand the holiness of the passage they have endured and know that the explanation of the mysteries which drove them to embark in search of answers throughout life is now writ large in constellations of clarity. The last stanza returns us to Melville, the 'mariner' whose 'Monody' this poem appears to be. Beyond the reach of the cynics and philistines who dismissed his work while he was alive he now resides in peace beneath the waves, his ghost uniting all those who have been lost at sea – the sea of human ignorance and misunderstanding. Eternity is beyond crude mortal computation; and it is for eternity that the sea guards the genius of its laureates:

> Compass, quadrant and sextant contrive
> No farther tides ... High in the azure steeps
> Monody shall not wake the mariner.
> This fabulous shadow only the sea keeps.[76]

Shortly before beginning 'At Melville's Tomb' Hart had sent a gift to the Rychtariks – one of the two masks he had been given by Susan's first husband James Light as souvenirs of the latter's production of Coleridge's 'Rime of the Ancient Mariner' which Hart had seen in February 1924. The mask he had sent the Rychtariks was of an angel but its partner he decided to keep for display in his room. 'The effect', he assured his friends of the gift they would receive, 'is unearthly', as was no doubt the effect – and ultimate significance – of the mask he retained.[77] A trophy of the literature of the sea, it represented a drowned sailor and was in effect a death mask: henceforth, mutely and sightlessly, it would look down from the wall in supervision of Crane's perpetuation of that literature – and in prescience of his final submission to the seductiveness of its pleadings.

For all its beauty, 'At Melville's Tomb' had a difficult journey from completion to publication. Perhaps such a fate was appropriate to a lyric originally prompted by the injustice of literary neglect but it was galling nevertheless to discover how widely his poetic aims and achievements appeared to be misunderstood, not least by those who should know better. Cowley, Tate and Brown, already perplexed by Hart's sexual interest in sailors, had begun to voice doubts about certain tenets of his artistic creed while the editors of literary periodicals seemed to delight, not in encouragement or acceptance, but in the dispensing of pedantic chastisement. The women, Hart felt, were particularly blinkered and bookish: Marianne Moore was now a favourite object of ridicule and Harriet Monroe, editor of *Poetry*, seemed equally spinsterish and unimaginative. So when, the following year, after receiving 'At Melville's Tomb', Monroe wrote asking how he could justify his poem's 'succession of champion mixed metaphors', Hart was happy to reply at length – glad of the opportunity to present to the literal-minded his conviction, axiomatic among poets, that poetry was exempt from the laws of logic that governed unmeasured writing and that it was by definition always about something more than any prose paraphrase of its contents. Insisting that Crane's 'ideas and rhythms interest me', Monroe was forthright in her curiosity:

> Take me for a hard-boiled unimaginative unpoetic reader, and tell me how *dice* can *bequeath an embassy* (or anything else); and how a calyx (of *death's bounty* or anything else) can give back a *scattered chapter, livid hieroglyph*; and how, if it does, such a *portent* can be *wound in corridors* (of shells or anything else). And so on . . .[78]

Hart thanked her for 'the good nature and manifest interest' her query revealed but insisted that he was 'much more interested in certain theories of metaphor and technique involved generally in poetics' than he was in defending his own lyric achievement. As a poet he was, he said, no doubt 'more interested in the so-called illogical impingements of the connotations of words on the consciousness (and their combinations and interplay in metaphor on this basis)' than 'in the preservation of their logically rigid significations'. Perhaps this policy gave the impression that his technique of composition entailed nothing more than 'juggling words and images until I found something novel, or esoteric' but the process was 'much more predetermined and objectified than that'. Suggestiveness was a legitimate resource in the writer's range: poets lived by 'nuances of feeling and observation' and to attempt to deny them that authority was 'to limit the scope of the medium so considerably as to outlaw some of the richest genius of the past'. Seeking vindication in precedent he pursued his argument, gleeful at the thought of exposing his adversary's inconsistencies. Was Monroe deaf, for instance, to 'the relations between a drum and a street lamp – via the unmentioned throbbing of the heart and nerves in a distraught man which tacitly creates the reason and "logic"' of Eliot's 'Every street lamp that I pass/Beats like a fatalistic drum!' Poetry was a metaphorical practice and one, moreover, which had to be progressive in its attainments:

> If one can't count on some such bases in the reader now and then, I don't see how the poet has any chance to get beyond the simplest connections of emotion and thought, of sensation and lyrical sequence. If the poet is to be held completely to the already evolved and exploited sequences of imagery and logic – what field of added consciousness and increased perceptions (the actual province of poetry, if not lullabyes) can be expected when one has to relatively return to the alphabet every breath or so? In the minds of people who have sensitively read, seen and experienced a great deal, isn't there a terminology

something like short-hand as compared to usual description and dialectics, which the artist ought to be right in trusting as a reasonable connective agent toward fresh concepts, more inclusive evaluations?

Poetry had to build on its past achievement, as did science – and Hart concluded his reply by reminding Monroe that even the latter discipline now resorted to metaphor. What else underlay the new age of 'relativity', which sought to calculate the extent of the universe as a symbol of time? Why should poetry shy away from abstractions and measurements which were not strictly logical when the new physics deployed evaluations 'quite as metaphorical, so far as previous standards of scientific methods extended, as some of the axioms in Job'?[79]

About the time Hart began writing 'At Melville's Tomb' Grace caught the train south, armed with letters of introduction from Ohio banks and determined, despite the repeated objections of her son, to invest the proceeds of the Cleveland house sale not in a savings account or in the Villa Casas but in the property boom then under way in Florida. She sold her car, 'Diana', to a man who turned up in response to her advertisement just as she was about to leave and wept at the thought of abandoning her old mother, who would travel south later once Grace had established herself. In Miami, noisy five-year-old child of the boom, she installed herself at the Hotel Strand and surveyed in horror the thrusting transience of the new world into which her restlessness had led her, assuring Mrs Hart on 16 October that the town reminded her 'of nothing so much as just what hell might be'. She proposed to invest her money in any property corporation that would take her on as a saleswoman and was optimistic of riches and success, even though it should have been obvious that not all the sharks in Florida lurked offshore. There were 'men men men everywhere, young & old, & it has been my very good fortune to meet a number of very high type ones'. There was no harm in the introductions: some potentially lucrative encounter might well come as a result of the wining and dining that went on in the evening and 'if these men down here like you they will let you lead them around by the nose'. She was going to investigate business opportunities in Palm Beach, Fort Lauderdale and Boca Raton, was eager to meet some of the 'very prominent Cubans [who] are in Miami at the present time' and proposed at the end of October to travel to the Isle of Pines to inspect the Villa Casas.[80] Hart wrote to Grace on 24 October, urging his mother once again to devote her time and money to the latter property rather than to Miami – 'it isn't the place for people like us'.[81] The same day he wrote to his grandmother, who was about to travel to the town of Winter Haven, but as soon as the Florida-bound train departed Cleveland Mrs Hart realized she was too fragile to travel alone and although she reached her destination it was only to succumb to extremely painful bladder complications that rendered her a lonely and fretful burden on her host.

Before Grace could establish contact with her mother, and long before she could justify an expedition that was rapidly becoming a traumatic and expensive fiasco, she too fell ill and remained in Miami, confined to her room at the Hotel Strand and too weak to write to anyone, until early December when she and her mother were reunited in Cleveland. Supposing her to have gone to the Isle of Pines, Hart wrote to Grace there but when no reply was forthcoming he assumed she was angry with him for counselling against investment in Florida – a suspicion that made his worsening financial anxieties harder to bear. By the end of October he was in debt all round; on 4 November, with nowhere else to turn, desperate for financial assistance but not diplomatic in his desperation, he wrote to CA, pledging that *White Buildings* had been accepted for spring publication by Boni and Liveright and certain that he would be employed again 'within two weeks'. As it was, reluctant to borrow more money from friends, he wondered if his father would lend him a small sum against his next job? He knew CA considered him a 'forlorn picture of shiftless indigence and feeble will' but perhaps he might be interested to learn that three critics reckoned his forthcoming volume the equal in importance of any poetic work issued in America since Whitman's *Leaves of Grass*. Was his father incapable of rubbing 'some of the prejudice' from his eyes, not only in order to see his son more clearly but also to understand that there were realms of achievement beyond commerce? 'If I never wrote another line my reputation would last as long as that of any living banker, and I shouldn't think you would care to be put down in the eventual biography for posterity as the disgruntled, narrow minded commercialist who went about apologizing for his son's "failure".'[82]

Replying with hurt dignity, Clarence Crane acknowledged that he and his son were always likely to have divergent ideas 'of what constitutes a wonderful existence' but although he continued to subscribe to the old wisdom – that 'You cannot catch flies with vinegar' – he nevertheless dispatched $50.[83] Hart replied with thanks and with an admission that following the sale of the house, and with his mother and grandmother beyond contact in Florida, he felt 'rather strange these days'. Once he got another job he would see matters less anxiously but at the moment 'I realize how few we are and what a pity it is that we don't mean a little more to each other.'[84] CA concurred, writing back: 'Families while broken up and discarded really do mean something to us after you grow old and feel the coldness of the outside world.' He wished his son well but continued to believe writing should be an avocation not a vocation. As for Hart being the greatest poet since Whitman, 'the greatest in your class since 1852, I can hardly see it that way, but probably I am not informed'.[85]

CA was forthright: money mattered, and if he pressed the point now more insistently than at any time since Hart had left Cleveland it was perhaps because he detected a vulnerability hitherto absent from his son's opinions. Hart too was edging towards reappraisal. Only three months previously he had told Waldo that

Cleveland would eventually become for him 'more a myth of remembrance than a reality, excepting that my "myth" of a father will still make chocolates here'.[86] Now, glad that his father had proved more substantial than myth, he saw that he had not only been constant geographically but financially – unlike Grace, one day flirting in Florida, the next vanished, for all he knew, on a course of tropical pleasure, her house sold, her money squandered, her mother abandoned, her husband-to-be in limbo.

Once again Hart repaid his debts and once again he was almost penniless, with no job and absolutely no idea where or how he was going to further the great task that lay ahead – completion of *The Bridge*. A few poems were circulating for publication, among them 'The Wine Menagerie', but if any magazine ever accepted them payment would obviously be slender. That poem, having been rejected by *Criterion*, was now awaiting a verdict at the *Dial*, but when Marianne Moore finally announced on 10 November that she wanted to publish it her terms were distressing: even though 'it is so much our wish not to distort or to interfere with an author's concept' she proposed drastic cutting of the work and a new title, 'Again'.[87] The thought of the surgery must have been agonizing but hunger dictated pragmatism and having worked so hard to perfect the poem Hart replied by return of post to signal acquiescence, declaring that 'inasmuch as I admire the sensibility and skill of your rearrangement of the poem I shall be glad to have it so printed in The Dial'.[88] He sent a catalogue of grievances to the Rychtariks on 1 December, mentioning that the 'nervous strain' of life at the moment had 'about floored me' and explaining that Moore had cut the poem beyond recognition and that he would 'never have consented to such an outrageous joke if I had not so desperately needed the twenty dollars'.[89] Then panic and artistic pride set in. How could he let such a crucial confession of drinking and desire be edited and reduced to something called 'Again'? In despair he turned to Matthew Josephson, who remembered Hart sobbing on his bed about the dilemma. As Josephson knew, 'most of [Hart's] friends could not afford to perform for him the full services of a psychiatrist which he required at intervals' but he took pity on the weeping figure and offered to retrieve the poem from the *Dial* for the original $20.[90] His efforts came to nothing, however – 'Again' appeared in the magazine in May 1926, when Kenneth Burke famously remarked that Moore had only succeeded in extracting all the wine from Hart's menagerie. Worse was to come; by the end of the year Hart's plight was so acute that even his newest poem had to be offered for sacrifice: 'At Melville's Tomb', complete with apologetic covering note, was submitted to Moore, 'at the risk of taxing your patience', on 30 November.[91]

Bracing himself for the next set of proposed excisions Hart may have wondered if he would ever again complete a poem that was not doomed to butchery – but bridges were not constructed for subsequent division and songs of American destiny could not fall beneath the sway of the myopic schoolmistresses who marked and corrected the nation's literary magazines. His bridge had to be built and now that the time had come to raise its span his need for sure financial foundations became unarguable. With no obvious alternative solutions, besides getting the job he seemed unable to secure, he would act on a wild suggestion recently made by Waldo Frank – and apply for the patronage of a rich man. On 2 December he telephoned Mr Sharpp, the business secretary of Otto Kahn, and when Sharpp suggested he send a letter instead Hart wrote to the banker and philanthropist the next day wondering if he was 'sufficiently interested in the creation of an indigenous American poetry' to lend him $1,000 'at any rate of interest within six per cent', with the $5,000 held in trust from his grandfather's estate standing as security, and promising that in the event of assistance he would retire to the country for a year of cheap living and work on *The Bridge*, which would represent 'a new cultural synthesis of values in terms of our America'.[92] On 5 December Kahn's private secretary, Mr Mutke, offered an appointment on either 7 December at 3.30 at the financier's office in Wall Street or between four and five o'clock 'tomorrow, Sunday', at Kahn's home, 1100 Fifth Avenue.[93] As Hart had recently told CA, his shoes leaked, his pockets were empty and for six weeks he had tramped the streets, 'being questioned, smelled and refused in various offices'.[94] This was not the time to delay, so on Sunday, 6 December he made one of his rare expeditions up Fifth Avenue, remote in more ways than one from Brooklyn and Greenwich Village, stopping at 91st Street outside one of the last palaces to be constructed along these marble miles, a gold stone replica not a decade old of a Renaissance *palazzo*, complete with *porte-cochère*, which was the scene of one of the most important encounters of his life.

Rigid in bearing and anachronistic in appearance, Otto Kahn may at first have seemed an improbable saviour of any kind of modern poetry, let alone American: German military service had stiffened his posture and Savile Row tailoring, a declaration of long-standing Anglophilia, was responsible for the unyielding and Edwardian formality of his clothes. With his spats, his cane, his starched rounded collars and Homburg hats he was familiar both to the residents of Carnegie Hill, where his dachshunds took the air, and to the commuters who saw him spend his morning nickel to travel to work by subway, a rose forever in his buttonhole. His destination was a twenty-two-storey building on Wall Street, headquarters of the investment bankers Kuhn, Loeb and Company, where he worked, as he was fond of remarking, in the service of a profession 'which is outrageously overpaid'.[95] He had another favourite maxim – 'I must atone for my wealth' – and philanthropy was his chosen means: by the time Hart met him he had received orders in recognition of his generosity from France, Italy, Belgium and Spain, indeed was thought to have been more decorated than any other American citizen, so great had been the extent and the ardour of his penance.

It was the munificence of enlightened cultural patronage which had characterized the liberal German-Jewish upbringing begun when Kahn was born in

Mannheim in 1867 to a family of Rhenish Jews who made a fortune in feather beds before moving into banking. As a boy Kahn proved an accomplished musician; in his adolescence he wrote blank verse dramas. Military service in the Mainz Hussars rendered him hostile to militarism; translation to England, where he worked in the London office of Deutsche Bank, transformed him into an Anglophile, a Savile Row dandy and a British subject. Both of his aunts had married Englishmen and maintained salons in the capital: by the time Kahn moved to America in 1893 he admired Pater and Carlyle, was acquainted with H.G. Wells, Henry Irving, Harley Granville-Barker and Herbert Beerbohm-Tree and was a close friend of the poet Richard Le Gallienne.

In New York he married the daughter of a partner at Kuhn, Loeb, an investment bank synonymous with railroad financing, and astonished Wall Street when, aged thirty and on Kuhn, Loeb's behalf, he restored the bankrupt Union Pacific Railroad to solvency and efficiency. He became the acknowledged authority on railroad management and investment and amassed a vast fortune through this expertise – by 1910, when he bought a Franz Hals for $500,000, he was in a position to outbid J.P. Morgan himself and by the time Hart was first admitted to his limestone palace its walls were hung with works by Botticelli, Cranach, Mantegna, Clouet, Boucher, Giovanni Bellini, Carpaccio, Lorenzo Lotto, Rembrandt, Corot and Canaletto. More than art he loved music, especially opera, and as chairman of the board of directors he overhauled the bureaucracy of the Metropolitan Opera and devoted almost $5 million of his personal fortune to its prosperity – although owing to the anti-Semitism of the Social Register he was unable to secure his own box for many years.

Kahn was the friend of Caruso and the sponsor of Ravel, Milhaud, Prokofiev and Stravinsky. He brought Diaghilev and Nijinsky to New York and persuaded Pavlova to dance in America, as well as managing her money for years afterwards. He helped Isadora Duncan, Paul Robeson, the *Little Review* and the Provincetown Players. He knew actors and publishers, speakeasy proprietors and showgirls. He was the hope and support of dozens of aspiring musicians, the lifeblood of the New Playwrights' Theatre, a champion of black art, a friend to many of the Algonquin wits and a significant contributor to the restoration of the Parthenon. He supported Theodore Roosevelt and the principle of federal regulation of business and during the Great War he urged German Americans to renounce their native in favour of their adoptive culture. Kahn became an American citizen in 1917 and with the peace laboured tirelessly for American assistance in European reconstruction. He opposed the League of Nations and Prohibition but supported American commitment to the gold standard. He spoke English with a soft German accent and was gentle, punctual and polite. There was, it seemed, scarcely a limit to his enthusiasm and generosity: to Georges Clemenceau he was the greatest living American and when he died in 1934 an announcement was delayed until after closure of the day's business lest his death depress the Stock Exchange.

Generous and culturally sophisticated as Kahn was he nevertheless relied on various informants to help him assess the innumerable pleas for help he received. Waldo Frank was among the advisers and he remembered being summoned to lunch at Kuhn, Loeb for his opinion about Paul Robeson and about Hart Crane. The following year he wrote a profile of this Jazz Age Maecenas for the *New Yorker* and noted that Kahn's face 'reveals no struggle' and that 'replete with experience, he is a child at sixty'. Frank found the millionaire's great house pompous but definitely had Hart in mind when he observed that Kahn was nevertheless at his best at home, 'offering an hour (and a check for a year's leisure) to some humble poet'. There was no insincerity to the benevolence because 'in helping, he is receiving what he needs. He looks at his Italian Primitives, at the illuminated manuscripts and at the bibelots on his Gothic tables with an easier eye.'[96]

Distracted by such splendours and no doubt nervous too, Hart seems to have been inattentive to the minutiæ of the banker's reckoning and his incomprehensible talk of insurance policies – all he knew, he later told Underwood, was that Kahn's remarks of encouragement and appraisal 'made me feel like nothing so much as a race horse'.[97] No other account of the meeting survives, but its outcome was soon public: the financier pledged assistance, and it was with great relief that Hart went out that night to celebrate with Laura Riding, who had decided to move to England and had booked passage for 27 December. The evening she and Hart spent at Sam's speakeasy in the Village was a farewell of sorts, and although they would be reunited briefly three years later it was this encounter that Riding chose to remember as the significant valediction: 'The kind of devotion we felt to each other that night was the real good-bye between us, simple and affectionate and clear, and of a quality utterly alien to the dazed, jerky, gossipy Greenwich Village atmosphere in which it took place.'[98] Marianne Moore wrote on 10 December, accepting 'At Melville's Tomb' on condition that Hart agree to the excision of the fourth stanza. 'May we ask very seriously … that you decline to give the poem to The Dial if you are unable to make this concession with heartiness.'[99] Thanks to Kahn's support he could not comply, and it was a pleasure to withdraw the poem. On 16 December Jane Heap wrote offering to assist him with his difficulties but Hart wrote back the same day enclosing 'Passage' for her consideration and explaining the nature of his recent rescue and his plan to go to the country for a year to work on *The Bridge*: 'Thank God, for once in my life I'm being paid for doing exactly what I want to do.'[100]

In the midst of these developments contact was re-established with Grace, but on terms less adoring on Hart's side than at any time previously. When she broke her silence of almost six weeks to announce that she hoped to return from Miami to Cleveland for Christmas he indicated frostily that he would not be joining her there: he had other plans and new opinions to go with them. He had gone through 'a good many realizations of various sorts – during the last six months', with Grace clearly involved in the reappraisal, and following her long silence in

Florida 'it was a shock for me to realize that you needed me so little'.[101] By the time he wrote to her, from the Hotel Saint George in Brooklyn, he was already in transit, preparing to move to a house that would become his closest approximation to a home for the next few years. In November, following the loss of his job at *Telling Tales*, Allen Tate had decided to retrench by moving upstate; he and Caroline rented a house half a mile from the Browns and invited Hart to join them. At the time, uncertain about developments in Florida and Cleveland and still committed to remaining in New York to find a job, Hart had hesitated. Now, however, it was the obvious course to take: rural winter isolation would give him the peace he needed to write but not the opportunity to squander Kahn's money, and the Tates sounded as though they would be happy to accommodate him until he could build for himself on the land acquired from Bina Flynn. So – once again discharging all debts except the largest, the money he owed to the Rychtariks – he accepted the offer and it was agreed that he should arrive on the last Saturday before Christmas. Tate wrote to say that he and Slater Brown would try to collect him from the station but if they were unable to drive to Patterson would Hart mind buying a few provisions – a broom, a pound of raisins, carrots, turnips and two pounds of dried apples – before finding his own way home? 'The upstairs room is ready for you,' he added, 'the finest room in the house, albeit not the warmest.'[102] Henceforth Hart would expect correspondence here: c/o Mrs Addie Turner, Patterson, New York, an address that held good for most of the remaining years of his life.

12

The Tates were very poor, even by the impecunious standards of their circle: although Caroline was working on her second novel, Allen was the principal breadwinner and his earnings, derived largely from book reviewing, seldom exceeded $40 a month. The Browns, eager for companionable neighbours, proclaimed the cheapness of the land and the abandoned farmhouses around Tory Hill and persuaded several friends to buy nearby properties – but not the Tates: 'We couldn't buy an extra Woolworth dinner plate,' Caroline lamented and even baby Nancy Tate was sent to live with her grandmother rather than endure the rigours of the literary life.[1] When economics finally drove them to the country, however, it was to the Browns' locality that their thoughts inevitably guided them, if not as prospective owners then as tenants, and by the time Hart caught the train to join them the week before Christmas they were settled in what Malcolm Cowley called 'a barnlike house half a mile from the Browns' cottage by a path that wound through abandoned fields'.[2]

Bleak though these conditions sounded they were mitigated by amenities the neighbours at Robber Rocks could only envy: an indoor pump next to the kitchen, a telephone within a mile's walk and a mailbox outside the door – and all included in the $10 it had been agreed they would pay each month for eight partly furnished rooms. The house had formerly been a dormitory for a nearby boys' school and was still divided into what its owner, Mrs Turner, called 'parts' which were inhabited by herself, her Aunt Julia and her various tenants. The aunt was eighty and deaf; she was garrulous in conversation with God and her confidences reverberated throughout the house, but she never spoke to strangers and history credits her with only one remark addressed to mortal ears: *'Great Expectations* – I've read that book twenty times and I still don't like it.'[3] Addie Turner herself was sixty, 'a character', in Tate's opinion, 'a New England farm woman and extraordinarily stupid but motherly and kind'.[4] Cowley remembered her 'whining voice and a moderately kind heart' while the novelist Nathan Asch, a subsequent tenant, recalled her 'intense black hair' and her incessant calls for her cat, Tiger.[5] She was often termed a widow but the reality was darker: eccentric as the household was it was not eccentric enough for her husband, 'Blind Jim', who wore bead neck-laces in the local asylum and – believing himself to be a girl – played the coquette with a fan.

Hart arrived burdened not only with the groceries Tate had requested but with rarer spoils – delicacies for the table, quantities of liquor and a new and much-remarked pair of snow-shoes bought for survival in any forthcoming inclemencies. Otto Kahn had already supplied $1,000 – with the same amount again eventually forthcoming – so it was no surprise to the Browns that Hart appeared in 'tremen-dously high spirits' which entailed expansive projections of achievement for the forthcoming year.[6] He was allocated his own 'part', which comprised three large rooms on the second floor above the Tates' quarters, and shown the pump room available to all members of the household and the adjacent kitchen dominated by a large wood-range for heating and cooking where it was envisaged he and the Tates would eat. He decided to use only two of his rooms: the largest became his study, in which, he told the Rychtariks, 'the sun streams every morning', while the room containing 'a fine old "sleigh bed"' would serve for sleep. He brought his small drop-leaf desk from Robber Rocks and arranged his treasures lovingly around the walls: daguerreotypes of Mrs Hart and a shawl she had knitted for him, as well as 'pictures and knick-knacks' which he told the Rychtariks 'look won-derfully jolly on the simple kalsomined walls and the books fairly glisten on the shelves'.[7]

One of the first letters to reach this new address came from CA. Only two weeks previously Hart had ended his last correspondence to his father with a plea – 'let's not argue any more' – and now the elder Crane conveyed assent.[8] He had carried his son's letter with him when business disappointments took him to Detroit and Chicago – embezzlement of company profits in the former and poor sales in the latter – and replied with 'fondest hopes that you will accomplish what you are striving for' as well as pledges of financial assistance and the promise of seasonal confectionery in the mail.[9] Hart wrote back on Christmas Day after a long walk in the hills. He had helped Caroline prepare cranberry and plum pud-ding sauces and now, from his second-floor study, surveying a valley 'white with the moonlight on the snow', he felt great contentment. He thanked CA for Christmas money and chocolates and also for the flowers he had sent Mrs Hart. He was looking forward to getting to work but in the meantime he and the Tates were laying down provisions against cold and snow. 'But once fixed, we'll be as independent as the proverbial pig on ice.'[10]

That same day he acknowledged a Christmas card from Wilbur Underwood and said how sorry he was that they had missed each other during the course of his friend's recent stay in New York. Hart doubted, however, that his companionship would have enhanced the Washingtonian's visit since he had been 'on the edge of a serious sort of breakup' before Kahn's assistance. For the next month he planned to 'vegetate, walk and read' and already he felt 'terribly old' and would be 'a perfect "white head" by thirty'. What a relief it had been to escape 'the rasping metropolis for awhile' – but even here its harshness could prove unsettling. He had taken up Whitman again: 'Specimen Days' had convinced him that 'no other American has left us so great a heritage' yet to realize 'how he is regarded in some quarters still seems incredible'. Only two days previously the *Nation* had published an editorial, occasioned by an exhibition of Whitman's writings at New York Public Library, that offered a reminder of how vulnerable even the glorious dead were to the strictures of a philistine and bigoted society. The infamous Ernest Boyd had recently charged Whitman with debauching the morals of a literary generation and now the *Americana Collector* had published an open letter to the library stating that the author of 'Calamus' was 'abnormal' and commending the determination of librarians in the great Eastern colleges to deter students from reading him.[11] Literature was a preoccupation of the country festivities: the Cowleys had come for the holidays and were staying in rooms adjacent to Hart's and the Josephsons were at Robber Rocks, where a large party was given one evening for all the friends around Tory Hill. Susan remembered snow blowing through the broken panes of the large room where the guests gathered and where Hart, at Cowley's suggestion, read aloud 'Voyages' II in his distinctive fashion: he always 'forgot himself' when he read his own poems and 'put himself into it' with his 'vigorous, strong voice'.[12] The poem had originally ended with the line 'The seal's findrinny gaze toward paradise' but when complaints had been voiced that the exotic adjective existed nowhere in any dictionary Hart had paused, always determined that his vocabulary should be lexically regular, however unconventionally deployed, before deciding on a substitution. Now the lyric invoked 'The seal's wide spindrift gaze' – and after completing his reading he invited opinions from the guests. Some found the original word more suggestive and rhetorically satisfying; others felt that its dubious standing necessitated deletion and in the end, though sure the term was not his own invention, Hart agreed. Only later did Slater Brown establish Hart's likely source as Melville – but by then the later version had become orthodox.

Another subject much discussed that Christmas was Oswald Spengler's recently published *The Decline of the West*. Hart would not read this controversial work until it began to appear in translation in 1926, and thus knew little of its contention, so fascinating to the rest of the group, that all cultures pass through cycles of growth and decay and that Western Europe, entering its terminal phase, would now embark on a period of technological and political expansion to compensate for its cultural decadence. Yet if he was behind in his required reading, if he was drunk, penniless, half-orphaned, a sort of ward of his friends, he was also emerging as the cynosure of the group, whose achievements were implicitly recognized as something to record, just as the evolution of his poems was seen as historically significant. When Malcolm Cowley returned to New York it was about Hart, rather than anyone else, that he chose to write a poem, 'The Flower in the Sea', a tribute its subject commended as 'flatteringly apocalyptic' when he wrote a letter of acknowledgement on 3 January 1926. He was 'just beginning to get down to work' on his own literary labours, he promised, now that he and the Tates had completed the laying in of supplies: they had prepared themselves as though for a veritable siege, 'though there may be the mildest of days ahead'.[13]

Storms as bitter as any that ever blighted the Connecticut hills lay in the future – to rage inside as well as out – but in the tranquillity that followed Christmas among his family of friends Crane surrendered himself to the nostalgia and introspection that always overcame him in the country and the resulting contemplations were committed to a poem begun now and completed in April, 'Repose of Rivers', last written of the lyrics which eventually appeared in *White Buildings.* Slater Brown recalled that it was a work deliberately written to please Marianne Moore – 'she always liked to have a lot of animals about her in poetry' – so when Crane came to evoke the mystery of memory and to project his escape from miserable past experience in private fantasies and oceanic freedom, he incorporated beavers and turtles for her pleasure to produce one of his loveliest and most elusive lyrics.[14] 'Repose of Rivers' has the aspect of a reverie, its sinuous recollections extending no further than the subtlest half-rhymes, its associations yielding one to another only elliptically, its structure finding an almost incantatory coherence in a prevalence of sibilants which evoke silence, the sleep of dreams and the susurrus of the waves by which he was haunted:

> The willows carried a slow sound,
> A sarabande the wind mowed on the mead.
> I could never remember
> That seething, steady leveling of the marshes
> Till age had brought me to the sea.

Breezes causing the branches near Mrs Turner's house to creek and moan carried strange associations of other trees, those which had towered above his childhood, and the wind which blew towards Patterson awoke its memories, whether set against the meads of rural Ohio or the tropical marshes he had passed on his first journey to the Isle of Pines. The sea which waits at the threshold of memory is not only the literal sea but the sea of experience – yet rather than cast himself upon its heaving waters the poet retraces his steps, back through memories which this time, forming the substance of the second stanza, are cruel and hellish: 'And remembrance of steep alcoves/Where cypresses shared the noon's/Tyranny; they drew me into hades almost.' How much, the third stanza tells us, he would have 'bartered' in order to learn the meaning of 'all the singular nestings in the hills', all the temporary lodgings in time when he thought himself settled only to move on again, and all the mysterious traumas he had undergone – 'The pond I entered once and quickly fled'. The fourth stanza, influenced by his recent reading of Whitman, and in particular by the latter's 'Once I Pass'd Through a Populous City', conjures 'that memory all things nurse' as the poet's reverie once again draws him towards the Caribbean. Having survived life in the polluted and licentious city he finds himself where 'The monsoon cut across the delta/At gulf gates': New Orleans, gateway to tropical America. And there, as though he can experience and imagine nothing more, he ends his poem, 'beyond the dykes', where no sound is audible apart from the sigh of the winds which range the endless and enticing waves – that 'wind flaking sapphire' that holds assurance of absolute peace: 'And willows could not hold more steady sound.' It is as though he has attained the wordless ecstasy beyond poetry and beyond the poetry which is the purpose of his life there is the sea, once again confronting him as it had done at the resolution of 'At Melville's Tomb', a blue infinity at the end of every prospect.[15]

The beginning of January proved very cold and even as he dreamed of Caribbean seas Hart informed the Rychtariks that he dressed each morning in 'boots, woollens and furs'. He had two oil stoves in his room, however, and he longed to use the snow-shoes he had bought before leaving New York, 'and so I pray for heavy storms'. Since the stoves downstairs consumed wood rather than oil there was always plenty of chopping to be done by those who could get warm no other way and the chores had already been allocated – at least to Hart's satisfaction: Caroline prepared lunch and dinner, Allen made the breakfast and 'all I have to do is wash dishes'.[16] The Tates themselves may have wondered when this arrangement had been agreed but for the time being they were happy enough with Hart's companionship, although their enthusiasm already fell short of Mrs Turner's. Addie 'worshipped' him, Caroline noticed, and she and her favourite tenant took to gossiping in the kitchen while she peeled potatoes. She listened sympathetically to the sad story of a 50-gallon drum of bad kerosene Hart had bought; she mothered him and became his confidante; she cleaned for him; she blushed and simpered girlishly when he took her round the waist and waltzed to the accompaniment of the phonograph; and when the Tates complained discreetly that Hart was not doing his fair share of domestic chores she was expressive in her loyalty: 'Well, Mr Crane is so sensitive and nervous he don't do those sort of things.'[17]

At first, however, these grievances remained insignificant and a routine developed: Hart spent the mornings in his room reading or writing letters and at lunchtime he would eat with the Tates. The afternoons were spent in a little further reading and writing and then a walk, and in the evenings he usually went to Robber Rocks. A pattern was also emerging in his drinking, as Tate recalled: he tended to get 'a little drunk' every night on the bootleg rum or whiskey which were the country's most readily available intoxicants and 'he liked rum particularly'. Hard cider was something to be avoided, however: it was 'very bad for him' because 'he would get very drunk on it, and be ill afterwards'.[18] The weekends tended to be more dissolute because there were usually guests from New York but on the whole 'it was rather a quiet time' as Mrs Turner's resident writers settled to their labours: Caroline to her novel; her husband to his reviewing for the *Nation,* the *New Republic*, the *Herald-Tribune* and the *New York World*, and to the composition of what became one of his most important poems, 'Ode to the Confederate Dead'; and Hart himself to the resumption of *The Bridge*, the closing section of which he had brought with him in provisional form from New York.

'Atlantis', as this final section was eventually called, was the earliest part of Crane's great epic to be conceived, although few of the lines written in the early months of the poem's infancy in 1923 survived in the peroration as it was published in 1930. The section's protracted composition and peculiar history – Crane built his bridge backwards by starting with its climax – go some way towards explaining its language, itself a structure of grandiose metaphor which signals the heroism of any doomed quest for lost or fabled cities besides generating a kind of euphemistic haze around the ultimate bridging Crane conceived, a bridging with another man which is the unspoken and unspeakable impulse behind much of his most ecstatic poetry. Although 'Atlantis' was substantially complete by the summer of 1926 it contains echoes of poetry and correspondence written two years previously at the height of his passion for Emil – notably elements of 'Voyages' and the letter he wrote to Frank about 'walking hand in hand across the most beautiful bridge in the world', a letter which seems to be almost a prose rendition of 'Atlantis' as it now begins, with the poet about to walk from Manhattan at night across Brooklyn Bridge:[19]

> Through the bound cable strands, the arching path
> Upward, veering with light, the flight of strings, –
> Taut miles of shuttling moonlight syncopate
> The whispered rush, telepathy of wires.
> Up the index of night, granite and steel –
> Transparent meshes – fleckless the gleaming staves –
> Sibylline voices flicker, waveringly stream
> As though a god were issue of the strings . . .

As he surveyed the winter landscape around Mrs Turner's, Emil and that passion seemed distant things and certainly inadequate as inspirations for the work in hand. But then 'Atlantis' was not a love poem: its purpose was to resolve and vindicate in a rhapsodic paean all the forms of bridging – between times, cultures and people – he would endeavour in his forthcoming vision. *The Bridge* when achieved would be a kind of metaphor for art itself – since every work of art marked a union between imagination and creation – and it remained a national epic in his mind because America herself was born of a fusion of European imagination and enterprise which made her singular among nations. Brooklyn Bridge, where he and Emil had so often walked, had been the conduit and the setting of the most important union in his life but it was also the first of the spans erected to link Manhattan to the rest of New York, greatest of the cities which greeted trans-atlantic voyagers. It was the means by which he and Emil had joined each other across the East River but it was also a pathway to the citadel of white buildings which shimmered across the water: 'Atlantis' begins with footsteps on a real bridge but in the second stanza that bridge has become transformed into an edifice entirely metaphorical:

> And through that cordage, threading with its call
> One arc synoptic of all tides below –
> Their labyrinthine mouths of history
> Pouring reply as though all ships at sea
> Complighted in one vibrant breath made cry, –
> 'Make thy love sure – to weave whose song we ply!'
> – From black embankments, moveless soundings hailed,
> So seven oceans answer from their dream.

Beginning work again in earnest on 4 January was not easy, as he explained to Mrs Hart the following day: 'From now on I hope to have the necessary inspiration to keep steadily at it. One really has to keep one's self in such a keyed-up mood for the thing that no predictions can be made ahead as to whether one is going to have the wit to work on it steadily or not.'[20] It was as though composition had become an act of will or auto-intoxication, a sedentary equivalent of tightrope walking in which all resources were focused on the far horizon to the exclusion of the chasms beneath. By faith he would cross the void between history and myth, between present and future, between experience and illumination, to reach his final Atlantis and to do so, he informed Frank a few weeks later, he needed a 'sym-phonic' manner that would liberate his 'condensed metaphorical habit' and enable him to 'induce the same feelings of elation, etc. – like being carried forward and upward simultaneously – both in imagery, rhythm and repetition, that one experi-ences in walking across my beloved Brooklyn Bridge'. The resulting eight-line stanzas of blank verse test their verbal construction to the utmost as they attempt what Crane told Frank was 'the convergence of all the strands separately detailed in antecedent sections of the poem' in order to make the bridge become 'a ship, a world, a woman, a tremendous harp'.[21] The first stanza, with its suggestion that 'a god were issue of the strings' prepares us for the celestial music of the third stanza, a music which commands the 'crystal-flooded aisle' of the great church that is the world before extending into space itself, 'The loft of vision, palladium helm of stars'. This music is ecstasy, and ecstasy outpaces time – 'Tomorrows into yester-year' – besides being the reward of all true visionaries, whether Crane or Jason and his argonauts, 'splintered in the straits'. The bridge becomes an epiphany, 'Tall Vision-of-the-Voyage', which can lift 'night to cycloramic crest/Of deepest day'. Its suspending strings comprise a 'Choir, translating time/Into what multitudinous Verb the suns/And synergy of waters ever fuse'. The visionary can now hear the great word of creation and that word is Love – 'Psalm of Cathay!/ O Love, thy white, pervasive Paradigm...!' The bridge is thus a 'steeled Cognizance', a way of comprehending divine purpose: it is a symbol of American cohesion but also a pledge of forgiveness of America's bloody history:

> Unspeakable Thou Bridge to Thee, O Love.
> Thy pardon for this history, whitest Flower,
> O Answerer of all, – Anemone, –
> Now while thy petals spend the suns about us, hold –
> (O Thou whose radiance doth inherit me)
> Atlantis, – hold thy floating singer late!
>
> So to thine Everpresence, beyond time,
> Like spears ensanguined of one tolling star
> That bleeds infinity – the orphic strings,
> Sidereal phalanxes, leap and converge:
> – One Song, one Bridge of Fire!...

It is a rhapsodic hymn – and if 'Atlantis' ends with a question it is a question expressing the disbelief of the visionary once the splendour of the vision has disappeared. The more glorious the visitation the greater the scepticism will be – but mortal doubt should never invalidate mortal scope for discovery and dream:

> Is it Cathay,
> Now pity steeps the grass and rainbows ring
> The serpent with the eagle in the leaves...?
> Whispers antiphonal in azure swing.[22]

Conditions for the composition of these raptures were not ideal. After Christmas Mrs Hart succumbed to severe gastric sickness; in the ensuing weeks she suffered great pain on scant sustenance and when Grace was not exhausted with nursing she was distracted with worry about the cost of the attendant medical care. There was nothing Hart could do but hope and wait and attempt to write. He sent reports of progress on 'Atlantis' to Cleveland – 'I've been at work in almost ecstatic mood for the last two days ... I never felt such range and symphonic power before' – as though the maintenance of normal correspondence might restore normality but in the second week of January his grandmother's condition remained acute.[23]

1. The young Harold Hart Crane. 'I'm going to be a poet.'

2. Hart's mother, Grace Crane, whose beauty was widely remarked.

3. Hart's father, Clarence Crane, a large and ambitious man whose solid frame belied an anxious disposition.

4. A shy and awkward romantic, Hart (*seated, front row left*) was already committing his aspirations to poetry when this Crane family group was taken, probably in 1915. His father is at the top of the picture and his mother is seated to the right in the middle row. Also present are Hart's grandfather Arthur Crane (*standing, second from left*), his great uncle Fred Crane (*standing, third from left*) and his grandmother Ella Crane (seated in the back row, second from right). In the foreground Byron Madden holds his daughter Betty while his wife, Bess Madden, looks on.

5. A postcard advertising the company which in its heyday ramified over several states and made a seven-figure fortune for Clarence Crane.

6. 1709 East 115th Street, Cleveland, Hart's home and surest sanctuary between 1908 and 1925. He has marked The Sanctum de la Tour which was the scene of his earliest poetic endeavour.

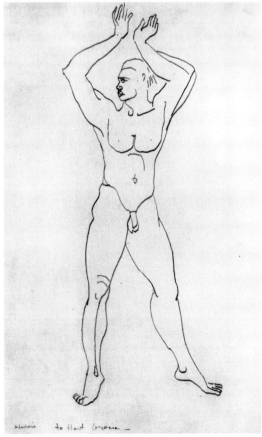

7. Hart met the sculptor Gaston Lachaise in 1923. He soon became his 'worshipful friend' and agreed to pose nude for this drawing during Christmas of that year.

8. Waldo Frank, Hart's most revered mentor. Shortly after their first meeting Hart wrote: 'I have not wavered in an enthusiastic conviction that yours is the most vital consciousness in America.'

9. Otto Kahn was ranked among the world's richest men when he became Hart's benefactor in 1925. A peripatetic and internationally famous philanthropist, he was honoured by the governments of France, Italy, Belgium and Spain.

10. After a hesitant beginning, Malcolm Cowley became one of Hart's closest friends, as well as one of America's most esteemed men of letters. He is shown here at his desk at the *New Republic* in the early 1930s.

11. Hart on the roof at 110 Columbia Heights, Brooklyn, where he moved in 1924. Behind him, and dominated by Brooklyn Bridge, is the vista which was his greatest inspiration. 'It is everything from mountains to the walls of Jerusalem and Nineveh.'

12. Emil Opffer on the same rooftop. Shortly after meeting him, Hart told Waldo Frank, 'For many days now, I have gone about quite dumb with something for which "happiness" must be too mild a term.'

13. Emil Opffer and (*left*) one of Hart's earlier – but platonic – passions, William Slater Brown.

14. William Slater Brown (*right*) faces Hart, while Allen Tate faces the camera, in a mock Wild West saloon in Times Square early in 1925.

15. Grace Crane in 1926 with her unsuspecting second husband, Charles Curtis. Hart was convinced his mother had remarried for all the wrong reasons.

16. A bathroom was being installed at Robber Rocks when Hart broke the unspoken rule and brought a sailor back to the country. Cheerfully improvising, Susan Slater Brown nevertheless did what she could to make 'Honey Boy' feel at home – or at sea.

17. Hart bizarrely dressed for his prodigious summer of 1926 on the Isle of Pines.

18. The weather was the hottest the islanders could remember and Hart would learn to his cost that hats were an essential accessory to Caribbean travel.

19. Hart's Parisian patrons Harry and Caresse Crosby encouraged completion of *The Bridge*. Prior to Crosby's suicide, which Hart hailed as 'imaginative, the act of a poet', they embodied the restless hedonism of the age.

20. One of the many distractions of Paris: Peter Christiansen, formerly of the Danish Royal Artillery, was Hart's lover in 1929.

21. Roy Campbell, photographed by Hart in the south of France in 1929. Hart's visit was not a success and Campbell complained that his guest 'could neither hold his drink nor control his abnormal "queer" nymphomania'.

22. The interior of Canary Cottage, Clarence Crane's last business enterprise and his son's last home in Ohio, was furnished with the elder Crane's collection of American antiques and served 'fine chicken dinners' in the village of Chagrin Falls.

23. With years of mutual incomprehension and intermittent strife behind them, Clarence Crane and his son pose happily together outside Canary Cottage in December 1930, shortly before Hart's departure for Mexico.

24. When Hart returned to Ohio in 1931 following his father's death he visited his cousin Helen Hurlbert in Warren. The picture she took on this occasion, with Hart holding a recently befriended kitten, recalled the promise made in 'Chaplinesque': 'For we can still love the world, who find/A famished kitten on the step'.

25. Hart and writer and bibliophile Sam Loveman, taken by Walker Evans in 1929. Though distrusted and often disliked by many of Hart's friends, Loveman proved a staunch support during Grace Crane's declining years.

26. David Siqueiros, photographed by Hart outside his house in Mexico. After commissioning his own portrait, Hart declared, 'The very soil of Mexico seems spread on his canvasses.'

27. Hart Crane, painted by David Siqueiros, 1931–2. Something in the poet's gaze was disturbing and Siqueiros rendered his sitter in almost devotional pose, with his eyes looking down at a book. In an ominous gesture, Hart destroyed the portrait in April 1932.

28. Hart's house at 15 Michoacán Norte in Mixcoac, on the outskirts of Mexico City. He was delighted, he relayed to friends in America, to be installed in 'my own home at last'.

29. Hart's principal servant Daniel Hernandez and his son outside the gates of 15 Michoacán. Hernandez had to go when he acquired a gun and then began to imitate his employer by returning home incapable with drink.

30. Dressed as a sailor from his beloved Marseilles, Hart poses in the garden of 15 Michoacán in the 'ancient silver pony bridle (bells and all!)' which William Spratling had helped him to acquire.

31. A tranquil moment in an otherwise notoriously tempestuous acquaintance: Hart with neighbouring writer and Guggenheim fellow Katherine Anne Porter in Mexico in 1931.

32. Hart and Peggy Cowley, the woman he proposed to marry, in Mexico in 1932, photographed at about the time he told her, 'I don't think that either one of us ought to urge the other into anything but the most spontaneous and mutually liberal arrangements.'

33. Peggy Cowley photographed by Hart in the Cathedral of Santa Prisca in Taxco at the time he was writing 'The Broken Tower'. 'Have you not heard, have you not seen that corps/Of shadows in the tower, whose shoulders sway/ Antiphonal carillons....?'

34. Still young and handsome but showing signs of dissipation: Hart in relaxed mood for the camera of Walker Evans, who remembered the poet's promise that his death, when it came, would be 'with a bang, by God'.

It was as much to take his mind off that crisis as to rest it from the labours of composition that he accepted a lift into New York on 10 January for five days of self-indulgence and city stimulus. He spent $100 in a Brooklyn antique shop on various tribal artefacts including a headdress, a ceremonial shield and spear and a libation cup, afterwards arranged in his room in a panoply vividly memorable to his friends, but the sums he disbursed in the sailor speakeasies are unquantifiable. For some reason he now pursued his nocturnal pleasures incognito – and it could have been as 'Mike Drayton', avatar of one of the lesser Elizabethan dramatists, that he met Jack Fitzin, a sailor with whom he spent what he later told Underwood were two memorable nights in Brooklyn. New York seemed extremely polluted after Patterson, not least because of the soft coal its inhabitants were now burning, and it was a relief to be back in the country on 15 January. The news from Cleveland continued to be dispiriting, however, and even as Hart confided to Waldo that he lived in daily expectation of the summons to his grandmother's deathbed, Grace wrote with anxieties about money after her mother's death, when she feared that despite marriage to Charles Curtis she might again have to work.

Setting aside 'Atlantis' Hart turned once more to *The Bridge* for distraction, and to the other end of its lyrical arc, but where to begin the beginning of America, which had existed as a legend in the European imagination long before Europeans had imposed that legend on Indian reality? Pre-Columbian history seemed secondary to his poetic ambition yet Christopher Columbus himself, who discovered the Americas only by accident and never set foot in the modern United States, was not entirely satisfactory as a point of narrative departure. In search of guidance, Hart immersed himself in eclectic preparatory reading – in Alfred North Whitehead's *Science and the Modern World*; Marco Polo's *Travels*; Arthur Sturgis Hildebrand's *Magellan*; William H. Prescott's *History of the Reign of Ferdinand and Isabella*; the *Oresteia*; Frank's *Virgin Spain*; Melville's *White Jacket*; George Francis Dow's *Whale Ships and Whaling*; Lawrence's *The Plumed Serpent*; and the history and philosophy of Sir Francis Bacon. Columbus's *Journal*, with its descriptions of his transatlantic expeditions, was inevitably a part of this education – but it was when Hart read the navigator's account of his first exposure to the West Indies that he was repeatedly struck by an auspicious familiarity. As he told Mrs Hart, 'It has reminded me many times of the few weeks I spent on [the Isle of Pines] to hear him expatiate on the gorgeous palms, unexpected pines, balmy breezes, etc. which we associate with Cuba.'[24] There was something deeply pleasing in the idea of these shared exhilarations: perhaps, after all, his narrative should begin by evoking the traditional father of American discovery. And if, when Hart started to write, he could visualize 'The first palm chevron the first lighted hill' the grateful voyager had seen four-odd centuries before he could also believe in Columbus – as he believed in himself – as a maverick dreamer ridiculed by urban sceptics for his faith in a fantastic ambition: 'I thought of Genoa; and this truth, now proved,/That made me exile in her streets.... Then faith, not fear/Nigh surged me witless.' As his imagination worked, however, it fastened not on a European's first astonished glimpse of a 'new world', as Columbus himself called it – unlike Milton, he would not describe Paradise – but once again on the fearful mind, itinerant and alone upon the awesome expanses of the sea: 'Into thy steep savannahs, burning blue,/Utter to loneliness the sail is true.'

'Ave Maria', as this second section became, is again written in blank verse with occasional rhyme and besides constituting another meditation on oceanic voyaging it sees Crane at his most confidently Elizabethan as he recreates the speculations and prayers of Christopher Columbus when he returns to Spain believing, after his first sight of the Americas, that he has discovered Cathay:

> Be with me, Luis de San Angel, now –
> Witness before the tides can wrest away
> The word I bring, O you who reined my suit
> Into the Queen's great heart that doubtful day;
> For I have seen now what no perjured breath
> Of clown nor sage can riddle or gainsay ...

Columbus prays for deliverance for his ship from the storm that rages as he sails eastward – 'Yet lost, all, let this keel one instant yield!' The divine Word which is the New World will be lost if he and his men sink: 'For here between two worlds, another, harsh,/This third, of water, tests the word ...'. But Crane's Columbus has faith and affirmation and he is sure, his terror notwithstanding, that his belief will grant him safe passage: 'Some inmost sob, half-heard, dissuades the abyss,/Merges the wind in measure to the waves.' As he ponders the wealth which will accrue from the New World to the Old – 'Like pearls that whisper through the Doge's hands' – he prays nevertheless that the new and virgin land will not be raped but accorded 'thy God's, thy Virgin's charity!' Glimpsing flotsam and vegetation, 'The jellied weeds that drag the shore', Columbus knows his return to Spain is assured and he addresses words of awe, praise and thanksgiving to God, 'incognizable Word/Of Eden and the enchained Sepulchre'.

Columbus has relied upon a compass, 'A needle in the sight, suspended north', just as Crane believed in the technologies of his own day, but his conviction has been indispensable to the successful deployment of newly developed scientific instruments. The New World has been discovered, we gather, by technology allied to belief, which will in turn yield 'the far/Hushed gleaming fields and pendant seething wheat/Of knowledge' of the American future. Columbus has realized his destiny in this world-transforming discovery and he can conclude his words of praise and thanksgiving, and 'Ave Maria' itself, with an ecstatic assertion that the globe will never contain the restlessness of the mortal imagination: 'still one shore beyond desire!/The sea's green crying towers a-sway ...'[25]

After slight alleviation in the middle of the month, the end of January proved 'very, very cold': 'We all go about shivering most of the time,' Grace was informed and Hart's hands were so stiff from numbness and wood-cutting that his handwriting was distorted.[26] The Tate household braved the frozen journey to Robber Rocks for a festive banquet on 30 January – baked ham, turnips, squash, pickles, mashed potatoes, cider and plum pudding – and Hart related to Grace the next day that the intense cold seemed to have ended. But then the snows for which he had so flippantly prayed fell with splendour and when he wrote to Gaston Lachaise a few days later to say how much he envied him a calling which could at least keep him warm while he worked he bemoaned the fact that 'wiggling a pen or tapping a typewriter is hardly as conducive to good circulation or warmth while every breath one takes comes out like a steaming snort from a dragon!'[27] The snow was so deep that for six weeks Mrs Turner's house was, in Malcolm Cowley's words, 'as effectively isolated as a lighthouse on a Maine island'.[28] Hart and Caroline developed severe chilblains, everyone slept with toboggan capes on their beds, Hart wore his grandmother's shawl even as his bad kerosene refused to burn, the postman became a fond memory, skis or snow-shoes were required for the expedition to buy milk, butter and eggs at the Jennings farm – and three strong yet divergent personalities began to sense the claustrophobia which is the real penance of country life.

For the time being Hart pursued his idiosyncratic literary programme and endeavoured to work. On 20 February he complained to his Cleveland friend Charles Harris that he was 'a little bored with the ultimate privacy of a rural winter' and that he was pining for cabs and cocktails, but the absence of distraction was at least beneficial for writing.[29] On 2 March, informing the Rychtariks that he and the Tates had had no mail delivered for six weeks, he continued to think that the advantages of the hard regime outweighed its disadvantages, although his mood regarding *The Bridge* varied: one day 'the project seems hopeless', another day 'the theme and the substance of the conception seem brilliantly real'. And if the final achievement disappointed it would at least be a brave attempt, 'a *huge* failure'.[30] A few days later, writing to Gorham Munson, however, Hart admitted the snow had become 'a burden'. Several sections of *The Bridge* were nevertheless 'in feverish embryo' and he continued to feel that if his great vision faltered it would be 'hugely and unforgivably, distinguishedly bad'. At least his writing, however extravagant, marked a divergence from the fashionable preoccupation with defeatism and death professed by Eliot and his poetic admirers. 'O the admired beauty of a casuistical mentality', which was ultimately satisfied with 'twelve hours sleep a day and archeology'. On the subject of his poetic convictions, would Munson mind sending him his essay 'Young Titan in the Sacred Wood', which contained the first critical appraisal of his poetry? 'And may I be frank – without seeming to reflect on any personal relationships of the past – in stating my reactions?'[31]

No sooner had Munson's essay arrived at the local post office than Hart saw the author himself in Manhattan – Grace had written to announce that she and Charles Curtis were planning to marry and summoned her son to Cleveland to help plan the arrangements. Travelling to the Midwest as usual via New York Hart stayed at the Hotel Albert – where the clerk proved reluctant to admit some of the companions he tried to invite upstairs – and saw several friends in the city, among them the Cowleys, before proceeding to a brief but tranquil stay in Ohio much enlivened by Grace's surprising skills with the cocktail shaker. As he subsequently told Cowley, he was 'released from the fond embrace of my relatives in Cleveland – only to fare into rather more than less spasmodic embraces in N.Y. – a one night spree – on my way back'.[32] The evening with Munson was not entirely satisfactory: once such close friends, the two writers had what Hart subsequently termed a 'rummy conversation', trying to resolve the differences of literary opinion exposed by Munson's essay.

In many ways the critic remained enthusiastic: Hart was 'the most richly endowed of our younger poets' and it was merely the cowardice of the major literary journalists and editors that had condemned him so far to appearing in 'the small impecunious and adventurous type of review'. At sixteen he had written 'on a level that Amy Lowell never rose from' and now he commanded an artistry 'that scarcely any other living American poet ever reaches'. Eliot's despair, which twisted 'the great curves of the beauty of former ages into the mean ugliness of our day', went unchallenged by all the younger poets apart from Crane, who alone 'attempts the reconciliation of mellow beauty with nascent beauty and affirms a delving upward for the new wine'. His verbal range and musical sense were unchallenged but he also possesssed 'that intense, dionysian, dancing, exalted energy that by sheer pressure lifts him to heights unattainable by less titanic poets'. Of course, he was not easy: 'His poems are ecstatic illuminations, the tensile expansions of his psychology. That is why they require the close application of the reader who must walk in patient labor over the ground the poet has flown by his genius.' At times, indeed, he was too impenetrable for his own good – and there were other reservations besides. There was something foreign to his ecstasies, 'as though Crane accidentally tapped some potential reservoir of emotions, purer and higher than those with which we are ordinarily familiar'. Munson could do nothing more than hint at the unorthodoxy of Hart's emotional nature but he was forthright about his intellectual attainments. 'Bluntly, he does not know enough.' In part it was a deficiency to be expected, since Crane 'does not read critically but as a poet seeking "shocks" to push on his own development'. Nor did his age help. Contemporary America offered 'an uncritical atmosphere', as a result of which 'he has dined on meager ideas' and been 'stranded in an arid region so far as currents of fresh, intelligent and alive thought go'. The fact remained, however, that he was 'a mystic on the loose' because his poetic flights sometimes lacked ballast. It was one thing to 'doubt the truth of appearances which the world shows us' or to have 'intuitions of the higher dimensions, of the dimensional character of time in particular', but without the rigour of some informing discipline there was always the possibility that one's 'cosmic intuitions may be merely furtive Peeping Tom glimpses through a smutted windowpane at the universe'.[33]

It was a measure of how important Munson had once been to him, as well as of the passion which governed his literary convictions, that Hart thought it worth while to reply to the essay's charges at length on his return to Patterson. Readily conceding 'my wholesale lack of knowledge' regarding the numerous ways in which man sought to judge and classify truth and experience, he patiently attempted to explain to his old friend why such a gulf of belief now yawned between them. Munson had made many comments about him in his essay which he found both pleasing and percipient – but overall he thought the work annoyingly flawed, partly because its author ascribed to him poetic aims which he never had and also because, if only obliquely, he imported the privileged information of friendship into his criticism. And there were basic divisions between their literary assumptions. For Hart poetry was 'simply the concrete *evidence* of the *experience* of a recognition (*knowledge* if you like)'. It was 'both perception and thing perceived' and there was no point in expecting it to arbitrate in human relations with the divine, 'be it Osiris, Zeus or Indra'; all it could do was give an intimation of spirituality, of 'the assumption of a godhead'. Indeed to ask anything specific of poetry was to subordinate it to science and philosophy, when science concerned 'all exact knowledge and its instruments of operation' and when philosophy attempted to derive from rationality.

Munson had invoked Plato – but Hart insisted that Plato, and by extension any other philosopher, survived in fame not primarily because of the truth of his philosophy, but because of the coherence of his arguments as he expressed them. Incidentally it was worth remembering that Plato had advocated the banishment of poets because they had attempted the classification of chaos on systems different from his own – so ancient was the distinction between the two arts. The difficulty for all thinking men of the modern age lay in 'the paradoxes that an inadequate system of rationality forces on the living consciousness'. He was far from opposing any new harmony of laws that could provide 'a consistent philosophical and moral program for our epoch' and if such a system existed he would no doubt already be writing 'under its "classic" powers of dictation', but it did not and he was certainly not endeavouring to promulgate any such system in his poetry.

In any event he was determined that his work would always avoid 'the employment of abstract tags, formulations of experience in factual terms', and depend instead on the 'more direct terms of physical-psychic experience', because to follow any other course would rob it of 'its impact' and render it simply 'categorical'. Implicitly and above all he defended the right to elusiveness. Fighting his other battle of poetics with Harriet Monroe he insisted that a poem always constituted more than its prose rendition; with Munson he reserved his right to be subjective, undidactic and subtle and to resist moral and ethical taxonomies, and Munson's attempts to fit him into philosophies that were wholly inappropriate 'drives me to the platitude that "truth has no name"' – although 'relativity' was currently its fashionable pseudonym.[34]

The following day Hart replied to Otto Kahn, who had written at the beginning of the year, acknowledging his protégé's seasonal greetings and expressing the wish that the poet, once 'relieved from material care for a while and settled in reposeful and healthful surroundings', would prove himself 'a master builder in constructing "The Bridge" of your dreams, thoughts and emotions'.[35] Hart responded with the news that he was 'flashing in a signal from the foremast', busy as he was with 'Ave Maria', 'for mid-ocean is where the poem begins'. Despite encountering 'many unexpected formal difficulties' in the execution of his vision, he remained confident the poem would be perfected 'probably by next December' and he was certain it would be 'a dynamic and eloquent document'. So far he had written about a hundred lines and was now working 'straight through from the beginning', struggling to reconcile all the 'many interlocking elements and symbols at work' that when fused would form a poetic narrative 'based on the conquest of time and knowledge'. 'Atlantis' was 'the mystic consummation toward which all the other sections of the poem converge' but he had already established the structure of the remainder of the poem and offered to send Kahn what he had so far written for inspection.

By present reckoning *The Bridge* comprised six sections: 'Columbus' concerned the conquest of space and 'Pocahontas' the fertile body of the American continent. The same continent's spiritual aspect was evoked by 'Whitman' and his dialogue with a dying soldier in a Washington hospital during the Civil War, while the involvement of blacks in American history, subordinate and unrecognized as they were, would be described in 'John Brown', in which a black porter on the Calgary Express would sing while making up berths. 'Subway' would illustrate the hell of modern times, in which machinery continued its encroachment on human life, and 'The Bridge' would be 'a sweeping dithyramb' symbolic 'of consciousness spanning time and space'. The first and last sections were written in blank verse 'with occasional rhyme for accentuation' but he would only decide on the forms appropriate to the other sections 'when I come to grips with their respective themes'.[36]

Kahn replied on 22 March, jauntily metaphoric and glad of the 'signal from the foremast'. He waived the offer of a preview but was delighted to learn more of the subject matter of *The Bridge* and happy to discover that 'the voyage is proceeding with favoring winds and seas, and with the good ship headed straight for its destination'.[37] By then Hart had a bad cold – caught, he assumed, in the overheated buildings of an arctic New York City – but whatever the origin of the infection it did nothing to stem the poetry's flow and as he continued to perfect 'Ave Maria' he felt himself, as he confided to Frank, 'adrift [in] a music that is almost a burden'.

He took the opportunity to congratulate his friend on *Virgin Spain* and reminded him that 'your discipline and your confidence are so dear to me'.[38] So impressed was he by Frank's new book that he ordered a copy from Laukhuff's for his mother, to whom he wrote on 28 March to say how much he had enjoyed his recent visit to Cleveland. Mrs Hart was at last recovered and relations with Grace had proved so harmonious that he was now sure 'you and I can share our understanding of things more and more as time goes on'. Of course there would be future misunderstandings between them but now he felt 'awfully proud of *you*, however less occasion I may have to feel similarly about myself'. He did 'some awfully silly things sometimes – most of which you don't know about' but his principal hope and desire was that 'you never will turn your back on me'.[39]

Snow persisted until the end of March but when at last the thaw came it served only to perpetuate the isolation confronting the three writers by choking the roads with impassable mud. For the Tates themselves the prolonged siege was frustrating but with no money to spend and with literary ambitions to meet they knew there was much to be said for seclusion. Caroline was determined to improve on her first novel, 'Darkling I Listen', destroyed once she sensed her husband's disappointment, and Allen, besides labouring on 'Ode to the Confederate Dead' and other poems, was committed to producing numerous book reviews; important among them at the end of March was his assessment of T.S. Eliot's *Poems: 1909–1925*. The undertaking had a significance for Tate beyond the courtesies commanded by Eliot's growing literary stature: he now looked upon the older poet as his mentor and earlier in the winter he had defied the snows to send twelve poems and an essay to Eliot at the *Criterion*. The latter replied in mid-March with words of encouragement which immediately galvanized his disciple into composition and when Hart wrote to Cowley at the end of March he included the news that Allen 'suddenly sprouted last week and has been going ever since' after Eliot intimated that he might publish some of his work in the *Criterion*. 'I wish I had a lyric or so to circulate like Allen,' Hart lamented, suddenly aware that the inspiration that had filled him since Christmas was ebbing.[40] If there was a hint of envy in his tone it was compounded by the literary divergence which he now sensed was developing between Tate and himself and acting to cool a friendship that had begun with such warm mutual esteem. Tate, after all, had almost been his discovery and it was through him that the Tennessean had met the New York writers who were now his circle of friends. In the early days of friendship he had looked upon Hart not only as a major new poetic presence in America but as a model and a personal inspiration – and now that position had been usurped, and usurped moreover by Eliot, whose literary pessimism Hart had repeatedly challenged, not only verbally but poetically. What, after all, was *The Bridge* but an attempt to revive the epic voice which Eliot had pronounced for ever still and to declaim in brave measures the mythic destiny of a land Eliot had found so prosaic as to flee? Disagreements resulting from these shifting loyalties had often emerged in conversations that occurred in the snowbound house but when Tate came to review Eliot's poems for the *New Republic* and to declare him the most important living poet he was effectively publishing his scepticism about Hart's own position and about *The Bridge* which was his daily preoccupation and vindication.

The rejection fell heavily. Hart had a great belief in his lyric gifts but the auto-didact in him never quite overcame the awed respect he felt for the university graduates he numbered among his friends. It was one thing for his poetry not to be understood by his parents but when friends who were also Phi Beta Kappa scholars or sons of the Ivy League professed themselves bemused he had to pause. With nowhere else to turn, he asked Munson what would become of his determination to reclaim heroic poetry when he was doubted by 'the only group of people whose verbal sophistication is likely to take an interest in a style such as mine'.[41] Then his inspiration disappeared altogether and he found himself in a mud-besieged house with two preoccupied cohabitants who had been made aware, like Munson before them, that Hart was not an easy visitor. As recently as January Tate had considered his fellow poet 'one of the finest men alive – if possible, finer than his poetry', but familiarity bred qualification.[42] He began to see that Hart was 'incredibly child-like along with his literary sophistication' and that he was 'frag-mented into many different persons', so that although his 'good side was very appealing and the reason why people were so fond of him' he was also 'not a con-sistent personality at all' and often sulked as 'the great neglected, misunderstood person'.[43] The fact was, as the other members of the group realized and Cowley pronounced, 'Hart had a greater thirst for fame than the rest of us, and it made him less patient in the face of hardship.'[44] It followed that he was restless when unable to write but also eager day and night to discuss his poetic aims and tech-niques and this tendency also began to annoy Tate, especially when Hart took to bursting into his study to debate some literary theory when he was searching for the *mot juste* of a poem or a review.

Once work on *The Bridge* halted, these interruptions increased – and were visited besides on Caroline as she struggled with her novel in the kitchen. As a kind of well-meaning child Hart saw no selfishness in his friendly overtures; in any case, the kitchen provided the easiest short-cut to the pump room where he kept his shaving implements. Rather than mention her grievances Caroline allowed them to fester and finally decided to put a lock on the kitchen door, thus forcing Hart to walk the long way round. When he responded petulantly by commission-ing Mrs Turner to do his cooking, and by using her kitchen for eating and shav-ing, the Tates took the unsubtle hint and started to catalogue what they saw as abuses of their hospitality, most grievous of which was Hart's failure to assist with chores around the house.

Malcolm Cowley had already noted that when he was staying at Robber Rocks Hart helped the Browns with such activities 'as a child might help them, for the fun of it'.[45] There was no sense of sustained obligation, however, particularly when other labours kept him at his desk, and once he was installed with Allen and Caroline, Hart confided to Cowley that he disliked chopping wood because it 'constricted his imagination', apparently not reflecting that such fastidiousness was bound to prove annoying in the course of a severe winter. Mrs Turner's doting indulgence of Hart's needs and whims added insult to injury, as did the growing suspicion that he was taking his complaints about the Tates and their dull domestic ways to the Browns – because once the hostile parties took to avoiding each other, and then to communicating through notes slipped under doors, Hart resorted increasingly to Robber Rocks for discussion of *The Bridge* and for afternoons of gossip, cider and sympathy. But the Browns knew better than to take sides and in any case they had work to do, so after a while they also tried discreetly to discourage Hart's tireless overtures. By 5 April, when the latter wrote to Munson, it was to express relief that the Cowleys were moving to the area in May: he looked forward to stimulating talk with Malcolm 'before I, the climate, the solitude, or whatever it is, drives him into the kind of shell that Brown and Tate seem to have retired into lately'. In the meantime, 'I drone about, reading, eating and sleeping'.[46] Caroline found his activities less innocuous: 'God save me from ever having another romantic in the house with me!' she pleaded, insisting that the interval of cohabitation with Hart Crane, adored and idolized as he was by Addie Turner, contained ample 'material for a Eugene O'Neill play'.[47] Without ever learning the true nature of Hart's early hopes for her husband, she may have drawn the parallel with other unsettling affections in mind: years later her novel *The Malefactors* would contain a scene in which the character clearly based on Hart propositions the character equally obviously modelled on Tate.

Tate himself found his friend's ambitions exhausting: 'Hart had a sort of megalomania – he wanted to be The Great American Poet.'[48] Hart on the other hand began to suspect a tacit conspiracy among his friends and to resent their scepticism as a clear cause of his problems with *The Bridge*. Thus when he complained to the Rychtariks on 11 April about difficulties with 'Ave Maria' he told them he could only be confident of Frank's proper appreciation because 'most of my younger associates and friends will probably be pretty doubtful about it. Well, one has to face such things with a confidence superior to a lot of contingencies.'[49] A quarrel was inevitable, and it occurred on 16 April when Hart and Mrs Turner, liberated at last by the recession of the mud and beckoned by the imminent spring, made an inspection of the back yard one morning before breakfast. The Tates later claimed they overheard Hart pointedly complaining about the mess made by Tate's log-chopping whereas Hart himself insisted that he and Mrs Turner were casually walking around when Tate's head suddenly appeared behind a door and he shouted, 'If you've got a criticism of my work to make, I'd appreciate it if you would speak to me about it first.'[50]

Inglorious as the drama was, it signalled Hart's need to move once again. Mrs Turner pleaded with him to remain and offered rooms entirely self-contained but he was determined to leave, particularly after the Tates slipped notes under his bedroom door in explanation of their annoyance. The essence of Caroline's complaint was that he was inconsiderate and overwhelming but her husband went to articulate lengths to persuade Hart that he mistook disagreement for personal criticism, that he was incapable of seeing points of view other than his own and that he claimed sanction for his extravagant stubbornness in literary precedent: 'You have often referred to a "demonic" possession, something like Marlowe's; that's quite all right; but you shouldn't act upon it in ordinary life, for you can't expect others to take it seriously.'[51] When Hart wrote to Grace to announce the rupture on 18 April he was clear not only that his behaviour was blameless but that Caroline, with 'the malicious nature of a person I thought to be friendly', was the real cause of the disagreement. The fight could scarcely have come at a worse moment: spring in Patterson would have been the perfect season to continue *The Bridge*, but now he had to pack his bags, and do so without sufficient funds remaining to rent an apartment in New York for the months of writing that lay ahead. As far as he could see there was only one solution to the emergency: would Grace allow him to go to the Isle of Pines, where he would be able to write without the distraction of other people or the worry of paying rent? She had always refused him before, but if she did so now, he threatened, 'I'm not sure how much farther away I'll go to accomplish my purposes. Perhaps to the orient, even if I have just enough to get there and no more.' But his mood was so grim, he told her, that he half contemplated even longer absences and wondered if he could best resolve his dilemma 'with powder and bullet'.[52]

Wherever he went he had to reply to the Tates first, as it seemed, to finish the business of friendship and to hope that 'my image, howsoever it stands in your recollections, shall be erased as speedily as possible'. But fluency failed him – and although he drafted two letters it remains uncertain whether he was sufficiently satisfied with either one to send it. Extant copies attest to his future plans and his immediate disappointment: he had rented the north-east bedroom from Mrs Turner under a separate term and proposed to store his possessions there indefinitely. He had never tried to reduce the Tates to menials in their own house and his only motive in commissioning Addie's assistance had been to ease their burden of work – and on the subject of motives he was distressed to learn that Tate's reason for inviting him to stay had arisen merely from concern for his repeated financial difficulties. 'Too deeply hurt to simulate any tricky indifference', he wanted to state how much he still admired Tate's poetry, not least because it remained untainted by that 'particular supine narcissism' with which Eliot had seduced his numerous admirers. Matters of literary taste aside, he admitted that as a cohabitant he left much to be desired. He acknowledged many 'gross errors of taste and many, many lapses of consideration' which had led him to invade their time and their privacy. The fact was 'I'm a comparative barbarian in many ways and certainly was not raised by the lack of education and social chaos that my family accorded my adolescence.' What early deprivations had begun, later life had compounded and if he was indeed selfish it was because 'I have lived quite alone, without any real social relations with people for many years'.[53] Yet in the end he knew there was more: other disapprovals, let them remain unnamed, lay behind 'the *real* causes you and Caroline have mounted against me'.[54]

Uncertain what to do next, Hart left for New York. Three weeks previously, with funds depleted, he had written to Kahn for further assistance and had received half of the $1,000 still outstanding from the original agreement. Even in the Caribbean $500 would not last indefinitely but the Isle of Pines still seemed to represent the cheapest immediate option for living, so he booked passage on the United Fruit Line's SS *Ulua*, which sailed for Havana on 1 May, and invited Waldo Frank to join him for the adventure. The Rychtariks had written asking if he could repay the $225 they had lent him to buy Bina Flynn's acres but the more he thought about it the more he realized he could spare only $100 at the moment. Grace, he told them, was making 'a terrible fuss' about his Caribbean proposal but he was sure his plan was the right one: once on the island he could live frugally and eke out his remaining funds in order to write *The Bridge* and in the meantime he hoped they would understand his position, withhold any just anger they might have and accept his word – 'I don't think I'm a dishonest person'.[55]

Although Grace claimed she opposed his plan to go to the island because of the 'whimsical temper' of Mrs T.W. Simpson, caretaker of the Hart plantation since the death of her husband, he knew what she really dreaded was the greater distance that would soon divide them.[56] But he wrote to Mrs Simpson to announce his plans and once Grace saw the strength of his determination she reluctantly capitulated. Hart wrote to her on 24 April, '*terribly sorry*' he had not been able to make her agree wholeheartedly to his plan but promising her that matters might resolve themselves 'much better than you may expect'.[57] Later that day he returned to Patterson to equip himself for the journey and for subsequent literary labour and once packed he transferred himself to Robber Rocks for his last night in the country. The Browns had offered to drive him to the early morning train to New York and just as light was breaking Susan went to the garden well to draw water for breakfast, glimpsing as she did so a herd of fifteen deer gathered at a hollow a hundred feet away. She beckoned Bill and Hart through the window and silently they joined her and for a moment the three friends watched in tacit delight until the animals sensed them and equally tacitly made for the nearby wood. 'We watched them leap, one by one, with infinite grace, over the stone wall at its edge. Hart was transfixed; then he burst into tears and kept embracing us in turn, saying how much he loved us and would love us "till his dying day".'[58]

Back in New York Hart learned that Waldo had accepted his invitation to the island but, as the more experienced traveller, proposed modifications to the

itinerary: the United Fruit Line transported its passengers to Havana in five days
but the New York and Cuba Mail Steam Ship Company (Ward Line) did it in four,
so Frank made bookings on the SS *Orizaba*, which was also sailing for Cuba on 1
May. Then Grace, ever impetuous, suddenly cancelled the matrimonial plans she
had made in Cleveland and arrived in New York with Charles Curtis, determined
that her son should witness her wedding. There was an emotional reunion at the
Hotel Albert and a whirlwind of nuptial excitement including a lunch with Gaston
and Madame Lachaise, a dinner with the Cowleys – and only one unpleasant altercation, which occurred when mother and son attended a performance of O'Neill's
The Great God Brown. Grace made a last attempt to dissuade Hart from leaving and
the resulting scene precipitated theatrical exits and penitent red roses the next
morning. Relations were sufficiently restored, however, for Mr and Mrs Charles
Curtis to make their way to the pier on May Day to wave the voyagers farewell.
Waldo studied Hart's new stepfather, who seemed 'like a comic opera version of a
loud American businessman – his shirts, his pants, his necktie, the jewelry, rings
and so forth'. As for his new wife, 'there was in Grace too this rather crude, bar-
baric strain, but in her it was attractive; she was a very live person'.[59] Hart himself
considered Curtis 'a good sport' for the way he had indulged Grace and himself
in their three days together in New York but privately, as the *Orizaba* pulled from
the pier, he wondered how content she would prove in her second marriage.[60] As
he confided to Waldo, the disparity in age worried him and try as he might he
could not rid himself of the suspicion that she had married for all the wrong
reasons.

PART FOUR

Cuba and California

May 1926–May 1928

*I could never remember
That seething, steady leveling of the marshes
Till age had brought me to the sea.*

'REPOSE OF RIVERS'

13

Hart's cares lifted on the voyage south, as smooth sailing gave promise of the approaching tropics. On 3 May, with the *Orizaba* off Florida, he told Grace of flying fish and reported 'the usual increasing blue' of the journey; and once below deck he could sample further delights, important among them the availability, novel to this poet of the Prohibition, of European liquor which was both legal and uncorrupted. In a ship half empty the two friends shared a cabin and apparently remained apart from their predominantly Cuban fellow passengers: Waldo Frank, tireless Hispanist as he was, pointed out one typically Castilian woman but Hart was unmoved – 'she doesn't send any thrills up my spine' – and contented himself instead with discussing *The Bridge* with his mentor and wondering how long he could survive on what remained of the $500 recently advanced by Otto Kahn.[1] In 1915 Hart's first exposure to the Caribbean had culminated in swallowed sleeping powders and attempted suicide but its waters had compensated him since with poetic inspiration – and if the bells off San Salvador now chimed unheard there would surely be other causes for exhilaration in Havana, where the *Orizaba* docked on Tuesday, 4 May.

Only yards away from the point of disembarkation was the spot where the US battleship *Maine* had been blown up in an act of atrocity that had ignited the Spanish-American War twenty-eight years previously. But the phantoms of golden galleons also rode at anchor in Havana Bay: what was recent history to the thought that Christopher Columbus himself had twice visited this very island or that the Spaniards had used it as the point of departure for their conquest of Mexico, or that there were thousands here whose ancestors had first come in search of El Dorado? The travellers stayed only one night in the city, at the modest Isla de Cuba hotel, and saw a show at the Alhambra before devoting the remainder of their time to sightseeing and exploration. The Alhambra reminded Hart of the National Winter Garden Burlesque in New York: the dialogue was beyond him but there was nothing esoteric about the accompanying pantomimes, which easily outdid the oft-proclaimed ribaldry of the Lower East Side. Havana itself, he informed the Browns a few days later, was 'hyper sensual and mad', without 'apparent direction, destiny or purpose' – e.e. cummings would surely love it. Waldo's fluent Spanish took them away from the familiar trails of the American tourist to cafés 'filled with blacks, reds, browns, greys and every permutation and combination of southern bloods that you can imagine' and through decaying quarters full of 'gratings and balconies and narrow streets with plenty of whores nodding'. Old crones hobbled around selling lottery tickets while buxom Jamaican women looked on and laughed. Fragrant cigars and abundant alcohol were a delight to the fugitives from puritanism but the 20 cent taxis aside, everything was expensive and Hart had to promise himself that he would return 'when cash is plentiful'. Maddeningly a fleet of American destroyers landed on Wednesday and the Browns were informed that the streets 'immediately became torrents of uni-forms'. But there was no possibility of delaying departure – how could Hart have justified such self-indulgence to his stern and high-minded cicerone? – and Wednesday evening saw the travellers catching the ferry from Batabanó to the Isle of Pines, the tiny satellite sixty miles south-west which Cuba had recently reclaimed.

Since the *Orizaba* had brought them to Havana a day ahead of their original plans, Mrs Simpson, the caretaker of the Villa Casas, was not expecting them – indeed was not expecting Waldo at all – and when they appeared she collapsed in a violent fit of coughing while in the background her garrulous pet parrot, Attaboy, screeched bizarre salutations: 'Damned poor dinner! Damned poor dinner!'[2] Adaptable in the extreme, she busied herself with settling her guests and installed Hart in Grace's old room on the front west corner of the house and put Waldo next door. Hart was amazed by how much he had forgotten – or uncon-sciously repressed – from his traumatic first visit: the indoor bathroom was new, but what of the great mango tree outside the back window of his room, or the sur-prising size of the house, or the magical arrival of the tropical dawn, or the aston-ishing variety of fruits – guavas, limes, kumquats, kashew apples, cassavas, breadfruit, coconuts, wild oranges, bananas, mulberries, avocados, papayas, mangos, tamarinds, pomegranates and grabanas – with which he at once began to dose his delicate and temperamental stomach? How could his memory have oblit-erated these marvels, his quarrelling parents notwithstanding? And how could he have believed his mother when she insisted that Mrs Simpson was a capriciously difficult old woman from whom she had all along wanted to protect him? 'Aunt Sally', as she quickly became known, endeared herself to the travellers almost at once and when Hart wrote to Grace on 8 May it was to commend 'her wit, her good sense and lack of all sentimentality'.[3]

The travellers had arrived at the height of the mosquito season but in the next few days, nothing daunted, they picked coconuts, bought fish, adopted a young owl that squeaked the way Peggy Cowley did when drunk and found a nearby beach from which to swim, although by the afternoon the water was almost too warm. In theory it was the rainy season but Aunt Sally was surprised by how dry the days had so far been. In the absence of tropical storms, she was able to show her visitors something of the island and one day they hired a car and drove to Jones' Jungle, a garden and arboretum developed over the last twenty-three years by an expatriate couple who impressed the poet as 'by far the pleasantest and most cultured people I have met on the island'. It was all the more poignant, then, to hear their story over the picnic prepared by Aunt Sally: since the reversion of the territory to Cuba the fears of all the foreign residents who had resisted Havanese control had been realized. Property values were falling and the Joneses explained that at any time Cuban bureaucrats could seize their land and offer no more than $5 an acre in compensation. Apart from their property they were penniless and their only income came from admission charges to the Jungle and from the little that Jones himself could charge as a taxi driver. Hart found their story 'pitiable to the point of tears', he told Grace, not least because the splendour of Jones' Jungle eclipsed anything he could imagine in the West Indies or North America and reminded Waldo, a seasoned traveller, of nothing less than an estate once seen in the Azores which had belonged to a Portuguese prince.[4]

On the evening of 18 May Waldo Frank returned to New York: his recent impressions, recollected as 'Habana of the Cubans', would appear in the *New Republic* in June and for the remainder of the summer, in the course of what became Hart Crane's greatest period of sustained lyric achievement, he was the keeper by letter of his poetic conscience. But with his departure Hart was suddenly alone with his destiny, further from home than he had ever been and for the first time in his life remote not only from friends but from American soil – here in this paradise of painful adolescent memories. In theory he need not be solitary: almost half of the 6,000 people who lived on the Isle of Pines were Americans and the principal town, Nueva Gerona, was nearby – so near that despite the heat and the mosquitoes it was an easy matter to walk there for the mail. But there was little besides to detain one: as he later told his Cleveland friend Charles Harris, there were just 'too many Americans of the Main Street variety'.[5] Local talk was of local interests; anxieties about Cuban sovereignty were about as far as speculation and philosophy could wander from routine discussion of the citrus farming, copper mining and marble quarrying which sustained the island's economy. A model prison had recently been constructed and the plantation bungalows were occasionally enlivened by news of fugitive convicts at large in the island's interior – a place where only the desperate or the intrepid ventured. For all its outstanding natural beauty the Isle of Pines was ultimately inhospitable and human habitation was restricted to the littoral, far from the mountains, the swamps infested with alligators and giant crabs, and the dense forests of pine, lignum vitae, cedar and mahogany which commanded the hinterland.

Christopher Columbus, on discovering the island in 1494, had named it Evangelista as he claimed the Caribbean for God and for Spain but the Catholic conquerors themselves, avid for gold and slave labour, found nothing here to enrich them and having paused at the pine-clad island to rename it they returned to Cuba and the territory remained forgotten until after the conquest of Mexico. With the consequent development of gold and argentine traffic between the New World and the Old, however, and the inevitable rise in piracy on the Spanish Main, the Isle of Pines came into its own as the impenetrable and ungovernable sanctuary of buccaneers and in time the legend arose that it was rich with buried treasure. So persistent was the story that when in 1883 Robert Louis Stevenson published *Treasure Island* he included a map of his eponymous island which was striking in its resemblance to the eighty square miles where Hart had also come, if not for buried treasure, then certainly for sanctuary.

At least there was Aunt Sally, and in the ensuing weeks she emerged as one of the most endearing figures in the poet's life. Frederick Swetland, a resident of the island, remembered her as 'a little, dried-up, sun-wrinkled wisp of a woman with sharp (dark?) eyes behind glasses, an active mind and an acid tongue and a warm heart'.[6] To Waldo she was both anachronism and archetype: 'Rustic America in a way, with all the spiritual qualities that you sometimes find among farmers' wives – whimsical, intelligent and a twinkle in her eye.'[7] With widowhood she had assumed her husband's responsibilities as caretaker of the Villa Casas but to make ends meet she also sold fruit, made pies and cakes to order and every week baked twenty loaves of bread for sale at 15 cents each. Her husband's life insurance provided her with a small stipend but she hoped she would expire before it did, otherwise, she explained, 'I guess I'll have to paint my legs yellow and pick with the chickens'.[8] Perhaps one day she would return to America and work for her nephew at his candy store in Kansas. If not, she could always plant fig trees: 'I'll at least have food and raiment and a fig leaf is all one really needs down here.'[9] She was nothing if not resourceful – 'The point of this pencil is about the shape of a Cayman nigger's nose but 'tis all I have' – yet in the numerous letters she sent to Hart following his eventual return to America one glimpses her financial insecurity, her isolation, her declining health and her fear of hurricanes and cyclones, as portended in the sunsets which she studied: the more vivid, the more ominous.[10] She knew other local widows but her daily companions were a cock and complementary hens and Attaboy, who mimicked her relentlessly and whose stony derision spared neither her chronic rheumatism nor her racking cough, which he imitated so uncannily that Hart sometimes thought Aunt Sally in two places at once. Despite these afflictions and in the face of all adversity she was cheerful, thrifty, hardy and sane, an indomitable woman whose contempt for self-pity and hysteria inspired the young poet she now took to mothering and stood in stark contrast to the ready palpitations of Grace Crane, whose dislike of Mrs Simpson was, it soon emerged, cordially reciprocated.

With Waldo gone the obligations of hospitality retreated and Hart and Aunt

Sally turned to practicalities. Dispiriting as it was to learn that property prices were falling on the island, Hart attempted to turn the depression to his advantage: why, his letters to Grace began to wonder, did she consider selling the Villa Casas when little or no profit could accrue from the sale? Given her dislike of northern winters she would always need some palmy retreat: surely it made more sense to repair and maintain the fabric of a house she already owned in the tropics rather than flit from one expensive hotel in Florida to another? But if she could be persuaded to agree, there was no time for delay: the Villa Casas was only a quarter-century old but it was already in a bad state of repair. The boundary fencing was collapsing and Hart saw at once that new gates were needed at the front of the property to exclude cows if not marauding pigs. It was five years since Grace had been to the island – did she know the house needed repainting, that its sunscreens had to be mended, that the pump which drew water from the well was out of order and that the wooden structure that supported the water tank was rotten? Most seriously, the roof was in desperate need of renewal and if the whole house was not to decay in the tropical rains Hart urged that the shingling be replaced, either with asbestos roofing or, better still, tiling. Unequal to this labour, he turned his handyman's zeal, short-lived but ferocious, to the accomplishment of lesser improvements beginning with the dense citrus groves that surrounded the property. He had noticed on arrival that the area immediately adjacent to the house was thicker with mosquitoes than anywhere else and deduced that the orange trees, many of which were dead or decrepit, were responsible, since the closeness of their planting fostered incubation. Wielding a machete under the blazing sun he eradicated as many as he could, to replace them with royal palms, which Grace was informed were 'the perfect sort of tree to have round a house, their ornamentation, stateliness and openairyness can't be surpassed'.[11] She wrote back approving the replanting and was eventually rewarded with 'Royal Palm', a sixteen-line lyric dedicated to his mother in which Crane serenaded this beautiful tree, 'Forever fruitless' and 'Uneaten of the earth or aught earth holds'. There was something sublime in its sterility: it avoided the cruelties of growth and decay, the monstrous press and toil of procreation, all magnified unbearably here in the tropics, to offer to the poet instead an example of autonomy and transcendence. It was

> beyond that yield
> Of sweat the jungle presses with hot love
> And tendril till our deathward breath is sealed –
> It grazes the horizons, launched above
>
> Mortality – ascending emerald-bright,
> A fountain at salute, a crown in view –
> Unshackled, casual of its azured height
> As though it soared suchwise through heaven too.[12]

The vegetation of the island, so strange and beautiful, so vivid, luxuriant and ultimately sinister, was a source of wonder for the duration of his tropical summer.
Even as the ferry from Cuba arrived by dawn he remarked 'the mountains,
strange greens, native thatched huts, perfume' and was put in mind of the South
Sea romances of Melville, another writer seduced by the tropics, before being distracted by the blossoming oleanders and mimosas, which made the air 'almost
too heavy with perfume'.[13] A few days later Hart sampled freshly picked mangoes
and in his first letter to CA from the island he extolled them as 'the most delicious fruit I ever tasted' and suggested, half seriously, that after the initial cost of
advertising they would prove a commercial triumph in North America, where
'people would come back for them like wildfire'.[14] Reading Lewis Spence's
recently published *Atlantis in America* had drawn him to prehistoric speculation
and in a letter to Susan Brown he shared his conviction that the mango tree was
'the original Eden apple tree'.[15] By way of elaboration he enclosed 'The Mango
Tree', a poem which aspired to the status of a calligramme, since in deference to
Apollinaire's term the shape it assumed on the page was the shape of the tree it
described.

Beautiful and bounteous as it was, however, there was something unsettling in
this ripe and waxing world and in his first letter from the island to Wilbur
Underwood he complained that his mind was 'completely befogged by the heat
and besides there is a strange challenge and combat in the air – offered by
"Nature" so monstrously alive in the tropics which drains the psychic energies'.[16]
There were immense skies and sudden prospects of purple and Prussian blue sea
framed by glossy foliage and unimagined flowers – but for much of the day it was
too hot to walk merely for pleasure. In any case, initial explorations completed,
where could he go? Nueva Gerona itself contained a City Hall and a Catholic
church, an American bank, a post office, a hotel, a small market, a shop or two
that sold the *Havana Post* but little besides to excite poetic fantasy.

A marble quarry in the mountains opposite the house proved slightly more
inspiring, and he took to walking there in the early evening, after the heat had
declined, to watch the chain gangs from the prison as they sawed the marble
blocks into slabs. A road led directly towards the quarry and then curved round
the foot of the palm-fringed mountain, while beyond blazed 'the sunset's tower-
ing sea', and at times, as he walked this familiar route, Hart pondered the tricks of
the fading light that left him alternately blinded and dazzled by mountainous
shadow and sun-reflecting ocean or else made it seem as though the island floated
above the embracing sea. Crepuscular distortions – yet they brought to mind the
other tricks and distortions of life, including the animal yearnings that seemed to
lead invariably to tears. Sexual desire was transient and treacherous and later, when
he revisited this scene and its attendant speculations in one of his loveliest minor
lyrics, 'Island Quarry', he thought how often he had longed to be as hard and
strong as the marble, which was insensate and as enduring as great art:

It is at times –

In dusk, as though this island lifted, floated
In Indian baths. At Cuban dusk the eyes
Walking the straight road toward thunder –
This dry road silvering toward the shadow of the quarry
– It is at times as though the eyes burned hard and glad
And did not take the goat path quivering to the right,
Wide of the mountain – thence to tears and sleep –
But went on into marble that does not weep.[17]

On 21 May, Cuban Independence Day, Hart indeed walked under goat escort when he returned from festivities thoroughly drunk on Bacardi. Recent routine had been broken, and with it the decorum observed since Waldo had first joined him for their excursion, and Hart was just sober enough to wonder as he reached the house what Mrs Simpson would make of his stubbed toe, his skinned knees and his altogether obvious condition. But she took it all in her stride: she had raised no objections to cigar-smoking and now, he relayed to Susan, it was established 'that I can drink as much as I damned please'.[18] Happily the house was big enough for him and Aunt Sally to avoid each other whenever they chose, so for much of the time he was undisturbed and unresented as he pounded the baby grand piano or read or wandered around in his island costume – sailor pants, T-shirt and hemp-soled shoes, the traditional footwear of the Hispanic peasantry, bought at Waldo's advice in Havana – or corresponded with distant friends, waiting the while for the instructions of the muse.

Inspiration was not encouraged when O'Neill wrote, somewhat enigmatically, to suggest that although Horace Liveright was not expecting him to write a foreword to *White Buildings* he was still awaiting further material from Hart himself. What could it mean, the poet asked Waldo on 22 May. Was Liveright's interest in publication now contingent on completion of *The Bridge*? Was he considering withdrawing from the arrangement? It was distressing to reflect that the typescript of *White Buildings* might soon begin its travels again, however determined Waldo remained to sell it. But then Susan wrote with news that cheered him greatly: Jack Fitzin, his sailor love from the previous January, had attempted to visit him at Mrs Turner's while on his way to spend leave with his family at Passaic, New Jersey. Hart had long known of the plan, since Fitzin had announced it by letter as soon as his ship reached the naval base at Norfolk, Virginia. Hart had sent a postcard from Havana to Passaic, in a bid to pre-empt what he feared might be an embarrassing encounter and he was grateful to the Browns for their care of his visitor. As he explained to Sue, he was sorry to have missed him, but it was to Underwood that he dilated more freely on this gesture of constancy, which was so different from the prevarications of publishers or the treachery of certain recently estranged friends:

I was very touched to hear that he had journeyed all the way from Norfolk – in memory of two evenings in Brooklyn last January. Immortally choice and funny and pathetic are some of my recollections in such connection. I treasure them – I always can – against many disillusionments made bitter by the fact that faith was given and *expected* – whereas, with the sailor no faith or such is properly expected and how jolly and cordial and warm the touseling *is* sometimes, after all. Let my lusts be my ruin, then, since all else is fake and mockery.[19]

The rains had arrived and Hart and Aunt Sally were kept busy moving pots and pans up and down between the attic and the sitting room, both of which were vulnerable to leakage. Then, suddenly unbearably restless, he succumbed to expatriate stories that Grand Cayman was an island paradise it was worth his while to explore and one, moreover, that lay only 150 miles, or two days' voyage, south of the Isle of Pines. He had written no poetry since arriving in the Caribbean – why not undertake an adventure, especially as the exhilarations of sailing might reawaken the dormant lyric urge? He booked passage on a schooner departing Nueva Gerona on 3 June and Aunt Sally made preparations for him: 'bread, cheese and cookies', he assured Grace. There was always the fear that he might be seasick once the voyage was under way but 'then I'll have at least found out that I'm a goodfornothing landlubber'.[20]

In the event the excursion was a nightmare beyond his worst imaginings: the sublime skies and sightings of a white fin shark and hundreds of the 'huzza porpoises' mentioned in *Moby Dick* were no consolation for the conditions on board. The schooner was 60 feet long but it was only after the vessel cleared Nueva Gerona that he discovered he would be sharing it with thirty-five other passengers, 'and all of them niggers', Grace was told, 'who proved to have no idea of ordinary decent cleanliness'. The drinking water tasted bad, there was no shade on deck against the merciless sun and it was impossible to venture below deck 'unless one could brave the stinks and fumes of a dozen odd sick and wailing nigger females'.[21] Such conditions would have been trying in the course of a regular voyage, but to compound the misery the ship was becalmed for two days under an equatorial sun that turned the sea, he told Waldo, into 'a blinding glassy gridiron'.[22]

But any expectation that arrival would entail deliverance was dashed while the schooner was still three miles from Grand Cayman: clouds of vicious mosquitoes descended on the ship, and in particular on its conspicuous fair-skinned passenger, and began a torment that ceased only when Hart was once again mid-ocean on the return voyage. As he later told the writer Yvor Winters, 'My northern blood was simply ice cream and strawberry tarts to those various families of tiny vampires.'[23] Exploration revealed that the island itself was a barren hades of huge insects, terrible heat and scant shelter. Its only hostelry was a sort of boarding house overrun by pious natives who sang hymns indefatigably and whose children roamed around screaming and shouting, and there was no possibility of escaping to the famous beaches because of the mosquitoes. For ten days he stayed inside, immersed for the third time in *Moby Dick* and covered in noxious insect-repellent; even so, by the time he boarded the schooner back to Nueva Gerona one side of his face and neck were, he informed Grace, 'so badly poisoned from the constant bites that they were quite swollen'. On the return voyage the ship was again becalmed for two days on a sea so still 'that you could see yourself in it like a mirror', and again there was no escape from the sun, so that by the time he returned, 'our island seemed like Paradise and Mrs Simpson like the goddess of Liberty'.[24] His sunburn, he told Waldo, was 'positively Ethiopian'.[25] More immediately worrying were the chest pains and the heavy sweating and breathing problems that began to afflict him at night; and what he described to the Browns as 'a double-barreled non-pareil ear-ache' then convinced him that he had aural abscesses and should seek medical advice in Havana.[26] Dr Agramento, a Columbia graduate, reassured him: he suffered from neither boils nor abscesses but a throat infection possibly caused by foul water and cartilaginous contusions inflicted by the sun. Aunt Sally syringed the ears and gradually the pain subsided even as the burnt skin peeled. Henceforth, however, a proper hat would have to be added to his bizarre island garb: beautiful though she was, Nature was not to be flirted with here.

But the tourist's tribulation was the poet's gain and later in the summer, once he had started to write, Crane distilled his impressions of Grand Cayman in two exquisite lyrics – 'The Air Plant', in which the outlandish organism of the title, rooted in the thin sand and dependent on that 'Angelic Dynamo', the hurricane, for salvation from 'the shark-swept Spanish Main', mirrors short-lived and vulnerable man, fearful of death and uncertain of redemption; and 'O Carib Isle!', a great and heart-rending disquisition into the value, not merely of poetry, but of the very vowels of human speech.[27] Hart Crane is one of the few white poets to have flourished in the tropics: there is little English or American poetry analogous to his Caribbean meditations, which often suggest a verbal counterpart to the paintings Winslow Homer completed in the West Indies thirty-odd years before. Both artists were inspired by a natural world more beautiful and more implacable than anything they had registered in the north; and both relied on meticulous observation of this world to support their apprehension of a sublime terrestrial force beyond human calculation or containment.

The tarantula rattling at the lily's foot
Across the feet of the dead, laid in white sand
Near the coral beach – nor zigzag fiddle crabs
Side-stilting from the path (that shift, subvert
And anagrammatize your name) – No, nothing here
Below the palsy that one eucalyptus lifts
In wrinkled shadows – mourns.

There was an American cemetery on the Isle of Pines but it was in the course of a visit to the graveyard on Grand Cayman, located near the shore of this bleak coral outcrop, that Crane was struck by the terror of it all – here where the remains of men and women as restless and displaced as he was himself lay, not in the final slumbering repose of elegiac tradition, but in a gritty necropolis far from home and fast sinking beneath a natural world at best indifferent and at worst hostile. The lily, that peerless flower so prominent in Christian iconography, is menaced here by a carnivorous spider which was beyond the patristic imagination while the small metallic noises of animal and insect activity – the prowling and the preying – are evoked in harsh and scuttling lines. The eucalyptus, ancient friend to the apothecary, is itself palsied here and there is no sign that anything mourns – indeed the only activity is provided by the fiddler crabs: Hart had read of Eliot's 'ragged claws scuttling across the floors of silent seas' but here he saw something more distressing – the sinisterly gregarious crustaceans that wound their way diagonally across the sand and the defenceless graves, disrupting as they did so the names of the dead spelt out in shells below each plot and leaving behind their indecipherable tracks that would inevitably obliterate sooner or later all human memorial.

This very erosion is implicit in the opening stanza's compressed syntax: 'Neither' was once the first word here, its insertion making sense of the animal catalogue that ignores all human piety. Struck by this mute indifference to human remains the poet contemplates the shell-edged plots themselves, 'Brutal necklaces of shells around each grave/Squared off so carefully', and comforts himself with the idea that he can at least count 'these nacreous frames of tropic death' and in so doing declare a human skill, a power of calculation, that can challenge the analphabetic wilderness. 'Tree names, flower names/Deliberate, gainsay death's brittle crypt.' Yet even as he tries to console himself with this human capacity for naming and ordering nature's inexorable activity he senses some ineffable force around and behind him that if it decides not to strike now will certainly do so presently: 'Meanwhile/The wind that knots itself in one great death – /Coils and withdraws.' As a result, 'syllables want breath': Adam named what he saw in Eden but in this coral hell, made up of the brittle remains of millions of long-dead creatures, the naming process is void. Despite his 'ambushed senses' the poet admits to himself that there is no 'Captain', no benign deity, in control of this 'doubloon isle/Without a turnstile'.

Rather than be interred in such a hades Crane hopes his spirit will be 'Sieved upward, white and black along the air/Until it meets the blue's comedian host.' His prayer remains unanswered: there is no escaping this fiery and inert world, which alternated diabolic stillness with the diabolic tempests all the islanders feared: 'Slagged of the hurricane – I, cast within its flow,/Congeal by afternoons here, satin and vacant.' Yet if this beautiful poem is unflinching it is also heroic and affirmative. Perhaps human principles of taxonomy were indeed powerless on

earth and perhaps all terrestrial things were no more than congealing flesh waiting for the hurricane's swift dispatch. But the oceans he was sure sang another
song and if poets were as expendable and as misunderstood as the hissing terra-
pins he saw each morning bound and ready for soup and slaughter in the
Caribbean markets there was still no denying their glory and privilege in hearing,
and seeking to relay, this other music of the waves:

> Let not the pilgrim see himself again
> For slow evisceration bound like those huge terrapin
> Each daybreak on the wharf, their brine caked eyes;
> – Spiked, overturned; such thunder in their strain!
> And clenched beaks coughing for the surge again![28]

Hart returned from Grand Cayman on 18 June to face financial anxiety once again.
The cost of the expedition and its subsequent medical expenses made serious
inroads into his savings and his regrettable priority back at the Villa Casas was to
sell his 20 acres back to Bina Flynn. The disappointment was softened by pleasing news from London: Edgell Rickword, critic, war poet, Rimbaldian authority
and editor of the *Calendar*, had agreed to publish 'Passage', 'Praise for an Urn' and
'At Melville's Tomb', but set against that development was the continuing uncertainty over *White Buildings*, and when he wrote to Waldo on 19 June Hart could do
no more than wearily acknowledge all his friend had done to bring the maiden
volume to publication and express his regrets that O'Neill had felt constrained to
promise a foreword it now looked as though he was bashful about writing. It had
been difficult for the poet to ask this favour in the first place and he would certainly not apply again – but his morale was low anyway. He told Waldo of 'emptied vision' and wanted to resist 'mere word-painting and juggling, however
fastidious'. He had thought that Kahn's patronage would free him to compose
epics he could never manage while committed to office employment but 'now I
know that much has been lacking all along'. But futility was more than his own
personal dilemma: 'I think the artist more and more licks his own vomit, mistaking it for the common diet. He amuses himself that way in a culture without faith
and convictions.' For some reason he simply could not write yet and whenever he
was poetically silent he was miserable – but he hoped Waldo would not think too
much about his problem: 'My judgements are too unsettled these days to make me
feel that I deserve much attention, much less the faith that you assure me of.'[29] But
of course he did need that attention and the following day he wrote to his con-
fessor again. He was now reading Spengler's *The Decline of the West*, he explained,
and its contentions, when combined with his own debilitated state and prevailing
inability to write, prompted him to believe the worst prognostications not only for
his art, but for all artists. For the last two months, he admitted, he had been
'confronting a ghostliness that is new' and now wondered if 'there is any good

evidence forthcoming from the world in general that the artist isn't completely out of a job'. No one cared any longer about vision or about poetic distillation of representative experience. What then was he doing trying to write his long bridging poem, which represented 'an act of faith besides being a communication'? He still wanted to achieve his great ambition but 'the whole theme and project seems more and more absurd'. How could he bridge the gulf between past and present when the dynamics of the construction could not cohere? After all, 'The form of my poem arises out of a past that so overwhelms the present with its worth and vision that I'm at a loss to explain my delusion that there exist any real links between the past and a future worthy of it.' All America cared about now was 'shorter hours, quicker lunches, behaviorism and toothpicks' – so much for Whitman's heroic vision of his country's future; so much for his own determination to celebrate a land of myth. In an unpoetic age there was no room for a poetic America: his vision was null and he speculated that 'a year from now I'll be more interested in working in an office than before'.[30]

He changed books and tackled *Don Quixote* and *Swann's Way*. Then at the beginning of July his luck changed: Waldo cabled to say that Horace Liveright had definitely decided to publish *White Buildings* in the autumn and a letter from Susan gave confirmation of the news and a fuller account of the decision. It appeared that about a month previously the publisher and James Light were guests at Otto Kahn's and at that stage, although he had the typescript of the book with him, Liveright was resolved not to publish it: he was unenthusiastic about the poems and as far as he could see nobody understood them. Three weeks later he was still in possession of the typescript, which was on his desk when Light and O'Neill visited him on business, and still against releasing it – but his guests urged him to reconsider, insisting that one day he would be proud of having published Hart Crane's first volume. Liveright reverted to his old position: if O'Neill would contribute a foreword he would relent, and after further murmurings and misgivings on the playwright's part the arrangement was concluded and the printer informed.

On 9 July Liveright himself wrote to Hart officially: *White Buildings* would appear in the autumn and the author would receive a royalty of 10 per cent on the first 1,000 copies sold. He enclosed a contract for signature and an advance of $100 and as a condition reserved the option on the poet's next two books. As Hart told Waldo, the wonderful news was 'not without results in piercing the miasma of these tropics' and about ten days later, with his ears recovered and his confidence restored, he began to write.[31] However hesitant his initial endeavours, within days his trepidation disappeared; Mrs Hart was informed that his mind had begun 'to swarm with ideas' and soon he was 'writing like mad'.[32] Personal experience and literary preparation – his memories, his reading, his nostalgia for New York, his conviction of poetic greatness, his very vision of America, which like all giants was best appraised from afar – suddenly and mysteriously coalesced in this house where once he had suffered, and sustained him during a period of lyric inventiveness that lasted for the next ten weeks. Circumstances even conspired to free his mind from anxieties about his mother. Her normally incessant correspondence had halted more or less completely since his arrival on the island: perhaps, after all, marriage to Charles Curtis was keeping her happily distracted. He missed her, of course, but in Aunt Sally he had the perfect surrogate: long years of island life had matured her self-sufficiency and she happily sewed, gardened, baked or gossiped with her friend Mrs Durham for all the hours she knew he needed solitude, emerging only in his intervals of disengagement with words of tart common sense or motherly encouragement.

The weather grew hotter and hotter but although Hart's sleep suffered he rose each morning charged with lyric strength: like Prospero's island kingdom, the Isle of Pines itself now seemed enchanted and like Shakespeare's wizard Crane seemed able to conjure its harmonies. 'I feel an absolute music in the air again,' he informed Waldo on 24 July, 'and some tremendous rondure floating somewhere.' He had completed 'To Brooklyn Bridge', the eleven-stanza 'Proem' to his great work, and happily insisted that the poem was 'almost the best thing I've ever written'. There was 'something steady and uncompromising about it' and in the excitement and ease of composition his birthday had passed almost unnoticed.[33] On the very day he turned twenty-seven Washington Roebling, former inhabitant of 110 Columbia Heights and the builder who had realized his father John Augustus Roebling's designs for Brooklyn Bridge, died in New Jersey aged eighty-nine, and with the appearance of his obituary in the *New York Times* the origins of the great arc retreated further into history even as Crane sought to project the structure into myth. From the desk in his room he could contemplate the mango tree at the back of the Villa Casas but what he actually saw was an icy harbour half a continent away:

> *How many dawns, chill from his rippling rest*
> *The seagull's wings shall dip and pivot him,*
> *Shedding white rings of tumult, building high*
> *Over the chained bay waters Liberty –*

He thought in his 'Proem' of the city life he had left far behind, with its cinema-going multitudes, its subways, its lonely suicides, Wall Street – above all he thought of its sentinel bridge, so familiar in his mind's eye as the sun rose over Long Island and gilded an edifice that was both granite and ethereal, motionless yet forever extensive:

> *And Thee, across the harbor, silver-paced*
> *As though the sun took step of thee, yet left*
> *Some motion ever unspent in thy stride, –*
> *Implicitly thy freedom staying thee!*

If the bridge was a marvel of engineering – 'How could mere toil align thy choir-ing strings!' – it was also a 'harp and altar, of the fury fused': its powers of join-ing and reconciliation were musical and as conqueror of the East River and unifier of mankind in the diverse citadels of New York it inspired a mystical if not a reli-gious reverence. 'Under thy shadow by the piers I waited.' How often, sheltering from falling snow yet hopeful of a nocturnal encounter, he had pondered the colossal riverside limbs of the structure and glanced at the skyscrapers across the water, only to see, late at night, 'The City's fiery parcels all undone'. Whatever the time and whatever the season, however, the Roeblings' structure maintained its vigil, its sublime arc adding to human wonder at the glory of God, its great curve conveying pledges of harmony and union from the raving Atlantic into the very heartlands of the pioneer:

O Sleepless as the river under thee,
Vaulting the sea, the prairies' dreaming sod,
Unto us lowliest sometime sweep, descend
And of the curveship lend a myth to God.[34]

The lyric was sent to the *Dial* for Marianne Moore's inspection but a copy also went to Waldo. From now on, to frustrate whatever cataclysms misfortune could unleash, he would send a duplicate of each newly completed section of *The Bridge* to Frank, the 'dear repository of my faith'. In the same letter he enclosed refine-ments to 'Ave Maria', now undergoing final revision, and exulted over the 'water-swell rhythm' that he remembered from his voyage to Grand Cayman and had now incorporated in the poem.[35] His heart was lifted still further in the third week of July when the protracted publication of *White Buildings* brought evidence that some of his friends were more stalwart than he had imagined. O'Neill had finally admit-ted what had long been clear: with the best of intentions he was unable to write the foreword demanded by Liveright – not least, he subsequently explained to Hart, because he was without experience as a journalist and had no training as a critic. Nothing he could say would adequately serve the poems or the poet and he was worried in any case that Hart 'might get the wrong angle on the position I took and that it might in some way put a spike in our friendship, or at least intro-duce an element of resentment'.[36] Hearing of the dilemma in Patterson, Allen Tate came forward and volunteered in noble service of the republic of letters to write an introduction which O'Neill could then subscribe. Since that plan was unacceptable to the playwright it was agreed that Tate should introduce *White Buildings* in his own name and when Hart returned his signed contract to Liveright, it was with assurances that everyone was well served by the solution finally adopted:

Tate understands my work thoroughly. He is a very acute critic of literature gen-erally, and poetry especially. I'm sorry that Gene didn't feel nervy enough to attempt some exposition of this mystery of mysteries, Hart Crane, but I feel fortunate enough in your final choice.[37]

Privately Hart was moved by Tate's gesture – it was 'truly beautiful' of him, he told Waldo – but when on 25 July he tried to write a letter of grateful acknowledgement words failed him.[38] Nothing had passed between them since the poet's stormy departure from Patterson and now he was humbled by Tate's reminder that if true friends disagree they also forgive; all he could do was stutter thanks for 'the extremity of your interest (may I say generosity or *friendship* without too much transgressing appropriate boundaries?)'.[39]

He was very happy that night, especially as a propitiatory breeze blew in from the sea, and he walked singing through the orange groves by the silver light of a moon so low it seemed intent on listening. The heat on the Isle of Pines was now, he told Waldo, 'prostrating', but better that than the cyclones currently raging off Florida.[40] Writing letters of thanks and reconciliation could be difficult but *The Bridge* progressed with ease: on 29 July he informed the Cowleys that 'Columbus has been cleared up' and having read Basil Lubbock's *The China Clippers* he was already working on a provisional draft of 'Cutty Sark', which would eventually constitute the fulcrum Part III of the final poem.[41] Its form was to be experimental – how else convey the meanderings of a drunken sailor as the preface to a celebration of the nineteenth-century tea clippers which raced the seas to China? – yet for all that its composition was pleasurable and he proudly entrusted a copy to the Cowleys, charging them to show it to nobody apart from Tate and the Browns. To Waldo alone he remarked that it was surely more than coincidence that 'when "Cutty Sark" was bobbing up' the *Orizaba,* which had speeded the poet himself over the waters, was simultaneously in the news for saving lives in the Florida cyclone.[42]

'No – I can't live on land – !' 'Cutty Sark's' drunken sailor declares, as he reminisces in a South Street saloon before getting ready to join his ship, and the narrator of the poem glimpses 'the frontiers gleaming of his mind'. In a section that would eventually be placed midway through *The Bridge* Crane wrote a brilliant piece of impressionistic poetry that evokes the ramblings of a rum-sodden mind as well as the swell and lurch of heavy seas – besides incorporating two voices, of Time and Eternity, which are heard throughout the larger literary structure. Several fragments of personal experience are embedded in these eighty-five lines, which begin in the 'present' of the South Street speakeasy and move to the 'past' of the Victorian tea trade, represented by the ships that were drawn, like Columbus before them, to Cathay: 'Cutty Sark', besides being the name of the British clipper that set a speed record for the trading route from England to China, was the name of Crane's favourite whisky, and the intoxicated South Street mariner is later bound for Antwerp, which was also lover Jerry's destination so many sailors ago.

As the seaman tells his story in the bar the background talk ebbs and flows – 'Murmurs of Leviathan he spoke,/and rum was Plato in our heads' – while a pianola tinkles 'Stamboul Nights', the words of which – as deftly quoted by Crane – suggest first the world of Time, '*teased remnants of the skeletons of cities*', and then the Eternity which *The Bridge* will eventually evoke: '*ATLANTIS ROSE drums wreathe the rose*.'[43] The poet leaves the sailor and the speakeasy behind and crossing Brooklyn Bridge he sees what Crane later described to Kahn as 'the airy regatta of phantom clipper ships', the description of which concludes 'Cutty Sark'. It had been 'a pleasure to use historical names for these lovely ghosts. Music still haunts their names long after the wind has left their sails.'[44]

On 30 July Hart wrote a long letter to Grace to thank her for the birthday gift she had sent and to urge her to write to Aunt Sally about her plans for the Villa Casas. He was well, he promised, despite continuing insomnia in the hot and noisy tropical nights, and assured her that he was avoiding unnecessary physical exertion in the sun. He had written over ten pages of *The Bridge* in the last ten days – 'highly concentrated stuff, as you know it is with me' – and was sure that by the time he returned to America the following May his labour would be over. He was happy, 'for the poem will be magnificent'. Aunt Sally was 'a perfect peach' and he was 'simply immersed in work to my neck, eating, "sleeping", and breathing it', with regular sessions on the baby grand whenever he needed to clear his mind of discarded rhymes and rhythms.[45] Reading was another indispensable distraction: Proust and Cervantes had given way to Nashe's *The Unfortunate Traveller*, Fielding's *Jonathan Wild* and Smollett's *Ferdinand Count Fathom*, all of which, he informed Underwood on 3 August, contained 'marvellous prose & observations, satire & diamonds' and provided him with 'good ballast for some of my rather transcendental flights'. Less satisfactory was 'that dirty sheet', the *New York Times*, to which he had just subscribed. 'If you knew the behind-the-scenes of their atrocious snobbishness & lick-spittle attitude toward writers and factions of writers!' he fulminated to his Washington friend, claiming that when *White Buildings* was published, 'I don't expect anything but shit from them'.[46]

That same day Hart sent copies of the 'Proem' and 'Ave Maria' to Kahn and another report to Frank, who was informed that his friend was now toying with the idea of appending notes to his poem, as Eliot had done with *The Waste Land*. Hart enclosed them in the letter, along with the latest version of the last section of *The Bridge*, now officially designated 'Atlantis', and a copy of Tate's foreword, which he considered 'clever, valiant, concise and beautiful', so much so that it was hard to imagine O'Neill could have produced anything comparable. Conviction and exhilaration prevailed: he felt, he said, as though he were 'dancing on dynamite' – all components of the poem were now 'moving forward at once' and he understood at last why bridges were raised from both ends simultaneously. He had built out now from near and far shores; still to be realized was the great central arc, which he proposed to call 'Powhatan's Daughter' and which would precede his accounts of the conquest of time and space which had yet to be written.⁴⁷ The good omens persisted on 5 August when Marianne Moore accepted 'To Brooklyn Bridge' without demur and sent payment of $40. Subject to reservations about one line (which the poet subsequently altered) Waldo also liked the lyric and was rewarded on 12 August with yet more instalments of the larger poem, including versions of the 'Three Songs' which eventually constituted Part V – 'Southern Cross', 'National Winter Garden' and 'Virginia'. Hart was now reading Leta Stetter Holingworth's *Prairie Years* in preparation for work on 'Powhatan's Daughter' and already knew he wanted that section to include poems about an Indian sacrifice and the Gold Rush of 1849. He leapt, he said, from writing one part of *The Bridge* to another, 'like a sky-gack or girder-jack', marvelling at the functioning of the creative memory, which in timely fashion had released 'impressions and concepts gathered the last several years and constantly repressed by immediate circum-stances'. Although only half finished, his poem was now longer than *The Waste Land* but Hart was satisfied – only an expansive scheme could easily contain all his accumulated ideas and reflections 'without the violences that mar so much of my previous, more casual work'.⁴⁸

On 19 August, writing to Waldo again, he was ready to admit that even Spengler's work, depressing though it had been to digest, had played a part in the intellectual and creative processes now bearing fruit. For the first time he could believe that 'every circumstance and incident in one's life flocks toward a positive center of action, control and beauty'. He lived, as never before, '*completely* in my work', convinced that the past existed in the present and certain that in handling 'the beautiful skeins of this myth of America' he could evoke both temporal states for their mutual illumination. As never before, he felt, he was an artist who built his artefact from inventiveness and inner conviction, rather than applying creative perfectionism to personal experience. His nights were enthralled by the most vivid dreams but even then he was aware of a ceaseless process of verbal elimination – 'sometimes words come and go, presented like a rose that yields only its light, never its composite form' – as though his imagination were temporarily invulner-able to the exhaustions of the body or as though the lyric impulse were both autonomous and self-perpetuating. The rains continued with a vengeance: pre-cipitation was daily and overpowering and 'the thunder rods jab and prospect in the caverns deep below that chain of mountains' Waldo no doubt remembered opposite the house. 'You can hear the very snakes rejoice, – the long, shaken-out convulsions of rock and roots.'⁴⁹

His own imaginative workings were also subterranean now – he had begun work on 'The Tunnel', the great poetic descent into the Hell of contemporary Manhattan which would constitute the penultimate section of *The Bridge* and its darkest hour, before the salvation entailed by the climactic 'Atlantis'. By 23 August, he told Waldo, it was almost done, even though the composition was 'rather ghastly, almost surgery', and most of it was drawn from notes he had taken in the subway 'while swinging on the strap at late midnights' on his way back to Brooklyn from an evening in Manhattan. Had Waldo noticed how 'throughout the poem motives and situations recur – under modifications of environment'? This symphonic repetition was very much his own design but sometimes he wondered if the themes of his work presented themselves independently of his creative faculties. Either way he was happy and assured his mentor that the surprises held for him by 'the organic substances of the poem' were among the 'greatest joys of creation'.[50]

'The Tunnel', besides establishing its author as a major practitioner in the principal twentieth-century poetic tradition – that of urban despair – continues this pattern of recurrence with the poet emerging one evening from a theatre in Times Square and making his way amidst the milling crowds to Columbus Circle. The scene is one of aimless nocturnal pleasure-seeking: the situation is Broadway, 'the great white way' of neon and legend which links Square with Circle but which also follows an ancient Indian trail long predating New York's street system. Echoes of antecedent Indian culture are thus introduced even as the poet walks to the noisy crossroads named after the man who discovered America. The poet takes the subway home and as he enters the station he deposits the coin which will crop up repeatedly in the poetic time-travel of a continent. The entrance to the subway 'yawns' in infernal manner, confirming what the epigraph from Blake – 'To Find the Western path/Right thro' the Gates of Wrath' – has already intimated: this is to be a journey in Hell where human beings avoid eye contact and where the snatches of conversation overheard as the train 'rivered under streets/and rivers' are both sordid and banal. The train stops at 14th Street and the poet reflects that Hell must be like these tunnels he now travels – darkly involved, endlessly repetitious and inescapable – but more chilling is the realization that he has resorted here before, and of his own volition. Just as the descendants of the visionaries who built America now scuttle around in trains talking in trite incoherence, so he who once believed in true and enduring love remembers brief encounters in the station men's room:

> The phonographs of hades in the brain
> Are tunnels that re-wind themselves, and love
> A burnt match skating in a urinal –

The doors close; the train continues; and now a vision: 'Whose head is swinging from the swollen strap?/Whose body smokes along the bitten rails?' It is Edgar Allan Poe, a misfit from birth, as Crane sometimes felt himself to be, another uneasy compound of Romanticism and Symbolism, a sacrificial victim of Whitman's great democracy – not because he wrote poetry the crowd could never comprehend but because he was dragged, incapable with drink, from polling place to polling place by a mob intent on using him for multiple voting. He was the first

American writer to dwell darkly 'in interborough fissures of the mind' and the first to exert a major influence on European writers. But sometimes the poet wondered if Baudelaire's verdict – 'America was Poe's prison' – might also apply to him. 'And why do I often meet your visage here,/Your eyes like agate lanterns – on and on/Below the toothpaste and the dandruff ads?' The train continues its journey downtown and the poet contemplates Poe's mysterious fate and wonders if in his last hours he denied the validity of his country's myth:

And when they dragged your retching flesh,
Your trembling hands that night through Baltimore –
That last night on the ballot rounds, did you,
Shaking, did you deny the ticket, Poe?

More passengers get off at Chambers Street: 'The car/Wheels off. The train rounds, bending to a scream,/Taking the final level for the dive/Under the river'. Now a 'Wop washerwoman', on her way home from cleaning some 'gaunt sky-barracks', arrests the poet's attention: is she perhaps a 'Genoese', like Columbus before her, and does she bring succour 'Back home to children and to golden hair?' The train now embodies the 'Daemon' of technology which has turned against its creators, and human beings themselves, as represented by the train's passengers, are 'caught like pennies beneath soot and steam'. The train oversees 'the muffled slaughter of a day in birth' and mocks sensate humankind – 'shrill ganglia/Impassioned with some song we fail to keep' – but just as it seems there is no hope of reprieve or escape from the meaningless mechanized hell of con-temporary reality the poet hears '– A sound of waters bending astride the sky/Unceasing with some Word that will not die...!' Emerging at last from the subway he finds himself 'Here by the River that is East'. He has been 'Tossed from the coil of ticking towers', and thus released not merely from the money-minded chasms of Manhattan but from the temporal world itself. He is back at Brooklyn Bridge where he began his quest for America at the poem's beginning: he marvels, as in a dream, at the reality of river life behind him – the tugs, 'the oily tympa-num of waters' and the lights and sounds that animate the night, but now he looks ahead – 'Tomorrow,/And to be. ...' As he stands by the water 'the hands drop memory' – pain and spiritual lethargy fall away and he apprehends the nearness of Atlantis. In a moment of almost magical stillness the poem ends with the benign and purging fire of deity evoked in three short declining lines: 'Kiss of our agony Thou gatherest,/O Hand of Fire/gatherest –'[51]

At the end of August, with all principal sections of *The Bridge* either carefully sketched or complete, Hart went to Havana for a vacation, knowing prior to departure that he could ill afford the excursion but eager, he explained to Grace, 'to see a few bad shows' and hopeful that a change of environment would

alleviate his acute hay fever.[52] In May Waldo's easy Spanish had assured his
smooth passage through the city but now, monoglot and alone, he played safe
and checked into an American hotel for a week of pleasure and distraction. His
brief visit here for medical relief following the arduous voyage to Grand Cayman
had left him with memories of 'a lovely city' which was 'full of white and gold
and azure buildings'.[53] Now closer inspection revealed a metropolis more geared
to carnival than any he had ever experienced: an estimated 7,000 bars appeased
the thirsts of this city of half a million and although the 'Distrito de Tolerancia'
of prostitution near the San José docks had recently been suppressed as detri-
mental to the island's birth rate, a flourishing race track, the Cuban national lottery, the famous Casino, even the cock-fighting, legally enshrined in the ring
opposite Havana Station on Jesùs del Monte Street, spoke well of a national
understanding that the keenest pleasures often entail elements of chance and
unpredictability.

Under the corrupt presidency of Gerardo Machado, with the island's economy
ravaged by inflation and global fluctuations in the price of sugar, foreign tourists
were well placed to enjoy Cuba's temptations and since Americans required neither
a passport to enter this Caribbean Sybaris nor a visa to remain they inevitably constituted the preponderance of visitors. Indeed by the mid-1920s the most fashionable elements of Chicago, Philadelphia and New York considered it imperative to
be seen in Havana at some stage in the social season which ran for three months
from early December, and American gossip columns reported regularly on the
appearance of Astors, Whitneys, Goulds and Vanderbilts, even Otto Kahn himself,
as they were glimpsed rubbing shoulders with the island's richest plantation
owners at the Casino or the Jockey Club or sipping 'Mary Pickfords' beneath the
palms at the Sevilla-Biltmore. In August, however, with hurricanes gathering on
the horizon, penniless poets and locals had the plazas largely to themselves –
which was perhaps why Hart came to remember this capital of the West Indies as
'almost a paradise'.[54] With funds low as usual there was a limit to the pleasures
open to him but on the night of 31 August a meeting occurred which redirected
the remainder of his stay as well as entailing so many unforeseen expenses that he
was compelled to approach CA for a $50 loan before he returned to the Isle of
Pines.

Thanks to Waldo's introduction Hart had no need to rely on his instincts,
increasingly acute as they were, when it came to finding city lowlife – with its
inevitable crowd of lonely onlookers – and after an evening at the Alhambra he
headed for Park Central and the possible rendezvous that had all along brought
him to Havana. He met a young sailor named Alfredo, whose ship, the *Maximo
Gomez*, was in Havana harbour, and although poet and mariner shared scarcely a
dozen words Hart was able to promise Waldo that this new romance was 'immaculate, ardent and delicately restrained – I have learned much about love which I
did not know existed'. Most Cuban sailors, he had already established, were 'ter-

rible', but Alfredo was somehow different, perhaps because his parents were Spanish. At any rate Hart now knew 'what delicate revelations may bloom from the humble' and in the course of 'three long and devoted evenings' of walks and drives along the Malecón, which must of necessity have been largely without conversation, he resolved to learn Spanish. As a preliminary step, and perhaps because it would be easier to explain away his sailor, he decided to move from his American hotel to a Hispanic one: once again, following Waldo's introduction, he knew just where to go, and took Alfredo to the Isla de Cuba, with its *grandes departamentos con servicio sanitario privado y elevador*, for the remainder of his stay. He left Havana for Batabanó and the ferry home on 3 September, but in the course of one last drink in the white, gold and azure city he assured Waldo from La Diana, *Gran Café, Reposteria (abierto toda la noche)* that he was 'much relaxed' after his holiday and anticipated having 'a fresh view of what I have written and have still to write – and with an internal glow which is hard to describe'.[55]

Havana had inspired in more ways than one: he now knew what he wanted to write once *The Bridge* was complete – 'a blank verse tragedy of Aztec mythology,' he told Waldo, 'for which I shall have to study the obscure calendars of dead kings'.[56] At some stage in the next few years he intended to travel to Spain to learn its language properly – but all dreams aside, reality was the ferry back to Nueva Gerona and the lonely island guarded by an old woman; the huge edifice of poetry that still remained to be perfected; remembered kisses in Cuba and the poignant thought that he might never see his sailor again. The picture darkened when he opened the mail from Cleveland: Grace had written twice in his absence with news that threatened to end the tranquillity crucial to composition. After only four months she and Charles Curtis had agreed to separate and here she was again reaching out for the prop who could never go to the divorce courts. He replied on 6 September and told her she was 'very brave' in the face of adversity and that he was 'proud of your spirit' but even as he urged her to stop thinking that everything was 'all over' he must have wondered how far he would have to travel to escape his family's troubles.[57] By the time he wrote again, on 19 September, Grace had already sent him two further letters complaining that he seemed unsympathetic and advising him that she was moving from Wade Park Manor to an apartment in Superior Road. On the contrary, he was sympathetic, he promised, but he was also 'attempting a titanic job' of creation 'and if anything of that is to be accomplished there must be some calm and detachment sought for'. Indeed calm would see them all through and in the meantime he begged her to stop thinking about 'melodramatic things like old ladies homes'.[58]

To make matters worse, Hart was penniless again. CA had either not responded to his appeal or else his reply had been lost to the Havana post office, which was notorious for opening any mail which looked as though it might contain currency. Both possibilities were distressing but rather than contact his father again Hart decided to approach Otto Kahn for the outstanding $500 of promised support, assuring him on 19 September, 'albeit with no excess of modesty, that [*The Bridge*] is already an epic of America'.[59] He advised the banker to send a cheque to circumvent post office larceny but Kahn was travelling and that plea, and a subsequent reminder, went unanswered.

So he was thrown back on Aunt Sally for support as he once again took up *The Bridge* and continued work on the section which would eventually become 'The River' and would continue the larger poem's passage back through time by linking the noisy twentieth-century America of advertising and mass consumption with the earlier continent of the European settlers.

Both worlds abutted the Mississippi River, river of time, great vehicle of all America's history, and the more he pondered this section the more he determined to embed in its lines a tribute to Aunt Sally herself, who was, he later told her, 'my idea of the salt of all pioneers'.[60] Conclusion lay some way in the future, but as he struggled with his rhymes, apparently abandoned by CA and Kahn, he knew he could depend on this stalwart friend who had proved herself to be 'the very elf of music, little wrinkled burnous wisp that can do anything and remembers so much'.[61] She loved to hear his Cuban dance records played loudly on the gramophone and would tap and twirl at her work in the kitchen. He by contrast loved to hear her reminiscences of New Orleans and Louisiana and eventually he set them for ever in the dialogue of 'hobo-trekkers' that animates the central section of 'The River':

> I heard a road-gang chanting so.
> And afterwards, who had a colt's eyes – one said,
> 'Jesus! Oh I remember watermelon days!' And sped
> High in a cloud of merriment, recalled
> ' – And when my Aunt Sally Simpson smiled,' he drawled –
> 'It was almost Louisiana, long ago.'[62]

The October issue of *Poetry* appeared, and with it 'At Melville's Tomb' and Hart's accompanying controversy with Harriet Monroe, to which the poet proudly drew Kenneth Burke's attention, convinced as he was that 'I come off very well with the woozy old spinster'. He took the opportunity of congratulating Burke for his recent review of Spengler's *The Decline of the West*, which was the only appraisal he had seen 'that doesn't swallow the whole hook and sinker in favor of [the reviewer's] private predilections'. His own views of time, history and cultural longevity had been dramatically modified since his arrival in the tropics and now he could assure Burke: 'You have to live in or under a Greek sky like this, down here, to know why the ancients had a different idea of the space or "futurity" of *blue* – than did the monks and denizens of the northern abbey's [*sic*], half the time fog-filled, of the *middle-ages*.'[63] And then out of that blue sky a letter from a complete stranger: Yvor Winters, a poet and linguist affiliated to the University of Idaho, wrote with expressions of admiration for Hart's poetry and with the request that he send copies of his latest work for him to read.

Hart was delighted by the overture and although he claimed he had neither the time nor the energy to comply with Winters's request he was happy to send a detailed reply on 5 October. He admired what little he knew of his fellow-poet's work and was particularly gratified by Winters's opinion of 'Faustus and Helen' ('one of the great poems of our time – as great as the best of Stevens or Pound or Eliot') which Winters's friend Harriet Monroe had published in *Poetry* as part of her public quarrel with Hart and his metaphors.[64] In a sense, however, it was not surprising that Winters saw the point of that earlier poem: as Hart now explained, the two of them were disciples of Whitman and the 'new Metaphysics' the latter had proclaimed in *Democratic Vistas* was apparent in both their work. One returned to Whitman repeatedly, and to Poe and 'my beloved Melville', for a 'renewed appreciation of what America really is, or could be' but when it came to contemporary poetry there was little to inspire. Cummings and Marianne Moore could be impressive, but Hart was sure Winters agreed that Amy Lowell wrote 'scullery permutations' and Carl Sandburg was nothing more than a hybrid conceived by the fusion of Hart's first literary acquaintance, the essayist and homespun philosopher Elbert Hubbard, and the ghost of Harriet Beecher Stowe 'on a slab of the sunburnt west'.[65]

Winters was nothing if not opinionated when it came to literature, as Hart would learn, and in due course would take issue not only with the latter's low opinion of his idol William Carlos Williams but also with the very axioms of Cranean poetry. Long before Hart's strictures could be acknowledged, however, the deliverance which the locals had dreaded and which had been implicit in the torrid summer, the hottest Aunt Sally could remember, suddenly smote the Isle of Pines with irresistible fury. As though invoked by 'O Carib Isle!', a severe hurricane reached the island on the evening of 19 October before blasting its way to Cuba the following day. Although the system weakened as it raged, its winds were still travelling at 130 miles an hour when it gained Havana on 21 October and by the time it spiralled out to sea it was judged to have been the most serious storm in eighty years: its voice, the *New York Times* reported, 'was a steady growl, increasing at times of its greatest violence to a shriek'.[66] When the winds had begun to rise ominously Hart followed Mrs Simpson's instructions and went round the Villa Casas closing shutters, retrieving objects from outside and positioning vessels beneath the known weak points of the roof. But when he and Aunt Sally saw the malevolence of the storm they took shelter with Attaboy beneath the biggest bed in the house and remained there for the duration, to reminisce above the sound of splitting walls, falling plaster and tearing gables. When the winds temporarily abated Hart would emerge for supplies of food and drink and on one occasion, driven by bodily needs, he ventured scantily clad into the garden, to leave an indelible impression on Aunt Sally's mind: 'The picture of Adonis striding through the tall grass garbed "a la natural" often comes to me and makes me wonder how we both came out so well.'[67] She who possessed great spirit and the instincts of a survivor thought she saw the same qualities in him and later promised 'I had rather go through a hurricane every day with you who could at least laugh a little'.[68] Whether or not she knew it, he had not always shown the same tenacity. Ten years previously, bent on self-destruction in this very house, he had miscalculated with razor blades and narcotics: now, cast within the flow of the hurricane, he need have calculated nothing beyond submission had he been eager for death. But now, great with poetry, he sheltered. Now Hart Crane chose life.

The following morning, with the worst of it over, these orphans of the storm emerged from their shelter and, placing cushions on their heads in case more of the house collapsed about them, they put 'Valencia' on the gramophone and danced a one-step celebration. Braving the ebbing tempest they walked into Nueva Gerona, unprepared for the destruction that greeted them: the streets were chaotic with damaged vehicles, uprooted wires and trees, dead animals, injured survivors and miscellaneous debris. Fernandez' Hotel was still serviceable as a makeshift hospital but most of the other prominent buildings, including the Catholic church and the City Hall, had either been badly damaged or razed and the ferry to Batabanó was floating in fragments where once the wharf had been. The town was without wireless communication with the outside world but rumour already had it that Havana was flooded and aflame. The truth, when it finally emerged, was no less distressing: power and water supplies in the city had been severed, the Maine Monument had been levelled, 200 bodies were thought to be floating in Havana harbour and in Cuba as a whole the death toll was put at 600, with 9,000 injured.

In New York a Cuban Relief Committee was established at the offices of J.P. Morgan and Company and in the light of President Coolidge's expressions of sympathy and condolence President Machado appealed for official aid in Havana to General Crowder, the United States ambassador to Cuba. On the Isle of Pines more than 1,400 people were rendered homeless and although the final casualty list as declared by Sheridan Talbott, the United States consul, was relatively small – three Americans and twenty-two others dead, with a hundred Americans injured – damage to property and agriculture was put at $2 million.[69] By any standards, catastrophe had befallen the islands but before Hart could assess the consequences for his own future he and Aunt Sally had to return to the Villa Casas to salvage what remained of his grandparents' distant dream of a place in the sun. Later, in 'Eternity', he would recall their puny efforts at reclamation and the scale of the devastation that mocked them:

Back at the erstwhile house
We shoveled and sweated; watched the ogre sun

Blister the mountain, stripped now, bare of palm,
Everything – and lick the grass, as black as patent
Leather, which the rimed white wind had glazed.
Everything gone – or strewn in riddled grace –
Long tropic roots high in the air, like lace.

Salvation sailed from the American naval base at Guantánamo Bay in Cuba: the destroyer *Goff* and the USS *Milwaukee*, with her complement of 458 men under Captain Clark H. Woodward, arrived at Nueva Gerona to re-establish wireless contact, replace telephone lines, organize a medical centre and supply the stricken island with more than 50 tons of food.[70] Much of this activity was inevitably focused on the beach, where able-bodied spectators gathered to watch the operations. In gratitude some of the local ladies set up trestles on the sand and provided refreshment for their rescuers and in gratitude of another kind a restless poet appeared with a camera: numerous photographs survive among Hart Crane's papers as evidence of his fieldwork – their clusters of sailors, laughing and friendly, dazzling in their white uniforms against the sea, apparently unsuspicious of the intensity of the poet's connoisseurship. He pursued some of them to a bar that was still in business and 'Eternity' provides a glimpse of the small talk that ensued and the larger ambitions it betokened: 'I stood a long time in Mack's talking/New York with the gobs, Guantanamo, Norfolk, –/Drinking Bacardi and talking U.S.A.'[71]

It was the one excitement in a dismal time: with his inspiration broken, his pockets empty and the Villa Casas uninhabitable for the foreseeable future it was clear he could not remain on the Isle of Pines and already, as though clawing him back, notification came from the American Embassy in Havana that inquiries about his welfare in the wake of the hurricane had been lodged in Washington, presumably by Grace. Aunt Sally offered to pay his fare back to New York and in the last few days on the island he slept only with the aid of large doses of Veronal. In pre-emption of the hurricane he had sent all recently written poetry to New York for safe keeping and now reluctantly he prepared to follow it, back to a family which expected unreconcilable things and to America which expected an epic. On the journey home, attempting to trace Alfredo in Havana, he ran into one of his fellow crewmen and learned through 'signs and contortions' that his sailor had sustained serious shoulder wounds and a broken arm in the course of the hurricane, which had sunk the *Maximo Gomez*.[72] Hart never saw Alfredo, Mrs Simpson or the Isle of Pines again: the Cuban sailor would write occasionally and Hart maintained an affectionate correspondence with Aunt Sally for the remainder of his life but this happy chapter, the most fruitful of his career, was closed. He had not finished with the tropics and the Caribbean had not finished with him but for now it was back to the North and to the friends who had anxiously been scanning newspaper lists of those injured in the hurricane. Among them was William

Wright, who wrote to Hart on 23 October: 'I am a bit anxious lest you should have mingled yourself and your Penates with the hurricane and sailed off to a Realm of Pure Poesy without further ado. Not that I think you have. With all your internal combustion, you oppose too much resistance to the cosmos; and you are too tough a knot spiritually to be much troubled by a mere physical tempest.'[73]

14

Hart returned to New York on 28 October and after registering at the Hotel Albert he set about ordering his affairs. He cabled Grace to assure her of his survival; she replied with her customary flair for drama to indicate that she had endured whirlwinds worse than any that had ravaged the Caribbean, having been admitted to hospital two weeks previously with 'things in terrible shape here'.[1] She also revealed, without specifying how or why, that she had enlisted the assistance of Otto Kahn – another conspicuous presence on Hart's list of people and problems to be addressed. The financier had returned from his travels to receive the poet's anxious pleas from the Caribbean and now sent word that he would be available for a brief interview at 1100 Fifth Avenue on the morning of Tuesday, 2 November. In the meantime, desperately worried about money, Hart wrote briefly but affectionately to CA to announce his return and to hint that the financial problems that had prompted his letter from the Isle of Pines were still unresolved. At least Waldo could be depended on for reassurance – he had seen the latest issue of *Poetry* and wrote to say he was thrilled by his friend's contribution: 'The Melville poem has a third stanza that is simply glorious. I feel, somehow, that Herman Melville must learn of this created recognition.'[2]

It was also encouraging to learn through Tate that Yvor Winters was concerned about his welfare following the hurricane and on 1 November Hart sent his new correspondent a brief letter of thanks saying that Winters should write to him henceforth care of Mrs Turner, since at the moment he was 'terribly rushed and undecided as yet as to exactly where I shall settle'.[3] That same day he sent 'O Carib Isle!' to Harriet Monroe, pointing out that the lyric was not a description of an event but an anticipation. 'Nevertheless, it is quite true to the *psyche* of the monster; and if you are convinced enough to want to publish it – I'm hoping you'll let me know as soon as possible. For don't we all, especially we refugees, (and poets besides, Grace a Dios!) don't we ALL need money?'[4] Whatever the state of his finances, however, his family would always be the same and with the apparent intractability of their problems confronting him more starkly than ever after his respite on the Isle of Pines he began to wonder, as he explained to Charlotte Rychtarik, how much more of his energy would be absorbed by difficulties he could never resolve. He was eager not to hurt anyone's feelings, 'but I think that unless I isolate myself somewhat (and pretty soon) from the avalanche of bitterness and wailing that has flooded me ever since I was seven years old' he would be deprived of the capacity to breathe, let alone write.[5]

Now Grace had even started to involve herself in his relations with Kahn, as he discovered when he arrived at 1100 Fifth Avenue to be told she had asked for the financier's assistance in establishing whether Hart had been among the hurricane's victims. The meeting was a short one; and beyond expressing mild surprise that *The Bridge* was not yet complete, Kahn reiterated his interest and goodwill and promised that the remaining $500 would be paid at once. So for the time being, whether or not his father chose to disregard his plight, Hart could rest more easily. Even as the poet and the banker were talking, however, Clarence Crane was writing to his son, enclosing not only $25 but also the reason for his prolonged silence: Frances Crane, the Irish beauty he had married eight years previously, had been diagnosed as having incurable cancer, 'and I have been so nearly crazed with grief from that day to this that I am in no condition now to write you a very satisfactory letter'. He was glad to learn Hart had survived the hurricane and that he was well and contented: 'If so, you are the only member of the Crane family who is'.[6]

Despite this awful news there seemed little to be gained by travelling to Cleveland: when he could do nothing to assist his mother or stepmother *The Bridge* had to remain his priority and so by the end of the first week in November Hart was back at Patterson and waiting for inspiration to revive. Since the Tates had returned to New York his reconciliation with Allen could go no further for the time being and he was thrown back on Addie Turner for companionship – and on Aunt Sally for comfort and Caribbean news. He wanted to settle his debt to her – $250 by his reckoning, for the fare back to New York – and she wanted him to focus his energies. 'Don't you dare give up for I have much faith in you boy and you must finish "The Bridge".'[7] Again and again between now and Christmas she wrote with news about the decay of the Villa Casas, which was gradually being dismantled by the elements and by thieving Cuban farmers. If the Hart fortunes were in decline, however, she was sure his own, with the publication of *White Buildings* now certain, were ascendant: 'So glad, so glad your book is coming out so soon ... I'm sure you are getting at last what you deserve[,] Praise; but don't let it spoil you, 'twas useless for me to write that – you are too reasonable and level-headed to be spoilt by well-merited praise.'[8] Less welcome was the letter Charles Curtis wrote on 10 November with a summary of his failed marriage to Hart's mother. Grace had been 'in a bad way', it transpired, for about six weeks owing to the move from Wade Park Manor and anxieties about Mrs Hart's health. She had quarrelled with one nurse before engaging another, had attempted to have her mother committed to hospital and had moved from her new apartment to the Hotel Statler and back again. Stress had led to anger; anger to acute pain in her legs; and now she was confined to bed. It was a pattern for which Curtis was wholly unprepared: 'As a result of the experiences of the last six weeks, and similar experiences at intervals of about a month ever since last April, I have given up every hope of ever being able to live with [Grace].' He had always refused to quarrel with her but now, on his lawyer's advice, he intended to seek a divorce. He waived all claim to the $2,000-worth of furniture he had bought for the new apartment and guaranteed to pay the rent there until 1 October 1927. Since Grace had asked him to move out two days ago he was staying with his daughter and now took the occasion of the last letter he wrote to the stepson he scarcely knew to express his 'feelings of disappointment and regret at such an unfortunate outcome'.[9]

It was as though he had never been away. The same remembered hills, already bleak and brown in an early winter, and the same family problems – no wonder Hart complained to Wilbur Underwood of exhaustion: 'I'm so tired I can't imagine ever leaving here or stirring again – too tired to write – as I was to talk when you saw me in town.'[10] He could be frank in his lethargy and depression with old friends but new acquaintances required greater efforts of enthusiasm. In any case Hart was genuinely elated by the interest shown in his work and life by Yvor Winters and the correspondence the two men now resumed constituted the poet's principal literary activity for the remainder of the year.

Hart always wanted intellectual, as well as emotional, sympathy and what appealed to him about Winters beyond his evident devotion to poetry was his apparent belief that Hart himself was now pre-eminent among its youngest generation of practitioners. More pleasing still, this was a conviction undistorted by the obligations of friendship and freely declared in *Poetry* and other such organs of wayward prestige. It was one thing for Tate or Frank or Munson or Cowley to applaud his latest lyric, but they imported personal considerations into their evaluations and New York's small literary world knew them to do so. But Winters was open to no such accusations: although his reputation in 1926 was steadily growing he was the most isolated figure in contemporary American letters, a man of transmontane objectivity who was forever excluded, as Hart felt himself to be, from the comfortable Ivy League brotherhood which commanded East Coast intellectual opinion. Unlike Hart, however, his senior by one year, Winters made a pugnacious virtue of this exclusion and in a life spent almost entirely in the American West he devoted much thought and time to criticizing what he saw as the easy orthodoxies of the Eastern universities. His remoteness made him a voluminous letter-writer and he maintained extensive correspondence with many figures in New York's literary world: at the time he began writing to Hart he was planning to abandon his position at the University of Idaho and move to Paris as a preliminary to establishing himself as a poet and linguist. But financial insecurity, aggravated by his own and his wife's history of consumption, kept him in the West and a year after his first overture to Hart he embarked on a course of study at Stanford Graduate School which marked the beginning of his lifelong association with that university. He had begun publishing his own poems while in a sanatorium for consumptives and by 1926 his work had appeared in many of the little magazines. At this stage, his critical judgements were still unformed and forgiving but in the course of the next few years of steady writing, frugal living and earnest study, as poet, critic and academic, he evolved a stern morality which was hostile to mysticism, ecstasy and romantic escapism, which insisted that good poetry involved the control of perception by the intellect – and which spared no feelings in the defence of those values.

In the autumn of 1926, with rational stoicism still ahead of him, Winters was concerned not only about Hart's poetry but about the practicalities of his life and in a letter sent to the Isle of Pines and forwarded to Patterson he urged him to get a job in teaching as a way of making ends meet. When Hart replied on 12 November, it was to insist that he was completely unequipped for such activity. He was without high school education, so Winters would readily understand that 'I'm not being merely modest when I say that my French is weak and my Spanish nil'. Nevertheless, he said, 'I greatly appreciate your interest', as well as Winters's determination to share his literary enthusiasms, paramount among which was William Carlos Williams. Hart knew and admired some of his lyrics and liked Williams 'much personally' but was reluctant to read his *In the American Grain*, despite Winters's fervent endorsement, in case its parallel subject matter upset his scheme for *The Bridge*. On the subject of poetry, had Winters read Edwin Muir's *transition*, the first study to expose 'the real weaknesses' of Eliot's poetry and criticism? Here was a book that offered a welcome antidote to the parochial strictures laid down by figures such as Harriet Monroe. Knowing Monroe as he did, Winters had been eager to learn what prompted her insistence that Hart explain 'At Melville's Tomb' before she would consider publishing it. Warming to the repetition of a favourite anecdote, in which by implication the complexities of modernist thinking were seen as a masculine preserve bewildering to literature's genteel spinsters, Hart explained that it was Ezra Pound who had lent *Poetry* its inquiry, courage and discrimination. Since his defection, Monroe was 'back on the ancient journalist footing where he found her', with her bigoted self-confidence unchallenged: 'She is the kind of person who would run up to Newton, and in behalf of all good easygoing "hopefuls" of the middle-west, would query, "But aren't you a little bit too mathematical, Sir Isaac?"' Enough gossip: Hart eagerly awaited the manuscript of poems Winters had promised and hoped they had not been lost for ever to the Havana post office. In the meantime here he was, in a 'vacant state of mind' and still a little shaken by the extremes into which fate threw him – 'winters in polar regions and summers under the equator'.[11]

Three days later another letter was forwarded from the Isle of Pines and Hart felt like shouting 'Eureka!' because of the 'most intimate sort of critical sympathy – not only with my work, but with my aims' that Winters revealed. Now Hart was convinced of the 'essential sympathy' that existed between his literary values and his correspondent's, especially in light of his familiarity with the list of favourite quotations from poetry that Winters had sent. Winters was eager to know how exactly Hart defined his current poetic undertaking – surely he could not conceive of attempting anything like a narrative epic, when that form was clearly incongruous to the modern age? Hart agreed – epics were too limited a form for the breadth of twentieth-century experience and belief (or disbelief); too limited, that is, 'until somebody actually overcomes the limitations'. Perhaps it was just simpler to discard altogether the traditional nomenclature: at any rate 'the old definition [of an epic] cannot cover the kind of poem I am trying to write except on certain fundamental points'. He was dealing with 'mythical' material in the epic tradition, to be sure, 'but what is "mythical" in or rather, of the twentieth century is not the Kaiser, the sinking of the *Titanic*, etc. Rather it is science, travel (in the name of speed) – psychoanalysis', along with 'the eternal verities of sea, mountain and river'. Once he started talking about his modern myth, he apologized, there was no stopping him because he was wrestling concurrently with so many problems of material and structure: yet he never doubted that the old narrative forms, and the rhetoric that went with them, were obsolete, never doubted either that 'the link-by-link cumulative effect of the ancients' had also been made redundant. Having said that, for all the complaints of the modernists, who insisted that narrative history was old-fashioned, life was lived chronologically. There were 'certain basically mythical factors' in modern Western life which 'literally cry for embodiment' and he was convinced these factors had to be presented 'in chronological and organic order' if they were to appear in 'their true luminous reality'. Thus it was with his account of 'the annihilation of time and space', which was not only 'the prime myth of the modern world' but also, implicitly, the legend of America. The early settlers had once bridged their vast continent by horse, wagon and railroad. Now telephone and radio linked the coasts and soon the American skies themselves would be conquered.[12]

Having decided against reading *In the American Grain*, Hart changed his mind and found much to admire in Carlos Williams's series of essays on Columbus, Pocahontas, the Spanish Conquest, the Puritans and the other episodes of the American story he had decided to consider in *The Bridge*. Writing to Waldo on 21 November he declared the book 'an achievement that I'd be proud of' and was intrigued to see that Williams had situated 'Poe and his "character" in the same position as I had *symbolized* for him in the "Tunnel" section'.[13] He longed for Waldo to visit Patterson for a weekend: the stimulating discussions that would ensue might rekindle his mind for continuation of *The Bridge*, which was at present neglected. Until they did meet he enclosed a 'little thing', a recently completed fourteen-line poem, 'To Emily Dickinson', which hailed as a fellow visionary with similarly heroic ambition the prolific Amherst poet who published so little: 'You who desired so much – in vain to ask –/Yet fed your hunger like an endless task.'[14]

A quiet Thanksgiving with the Browns was made happier by Harriet Monroe's acceptance, with accompanying payment, of 'O Carib Isle!' Winters wrote again, this time with corrections of Hart's Latin and Spanish in parts of *The Bridge*, and then a second letter arrived from Alfredo, and Hart told Aunt Sally on 5 December that he had 'a great time' translating it with the aid of a small dictionary.[15] She wrote to him the same day with a possible solution for the future of the Villa Casas: she had found a potential tenant who proposed to restore the house and pay $10 a month to inhabit it, and she was now convinced Grace should either accept this arrangement or sell the property as soon as possible. But Hart had heard nothing from his mother for the best part of a month and knew her silence could only mean displeasure. Already it was below zero, there was snow on the hills and as he lay awake at night he could hear the water in the jug on his wash-stand click into ice. Although he could hardly wait for the appearance of *White Buildings* the prospect was nerve-racking nevertheless – yet the two people in whose eyes the publication should have counted as a major vindication, his mother and his father, were as usual distracted with problems of their own. By the time he wrote to Underwood on 16 December gloom had turned to depression and depression to sickness. He had tonsillitis, he was lonely, and it seemed as though 'nothing but illness and mental disorder' prevailed in his family. He was disin-clined to rush to Cleveland to nurse woes with which he had no sympathy and saw no point in bolstering the faith in Christian Science his mother and grand-mother professed when he had long since discarded its tenets as 'crass and cheap'. To go there would mean 'tortures and immolations' beyond description yet to remain entailed wondering why there seemed to be 'no place left in the world for love or the innocence of a simple spontaneous act'.[16]

Grace broke her silence with a letter just before Christmas, but by then Hart's nights alternated between insomnia and a sleep which he told his mother was ani-mated by 'an endless reel of pictures, startling and unhappy – like some endless cinematograph'. Not the least of his worries was the future of *The Bridge*: at the moment his mind was like 'dirty dishwater' yet it was imperative that he recom-mence work on his great project. 'So much is expected of me via that poem – that if I fail on it I shall become a laughing stock and my career closed.' He said he was glad she had taken up Christian Science again but insisted she should treat it as a philosophy of life rather than simply a cure in times of trouble – and while they were on the subject of philosophies of life, he begged her to think twice before resorting to resentment, self-pity and anger, the very demons he also struggled to vanquish. 'I know they are demons – they never do me anything but harm.' It was not his most buoyant letter, as he was aware, but he still had tonsil-litis and what looked like being 'a very melancholy Christmas for all of us' lay ahead.[17] In the event the festival was tranquil rather than miserable: along with the Browns and visiting New Yorkers he spent Christmas Day just down the road from Addie Turner's at the house of Eleanor Fitzgerald, business manager of the Provincetown Players. Horace Liveright sent a copy of one of his best-selling biographies of the year, Emil Ludwig's *Napoleon: The Man of Destiny*, but the only old friend from the outside world to remember him was Wilbur Underwood, who sent a book of poems and some old copies of the London *Times*. Winter in Patterson meant almost complete seclusion so it was always refreshing to hear news from beyond the hills. Hart hoped Underwood would write again and was particularly eager for more details of the 'brass-buttoned-tattooed vision' his friend had recently taken back from New York to Washington.[18]

Frances Crane died on 3 January 1927 but with CA distracted with grief Hart only heard the news three weeks later when Mrs Hart wrote to tell him. He had pre-occupations of his own, among them the imminent appearance of *White Buildings*, advance copies of which had appeared at Patterson early in December. It was, he told his mother, 'a beautiful book', but in his excitement he spoke prematurely: at the end of December Allen Tate inspected the volume, only to demand its retraction when he saw his name misspelled on the title page.[19] In view of the unstinting assistance he had already given, and his current efforts to secure the book's publication in England, neither Hart nor Liveright could deny him but when the poet wrote to Tate early in January it was with the complaint that everyone in Cleveland was tired of waiting. 'Lord! is there anything else that can happen to that book? How long will it take them to put in those new title pages, I wonder?'[20] At least there was interest overseas and on 6 January Hart wrote to Liveright to inform him that Edgell Rickword, 'acting as advisor for Wishart & Co., a new publisher starting up this spring', was interested in publishing the book in London. 'Rickword is editor of The Calendar, as good a quarterly as The Criterion and of growing critical influence in England.'[21] The following day he wrote to Rickword himself to praise his biography of Rimbaud, which he had found 'sympathetic and critically stimulating', and to submit 'O Carib Isle!', 'Cutty Sark' and 'The Harbor Dawn' for possible inclusion in the *Calendar*. If Rickword decided to publish the poems Hart hoped he would reproduce 'Cutty Sark' as close to its typescript form as possible. It was a 'cartogram', if he could so style a variation of the calligramme: 'The "ships" should meet and pass in line and type – as well as in wind and memory, if you get my rather unique formal intentions in this phantom regatta seen from Brooklyn Bridge.'[22]

Winters of course got the intentions, not of *The Bridge*, this time, but of *White Buildings*, a copy of which reached him on 10 January. He read the collection quickly, prior to beginning the review he had promised Hart he would write, and was astonished by its contents, as he told the poet the same day: 'I withdraw all minor objections I have ever made to your work. I have never read anything greater and have read little as great.'[23] By now, with stage fright taking the form of revisionary perfectionism, Hart was going through the collection and finding fault with individual lyrics. He was 'elated', he told Winters on 19 January, to learn that he thought so highly of the book and in the meantime he had resumed his labours on *The Bridge* and was working on what became 'The Dance'. Sending Winters a provisional draft of the lyric he once again solicited his assistance: with his knowledge of Indian tribal lore and language, could the critic give him any advice about the name 'Maquokeeta', which he had borrowed from an Indian cab driver in New York and proposed to incorporate in the final poem? Did the name have any symbolic or philological connotations he should know about before adopting it?[24]

Yet for all this show of purpose Hart began the year in a listless mood. He had been delighted to receive a New Year's greeting from Jack Fitzin in Gibraltar but with the cessation of Alfredo's letters he knew that romance had died. By the middle of January it was 16 degrees below and the Caribbean seemed desperately remote; in fact all that appeared to remain of that happy time was a bodily vulnerability to the cold that saw him plagued with chilblains and rheumatic pains on top of tonsillitis. In order to keep warm he and Mrs Turner spent much of their time together in one room: she cooked, washed and mended clothes for him, all for $7 a week, besides providing the inestimable services of companionship. Now that the Tates and the Browns were in New York for the winter Hart was unbearably lonely and besides his expeditions to the bootlegger his days in the kitchen with Addie represented the total of his human companionship. Since his funds were all but exhausted he would soon have to return to New York to look for work but the knowledge that such an upheaval lay ahead left him incapable of concentrating on *The Bridge*. With that enterprise once again at a standstill he wrote letters, read into the night, got up late and attempted to learn Spanish, as daydreams of a life in Havana or Cárdenas, Guadalajara or Toledo continued to haunt him. As he admitted to Underwood, 'all this is a dream' – but the more he surveyed the white hills or trudged through the snow for illegal liquor the more he felt drawn to 'someplace where there is *some* liberty of action, where one can take one's time – and perhaps have something to drink'.[25]

Only a few years previously Hart Crane had thought and written in terms of transcendence. Now his thinking became increasingly escapist. He tried to learn a language, not as Winters did, for the linguistic exercise, or for the literature it would make available, but because it gave a focus to the sense of exile with which he had been born and which he had now begun to admit to himself. Drinking offered another exit from an unsatisfactory present and one which proved easier of proficiency than Spanish. In 1927, the year in which alcoholism finally took hold, this twenty-seven-year-old knew there were good reasons beyond the financial why he no longer lived in New York. In the metropolis, as he told Winters, 'approach me at any hour but the "morning after", and I'm all for the

Mermaid again. I've worn out several kidneys and several bladders already on bootleg rum, but I seem always ready to risk another.'[26]

But whatever sense and self-preservation dictated, by the beginning of February Hart had been isolated in the country for three months and when Macaulay Company publishers invited him to a party in New York to mark the launch of the *American Caravan*, a yearbook of American letters, he caught the train without hesitation. Paul Rosenfeld, Alfred Kreymborg and Van Wyck Brooks, the editors of the *Caravan*, hoped to include 'Ave Maria' in the first volume, scheduled for publication in September, so it was as a potential contributor that Hart attended the party, which was given, Grace was informed, 'in a huge but unbelievably vulgarly furnished and expensive apartment on West End Avenue'. Literary New York was out in force, wine, cocktails and highballs flowed, and 'I had my share'.[27] Rosenfeld had been so impressed on first reading 'Ave Maria' that he had called its author long-distance in his determination to secure the poem. Since Liveright had the option on Hart's next two books, copyright commitments prevented immediate agreement but the poet had also arranged to see his publisher while in New York to discuss expected reviews and sales of *White Buildings* and he hoped in the course of the meeting to come to an arrangement which would accommodate the *Caravan*, which was after all to represent all that was best and brightest in current American writing.

Boni and Liveright occupied a brownstone at 61 West 48th Street in the heart of Manhattan's speakeasy district: there were six illegal drinking establishments on the same block and every one of them was said to be used as an unofficial branch office by Horace Brisbane Liveright, who was considered by Gorham Munson to be 'no less in tune with the Zeitgeist than were Scott Fitzgerald, Edna St. Vincent Millay and John Barrymore'.[28] There was an appropriateness to the fact that the most important poet to emerge in America in the 1920s should appear under the aegis of the age's most innovative publisher – a collaboration almost foretold in 1919 when Hart, at the suggestion of Padraic Colum, had applied to Liveright for a job as a proof-reader. The company was then only two years old, its chief executive conspicuous in a profession still dominated by gentiles – but Horace Liveright was a showman by nature and it was his theatrical personality, as much as his chancer's instinct, that gave Liveright its glamour, recklessness and imaginative extravagance and enabled it, during his twelve years of management, to change for ever the nature of American publishing. He was a charmer, handsome and flirtatious, and Waldo Frank, a Liveright author, remembered his 'very sharp warm eyes' and the fact that 'he had something of Madison Avenue about him – that is, he was casual and lordly and princely and slick'.[29]

Liveright and his original partner, Albert Boni, had established their publishing fortunes with the foundation of the Modern Library, a collection of reprints of classics, ancient and modern, at 60 cents a volume, which brought them a net profit of $10,000 at the end of their first year. Such success was remarkable in a house without a backlist but it was not in Liveright's nature to rest on his laurels: it was as a gambler and a socialist that he released Trotsky's *The Bolsheviki and World Peace* and found himself the publisher of a best-seller. John Reed's famous account of the Russian Revolution, *Ten Days That Shook The World*, soon joined the company's catalogue but literature remained a major commitment, even though some of Liveright's authors, such as Theodore Dreiser and Eugene O'Neill, took some years to repay initial investment. Liveright revived the American fortunes of Stendhal and Zola as well as introducing his compatriots to Freud with publication of the latter's *General Introduction to Psychoanalysis*. He brought out the earliest works of such writers as Dorothy Parker, e.e. cummings, William Faulkner, Ernest Hemingway and Lewis Mumford and although Random House outmanoeuvred him to publish *Ulysses* it was Liveright who first published *The Waste Land* in book form and it was Liveright's desire for more bulk in the publication that led to Eliot's inclusion of his famous notes.

He fought censorship more tirelessly than any other publisher and made regular appearances in court to answer for the alleged obscenity of his authors. He was the first white publisher to underwrite the Harlem renaissance and it was he who released those quintessential testaments of the age, *South Wind*, *Miss Lonelyhearts* and *Gentlemen Prefer Blondes*. He supported the career of Ben Hecht, most prominent novelist of the Chicago renaissance, until a bitter quarrel and Hecht's departure for Hollywood and a career in screenwriting. Hecht exacted revenge with a screenplay about the New York literary world and in the film that resulted, *The Scoundrel,* the character clearly based on Liveright was played by Noel Coward in his first major screen role. Coward attended Liveright's famous parties, where the publisher's notorious generosity with bathtub gin or with more aromatic refreshment just smuggled off the boat was enjoyed by such regular guests as Carl Van Vechten, Dorothy Parker, Paul Robeson, Alexander Woollcott and George Gershwin. Louis Kronenberger never forgot the sight of Hart at one such occasion, 'violently plastered and very pugnacious'.[30] Otto Kahn himself was sometimes to be glimpsed at these riotous events, his Edwardian capitalist's attire incongruous against the Italian Renaissance furnishings of the Liveright headquarters, and was known to advise the publisher on the stock market speculations he often pursued in order to make ends meet. It was this same love of living dangerously that drew Liveright into theatrical production: his earliest venture, New York's first *Dracula,* starring Bela Lugosi, brought him renewed fame and fortune, but a series of later miscalculations, when Liveright's judgement was fast dissolving in severe alcoholism, proved his professional undoing and the career of this great impresario of the Jazz Age, Ezra Pound's 'pearl among the publishers', ended in 1932 with his death at forty-nine.[31]

An agreement was reached, 'Ave Maria' duly appeared in the *American Caravan* in September and Hart was able to congratulate himself on his association with the publisher who at this stage also represented Eliot, Pound, e.e. cummings, Robinson Jeffers, H.D., Edgar Lee Masters and Dorothy Parker. His involvement with Liveright made no money for either of them but nevertheless proved friendly and mutually affectionate – indeed although Hart never knew it his publisher in effect subsidized both *White Buildings* and *The Bridge*. It was a facility Liveright was known to extend to some of his more favoured and less lucrative authors – but when it came to another service he was said to provide, arranging women for lonely writers in New York for a night or two, Hart had neither curiosity nor need, being quite capable of making alternative arrangements. His last two nights in the city were spent on the Hoboken waterfront – 'it's for men only', the Browns were informed – where beyond Front Street there were three speakeasies in a row providing beer at 15 cents a go and gin and Irish whiskey cheaper and smoother than anything to be had in Manhattan. It was as 'Mike Drayton' that he undertook these journeys and as the Elizabethan playwright reborn that he met 'a wild Irish red-headed sailor of the Coast Guard' who took him to 'coffee dens and cousys' on Sands Street and then to an opium den deeper in Brooklyn.

Whatever attempts he made to find work in New York came to nothing but his return to Patterson was softened by the discovery of six cards awaiting him from Jack Fitzin 'with much more than the usual brief greetings'. Reading material of another order was available in the form of Hemingway's *The Sun Also Rises*: when Hart read this 'brilliant and terrible book' he told the Browns it owed its success to the repeated mention of alcohol, which on almost every page appealed to the nostalgic thirsts of the Prohibition.[32] Eugene Jolas, the Franco-German-American writer and editor, wrote from France to say he had received a copy of *White Buildings*: as Allen Tate had promised, the book was 'immense' and he intended to review it in *transition*, the magazine he and Elliot Paul were soon to begin publishing in Paris.[33] Subject to Hart's approval he hoped to include 'O Carib Isle!' in the first or second number: in the event eight of the nineteen lyrics Crane published in 1927 appeared in *transition* and Jolas was later to prove an important guide to the boulevards, and the expatriates, of Paris.

By the third week of February, although only just returned from New York, Hart was more restless and lonely than ever, not least because the snow was so deep that at times he thought the roads would still be impassable at Easter. No mail got through for over a week but he was nevertheless plagued with guilt about Winters, who continued his relentless letter-writing and patiently awaited a response to two recent offerings which had been gathering dust at Patterson for days: 'Dynamism', a set of notes on poetic theory, and the manuscript of *Fire Sequence*, the collection of lyrics on which he had been working over the course of the last few months. Hart returned the notes on theory on 23 February and told his fellow-poet his 'scientific viewpoint is pretty much hugger-mugger'. Perhaps Winters found his doctrine poetically helpful but as far as Hart himself was concerned there was something suspect in any one comprehensive theory of existence: 'No such incantation can lay life bare, or bring it a bit nearer – for me.'[34]

Assessing *Fire Sequence* three days later, Hart reminded Winters of how astute he could be as a judge of poetry: although there were numerous verbal felicities and intellectual rewards to be found in the lyrics involved he questioned their author's underlying aims and wondered at his dependence on science as the touchstone of existence. Irrespective of the technical success of some of the poems, he found 'a kind of moral zeal – a preoccupation with the gauntness and bareness of things' which marred the persuasiveness of certain lines. Was Winters perhaps too obvious in his trenchancy, too reductive in his demystification? 'Laying Life bare is all very well, but I think the Lady is best approached with a less obvious or deliberate signal than an upraised axe.' For the first time Hart glimpsed the possibility of his error: perhaps after all he and Winters were not literary co-religionists, striving with parallel faiths to evoke and describe eternity. 'You want to strike directly inward, whereas I never consciously premeditate striking at all; I am interested mainly in a *construction*, autonomous, – the validity of whose abstract "life" of course, is dependent on organic correspondences to Nature.'

There was nothing he could teach Winters about logic and incisiveness but his own purpose was different: he wanted to construct rather than to penetrate or dismantle. 'In this sense *White Buildings* has two symbolic meanings, or connotations, its primary one being metaphysic-mechanical: it is only secondarily "Woolworthian".'[35] His lyrics were edifices rather than incisions – but because Crane understood elusiveness as a literary virtue and as a condition of existence they were necessarily constructs of apparently shifting stability and permanence. Built upon observations which he hoped were true to nature, they were held together with metaphors that could suggest without ever insisting. They depended for their life not only on the passion of the poet as he wrote them but on the responsiveness of their readers, who might sometimes connect the metaphors into a strong and coherent structure while at other times taking meaning on trust. Thus it was with skycrapers: sometimes the Woolworth Building seemed no more than a cloud castle when the elements misted pedestrian vision; and sometimes it seemed solid as a rock in the morning's diaphanousness.

By the end of the month Hart had to tell Addie he was penniless but she assured him he could stay as long as he wanted on credit. His friend Isidor Schneider, a poet and an editor at Boni and Liveright, wrote with news of a possible job at the *New Yorker* but what use was such information when Hart lacked the price of a train ticket? To add to the gloom, he had recently learned there was less to Kahn's munificence than met the eye: the financier had taken out a $2,500 life insurance policy on his behalf to cover the sums advanced, 'which, of course I was dumb bell enough not to understand when he proposed it', Hart complained to Waldo, with the result that he had to pay $60 per annum to the Kahn estate for the rest of his life. Aunt Sally was outraged on his behalf: 'Kahn another idol smashed but as you say 'tis amusing, yes downright laughable when one thinks how the rich do protect themselves when they *give* a poor devil anything. They don't know what the word means 'tis all barter & trade with them.'³⁶

Hart was less strident and contented himself with telling Waldo the scheme represented 'a new way to avoid income taxes and become heroic – both at once, if you get what I mean'.³⁷ In other words Kahn won the prestige of philanthropy while offsetting his patronage against tax. There was no use hoping CA would help with money: Hart had heard nothing from his father since November and was now sufficiently depressed – and irritated – to tell Mrs Hart that the imminence of *White Buildings* 'has so angered him that I need not expect to hear from him again'.³⁸ Three weeks later, with silence from that quarter continuing, Hart's position had hardened still further and now he told Grace CA seemed to him 'as thorough a specimen of abnormality as I have ever heard of'. Until his father replied to some of his letters he had decided not to write any more and he had given up trying to fathom his values and reactions. 'He probably likes to build up the picture that he's creeping around in utter disgrace on account of the public "disgrace" his son has made of himself.'³⁹

In fact Clarence Crane – taking Veronal in order to sleep – was still too miserable to follow his son's fortunes when March arrived, and with it the first intimations of a thaw. To the distant roar of melting snow Hart walked over to inspect Robber Rocks and reported to the Browns that the house seemed in good order and that 'spring gurgles'.⁴⁰ The sooner he could tempt some of his friends to return from their New York hibernation the better – but it would be another few weeks before he would see Bill and Sue, who were about to embark on a banana boat for two weeks of Jamaican sunshine. The inexpensive holiday had been organized by Emil – but Hart was too poor now for such escapes, too poor even to go to New York for the farewell party given for the Browns by Laurence and Peggy Vail at the Brevoort Hotel. Loneliness was compounded by yet another sickness, this time conjunctivitis, which limited his reading and writing and eventually forced him to walk into a nearby town for medical attention he could ill afford. 'I suspect it's all more or less due to the nervous strain,' he told Aunt Sally, insisting that 'circumstances are far from encouraging whichever way I look'.⁴¹

Fears about the reception of his first book were not alleviated by the fact that magazines seemed to take so long to decide whether or not they wanted to publish the latest sections of *The Bridge*. At the end of February, desperate for cash, he had sent his newest version of 'The Dance', which was to form the fourth lyric in 'Powhatan's Daughter', to the *Dial*, despite misgivings outlined to Tate that Marianne Moore would probably 'object to the word "breasts", or some other such detail'.⁴² Two weeks later he had heard nothing from her and again confided to Tate his distress that contemporary writing should be entrusted to such timid guardians as the editors of the literary periodicals: 'What strange people these old virgins (male and female) are. Always in a flutter for fear bowels will be mentioned, forever carrying on a tradition that both Poe and Whitman spent half their lives railing against – and calling themselves "liberals".'[43] In the event the *Dial* did accept 'The Dance', although Moore was hardly enthusiastic when she reported her decision to James Sibley Watson. The poem seemed to her 'vapid and pretentious – not well reefed ... the thought, the rhythm, and the syntax "yield" where they shouldn't yield, and the climax scarcely apologises for much that is unpractised'.[44]

By the time Hart wrote to Tate again he was still unaware of Moore's decision and still miserable about contemporary writing, its custodians and its exponents. How he envied 'buckandwing dancers and the Al Jolsons of the world': besides being free of 'milksop' editors they at least gave pleasure to others. But who now cared for poets, or philosophers of any hue? There was 'no place left for our kinds of minds or emotions' – and no point in continuing with the 'mock ceremonies' of poetry if neither truth nor pleasure was to be had in the process.[45] His pessimism about the status accorded to poets in a busy age seemed confirmed when advance copies of the *New Republic* arrived to reveal that Waldo's review of *White Buildings* had been edited. To Hart's partisan eyes it now seemed much less enthusiastic, not least because it had been shorn altogether of its bold (and quotable) peroration: 'Yet already White Buildings gives us enough to justify the assertion, that not since Whitman has so original, so profound and – above all, so important a poetic promise come to the American scene.'[46]

On 19 March the *Dial* conveyed its acceptance of 'The Dance' and Hart's spirits rose: at least now he would be able to repay his debts to Addie and to the doctor. He had ordered some new glasses, having lost his last pair at the Villa Casas, and his vision was much better – although he remained unsure whether that was because the blinding snow had finally gone or because his nervous crisis seemed to be in abeyance. As he reminded Grace, however, when he wrote to her that day, mood and climate were contingent: 'My spirits react entirely too much to the endless gloomy days we've had for so long.'[47] Winters was also due a letter, especially now he had praised the 'Three Songs' destined to become Part V of *The Bridge*. But the more Hart thought about his ambitious poem, the more he wondered when it would be completed. Without undertaking such a venture it was impossible, he told Winters, to conceive 'what endless problems arise in carrying forward the conception of a theme like the Bridge', the 'multitudinous aspects' of which required much more than 'ordinary mental logic' for satisfactory fusion. The 'embryonic Idea' of the poem had been with him for six years before he wrote a line and now he wondered if another six years would elapse before he was ready to commit his mental scheme for the rest of the poem to paper. 'Logic or no logic, I can never do anything that is worth while without the assent of my intuitions.'

The next stages of the poem were clear in his mind but what he could only term the 'temperature', by which he meant 'the condition for organic fusion of experience', was not yet right and the only way of readying oneself for that condition was to exist, as far as he could see, in a state of 'alert blindness'. He loved 'aesthetic speculations' but no amount of theorizing could replace or induce the 'necessary assimilation of experience' which was always the artist's principal challenge. How that assimilation was then used was a matter for the individual artist's choice: some, like William Carlos Williams, whom Winters so admired, opted for endless repetition of the classic truths but Hart himself, with his 'more or less religious attitude toward creation and expression', hoped always for 'revelation – or what seems revelation to me'. On the subject of Winters's idol, although, with the exception of a fragment called 'Paterson', he liked almost everything he had written, he was also haunted by the thought that there was something too 'casual' about his 'observations and emotions'. This reservation could apply to much of Whitman but in his case there was also some sublime yearning, some 'rhythm that almost constantly bespeaks the ineffable "word" that he has to speak'. It was a force which transcended logic and 'one either grasps it or one doesn't' but it separated him for ever from a poet such as Williams, who was admittedly capable of placing remarkable metaphysical constructions on personal experience but who for all that seemed acquiescent, 'bent on appreciating the best that is given to him', without aspiring to more.

Hart also found him deficient in his understanding of metaphor, which existed to 'convey and even accentuate the reality of its subject' and then 'locate and focus the value of the material in our complete consciousnesses'. It seemed to him that Williams was all for fancy at the expense of the imagination; but perhaps he and Winters would have to agree to disagree. He wanted to finish his letter before the postman came and did so with a challenge – how he longed for his friend to give more serious thought to the work of e.e. cummings: 'the sensibility of the man is equal to Donne's – and if he had only cared to take a little more pains and organize – he'd be superb'. Finally, *Fire Sequence* deserved a higher opinion than its author appeared to hold. Winters was 'more essentialized and certainly as adept' as Carlos Williams, even if 'you haven't quite the range'.[48] With that he signed off, apparently unaware that after spending several paragraphs in the subtle denigration of Carlos Williams it was hardly tactful to point out that for all his limitations he still had a breadth his friend could never equal.

After elaborate farewells the boat on which the Browns embarked for Jamaica was hit by a tug as it made its way to sea down the East River and after a day spent steadying themselves on the tilting vessel as it lay off Liberty Island the disappointed travellers returned home and thence to Robber Rocks. Hart was delighted to see them and celebrated, Sue remembered, 'by applying himself heartily to the hard cider in our cellar'.[49] One thing led to another – including, to begin with, a bibulous discussion about Plutarco Calles, since 1924 the President of Mexico and now prominent in American headlines owing to his determination to enact recent land reforms requiring all non-Mexican holders of oil rights to exchange those rights for fifty-year leases. In general, whatever the extent of his

anti-clerical legislation and the ruthless persecution of priests it entailed, intellectual opinion in the United States admired the tenor of Calles's domestic policies
and saw in his agrarian reforms, his amortization of the public debt and his commitment to the education of the peasantry the credentials of a true progressive.
Once American oil interests were threatened, however, the Coolidge administration, and in particular Secretary of State Frank Kellogg, took a less charitable view:
Calles was denounced as a Bolshevik and in Washington armed intervention, that
increasingly popular expedient for the redress of American grievances, only
recently adopted in Nicaragua, was urgently advocated.

    Although a Laodicean in religion and politics Hart followed the affair in the
Nation and the *New Republic* – both sympathetic to Calles and clarion in their calls
for a peaceful settlement – if only because his friends were now regular contributors to their pages. That night, inflamed by what he later described to Tate as
'highly combustible nectar', and with the claims of liberty and reform still ringing
in his ears, he left Robber Rocks hell bent on writing a letter to the Mexican
President to assure him of his admiration and urge him to defiance of American
intervention.⁵⁰ As he described the ensuing events to Winters, he settled to his
typewriter but was soon so infuriated by his – or its – inability to write Spanish
that he hurled the machine from the window and would have sent the lamps after
it had not Mrs Turner interceded, only to be 'swept to the floor in attempting to
restrain me', after which Hart 'howled imprecations against Coolidge'.⁵¹ By the
time the Browns left Robber Rocks the typewriter had been retrieved from the
mud and in New York Bill, ever urbane, persuaded Smith Corona to supply a new
typewriter in exchange for the old and mud-clogged machine before he and Sue
set out once more for Jamaica. With their departure the spring retreated: tempera-
tures plunged in Patterson and when Hart wrote to Underwood on 21 March the
valley's choir of birds had been replaced by 'the cold wind full of icicles'. A
sudden longing for green things had led him to plant lettuce in the cold-frames
and Addie had promised to cook cowslips as soon as they sprouted. 'I never ate
any – but they sound to me always as good as some Shakespearean lyric.' Once
again he felt 'melancholy' but promised his friend 'I shall revive with the first
sunny day'.⁵²

    Six days later he was happier again: 'Aunt' Harriet Monroe had accepted 'Cutty
Sark' for *Poetry* and when Hart sent her the latest version of the poem there was a
teasing tone to his explanation of technique as well as a laughing acknowledgement of his notoriety as a dockside ne'er-do-well. The absence of punctuation in
the poem seemed as 'simple as heaven' to him. 'Of course if none of your readers
has ever been so drunk as you and I have (or so delirious) they will never understand the Manhattan waterfront nor realize that commas don't occur in night-
mares, utopias, nor hemorages [*sic*].' His aim was to evoke 'the blurring of the
faculties in a gin-rum-soaky atmosphere' and however successful he had been the
result, he told Monroe, 'can't be half so hard on your readers as Molly Bloom's

soliloquy at the end of "Ulysses"'.[53] If he seemed to be doing nothing to *The Bridge* but refining its existing lyrics he had at least come up with a plan that might stimulate fresh inspiration besides helping to sell the poem when complete: a biography of the late Washington Roebling. There was an editor at Macaulay who might be interested in the scheme and Hart wondered if Tate, when he was next in the vicinity, could check at the 42nd Street Library to see whether much had yet been written about this man, 'a true Spenglerian hero'.[54] A book about the Roeblings was indeed published in 1931 but Hart's idea unfortunately came to nothing – so posterity will never know whether he thought it merely a coincidence that both John Roebling and Grace Crane subscribed to spiritualism and Christian Science and that both were the parents of bridge builders without precedent.

By the end of March he was too distracted to pursue any scheme for long. *White Buildings* was on sale, reviews had at last begun to appear and he shared with Tate, whose foreword was much praised, his conviction that 'this is the last time in our lives to be badly discouraged'. He detected 'many salutary signals', portents that at last 'the ice is breaking – for both of us'. Their ideas and the manner in which they expressed them had begun to awaken public curiosity and if their advance towards fame was slow it was also sure and would not be reversed by changes in intellectual fashion. If only they were clairvoyants they would be able to see their future fame and fortune and be amazed: 'We wouldn't believe the developments of the next five years if they could be detailed now!'[55] True enough – but by the end of 1932 only Hart Crane's friends would be available to count life's strange surprises.

Liveright printed 500 copies of *White Buildings*, the slender volume of fifty-eight pages that for the price of $2 finally brought before the public Hart Crane's selection of his finest lyrics. There was nothing of *The Bridge* here, of course, but his two other poetic sequences, 'For the Marriage of Faustus and Helen' and 'Voyages', were included along with twenty-one other poems. The back cover bore a photograph of Ezra Pound and an advertisement for his *Personae*, as well as the endorsement O'Neill had agreed to supply in lieu of the foreword he had promised but never delivered: 'Hart Crane's poems are profound and deep-seeking. In them he reveals, with a unique power, the mystic overtones of beauty, which move words to express vision.' The book's epigraph was from Rimbaud – *Ce ne peut être que la fin du monde, en avançant* – and its dedication was declared to Waldo Frank, who accepted the tribute imperturbably: 'With most of Hart's friends the basis was anything but the deep common vision which we shared, each in his own idiom. He was a divided personality of course: and he would come to me precisely when the exigencies of this vision moved him. When he was with me, he was most deeply himself: the poet.'[56] Advance knowledge of the dedication had prevented him from offering to write the preface when O'Neill withdrew; but Tate's foreword filled the breach well, mentioning Hart's early debt to Imagism and the ambition that transcended it and commending the personal and idiosyncratic nature of the poetry, which indicated a 'fresh vision' of the world and one its author captured in a 'new creative language'.

A total of 121 copies were sent to reviewers and editors, with Hart himself proving to be one of the book's best customers: signed editions were dispatched to the Rychtariks, the Browns, Grace, Bill Sommer, Aunt Sally and other friends besides. Mrs Simpson at least promised to do what she could in the way of promotion in Nueva Gerona: "Tis a very pretty little book and I shall prize it very highly for both the donor & the writer's sake. I showed it to several and they all admired it ... they also wish to borrow it but I am going to ask them why not buy a copy for themselves?'[57] Cleveland, Grace related, was yet more curious – 'the jewish womans book club of this city are discussing you at their meetings and considerable local interest is manifesting itself' – so much so that opinions were exchanged even in rural Ohio, much to the poet's amusement.[58] As he explained to his mother, 'When I read about Mrs Jackson taking a copy to read to the Garrettsville Federated Women's Clubs I rocked with laughter! The poor dears will never, NEVER know what in hell to make of it all!'[59] Nor, it seems, did the *Cleveland Press*, which contented itself, beneath the title 'Hart Crane bon-bons are acclaimed', with quoting Charles Brooks's 'Hints to Pilgrims', along with the explanation, 'Crane's candies, with which the Cleveland family's name is more familiarly identified, weren't so sweet to young Hart Crane. He preferred poetry, particularly his own.'[60]

Whether or not Hart expected anything else from the Ohio newspapers his hopes regarding the metropolitan press were high: *White Buildings*, he had assured Grace as long ago as January, 'is going to get some excellent and laudatory reviews'.[61] A few days later Waldo received similar assurances: a satisfactory appraisal had already appeared in the *Herald-Tribune*, *Poetry* would be sure to review him soon and he knew for certain that Mark Van Doren and Yvor Winters were going to assess his book in the *Nation* and the *Dial*. In the *New York Sun* Herbert Seligmann recognized that 'Hart Crane deals with forms of experience one cannot but feel to be intimately his own', with the result that his work 'is for those to whom poetry means personal activity, who are devoted to concentrated word music'. Warning that it 'is nowhere easy, neither lightly written nor hastily to be mastered', he nevertheless insisted that 'throughout the poems are many lovely and distinguished lines, testimony not only to a finely trained ear but to an invention that achieves abstract utterance by ellipsis and the excision entirely of what is inconsequent'.[62] It was a lengthy review for a first volume and one which Hart considered 'sincere and just', and for the time being, he assured Waldo, 'I certainly feel myself very fortunate, considering the type of stuff in WB.'[63]

An impartial observer would have maintained this position two months later: for a collection of poems, and challenging poems at that, *White Buildings* received extensive, and often cautiously enthusiastic, attention. But Hart was neither impartial nor prone to modest expectations and overall reaction to the book fell short of his hopes. The *New Republic* had delivered the first blow by editing Waldo's sympathetic analysis, with its crucial references to Whitman, although what remained was enough to impress most readers with the force of Frank's admiration. He considered the lyrics to be 'as distinct from those of other contemporary American poets as one metal from another'. Crane was 'a mystical maker' who belonged to the school of poets 'who create their world, rather than arrange it'. The result was a poetry too personal for morality: 'You will find in the successful poems of this man no statement: for statement is judgement, and the ingredients of his poems antedate judgement, being indeed the "protons and electrons" of his vision.'[64]

Unsurprisingly, Frank was the only commentator who pursued the visionary theme so insistently and the other reviews largely concentrated on Crane's verbal complexity and varied in enthusiasm according to whether or not the critic in question had had the ability, or the determination, to wrest meaning from the private and ecstatic responsiveness of his art. The *Saturday Review of Literature* had had neither: 'Mr Crane's poetry is intensely mannered, intensely self-conscious. It, too, is aloof, intellectual. It often rapes language under the impression that it is paying expression the highest possible compliment by being almost understandable.' In sum, 'We haven't the slightest idea what a good deal of it means.'[65] In the Literary Supplement of the *New York Herald Tribune* Genevieve Taggard went further and derided Crane's 'mannered obscurity, his slightly faked sonority' – devices which betrayed the poetaster.[66] In the *Nation* Mark Van Doren registered the splendour and persuasiveness of some lyrics while confessing bewilderment about the arguments of others.

Given his low expectations of the *New York Times*, it came as no surprise to Hart to find his work treated in an omnibus review which also considered recent writing by John Crowe Ransom, Langston Hughes, James Rorty, Humbert Wolfe, Richard Aldington, John Drinkwater and Ford Madox Ford. 'They often bunch them that way,' he assured his mother – and himself.[67] Yet this was honourable company for any poet and on closer inspection Hart found that Herbert S. Gorman had proved equable and even-handed: he had placed *White Buildings* in the same category as the work of John Crowe Ransom: both poets were 'intellectual' and 'the emotions they handle have been translated in passing through the brain'. Crane's poetry was more abstruse, 'Yet the line structure is so beautiful in itself, the images so vividly conceived, and the general aura of poetry so indelibly felt that the general reader will move pleasurably among the impenetrable nuances.'[68]

The *Boston (Massachusetts) Transcript* wondered how poetry could prove simultaneously so hard to understand and yet so haunting. It found 'a persistent rigorousness of technique administering to vision' in Crane's work, which it declared to be 'affectingly interesting and profitable'. Furthermore, 'if nearly each poem is ten times a palimpsest, all this is at the antipodes of sentimental slovenliness'.[69] That newspaper owed him no favours: nor, strictly, did the *Dial* – but association surely counted for something and after sending the latter publication a series of lyrics any self-respecting literary periodical should have felt honoured to publish, Hart not unnaturally expected some recognition of his endeavours. But Marianne Moore decreed otherwise. When Winters sent his review to her she returned it with a covering note rebuking his excessive enthusiasm and instead published a notice which compounded the insult of brevity and anonymity by accusing Crane of 'what one might call high class intellectual fake'.[70]

Hart shared Tate's suspicion that Conrad Aiken was the author but what did the identity truly matter? The man was 'full of poison' but he still had a right to his opinions and all Hart could do was console himself with the thought that for years William Blake had been dismissed as insane.[71] A major consolation came from London where the *Times Literary Supplement* published a review Hart considered 'the most satisfactory newspaper mention we have had'.[72] Acknowledging that Crane was compelled to answer 'our present complex urban civilization', the estimate judged that 'at least he recognized the necessity of deepening its analysis until it has its roots in vision'. He had 'a quality of vision as well as of styles, the capacity, in short, to assimilate a conscious psychological subtlety in an act of creative imagination'. Sometimes the effort required to comprehend his meaning 'kills the possibility of aesthetic response' but as a whole 'in single lines of arresting and luminous quality and in whole poems, Mr Crane reveals that his originality is profound'.[73]

It was left to Yvor Winters, however, to reassure Hart that if most great men are misunderstood in their day there will always be one dissenting voice of unequivocal praise, and now it sounded from California. After Marianne Moore had rejected his review Winters revised it and dispatched it to Harriet Monroe and when Hart opened the April issue of *Poetry* he felt sure he would never find a greater apologist. His own and Winters's literary ambitions might be divergent but at least the latter understood what he was trying to achieve – and being neither a trimmer nor a lackey to East Coast literary sectarianism he was prepared to give him public praise for his ambition. Winters placed Hart in a visionary company: despite 'an occasional tendency to slip into rather vague rhetoric' he considered him to be among 'the small group of contemporary masters'. One of 'the five or six greatest poets writing in English', he deployed 'steely tangible imagery' and could summon 'an infinitude of metaphysical and nervous implications'. In particular Winters commended 'Voyages' II, the conclusion of which he considered merited Crane's comparison with 'no one short of Marlowe'. No wonder he admitted to having watched 'Mr Crane's progress for about eight years, with mixed feelings of admiration, bewilderment, and jealousy'. Although this was a qualified version of the eulogy sent to Marianne Moore it still unsettled Monroe. She decided to publish it intact but the footnote she appended was deflation enough: 'It seems a bit hazardous ... to hurl the adjective great at any contemporary. However, the left wing, in any cause, has always flown with conviction and audacity, and it has seemed best not to attempt any clipping in this instance, but to admit an analysis of Mr Crane's artistic motive and style as offered by a poet in complete and enthusiastic sympathy with his art.'[74] Hart was too happy to care what Monroe thought and in gratitude sent Winters what he termed 'a little two-dimensional toy' he had made one day, of a man with a halo descending a mountain and carrying as he did so a guitar or fiddle. Hart's 'Musician Apostolic' delighted its recipient and remained on his study wall for the next forty-odd years, even though long before then Winters had recanted his enthusiasm for Crane's poetry and Hart himself had revoked his opinion expressed that spring of publication, that Winters, along with Tate, had 'more courage than any ten other men I could pick'.[75]

15

In the first week of April Hart returned to Cleveland for a visit undertaken to comfort both his parents as they faced their respective domestic crises. The idea, and the train fare, had come from CA, who wanted to see his son before leaving on 1 May for northern Canada, where he proposed to escape his woes in the inspection of a mining property near Hudson Bay in which he had recently acquired an interest. Well before then, on 19 April, Grace was due in court for her divorce hearing and her letters of recent weeks, with their references to loneliness, exhaustion, the malicious gossip of friends and fears of an impecunious old age, gave Hart an idea of the mood he could expect on arrival.

For the next two weeks he divided his time between two miserable households, distracting his mother and grandmother by day before returning to console CA each evening. It was the first time since 1916 that he had slept under his father's roof but if there was awkwardness in the transition it was alleviated by the presence in the house of CA's niece Fredrica Crane, who was much struck by the way her cousin declaimed *Dr Faustus* or stormed the keyboard of Frances Crane's Steinway grand. There were few other diversions: Hart saw none of his old Cleveland friends and even a pilgrimage into the commercial section of the city, to search for the resonantly named American Bridge Company, housed, as far as he remembered, in the Guardian Building, proved disappointing. For all Hart's attentions, Grace's mood deteriorated as the hearing approached but in a surprising departure from family tradition she decided he should be spared as much of the anguish and embarrassment as possible and when CA invited Hart to join him on a business trip to New York she urged her son to accept, even though the expedition was scheduled to begin the day before her court appearance.

The two men smoked cigars together on the east-bound train before registering for two nights at Manhattan's Hotel Roosevelt and by the time they went their separate ways CA, as though signifying an end to years of mutual disapproval and distrust, had offered his son an allowance to cover future board and lodging. If he had not always understood or approved Hart's chosen career he could not deny his perseverance in the face of its obstacles, or the published fact of *White Buildings*. In any case, for the time being at least, however wayward his son, he was also his only emotional support. Hart was equally eager for reconciliation: with time had come an understanding that much of his ambition and determination had been inherited from CA, and with that understanding came redoubled affection. A few days later he declared their New York stay to have been 'the most satisfactory visit we have ever had together' and one which he trusted had gone some way towards alleviating CA's gloom, however temporarily, 'for it is a good thing to be of some use to one's father, especially when he's been so good to me as you have'.[1] Nevertheless it was with silent thanks that he returned to Patterson; as he explained to Winters, after 'a mad harrowing two-weeks with the bevy of my family' he felt 'tired and much "reduced"'.[2] Nor did news of the divorce hearing prove uplifting: the *Cleveland News* and the *Cleveland Press* found such sensationalism as they could in the tawdry end to Grace's matrimonial hopes, enacted before the Common Pleas court, and implied that she was an exacting, spoilt and extravagant woman for finding insufficient the $150 a month 'pin money' Curtis had allowed her when they were married and the $250 a month he had paid her since their separation.

Relief at being back in the country was quickly followed by restlessness. The woods, Hart told Grace, were spangled with 'shad-blows and the loveliest cowslips' and Mrs Turner, delighted to resume her ministrations, 'has been cooking me bushels of fresh dandelion greens' – but immemorial inspiration of poets though it was, the spring failed to revive him.[3] Turning to *The Bridge* again, he worried that the poem's last two sections required yet more attention: writing to Winters to thank him for some photographs of paintings by Polelonema, a Hopi Indian artist, he wondered if 'The Tunnel' needed 'a certain sort of sensitizing introduction' in order to ensure 'the fixation or due registration of the subsequent developments of the theme'. As for 'Atlantis', if it aspired to Pater's idea of 'frozen music' he suspected it was also 'too subjectively written' to 'legitimately explain or condone'. Perhaps before attempting to appreciate its meaning and technique everyone should walk across Brooklyn Bridge 'to get the marvellous feeling the webbed cables give (as one advances) of a simultaneous forward and upward motion'.[4] As if these uncertainties were not enough, 'The River' still awaited him; but however willing the spirit the flesh was weak – or else distracted – and his thoughts wandered back to New York and to the waterside shadowlands he had been too busy to revisit during his time with CA.

At the end of April he caught the train and registered (thanks to his father's allowance) at the Hotel Albert and on 4 May, shortly before returning to Patterson, he detailed his recent adventures for Underwood: 'A great time yesterday afternoon on the USS *Shawmut*, marvelous old Johnny Walker and Bacardi from the officers – such hospitality!'[5] An undated set of directions in one of Hart's notebooks testifies to the intrepidity of the pleasure-seeker: 'USS *Shawmut*, Dy[c]kman St. Broadway to 241 St Station. Get off at Dy[c]kman St. Take any boat to *Shawmut* from Dy[c]kman Ferry.'[6] His letter to Underwood had more than revelry to report: he was 'in love again' and when he thought about his new sailor he felt as though 'Apollo himself may have been sojourning in Gob blue – but that aloof rather chilly deity would hardly have qualified so well'.[7] Yet it was not aboard the *Shawmut* that the poet had lost his heart: his new love was a sailor named Evered in the quartermaster's division of the USS *Arizona* and by 12 May, when Hart resolved to return to New York to see him, the two men had exchanged letters. By now Evered was routinely considered divine – it is as 'Apollo', 'Phoebus Apollo' or 'Phoenix' that he survives in correspondence – and Underwood was assured that he 'has brains as well as beauty'. Indeed in support of his claims that Apollo was not just a god but a thinking god Hart quoted the end of his last letter for the edification of his friend in Washington: 'If you are in the city I should like very much to see you. I cannot come to you; for the last silver dollar is squandered and gone. Yet, omnia vincit amor. It is a little life and tomorrow – we may die. Dum vivimus, vivamus. May I see you? A morte, E.'[8] A series of farewells and reunions intensified by contraband alcohol, the affair progressed satisfactorily, so much so that in the third week of May, with whatever excuses to the doting Mrs Turner, Hart invited his sun deity to Patterson. Again it was Underwood who was vouchsafed a glimpse of the godhead: 'I brought my phoenix directly back with me to the country – in company with two quarts of Johnnie Walker – and he spent the weekend with me under the apple trees. Life is worth living at times.'[9] But to love sailors is to love those who must leave, and in the first week of June the *Arizona* and her resident Apollo returned to California, presumably to the naval base at San Diego, and Hart told his confidant in Washington, 'I'm still in a doting daze.'[10]

He also mentioned his passion to Winters – 'I am disabled from everything but the alphabet, having fallen anew into love' – but only as an excuse for further delays with *The Bridge* and certainly without supplying any details.[11] Otherwise he tried to keep Apollo a secret, as he was to do with several of his successors, for both superstitious and practical reasons. To expose love to public knowledge was not only to taint it but also to tempt providence – but beyond these considerations there was the certainty that his friends, at least his heterosexual friends, for all their liberal protestations, would not understand, which is why he came to depend so much on Wilbur Underwood, who could be trusted to maintain discretion and to avoid the smug sympathy shown by the couples when another of his dangerous liaisons foundered. Not that the Tates, the Browns and the Cowleys were unaware of Hart's other life and his interest in the sort of men they would never in ordinary circumstances meet: Lorna Dietz remembered many conversations about his sexual activities in the course of which Hart would often begin 'a diatribe against some "gob" who'd stolen from him, or sponged on him' or how he would be 'contemptuously bawdy' about the sailors he met for one-night stands. However, 'when I asked him why he was so intimate with them if he felt that way, he told me the only thing he liked about them was their uniform – that beautiful waist-line'.[12] Susan Jenkins Brown was also forced into confrontation and never forgot the evening she and Hart were walking through Times Square after the theatre and 'two loutish, pimply-faced lads in gobs' uniform passed us, white hats squeezed down unbecomingly over one eye, accentuating a moronic appearance'. Left to her own devices she would probably never have noticed them, but not so her companion, who seized her arm and whispered: 'Look at them, Sue! Aren't they bursts of beauty!'[13] Aware that he would never fit within society's norms and uneasily defiant about his incongruity, Hart oscillated between considered discretion and a brazen vulgarity that fuelled the Patterson crowd's worst expectations. It was indeed hard to know what to make of it all: were Hart's sailors no more than adjuncts to a physical appetite that seemed both voracious and indiscriminate or were they supporting players in a greater quest for love? Either way, his married friends found something increasingly uncompromising, even provocative, in his sexuality and sought decorum and security in tacit rules of conduct. It was one thing for Susan to be confronted by Hart's sexuality in Times Square but in the country it was a different matter and this time she moved to contain an awkward juxtaposition. The sailor in question was called Jack Woodruff, except by his admirer:

Hart called him 'Honey Boy'. It was the only instance of his breaking the understanding we had with him that he was not to bring any sailor pick-up to the country. He did it when both he and the boy were pie-eyed: coming up on the late train from NYC and having a taxi to Mrs Turner's. Hart did not demur when we took the sailor to our house the next morning, where we entertained him for the day ... gave him dinner and then drove him to the train.[14]

Hart was becoming a social challenge and his sexual activity was integral to the threat he posed. He told his married friends he found heterosexual relations 'funny', without specifying whether he meant comical or bizarre, and he reversed the conventional wisdom by which love is made official and public and its physical expression left undescribed. Slater Brown noted the paradox: as far as he knew about Hart's loves he sensed that 'they were pure things to him, they needed no apologies or explanations and when they weren't rebuffed [he] was happy in them'. The transient side to his nocturnal life, however, 'Hart attempted to conceal behind bravado and defiance', a policy which entailed ever more lurid accounts of the 'uptown fags' he encountered as well as of 'those sordid and drunken pick-ups on Sands Street, the lowest type of sailor whom Hart plied with liquor and paid money to'.[15] There was an element of equivocation, of dissociation, which was unsettling in a man and poet who hoped to bridge the contradictions of existence

– yet if Hart was equivocal about his sexuality it was because his social and moral environment made him so. Perhaps once again America, in many ways his inspiration, was also his inhibition: after his experience in Cuba with Alfredo he began to think it would be easier to live the sort of physical and emotional life he wanted abroad. But for now all he could do was to channel the complexities of sexual desire into poetry. 'Thou Canst Read Nothing', completed at some stage in the mid-1920s and never published in Hart's lifetime, is written in what Allen Tate, in his introduction to *White Buildings*, termed Crane's 'grand manner' – a manner of Elizabethan courtliness which reads strangely as a description of nocturnal cruising and seems almost to ask approval from his literary friends for an activity they regarded with profound ambivalence:

Thou canst read nothing except through appetite
And here we join eyes in that sanctity
Where brother passes brother without sight,
But finally knows conviviality ...

Go then, unto thy turning and thy blame.
Seek bliss then, brother, in my moment's shame.
All this that baulks delivery through words
Shall come to you through wounds prescribed by swords:

That hate is but the vengeance of a long caress,
And fame is pivotal to shame with every sun
That rises on eternity's long willingness ...
So sleep, dear brother, in my fame, my shame undone.[16]

In the third week of that amorous May Hart spent a few days as the guest of Gaston and Madame Lachaise and when John Dos Passos and two friends passed by in the course of a walking holiday a game of croquet was convened, only to be dominated by talk of Charles Lindbergh, whose successful landing outside Paris made him the first man to fly the Atlantic. Several pilots had recently died attempting the same feat: Lindbergh's endeavour rendered the world a smaller place even as it made him an international hero. Hart looked on, as he told CA, 'a little jealous' of the great aviator: 'Time and Space is the myth of the modern world ... and it's interesting to see how any victory in that field is heralded by the mass of humanity. In a way my Bridge is a manifestation of the same general subject.'[17] Although Lindbergh was the talk of nations, he failed to inspire Hart when he returned to his typewriter. Instead he planted a vegetable garden as a distraction, only to see his labours washed away in a prolonged spell of heavy rain, and it was in a mood of continuing listlessness that he told Underwood, 'I am almost tired of being a poet!'[18]

His calling looked even more thankless when Yvor Winters wrote with approving reference to Edmund Wilson's recent essay in the *New Republic,* 'The Muses out of Work', in which the great panjandrum surveyed American poetry written in the last year and chastised its practitioners for having no engagement with the outer world: 'Does it really constitute a career for a man to do nothing but write lyric poetry? Can such a man expect the world to be concerned with what he has to say?' It was annoying enough for Hart that the most influential literary critic in the United States should promulgate opinions his own father would have endorsed – but worse was to come. Although Wilson cited *White Buildings* as being one of only two significant collections of poetry to emerge in the last year (the other being *The King's Henchman,* by his intimate friend Edna St Vincent Millay) the terms of his enthusiasm were scarcely likely to swell Hart's royalties: 'Mr Crane has a most remarkable style, a style that is strikingly original – almost something like a great style, if there could be such a thing as a great style which was, not merely not applied to a great subject, but not, so far as one can see, applied to any subject at all.' Although Hart's work evoked the lyrics of Rimbaud, his emotions and his syntax were vague: 'His poetry is a *disponible,* as they say about French troops. We are eagerly waiting to see to which part of the front he will move it: just at present, it is killing time in the cafés behind the lines.'[19] After unending money worries alternating with the lonely struggle for the right epithet this easy dismissal was bound to rankle; Winters's letter, now lost, clearly added insult to injury, especially as he seems to have taken it upon himself to lecture Hart about his personal life. He knew from recent letters that the poet from whom he expected great things got so drunk as to throw typewriters out of windows before falling in love and using the condition as an excuse for not writing. Furthermore he had been disappointed by 'The Tunnel' and by 'Atlantis'; it was time he did not only his friend but also poetry in general a service by reminding Hart that the aspiring poet should strive first to be 'the complete man'. With Apollo just about to leave and with his conscience plaguing him about 'The River', Hart was in no mood for lectures and on 29 May he sent Winters a long and aggressive letter of self-justification which foreshadowed graver differences.

'You need a good drubbing for all your recent easy talk about "the complete man", the poet and his ethical place in society.' It was all too easy, Hart insisted, for a figure such as Wilson, 'born into easy means, graduated from a fashionable university into a critical chair overlooking Washington Square' to 'sit tight and hatch little squibs of advice to poets' in an essay that had been 'just half-baked enough to make one warm around the collar' (even though his own background was much more prosperous than Wilson's and adolescent idealism alone had stood between him and the Ivy League). How could a man as rigorous as Winters second such glib pronouncements? In principle, he agreed, there was much to be said for the idea of 'the complete man' in an age characterized by a 'horrid hysteria for specialization'. He also believed in principle in the idea of 'some definite ethical order'. But it was worth remembering that Munson and others had wanted to make themselves into complete men too and that after disappearing behind 'the portals of the famous Gurdjieff Institute' and putting themselves through 'all sorts of Hindu antics' they had discovered 'a good substitute for their former interest in writing by means of more complete formulas of expression [and] have ceased writing now altogether'. Of course Hart considered catholic openness, the universal view, to be desirable, but it was a greatness given to very few. He himself lacked it but he could at least recognize his deficiency: 'I doubt if I was born to achieve ... those richer syntheses of consciousness which we both agree in classing as supreme; at least the attitude of a Shakespeare or a Chaucer is not mine by organic rights, and why try to fool myself that I possess that type of vision when I obviously do not!' He had 'a certain code of ethics', although it was not reducible to an exact formula, and he considered 'a certain decent carriage and action' indispensable 'in any poet, deacon or carpenter'. And for the record, he regretted none of his actions, including those which resulted from his sexuality. Since Winters had invoked the subject of personal morality and its governing standards, Hart insisted that 'I reserve myself the pleasant right to define these standards in a somewhat individual way'. It was dangerous to judge artists by what was known of their private lives and if Winters thought Leonardo might have achieved more if he had been resolutely heterosexual, he was living in a dream world: 'I don't think your reasons for doubting his intelligence and scope very potent – I've never closely studied the man's attainments or biography, but your argument is certainly weakly enough sustained on the sole prop of his sex – or lack of such. One doesn't have to turn to homosexuals to find instances of missing sensibilities.'

In any case, what was 'a complete man'? Was Winters unable to see that 'the whole topic is something of a myth anyway' and that it enshrined an idea 'consequently modified ... by each age in each civilization', which was why Tom Jones embodied eighteenth-century England's ideal even though he knew nothing of calculus or Darwinian theory? Despite these deficiencies, he offered a more rounded figure than Thomas Hardy's more recently sketched protagonists. Hardy's poetry was a marvel – 'I think him perhaps the greatest technician in English verse since Shakespeare' – but in his novels 'not one of his characters is for one moment allowed to express a single joyous passion without a forenote of Hardian doom entering the immediate description'. In view of this variability of definition it was particularly ridiculous to expect Hart to become some paragon of completeness. In any case, 'I don't care to be credited with too wholesale ambitions, for as I said, I realize my limitations, and have already partially furled my flag'. Winters was a 'meticulous and sensitive reader'. Hart was prepared to concede the flaws the critic found in his poetry but hoped to extend his 'scope and viewpoint', even if he was not prepared to 'trust to so methodical and predetermined a method of development' as Winters recommended. They could both agree that there were no 'shortcuts across the circle' – but the experience which fed literature could not be bought; it could only, as it were, be experienced, and by each man in his own rhythm. 'One can respond only to certain circumstances, just what the barriers are, and where the boundaries cross can never be completely known. And the surest way to frustrate the possibility of any free realization is, it seems to me, to wilfully direct it.' Personal conduct was not an area for external legislation and Hart was not about to forgo any experience just because Winters thought he should, even if the latter considered him 'aimless and irresponsible' as a result.

Nor could he help it if Winters considered him 'a metaphysician', even though he was nothing of the sort, never having read 'Kant, Descartes or other doctors'. Because 'the first poem I ever wrote was too dense to be understood' he had been labelled metaphysical and critics continued to apply the term because it was easier than bothering to read each fresh poem closely before deciding how to define its author. The fact was that Hart's poetry was slender in volume and dense in content for good reason. 'I write damned little because I am interested in recording certain sensations, very rigidly chosen, with an eye for what according to my taste and sum of prejudices seems suitable to – or intense enough – for verse.' Winters had inferred much of his personality from his poetry without reflecting that although his writing was reflected in his character, not all of his character was reflected in his writing. One day, perhaps, he would write prose and would then expose 'a much thicker slice of myself'. In the meantime he would try to ensure that his work approximated to 'a true record of such moments of "illumination" as are occasionally possible', and that it attained to that 'sharpening of reality' which poetry alone could capture. 'That is one reason above all others – why I shall never expect (or indeed desire) *complete* sympathy from any writer of such originality as yourself.'[20]

Annoying as Winters's letter had been, it at least served to put Hart on his mettle and may even indirectly have revived poetic energy, since by the middle of June he had recommenced work on *The Bridge*: finally 'The River' had begun to flow. No sooner had he started to expand the tentative version begun a year ago on the Isle of Pines, however, than severe hay fever struck and he set the work aside again and read Charles M. Doughty's *Arabia Deserta*. Sneezing and blindness notwithstanding he struggled into New York when a postcard from Jack Fitzin proclaimed that the sailor and his ship were returned from their long voyage in European waters. Aunt Sally, apparently conversant with many of the below-deck details of Hart's life, was told of the reunion: 'He was standing up on the forward deck when I saw him from the pier head, and after taking me all over the ship (a destroyer) we had a very pleasant evening, taking in a movie on hunting in a jungle, full of marvelous tiger close-ups and elephant stampedes.'[21]

Hart was back in Patterson by the end of the month and on 1 July, despite their recent altercation, he sent Winters a complete version of 'The River', 'my long struggle with an attempt to tell the pioneer experience backward'.[22] The lyric was to be placed between 'Van Winkle' and 'The Dance' in the completed sequence and took up the last lines of the former poem, with their reference to a 'car-change'. Now that change has been made and the narrator finds himself on board the '20th Century Limited' as it roars into the interior of the continent, the frenzy of the train's motion and the blurred vision from its windows constituting an evocation of contemporary America. Unable to bear the dizziness and the dissonance the narrator leaps from the train and joins 'three men, still hungry on the tracks, ploddingly/watching the tail lights wizen and converge, slip-/ping gimleted and neatly out of sight'. At once, as the poem modulates into its second movement, he senses an older, slower America, in which the laborious technology of the pioneers was used to subjugate a vast continent peopled, and named, by races subsequently dispossessed:

> The last bear, shot drinking in the Dakotas
> Loped under wires that span the mountain stream.
> Keen instruments, strung to a vast precision
> Bind town to town and dream to ticking dream.
> But some men take their liquor slow – and count
> – Though they'll confess no rosary nor clue –
> The river's minute by the far brook's year.
> Under a world of whistles, wires and steam
> Caboose-like they go ruminating through
> Ohio, Indiana – blind baggage –
> To Cheyenne tagging ... Maybe Kalamazoo.

The narrator has joined three 'Hobo-trekkers' who remind him of the 'Rail-squatters ranged in nomad raillery,/The ancient men', he used to see behind his father's maple syrup cannery. Although they appear to be 'Holding to childhood like some term-less play', although they are 'Blind fists of nothing, humpty-dumpty clods', these homeless men are possessed of 'Strange bird-wit, like the elemental gist/Of unwalled winds they offer'. Sending the poem to Aunt Sally, Hart explained that 'these hobos are simply "psychological ponies" to carry the reader across the country and back to the Mississippi' and in their presence the narrator ventures further into the heart of America.[23] As he does so he becomes increasingly aware of its precedent cultures: 'Papooses crying on the wind's long mane/Screamed redskin dynasties that fled the brain,/– Dead echoes!' Now he comprehends the continent as a body of other legends – instead of the America of commerce and pioneers he sees the world that came before it, embodied now by Powhatan's daughter, Pocahontas:

> I knew her body there,
> Time like a serpent down her shoulder, dark,
> And space, an eaglet's wing, laid on her hair.

To contemplate the Indian peoples was to reflect on the pillaging of their conquerors, who had cast down the ancient American gods and had plundered and felled their vast forests in order to make way for the railroad tracks which had in a sense created and bound together the industrial United States. The thought of the railroads reminds the narrator of the train he left and which now, in southern Illinois, he rejoins, only to see 'Pullman breakfasters' journeying towards the confluence of the Ohio and Mississippi rivers. Another lost America, the land of steamboats, is briefly evoked, before the poem moves into its concluding section, in which eight confident quatrains celebrate the Mississippi, river of time and river of American destiny:

> You will not hear it as the sea; even stone
> Is not more hushed by gravity ... But slow,
> As loth to take more tribute – sliding prone
> Like one whose eyes were buried long ago
>
> The River, spreading, flows – and spends your dream.
> What are you, lost within this tideless spell?
> You are your father's father, and the stream –
> A liquid theme that floating niggers swell.

All American history is dissolved in these mighty waters: besides the blacks enslaved by the contiguous cotton plantations there are the 'tall ironsides' of the Confederate and Union forces as well as the bones of Hernando de Soto, Spanish explorer and first European ever to see the Mississippi. The river is the great artery of America and 'drinks the farthest dale' before flowing past New Orleans, 'the City storied of three thrones'. The Spanish, the French and the Americans all at one stage claimed sovereignty here – but every national and temporal dominion is melted by this great tide as it prepares to flow from terrestrial confinement into the Gulf of Mexico. It is a release which is also an agony, a liberation which is also a death, enacted, like so much in Crane's life and imagination, against the Caribbean:

> Ahead
> No embrace opens but the stinging sea;
> The River lifts itself from its long bed,
>
> Poised wholly on its dream, a mustard glow
> Tortured with history, its one will – flow!
> – The Passion spreads in wide tongues, choked and slow,
> Meeting the Gulf, hosannas silently below.[24]

Since he had included a reference to Aunt Sally in 'The River' it was only natural that he should supply her with an explanation of the poem's purpose in *The Bridge* and the logic with which it yielded to the poem that succeeded it, 'The Dance'. His aim had been to 'unlatch the door to the pure Indian world' and thus to make readers feel they had been 'led back in time to the pure savage world, while existing at the same time in the present'. This sense of temporal fusion had been 'a very complicated thing to do' and had entailed more work than any other section of the larger poem so far.[25]

He was pleased with his description of the Mississippi and confident that readers would understand the thrust of *The Bridge*'s temporal retrogression, which reached its furthest extent in 'The Dance', a lyric of twenty-six stanzas rhyming on alternate lines which evokes the lost Indian world, a celebration of which Crane considered – remarkably, for his day – to be indispensable to a mythic understanding of modern America. As he explained to Kahn, 'Powhatan's Daughter' as a whole concerned the fusion of indigenous and invading cultures. Yet although he invokes Pocahontas Crane has nothing explicit to say about her destiny, which transformed her from an Indian princess to a Christian convert, wife of an English settler and mother to his son, who is known to legend as the first American offspring of European and Indian. The fact was that if he depended on history and chronology he would compromise the symbolic force of *The Bridge*. Pocahontas, he reminded his patron, 'is the mythological nature-symbol chosen to represent the physical body of the continent, or the soil' and the central movement of *The Bridge* was 'mainly concerned with a gradual exploration of this "body" whose first possessor was the Indian'.[26] Although undescribed, however, the princess is a significant presence in 'The Dance', where Crane drew on boyhood memories of Ohio for the sequence of exquisite stanzas which describe his journey over mountains and waters and centuries to the Indian past:

> Over how many bluffs, tarns, streams I sped!
> – And knew myself within some boding shade: –
> Grey tepees tufting the blue knolls ahead,
> Smoke swirling through the yellow chestnut glade …

Having reached pre-European America he discovers a tribal dance in full progress and at its centre Maquokeeta, an Indian chieftain, bound to the stake and about to be sacrificed to the flames. In deft metaphorical compression the might of industrial America is foretold in the feathers of his ceremonial headdress: 'A cyclone threshes in the turbine crest,/Swooping in eagle feathers down your back.' Taking upon himself the white man's burden of guilt for the slaughter of the Indian tribes the narrator leaps into the flames and in a passage of supreme descriptive beauty he evokes the torments of destruction – 'I could not pick the arrows from my side' – the ensuing redemption in which he and Maquokeeta become one and their consequent liberation from mortality. Translated into a star, the Indian surveys lands conquered by the white man: but the invader knows nothing of Pocahontas, who embodies the aboriginal spirit of America. 'She is the torrent and the singing tree;/And she is virgin to the last of men.' Whatever the devastation caused by Europeans she is still honoured by the ghost of the Indian chieftain, now become a fusion of time and space, and as the poems ends 'her perfect brows' are laid to his in mystic marriage and the narrator is left to proclaim the covenant he made with the Indian and the divine harmony that ensued:

> We danced, O Brave, we danced beyond their farms,
> In cobalt desert closures made our vows . . .
> Now is the strong prayer folded in thine arms,
> The serpent with the eagle in the boughs.[27]

Aunt Sally was delighted with the latest instalments and flattered to find her name immortalized in the masonry of *The Bridge*: 'I think of you a kid yet only 28 years and yet you have done more than many twice your age.'[28] For once Hart also felt self-congratulatory. As he told Winters, he was convinced 'The River' 'flows much more evenly' than any piece of similar length he had attempted 'and I think that it forms an interesting contrast to the rapid foot-beat of the Dance that follows'. He had tried 'to give it the racial tang of the Great Valley without lapsing into Sandburgian sentimentalities'. He would await the austere critic's verdict but in the meantime he felt huge relief that two of the most difficult components of his great poem were finished: the labour had 'weighed so heavily' on him for such a long time 'and contained so many apparently insurmountable difficulties that I was becoming very depressed'.[29]

That summer, in a dramatic concession to the modern age, Mrs Turner had a telephone installed. Henceforth Hart would feel less isolated from his friends – but also, less happily, from his family. Having gone to Chicago after her divorce Grace spent several uneasy weeks waiting to hear how much she was to be awarded in alimony. Consumed by restlessness and afflicted by various malaises she pined for the security she had renounced – a home of her own – and now beheld all men with scepticism and marriage itself with repugnance. She saw a psychoanalyst for the unusual purpose of establishing the sort of job she was best fitted to do but rather than putting the results of the 'vocationgram' to good use she went back to Cleveland and moved herself and her old mother once again to a small apartment overlooking the John D. Rockefeller estate at 13800 Superior Road. The distress of recent publicity made her long to escape Cleveland for good and she toyed with the idea of a summer in Patterson as a preliminary change of scene. Hart found various excuses to deter her, including the extensive and exhausting presence at one stage of the Laurence Vails and their six children, but then Mrs Hart once again became gravely ill and all Grace's attentions returned to nursing. When alimony was finally awarded the sum was modest – $150 a month for two years – and thereafter, the stigma of divorce permitting, she would have to find a job.

CA's position seemed no more enviable: his depression continued, despite his recent visit to Canada, and on some mornings, he told his son, he cried all the way to work. 'To me, life is just one big, black cloud.'[30] Financial anxiety compounded emotional despair – recent wholesale and retail confectionery sales had been disappointing but a life devoted to hard work afforded few alternative sources of consolation. He continued to send his son $50 a month but his accompanying letters spoke in accents of melancholy and regret that were new to their recipient. 'I know you are not interested in things I am doing,' he told Hart that summer, 'and so much of my life is now in ship-wreck I cannot say the example is a good one for you to follow. About all that the Lord can do with my soul when it comes to the final accounting is to say that I worked hard and accomplished little.'[31] Never a defeatist, however, he continued to explore other ways of distracting his mind and spreading his liability and was now determined on a new scheme: the acquisition of a rural roadside tavern in which he could serve 'fine chicken dinners' to 'the high class business in this section of the country'. Although the right property had not yet materialized he knew he wanted Hart to return to Ohio to live and work with him in this next venture and promised, 'I would not ask you to do the cooking or to milk the cow.'[32] He eventually settled on two adjacent properties surrounded by maple trees in the village of Chagrin Falls; once extensions and renovations had been completed he proposed to live there himself and hoped to be open for business in September. First, however, the establishment had to be christened and with the Cranean love of punning CA was already contemplating a play on his name – but when 'Crane's Nest' was ventured he changed his mind. 'The name is Canary Cottage,' he told his son. 'Nests get foul so easily.'[33]

Whatever it was called, Hart knew he could never live there: curtailment of freedom was much too high a price to pay for financial security and he delicately reminded CA that every summer the surrounding cornfields would render him incapable with hay fever. Happily, relations between father and son were now sufficiently harmonious for CA to accept the excuse even if he doubted it and he pledged continued financial assistance in order that Hart could 'show your mettle as a writer'.[34] By the middle of August, however, with poetic inspiration once again unavailing, Hart's morale was in decline. He gardened, played croquet and drank cider but the imminence of autumn entailed bleak decisions: should he spend the coming winter in cheap but snowbound isolation with Addie and her cats or would it be better to return to New York, where he would need a job to survive? These were depressing alternatives, and even though T.S. Eliot wrote to say he wanted to publish 'The Tunnel' in the *Criterion* there was no mistaking Hart's mood when he wrote to Underwood: 'It's no use to tell you how futile I feel most of the time – no matter what I do or conceive of doing, even. Part of the disease of modern consciousness, I suppose.'[35] The old dream of combining work with travel sent him to New York at the beginning of September in search of a job as a waiter on an American shipping line but by 12 September he was back at Patterson and once again writing to Otto Kahn for help. Presuming his patron's 'continued interest in the progress of *The Bridge*', Hart dispatched a copy of the work as it now stood and attempted to explain his poetic logic, especially with regard to 'Powhatan's Daughter'. He wanted the banker to understand that he was not attempting a lyrical history of the United States but a poetic distillation of America, and one which revealed 'the continuous and living evidence of the past in the inmost vital substance' of their own time:

Consequently I jump from the monologue of Columbus in 'Ave Maria' – right across the four intervening centuries – into the harbor of 20th-century Manhattan. And from that point in time and place I begin to work backward through the pioneer period, always in terms of the present – finally to the very core of the nature-world of the Indians. What I am really handling, you see, is the Myth of America.

The work had entailed the identification and fusion of thousands of strands of meaning as well as great reserves of patience, since on many occasions he had been obliged to wait 'until my instincts assured me that I had assembled materials in proper order for a final welding into their natural form'. He hoped Kahn would understand that although the poems could stand discretely they were all ultimately interdependent, rather like the frescos of the Sistine Chapel. He gave an account of the sections now finished – 'The Harbor Dawn', 'Van Winkle', 'The River', 'The Dance' and 'Cutty Sark' – and summarized 'Indiana' and 'Cape Hatteras', which were projected but not yet written. 'The range of *The Bridge* has been called colossal by more than one critic who has seen the ms,' he explained and as proof of the interest his project had aroused he listed the magazines which had accepted individual poems for publication. 'I have been especially gratified by the reception accorded me by The Criterion, whose director, Mr T.S. Eliot, is representative of the most exacting literary standards of our times.' Such recognition was reassuring – but once again Hart needed help: having failed to get a job at sea he wondered if the financier would consider putting in a good word for him as an advertising copy-writer at the publicity department of the Metropolitan Opera, 'where I am certain of making myself useful'. Better still, would he consider advancing him another $800 or $1,000? 'There is no monetary standard of evaluation for works of art, I know, but I cannot help feeling that a great poem may well be worth at least the expenditure necessary for merely the scenery and costumes of many a flashy and ephemeral play, or the cost of an ordinary motor car.' If Kahn felt so inclined, Hart could envisage a rapid conclusion to his labours: with additional support he would go to Mexico or Spain to work and trust to that liberation of the imagination he had experienced on the Isle of Pines, where 'the "foreign-ness"

of my surroundings stimulated me to the realization of natively American materials
and viewpoints in myself not hitherto suspected'. In the end, however, speed of
composition was of secondary importance: 'The Aeneid was not written in two
years – nor in four, and in more than one sense I feel justified in comparing the
historic and cultural scope of *The Bridge* to that great work.'[36]

Kahn replied on 19 September, pleading 'overwhelming demands' on his time
as an excuse for not responding to *The Bridge* in critical detail. Nevertheless the
poem as it stood confirmed him 'in my opinion of your great and singular talent'.[37]
He offered to talk to Mr Guard, head of publicity at the Metropolitan Opera, and
proposed interim assistance of $500. A different vote of confidence came from
Paul Rosenfeld, who wrote following publication of the *American Caravan*. He was
sorry to learn that Hart was 'going to be forced out of your laboratory again' by
the need for work and – in a tribute to the other myth the poet so painstakingly
constructed, that he battled daily against the indifference of a miserly Clarence
Crane – he added, 'Your father must be a very uncultivated man.' He was pleased
Hart had liked the *Caravan* – 'if it impresses you and the rest of the one hundred
and seventy four persons comprising American culture, we shall be successful well
nigh beyond our deserts' – and declared his continuing admiration for 'Ave Maria':
'Some of the moments are almost as grand as Marlowe.'[38] But before Hart could
decide whether or not to continue his job-hunting in New York Grace intervened:
she had determined to move herself and Mrs Hart to Los Angeles, in the hope that
the benign climate, coupled with the support of nearby relations, would hasten her
mother's recuperation. A letter from CA followed, to reveal that Grace had applied
to her former husband for Hart's train fare to Cleveland, and so at the end of
September the latter found himself back in Ohio once more and busy helping his
mother, at her most lachrymose and nervously indecisive, with yet another move
while his grandmother looked on, impassive now with frailty.

Exhausted and depressed, Hart returned to Patterson – but by the second week
in October he was in New York and staying with Sam Loveman at 110 Columbia
Heights: the idea now was that he would work for the next two months and then
sail for Martinique, there finally to complete *The Bridge*. When he met Kahn for
another interview, however, his patron's mood of generosity was such that plans
altered once again. The financier was so anxious, CA was informed, 'that I keep
on with the composition without interruption until it is finished' that he had
offered $300 to pay for Hart's ticket to the Caribbean, on the understanding that
once he reached Martinique the poet would be maintained by his father. His
monthly allowance of $50 would prove ample, Hart assured CA – besides, he
hoped while on the island to learn French and Spanish, 'which will make it possible for me [to] earn my living up here later by translation work'.[39] He reserved
passage for 20 October on the Furness-Bermuda Line and despite a terrible hangover was able to write to the Browns asking them to retrieve certain items still at
Mrs Turner's for use in the tropics: 'The two white dungarees and the one blue,

also the soiled grey suit I wore around the country this summer. And the Bennet's French grammar.'[40]

Acknowledging his son's new plan CA dispatched two months' allowance on 13 October 'in order that you may have plenty of cash to start off with', but once again, with departure only a week away, Grace interceded.[41] Writing from southern California she declared herself on the verge of a nervous breakdown as a result of attempts to secure accommodation for herself and her mother and begged Hart to remember that his grandmother's condition was now extremely fragile and that two of them might be needed to nurse her if she took a sudden turn for the worse; whatever happened, he must remain in the United States. So Hart cancelled his reservation and took a job in a Manhattan bookstore and wrote wistfully to Underwood of the 'truly golden Carib primitives' duty had obliged him to forgo.[42] New York had its consolations, of course, as Sam Loveman was well placed to observe. He discovered that Hart was friendly with 'a very rich Scandinavian' who kept a boat on the Hudson 'and Hart would occasionally invite some of his sailor friends up there'. One day Loveman returned to Columbia Heights to find Hart sitting on the bed reading passages from *Moby Dick* and *The Bridge* 'to a stoker, a stocky rough stoker I think from the battleship *Wyoming*' whose hands, unsurprisingly, 'were grimy from the coal'. He was listening, Loveman remarked, 'with rapt attention' but clearly 'couldn't understand a word'. The reading ended and Hart urged Loveman to join the two of them on board the boat in the Hudson: the three men set off together but Loveman returned as soon as possible, since 'the atmosphere [aboard] confused and somewhat disheartened me'.[43] Perhaps it was in the course of one of these sailing parties around Manhattan that Hart met the 'sailor kid' he described to Underwood at this time, 'A kind of gamin who wakes up after the third – and asks me who's my doctor. "Why?" "Because I'm love sick about you." He'd wear me out if I'd let him. His affection also includes a certain amount of gold-digging. But he's worth it.'[44]

With such additional expenses Hart's earnings from the bookstore proved very useful. But although at first he considered himself lucky to have found the job, in no time he grew to hate it and his hours of freedom, Loveman noted, were marked by heavy drinking or else by ever more frequent sprees along the waterfront. Sue recalled that he complained to all his friends 'about his physical and mental sufferings in the small, dimly lit bookstore' and once again, in a refrain ever more familiar to those who knew him, he insisted that he was 'caught like a rat in a trap'.[45] This time it was Eleanor Fitzgerald who came to the rescue by introducing Hart to her friend Herbert Wise, a wealthy thirty-four-year-old neurotic who on medical advice was planning a six-month stay in California following a nervous breakdown and was in need of sensitive and well-read companionship for the duration of his sabbatical.

There was an interval of probation, of lunches, dinners and drives, but by 3 November it had been decided: Hart was to travel to southern California as the millionaire's secretary and companion and had been charged with ordering large quantities of books for the expedition. Wise also proposed to take his car, chauffeur, nurse and valet on the transcontinental journey but from the outset it looked as though Hart would enjoy a special position in the *ménage*. As Grace was told, 'He has travelled everywhere, and if our friendship proves to be a success there is a possibility of its including such things as travel with him in Europe.' Wise professed a great interest in Hart's poetry and had promised to give him 'almost complete freedom' to pursue his inspiration. In the meantime the poet had been warned by his new employer's physicians 'to exercise as sedative an effect on him as possible'.[46] Had Grace been a different sort of woman she might have found this letter rather curious: the details of Hart's probation sounded more like a courtship than anything else and the idea of his exercising a calming effect on anyone was fantastic, when all his life he had demanded response and reaction. Preoccupied as she was with her own new Californian life, however, Grace left no comment – and she was ignorant of the other anomaly of the situation, whereby although she heard all about Wise, he knew nothing of her, or of the fact that the poet's mother, formerly introduced with such pride to all his friends, would be a fellow resident of Los Angeles.

Sue met Wise before the millionaire and his entourage departed for the West and found him 'a frail, quiet, reticent man'; he and his resident poet 'hardly seemed compatible'.[47] By then Hart was racing around New York in a state of boisterous exhilaration, scarcely able to believe the good fortune that had redeemed him. He visited the Manhattan offices of *Poetry* and so came face to face at last with Harriet Monroe, who remembered him 'as a powerful, athletic figure, who was inclined to laugh at the luxurious way' in which Wise travelled.[48] He bought numerous gifts for friends and told his mother he was looking forward to practising his tennis in California's eternal summer. To Underwood he confided other expectations: he had heard that southern California was 'Arcadia in more ways than one', and with the *Arizona* now lying at anchor in Los Angeles harbour, 'Possibly I shall encounter the Phoebus Apollo of last spring'.[49] Drunk more often than not, Hart mislaid his train ticket several times before departure, which was scheduled for 17 November, but degradation took a new turn following a drinking contest with e.e. cummings and his second wife, Anne, as a result of which Hart found himself drunk enough to attract the attention of the law. What exactly he was doing to arouse police disapproval is lost to history but at about three in the morning he found himself being driven to Brooklyn's Clark Street Station to be locked up for the night. Drunk as he was, he took precautions, 'slyly en route tossing all evidence such as billets doux, dangerous addresses, etc., out of the window', he told the Browns. The next morning, after making 'an impassioned speech to a crowded court room', he was released without even a fine and was soon roaring with laughter as cummings related the events of the night before over afternoon beer. 'I never had so much fun jounced into 24 hours before,' he assured Bill and Sue, who were unconvinced by the claim as well as being fully aware of how desperate Hart always was to impress cummings.[50]

> He was completely dazzled by EE's mental and imaginative velocity, he played up to [him] and in his presence tried to imitate him. He admired EE's poetry almost to excess ... [and believed] that he had brought poetry to such a state of technical perfection that there was nothing beyond. This violent admiration every so often would, when Hart was drunk, turn into the most violent abuse, largely because he courted EEC's friendship and was persistently greeted with diffidence.[51]

Happily Hart was involved in no more bids to woo his fellow poet – or anyone else – before the day of departure arrived and he finally boarded the train that would take him across the continent. '*Ain't we got fun!!!!*' he wrote Grace, using the refrain of a popular song to evoke the spirit of forced hilarity that was becoming a feature of his correspondence.[52] Aunt Sally, when informed of Hart's new career, was inclined to agree: 'Hoping you have a glorious time and that your *boss* will fall so deeply in love with you that he'll want to keep you on forever.'[53]

16

California was a distant place then: it took Wise and his retinue five days to cross America – but on 21 November they finally emerged from the train and made their way to 2160 Mar Vista Avenue, a property Wise had rented north of Pasadena, in the foothills of the San Gabriel Mountains. Hart's new home, an extensive villa in the Spanish style built around a courtyard with fountain, belonged to the president of American Express and was, the poet complained, 'all bathrooms and bad furniture'.[1] Its gardens were luxuriant with oleanders, roses, camellias and acacias and beyond lay the poppy fields and citrus orchards of Altadena, a rural settlement with air resinous from the contiguous forests. The Mount Wilson Observatory stood sentinel in the peaks behind the house, its telescope the largest in the world, and below, stretching between the poet and the Pacific Ocean, lay Los Angeles, which only thirty years before had been an outpost, its shacks engulfed by orange groves, its surrounding canyons a home to the coyotes that howled by night. With the advent of the railroads and the discovery of oil, however, it had become the destination of the greatest internal migration in American history: huge influxes, of every race and religious denomination, arriving to take advantage of the city's plentiful electricity and famously therapeutic climate, built suburb upon suburb of bungalows. In Hart's day Los Angeles was a boom town of more than a million inhabitants which attracted a further 100,000 new residents every year, among them Grace and Mrs Hart, now settled a few miles south-west across the great Los Angeline coalescence at 1803 North Highland Avenue in Hollywood. They had come to a city already dominated by one industry: four-fifths of the world's films were now made here and many of the newest immigrants aspired to join the ranks of the millionaire film stars whose villas, palaces, castles and follies had begun to lend an air of unreality to certain zones of the city and whose activities, public and sometimes private, commanded an idolatrous audience. Not since antiquity indeed had gods moved so freely among men – but as Hart was to discover, some film stars were more approachable than others.

He was remote from this wonderland in the pampered isolation approved by Wise's doctors. Fragile, highly strung and indecisive as he was, however, Hart's new employer was far from being either an invalid or a hypochondriac: having been given money by his father Nathan Wise, whose tobacco distribution company, Metropolitan Tobacco, had made him a millionaire, Herbert amassed a further fortune on Wall Street, where he was advised by a young stockbroker named Irving Sartorius with whom he later went into business. He lost his fortune in 1929, only to recoup and increase it in the 1930s and 1940s, but he found time besides to devote to Jewish philanthropy and to his own literary enthusiasms. He wrote a play, 'Mr Jefferson', and along with Phyllis Fraser he co-edited *Great Tales of Terror and the Supernatural*.[2] His nephew Bennett Cerf, who founded and for many years incarnated Random House, called him 'the greatest influence on my young life'. He was 'never terribly strong' but his physical frailty could not disguise the fact that 'he was one of the most brilliant people I have ever met – absolutely brilliant. I felt he knew everything.'[3] As Hart had told Underwood before leaving New York, Wise wanted 'a secretary who can talk to him about Eliot, Spengler, metaphysics, and what not' – but it was only with the establishment of a routine at Mar Vista Avenue that the nature of that 'what not' began to emerge.[4]

Wise was not content with gentle distraction: he wanted to meet film stars and to give parties and soon Hart concluded that he had 'a furious love of excitement'.[5] In a city as elusive as Los Angeles it was at first hard to know where to look for potential guests sufficiently stimulating, but Hart had two significant contacts: although it was many years since he had seen Charlie Chaplin, the actor had been so friendly and sympathetic it was hard to imagine, if he could be found, that he would prove any different now, especially after the compliment of 'Chaplinesque'. Hart also wanted to see Alice Calhoun, an old friend from Cleveland two years his junior who had become a star of silent films. He had had no dealings with her since 1919, when writing stories for films had briefly seemed a plausible way to subsidize his poetry: Calhoun played her first major film role that year and since then, through Vitagraph in New York and Warner Brothers in Hollywood, she had made forty-three films, the most recent of which was *The Isle of Forgotten Women*. There were other calls to make before Hart ventured to Hollywood, however: Yvor Winters had suggested he contact Elizabeth Madox Roberts, a writer he had originally befriended at the University of Chicago whose first fiction, *The Time of Man*, set in the novelist's native Kentucky and published the previous year, had won international acclaim. Sadly, the meeting was not a success: she reminded Hart of 'a sibyl writhing on a tripod' and Winters was informed, 'I never felt that society could torture any human being so much before'.[6]

After this brief reminder of the reclusiveness and austerity necessary to literary creativity, the over-staffed splendour of the Wise establishment appeared unsettling, if not oppressive. Having survived the transcontinental journey, the millionaire's nurse, valet and chauffeur were now joined by a Viennese cook and a butler and every evening Hart sat down to a dinner that began with caviar and concluded with port. For good or ill, Patterson's turnip stews and brutal winters were far away and he told Isidor Schneider he was 'adding an irresistible five pounds to my pulchritude each day'.[7] The resources of an extensive cellar were complemented by the services of a bewildering assortment of bootleggers – an ideal situation in an environment where, Hart informed Slater Brown, 'one can't seem to wake up ... without the spur of scotch or gin'.[8] Having gone to California determined to perfect his tennis in the intervals between writing, Hart found himself undone by luxury and ease, a situation which boded ill for the peace of mind of a man whose thirst for alcohol was equalled only by a capacity for guilt in the face of inachievement. But should he be working for his own satisfaction or for Wise's? Was he a guest or an employee? Unable to decide he nevertheless informed Winters within a week of arrival that 'my situation demands a good deal of egg-stepping' – and the awkwardness inevitable in his uncertain position was compounded by the fact that Wise seemed to have more than a merely intellectual interest in his resident poet, an interest that emerged when their relations entered on a new phase of voyeurism and vicarious gratification.[9]

Underwood had guessed Wise's sexual nature at once and assumed that Hart was having an affair with his employer. Not so, the poet assured him, and 'when I become a concubine you shall be told all the dirt'. He was merely a diverting presence to have around the house 'and my calls were never made between the sheets'. However, one of his 'duties' at Wise's 'was to dash out every week end and come back with some sort of story of my adventures – and adventures there have been, too numerous to describe!'[10] Later, when Hart's restlessness had become acute, his status seemed little superior to the clownish but now, licensed to please himself in order to please others, he set out to discover what pleasures southern California could offer. One of the earliest excitements entailed a reunion: 'Everywhere such beautiful bodies, faces!' he told Sam Loveman on 1 December. 'Saw Evered last week end – went down to San Pedro in fact and on to the *Arizona*.'[11] His meeting with Phoebus Apollo had led to an exhilarating discovery: the fleet was in, and soon friends in New York became familiar with 'the pool rooms down at San Pedro where the battle fleet rides close at anchor'.[12] But it was scarcely necessary to go all the way to the docks for pleasure. 'The number of faggots cruising around out here is legion,' Underwood was assured. 'Half the movie stars are addicts, and Pershing Square in the center of Los Angeles is an even livelier place than Lafayette in Washington.'[13] Wise was duly apprised of this Hollywood gossip and on 8 December Winters was informed (without precise details) that 'movie studios have so far occupied a good deal of the time, mainly owing to my boss's curiosity in that direction'.[14] A few nights later Hart coincided in a restaurant with Charlie Chaplin and reported to the Schneiders that he hoped 'to lure him to our villa "under" Mount Wilson'.[15] Wise, Waldo was told, 'was simply wild to meet him and entertain him', but although Hart sent him a copy of

White Buildings and even tried to contact him on the telephone the actor kept his distance. 'He was simply too busy otherwheres to be interested ... and all the stars have built walls of mystery about themselves as impregnable as Carcassonne!'[16]

Not quite all, it turned out. Wise started to entertain and long afterwards, when Hart had returned to the East, the accounts he gave of the millionaire's parties left a great impression on the novelist Nathan Asch:

> From what Hart told us, I built up a picture of Hollywood as a voluptuaries' dream place where all the senses are satisfied ... I thought of where he lived with his rich patron as a sort of incense-laden seraglio, with couches on which reclined beautiful youths, and where even the ordered spaces of time meant nothing, so that day and night did not have ordinary connotations; breakfast was not served in the mornings, and the first meal of the day was not breakfast; liquor flowed, and bodies met and penetrated, prick entered ass hole, was licked by a mouth, in an atmosphere of music; and this Hart told us, once during a party at his boss's place, he found himself in the bathroom with a strange and beautiful looking man, worn looking too, who insisted on going down on him, and when he raised himself, showed himself to be the famous and already ageing star Ramon Novarro.[17]

The womanizing Chaplin did well to stay away: these were definitely not his sort of parties. Whether or not other famous actors exercised the same forbearance one can never know: if Hart could not immediately recognize Ramon Novarro, world famous after *Scaramouche* and *Ben Hur*, there is no establishing which other great screen lovers pursued him. He told several friends it would be safer to describe many of his Californian antics in person rather than commit the details to letters but he did give Slater Brown an account of the sort of 'Hollywood fays' whose company Wise seemed to find so diverting. 'I never could stand much falsetto', Hart insisted, adopting the tones of the celebrated female impersonator Bert Savoy to indicate his aversion to the arch *badinage* which was popular in the film world's demi-monde: 'Whoops! and whoops again, dearie, and then more warbling, more whiskey and broken crockery and maybe broken necks, for all I know.' Wise's present favourite had played Ariel in *The Tempest* before appearing in *Peter Pan*, 'and though she still makes the welkin ring I fear her voice will never do again. She has adopted the pronoun "we" to signalize her slightest thought, whim or act', and had been so upset on discovering that Hart had written a poem dedicated to Chaplin that 'she' immediately demanded a compensatory sonnet to her own loveliness. Even in the best of circumstances Hart was no court poet – and the storm that erupted when he refused to comply led Wise to suggest he might like a change of scene. By 19 December Hart was therefore happily on his own at the Breaker Club in Santa Monica and taking daily walks on the beach.

What a relief to watch the gulls and the pelicans and to chance upon stray eccentrics on the sand – one of whom had engaged him in a long conversation about Spengler, Kant, Wyndham Lewis and T.S. Eliot and turned out to know a friend of his and Brown's. But other encounters were also vivid in his mind. A few days previously, and much the worse for wear, he had gatecrashed a party at the Biltmore Hotel in downtown Los Angeles with an aviator named Chuck Short he had picked up shortly before. The two of them danced 'with fair ladies of the haute mondaine' and succeeded in getting their waiter drunk before being ejected, whereupon the pilot executed a Highland fling on Main Street and Hart, not to be outdone, drunkenly performed the 'gotzotsky' cossack routine long familiar at Village parties. His involvement with Short was brief but enjoyable and opened his eyes, he informed Brown, to the various uniformed alternatives of pleasure: 'After a good deal of "sailing" since arriving here – I am now convinced that "flying" is even better.'[18]

Although in some ways California had pleasantly surprised him, in general Hart found cherished prejudices confirmed: it was a vacuum, he told the Schneiders, a 'great pink vacuum' which amounted to nothing but 'miles and miles of marvelous blvds and pink sunsets and millions of happy vegetables aroused only on the rumor that somebody is sinning'.[19] For the time being he was stuck there, although it was somewhat worrying that in the month since his arrival he had written nothing but letters and had read only two books, I.A. Richards's *Principles of Literary Criticism* and Jessie L. Weston's *From Ritual to Romance*. *The Bridge* lay scaffolded and untenanted and poetry itself, the practice of which was integral to Hart's bravura self-definition, lay drunkenly discarded. But news from Yvor Winters roused him: the critic's parents lived at Flintridge outside Pasadena and Winters and his wife were planning a Christmas visit. Hart was delighted by the prospect but he would have to sober up – Wise and his Petronian revels would hold no appeal for the man with whom Hart had now been corresponding for over a year. He paid his first visit one afternoon and had tea with Winters and his wife in the latter's room: convalescing from tuberculosis, Janet Lewis was confined to bed until four each day and after a while the men withdrew to continue their discussion of poetry elsewhere. She found Hart charming but formed the distinct impression, as her husband declaimed and then discussed the major modern French poets, that he was timid with the language and familiar with its literature only in translation. Winters was more forcibly struck by their guest's appearance: the twenty-eight-year-old poet's hair was greying rapidly, 'his skin had the dull red color with reticulated grayish traceries which so often goes with advanced alcoholism, and his ears and knuckles were beginning to look a little like those of a pugilist'.[20] Hart stayed for dinner and later Winters's father drove them down Pasadena's famous Christmas Tree Street: Hart shared the back seat with Winters and the sight of the trees, actually Himalayan cedars, lit and festooned for the season, prompted him to a dramatic recitation of his poem 'The Hurricane', which he had sent to Winters in its pristine form:

Lo, Lord, Thou ridest!
Lord, Lord, Thy swifting heart

Naught stayeth, naught now bideth
But's smithereened apart!...

Whip sea-kelp screaming on blond
Sky-seethe, high heaven dashing –

Thou ridest to the door, Lord!
Thou bidest wall nor floor, Lord![21]

There were three subsequent meetings, all of which proved enlightening and mutually enjoyable. Winters, not a man given to lyrical enthusiasms, declared twenty years later that Hart was 'not a fool' and that he would 'gladly emulate Odysseus, if I could, and go down to the shadows for another hour's conversation with [him] on the subject of poetry'.[22] Hart was inspired by his friend's readings and exegesis of Rimbaud, Baudelaire and Valéry but astonished when the critic proffered specimens of his own recent poetry – the sonnets he now wrote were a dramatic divergence from the free verse he had previously espoused and indicated the radical changes that were shaping Winters's poetic convictions. Hart took the poems home and dutifully studied them but when he sent their author his opinions, just as Wise and his retinue were preparing for a day at Santa Monica, he trod carefully. 'They have a fine, hard ring', but somehow he was unconvinced: they seemed altogether 'too skeletal – i.e like a chemical formula rather than its concrete demonstration, which is an equivalent for what a poem ought to be in terms of metaphor.'[23] Perhaps the most significant result of this period of contact between the two writers, however, was Hart's introduction to the poetry of Gerard Manley Hopkins, which Winters read aloud from the posthumous collection assembled by Robert Bridges. The Victorian Jesuit's techniques of alliteration, internal rhyme and sprung rhythm were a revelation to Hart, who subsequently told Winters he had never before suspected words could retain their literal signification while at the same time approximating so closely to 'a transfiguration to pure musical notation'.[24] Unfortunately the collection was out of print, so Hart charged bibliophile Sam Loveman with finding a copy for which he declared he would pay as much as $10, the price of a month's rent at Mrs Turner's. Hopkins had taught him 'that I am not so original in some of my stylisms as I had thought' and if Loveman proved unable to find a second-hand copy Hart was resigned to laboriously typing out all the poems, 'for I've never been so enthusiastic about any modern before'.[25] When Bennett Cerf came to visit his uncle, Hart tried to persuade him to instigate a Hopkins revival in America, but to no avail: the young publisher seemed to have 'no ear nor mind for any poetry' and for all his urbane charm struck the poet as 'very superficial; a "type" all too common in every metropolis nowadays'.[26]

Winters and his wife returned to northern California. Hart and the critic never saw each other again but at least now they were back on terms of mutual esteem. In a review he was preparing for *Poetry* of *Fugitives: An Anthology of Verse* Winters decried the influence of T.S. Eliot on contemporary poetry and urged aspiring young American writers to look to 'the spiritual *and* formal values of two poets – Hart Crane, and especially that of the most magnificent master of English and of human emotions since Thomas Hardy, William Carlos Williams'.[27] When the American expatriate writer Kay Boyle attacked Hart's poetry in *transition* Winters came to his defence in a letter which the magazine published – a gesture which gratified Hart even more than Laura Riding's apparently benevolent appraisal of *White Buildings*, also published in *transition*. As far as he could see, Riding admired his work but the arguments of her approbation were so tangled that Hart asked Winters if she was 'trying to evolve a critical style from Gertrude Stein?'[28] If this was the best the little magazines could manage in the way of comment he wondered why he ever strayed from the literary supplements of the daily newspapers. Following publication in the *Criterion* of 'The Tunnel', William Rose Benét had tossed a garland of sorts in December in the column of literary gossip he wrote for the *Saturday Review of Literature*. Benét's remarks were as usual grudging and facetious but at least they were clear: allowing that many poems had been written recently about travelling underground and over rivers, 'we give Crane best'. 'Of course [he] has, ere this, been puffed and boomed almost *ad nauseam* by the *literati*. But here we perceive some reason for it. His poem is in no sense great, or, perhaps, even near-great, but it is his own and extremely interesting.'[29] A few months later, on 10 March, Benét was in less charitable mood and his compliments were correspondingly more oblique: 'Mr Moon's Notebook' was devoted to a prolonged and fatuous pastiche of Cranean tone and technique.

In the early weeks of 1928 Winters's unswerving commitment to literature continued to inspire Hart and turning to books as to an old friend he read *Wuthering Heights* – with Heathcliff giving particular pleasure; *Sodom and Gomorrah*, the latest volume of Proust; *The Counterfeiters* by Gide; *Time and Western Man* by Wyndham Lewis; *Trinc* by Phelps Putnam; *Streets in the Moon* by Archibald MacLeish; and *Messages* by Ramon Fernandez, which he assured Bill Brown was 'insufferable'.[30] Every week he read the *New Republic* and the *Herald-Tribune*, searching their pages, he told the Browns, 'for the names of our "rising generation"', and he even instigated a correspondence with the Spanish critic Antonio Marichalar, who wrote a Madrid letter for the *Criterion* and whose review of *White Buildings* had appeared in *Revista de Occidente*.[31] With his usual extravagance Wise had bought recordings by Victor of all the great composers so Hart informed Loveman he was living 'on intimate terms for the first time with Brahms and Beethoven – the two most exciting of all to me'.[32] He spent long hours sunbathing at Long Beach and Venice; he swam; and again and again he turned to *The Tempest*, 'that crown of all the Western World', only to find himself homesick for 'the dear hills of Connecticut' where he was accustomed to read Shakespeare.[33] If Hart Crane never actually loathed Los Angeles he was profoundly, and permanently, unsettled by it and he deprecated it in letter after letter to friends in the East. Everything there apart from the remorseless sunshine seemed to elude him: friendship, purpose, poetic inspiration, even Charlie Chaplin. He was imprisoned by the city's uncentred and straggling size, so impersonal after the intimacy of Manhattan, and bewildered by the all-pervasive posturing. 'One can generally "place" people to some extent,' he told the Cowleys, 'but not in Los Angeles. Wherever he turned he was appalled, whether by the spurious architecture or the radio evangelism of Aimée McPherson. 'The peculiar mixtures of piety and utter abandon in this welter of cults, ages, occupations, etc. ... make it a good deal like Bedlam.'[34] Indeed, he told Underwood, 'If it weren't for the Fleet I should scarcely be able to endure it.'[35] But if sailors could mitigate the day-to-day unrealities of the city they were powerless to change the way Hart saw it symbolically. He had conceived of his country as the physical expression of a myth and its people as the privileged inheritors of European idealism – but that was before Los Angeles. Here a continent was finally bridged and here the frontier had been closed. Here the logic of Manifest Destiny was fulfilled and here the mighty west-bound migration which defined America's pilgrim history had culminated – here in this seaside town of tawdry make-believe.

By the beginning of February Wise had begun to indicate that he wanted Crane to accompany him on his next trip to Europe: the opportunity was almost too wonderful to contemplate, even if Hart was beginning to tire of what he described to the Browns as his employer's 'interminable psycho-analysis of every book, person, sausage and blossom'.[36] The entertaining meanwhile continued, and when 'fairy God Mother' Hart wrote to the Browns on 22 February to congratulate them on the birth of their son Gwilym the future formalities of Christian guidance were the last thing on his mind. Sending what he termed 'a paean from Venusberg' while drinking his ninth Scotch he enclosed a photograph of 'a most affectionate red-haired mariner' with whom he had just spent a night. 'These western argosies, at roadstead far and near', what parades of 'pulchritude and friendliness' they promised – not that one had to venture far to meet the members of these argosies, who were often the most popular (and co-operative) guests at a party. 'I have met the Circe of them all – a movie actor who has them dancing naked, twenty at a time, around the banquet table.' For those whose preferences extended to something out of uniform Hart recommended a walk down Hollywood Boulevard, where there were 'little fairies who can quote Rimbaud before they are 18'. But it was in private houses that the wildest distractions were to be had: with his very eyes he had seen Betty Compson, prolific actress of the silent screen, 'shake her tits – and cry *apples* for a bite!'

Even if he did travel to Europe Hart doubted he would discover anywhere that
competed with Hollywood for depravity: 'O André Gide! no Paris ever yielded
such as this – away with all your counterfeiters!'[37] It was perhaps through this
Circe that the poet befriended one of his Los Angeles lovers, a sailor named Paul
Henderson who was a member of the crew of the USS *Pennsylvania*. Henderson
was in turn a friend (or more) of an actor who lived at Echo Park in Los Angeles
and signed himself 'Comtesse de Segur' in the letters he sent to Hart – camp and
coded letters that evoke the twilit Hollywood into which the poet had strayed, a
world where minor actors jostled for bit parts and squabbled over sailors in the
long wait for fame. The 'Comtesse' was also involved at one stage with an actor
named Fisher, who in turn became Wise's lover. The intricacies of these shifting
relations, as indicated in the Comtesse's letters, are now impossible to disentangle
but the tone of the correspondence testifies to an aspect of Hart's Californian life,
a life which was far removed from the days when the visionary company had
assembled to discuss higher awareness or the post-war crisis of poetry:

> And how do you do, Madame Wise? How are your diseases and your great
> villas, and your retinue and your lovers? John had some dirt and left the
> menagerie. Miss Fisher had her nose broken thru the wind shield and served 30
> days on one count.... Hart don't send me postal cards because they go to
> Mothers office & she reads them & when you write mark letter privé. Savez?
> ... La Wise is a building of a villa in Pasadena, I hear & still has that poor little
> faggot with him ... Paul will write you any day now. He sure has a gorgeous
> friend that came with him but they're both in N York now & they will be dis-
> appointed not to see you but I gave them some addresses. My God Hart I am
> so tired of it here – nothing but bloody movie news in the papers, movie every-
> thing.[38]

There was a slogan, familiar in those days from the advertisements for Pear's
Soap, which declared, 'He won't be happy till he gets it', a slogan Hart considered
admirably applicable to Wise and his desperate longing for a lover. As he explained
to the Browns, however, 'when [Wise] finally secured a quite cultured little piece
of Pear's Soap ... to console him in all ways at once, then I began to feel
altogether too extraneous for words.' Weeks of restlessness and declining morale
aggravated this sudden feeling of irrelevance, to say nothing of 'the tip-toeing
[and] solicitous, willy-nilly uncertainty of everything'.[39] The projected expedition
to Europe would entail many distractions from this dissatisfaction – but when
Grace heard of the scheme she once again begged her son to remain in America
in case his grandmother suddenly declined. Whether or not Wise and Hart had a
row it is now impossible to say – the millionaire is conspicuous by his complete
absence from the extant correspondence sent to the poet – but the latter came to
the conclusion he must leave Mar Vista Avenue and on 20 March, with nowhere

else to go, he moved to his mother's house in Hollywood. It was, as he admitted to Schneider, something of a transformation, since it took him 'from courts and halls and stucco walls to a very modest bungalow' situated in a stretch of other modest bungalows long ago demolished when Highland Avenue was widened for traffic: wood-shingled structures from 1915, their functional aspect prettified by poinsettias, rambling roses and ivy.[40] Here Grace lived in circumstances already ominously claustrophobic with Mrs Hart and the maid they had brought from Cleveland and it was here that Hart had visited his mother and grandmother twice a week despite the two-hour journey from Altadena.

On the whole, mother and daughter appeared content in California: perennial blossoms and oceanic proximity delighted them and the warm dry climate had left Mrs Hart, now eighty-nine, in better health than at any stage in the last three years. She was frail nevertheless and her condition necessitated not only her daughter's constant attendance but also the ministrations of various doctors whose bills, combined with the maid's wages, made such inroads into Grace's income that her slender portfolio of shares was slowly being sold to cover the deficiencies of alimony. She had a scheme, however, that would surely redress her own and her son's financial difficulties: Hart must become an actor – and she had no doubt that with his extensive connections in Hollywood a propitious route to fame and prosperity would soon open.

The radiant vistas of European travel dissolved in these oppressive surroundings and the skeletal structure of *The Bridge* faded further into the mists of hopelessness. Suddenly Hart felt as though life had trapped him, here in this lonely city where his mother was either a fellow-prisoner or else his gaoler and where his friends all seemed so far away. There was one cheering prospect, however: Emil had taken a job as a waiter on the SS *California* with the specific intention of working his way to the West Coast to see his former lover and his ship was due in Los Angeles on Saturday, 24 March. Sadly what should have been a joyous reunion turned into a near-tragedy of errors, albeit one which had long been the implicit danger of Hart's nocturnal roamings.

The meeting had been planned before Hart left Mar Vista Avenue but Opffer never received his friend's letter advertising a change of address and knew nothing of the poet's suggestion that they should meet at the dockside. When the *California* arrived – ahead of schedule – Emil therefore went straight to Altadena to meet Hart who was meanwhile heading for San Pedro clutching celebratory bottles to begin what turned out to be an eight-hour vigil. By the time Emil returned to the docks via Altadena and North Highland Avenue Hart, as he later informed the Browns, had almost finished 'a half pint of alcohol which I had brought for our mutual edification, and [Emil] had completely emptied a quart of Barcardi'. At that stage of intoxication there was nothing for it but further drinking, so at last reunited the two friends headed for a speakeasy and 'with much "skoling"' proceeded to order 'many bottles of dubious gin and whiskey', assisted by 'three or four still more dubious "merry andrews'" who had joined, or been invited to join, their table. At midnight the speakeasy closed and the rowdy group roamed the surrounding streets until one of the anonymous revellers suggested they hire a hotel room in which to continue drinking. For once money was no object: Emil had just been paid and in the bar they had all seen him 'flashing a fat payroll'. He and Hart were by now 'reeling but refractory' – but the poet was just lucid enough to register the dark and deserted streets and the mood of the unknown men and his own sudden foreboding. A second later he realized he and Emil were being quietly separated and a second after that, just as Hart tried to break free to raise the alarm, 'all five started slugging us'. A lone car turned the corner and their assailants fled, but not before both men had been robbed of everything and badly beaten, Emil almost to the point of unconsciousness. Hart somehow found his way to a police station to depose an account of the attack before returning Emil to the *California* with the aid of several of his shipmates and then seeking shelter for himself at a Salvation Army hotel. It was five the next afternoon before he finally returned to Hollywood, by which time the *California* had departed for San Francisco: Hart would have to wait until the ship passed through Los Angeles on its return voyage before seeing his 'Goldylocks' again.

In the meantime, he told Winters, he was 'worried sick' about his condition and confessed to the Browns that 'when I left [Emil] in his berth in the "glory-hole" of the *California* last Sat. night he looked as though he were nearing the Pearly Gates'.[41] It was all very well to tell Winters the incident was like 'an episode from Cervantes' but Hart implied the full sordidness of the situation when he told Bill and Sue that whatever happened Emil's mother and stepfather must not be informed.[42] Unfortunately it would be very much harder to evade, or delude, his own vigilant and possessive mother but whatever Grace thought when Hart returned dishevelled, bruised and stale with drink she now knew better than to be bluntly interrogative. The adoring son with the golden future on whom she had placed such great hopes a decade ago was not always apparent in the twenty-eight-year-old man with greying hair and reddening face whose poetry and drinking bewildered her – and as she subsequently admitted to Sam Loveman, silence often seemed the surest way to maintain domestic harmony: 'When Hart was in California I realized as never before that something had to be done to change his course. But I never said much, just a guarded word here or there ... was all I knew he would stand. He resented any criticism from me, no matter of how kind or friendly a nature, and I grew to withhold it all.'[43]

The poet was therefore not at his best when on the morning of 26 March he attended an interview with Otto Kahn, who was in Los Angeles on business and staying at the Ambassador Hotel. Hart had once again solicited his patron's assistance shortly before leaving Wise's employment and hoped that in the course of his own dealings in California Kahn would extend further funds or the offer of some judiciously placed word of recommendation. This time the financier chose the latter course and undertook to secure the poet an interview for some sort of writing job in the film world – and since even in Hollywood Kahn could invoke old and influential affections in support of his cherished causes he promised to speak to Jesse Lasky, who ran the entire California side of Paramount Pictures and whose partner in New York, Adolph Zukor, had been a friend of Kahn's ever since 1919, when the banker prevailed upon Kuhn, Loeb to invest $10 million in Paramount's plans for expansion. While Kahn was listening to the latest details of Hart's plight on one of the hotel terraces a newsreel team suddenly appeared and filmed their discussion, 'and for all I know', Hart told the Browns, 'we may be thrown upon the screen together all the way from Danbury to Hong-Kong and Mozambique! I'm wearing horn rims now so don't be shocked.'[44] Thus Kahn conferred fame even on his supplicants – but now he promised more and the consequence, as Hart subsequently told Bill Brown, was a meeting thousands in this wayward city could only ever dream of engineering: 'If I can hold on until the middle of May I'm due for an interview with Jesse Lasky (HIMSELF) and maybe through that entrée I can creep into some modest dustpan in the reading dept. of Paramount.' But that was still weeks away, and even if the interview yielded satisfactory results, what was the point? Did he really want to live with his mother anywhere, least of all in this city, when his life, his friends and his convictions all resided in the East? And then news came that the fleet which had done so much to alleviate his distress was to leave for Hawaii: now not even sailors could distract him, he complained to the Browns, from 'the full inconsequence of this Pollyanna greasepaint pinkpoodle paradise with its everlasting stereotyped sunlight and its millions of mechanical accessories and sylphlike robots of the age of celluloid'.[45] He was desperately lonely and during the course of southern California's subtle spring he contacted friends who had not heard from him for months – though without attempting to put a brave face on his deepening gloom.

Writing to Isidor Schneider on 28 March to thank him for sending Isadora Duncan's autobiography, *My Life*, published the previous year, Hart mentioned that he was 'prospecting for some scenario or other mechanical work with the movies' but his tone was melancholy, his only news was of recent reading and even that recreation had failed to inspire him. The spiritual malaise of the post-war world was much in fashion with writers and publishers and perhaps because he had once thought that the new age of mechanization would revitalize life and literature Hart read much that was written in investigation or as cure of this malaise, only to find himself frustrated or depressed by 'all these Whiteheads, Bradleys, Fernandez, Wyndham Lewis-es, etc., who keep drumming up new encyclopedias of the Future, Fate, etc.' Part of the problem was that they were all 'so formidable, bristling with allusions, statistics, threats and tremors, trumpets and outcries on the least splitting of a hair which I can't locate through the labyrinth of abstractions. I'm afraid I'd better give up trying to make any headway in their directions – or else relinquish all attempts to do any writing myself.' The fact was that he found himself bewildered and paralysed by this intellectual gloom about the future: the artist created in response to his understanding of the present – or perhaps the past – but to attempt to outstare the inscrutable tomorrow was to invite creative defeat. 'It seems as though the imagination had ceased all attempts at any creative activity – and had become simply a great bulging eye ogling the foetus of the next century.'[46]

He wrote to Waldo a few days later and said how sorry he was that correspondence between them had tailed off: giving a digest of his recent news he declared he was 'by no means settled in my present environment' and was not at all 'happily disposed'. Nor could he take comfort from the conviction of an imminent spiritual awakening of America, once the hope that had bound him in friendship with Frank and Munson. Again he mentioned the pessimistic forecasts of Lewis and Fernandez – perhaps Waldo could challenge them intellectually but Hart himself felt impotent: 'These Godless days! I wonder if you suffer as much as I do. At least you have the education and training to hold the scalpel.'[47] Munson had sent him a copy of his recently published *Destinations*, the collection of essays which contained 'Young Titan in the Sacred Wood' along with studies of various prominent contemporaries including Theodore Dreiser, Marianne Moore, Wallace Stevens and William Carlos Williams, and when Hart wrote with thanks and appraisal his tone was the same. He agreed with Munson's call for 'more definite spiritual knowledge and direction' but wondered how on earth it was to be realized. 'The spiritual disintegration of our period becomes more painful to me every day, so much so that I now find myself baulked by doubt at the validity of every metaphor I coin.' Regarding Munson's studies of individual writers, he admired his estimation of William Carlos Williams but knew too little of Theodore Dreiser to agree or disagree with his friend's judgement. 'As for Hart Crane, I know him too well to disagree on as many points as I once did, two years ago when I first read the essay.' He was grateful for the book's attention and thought that Munson's assessment of his technical aims in *The Bridge* was so persuasive that it had 'recently revived in me some conviction of "reality" here and there in my scrap heap'.[48]

A sense of intellectual futility was not his only complaint: though living in his mother's house he felt a desperate homesickness. When Bill Brown wrote to say that he and Sue had opened up Robber Rocks for the summer it made Hart ache with nostalgia and longing: 'Things like that croquet game in the rain, the afternoon at the cider mill, the skeleton surry ride and the tumble down the hill!'[49] To Underwood he was more succinct: he 'longed for the east', for his friends and for the modest life he had known 'out on the farmstead in Connecticut'.[50] In his desperation, having discovered that Underwood's old friend Alice Barney was living in Los Angeles, Hart had telephoned her and secured an invitation to her next soirée, which he hoped would be rather different from the usual Hollywood party. Mrs Barney was, after all, not only the widow of an Ohio railroad millionaire but also the mother of Natalie Clifford Barney, friend to Rémy de Gourmont, Radclyffe Hall and Lord Alfred Douglas, whose celebrated and conspicuously lesbian salon at 20 rue Jacob intrigued Proust and Colette and rivalled the hospitality of her great friend Gertrude Stein. Alice Barney's circle proved pedestrian by comparison, however, and having gone in expectation of grandeur, anachronism and all things Proustian, Hart was disappointed. Though naturally high-spirited and gregarious he now cut a lonely figure even at parties. His great-uncle Cassius and uncle Ralph Crane were living in Los Angeles at the time and the latter, who never knew Hart well, remembered clearly how solitary and incongruous he could seem, especially in CA's borrowed tuxedo:

> His father was a very large man. We were invited to some swell reception and he arrived at our place with this dress suit on[;] only a man with a great sense of humor could have been seen in public with it on. He looked [as though] he had two pairs of pants on with the cuffs turned up about six inches and the sleeves of the coat almost to the tips of his fingers. He made a lonely wall flower as he could not stand up without pants falling off unless he had his hands in his pants pockets. . . . I have an idea he was a sort of loner.[51]

As for CA, Hart and his father had maintained an intermittent but affectionate correspondence since the poet's departure for Los Angeles. When Clarence Crane wrote to his son at the end of March he qualified his accounts of the confectionery business and life at Canary Cottage with a benign scepticism about California and its famous charms. He had recently received a letter from Grace 'in which she indicates she is roaming around among flower beds and enjoying life to the fullest in Hollywood' but to Hart he confided his hope that 'she won't pick up a bumble bee in her quest for happiness'.[52] Replying to CA shortly after Easter, Hart relayed Grace's assurances 'that she now knows the buzz of bumble-bee from afar, and needs no further warnings!' Aware of his father's laconic attitude towards their Californian life he was eager to assure him not only of Grace's contentment but also of his own. Jobs were hard to find, it was true, but Kahn would facilitate some salvation and there were many happy distractions: the previous Sunday he had joined Ralph and Cassius and 50,000 others for an Easter Sunrise service at the Hollywood Bowl; and any day of the week saw him delighting in Hollywood's more worldly distractions. As he promised CA, 'There's a regular stampede of trim ankles, silken calves, dimpled knees and laughing eyes.'[53]

Yet if for CA's benefit he was a happy heterosexual Hart had decided it was time Grace knew the truth, although the occasion of his revelation and its underlying reasons are now irrecoverable. Grace later claimed his declaration occurred during the course of a weekend she spent at Altadena but she is contradicted not only by Sue Brown's memory (which situates the admission, described by Hart in a letter that later vanished, in the period spent in North Highland Avenue) but also by probability. There is nothing in Hart's extant correspondence to suggest that Grace ever went to Mar Vista Avenue but even if she did it is hard to imagine that her son would needlessly confront her with information he had chosen to conceal for years, information moreover that could easily have provoked an embarrassing confrontation in front of Wise and his concubines. Once he moved, however, to a claustrophobic bungalow fraught with financial anxiety and the apprehension of Mrs Hart's approaching death, Hart found himself in a situation where concealment was bound to prove both more difficult and more nerve-racking and where the temptation to resort to frankness, if only to simplify life, was consequently greater.

Perhaps years of relative freedom from maternal scrutiny had left him disinclined to perpetuate a tiresome fiction or perhaps he assumed Grace already knew and was only waiting to be told. Perhaps he acted pre-emptively: she was bound to find out sooner or later, so better from him than from anyone else. Perhaps there was something in his manner with Emil, whom he introduced to Grace and Mrs Hart when the Dane passed through Los Angeles on his way back to New York, that spoke to his jealous mother of more than old friendship or perhaps his condition after the attack in San Pedro was more incriminating than any amount of inventive alibis could conceal. For whatever reason, however, Grace at last knew – but her account of her reaction to the news is once again at variance with Sue's, since she later promised Sam Loveman, to say nothing of Hart's first biographer, that she received the news, if not happily, then at least with composure: 'The Cranes never knew about the struggle I have had [with Hart's drinking] nor of his emotional persuasion of which he calmly told me himself while in California. It was a great shock to me but he never knew it & it took me a long time to get my mind adjusted to the condition.'[54] Sue's recollection, again based on the lost letter, is of a confrontation much more melodramatic in which Hart blamed Grace for his sexuality and in which 'mother and son hurled insults at each other'.[55] Later Grace would claim that she read various studies of psychology and sexology with a view to understanding her son's erotic and emotional temper. Later still she seems to have convinced herself that she could remain his sweetheart when no other woman could ever usurp her position. But at the end of April these stages of equanimity were remote and if Hart had thought he was too old to live dishonestly under the same roof as his mother she soon gave him cause to reconsider.

Describing subsequent events to the Schneiders Hart declared that 'excessively hysterical conditions' developed at North Highland Avenue and that 'altogether it was intolerable'.[56] Mrs Hart was too frail for anything beyond observation at these dramas but mother and son were old partners in reciprocal manipulation and were both sufficiently histrionic to sustain anguish and mutual recrimination unaided. He complained, to Zell, that he was 'treated like an absolute two-year-old [and had] to emulate both Mary Baker Eddy and Douglas Fairbanks at once, run errands for corset strings, hair nets etc. besides undergoing the weekly round of hysterical scenes'.[57] Grace in turn complained of his drinking: after all, however tempting a refuge alcohol was, the scale of Hart's consumption only exacerbated existing problems, as she explained to Sam Loveman:

> He never needed much persuasion to go on one of his sprees – and when once well started one never knew just how it would end.... With mother sick unto death and requiring constant attention night and day and at all times when he was affected, trying to screen his condition from her [*sic*] – for they simply idolized each other. I never allowed myself to chide him when such conditions were evident. I just tried not to notice it, and waded through the scene as calmly and pleasantly as though things were quite normal. I knew perfectly well how 'touchy' he was at such times, and upbraiding him would be likely to produce most any kind of scene.[58]

Yet beyond the bottle there were few other escapes from this prison, especially now that Grace, aware of where and how Hart liked to relax, tried to keep him at home in the evenings, if necessary by taking to her bed with complaints of emotional exhaustion, so that he was forced to alternate with the maid in cooking and cleaning and taking Mrs Hart backwards and forwards to the bathroom. Slowly but surely a suspicion developed that as his mother's life constricted with age and insolvency her attempted hold on him would grow more obsessive: present measures to protect him from danger on the seafront would extend in time to protection from all comers who threatened her emotional sovereignty – yet the freedom to love was integral not only to life but to poetry. What he described to the Rychtariks as 'incessant hysterical fits and interminable nagging' became part of daily routine until one day, after a particularly difficult confrontation, Grace asked him to leave.[59] The crisis passed but a few scenes later she reiterated her request and this time he took her at her word, only to discover when he began to pack that his mother's interpretation of the teachings of Christian Science allowed her not only to challenge disease with willpower but also to induce it. As he related to Zell, 'On seeing my intentions ensued such an outbreak that before I could leave the house was full of sympathetic neighbors, Grace was on her way to the hospital (having worked up a really serious kidney disturbance) and I was left with the pitiful figure of Grandma, a trembling spectre of terror.'

Once it had been raised, however, the idea of departure became irresistible, not least because he now understood he could no longer live in proximity with his mother. Yet if it was impossible to remain under a narrow roof with a tireless emotional monopolist it was also hard to explain his decision to leave to a woman who dreaded more than anything the abandonment she invariably provoked: during the course of Grace's twenty-four hours in hospital Hart realized that the only way he could leave without further scenes and phantom prostrations was in secret. He paid the hospital bill and with what remained of his savings he bought a one-way ticket to New York. The day of departure – 15 May – approached and he packed gradually and stealthily between supervising Mrs Hart and his mother. Grace's recovery advanced slowly: again he suspected an act, and to Zell he mentioned his conviction that she was protracting recuperation day by day to ensure that he was reduced 'to a kind of idiotic jelly of sympathetic responses'. She was up and about again by 13 May, her renewed mobility greatly increasing the danger that his scheme would be discovered: he dissembled too, if only to outwit her, and as she staged recovery he performed his quiet and casual routine. In fact he was sick with nervousness and insomnia by the time the cab drove up with darkened lights and he slipped out of North Highland Avenue for good, never to see his mother or grandmother again. In so far as he had a home it was New York, cruel as it was, he told Zell, 'but far better for me than either of my parents'. As for Grace, 'I think it is suicide for both of us to try to live together again. I say this without any exaggeration.'[60]

PART FIVE

London, Paris and New York

May 1928–March 1931

Then glozening decanters that reflect the street
Wear me in crescents on their bellies. Slow
Applause flows into liquid cynosures:
— I am conscripted to their shadows' glow.

'THE WINE MENAGERIE'

17

Grace discovered a note on her son's pillow informing her simply that he had 'gone East',[1] and until she heard from him two weeks later she feared the worst, including, as she told Loveman, 'imprisonment at San Quentin, because of his daily visits to some bootlegger acquaintances he had made'.[2] In fact he was retracing his own earlier journey, and the journey of countless pioneers, travelling east by train across New Mexico and Texas to Louisiana and gloomily contemplating the painful impermanence of human relations. Was there any affection that did not end in disappointment or betrayal? And without sure love was life any less barren than the desert beyond the carriage window? They were unanswerable questions that echoed in the melancholy inconclusiveness of 'A Postscript', the poem that described his flight from his mother, the ominous title of which suggested that now he had fled her his life was to be a mere coda to the precedent days of hope and poetic conviction:

> Friendship agony! words came to me
> at last shyly. My only final friends –
> the wren and thrush, made solid print for me
> across dawn's broken arc. No; yes ... or were they
> the audible ransom, ensign of my faith
> toward something far, now farther than ever away?

The train stopped at San Antonio and again at Houston – after the desolate landscape of western Texas it was a relief once more to see flowers, cattle and human activity, although the sight of people brought back to mind the broken covenant of maternal affection and the memory of that older mother he had known in the West Indies who had demanded nothing and never forsaken him:

> Remember the lavender lilies of that dawn,

their ribbon miles, beside the railroad ties
as one nears New Orleans, sweet trenches by the train
after the western desert, and the later cattle country;
and other gratuities, like porters, jokes, roses ...

Dawn's broken arc! and noon's more furbished room!
Yet seldom was there faith in the heart's right kindness.
There were tickets and alarm clocks. There were counters and schedules;
and a paralytic woman on an island of the Indies,
Antillean fingers counting my pulse, my love forever.[3]

After the aridity of the desert and the ahistorical void of Los Angeles, New Orleans, where he spent a day before embarkation for New York, seemed like an oasis. Some journalists from the *Times-Picayune* who were also admirers of Hart's poetry showed him the town and treated him, he told CA, 'like a senator'. He ate the local specialities, he visited absinthe speakeasies and by the end of the guided tour he was already dreaming of spending a winter there: never before, he told Winters, not even in Salem, Massachusetts, had he felt so 'surrounded and permeated' by 'old' America. Yet although the French Quarter was irresistibly romantic it was also, he knew, alien to the plainer poetry of the United States: 'I suppose pewter is the more representative, and the old tarnished gold of Orleans belongs rather to the traditions of Martinique than to the spirit of the Minute Men.'[4] The voyage from New Orleans to New York began with a five-hour journey down the Mississippi Delta which Hart assured CA marked 'one of the great days of my life', not least because it vindicated the closing lines of 'The River', which had been written from imagination, not experience. As his ship finally reached the Gulf of Mexico he knew the surrender implicit in the confluence of river and sea and assured his father that 'there is something tragically beautiful about the scene, the great, magnificent Father of Waters pouring itself at last into the oblivion of the Gulf!' A voyage of five days followed: it was a relief to discover he no longer suffered from seasickness; a greater relief that meals were included in his ticket, since by the time he walked down the gangplank back into New York he had only $2 in his pocket.

Despite his insolvency, Hart was happy to be back and to see old friends, among them Waldo, who advanced him the money to return to Patterson, whence he wrote on 14 June to inform CA of his return. Carefully avoiding all reference to disagreements with Grace, Hart restricted himself to pleasantries about New York – 'people aren't as indifferent and impersonal there as they are in the west despite all the slogans and catchwords to the contrary' – and tentative applications for financial assistance.[5] Replying four days later CA expressed surprise at Hart's sudden return but if he had shrewd suspicions that his son had also found it impossible to live with Grace he kept them to himself. His confectionery business

was continuing to decline but Canary Cottage, besides keeping him happily occupied, had started to pay its way: takings for the previous day totalled $700 and it
now looked as though the concern would break even in its first year. He was therefore more than happy to send his son money, confectionery – a two-pound box of
Crane's 'Cartier La France' chocolates to satisfy not only Hart's sweet tooth but
also Addie's – and a piece of paternal advice: 'You are getting to be a big boy now,
so don't go around with your pants unbuttoned, and write your old decrepit father
whenever you have a stamp with which to mail it.'[6]

Mrs Turner's roses were in bloom and Hart succumbed at once to hay fever but
he was determined nevertheless to recommence work on *The Bridge*, so much so
that when Waldo invited him to spend part of June or July in Maine he declined.
With the Browns and the Josephsons nearby for the duration of the summer, however, and with Nathan Asch and his wife now installed as Mrs Turner's new tenants there were numerous distractions – and once Grace discovered his
whereabouts and began a steady flow of reproachful or imploring letters Hart's
concentration ebbed further, even as his need for the reassurance of drink and conviviality increased. Malcolm and Peggy Cowley also made daily, if agreeable,
claims on the poet's time: earlier in the year they had bought a disused farm with
60 ragged acres about half a mile away from Addie's at Sherman, Connecticut, and
Cowley remembered many afternoons of 'walking in the woods with Hart, and
the talks about poets and poetry'.[7] Both men were regular participants in the croquet tournaments convened at Robber Rocks but if Hart was in the mood for more
strenuous exercise great temptations lay in the hills, where numerous bootleggers,
including a Wall Street bankrupt and a cashiered army officer named Wiley Varian,
provided the locals – artists and farmers alike – with beer and applejack. Thirsty
customers might often arrive at these makeshift dispensaries to find an impromptu
party in progress but, lawless as they appeared, these festivities were regulated by
proprieties far stricter than anything Hart had been used to in Hollywood. Bill
Brown remembered how the poet 'came within an ace of being unmercifully
beaten up by some drunken and outraged farmers when [he] announced in so
many words that he was a c[ock] s[ucker]. The wife of the speakeasy proprietor
saved him that night, but the men there were ready to tear him into little pieces,
not only because Hart was a self-announced fairy, but because he had announced
it in foul language before a lady.'[8]

Nathan Asch later wrote a cycle of stories entitled *The Valley* about life around
Tory Hill but in his first months at Mrs Turner's he was struggling to complete his
third novel, *Pay Day*. Although a friend of Malcolm Cowley, he was as yet unfamiliar with the customs of the local crowd and wary, now and always, of Hart,
who struck him as being 'childish and erratic and perverse and perverted'. One
day, however, when the poet knocked on his door and suggested a walk to Wiley
Varian's, Asch assented and they set out on the two-mile expedition to Birch Hill
'over the unscraped, ungraded road, past long abandoned and now stone-scattered

tobacco fields', passing as they did so 'shacks in which the farmers ... seemed settled as impermanently as squatters'. Although Varian ran his operation with his wife, Asch thought them an ill-matched couple and he soon suspected the boot-legger 'hated women because he had her'. Since 'Hart felt nothing at all about women' he and Wiley 'hit it off pretty well, [with Hart] drinking up Varian's gin that he mixed out of alcohol tins in the woodshed'. Other drinkers arrived and Mrs Varian served them 'in her silk dress, with the whalebone stays of her corset showing, with her hips wriggling, delighting the mountain derelicts'. After a while Asch was ready to leave, but not so Hart, who 'did not come back for two or three days ... and when he did there was quiet for another day of his sleeping it off'. Even then Asch remained cautious: he suspected Hart of being in love with Cowley and it must have been galling that while he and his wife were no trouble to Mrs Turner she preferred the poet any day: despite the loud music, the overdue rent, the drinking and the drama, 'she loved him and fussed over him and was mis-treated by him and was his victim'. It seems that Asch never entertained the idea of complaining to the poet about the late-night typing audible through the wall that divided them, or the loud incessancy of Dvořák's *New World Symphony*; after all, Hart was 'so wrapped up in his many troubles that he did not have time to think of anybody else'. He struck the novelist as being 'the most uncurved and unflowing and uneasy guy' who had about him the look 'of some soda jerker or filling station attendant' with 'the same crew cut, the same sticking out ears, the same awkward arrogance of stance, and the same unpoetic look about him'. As for his poetry, Asch listened to Hart's explanations of what he was attempting to achieve in *The Bridge*, 'but I did not know what the hell he was talking about'.[9]

Asch would no doubt have been delighted to learn that his troublesome fellow-tenant was eager to leave Addie's: old dreams of owning a patch of this adopted homeland had returned and on 3 July Hart wrote to CA asking his father to lend him the money to buy a cottage nearby and offering the $5,000 in trust under grandfather Hart's will as collateral. Clarence Crane replied on 5 July, sorry to dis-appoint: he had a large mortgage and a bank loan to repay every three months and until Canary Cottage had broken even he had no financial surplus. To make mat-ters worse his confectionery business now seemed to be in irreversible decline: since the war high taxes, economic depression and commercial miscalculation had bedevilled his empire and over the last six years company losses had consumed half his worth. On 18 July he wrote again 'really very sorry' not to be in a pos-ition to help but he hoped Hart would understand: there were now staff problems at the Cottage and poor sales had persuaded him to sell the Crane store in Detroit.[10]

So Hart turned twenty-nine on 21 July with no prospect of stabilizing his domestic arrangements – not that he allowed the fact to diminish festivities. In a summer of parties his was the wildest and the most drunken: Asch remembered how he felt 'both sillily self-conscious and utterly unself-conscious' as the drink flowed and the revelry became more abandoned: 'We did not speak to each other, but rather each of us howled out, and we did not dance with our wives or even with each other, but whirled around Hart's room, faster and faster, as if we were truly possessed.' Another of Asch's memories of that summer is of Mrs Turner hiding in the kitchen, clutching her cat Tiger and moaning 'Oh, Mr Crane, Mr Crane', as Hart rampaged drunk and destructive through the house.[11] As a result of drunken violence stemming from his birthday or another occasion within the next couple of days she decided she could bear it no more and told Hart he must leave. Eleanor Fitzgerald offered him shelter nearby at Gaylordsville but the blow fell hard. He wrote to CA on 25 July with his new address but since there was no question of telling his father the real reasons for the move he explained that Mrs Turner had no longer felt able to extend credit. Too poor to travel to New York to find employment, he told his father he was now thinking of getting a job working on the nearby roads and had 'never felt quite as humiliated'.[12] CA replied two days later at a loss to understand. What had happened to the $50 he had sent two or three weeks ago? He enclosed another cheque for the same amount along with a lecture. 'Of course you don't know where to turn. You don't seem to have enough of the earnest side of life in your make-up.' He was far from recommending his own example, of all work and no play, as a pattern for life but once again he begged his son to see how hard it was 'to live in this world and be a good citizen without paying your way in the legal tender of the realm'. And however gifted as a writer Hart was, 'if writing does not pay you a dividend then you have to do something else'.[13]

If CA was concerned about his son's finances, Hart's friends were worried about the drinking. Cowley noticed 'that his bristly hair was turning gray and that his face was redder and puffier. Those were signs of a physiological change, from being a "heavy social drinker", as we had always known him, to being a "problem drinker".'[14] But if the physical self-punishment was alarming, the underlying restlessness and loneliness seemed more poignant. Cowley woke up in the middle of the night after 'a fairly gay evening at the Browns'' to find that Hart was asleep face down between him and Peggy, 'embracing both of us'. Silently they disentangled themselves. 'Hart rose, also without a word, and dressed in the faint glow of starlight from the window; then he groped and grumbled his way down the breakneck stairs. We never asked him how he got home.'[15] Cowley did offer practical assistance when the poet determined that he would have to find work in New York: it was agreed that for several weeks, until he found a job and his own place, he could stay at the Cowleys' empty apartment at 501 East 55th Street. On the way into the city Hart spent a few days with Charmion von Wiegand and her husband at Croton-on-Hudson but when Charmion went to the station to collect her old friend she was shocked by his appearance. Thinner now and with much greyer hair, he had 'aged tremendously' and she concluded that he had 'been through a very suffering period', besides noticing that 'his gestures had become pansy'.[16] It was from her house that Hart wrote to CA on 2 August with thanks for the last cheque: having discharged his debts he was left with $15 and was going to New York 'without any prospects whatever' and was resigned to taking 'anything on land or sea that I can grab'. Eventually, he promised, he would have a place of his own in which to settle himself and his chattels but in the meantime all he could do was thank CA for his continuing support, doubly magnanimous in view of his father's abiding incomprehension. 'I know, you think I'm just lazy.' There were other factors involved, however, and perhaps he would explain them one day, when he might also prove himself 'less trivial and inconsequential than you think'.[17]

He wrote again on 14 August: installed at the Cowleys' he was preparing his own food and doing his best to remain presentable 'without the help of a flatiron' but his shoes were giving out as fast as the latest round of loans advanced by friends, the heat was terrible and although he longed to learn a trade such as type-setting or linotyping he was now reconciled to finding work as a plumber's or mechanic's help. 'The way things are going now I'll consider myself lucky to get anything.'[18] Horrified to learn of his son's predicament, CA sent $40 on 16 August to cover his prompt return to Ohio. Three days later Hart wrote back, hoping his father would understand: he had spent the money on 'immediate necessities' and was going to remain in New York, having found temporary work clerking and cat-aloguing in Sam Loveman's new bookstore.[19] To Winters he complained of job-hunting and life 'in the big simmering gluepot Metropolis' but his luck appeared to turn towards the end of August when he got a better-paid temporary job that might lead to greater things at Griffin Johnson & Mann, an advertising agency at 18 East 48th Street, the vice-president and copy director of which was his old boss from Corday and Gross, G.W. Freeman.[20] He wrote to Cowley after his first day, relieved that it seemed 'a very decent outfit' but aware that he might only be employed there for a few weeks. In any case, 'I'm expected to perform prodigies but I feel as rickety as a cashiered Varian.' At least now he could rent an apart-ment: he intended to begin his search the next day around Columbia Heights but if Cowley suddenly came to New York he would find the key to East 55th Street 'under the linoleum in front of the door'.[21] He duly found accommodation in Brooklyn at 77 Willow Street and complained to Winters that his mind was 'mostly a flat blank these days', devoted as it was to preparing copy for Caloroil Heaters, Fos-For-Us Mineral Mixture animal food and Flowers of Love Wedding Rings.[22] But by the time he promised the critic he was looking forward to right-ing himself financially Grace had sent news from California – a cable dated 6 September – that would alter not only his prosperity but with it the future direc-tion of his life: 'Mother passed away tonight funeral here advise later Grace.'[23]

If Hart lacked the time and the money to attend Mrs Hart's funeral he was also disinclined to face Los Angeles and his mother. Instead he sent flowers and sympathy and on 9 September, when he sent CA news of his grandmother's death, he also suggested that Grace might appreciate a little financial support. Diplomacy was not a strength among Harts or Cranes, however, and if his father's reply was prompt it was hardly tactful: he declined to extend any monetary assistance to his former wife and as for Mrs Hart's death, 'this had to be expected for she had long since lived out her usefulness, either to herself or to others'.[24] Hart's own finances were suddenly dramatically improved: he was now set to inherit the $5,000 held in trust under the terms of his grandfather's will and with that money he would be free at last to buy a home of his own in which to finish *The Bridge*. But Grace had other ideas and although her letters from this period have disappeared, along with Hart's replies, all his friends were familiar with her plan, that he should live with her in California, where his inheritance would support them both.

At first the scheme was broached gently and with appeals to his sympathy but the tone gradually changed and then in the middle of September she stopped writing altogether. As if this cessation was not distressing enough, a letter arrived from the Rychtariks wondering when Hart was going to repay the $125 still outstanding of the $225 they had lent him to buy his Patterson acres three years previously. It hurt to think they had found him negligent in an area where he was normally scrupulous but at least now he understood why he had heard so little from them. Replying on 16 September, he promised that with the release of his Hart inheritance he would repay in full. However, 'You don't know how often I have thought of you and regretted the circumstances of your recent loss of interest in me.'[25] That same day, as a mark of his continuing loneliness, he wrote to William Carlos Williams out of the blue wondering 'why in paradise we don't once in a while get together'.[26] As far as the latter was concerned there was a good reason: 'I was a bit off homos and had heard that he was fairly assertive on that score.'[27] But more than naïve bigotry informed his decision: Williams coveted the poetic laurels of America and Hart, by writing an epic poem about their country, was inescapably a rival, worse still a rival with an important circle of admirers whose loyalty Williams had bemoaned earlier in the year to Ezra Pound: 'They say Hart Crane is – this or that – a crude homo.... Others think he is God Almighty which naturally offends anyone, like myself, who pretends to the same distinction. Best poet in U.S. say the Kenneth Burkes, Gorham Munsons, etc. I dunno. Ivor [*sic*] Winters is plum gaga over him.' Pound sent solace from Italy: Munson, Burke, Winters and Crane were nothing more than mediocre and mutually admiring and if their arbitration mattered in New York they were provincial and insignificant when compared with intellectual opinion in Europe. Williams remained unconvinced. Although Crane and his allies were 'cock suckers' the fact remained that Hart himself 'is supposed to be the man that puts me on the shelf'. In fact he was 'just as thickheaded' as Williams himself and 'quite as helplessly verbose at times', besides emerging 'into clarity far less often'.[28]

Williams would have found his assertion of the mutual admiration of Hart's circle confirmed by a review Winters was then preparing for the *New Republic* of Allen Tate's *Mr Pope and Other Poems* which the critic used as an opportunity to compare the latter's ambitions and achievements with Hart's. While conceding that 'Crane is aware only of those values that pertain to himself as an absolutely isolated phenomenon' and that he was able 'to countenance certain metaphysical illusions', Winters remained convinced of his greatness. He admired Tate too, but so far he was the lesser poet: 'Crane's quantitative achievement is much greater, and in all likelihood, Tate has not yet quite equalled the quality of Crane's best work; but on the other hand Tate's field of awareness, his general intelligence, is broader and better disciplined.'[29] Hart was moved by the tribute, but in his letter of acknowledgement to Winters he resented being put in some sort of 'all American Lyric Sprint' with other writers, since competitiveness was alien to his idea of creation. Tate, he felt, had 'a very complex mind and possibly a wider grasp of ideas than I do' but for all that Hart felt he had come no nearer to resolving the confusions of life as he saw them than 'to simply state the dilemma in a highly inferential manner', which is what poets usually had to do. What had always divided them poetically was Hart's 'avowed (and defended) effort' to attain to a kind of 'positive synthesis' and thus to transcend Eliot and his defeatism. Yet if Winters thought of Hart as living by illusions he misread him: 'I mean, stoicism isn't my goal, even though I'm convinced as much as you and Tate are of the essentially tragic background of existence.' It was all too easy to acquiesce in life's disappointments and tragedies, to reflect, as the Stoics did, that if everything else in life passed away one's endurance at least would continue. One had an obligation to resist, to affirm – 'call it all illusion or not'.[30]

If to Winters he was positive and courageous, to Underwood he confessed a different mood: 'I'm doing no writing – America seems so comfortably dead – you see it in millions of faces – that there's nothing left to struggle for except "respectability". Occasionally some sailor gives me a jolt – but I guess I'm getting old.'[31] As Grace persisted in silence he turned for companionship to his women friends, especially those divorced from writing and its rivalries, but misery and self-doubt often made him a heavy responsibility. Lorna Dietz remembered that he became 'a little dependent on me and was forever coming over at ghastly hours or calling me up on the phone'. He proposed marriage repeatedly: they would have a daughter called Thérèse but at the same time would 'not interfere with each other's liberty'. She was not tempted: Hart had begun to 'flaunt his vices', he was developing 'a persecution complex' and had become 'petty about money' besides. 'He became a great nuisance to have around for any length of time because he was forever crying his wrongs, making scenes, and monopolizing all one's thoughts, time, energy, emotions to no purpose, and leaving one exhausted.'[32] His weekend visits to Charmion's house continued but here too he outstayed his welcome in the course of an evening of manic dancing and violent inebriation. At one stage he interrupted his own frenzy to produce photographs of sailors he had loved whose loyalty he then proceeded to contrast angrily with the inconstancy of family and friends. Women above all were treacherous and after comparing their flabby forms to the muscular hardness of the male he collapsed, to be taken upstairs unconscious by Charmion and her housekeeper.

Suddenly on 15 October Grace broke her silence with a cable: 'Come at once desperately ill at home only you can help Zell in New York answer at once.'[33] Although the summons arrived at four in the morning Hart immediately attempted to trace his godmother at her regular Manhattan hotels to see what advice or information she could apply to the drama. Sam Loveman was about to leave for Cleveland; he too might soon be able to shed light on his mother's latest predicament. But what immediate steps should be taken? Grace knew perfectly well that even if he had the money for a ticket it would still take him a week to travel to the rescue but the more he read the cable the less convincing it seemed and without supplying reasons he replied simply, 'Cannot possibly come'. In some ways he hoped she was 'desperately ill' – because sickness was more becoming in a mother than dishonesty – but he was haunted by the suspicion that she was trying one trick after another to get him back to Los Angeles, there to subjugate him with her exactions and possessiveness. A few days later an actor friend from Hollywood strengthened his suspicions when he mentioned in a letter that 'Grace and I have been having the nicest times'. A few days after that the plot thickened further with the arrival of another mysterious message, this time, he told Zell, ostensibly written and signed by Grace's nurse and insisting, 'in the weirdest language', that his mother was 'very ill' and that 'I would greatly regret it if I did not come to California at once'. Desperate for guidance he turned to his godmother and in the course of a long letter written in the second half of October, which also described his last days in Los Angeles, he asked her to investigate. In the meantime, having contacted the Guardian Trust Company in Cleveland with a view to establishing what progress was being made with the execution of Mrs Hart's will, he learned from the assistant secretary Edward A. Stockwell that Grace had declared by cable that illness incapacitated her from signing the papers which would release her son's inheritance. Stalemate: so Hart determined to cease writing to his mother until she answered some of his letters or, he told Zell, until he was 'more firmly impressed with signs of sincerity on her part than she has so far offered'.[34]

In the course of these dramas Hart moved from Willow Street back to his old address at 110 Columbia Heights. 'Rooming houses depress me terribly,' he told Winters but here at least he was in familiar surroundings and in theory the view of the harbour was conducive to reading and writing.[35] By the third week of October, however, when he wrote to Charlotte Rychtarik, he knew Griffin, Johnson & Mann could give him no more work and as he faced yet again the dismal round of job interviews he complained to her: 'I haven't had a creative thought for so long that I feel quite lost and *spurlos versenkt*.'[36] A new friend found a solution, if not to his poetic difficulties, then at least to the practical ones. At some stage in the autumn, when walking beneath Brooklyn Bridge, Hart saw a young man with a small camera who appeared equally exhilarated by the colossal overarching structure and the prospect of skyscrapers beyond. His fellow pilgrim was the twenty-four-year-old Walker Evans, who that year had acquired not only his first camera but also the aspiration to develop a pure and documentary form of photography which was distinct from the commercialism of Edward Steichen and the flamboyance of Stieglitz. This ambition informed the projects that made Evans famous in the 1930s – his photographs of Cuba, of the American School of Ballet, of the antebellum architecture of the South, above all of the rural poor during the Depression – and took him to the front rank of twentieth-century photography. Like many others of Hart's generation he found poetry in the quotidian furniture of the United States, in the billboards, the subways, the Main Streets and the machinery, and recorded his observations with such unassuming authority that his camera still influences the way we imagine inter-war America – a country Evans seems to have invented as much as recorded. These triumphs were still in the future when he and Hart became friends but already the young man with the $6 camera had lived in Paris, and on returning to America had befriended the precocious Lincoln Kirstein and the writer and *saloniste* Muriel Draper. Like Hart he thought himself unwanted and incongruous in a society governed by commerce, like Hart he had a possessive mother, and like Hart he was alternately a puzzle and a disappointment to a father who lived in Cleveland and was not only acquainted with CA but also shared his conviction that what was good for business was good for America. The poet and the photographer had many grievances to share and soon they took to visiting junk shops together and exploring the ethnic enclaves of Lower Manhattan. Evans moved to rooms nearby in Columbia Heights and as the friendship between the two men deepened he discovered that photography was a subject on which Hart could dilate freely 'in his raving way' and that his laughter 'could fill a room'.[37]

To pay the rent Evans was working from six to eleven every evening checking stocks at Henry R. Doherty and Company in Wall Street and when he learned of Hart's plight he contacted Talbot Brewer, the personnel manager of the company and also his brother-in-law, and secured his friend a job. The work was welcome but inevitably uninspiring and much of Hart's day was devoted, as he soon told Malcolm, to 'sorting securities of cancelled legions ten years back' with 'chewing gum for lunch'.[38] As Cowley well knew, this meagre diet was broken intermittently at an Armenian restaurant in Washington Street where, at Kenneth Burke's suggestion, their circle had become accustomed to gather. Since Doherty and Company was nearby, Hart often joined Burke, Cowley, Bill Brown, Isidor Schneider, Matty Josephson and other occasional guests for lunch. The conversation, inevitably enough, was generally literary, but once a digression led to the subject of death and then to the disposal of mortal remains. Hart declared himself horrified by the thought of burial – as he put it, 'the worms crawl out, and the worms crawl in' – and expressed a preference for cremation. Bill Brown told him that one day he would need to leave explicit directions, whereupon the twenty-nine-year-old dictated a will expressing his wish that 'upon the occasion of my demise ... my mortal remains shall be committed to the flames'.[39]

The Browns had recently moved and Hart frequently resorted to their new house in East 12th Street, where he danced, drank, complained about Grace and listened over and over again to Sue's collection of records; his particular favourite at the time was Marlene Dietrich's 'Ich bin von Kopf bis Fuss auf Liebe eingestellt'. Other distractions were more altruistic: he was in regular contact throughout the autumn with Malcolm Cowley in connection with a project first broached weeks earlier in the country – the publication in one volume of the sixty or so poems Cowley had written over the course of his literary career. The two friends had spent hours reviewing the lyrics during the summer and in the ensuing weeks, suspecting that Cowley would be deterred by shyness and extensive journalistic obligations, Hart appointed himself editor of the projected volume. Scrupulously re-reading the entire corpus, he hinted at lines he felt could be improved; and since any collection should always be structured, he proposed a sequence for publication, capping his labours by devoting two whole days to the production of a typescript which, unknown to Cowley, he intended to submit to Gorham Munson in his capacity as editor at George H. Doran. *Blue Juniata* appeared the following year, under a different imprint and according to its author's sequence rather than Hart's, but Cowley never forgot his friend's generous and instigating enthusiasm, even if by then Hart was overseas and changed for ever by disillusionment with his mother.

Since his last correspondence with Grace, Mrs Hart's estate had continued in limbo, despite Hart's attempts to expedite matters with the Guardian Trust Company. As Mr Stockwell reminded him again on 16 November, however, the Trust could do nothing unilaterally: since Grace was a co-trustee of the estate her signature was indispensable to execution and 'I would suggest that you write her personally on this subject in order to avoid further delays.'[40] But relations between mother and son were fast approaching open hostility and having discovered the futility of correspondence Hart now considered legal action. Sue introduced him to her friend Arthur Garfield Hays, a lawyer later famous for defending Georgi Dimitrov, the Bulgarian communist accused of involvement in the Reichstag fire, and Hays, as Hart described events to the Rychtariks, 'directed his guns on the bank'. Grace also changed strategies and now prevailed upon friends and former neighbours to write to her son urging him to return to California, 'so that I never came home from work without wonder – and trembling about what next I should find awaiting me'.[41] At the end of the third week in November he telephoned the Guardian Trust to complain of his mother's behaviour and to demand an immediate $500 advance on his inheritance, the rest to follow within a week. Stockwell now revealed that for all her claims of incapacity Grace had sent the Trust a five-page letter insisting that Hart's inheritance should be withheld unless he joined her in California. Perhaps aware that Hart had taken legal advice, however, or else feeling uneasy about Grace's prevarications, Stockwell agreed to the poet's request for an advance and confirmed his decision in writing on 22 November. He quoted part of Grace's letter to the Trust – 'Hart owes me something for the years I have stood by him' – as well as offering discreet sympathy for his dilemma, albeit in terms Hart must have thought took understatement to the point of comedy: 'It seems to me that you, personally, are in a far different position as regards your own mother and her possible weaknesses than anyone else in the world.'[42] A few days later Hart cabled Grace and again demanded her signature. As he told Zell on 29 November, his mother replied 'with the most hysterical and mysteriously worded abuse that I have ever received', insisting that she had signed and airmailed the papers two weeks previously and broaching her conviction that CA and Stockwell should discuss between them whether or not Hart's drinking disqualified him from inheritance. The threat was coarse and absurd – but if his mother felt like black-mailing him who knew how long she would keep other aspects of his dissolution from his father? The greater the distance Hart put between himself and her the better, but even after his inheritance was finally paid he knew he would remain perplexed by Grace's actions, as he admitted to Zell: '[She] will probably never hear from me again. Nervous strain or simply hysterics could never explain the underhanded and insatiable vanity that has inspired her to attempt to crush her nearest of kin. And all for a bucketful of cash!'[43]

The stress of the situation, combined with his favourite means of escape, boded ill for Hart's career in Wall Street and one letter to Cowley concerning *Blue Juniata* written before Hart left for work one morning was indicative in its hung-over incoherence of his prevailing mood at the end of November. Referring to what he termed 'the usual recent maritime houreths' Hart revealed he had spent the evening before with his Danish millionaire friend on Riverside Avenue and then the night with 'a bluejacket from the Arkansas'. He was 'full of Renault Wine Tonics' and 'raving like a'mad [*sic*].'[44] When he finally left Doherty, after less than a month, he did so in dramatic fashion, arriving late, clearly still drunk and in yes-terday's clothes, and banging his fist down on a pile of stocks and bonds as the startled office looked on. 'There's Scott's Emulsion!' he roared. 'There's Scott's Emulsion. I never took a drop of that and I never will as long as I live!' He walked through the silent office, roared 'Never!' as he turned in the doorway and walked out for ever.[45] With Guardian Trust and Grace about to yield he had no further need of a job; in any case he would now finally be able to travel and determined to put an ocean as well as a continent between himself and his mother, he booked passage for England for 8 December. Herbert Wise, having returned to New York from Europe, took his former secretary to see Jerome Kern's *Showboat* at the Ziegfeld Theatre and a few days before departure Hart told Cowley that he and Lorna had been 'on the best bat ever' the night before. Once again he proposed to Lorna, and 'two cops came in and joined the party at three o'clock'.[46] The 'bat' occurred at Sam Loveman's but what Hart failed to tell Cowley was that Lorna had to sit on his chest to prevent him from smashing all Loveman's porcelain, before eventually soaking him in a bucket of cold water.

The drinking continued until Hart's last hours on American soil: on the eve of his departure he gave a party at Bauer's on lower Third Avenue and all the gang – the Browns, the Schneiders, the Munsons, the Cowleys, Walker Evans, Lorna, Charmion, Sam Loveman and others – watched him perform the 'gotzotsky', hammer 'Too Much Mustard' on the piano, recite his favourite dirty limericks, whirl the women around the dance floor and generally perform the role of happy and expansive host. To Lorna he seemed 'all laughter and happiness that night'.[47] But Solomon Grunberg, a new friend Hart had met through Sam Loveman, took away different impressions. Among the last to leave, he saw his host, publicly so ebullient, weeping bitterly because e.e. cummings had not turned up.

Despite the high winds and sleet that set in as the RMS *Tuscania* began her transatlantic crossing Hart's spirits soared: the ship rose and fell across great grey waves but he paced the quarterdeck and ate insatiably, a stranger to seasickness despite the turbulence and a student of Melville in moments of repose. He had money in his pocket – more than ever before – and he was sailing for promised lands, for the London of Shakespeare and Marlowe and the Paris of Rimbaud and Baudelaire. It was inconceivable that inspiration would elude him in such circumstances and in the meantime, as he told Loveman on 9 December, he had been assigned 'the one nearly handsome English waiter in the salon [*sic*]'. He was getting used to the tough food, the hangovers left by bootleg gin were clearing his system and the Irish whiskey served on board reminded him of Poe's balm of Gilead.[48] By the time the ship was off the coast of Ireland he had renamed it the 'Rumrunia' and to Bill Brown he explained why: rum was now the favourite drink with everyone aboard, its popularity extending from the quarterdeck to the fo'c'sle, 'where, as you might imagine, I've paid my respects'. As the only American among the Canadians, Australians and various Britons in tourist class he was an exotic, a status he enjoyed almost as much as the moment related to Charmion when 'one old squire' mistook him for a Cambridge man.[49] Alert for prototypes of literary eccentrics he glimpsed Falstaffs, Pickwicks and Mrs Gamps among his fellow passengers – and then proved himself their equal in peculiarity at the costume ball which was held mid-voyage, in which he distinguished himself, he told Brown, in 'flaming red coat, sailor hat, dress breeches – all lined with rum and brandy!'[50] After a rough start the crossing had proved exceptionally smooth for the time of year and although the ship was due to stop at Le Havre and Plymouth before finally reaching London, in many ways he wished the voyage had been longer. Yet he was impatient for arrival. As he told Underwood: 'Hope the King doesn't kick off until after Christmas, for I'm promised Merrie England verily.'[51]

By the time he arrived in London, however, he was fighting influenza with qui-
nine and Jamaica rum and the raw damp of an unfamiliar climate, combined with
the uncomfortable accommodation and indigestible food provided by the Royal
Hotel in Woburn Place, marked an inauspicious beginning to his first experience
of life outside the Americas. To make matters worse London, he told Isidor
Schneider, was 'the most expensive place I can imagine – more even than New
York'. Determined to enjoy himself, nevertheless, he set out to explore and by the
time he wrote to Waldo on 28 December he was already thinking of settling in the
city, not least because 'there is something genuine about nearly every Englishman
one meets'.[52] Long and solitary excursions were punctuated by meetings with old
soldiers or Australian charwomen: he marvelled at the winter greenness of the
parks and at the treasures of the National Gallery, where El Greco's *Agony in the
Garden* had the force of an epiphany. He was in 'a city for the etcher', he told
Schneider, as he patrolled the centre of the imperial capital, with its grey-streaked
and majestic façades.[53] But another, more notorious, London beckoned in the east,
where Jack the Ripper had stalked and Marlowe had met his death; and mindful
of Harry Candee's vivid anecdotes Hart made his way to Limehouse. Whatever
dangerous expectations he carried with him were disappointed by reality: he found
a pub, drank Scotch and soda enthusiastically and played a game of darts, but the
young toughs were hardly tough enough and the greatest danger, he explained to
the Rychtariks, was posed by the weather: 'The damp, raw cold was like a knife in
my throat.'[54] Besides solitary expeditions there were social commitments to be
honoured: he hoped to meet his principal English champion, the editor, poet, critic
and journalist Edgell Rickword, one year his senior and blind in one eye following service in the Great War, and also Paul Robeson, who was appearing in *Show
Boat*. Robeson was soon to move to Paris, but in the meantime he and his wife
Essie were installed in some splendour in a house rented from a former ambassador to Turkey and Hart was happy to see the actor on several occasions.

Hart's most important friend in England was already leading a life more dramatic than anything to be seen in the theatre. Since moving to London three
years previously Laura Riding had begun her turbulent thirteen-year involvement
with the poet Robert Graves: in 1929 they would move to Majorca but when
Hart contacted his old friend he found she was dividing her time between her
flat in Hammersmith and the nearby houseboat moored on the Thames which
Graves shared with his first wife, Nancy Nicholson, and their four children. In
1927 Riding and Graves had established the Seizin Press prior to collaborating
on *A Survey of Modernist Poetry* and *A Pamphlet against Anthologies*, completed earlier
in 1928. Literary partners and profound influences on each other's work they may
have been, but their emotional relations were often difficult and only five months
after Hart's visit Riding staged a spectacular suicide attempt from a third-floor
window in Bloomsbury which left her with a pelvic bone broken in three places.
In retrospect it was perhaps not the best time for even the most undemanding

guest to visit, but at first Hart was delighted by the welcome Riding extended. When she heard he was unwell she insisted he leave his Bloomsbury hotel so that she could nurse him in her flat and once introductions had been made to Graves and his wife it was agreed that Hart should spend Christmas Day on the houseboat. So began what he described to Loveman as 'the most unique Xmas I ever had' – in the course of a long walk by the Thames he admired the swans and the 'beautiful fleets of hardy rowers'[55] and at the houseboat, 'at Hammersmith in front of Wm. Morris' old headquarters' he enjoyed 'a most luscious plum pudding'.[56]

Over the next few days, however, moods deteriorated: Riding, Hart found, had a 'hysterical temper'[57] and she considered him 'most drunkenly unfair to Robert Graves as a poet'.[58] As far as one can see, Hart's relations with Graves were considerably easier: they discussed Gerard Manley Hopkins and Graves applied himself to finding a copy of his poems to give to Hart. The book turned up after the latter had left for Paris and Graves was pleased to send news of the discovery, adding, 'whenever I see a sailor I think of you tenderly'.[59] Riding took a sterner view: she, or Hart, or both, had changed since their happy friendship in New York and now she found him 'so naively-egotistically absorbed in his own work that in self-protection one listened only to a small part of what he said about his work'.[60] When she could distract him from his own literary ventures to consideration of hers she felt 'he did not understand in the least what I was doing and thinking and writing' and his responses oscillated 'between moods of great affection for me and moods of incoherent attack on what he felt to be the severity of my literary and other points of view'. She deduced that Hart felt 'cheated and hurt' by the newly ordered tenor of her life, when a few years previously 'we had both been involved in the same deceptively enthusiastic disorder'. His excessive drinking and promiscuous spending alarmed and annoyed her and although one evening, in the course of dinner at Gatti's restaurant, he revealed he was carrying a volume of her poems he was still unable to placate her. He stood up and began reading some of the lyrics in his 'peculiarly ecstatic way', in particular 'Sea, False Philosophy', but his rendition was not to its author's liking. 'He revelled in its application to himself and was moved to learn that I had written it with him in mind; yet he was completely blind to its implications.'

On New Year's Eve a large group which included the two American poets went dancing and then to the circus in Olympia. Riding was dismayed to find Hart 'drunker than I had ever seen him' and noted that when he executed one of his vehement solo dances the exertions did nothing to soothe his spirit. 'He grew more and more furious with me, reaching a mysterious climax with the words: "I'll show you! I'll go back to America and marry Lorna!"' It must have come as a relief to all parties when Hart made plans to leave for Paris on 7 January: celebration of some sort was in order for his last night in London so Riding organized an outing to the Palladium where she and Hart would be accompanied by her friend

Norman Cameron. At first all went well; until the interval he was 'drunk, but gentle and affectionate'. Then he convinced himself he had been given the wrong change at the box-office and Riding had to sort the matter out. Shortly after that his hat disappeared, only to reappear several rows ahead. Sensing that his concentration was irretrievably lost she took him to the bar 'and whom should Hart see but two American sailors!' He borrowed money and was gone. Next morning, she saw him off at the station: there was no sign of the sailors and Hart himself was 'sober, blank, trying hard not to be irritable about everything'. They never saw each other again but even as she watched the departing train Riding sensed it was a valediction, their warring prides and immoderate personalities necessitating 'a sort of fundamental goodbye'.[61]

18

Paris at last. When Hart arrived in the French capital in the second week of 1929 he graduated to full membership of a Francophile literary generation for whom the city remained an elysium of the arts. Proust had died and Pound had gone to Italy; but Joyce, Picasso, Brancusi, Matisse, Valéry and Stravinsky remained, and to visit at least once in a lifetime the city that sheltered or inspired them was crucial to the curriculum of every American artist and writer. Hart was a belated pilgrim: his friends knew the city already and since the war his country-men had been arriving in such numbers as to make their presence seem like an occupation. In the middle of the 1920s an astonishing 32,000 American expatri-ates lived in Paris, sometimes as beneficiaries of a favourable exchange rate, some-times as fugitives from Prohibition, sometimes as members of the colony of millionaires who shunned the Left Bank in favour of the Ritz, the American banks in the Place Vendôme and the *couturiers* in the rue de la Paix. The majority were artists, of varying degrees of integrity and accomplishment, who lived for truth and beauty in Saint-Germain and Montparnasse and each night congregated to trade reputations and beg loans in the Dôme, the Rotonde and the Sélect, those great expatriate watering holes which three years previously had supplied much of the setting and many of the characters for Hemingway's first novel, *The Sun Also Rises*. No sooner was it famous, however, than the carnival faced closure: the Wall Street Crash which occurred at the end of 1929 marked closing time in the bars and Harold Loeb looked on as the Greenwich Villagers sailed home: 'One by one we went on to recognized achievements or succumbed to the attrition of our dreams.'[1]

Hart arrived at the Hotel Jacob at 44 rue Jacob with two letters of introduction: Laura Riding had commended him to Gertrude Stein, whose salon in the rue de Fleurus was sooner or later attended by every visiting American, and Waldo had written to André Gide, albeit in the hope of doing more than merely projecting his friend into serious French literary circles. He had often remarked to Gorham

Munson, 'If Hart would only fall in love with an older disciplined homosexual, someone like André Gide, whom he would enormously respect as well as love, then he would probably acquire discipline by contact.'[2] In view of Hart's (and Gide's) known sexual interests the scheme was naïve, but neither one could deduce it from the letter of introduction Waldo supplied: 'Hart Crane, un de mes meilleurs amis, est selon le jugement de beaucoup de nous, l'unique poète de notre génération en Amérique. Il a besoin de vous connaître'.[3] In the event, as an incurable monoglot, Hart was largely restricted to socializing with the English-speaking colony: it was in the Sélect that he encountered the American poet Forrest Anderson, who was immediately struck by his 'vital and immediate' presence. The two writers returned to the Hotel Jacob and Anderson recalled watching the snowflakes falling in the courtyard as he and his compatriot drank *ron negritas* and listened to Manuel de Falla's *El Amor Brujo*. Hart showed him a new acquisition, 'an old-fashioned inkwell flanked by two French navy anchors, their flukes forming the penholders', and produced, with 'boyish pride', a photograph recently given him by Eugene O'Neill.[4] Together they ate bouillabaisse in Saint-Germain, explored 'the boîtes in the Rue de Lappe, frequented by *marins en permission*', and visited La Sainte Chapelle, which made such an impression on Hart that when he sent a postcard to Underwood a month after his arrival he chose a picture of the church's interior and described it as 'the greatest work of art here, I think'.[5] For guidance among the city's expatriate writers Hart turned to Eugene Jolas, whose *transition* had helped establish his Parisian reputation. Jolas was an enthusiastic cicerone and determined to introduce the newcomer to his literary world, which included Glenway Westcott, Ford Madox Ford, Edgar Varèse, Klaus Mann, Emma Goldman, Eugene MacCown, René Crevel and Kay Boyle. But there was one man in particular he wanted Hart to meet, one man whose demonic yet discerning sponsorship might impel the obviously distracted poet to turn once more to *The Bridge*.

Harry Crosby was rich, handsome and well-born, but when enemies and acquaintances later compared him to a character from the pages of F. Scott Fitzgerald they were thinking less of these undoubted virtues than of the unresolved aspects of a personality that appeared to encapsulate its restless age: the insatiable appetite for fleeting sensation and the directionless rebellion that most often expressed itself in provocation and extravagance. Born in 1898, he was grand where it mattered, in Massachusetts; it was a measure of the levelling quality of expatriation that Hart had to leave America in order to befriend a member of its patriciate. Through his mother Crosby was situated at the heart of the intricate cousinships of Old Boston while his father was related to the Van Rensselaers, sometime patroons of New York and great landowners of the Hudson Valley; Revolutionary War generals, state governors and signatories of the Declaration of Independence littered his ancestry and through both his parents he claimed kinship with Alexander

Hamilton. He emerged from the Great War with the Croix de Guerre and a Gothic imagination forever haunted by the carnage he had witnessed: Harvard seemed tame and futile by comparison and he took to heavy drinking. In 1920 he met Polly Peabody, the daughter of a distinguished, if impoverished, family from New York City: the scandal that ensued when he married this divorcée seven years his senior drove the couple to Paris, where they established themselves in eighteenth-century splendour at 19 rue de Lille. Having worked in a bank in New York, Crosby was just about qualified to contact his mother's brother-in-law, John Pierpoint Morgan Junior, to secure a job at Morgan, Harjes & Company but with a handsome $12,000 a year of his own he hardly needed the work and in no time had retired to devote himself to what now became the twin idolatries of his life: literature and sun worship.

Crosby read tirelessly, especially among the French Symbolists and the English Decadents, and held Rimbaud, Huysmans and Wilde in particular esteem. A prolific writer, he produced a large, if undistinguished, body of poems and prose-poems in adoration of the sun god who regulated his hours of solitude. He befriended his father's cousin Walter Berry, a distinguished international lawyer whose library was among the most important in France and whose correspondents included Henry James. Proust dedicated *Pastiches et mélanges* to him but Berry's closest literary association was with Edith Wharton, whose literary mentor and great love he became. She disliked the Crosbys, especially after she and Harry discovered they were conflicting beneficiaries in Berry's will. Indeed to those not of their court they were a vulgar and futile couple: if Harry's writing was banal his personal habits – gambling, wearing his wife's underwear, painting his fingernails, wearing black gardenias with black suits and drugging himself daily with opium and immoderate amounts of alcohol – seemed puerile and exhibitionist and were a great worry to his parents, especially after the arrival of one recent telegram, PLEASE SELL $10,000 WORTH OF STOCK. WE HAVE DECIDED TO LEAD A MAD AND EXTRAVAGANT LIFE. Nevertheless by the time Hart arrived in Paris an element of stability had entered the lives of this wayward couple: Polly had renamed herself Caresse and she and her husband now divided their time between Paris and their country property at Ermenonville near Chantilly, the Moulin du Soleil, which stood on the estate of Armand de la Rochefoucauld and had at various stages been occupied by Jean-Jacques Rousseau and the alchemist and magician Count Cagliostro. If in marriage Harry and Caresse were openly promiscuous, in death they would be joined, since in deference to another of Crosby's obsessions, with suicide, they had already agreed a date for their joint self-destruction – 31 October 1942, the date of the earth's closest orbital proximity to the sun. Meanwhile they were committed to the Black Sun Press, which they had founded in 1927 as a non-commercial publishing vehicle for their own writings, only to see it develop into a small but distinguished imprint responsible for costly editions of work by writers such as Ezra Pound, James Joyce, Marcel Proust and D.H. Lawrence.

Jolas alerted Crosby to Hart's arrival in Paris, a lunch was organized and Crosby's response was all that could be desired: establishing that Hart liked Cutty Sark whisky he invited him for dinner that evening and announced to Caresse on returning home that he had met 'the most wonderful poet'.[6] With a growing reputation as a writer and an enemy of convention Hart was quickly welcomed into the Crosbys' circle. On 19 January Crosby's diary recorded a meeting with Jolas at Les Deux Magots, 'where we found Hart Crane and all three of us to Prunier for oysters and anjou'. That night Crosby read *White Buildings*: such was his excitement that he noted in his diary, 'Today is the first day this year I have not walked to the Pôteau de Perthe or climbed to the top of my Suntower.'[7] On 23 January Hart was invited to the rue de Lille for lunch and when the subject of poetry was inevitably raised he indicated to Crosby that 'he will let us edit his long poem on the Brooklyn Bridge ... it is not yet finished (he is thinking of going to Villefranche to finish it)'. At lunch a few days later spiritual parallels emerged between them as Crosby listened to his new friend's sexual adventures: 'Hart Crane for luncheon and a long talk on poets and sailors he is of the Sea as I am of the Sun.'

Besides this shared fascination with absolute forces of nature both men longed to span the untranslatable divide: Crosby himself had written a poem called 'The Bridge' – 'There are Bridges (O let us be builders of bridges) between the Sun and her worshippers' – and by the third week in January he was determined to spur completion and publication of Hart's similarly titled work. The latter was invited to the Moulin for the first weekend in February and Crosby's diary recorded 'much drinking of red wine and [Hart] reads aloud from Tamburlaine and he is at work on his long poem The Bridge'.[8] It was in the country that the Crosbys' hospitality attained its most riotous prodigality and made of the Moulin a Xanadu the rich and famous flocked to visit. Douglas Fairbanks and Mary Pickford were frequent guests, as was George V's youngest son, the Duke of Kent. Salvador Dali, another regular presence, remembered a 'sensational library', an 'enormous quantity of champagne cooling, with sprigs of mint', and a stable converted to a dining-room and 'filled with tiger skins and stuffed parrots'.[9] On 3 February Crosby's diary recorded:

Mob for luncheon – poets and painters and pederasts and lesbians and divorcees and Christ knows who and there was a great signing of names on the wall at the foot of the stairs and a firing off of the cannon and bottle after bottle of red wine and Kay Boyle made fun of Hart Crane and he was very angry and flung the American Caravan into the fire.[10]

Before the weekend was over Hart had distinguished himself still further by seducing the young comte de la Rochefoucauld, who was shortly to be married. Nevertheless by the time he returned to Paris the Crosbys had extended an open invitation to the Moulin and it had been agreed that when *The Bridge* was finished the Black Sun Press would publish it in a private edition, with a colour reproduction of one of Joseph Stella's paintings of Brooklyn Bridge as a frontispiece.

'It takes a book to describe the Crosbys,' Hart informed Cowley on 4 February, wondering if it was novelty alone that endeared him to them. He was already 'dizzy' with meeting new people and there seemed to be no occasion in the day not marked by drinking. 'And as lions come these days, I'm known already, I fear, as the best "roarer" in Paris.'[11] He visited Gertrude Stein, 'despite my indifference to most of her work', but on 7 February he reported to Waldo how delighted he had been by her personality and her collection of Picassos. He knew, though, that he was 'being seduced by the astonishing ease of life' in the Crosbys' circle: the free-spending and cosmopolitan hedonism was as alien to his upbringing as to his experience and he realized that 'Paris really is a test for an American'. It was all very well to proclaim the city 'the most interesting madhouse in the world' but the fact was that 'it has been over a year since I have written anything longer than scratch notes for The Bridge'.[12] Nor had he made use of the other letters of introduction Frank had supplied – to Louis Aragon, Philippe Soupault and Valéry Larbaud. Aragon's address was written in the notebook he kept at the time, to be sure, along with those of Jane Heap, Laurence Vail, Gertrude Stein and Emma Goldman, but the names of less prominent personages – 'Raymond Magille, Compagnie des disponibles, 1er Depot des Equipages, Cherbourg' or 'Paul Mendes, matelot chauffeur' – give an indication of other ways Hart had found of distracting himself from the poem he had travelled so far to complete.[13] The same notebook recorded details of alternative avenues into an all-male world: addresses for the Bains de Panthéon and the Bains de Penthiève. All such pleasure entailed risk: whatever fears or symptoms drove Hart to take a test for syphilis on 9 February in a clinic on the Boulevard Saint-Germain were discounted, however, when he proved negative.[14] What they knew of their friend's excesses the Crosbys accepted: genius was entitled to licence and as long as he transmuted experience into poetry they were happy. For all their wild self-indulgence, however, Harry and Caresse took the Black Sun Press seriously and as the days went by without any apparent progress on *The Bridge* which they had undertaken to publish they determined that Hart needed protection from Paris and its distractions.

It was therefore agreed that after spending the next weekend at the Moulin he would remain behind in solitude to begin work on 'Cape Hatteras'. It was snowing when he arrived at Ermenonville with Jolas and his wife, but nothing could deter Crosby's hospitality and his diary recorded 'a great drinking of red wine and the Empty Bed Blues on the Graphophone and a magnificent snowball fight and we rode donkeys and we pulled the old stagecoach into the centre of the courtyard'.[15] There was makeshift polo with donkeys and golf clubs and skating on the lake near the château and then oysters, absinthe and opium when the February light faded. Monday must have come as something of a relief: Harry, Caresse and their guests returned to Paris and in the harshest winter in recent memory Hart found himself once again alone with his self-appointed task. Eager that he should be spared all distraction the Crosbys left servants to address the domestic practicalities and for the sake of inspiration they replenished the supply of Cutty Sark. The snow-blanketed park of the château, evocative, Hart found, of *Pelléas et Mélisande*, was available for exercise but in theory there was nothing else that could distract him from work on the next section of *The Bridge*, which was to celebrate man's conquest of the air and the guiding genius of Whitman. Hart informed the Rychtariks that the Crosbys had promised a Black Sun edition of *The Bridge* 'on sheets as large as a piano score, so none of the lines will be broken' – yet despite that incentive and the fact that he knew what he wanted to say the poet found after a year without writing that words eluded him.[16]

The weekend arrived again and with it the Crosbys, to discover their guest had made more impression on his surroundings than on 'Cape Hatteras': furniture from all over the house had been moved into his room at the Moulin, which was now littered with books and photographs of sailors, and in the village, scene of purchases on his hosts' credit, umbrage had been taken by both the postman's daughter and the baker's son. Hart's second week of solitude proved more productive, and by the time the Crosbys returned for the last weekend in February he had completed a provisional version of the new poem. Sensing the temporary end of inspiration he returned to Paris on Sunday night, sharing the journey back with Caresse and another guest, Constance Coolidge, and causing an unscheduled stop by instructing Auguste, the Crosbys' chauffeur, to halt the car, whereupon he walked to the front of the vehicle and solemnly urinated into its headlamps.

Back in the capital the revels continued. Crosby organized a party on the Seine on 26 February which was duly incorporated in another characteristic diary entry: 'Party on the Boat – Kay Boyle Laurence Vail Evelyn Nada Carlos Hart Crane a Dolly Sister Croucher and C[aresse] and Hart Crane tattooed his face with encre de chine ... and I was glad for a pill of black idol.'[17] Far from exhausting his novelty it seemed so far that the poet could do no wrong with Harry or with Caresse. She indeed had developed a particular fondness for him – he was 'cocky', his voice was like 'a foghorn far at sea' and if his manner appeared somewhat coarse in Paris it could never conceal his generosity and enthusiasm: 'Hart was stocky and bristly like a young porcupine. He had a lot of gusto and a Rabelaisian laugh. He even held his belly when he laughed.'[18] She noted his generosity: he regularly endeavoured to repay their hospitality with gifts – a necklace for her; moccasins bought from a sailor for Harry; or best of all a manuscript copy of 'O Carib Isle!', which Crosby acknowledged with raptures on 1 March: 'I am so damn glad to have this poem in MSS – someday when we are all dead they will be screaming and cutting each other's throats for the privilege of having it. It is sure as Kubla Khan is sure as Blake is sure as Ozymandias and Anabase are sure.'

Crosby had arranged to fly to Croydon near London on 2 March and suggested that in the absence of other commitments Hart might like to accompany him: they would depart at 6.30 in the morning and return to Paris at four, 'just in time for your sailor'.[19] Despite the fact that he had never flown before, Hart declined the opportunity but he was eager to return to the Moulin for the weekend, as he indicated when he wrote to Crosby to acknowledge the latter's praise for 'Cape Hatteras'. Harry's enthusiasm had proved 'very stimulating' and Hart promised to 'add a few more paragraphs to the flying machine'.[20] On 3 March, with Crosby suffering from the grippe, Hart paid a visit and the invalid recorded another conversation 'about sailors and hurricanes and about the Bridge and about how Otto Kahn gave Crane money'.[21] The poet did indeed return to the Moulin on several occasions in the coming weeks, not the least of the attractions being the Crosbys' new chauffeur. Auguste had been dismissed for reckless driving but Caresse was exposing Hart to temptation when she employed Lucien simply because he was handsome: his looks 'combined the elegance of a gazelle with the muscular charms of a Carpentier' and she noted the poet's 'misty eyes' as he appraised him one evening.[22] Hart's reputation for indulgence and excess was now widespread: letters from Paris friends alerted the Browns to one worrying escapade after another but nobody was more succinct than Laurence Vail, who informed them: 'Your friend Hart Crane is a great success here. C'est pas un homme – c'est un ouragan.'[23] By now the hurricane was ready to spiral elsewhere and in the third week of April, with Harry and Caresse planning a visit to Berlin, Hart decided to bring forward the spring by travelling to the South of France. He stayed with the Crosbys for two days prior to departure in a room freshly redecorated for Polleen, Caresse's daughter by her first marriage, who was soon expected home for the Easter holidays. The room was now all pink and white and patterned in rosebuds and when Caresse pictured Hart, 'with his sailor's duffle bag and his hobnailed shoes', she smiled at the incongruity, never thinking of the indelible extent to which he would make himself at home: on his last night he brought back a chimneysweep whose black palms and footprints patterned the entire room.[24]

On 19 April Hart caught the night train south and made his way to Collioure, a fishing village in the eastern Pyrenees the radiant light of which had enticed Braque, Matisse, Juan Gris and a thousand lesser landscapists. He registered at the Hôtel Bougnol-Quintana, inspected the twisting lanes, the local beaches and the vineyards that reached into the mountains behind and sent word to the Crosbys that in view of favourable first impressions, 'it looks as though I might stay awhile'.[25] On 23 April Caresse wrote to say she and Harry were inclined to publish *The Bridge* as it stood: why add to a poem which already seemed 'eternal and it is alive and it is beautiful'? Hart considered the work incomplete only because he knew what else he wanted to write – but if those additional sections were so important (and if they were ever written), why not include them in a later edition?

'I feel that if you published it now it would give you a fresh impetus for the rest!'[26] Hart replied two days later, relieved to be free of inhibiting deadlines and happy to learn that *The Bridge* already appeared complete. But immediate publication frightened him and he proposed a compromise: consignment for publication on 1 September, whether he had written anything else or not. As the Crosbys said, it would always be possible to release an extended version of the poem in subsequent editions. 'For all I know, the Bridge may turn into something like the form of Leaves of Grass, with a number of editions, each incorporating further additions.' In the meantime 'that suspended feeling that cities generally induce' was being alleviated by the combination of season and surroundings: across the countryside countless fruit trees blossomed beneath a sky filled with swallows returning from their African winter.[27] Collioure itself was very beautiful but a victim of its charm: painters were everywhere, unsettling him with their diligence and industry, and as the days grew warmer he felt increasingly lonely and unsettled. He sent brief notes to Bill Brown, asking why he never wrote, and to Gertrude Stein, reassuring her that the smell of sewage was not as noticeable as she had warned him it would be, and then on 1 May to Isidor Schneider, admitting that he would never want to settle in France in town or country: 'For even here by the blue inland sea, with ancient citadels and fortifications crowning the heights of a lovely white-walled village – I can't help thinking of my room out there in Patterson.'[28]

On 3 May he crossed into Spain and saw bullfighting at Figueras and a few days later, weary of painters and all things picturesque, he left Collioure for Marseilles, least loved of Mediterranean cities but to Hart a revelation. Here in this great seaport of unsung architecture and insignificant museums there was a happy absence of painters and of anything that might attract them – the city's art, for those who could see it, lay in its street life, which Hart surveyed with relish. Since antiquity seafaring peoples had come here in the name of commerce to create a city of polyglot vitality which traffic with French North Africa both expanded and spiced: a pleasing variety of thuggish exotics animated the fish market and the *vieux port* and dangerous temptation beckoned down every pungent alley. 'Marseille's a delightful place – to *me* – and I want to stay a week or two longer,' he informed Crosby on 16 May.[29] There was a Danish cruiser in the harbour, a gratifying number of brothels, which he spent an evening exploring in the company of an English sailor, and numerous bars along the waterfront in one of which he may have met Demetrius Mattoi, a Corsican sailor whose affections were a temporary delight, and André Gaillard, a sailor with Compagnie Paquet in Marseilles. Nearby Toulon, another significant port and Mediterranean home of the French Navy, proved well worth the journey, as further entries in the notebook testify: 'Lucien Bertrancourt, Matelot Mechanicien, Abord du "Thionville", Toulon'; 'René Arzalier, Matelot Electricien, Abord du "Jean-Bart", Toulon'; 'Paul François Falconetti, Matelot Electricien, 5e Depot Des Equipages de la Flotte, Toulon'.[30]

Delightful as these distractions were, however, Hart could not long escape his problems: as usual he was suffering from hay fever, despite the nearness of the sea, and financial calculations suggested he would be unable to support himself in France for more than another two months. As for *The Bridge*, although letters to the Crosbys mentioned the possibility of an accompanying gloss – 'Shall we try to help the poor public or not?' – the fact was that most of the day not devoted to sitting in the seafront bars talking to sailors was spent in the seafront bars drinking Pernod.[31] Having thought he had rid himself of artists he was spotted one morning 'running up and down the Canebière in search of some phantom or other' by Marsden Hartley, a painter he knew slightly from New York. At their first meeting they had discussed the nature of 'absolute music' but now Hart wanted to talk about *The Bridge* before trying to persuade Hartley to accompany him to Martigues, where he proposed to visit the South African poet Roy Campbell and his wife, Mary. Hartley liked Hart: 'He had a nice boisterous energy about him, he laughed out of his very vitals when he laughed, he chewed his black cigar in the manner of a barnacled beachcomber, he had a burly sort of charm.'[32] Nevertheless, he held back. Hart told him his mother frequently threatened suicide and there was something in the poet before him that portended turmoil and distress. He was a 'nice boy but a little flagrant in his methods', he reported to his friend Adelaide Kuntz, but in the end it was not so much the poet's predatory sexuality as his 'private hysteria' that Hartley found disquieting.[33] His temperament suggested 'an inordinate lust for masochism – mainly to force dramatic excitement – or what he liked to call the quiver of life'. There was nothing intentional in the turbulence he unleashed, 'but he seemed to demand succour from those he admired and much endurance. Hart was never mean – but some people are born that way and seem to have to make their friends pay for their love and affection.'[34]

Suspecting they had little in common beyond their nationality and their sexuality, Hartley resisted the poet's invitation to Martigues. Travelling alone, Hart discovered a scene of desolate beauty: the fishing village on the Rhône estuary where Campbell and his wife rented a house straddled canals which linked the Etang de Berre with the sea while all around were flatlands roamed by wild ponies and cattle and the cowboys who herded them. At first all went well and Hart's relief at being back among English-speaking society communicated itself even to Campbell's daughter Tess, who remembered him as having 'a very generous and expansive nature'. Her sister Anna was disappointed that he looked 'more like a bank clerk than a poet' but thought that Campbell took to Hart at once and 'loved him, I think, like a brother'. One evening her father rolled in some thyme bushes as they were walking home from the lake: Campbell called this procedure 'getting scented before dinner' and was delighted when Hart showed equal enthusiasm for the ritual.[35] But he was not a country creature or a practised family guest and once the wine started to flow the South African began to comprehend the alarming extent of his visitor's incongruity:

He was an extraordinary, tragic creature who appeared in those classical surroundings like a mad howling dervish, always weeping, or exalting beyond
himself. He could neither hold his drink nor control his abnormal 'queer'
nymphomania: he made himself a public laughing-stock everywhere among the
sailors and fishermen, by making advances to them. . . . He was charming when
sober, which was seldom: he read his wonderful poems like an angel, and we
were very fond of him, but he needed a keeper.

In the absence of such a custodian, Hart soon sought out the more adventurous
fishermen and duly imported lice into Campbell's house. He missed meals without consideration or warning or attended them intoxicated, insensitive and belligerent with homesickness. 'He had only one religion,' Campbell noted, 'the
Almighty power of the U.S.A. He believed in Whitman's vision of it altogether.
When drunk, this puny, flatfooted fellow would boast for hours about how with
seventy American marines he could conquer Europe. . . . He was forever comparing poverty-stricken Martigues with the glory of his native skyscrapers and
Brooklyn Bridge.'[36]
    In that case, his hosts appear to have decided, their patience abused and
exhausted, Hart might as well be on his way and having been invited to stay, he
was now invited to leave. 'We had to get him to go away but we parted friends,'
Campbell recalled, without indicating how such a delicate extrication could be
achieved with a guest who was obviously as vulnerable as he was volatile.[37] In the
fancifully vicious correspondence he maintained with his friend Wyndham Lewis,
Campbell described Hart 'crying like a big fat baby' as he 'put his typewriter into
one of his hands and the valise in the other and gave him a kick behind to get him
moving'. Why stand on ceremony with such a figure? He was after all 'a disgrace
both intellectually and morally, a howling, ugly-looking, lachrymose devil, like
nothing I have ever seen before. . . . I have never seen such a preposterous mixture
of a swashbuckler and a whining coward.'[38] The reality was probably less dramatic,
but in whatever circumstances Hart left, it was understood all round that he would
not be coming back. Some weeks later, after his return to America, he sent the
Campbells a postcard, 'still begging our pardon!!', Lewis was informed, and declaring that 'he was going to "hurl" himself off Brooklyn bridge: but the silly ass seems
to have forgotten to do so'.[39] Campbell may have wanted to impress Lewis with
his vitriol but no such ambition informed his meeting with Nathan Asch, when he
was travelling in the South of France a whole year later. Nevertheless, Asch was
amazed to note, the South African looked back on Hart's visit as a 'continual
senseless storm' and 'could not even talk about [him] without indignation'.[40]
    By 11 June the wanderer was back in Marseilles and anxious about ebbing time:
the Black Sun deadline was fast approaching, as was insolvency. Before going to
Martigues he had begged a loan from Allen Tate to enable him to return to Paris
and when he sent acknowledgement to his friend, now in France on a

Guggenheim fellowship, it was with the rueful admission that he had nothing beyond 'a coat of tan' to show for his last two months. 'I've really just "bummed around".'[41] By 28 June he was in Paris once more, his return marked by Crosby's diary: 'Hart Crane back from Marseille where he had slept with his thirty sailors and he began again to drink Cutty Sark.' On 29 June Crosby came home to find Hart there again and once more turned to his diary: 'Hart Crane was there very drunk (no more Cutty Sark left) and at last he left and so with C[aresse] to the Ambassadeurs.'[42] The next day, whether by impulse or long-standing plan, the Crosbys left: Hart arrived to find the house deserted and sensed his welcome was wearing thin. On 1 July, explaining that 'a thick fog' still clouded his last hours with them, he sent a letter that promised his patrons he was 'through playing around' and assured them he would devote the rest of his time in France to completion of *The Bridge*. Paris would be 'more lonesome than I thought' without them but he knew now he had little time left there.[43] Although he had more than $2,000 in a bank in New York, in France he was penniless, having exhausted his supply of traveller's cheques: he had no alternative but to return home yet to achieve even that he would have to borrow.

He had a new romantic interest – Peter Christiansen was another Dane but although he was young and handsome with equestrian skills acquired in the Danish Royal Artillery he was entirely impecunious and could do nothing to improve Hart's finances. Mr and Mrs Willard Widney, American expatriates whose friends included Ford Madox Ford, Hemingway and the painter Pavel Tchelitchew, were happy to include Hart in their circle, although Widney found his increasingly excessive behaviour a challenge to tolerance and generosity: 'He had a fierce megalomania, and when he had been drinking hard it became damned offensive.'[44] Widney was an enthusiastic sports spectator who regularly took groups of friends to boxing matches; Hart made one such occasion memorable with his admission, 'Boxing matches always make me feel homosexual.'[45] Conspicuously not invited to the Moulin, he stayed instead with the painter Eugene MacCown at the Villa Seurat at 101 rue de la Tombe Issoire and returned home very drunk most nights. He appeared as one of the signatories to a manifesto written by Eugene Jolas and published in *transition*: 'Revolution of the Word' demanded the excision from the language of 'monotonous syntax' but Hart would later repudiate its claims and blame his subscription on drunkenness. Occasionally he saw the Tates but Allen found him 'far gone in drink' and was inclined to keep his distance. He and Hart did spend one afternoon at Les Deux Magots, however, but happy observations about Paris, which the Tates loved and never wanted to leave, soon gave way to family grievances. 'He talked about his mother a great deal more than he ever had before. He was very bitter about her.' Hearing how Grace had threatened blackmail as a way of getting at his inheritance Tate was confirmed in his old opinion: 'I always thought he had the most appalling family I ever heard of.'[46]

Another café, another unedifying scene: Stuart Davis, an American painter, looked on as Hart, 'very drunk', surrendered a new Burberry coat to the waiter because 'he had no money to pay for a table full of saucers'.[47] And then another: this time the drama which precipitated his inglorious return home, with the Tates once again involved. Various Americans had congregated a day early for Fourth of July drinking at the Closerie des Lilas but Hart appeared reasonably sober when he decided to leave the group and wander off alone down the Boulevard du Montparnasse. He stopped at the Sélect and continued drinking, only to discover when ready to leave that he was unable to pay the bill. Madame Sélect, who resented hard-drinking Americans even as she depended on them, rejected Hart's promise to return the next day with payment as well as his offer to borrow money from a bartender he knew across the street. Matching her in unreason, he began to shout denunciations of French waiters and café proprietors and as a comic scene developed into an ugly confrontation other Americans in the bar, among them Eugene MacCown, began a collection to pay the bill. Madame, however, was determined on exemplary and humiliating treatment and ordering a waiter to detain Hart, she called for the police. A brawl ensued: waiters, and then a policeman, were sent sprawling by this poet who was rather less puny than Roy Campbell supposed, and it was only when Hart was clubbed insensible that police reinforcements were able to drag him away by his feet to the waiting vehicle. At La Santé he was thrashed with a rubber hose, thrown into a cell and held incommunicado for 'outrages violences ivresse'.[48]

Rumours that an American, identity unknown, had been detained at La Santé spread first to the French press and thence to the Paris offices of the *Herald-Tribune* but Hart's rescue only really began when Whit Burnett, a young journalist with the *Tribune*, telephoned Eugene MacCown wondering what was to be done. A defence fund was established, to which Willard Widney contributed 1,000 francs, a lawyer hired and a delegation convened: e.e. cummings, recently arrived in Paris, headed the group of writers who petitioned the Chief Prefect of Police on Hart's behalf, only to be told that since the prisoner had struck a police officer it would be impossible to release him without a trial, which was scheduled for 10 July. Meanwhile character references were solicited from Cocteau, Gide, Jane Heap, who now published the *Little Review* in Paris, and Jean Paulhan, who wrote on 9 July on behalf of the *Nouvelle Revue Française*: 'Monsieur – Assurez le poète Hart Crane je vous prie de la sympathie que nous éprouvons tous pour lui à la nrf. J'éspère bien vivement qu'il nous sera rendu demain soir, acquitté. Recevez, monsieur, l'assurance de mes sentiments empressés.'[49] That same day the Crosbys returned to Paris to find a letter from Kay Boyle alerting them to what had happened. Harry prepared to pay whatever fines were levied and was in court with MacCown the next day when, after six days in prison, Hart faced his trial. 'When the Judge announced that it had taken ten gendarmes to hold him (the dirty bastards, they dragged him three blocks by the feet) all the court burst into laughter,' he informed his diary. 'After ten minutes of questioning he was fined 800 francs and 8 days in prison should he ever be arrested again. A letter from the Nouvelle Revue Française had a good deal to do with his liberation.' Legal formalities required that Hart be returned to La Santé and Crosby spent an eventful day involving lunch, a consideration of the day's racing and a near-encounter with an American girl in the bar at the Ritz before collecting his friend from gaol towards 9 p.m. Hart, he noted, was the last prisoner to emerge and was 'unshaved hungry wild'. Freedom's first pleasure was a drink: Crosby and Burnett toasted Hart and his liberation in the bar of La Bonne Santé opposite the prison, after which they all drove to the offices of the *Herald-Tribune*, where Burnett wanted to write up the story. Later on Crosby took the poet 'to the Chicago Inn for cornbread and poached eggs on toast ... and Hart said that the dirty skunks in the Santé wouldn't give him any paper to write poems on. The bastards.'[50]

On 11 July Hart accompanied Crosby when he bought the poet's tourist class ticket back to New York on the USS *Homeric*, scheduled to depart six days later. His notoriety would precede him, thanks to the *New York Times* and its coverage of misadventures:

Amid the joyous laughter of the whole court, Hart Crane, an American citizen and a poet, promised the magistrate in the Thirteenth Correctional Court in Paris today that in the future, while in France at least, he would be dry.... 'For your own safety, I think that while you remain in France you should promise to keep the law of your own country and remain dry.' Mr Crane promised.[51]

That night Hart celebrated in Montmartre and was 'rather the worse for wear' when he arrived at the rue de Lille the next morning to dictate parts of *The Bridge* to a typist. He read his poems aloud, Crosby noted, 'and declared there was no greater poet', but his claims seemed poignant in view of his hung-over condition, made more comical by 'all sorts of stars and anchors pinned to his sweater'.[52] Later in the day he wrote to Roy Campbell to thank him for his hospitality – 'those hectic nights of universal confession which marked my sojourn with you and Mary' – and to tell him Crosby admired his poetry. And, he asked, 'I hope you will remember me to the Sun of Provence, who is the real Jove of the not only ancient but modern intelligence.'[53]

As his departure drew near he said farewell to the friends he was leaving behind, including Allen Tate, who found him 'very indignant about the French; France had become a hell after being a paradise a week before; and the first thing he shouted at me was that the frogs ought to pay the war debt!'[54] Anxious about Peter Christiansen's future he commended him to Crosby and hoped the latter would guide him towards some kind of work: he was 'honest, industrious, and will do anything that's honorable'.[55] On 17 July Christiansen and Crosby presented Hart with a farewell bottle of Cutty Sark and saw him board the *Homeric* for a homeland that suddenly seemed preferable. This was the traditional wisdom of expatriation but Hart Crane learned in a hard school and there was a bitterness in the tone with which he thanked Jane Heap for the character reference she had submitted for his trial: 'I have to laugh, Jane.... We Americans have got something they can't understand – any more than we could ever come to understand their pettifogging.'[56]

Even in Marseilles, suggesting to Crosby that 'Europe isn't my cure, after all', Hart had had intimations of this dissatisfaction.[57] Once at sea, however, his ambivalence returned: where did he belong, especially in view of the anxiety, divulged to the Rychtariks at the beginning of his French adventure, that 'my mother has made it impossible for me to live in my own country'?[58] The voyage was smooth but the notebooks which recorded the names of French sailors also contained sequences of words that may have occurred to him as he contemplated the waves – fragments for possible inclusion in lyrics which identified the divine mystery of the sea as well as the violence of the deliverance it could offer: 'The sea reflecting God'; 'Clouds billowing as agonists'; 'Harsh mark of the sea up from the elbow'; 'Guillotines of million mirrors'.[59] He read Donne and John Masefield and in mid-ocean he marked his thirtieth birthday, not with the bottle of Cutty Sark, exhausted after three days, but with bourbon and soda, a drink so associated with the Isle of Pines that it caused chimerical palm trees to wave on the horizon. Celebrations continued the following evening in the first-class bar, at least until he was ejected, and on 23 July he wrote to Crosby to congratulate him on his *Transit of Venus* poems and to assure him that 'the nearer we get to America the more "creative" I seem to feel'.[60]

The *Homeric* docked on 24 July but Hart's initial emotion was not one of inspiration but of shame and awkwardness in the wake of his recent humiliation. He wrote a long letter to Aunt Sally and in recognition of her birthday greetings he enclosed $25 and a recent photograph, which pleased her less than his news and his money: 'I got the letter with your picture but must say I didn't like the picture very well some how it didn't look like my boy poet. Are you really gray Hart?'[61] For days he lay low, his nervous anonymity broken by a chance encounter with Bill Brown. Together they returned to East 12th Street, where the latter noted his friend's erratic condition: 'He seemed ashamed of his wasted life in Paris and didn't like to own up to the fact that he had done not a lick of work while he was there. This remorse disappeared instantly after he had had a drink – a fact which led me to believe that drink was no longer a problem with him, it was a solution.'[62] Sue observed his changed appearance – 'complexion red and somewhat mottled, hair grayer, figure slightly puffy' – but when she scolded him for not getting in touch earlier she elicited a tearful admission: 'I thought you would never want to see me again.'[63] Having secured forgiveness in New York Hart returned to Patterson and to Mrs Turner, who also overlooked his misdeeds and permitted him the use of his old rooms and here he resumed work on the gloss notes for

'Powhatan's Daughter' as it would appear in the Black Sun edition of *The Bridge*. By 8 August they were complete and he dispatched them to Caresse with the assurance that he was back at work on the sections of the poem that remained to be written. In accordance with other promises made to the Crosbys he was also busy in New York investigating reproduction rights to Stella's paintings of Brooklyn Bridge held by Brooklyn Museum. Wandering the beaches of Brooklyn and Queens he found them, he told Caresse, 'packed with pulchritude', and at some stage in the following week he decided to rent somewhere in New York.[64] On 20 August he moved into a small furnished apartment at 130 Columbia Heights and a week later, in his first letter to Underwood since returning to America, he told of numerous house-warming parties involving friends recently made among the crews of the *Milwaukee*, the *Wyoming* and the *Cincinnati*. The Brooklyn Navy Yard was conveniently nearby and the janitor in Hart's building supplied a further incentive to hospitality by selling corn whiskey at $6 a gallon.

The Crosbys might have been disheartened had they known how much there was to distract Hart from his literary obligations. Yet despite all temptation he continued to apply himself and when he wrote to them again on 30 August it was to announced that 'Cape Hatteras' was now 'being worked out rapidly, and the aeronautical sections which you so much admired have been improved and augmented considerably'.[65] The poem contained lines longer than those of any other section of *The Bridge*, and in order to preserve them unbroken he now proposed publication on larger pages. Brooklyn Museum had given permission for inclusion of any one of its Stellas as a frontispiece but subsequent research had established that an engraved colour reproduction would cost $200. Presuming that to be prohibitive, he was now considering using a photograph of one of the paintings instead.

T.S. Eliot and Henry Seidel Canby solicited contributions to the *Criterion* and the *Saturday Review* and then the September issue of *Vanity Fair* appeared, and with it a picture of Hart, taken by Man Ray, which was included in an article about contemporary American poets. 'Singers of the New Age: A Group of Distinguished Young Poets Who Have Found Fresh Material in the American Scene' celebrated Joseph March, Robinson Jeffers, Stephen Vincent Benét, McKnight Black and Hart, 'an acknowledged leader among the younger Americans' whose poems were 'as aspiring and as clear-cut as the skyscrapers of which he writes'.[66] Caresse sent first proofs of *The Bridge*, which he acknowledged on 6 September: despite anxieties that there were too few words to each page he was delighted, especially now that a larger typeface had been adopted. He was working, he promised her, 'like mad' since moving into an apartment where he could keep his own hours and promised 'the final version' of 'Cape Hatteras' in a few days. 'It looks pretty good to me, and at least according to my ideas of the Bridge this edition wouldn't be complete or even representative without it.' Thereafter 'Quaker Hill' and 'Indiana', the final sections to be written, 'will come in quick succession' – indeed he promised a finished text by the second week in October.[67] Ten days later he sent her the completed version of 'Cape Hatteras'. There would be no further modifications, he promised, and altogether he felt 'pleased with the way I've been able to marshal the notes and agonies of the last two years' effort into a rather arresting synthesis'.[68]

Arresting perhaps, but 'Cape Hatteras' has always been one of the least-admired components of *The Bridge*. At 235 lines it constitutes Crane's longest poem – a celebration of the conquest of the air and a proclamation of Walt Whitman as sovereign exponent of the mythic destiny of America. Unfortunately its place and purpose in the grand scheme called for descriptions of places and situations that Hart had never experienced – a major challenge to a poet who was responsive rather than speculative. There are beautiful words and images here but they are overwhelmed by the metaphorical bravado Crane deployed to cloak the fact that he had never been to Cape Hatteras or flown or seen any kind of combat, terrestrial or aerial. Whitman himself supplied the epigraph – '*The seas all crossed,/ weathered the capes, the voyage done …*' – which anticipates the final satisfaction of the questing impulse and the unification of peoples and ages which is the underlying impulse of *The Bridge*.

As the poem begins, Crane presents his readers with prehistory: we glimpse a dinosaur and then Atlantis itself, 'the eastern Cape', sinking beneath the waves, 'While rises in the west the coastwise range' of what will become America. Leaping across ages the poet introduces those questers who have sought the lost continent 'round the capes, the promontories/Where strange tongues vary messages of surf/Below grey citadels'. Columbus was such an adventurer, as was Crane himself, whose spiritual questing ended with a return to America, 'to read you, Walt, – knowing us in thrall/To that deep wonderment, our native clay'. Another leap in time: for Columbus the sea was the final frontier but for twentieth-century man it is the air: 'And from above, thin squeaks of radio static,/The captured fume of space foams in our ears'. Since the poet's birth thirty years before, the Wright Brothers and then Charles Lindbergh had fulfilled man's immemorial designs on the air. Yet if Hart and his contemporaries were living at a time of outstanding scientific inventiveness and change – 'The nasal whine of power whips a new universe' – they were also the witnesses to human destructiveness of ever greater ingenuity. No sooner was the aeroplane invented than it knew 'the closer clasp of Mars' – but no poet who emerged from the trenches of the Great War evoked its technically advanced carnage with the verbiage Crane now deployed to describe battles in the sky:

> Behold the dragon's covey – amphibian, ubiquitous
> To hedge the seaboard, wrap the headland, ride
> The blue's cloud-templed districts unto ether...
> While Iliads glimmer through eyes raised in pride

Hell's belt springs wider into heaven's plumed side.
O bright circumferences, heights employed to fly
War's fiery kennel masked in downy offings, –
This tournament of space

In an echo of the sacrifice in 'The Dance', an aeroplane, exposed by searchlights, is shot down and its pilot, his 'eyes bicarbonated white by speed', plunges to destruction. 'Thou sowest doom thou hast nor time nor chance/To reckon – as thy stilly eyes partake/What alcohol of space'. As the sacrificial victim, however, the pilot is also a potential redeemer, a seer whose vision will transcend terrestrial boundaries:

Remember, Falcon-Ace,
Thou hast there in thy wrist a Sanskrit charge
To conjugate infinity's dim marge –
Anew. . . . !

Yet if America herself is to redefine infinity she must first of all renounce her bloody history and if anyone can guide her towards peace and fraternity it is Whitman: 'O, upward from the dead/Thou bringest tally, and a pact, new bound/Of living brotherhood!' Whitman, who witnessed the horrors of the Civil War, has kept a record of all his country's carnage: 'Thou, pallid there as chalk/Hast kept of wounds, O Mourner, all that sum/That then from Appomattox stretched to Somme!' In order to atone for its bloodiness America must first confront it, and with Whitman's mediation this confrontation and expiation can be achieved. As the poem moves towards its climax, Whitman is identified not only as the supreme myth-maker of America and the redeemer of its cruelty but also as Crane's personal inspiration:

Our Meistersinger, thou set breath in steel;
And it was thou who on the boldest heel
Stood up and flung the span on even wing
Of that great Bridge, our Myth, whereof I sing!

In the most lyrically successful passage in 'Cape Hatteras' Crane recalls the year he first read the work of this great inspirer – 'O, early following thee, I searched the hill/Blue-writ and odor-firm with violets' – before naming him now a 'Vedic Caesar' who reposed conviction 'Beyond all sesames of science' in the 'something green' of earth's annual regeneration. With Whitmanian guidance the aeroplane, symbol of America's technical genius, need not simply be an engine of destruction and in the penultimate stanza it is enlisted 'To course that span of consciousness thou'st named/The Open Road'. It has become a symbol of man's reborn and questing spirit and as the plane becomes airborne Crane assures Whitman, 'thy vision is reclaimed!' It was a vision of brotherhood, of healing and union, and as the dead poet extends a hand to his living disciple they set out together across the 'rainbow's arch' that rises above the 'ghoul-mound' of modern America, an invitation to future visionaries and also an inspiration:

> yes, Walt,
> Afoot again, and onward without halt, –
> Not soon, nor suddenly, – no, never to let go
>   My hand
>   in yours,
>   Walt Whitman –
>   so –[69]

The heat persisted in New York well into September so Hart divided the early autumn weeks between Patterson and the city – a vivid presence in its many cultural lives. At a party given by Paul Rosenfeld he shocked the painter and art critic Fairfield Porter by dismissing Edmund Spenser as 'an unreadable poet' and *The Faerie Queene* as 'impossible'.[70] When Rosenfeld began soliciting material for the fourth edition of the *American Caravan* he assured Hart he was the first writer to be contacted: 'We would feel not only happy but honored if you gave us the privilege of presenting one or all of your new cantos.'[71] Discussing death one night in a cab with Walker Evans Hart foretold a dramatic ending for himself: 'When it comes, it will be with a bang, by God.'[72] He was the poet sought out by Angel Flores, bilingual editor of the *Alhambra* magazine, as a kind of living monument when an important visitor came to New York. Federico García Lorca, a year older than Hart and with a mortal term only slightly longer, had established his reputation the previous year with his *First Book of Gypsy Ballads* and was now in New York to gather the impressions that would subsequently be recorded in *Poet in New York and Other Poems*. With Flores as interpreter, Crane and Lorca discussed Whitman and America before turning to more immediate interests – the sailors in the Brooklyn bar in which they met. When the Crosbys' friend Gerald Wallop, later the ninth Earl of Portsmouth, arrived in New York he naturally contacted the wild poet he had first met in Paris. Hart 'took me under his wing for a short embarrassing drunken interlude' and gave the visitor 'the same Paris feeling of living fully in today'.[73] On 25 September he took Wallop to visit Otto Kahn but instead of recognizing a great poet and an English lord the footmen at 1100 Fifth Avenue saw only two drunks and the visitors were rebuffed. Hart left his patron a note promising he would soon attempt to deliver a Black Sun edition of *The Bridge*, 'providing your lackeys are not quite so imposing and insulting'.[74] At Mrs Turner's, meanwhile, he found that the quarters previously occupied by the Tates and the Asches were now inhabited by the artist Peter Blume, who was then at work on two large canvases, *Parade* and *South of Scranton*. Blume noted Hart's 'volcanic enthusiasms about a great number of things, art and music among them' and found that 'his perceptions were unusually interesting, especially when he was sober'.[75] The poet's large personality apart, it was difficult for Blume to ignore his neighbour, not least because 'I could hear everything through those thin walls which separated us'.[76] Struggling now to complete 'Indiana' and 'Quaker Hill' ahead of the Crosbys' deadline, Hart typed late into the night, playing repeatedly the work of his favourite twentieth-century composers, or else such songs as 'You're the kind of man needs a kind of woman like me'.

Whether in New York or Patterson, Hart drank relentlessly and by the middle of October Evans, Brown, Loveman and Lorna Dietz were all accustomed to late night calls or even visits in the small hours which were prompted by one drunken drama or another. He was 'a wreck',[77] he later admitted to Sam Loveman, when he decided to return to Addie's in the third week of October and conceded to Lorna that 'I know I need a little "reserve" after the way I've been acting'.[78] For a while departure from New York seemed to calm him and he completed 'Indiana', but peace and progress were dispelled once more when he learned – possibly through Loveman – that Grace knew he had returned to America and was determined to visit him in the East. At a drinking session with Peter Blume shortly afterwards the two men consumed a gallon of bootleg wine but if Hart drank to forget, he misjudged himself: shortly afterwards Blume heard shufflings and mutterings next door and then Hart reappeared and invited him to inspect some photographs of his mother taken at various stages in her life. The early portraits, the poet insisted, 'show a lady' but the most recent studies, including studio portraits taken in Hollywood, revealed 'an old bitch'.

Blume went to visit Malcolm Cowley but when he returned an hour or so later mayhem prevailed: Addie was standing outside, terrified, while Hart was on a rampage of destruction on the upper storey. Blume knocked the poet to the ground and pinioned him with a knee on his stomach but before the fury subsided Hart swore from the corner of his mouth: 'You can keep me down but not *The Bridge*. It's on its way to Paris.' Later that night and much calmer the poet broke the silence of a year and telephoned his father, but whatever imagined reproaches had deterred him from calling earlier were not forthcoming. On the contrary CA was pleased to hear from the prodigal, not least because he had important news to relay: he was going to marry again and hoped his son would mark the event with a visit to Ohio. When Hart went to Blume's room once more, however, it was not to report the fact that he was soon to have another stepmother but to declare his relief at restoration of the relations that meant so much to him: 'I've just spoken to my father on the telephone. Do you know what it means to speak to one's father?'[79]

At the end of October Hart returned to New York to find a cable from the Crosbys offering him a simple choice: he must decide at once whether he wanted

The Bridge to appear before Christmas, complete or not, or in February. Fragile from recent excesses and apprehensive about his mother's movements and intentions, he was disinclined to face the decision and sought counsel from friends. Lorna advised him to put his father first and when he called CA again and the latter urged him to return to Ohio – 'We'll talk it all out when you come home' – the matter seemed settled and he cabled the Crosbys: 'DEFER PUBLICATION'.[80] As he explained in a letter written on 29 October, he wanted to see 'at least the bulk of the poem in proofs' and since 'Quaker Hill' was still unfinished there seemed no point in pressing ahead with immediate production. Harry and Caresse were due in New York soon and their visit would provide a useful opportunity for discussion of final details 'with no chance of misunderstandings'. For all its delays 'Cape Hatteras' had pleased them and he hoped they would also consider it had been worth waiting for 'Indiana', the significance of which was so important to *The Bridge* as a whole. What he had struggled to evoke in this newest addition to the large poem was the 'metamorphosis of Pocahontas – the indian into the pioneer woman, and hence her absorption into our "contemporary veins"'. Now the lyric had been completed he felt 'it does round out the cycle, at least historically and psychologically – one leaves the continent surrounded by water (pure space) as one found it in the first place ("Harbor Dawn"), and "Cutty Sark" quite logically follows as "space" again'. But more than anything he longed to be rid of the poem completely. For five years now he had lived with *The Bridge*: 'You can't imagine how insufferably ponderous it has seemed, yes, more than once!'[81] Even as he wrote, events were occurring the other side of the East River which would put an end to the world in which Hart had developed as a poet and conceived his literary ambitions. On Black Tuesday, 29 October, after several days of nervous trading, Wall Street crashed. The previous week had seen panic selling, expectant crowds outside the New York Stock Exchange and the suicide of eleven prominent financiers, but by the time Hart sealed the last letter he would ever send to both Crosbys in France 40 per cent of the total value of Wall Street stocks had been lost.

The implications of the collapse would change the thinking of Hart's literary generation, although the poet himself, with no more than a walk-on part in the literary scene of the 1930s, left no comments behind about the bankruptcy of capitalism. CA was no doubt watching events on Wall Street more closely, but when Hart arrived for a two-week stay at Canary Cottage he found his father in expansive and optimistic mood, largely thanks to the presence of the woman he was soon to marry. Elizabeth Agnes Meacham had first come into his life as a travelling sales representative whose job entailed selling decorative maps to the offices and boardrooms of Cleveland. Later she worked for the Crane Company and her suggestion that it sell food in some of its premises as well as confectionery eventually led to the opening of The Dinner Bell in Hudson, Ohio, and Canary Cottage in Chagrin Falls. A mere six years older than her future stepson and educated at

Notre Dame Academy in Cleveland, where her future sister-in-law Alice Crane taught music, she was a capable and sensible woman whose generous and easy-going nature offered what youthful impracticality had long needed: the makings of a sympathetic ally. Thanks in part to Bess's presence Hart's visit was entirely happy: it was agreed that a bedroom should be permanently reserved for him at the Cottage and when he wrote to Sam Loveman on 11 November to indicate that his welcome had been as warm as the six great fires that blazed in the property, he added, 'Feel as though I had a home at last.'[82] Canary Cottage had been named after a play CA had seen on Broadway and its furnishings replicated the stage set: writing to Bill Brown, Hart enthused about 'Father's collection of early Am[erican] clocks, desks, chairs, tables, beds and highboys' and wished his friend 'were here for some of the superb duck and chicken'.[83]

Before he could become accustomed to such ease, however, and before he had visited Bill Sommer or the Rychtariks, Grace reappeared on the horizon – she was bound for Cleveland but according to gossip among the Harts and the Cranes she hoped to spend Thanksgiving with her son. He in turn hoped to spend it with CA and Bess but news of his mother's proximity made him return at once to New York, where he spent the holiday alone and in such agonies of apprehension about the revelations his mother could unleash if she met his father that he developed back pains for the next three weeks. But when on 26 November CA sent him an account of Grace's movements he learned he was in the clear after all: his mother had indeed arrived in Ohio but when she called her former husband to arrange a meeting he declined to see her and when she asked if he was at all interested in her welfare, 'I told her I was not in any particular'. As promised, CA had withheld Hart's Brooklyn address and was now convinced that Grace should undergo examination to determine her mental, as well as her physical, condition, and assured his son that he would be 'fully justified in signing such papers' as were needed to facilitate the procedure.[84]

Once again dividing his time between New York and Patterson and mindful of the Crosbys' imminent arrival, Hart managed – despite intense anxiety and corollary drunkenness – to resume work on 'Quaker Hill', the last section of *The Bridge* to be written and the poem that described more fully than any other his feelings for the Patterson neighbourhood which was his adopted home. By evoking the history of this southernmost corner of New England and contrasting it with present reality, 'Quaker Hill' would illustrate the decadence of contemporary America and thus prepare the way in *The Bridge* for 'The Tunnel', the vision of modern Purgatory which yields in turn to the redemption and climactic ecstasy of 'Atlantis'.

By instinct, Crane was not a poet of place: his finest lyrics, whether considering love or fame or death or desire, scintillate in an unstable ether of mood and aspiration which transcends geographical, indeed terrestrial, considerations and even poems which appear to consider location, whether the Africa of 'Black Tambourine' or Porphyro's Akron, on closer inspection turn out to be preoccupied with exile and incongruity. Crane was born with this sense of displacement but as he grew older he learned to reckon it the condition of artists in a mercantile world and to idealize those figures he considered his fellow outlaws. Among them was Isadora Duncan, who supplies one of the epigraphs to 'Quaker Hill': 'I see only the ideal. But no ideals have ever been fully successful on this earth.' Over-experienced at thirty and with greying hair to show it, the poet who had first walked these hills six years before now understood more than ever the wisdom of Duncan's remark. But there was another lesson he had come to learn at first hand: the years, as they silently steal by one behind another, take away more than mere ideals. Life is about loss and the awfulness of loss, and to prepare the reader for his meditation on this theme Crane incorporates another epigraph, this time from Emily Dickinson, whose 'Summer's Obsequies' mourned the autumnal beauty which each year reminds man of his own brief season: 'The gentian weaves her fringes,/The maple's loom is red.' The grazing cattle Crane surveys in the open-ing lines of 'Quaker Hill' are untroubled by such intimations of mortality, how-ever: 'These are but cows that see no other thing/Than grass and snow.' Their acceptance of life's uncompromising terms is placid and instinctive: 'awkward, ponderous and uncoy', they have grazed these meadows since first introduced by the Quakers who were the locality's earliest white inhabitants. With what high ideals that sect first settled this countryside – yet all that remains of them now is their name, spoken so glibly by the colony of summering artists and writers 'who press the cider mill' and who 'with pledges taste the bright annoy/Of friendship's acid wine'. What drunken fun these fields had seen; though ever sensitive Crane cannot forget there were times 'when/The jest is too sharp to be kindly'. From all directions ghosts – of 'scalped Yankee's', 'slain Iroquois' and 'Dead rangers' – watch the festive artists who will one day join their spectral ranks, while above all stands Old Mizzentop, the 'palatial white/Hostelry' perched on the summit of the highest hill and the relic of a grander age, now silently awaiting demolition, its 'Long tiers of windows staring out toward former/Faces ... like eyes that still uphold some dream/Through mapled vistas, cancelled reservations!' Nobody, we are reminded, 'holds the lease on time and on disgrace'. However high their ideals, all those who once claimed this country have been superseded and all Crane can foresee, for Patterson and for the America of history and altruism, is tourism, gen-trification and money-making:

> This was the Promised Land, and still it is
> To the persuasive suburban land agent
> In bootleg roadhouses where the gin fizz
> Bubbles in time to Hollywood's new love-nest pageant.
> Fresh from the radio in the old Meeting House

(Now the New Avalon Hotel) volcanoes roar
A welcome to highsteppers that no mouse
Who saw the Friends there ever heard before.

If this rural neighbourhood he had come to love was doomed, a prey to rising land values and weekending New Yorkers, what of Crane himself? Born, he felt, to 'Shoulder the curse of sundered parentage', he struggled to reconcile the ideals with which he had begun to build *The Bridge* with the disappointments time had since inflicted. Who would have thought when he first conceived his epic that he would now live in dread of 'the postman driving from Birch Hill/With birthright by blackmail'? Bitterly estranged from his mother, he now valued love more highly as the purpose and explanation of existence and wondered if the heroic vision with which he had once tried to interpret life was either apt or valid:

So, must we from the hawk's far stemming view,
Must we descend as worm's eye to construe
Our love of all we touch..?

The end of *The Bridge* was at last in sight but suddenly the poem seemed to belong to past ages. The bolstering forces of his personal life – the new philadelphia of visionary artists he had once honoured, the passion for Emil, the demanding inspiration of maternal love – all seemed long distant and when he looked at America herself he saw, not the manifestation of a myth, but the growing lines of unemployed men stretching all the way from ruined Wall Street to the never-never land of Los Angeles. So what remained? In theory, love, the eternal consolation of poets – although sometimes he felt so solitary and misunderstood that the idea must have seemed no more than a grand abstraction. 'Leaf after autumnal leaf' fell as the poet brought 'Quaker Hill' to its close. Standing among 'dim elm-chancels hung with dew', he remembered 'that stilly note/Of pain that Emily, that Isadora knew', and realized he was listening to the cry of the whip-poor-will, the bird that sings before the dawn. In the context of *The Bridge* the bird's chorus gives the poet the courage to face the dreadful journey through 'The Tunnel' that follows and sounds an intimation of the redemptive harmonies of 'Atlantis'. In the context of Hart Crane's moods, however, the nocturnal music which 'unhusks the heart of fright' reminded him there was a poetic virtue even beyond love, and that was courage, the courage to continue singing in the night, like the whip-poor-will whose note

Breaks us and saves, yes, breaks the heart, yet yields
That patience that is armour and that shields
Love from despair – when love foresees the end.[85]

This haunted countryside was at its busiest and brightest in the year's last months: the leaves turned vivid for their annual fall and wagon convoys transported the apple harvest into Connecticut to the cider mill at Sherman. Malcolm Cowley remembered 'the smell of fermenting cider on all the back roads' and the strange accompanying rites that occurred when 'old people came out of their houses for a sort of saturnalia' before the first heavy snow. 'One passed groups of them by the roadside, hairy men in rags who sang in cracked voices or shouted obscenities. Once I saw Hart among them, reeling and shouting with the others.'[86] Cowley had many problems of his own to distract him from the spectacle of his friend's disintegration. Although the year had been marked by the successful publication of *Blue Juniata* – 'not even Hart Crane can surpass Mr Cowley's verbal excellence', Horace Gregory had insisted in the *New York Sun* – the critic nevertheless felt oppressed by personal and professional difficulties.[87] Tired of being what he termed 'the unfaithful slave of the typewriter' he had struggled financially for most of the year, finally surrendering journalistic autonomy in October for the position of literary editor at the *New Republic*.[88] New York, which had once seemed so exciting, had grown stale even as its feverish Jazz Age pace had quickened, and to Edmund Wilson, his predecessor at the *New Republic*, he regretted 'too many parties; too much seduction, sodomy, cunnilinctus and abortion; too much money spent; no sleep.'[89] Worse still, he and Peggy, a decade married, were drifting apart. 'She had casual affairs, and I had less casual ones', and soon he realized it would be impossible to reconcile his new burden of work with her bohemian love of late hours and domestic irregularity.[90] He and Hart therefore had much to discuss in the course of a walk they took one winter day in Patterson, but as usual Hart's problems seemed to require more urgent attention. As they stumbled 'in the frozen ruts of the road that led up Hardscrabble Hill' Cowley reflected that he had 'always refrained from interfering in Hart's life' but now, aware of the literary and personal challenges that faced his friend, he resolved to speak:

> I said, bringing the words out haltingly, that he had been devoting himself to the literature of ecstasy and that it had involved more of a psychological strain than most writers could stand. Now, having finished *The Bridge*, perhaps he might shift over to the literature of experience.... It might be years before he was ready to undertake another group of poems as ambitious as those he had just completed. In the meantime he might cultivate his talent for writing quiet and thoughtful prose. Hart cut me short. 'Oh, you mean that I shouldn't drink so much.'[91]

The reception the Crosbys encountered from Harry's parents when they arrived in America in late November was less than rapturous. The recent and notorious telegram authorizing the sale of $10,000-worth of stock was far from forgotten and occasioned a bitter quarrel between Crosby Senior and his son. When Stephen and Henrietta Crosby chastised Harry, however, and urged him to behave with more responsibility towards his name, his class and his fortune, they found him beyond contrition: 'For the poet there is love and there is death and infinity,' he informed them, 'and for other things to assume such vital importance is out of the question and that is why I refuse to take the question of money seriously.'[92] Despite the dissension, the Stephen Crosbys and the Harry Crosbys together attended the Game – the annual football match between Harvard and Yale – after which Harry went to see his mistress, Josephine Bigelow, while Caresse departed for New York, where she registered in suite 2707 at the Savoy-Plaza Hotel before organizing a rendezvous with Hart under Brooklyn Bridge. Harry joined her a few days later and on 7 December the couple were the principal guests at a party Hart threw in Brooklyn Heights to mark the completion of *The Bridge* and to introduce his Parisian patrons to his friends in New York.

Walker Evans, the Cowleys, their friend Margaret Robson, e.e. cummings, Harry Marks, American distributor for the Black Sun Press, William Carlos Williams and assorted sailors fêted the glamorous couple, bound for France aboard the *Berengaria* on 13 December, and toasted Hart and the Brooklyn Bridge, which Caresse remembered as being 'drawn like a netting across his window'.[93] Cowley forgot his troubles in contemplation of the millionaire Hart had so often described: 'Harry smiled a lot – you remembered his very white teeth – and had easy manners, and without talking a great deal, he charmed everyone.'[94] Margaret Robson listened to his impassioned theories about the 'complicated splendours of love and death, and of a great love that somehow should be fulfilled in his own death' as she and Crosby went to Pineapple Street to replenish Hart's dwindling supply of gin.[95] Caresse remembered a sailor asleep on the stairs: it was 'a wild party' and Harry's 'hair bristled like thorns and his eyes blazed like twin suns'. Cummings produced a pack of cards and invited Crosby to choose one. The latter said 'Ace of Hearts', crossed himself and pulled out – the Ace of Hearts. As Caresse recalled, without specifying why that particular card should have seemed as ominous as the traditional death card, the Ace of Clubs, 'There was a silent second torn from a doomed tomorrow, as inwardly all of us crossed ourselves.'[96] Hart himself broke the silence by reciting a line from one of Crosby's poems: 'Let the sun shine! And the sun shone!'

On 8 December many of the guests reassembled at a party given by Harry Marks. The following morning, when they were still in their hotel suite, Crosby suddenly suggested to Caresse that they should leap together from the window, thus achieving their joint 'sundeath' on a radiant winter day. Anguished and afraid, she held her husband back. But in reply to her pleas – that they had too much to live for – he replied: 'There is too much – I cannot endure it all.'[97] On 10 December they went their separate ways – Caresse to have tea with her mother-in-law and Mrs J.P. Morgan, and Harry to see Josephine Bigelow, whom he knew as 'The Fire Princess'. They agreed to meet again at Mrs Morgan's before accompanying Henrietta Crosby to the Caviar Restaurant, where they had arranged to join Hart and Margaret Robson, who would accompany them to the theatre to see Leslie Howard playing the part of a ghost in a comedy called *Berkeley Square.* Crosby failed to appear at the Morgan mansion, so the party set off without him, only to begin eating in a state of growing apprehension as Caresse decided to break the rules of tolerance she and Harry observed and telephone Harry's friend, the painter Stanley Mortimer, at his mother's house. She knew that earlier in the day Harry had met the Fire Princess at Mortimer's apartment in the Hotel des Artistes overlooking Central Park and now she asked Mortimer to help trace her husband. He agreed to return to his apartment to see what had become of Harry but when he called back, just before the party proceeded to the theatre, he had no satisfactory news: his front door was bolted from within but as soon as he gained access he would call again. At the Lyceum, Hart left his seat number at the box-office, explaining that an important call was expected, and when the summons came at ten o'clock he took the dreadful message: Crosby and his Fire Princess were dead in bed, both with bullets in the head, and the gun was still in Crosby's hand. It looked like a suicide pact. They rushed from the theatre to find a crowd of policemen waiting for the elevator in the lobby of the Hotel des Artistes but when Caresse, Mrs Crosby and the others tried to follow them, they were detained and Margaret Robson remembered 'seeing the dial showing the floors, going up and stopping on the ninth – like a movie sequence of a detective story'.[98]

The deaths caused a sensation. Press coverage was extensive and imaginative – what journalist could resist the revelation that Crosby's toenails were painted red? – and although the precise sequence of events in Mortimer's apartment that afternoon was never established autopsies indicated that Crosby killed himself at least two hours after shooting Mrs Bigelow. By due legal process the deaths were ruled a double suicide, a verdict neither Caresse nor any of the dead man's close friends felt inclined to contest: after all, Harry had often endorsed the opinion of William James, that when a man takes his own life, 'the fact consecrates him forever. Inferior to ourselves in this way or that, if yet we cling to life, and he is able to "fling it away like a flower" as caring nothing for it, we account him in the deepest way our born superior'.[99]

19

The funeral was hastily arranged since Caresse, whether eager to escape the scandal or to distract herself with practicalities, had decided to follow existing plans and return to France, and the Black Sun Press, on 13 December. Aware that Mrs Crosby was to sail with her, Hart was nevertheless eager to convey his own sympathy and support and after struggling to convey both in an incoherent telegram he decided to send flowers to the *Berengaria*. 'All the way across the ocean,' she later thanked him from Paris, 'they were lily orchid gardenia courage love invulnerability and they helped so much.'[1]

In view of her determination that *The Bridge* would still appear as scheduled the least Hart could do was to pledge his own dependability: he therefore promised she would have all final revisions before 1 January even though the circumstances for perfectionism were hardly ideal. Crosby's suicide, he told Charlotte Rychtarik, 'threw me flat',[2] and when he wrote to Allen Tate on 14 December to accept his offer to proof-read *The Bridge* before it went to press in Paris he admitted he was 'all broken up about Harry' and hoped the brevity of his letter would not be misconstrued.[3] Tate was not the only friend involved in the production: expense and practicality had ruled out the reproduction of one of Stella's paintings as a frontispiece – the Black Sun edition was now to appear with photographs of Brooklyn Bridge and East River traffic taken by Walker Evans. It was to be dedicated to Otto Kahn, who told the poet that while in principle he was uneasy with the idea of such tributes he was prepared in this instance to acquiesce, since 'you and *The Bridge* do not come within the four corners of general rules'.[4] In a final exertion of lyric determination Hart devoted the two weeks that followed Crosby's death to reworking 'Quaker Hill', pausing on 23 December to sign his contract with Liveright and receiving in return a $200 advance and a promise that the publisher's edition of *The Bridge* would not appear before 1 April in deference to the labour and conviction of the Crosbys. On 26 December he completed the modifications and rushed to get them aboard the Cherbourg-bound *Mauretania*.

Revision had taken longer than expected but he knew Caresse would understand. 'You can now go ahead and finish it all,' he promised.[5] At last, for her – and for him – it was over.

Margaret Robson had been invaluable in the last trying weeks of preparation. Convinced of Hart's poetic stature she had devoted long hours to sorting and retyping the numerous loose sheets of paper that constituted her friend's lyrical arc before preparing a final copy to go to press. He named her 'Little Miss Twidget' in recognition of her devotion but knew there were other accolades she would have preferred. Neither the first nor the last woman to attempt his conversion, she frankly admitted she was in love with him and did all she could to help him to a change of heart. She faced formidable competition, however: at some stage since his return from France Hart had become involved with a young sailor from Alabama named Bob Stewart, who had enlisted in the Navy in 1927 and served aboard the USS *Milwaukee*, the vessel (and crew of which) Hart had admired from tempest-torn Nueva Gerona.[6] Like two orphans, the poet and the sailor spent Christmas together, relying on what Hart described to Caresse as 'incidental gin' to alleviate the dullness of the day itself as well as the sadness of imminent separation: after 2 January, when Stewart rejoined the *Milwaukee* for manoeuvres off Guantánamo Bay, they would be unlikely to meet again before June.[7] At some stage now or later he introduced his sailor to Sam Loveman, whose verdict – 'one of those uneducated but innately fine human beings for whom Hart conceived a sort of Whitmanian affection' – was somewhat evasive but broadly approving. Stewart, he noted, 'tried desperately to make Hart stop drinking and once, during one of Hart's jamborees, burst into tears and said that he could not stand what he was doing to himself'.[8] With the sailor's departure he and Hart began a prolonged and frequent correspondence – among the papers left behind by the poet after his death there were more letters from Stewart than from anyone else and if the only one that survives, written from Cuba early in 1930, suggests their destruction was no loss to epistolary art it at least vindicates Loveman's claim that Stewart cared for Hart's welfare. Describing shore leave in Florida and insisting he will not disembark in Jamaica because there are 'too many negroes there', the sailor rebukes his lover for waiting 'too long to write' before proceeding to his condition as publication of *The Bridge* approached:

> You haven't gotten a job yet. Well, I won't say what I think of you Hart but I'd like to. I'd like to see your book, Hart. Don't forget the copy your [*sic*] going to send me Hart. I guess I'll have to have some pictures made & send you one, really I haven't even one picture of myself at the present. You know I don't like to have my picture taken.[9]

There was a seriousness to the involvement that was apparent even to friends Hart did not introduce. They noticed the way he read the shipping news in order to follow the *Milwaukee* and Lorna Dietz remarked that Stewart was 'the only sailor [Hart] ever referred to affectionately in my presence'.[10] Whether or not friends understood, Grace, when she finally learned about Bob Stewart, was profoundly bewildered. 'Of course I can understand how their friendship began,' she told Loveman, 'but how Hart could have any deep seated affection for him, such as craving his regard, or depending upon him for any spiritual support, is beyond me.'

> In fact it is all very disgusting to me. Hart had so many other friends, that were stable and intelligent also, who would have been only too glad to help him to keep balanced.... Poets must be strange creatures! I am sure that no person that had no more education or understanding of life, than this Bob has, could ever bring much comfort to me.... Could it have been that Hart's nature was so starved for affection and approval that he sacrificed all other requirements for that, when he found it? That is the only construction I can put on it, and if so, how pitifully pathetic.[11]

Stewart duly rejoined his ship and only hours later, when he wrote to Caresse, Hart was 'already missing him a lot'.[12] As 1930 dawned, however, there were many other anxieties to distract him, with money as usual prominent among them. At the beginning of January financial considerations moved him down the road to cheaper lodgings: he kept his old telephone number, MAIN 8083, at 190 Columbia Heights but the view from this furnished basement could hardly prove inspiring. His inheritance was dwindling at an alarming rate, even as the lines of jobless men threaded their way around New York, but recent income from his poetry could hardly sustain him. The Crosbys had advanced $250 against Black Sun earnings from *The Bridge*, but after he had reimbursed Caresse for his voyage back from Paris only $50 remained. On 4 January, even though he had only just received Liveright's advance, he wrote to the publisher explaining that until he could find work 'I'm very hard put to it for necessary funds' and wondering if more money, 'to the extent of $300 or so', could be advanced. As an inducement he added that the London publisher Jonathan Cape was apparently 'very interested in "The Bridge", although he hasn't as yet seen the complete manuscript'.[13] Also that day Hart wrote to Henry Seidel Canby, who was keen to publish 'Cape Hatteras' in the *Saturday Review*. The 'Canby Crap Can' had been one of his favourite objects of abuse for some years but this was no time for pride and he told Canby, 'I am in need of whatever returns I can make from my work right now. So I would appreciate it if you could let me know very soon whether you can use "Hatteras".'[14] Liveright replied on 6 January, sympathetically but firmly reiterating the terms of the contract and suggesting that Hart broach money matters with the company treasurer, Arthur Bell. Five days later, however, with a gesture that went far towards explaining his popularity among authors, he sent a telegram of reconsideration: 'My conscience has been bothering me since I wrote you on Wednesday if you'll come in some time Monday morning I'll be glad to give you [an]other two hundred.'[15] With *The Bridge* on the Black Sun presses at 2 rue Cardinale, Hart worked at a poem in honour of Harry Crosby which Caresse and Eugene Jolas hoped to include in a special issue of *transition*. When he sent 'The Cloud Juggler' to Paris, however, it was with an apologetic letter: he knew the lyric was uninspired and promised he would not take offence if Caresse excluded it from the memorial publication.

On 14 January, after a hiatus of thirteen months, Hart resumed correspondence with Yvor Winters when he wrote to congratulate him on his recent essay in the *American Caravan* and on *Gyroscope*, the magazine Winters had started the previous year. Although Hart had no expectations that the latter would review *The Bridge* he admitted he had asked Caresse to send him a copy of the Black Sun edition, 'physically one of the most beautiful libros I know of'. Meanwhile he hoped his long silence would not be misunderstood but labours of completion had left him reluctant to conduct correspondence involving 'any further controversies, metrical, theoretical, ethical or what not'.[16]

Whether or not he was convinced by these claims, Winters's own enthusiasm for poetics and philosophy had, if anything, increased. While Hart had been roistering around Paris he had continued to write poetry and had pursued a course of reading and contemplation which resulted in the realignment of his aesthetic loyalties. During a prolonged sabbatical he had reconsidered the nature of life and art and emerged a rational stoic who distrusted mysticism as escapist and disingenuous. He began to write critical prose as well as poetry: the essay Hart admired, 'The Extension and Reintegration of the Human Spirit, through the Poetry Mainly French and American since Poe and Baudelaire', formed the kernel of his first book, *Primitivism and Decadence*. Furthermore he had begun his short-lived magazine, *Gyroscope*, the 'Statement of Purpose' of which had promulgated his new position. Henceforth he opposed 'all doctrines of liberation and emotional expansionism', all 'religious expansionism' and 'doctrines which advocate that the poet "express" his country (Whitmanian Rousseauism) or his time'.[17]

If Hart had read the manifesto attentively or applied its logic to his own work he would have foreseen the disagreements that loomed, if not the manner in which they were expressed: intellectual re-education had left Winters implacable and it was inevitable that the poetry of Hart Crane would now be subjected to the ruthless critical inquiry he applied to the insensate dead, an inquiry that took no account of authorial vulnerability or the expectations of friendship. Contrary to Hart's assumptions, Winters did want to review *The Bridge* and when the poet wrote again on 27 January it was to supply the details he would need for his byline: the Black Sun edition was to appear on 1 March, with 200 copies on Holland Van Gelder at $10 and fifty autographed copies on vellum at $25. The Liveright edition would appear on 1 April at a cost of $2.50. The mathematics of it all interested him less than the reviews, but with notices now promised by Tate, Cowley, Schneider and Winters, he was convinced that coverage would not only be extensive but sympathetic.

Preparations continued in Paris. Caresse was now ready to send out the review copies, the vellum edition, and a further twenty-five complimentary copies destined for opinion-mongers and cultural arbiters: T.S. Eliot, Rebecca West, D.H. Lawrence and Jonathan Cape were transatlantic exceptions in a largely American group. She was 'so excited' and 'wanted this edition to go down in history as a super-beautiful one in every way'.[18] Hart was now developing stage fright: sleepless by night, he read or roamed around exhibitions or thought about getting another job during the day before proceeding to whatever gathering the evening held in store – whether a Liveright party, or a dinner at the Hotel Roosevelt in honour of Waldo Frank, or a party at the Ritz to launch *Men, Marriage and Me*, the autobiography of the much-married screen actress Peggy Hopkins Joyce, who was the inspiration for Anita Loos's character Lorelei Lee.

The Black Sun trade editions were shipped at the end of February and on 6 March Hart went by appointment to Kahn's office to present his Maecenas with a specially bound copy ahead of the first reviews. But then it transpired that in contravention of his understanding with both publishers, literary editors of the various newspapers were inclined to withhold all notices of *The Bridge* until the appearance of the Liveright edition. It was a decision in which Hart had no involvement, but it was he who had to answer Caresse's rage when she wrote from a London clinic following a physical and emotional collapse. She was '*furious, really furious*' when she had worked so hard to produce the Black Sun edition six weeks before the release of Liveright's and when the critics Hart knew had promised they would write about the Paris edition separately. It was 'one of the most unkind and disloyal things' she had ever encountered: 'That is the way the world is run over there, I know, and it makes me contemptuous and disbelieve in human relations.'[19] It was not an easy letter to answer and Hart waited more than two weeks before assuring her that he had acted in good faith and that he was unable to influence literary editors, since 'as author of the book, I have certain boundaries of modesty to observe'.[20] In the interim, with 'distressing forebodings about the next meal', he wrote to Kahn for financial assistance or a word of recommendation. However acute his situation appeared, he wanted the financier to understand that he sought nothing more than temporary assistance: many reviews of *The Bridge* would be 'highly favorable' and he was confident that 'the resulting réclame' would soon lead to work in editing or advertising.[21] Kahn replied two days later with a cheque for $100 and apologies that he could not be more liberal, 'but I find myself overwhelmed with demands and commitments'.[22]

By the time Hart left for Patterson in mid-April the first reviews had appeared, with Herbert Weinstock opening the praise in the *Milwaukee Journal*. *The Bridge*, he felt, restored to American literature 'the spaciousness which it has lacked since Whitman and Melville'. If *White Buildings* had 'suggested to many careful readers that a truly major poet was beginning to speak in the United States', *The Bridge* confirmed that volume's promise and Weinstock insisted 'it must be recorded somehow, somewhere, to the credit of our era if it recognizes Hart Crane and rightly praises him instead of leaving his reputation lying about to be resurrected by our descendants'.[23] Vincent McHugh in the *New York Evening Post* was less emphatic but suggested there was splendour as well as inevitability in the imperfections of *The Bridge*. 'To propose so enormous and complex a mystical synthesis is almost to invite failure.' Nevertheless, 'this is perhaps the most remarkable attempt at an orchestrated modern American poem since Eliot's *Waste Land*'.[24] Horace Gregory in the *New York Herald-Tribune* gave the impression that *The Bridge* defeated his powers of classification. Insisting that Crane's poetry was betrayed by prose explication and that his work as a whole required literary sophistication despite its non-intellectual content, Gregory found that there was no one else writing in 1930 'with like emotional intensity'. If it was 'impossible to predict a future for Hart Crane', the publication of *The Bridge* had nevertheless vindicated his promise as 'an important American poet'.[25] In the *Nation* Granville Hicks was also preoccupied by the intensely poetic nature of Crane's writing: 'If it is the essence of poetry to say that which cannot be said in prose, Mr Crane's rank as a poet is extraordinarily high.' One could conceive of other poets who surpassed him in certain ways but there was no one else 'who can do as many things as well as he can'. *The Bridge* would be subjected to much critical scrutiny over the years, 'and it is probable that that scrutiny will find in it a greatness beyond the reach of a reviewer's superlatives'.[26] In the *New York Times Book Review* Percy Hutchinson suspected 'there is certain to be no unanimity of opinion' regarding *The Bridge* and wondered if 'clearness, in the usual acceptance of the term, is not desired by Hart Crane'. There was perhaps a new poetic technique underlying the work – a technique Hutchinson was tempted to call 'cubism in poetry' which entailed 'the piling up of startling and widely disparate word-structures so that for the mind the cumulative result is very like the cumulative result of skyscrapers for the eye when looked on through a mist'.[27]

For a poem, and an ambitious one at that, these opinions were doubly handsome in view of the fact that they appeared, not in recondite literary journals, but in major newspapers with wide circulations. Yet they mattered less to Hart than the published verdicts of his friends and it was these he awaited when he returned to New York in May. Meanwhile against expectations Bob Stewart appeared on shore leave and then Demetrius Mattoi, one of his Marseilles sailors, wrote from Corsica: 'Comme je me trouve encore à Cargesc je vous écris cette petite carte.... Peut-être que je vais à Pers vers le mois de juillet mais je ferai aller retour à Paris. J'attends avec patience votre charmante réponse ici à Cargesc puis on s'écrira plus souvent.'[28] Not all men of the sea were made remote by distance or linguistic difference: through Emil, Hart had got to know a one-time sailor with literary aspirations, an association with the underworld and a shifting identity to match, known variously as 'Carl Carlsen', 'Bobby Thompson' and 'Tommy', and for a while, Bill Brown noted, Hart and this dodger and survivor of the waterside world were 'very close'.

Easygoing as he was, Brown viewed the association with misgivings: 'Tommy', as he knew him, appeared to be 'a queer shadowy figure who seemed to have emerged from the underworld' and who was 'devoid of any moral sense'. He and Hart went drinking together in Sands Street, but Tommy confessed to Brown that 'he drank only when he couldn't procure drugs'. Inevitably short of cash, he also admitted that 'on several occasions he rolled Hart for whatever money he had'. Hart himself was either blind or indifferent to these tendencies and happily supplied letters of introduction to Robert Graves and Roy Campbell when Tommy went to Europe. Brown was amused to learn that he was received 'as a gifted American writer' but suspected he realized 'his association with the underworld was his main attraction among literary people'.[29] Through Emil, Tommy also met Eugene O'Neill and Walker Evans: the latter dismissed him as 'just another one of Crane's characters; a sphinx without a secret' but nevertheless suggested that he try and sell some of his short stories to *Hound and Horn*, and accordingly put him in touch with the young Lincoln Kirstein, then a contributing editor to the magazine.

'Who was Carlsen?' Kirstein would wonder, almost fifty years later. 'I never really discovered, much as I longed to know.' What he did establish, in the course of a brief affair in the early Thirties, was that Hart's was still a strong presence in the house Carlsen inhabited in lower Manhattan near the Hudson River. A two-storeyed, early nineteenth-century clapboard structure, the property seemed to Kirstein as though it had been awarded Carlsen 'by the guardian angels of Whitman and Melville'. The central house in a terrace of three, it was set back behind a gap in the street; on entering the single downstairs room one of the first items Kirstein noted, along with three odd brass candlesticks and a model ship inside a bottle, was 'a portrait of Crane, by Walker, in an old cork mat'. The room itself was 'bare, spotless, shipshape tidy' and could have been comfortable 'as a whaler's cabin anchored in Nantucket, New Bedford or Sag Harbor'.

Carlsen's appearance was fully consonant with the surroundings Hart would have found so pleasing: 'He wore well-worn, crisply laundered, old regulation U.S. Navy bell-bottoms, with a drop fly and thirteen buttons, in honor of the thirteen original colonies'. If the physical details of Hart's other sailors are lost, thanks to Kirstein we have a portrait of Carlsen which, though drawn with eyes much fonder than Brown's, is valid nevertheless: in his late thirties and with blond hair close-cropped, he was 'clean-shaven, leathery, no extra flesh, and apparently hard-bitten'. Hart's charms for Carlsen were of a different order altogether: Kirstein suspected he was dazzled by the poet, who had entered his life like some Prospero, 'transforming Manhattan and Brooklyn into enchanted islands'. In awe as he was, Carlsen proved slow to speak of Hart to the younger man: 'He shied away from mention of violence or perversity. For these there were no apologies ... such was the fiber of genius that Crane was licensed to play as he pleased. Crane was above praise or calumny.'[30]

Despite Carlsen's companionship – or because of it – Hart was more drunk and restless in New York than usual. Suddenly nostalgic for France, he cabled Caresse that he was about to embark for Paris, only to write an ashamed retraction the following day that mentioned an astrologer's recent promise 'that I'm due to be near the water, salt water, and perhaps on it'.[31] His friend Eda Lou Walton gratified him by announcing that she intended to include *The Bridge* in the course of contemporary poetry she taught at New York University and Radio WNYC invited him to give a five-minute reading from the poem on 24 May. Not for the first time, however, and certainly not for the last, the sea interceded in Hart's life: a shipwreck off the coast commandeered the ether for important messages with the result that all local radio programmes were cancelled. The overture was never repeated, and since an age without television depended entirely on radio to register the speech of contemporary celebrity, we have no record of Hart Crane's voice, the enthusiastic modulations and Midwestern inflexions of which always struck his auditors. In that sense, and remarkably for a twentieth-century poet who was familiar with technology and excited by its progress, he is as irrecoverable as any of his Elizabethan idols. With time on his hands that evening, Hart paid a call on Sam Loveman and found him once again entertaining H.P. Lovecraft, who was saddened to note that although the poet had shaved off his moustache he was now 'more weather-beaten & drink-puffed' than ever:

> When he entered, his discourse was of alcoholics in various phases ... but as soon as a bit of poetic and philosophic discussion sprang up, this sordid side of his strange dual personality slipped off like a cloak, & left him as a man of great scholarship, intelligence, & aesthetic taste, who can argue as interestingly & profoundly as anyone I have ever seen. Poor devil – he has 'arrived' at last as a standard American poet seriously regarded by all reviewers & critics; yet at the very crest of his fame he is on the verge of psychological, physical & financial disintegration, & with no certainty of ever having the inspiration to write a major work of literature again.[32]

That it was a major work appeared to be the consensus among *The Bridge*'s critics. In the *Saturday Review of Literature* Louis Untermeyer, remarking 'the accepted distortion and telescoping of time-space which has become, it seems, part of every modernist's equipment', singled out 'the apostrophic power, the strangely turned but undeniable eloquence which makes *The Bridge* an important contribution to recent American poetry'.[33] In a second review in the same publication William

Rose Benét protested that Crane 'does things to the English language that make us wish to scream in torment' but hailed him nevertheless as 'an outstanding modern writer' whose unsustainable ambition seemed almost integral to his stature: 'Some of Mr Crane's most successful moments are due to his sheer recklessness; he is an unbaffled though not always a successful Prometheus.'[34] And in *Theatre Guild Magazine* Mark Van Doren, doubting that Crane would ever 'have anything to say to ordinary men', acknowledged him 'that thing which we have been hearing about from France, a "pure poet" '.[35] Isidor Schneider, commending Hart for his lack of verbal and literary inhibition, dispensed generous bromides in the *Chicago Evening Post*[36] while in the *New Republic* Malcolm Cowley trod gingerly: 'The River', he wrote, was 'one of the most important poems of our age' and was almost rivalled in quality by 'Ave Maria', 'Cutty Sark' and 'The Dance'. Declaring *The Bridge* 'a unified group of fifteen poems' he judged it overall to be a qualified triumph. Its flaws struck him as 'obvious' – but he would not be the one to describe them: 'The faults of "The Bridge" I shall leave to other reviewers.'[37]

Since Cowley had always seen writers as inseparable from their work it followed that he would consider their vulnerabilities in tandem with their art. Not so Winters, whose assessment appeared in the June edition of *Poetry*. Allowing for the fact that Crane's was 'a genius of high order', Winters dismissed *The Bridge* as 'a form of hysteria' in which its author had endeavoured 'to emotionalize a theme to the point where both he and the reader will forget to question its justification'. He praised 'The River' and 'The Dance' but found 'Cape Hatteras' 'desperately sentimental' and 'Indiana' 'mawkish and sentimental'. There were lines of exquisite strength, of 'pure electricity', but the poem lacked 'restraint', it depended on 'moment-to-moment inspiration' rather than cogency and it declined to expose ecstasy to rational inquiry: in short it was a monument of foolish anti-intellectual writing. There was an element of justice in these strictures but the pomposity and didacticism of the article would have annoyed a complete stranger let alone a friend and there was no excuse for Winters's most extravagant claims: to say that 'the flaws in Mr Crane's genius' were 'so great as to partake ... almost of a public catastrophe' was ridiculous and unreasonable, especially when he had known about *The Bridge* and the aims of its author for over three years. And here lay the principal hypocrisy – his review fell between the two stools of loyalty and objectivity, because Winters knew too much and disliked what he knew. He understood perfectly well that *The Bridge* was not concerned with complexities of human emotion but with a myth and the society that myth had created. It was therefore irrelevant to complain that only one poem in the entire sequence 'endeavours to treat clearly of an individual human relationship' and insolent to suggest on that basis that Crane was 'temperamentally unable to understand a very wide range of experience' and that even his best lyrics thus had about them 'something of the fragility of innocence'. The fact was that it was not Hart's breadth of experience – so much wider than his own – that Winters questioned, but the validity of the

experience itself: how could Crane's sexual disposition allow him an understanding of his fellow beings or permit him a mature comprehension of the human
emotions?[38]

Hurt and angry, Hart replied on 4 June, conceding that Winters had the right
to change his mind, even to print opinions which were at variance with much that
they had privately agreed in correspondence over the last three years, but wondering whether Winters's probity as a critic was enhanced 'by permitting your own
special notions about the author's personality to blur the text before you'. As far
as Hart could see he had taken 'a good many of my ethical and privately expressed
aesthetic convictions' and then adopted 'exaggeration, misappropriation – or just
confusion' to substantiate his own prejudices about the poem, without bothering
to read it carefully or systematically. It was obvious from what he said about
'Indiana' that he had misread it; and if he now liked 'The River' less than he had
done before simply because it was part of a longer poem that enshrined the genius
of Whitman, so be it. What annoyed him, however, was that 'you ascribe, again
and again, quite different objectives on my part than anything said in the text
could reasonably warrant' and then 'on the same basis, pronounce the performance
botched'. Winters knew Hart had never intended to write an epic in the orthodox
sense, not least because 'I doubt that our present stage of cultural development is
so ordered yet as to provide the means or method' for such a treatment. And why,
in his reading of 'The Dance', did Winters 'confuse the intentionally relative with
some interpolated "absolute"' of his own? Hart had not set out to offer 'some law
of the Medes or Persais [sic]', merely to evoke 'an identification of myself (or the
reader) for the moment with the Indian savage while he is in process of absorption into the elements of the pure nature-world about him'. Of course they would
have to agree to differ about Whitman – but Hart began to wonder, as Winters's
vision 'develops, narrows, or focuses' (and he could choose whichever verb most
appealed), whether it had shifted altogether from poetry towards some 'pseudo-
philosophical or behavioristic field of speculation'. Munson had gone that way
already, but Hart knew, not least because of the '"moment-to-moment" inspira-
tional limp' Winters had already ascribed to him, that he would not be following
them. It had taken more than five years 'of sustained something-or-other' to complete *The Bridge*, and 'with more actual and painful "differentiation of experience"
into the bargain' than he suspected Winters himself would ever risk. Of course –
eternal cry of all artists – the result had fallen short of the original heroic vision,
but for all that he knew he was more than just 'the wreckage' Winters beheld, and
that his lyrical flights outdistanced 'the cog-walk gestures of a beetle in a sand
pit'.[39]

Winters's review terminated the correspondence and the friendship: the two
men had been brought together by the written word and the written word duly
estranged them, but for Hart it was a bitter and humiliating episode and one he
was unable to forget. He sent Allen Tate a copy of his rejoinder, which he told

Isidor Schneider he had been forced to write lest Winters interpret his silence as acquiescence. Henceforth, he joked, he would not address subjects beyond Winters's experience or approval: 'Poets should defer alluding to the sea ... until Mr Winters has got an invitation for a cruise!'[40] Tate replied on 10 June: Winters, he reassured his friend, was perplexing – astute about poetry but often loyal to mediocre poets, highly intelligent yet obtuse about human relations, devoid of tact or humour but with 'a certain nobility of character'. Difficult as he was, however, Tate shared several of his reservations about *The Bridge* and the laurels it bestowed:

> Your vision of American life comes from Whitman, or from the same sources in the American consciousness as his. I am unsympathetic to this tradition, and it seems to me that you should be too. The equivalent of Whitmanism in the economic and moral aspect of America in the last sixty years is the high-powered industrialism that you, no less than I, feel is a menace to the spiritual life in this country.[41]

Gentler than Winters, and more tactful, Tate was nevertheless disinclined to praise a poem he found unsatisfactory simply for the sake of its author's feelings and when his review appeared in *Hound and Horn* at the end of June it found certain lyrics supremely beautiful but *The Bridge* as a whole symbolically and structurally incoherent. Indeed philosophically it seemed no more than 'a sentimental muddle of Walt Whitman and the pseudo-primitivism of Sherwood Anderson and Dr. W.C. Williams, raised to a vague and transcendental reality'. Like Winters before him, he worried that the poem lacked intellectual incisiveness: it represented the 'rejection of a rational and qualitative will' and as such continued 'the main stream of romanticism in the last hundred years'.[42]

Once again, rather than risk appearing to agree by remaining silent, Hart acknowledged Tate's 'admirable review', his glum and wounded tone indicating just how unadmirable he had found it. Even if his friend had been right to place *The Bridge* at the end of the Romantic tradition, a tradition Hart himself was by no means convinced was spent, at least he indicated the significance of the poem as a link to whatever new poetry was emerging. Increasingly, however, Hart was convinced that poetry of any kind would be undervalued – not least by critics: Winters, Munson and other such commentators were no longer interested in poetry but in some 'cure-all' that could 'sum up the universe in one impressive little pellet'. His own work was, he fully conceded, 'too personal' to qualify as a philosophical panacea – but by the same token were not Coleridge, Keats and Marlowe also damned? And he promised now that if he did write any more poetry it would be 'at least as personal as the idiom of *White Buildings*'. Tate had rebuked him for 'sentimentality in my attitude toward Whitman' and he admitted that the address delivered in 'Cape Hatteras' 'exceeds any exact evaluation of the man'. But why argue about him anyway, when Tate appeared never to have read *Democratic*

Vistas and the poet's numerous other pronouncements against industrialism and materialism, 'of which you name him the guilty and hysterical spokesman'?[43] In reply Tate urged Hart to read the review more than once, since 'a first reading emphasises what we are looking for or don't want to see'. His predictions about the Romantic movement had been tentative, he stressed, but as for Hart's promise – or threat – that in future he would write lyrics in the personal manner of *White Buildings*, Tate was happy: 'You have never surpassed certain poems of the first book, and I think it is something of a compliment to believe that you never will.'[44]

Looking back on this period, Malcolm Cowley remarked that Hart was now 'running through his friends and admirers like an heir through his rich estate' as the fluctuations in mood triggered by feelings of failure and intellectual ostracism led to one drinking bout after another. He was no longer invited to many large parties after the way he had repaid the hospitality of his country neighbour Montgomery Schuyler by drunkenly smashing his collection of records, attempting to throw his phonograph from an upstairs window and then demanding, 'My father is a millionaire. Who is *your* father?'[45] Despite this insult Schuyler included Hart among his Fourth of July guests, as did Slater Brown and Peter Blume, but if these friends were apparently spared drunken scenes, Addie was not. One evening in early July, when Hart stormed drunkenly from the house to visit a bootlegger, she locked him out: he regained access by smashing in a door and window, after which he lurched around the house with a smoking lamp, threatening reprisals. Claiming she intended to sell the house, Addie told him to collect his possessions and leave – for good – so he moved himself and his treasures to Eleanor Fitzgerald's house twenty minutes' walk away at Gaylordsville, Connecticut. He made the move seemingly without remorse, dismissing the old woman and the farm that had sheltered him for years with a shrugging explanation to Tate that he had always been slow 'to relinquish some hold or connection that has long since ceased to yield me anything but annoyance'.[46]

Fitzi knew she was taking in a difficult guest but no sooner had Hart arrived than he announced his plan to spend two weeks in New Hampshire where he would celebrate his birthday at Joy Farm as the guest of e.e. cummings and his wife. On 17 July he sent instructions to Lorna, who was in New York but due to accompany him to New Hampshire, to get 'two quarts of alky at the French place, 327 West 26th. It's only two bucks a quart there – and I'll halve the cost with you'.[47] The expedition appears to have been no more than partially successful: far from seeking tranquillity in New Hampshire, Hart and Lorna turned their back on views of Mount Chocorua to play the Victrola and one night, haunted by feelings of inferiority to cummings, Hart woke the entire house by persistently asking Lorna if she thought their host liked him or merely tolerated him. Insecurity was aggravated by pain from a rotting tooth and then by an attack of boils that developed under his arm: by the time he returned to Gaylordsville the limb was too swollen to allow for much writing or typing. Awaiting him were birthday greetings from Aunt Sally – who revealed that the Villa Casas had been stripped of its contents and was occupied by squatters – and from Grace, who enclosed a recent photograph of herself along with congratulations on *The Bridge* and announced that she was now working at a hotel in Oak Park, the Illinois suburb where she had been born.

Her news did nothing to dispel the gloom that settled on her son as the summer advanced. He read the *Divine Comedy* and told his and Loveman's friend Mony Grunberg that Dante had made him realize 'how much more than ever I have to work to accomplish anything'.[48] Little wonder that Peter Blume, who saw much of him while he was at Fitzi's, was convinced 'his depressive side was becoming deeper and more pronounced'. Blume remembered sitting with him 'on the side of Fitzi's house by the pump' and listening as Hart complained of being 'all pumped out' after publication of *The Bridge* and doubtful that 'he could ever write a word of poetry again'.[49] He quarrelled with Fitzi, whose dog he kicked because it barked while he was listening to jazz records, and with Emil, who came up one weekend between voyages and politely suggested that Hart should put his enema bag away when not using it rather than leaving it for all to see in the garden privy. As Emil knew, Hart had always suffered from constipation – but if the poet's body had remained the same, the temper and self-esteem were increasingly volatile. He was bitterly affronted by the suggestion and went to Sue Brown in tears: 'I'm just trying to keep myself sweet and clean, Sue!'[50] An empty present threatened a miserable future: without money or project Hart felt doomed once more to enlist in New York's army of hacks and copy-writers unless he could think of an alternative. But he – or else a friend – did, and on 5 August he sent for the papers needed to make formal application for a fellowship from the John Simon Guggenheim Memorial Foundation.

Established only five years previously by Senator and Mrs Simon Guggenheim in memory of their dead son 'for better understanding among the citizens of the American republics', the Foundation disbursed annual fellowships to scientists and artists and others whose pursuits 'dignify, ennoble and delight mankind'. On 8 August Henry Allen Moe, the Foundation's chief administrative officer, dispatched explanatory literature and an application form for fellowships for 1931–32 and Hart set about answering its requirements. Applying for a fellowship in 'creative writing', he supplied as referees Waldo Frank, Louis Untermeyer, Otto Kahn, Edmund Wilson, Paul Rosenfeld and Henry Seidel Canby. His academic, professional and technical accomplishments, as given in answer to the form's questions, looked meagre and he erred on the side of self-flattery when describing his linguistic aptitude: 'French. Can read, speak and write moderately well. I studied German while in high school, but through desuetude have lost what proficiency I had attained.' As for his career in advertising, he supplied summary details before explaining, 'Inasmuch as this sort of work is so alien to any interests or qualifications pertaining to the realm and object of the Guggenheim Fellowships – as well as to my own creative concerns – it would seem irrelevant to cite particular dates and tenures.' Hart had no specific literary ambitions in the summer of 1930 but since the Foundation required applicants to describe their plans for study, and since overseas residence was a condition of subsidy, he had to extemporize. His application, he claimed, had been spurred by the desire to combine freedom for literary composition with European study. 'I am interested in characteristics of European culture, classical and romantic, with especial reference to contrasting elements implicit in the emergent features of a distinctive American poetic consciousness.' Europe had already given him some poetic stimulus, as elements in *The Bridge* might attest. Now he hoped to return there, and to combine his 'creative projects' with 'modern and medieval French literature and philosophy' which 'interest me particularly'.[51]

He completed and mailed the application on 29 August 1930 and resigned himself to waiting: the new fellowships would be announced in March. In the meantime his referees submitted their endorsements; four were perfunctory but Waldo Frank hailed his friend as 'perhaps the profoundest poet of our generation'[52] and Rosenfeld, in the course of a long panegyric, described Hart as 'the most promising figure on the poetic horizon in America', whose lyrics 'seem destined to figure in future anthologies by reason of their sheer poetic inspiration'.[53] Some weeks later, ever loyal to the cause of letters, Allen Tate took it upon himself to write an unsolicited reference which asserted that 'of all the poets who have applied [Crane] is the best' and insinuated that the Guggenheim would almost have to answer to history if it failed to assist him: 'Perhaps it would be nice for the Foundation to have his name on record fifty years from now. It would be hazardous to say so much of any of the rest of us.'[54]

The recommendation was written from Benfolly, the house in Tennessee to which Tate invited Hart at the end of the summer. The southern life the property embodied was alternately a subject of facetiousness and outrage to the poet from Ohio and Tate knew that when drunk Hart was likely to 'reproach me for being Southern'. Worse still, 'He imagined me (in his own words) "beating negroes until their backs bled". He meant it, and that just about took the measure of [his] sense of political and social reality.'[55] Now, however, was not the moment for enlightenment. As Hart explained when declining Tate's offer, he had to get some kind of job soon, 'or at least be on the scene of interrogation, prison, palace, and supplication'.[56] Despite their recent differences, he would remain at Fitzi's until she closed her house and returned to New York for the winter. It was from Gaylordsville that Hart sent an inscribed copy of *The Bridge* to John Roebling, whose grandfather and father had designed and built Brooklyn Bridge, along with a letter that described the East River span itself as 'the matchless symbol of America and its destiny' and expressed the hope that Roebling would find the poem 'in its way as ambitious and complicated' as the structure which had inspired it.[57] Incapacitated by illness, Roebling left the reply to his wife Margaret, who informed Hart on 23 August that Roebling already owned a copy which he was in the habit of reading aloud to his family. 'It is a cause of gratification to the family that the Brooklyn Bridge which is very near to their hearts should have inspired so remarkable a poem.'[58] *The Bridge* went into a second printing in September but it would be a long time before its author saw any remuneration. Desperate for funds again, he applied to Kahn for assistance on 9 September but the financier was in Europe and his dependants went unheard – by the time Hart and Fitzi returned to New York at the end of September the poet told Mony Grunberg that poverty 'engrosses, nay inundates me'.[59] During the summer he had relinquished his basement in Columbia Heights as an economy, so he was now compelled to stay in Fitzi's spare bed at 45 Grove Street before moving to a cheap room at the Hotel Albert and then a cheaper one at the Hotel St George in Brooklyn. His mood was improved at the beginning of October when it was announced in *Poetry* magazine that *The Bridge* had been awarded the Helen Haire Levinson prize of $200 and another stroke of luck soon followed, when two acquaintances at *Fortune*, Russell Davenport and Archibald MacLeish, suggested to their editor, Parker Lloyd-Smith, that the article he envisaged to mark the imminent completion of George Washington Bridge should be written by the acclaimed laureate of bridges himself. Lloyd-Smith liked the idea and proposed, after meeting Hart, that he might also like to write about J. Walter Teagle, the president of Standard Oil of New Jersey.

With notebook in hand Hart made several visits to the site of the construction over the Hudson River and if, as Slater Brown speculated, he was plagued by 'an awe-inspiring hangover and a sulphuric breath', he managed nevertheless to interview engineers, speak to crane operators, and ascend the bridge's towers in the construction elevators. Indeed enthusiasm gave way only once, when he declined to cross the span on its temporary catwalk 200 feet above the water.[60] When completed the following year George Washington Bridge seemed to Le Corbusier the most beautiful bridge in the world – but inspiration completely failed Hart and with no more than jottings to show for his fieldwork he began the second article, conducting what he considered a successful interview with Teagle, despite a black eye sustained the previous evening at a party. Again, however, it was at the typewriter that problems began: as he told William Wright, 'when I come to write it up in a typical *Fortune* style the jams gather by the hundred'.[61] In the course of these frustrations Wilbur Underwood arrived in New York, followed shortly afterwards by Bob Stewart. Underwood was assured that the air assumed 'a pleasant warmth' as a result of Stewart's advent but Hart's concentration was bound to suffer and when he completed his essay on George Washington Bridge it was rejected by Lloyd-Smith.[62] By 20 November he was ready to submit a rough draft of his article on Teagle but since acceptance and payment could still lie weeks away he asked Underwood for a loan of $10 before turning to Wright for money the following day. 'Unmitigated anxiety has a highly corrosive effect on the resilience of the imagination,' he informed his boyhood friend, at the same time acknowledging that he was far from being alone in his distress: 'New York is full of the unemployed, more every day, and the tension evident in thousands of faces isn't cheerful to contemplate.'[63] In reply Wright praised his friend for 'living life dangerously' for the sake of his art, thus soothing his pride prior to lining his pockets: he enclosed two cheques, one for immediate needs, the second for use if *Fortune* failed, as well as a practical suggestion – had Hart ever considered teaching? The poet replied on 29 November, touched and amused that Wright had applied such a 'Nietzschean' interpretation to his 'almost chronic indigence'. The fact was, however, that 'my exposures to rawness and to risk have been far too inadvertent, I fear, to deserve any such honourable connotations'. The Teagle article was now awaiting approval but in the event of rejection he was resigned to selling books for Doubleday-Doran. With the Depression, there was no work to be had in advertising and as for Wright's suggestion that he teach, 'You may have forgotten that I left East High without even a diploma ... so who am I, therefore, to rule a class!'[64]

Lloyd-Smith returned the rough draft of the Teagle article for modifications but it was lost in the mail, or so its author insisted, and with its disappearance Hart's career in journalism ended. Thanks to Wright's second cheque, as well as an emergency $100 lent by Liveright, he survived in New York for another two weeks, finding comfort alternately in the company of Lorna, Loveman, Slater Brown and Margaret Robson, or else in the gallon of whiskey he now kept permanently at the foot of his bed. In December Sinclair Lewis, the first of his countrymen to be so honoured, was awarded the Nobel Prize for Literature but if American writing finally seemed to have attained international legitimacy New York was a bleak place for its practitioners and on 12 December, having exhausted his list of possible creditors, Hart telephoned his father to say he was coming home for Christmas.

Glad of an extra pair of hands in a busy season, CA put his son to work wrapping packages in the Crane store on Euclid Avenue in Cleveland, where for the next two weeks Hart drove each morning from Chagrin Falls. Christmas itself passed peacefully and when he wrote to Sam Loveman on 29 December it was to report his 'maidenly complexion and a bulging waistline'. He was using the new Canary Cottage stationery and assured Loveman that its anodyne slogan – 'The place to bring your guest' – would have been changed to something more assertive had he been consulted: 'The fourth word would still have begun with "b" but there would have been more action implied in the order of the other letters sustituted, or I'm no befriender of monks and monkery.' But this was no time for flippant ribaldry – he had no idea what sort of work he would do next or when he would return to New York. He had given up drinking on arrival in Ohio and his metropolitan excesses now seemed very far away. For himself, and for everyone, the future seemed serious and uncertain: 'Gone is that glittering eye of Sands St. mid-nights, erstwhile so compelling; and the ancient mariner is facing the new year with all the approved trepidations of the middle west business man, approved panic model of 1931.'[65] Once the holidays were over Hart assumed the duties of handyman and waxed, polished, repaired and decorated any corner of Canary Cottage that fell short of CA's exacting standards as well as making frames for the reproduction paintings his father sold as a subsidiary business. Left holding the fort when the elder Crane took his wife on a three-week honeymoon to Cuba, he wrote regularly to friends in New York and was pleased to learn his fame was not entirely forgotten when the *Nation* included him in its Honor Roll for 1930 for *The Bridge*, 'a poem unusual in technique, original in imagery and affirmative in tone'.[66] And on 21 January the Guggenheim Foundation requested copies of *White Buildings* and *The Bridge*: it was a good sign, but to Mony Grunberg he admitted 'to a certain tremorousness' as the date for the announcement of the new fellows approached.[67]

He read – Spinoza, Blake, James Branch Cabell's *Jurgen*, and John Dos Passos's *42nd Parallel*, which had also been commended by the *Nation* and which struck Hart as 'good' even though 'Dos has yet to create a full portrait'. He paid courtesy calls on aunts and cousins nearby and although Bill Sommer refused to see him – for reasons never clear – he was still welcome at Laukhuff's, so once a week he went into Cleveland, to buy books, use the library and attend a concert with the Rychtariks. He received numerous letters from Bob Stewart, who was now looking forward to leaving the Navy in March, he read former President Calvin Coolidge's daily advice in the newspaper and he listened to WJZ and WEAF radio. His bad tooth was extracted, he repaid some of the money he owed William Wright, once in a while he saw a film and after their return he spent quiet evenings with Bess and his father. CA liked to pontificate about the Depression and as he and Hart sat together, with discord and their respective triumphs behind them, the poet began to suspect that Clarence Crane was almost happy in the national unhappiness. 'My father, you can visualize his type, is actually "enjoying" the depression, or at least his incessant howls about it,' he complained to Lorna. 'Despite the losses personally involved, I think he will actually be disappointed if matters improve in less than five years.'[68] CA assumed his son had come home for good but by the middle of February Hart was restless and when he listened to Roxy's Sunday morning concerts he thought nostalgically of how he and Loveman had once heard them together, 'both looking out that window on the harbor'. He particularly disliked Sundays – so many people at Canary Cottage and so little time to himself – but 'no one is to blame', he told Loveman, 'I don't mean that at all. I've really been treated very squarely considering the family prejudices and limited imagination.'[69]

Yet if he was restless in Ohio, Hart also wondered how at home he would feel if he ever returned to New York. The letters his friends wrote and the opinions they published in their various magazines alerted him to the shift in intellectual opinion which was gaining momentum as the Depression deepened. The days when artists devoted themselves to art were over, it seemed, and now, as everyone sought solutions to economic, rather than aesthetic problems, loyalties were dividing around causes which held no interest whatever for this apolitical poet. 'When they get it all decided, Capitalism or Communism,' he suggested to Waldo on 19 February, 'then I'll probably be able to resume a few intensities.' Until that time, however, 'I can't muster much of anything to say to anyone.' Suddenly he felt isolated and outdated, a 'disappointed romantic' who remembered the days when America's literary future seemed so bright and when poets disputed the future of poetry, not the identity of the next President. What had changed and where had he gone wrong? Had he made 'too many affable compromises' in his self-appointed task to identify and articulate his country's mythic nature, or was America herself now different?[70] The present messy reality was certainly far different from the destiny he had envisaged when he conceived *The Bridge*. Perhaps he had been foolish to doubt Spengler; perhaps after all decline was inescapable, even for the United States. He longed to leave Ohio but not if it meant running to New York. His escape had to be more distant and ambitious but unless the Guggenheim selected him he was unable to see how he could escape or where he could go. On 28 February the Foundation asked how much money he thought he would need if awarded a fellowship. In reply he suggested a total of $2,550 – $400 for travel, $1,300 for living expenses, $300 for tuition, $250 for books and $300 for miscellaneous costs – and as March dawned he steeled himself for the announcement. Finally on 13 March Henry Allen Moe wrote to say that his application for a fellowship had been successful and that he had been awarded a grant of $2,000, the maximum allowed to bachelors that year. Bess Crane knew her stepson 'had been watching the mail very closely that week'. One evening, 'I saw him hurrying up the walk, and calling "Father, Father, I got it", and throwing his arms around his father, both of them laughing and crying like children.'[71]

PART SIX

Mexico

March 1931–April 1932

I am not ready for repentance;
Nor to match regrets. For the moth
Bends no more than the still
Imploring flame.

'LEGEND'

20

Hart was jubilant. At a stroke he had been rescued from insolvency and indirection: at a word *The Bridge*'s reception was redeemed and a lifetime of aspiration to fame and greatness was vindicated. Knowing nothing of the rivalry he had outdistanced – and the Foundation had received more than 700 applications from the United States alone – he wrote to Henry Allen Moe on 16 March to acknowledge the award and spoke of 'a stimulating sense of pride and gratitude' at 'this evidence of trust in my abilities and character' and pledged his 'utmost efforts' to justify the Foundation's decision. Situated as he was 'among the vast horde of the unemployed', and with 'nothing of consequence' to detain him, he hoped to sail for France 'for constructive work and study' before the middle of April.[1]

News of the honour was published in the Cleveland press but the knowledge that Bob Stewart was passing through New York on his way to beginning civilian life in Alabama intensified Hart's restlessness and without stopping to relish his local fame he left for the East, seen off at Cleveland station by CA, Bess and the Rychtariks. Since it had been agreed that his fellowship would run from 1 April, he soon moved on to Connecticut to pack, and because Fitzi was still in New York he stayed at Matthew Josephson's farm at Sherman, which had been rented for the winter by Peter Blume and his wife. Muriel Maurer, a young fashion editor, arrived for the weekend, as did Malcolm Cowley, and later that day the Blumes and their guests found themselves involved in Hart's travel preparations, which in Cowley's eyes acquired the aspect of a valedictory ritual. His possessions were scattered all over Tory Hill: now, preparing to leave America for a year, he decided to entrust his greatest treasures – assorted books, the trophy of African arms and a silver-bronze 'Sea Gull' sculpted by Gaston Lachaise – to the Blumes and to distribute other items among his friends. Muriel received a vermilion sash, Blume was given CA's old evening clothes, his wife acquired a sailor's shirt and a pea jacket, and Cowley himself was given a belt embossed with a large brass anchor. He noted that the donations were made 'with a warmth and thoughtfulness that made them precious' but there was a strange finality to the ceremony, 'as though we were Roman soldiers casting lots for his garments'.

The evening passed uneventfully, not least because the Blumes, mindful of last summer's dramas, poured their guests one drink each and then removed the bottle, the disappearance of which Cowley was surprised to note Hart watched 'in unaccustomed silence'. The following morning, while Blume worked at *South of Scranton*, the two writers set out for a walk and a talk – their first in many weeks and, it turned out, their last. In February Malcolm and Peggy had separated: if painful, the decision had been friendly, but Cowley felt stale and trapped, despite his recent promotion at the *New Republic*, and longed more than anything to forget his woes by travelling to Europe to write a book. Yet when he considered Hart, who now confronted that very opportunity, he found him pensive if not dejected: 'He talked without bitterness about the critics who had condemned *The Bridge* and wondered if they weren't partly right; "But – " he said, and left the word hanging.' In retrospective mood, 'he seemed to have acquired the tired wisdom about himself that is sometimes revealed by dissipated men'. As for the Guggenheim fellowship, it appeared already to have become a worry as well as a blessing: experience had taught him how distracting France could be, and for all his claims to the Foundation he had no real idea what he would do there. On the spur of the moment Cowley suggested Mexico instead. Having recently returned from a visit there, he spoke evocatively of its varied landscape and fused cultures. Cigars, rum and servants were cheap and if hearsay was anything to go by, 'the sexual customs of the Aztecs were much like those of the Arabs'. Hart 'took a few steps in silence'. How can he have been so obtuse? France was not his domain – why else had he achieved so little there? He was and always had been an Americanist, and now he thought about it his next project had been staring him in the face since the inspired summer of 1926, when he decided to write a blank verse tragedy about the Conquest of Mexico. 'Suddenly,' Cowley recalled, 'he started talking about the long poem on Cortez he had planned to write' and then recited four lines of the poem which 'seemed to open gates for him'.

Continuing their cautious hospitality, the Blumes provided nothing to drink at lunch but Hart nevertheless began an enthusiastic monologue involving Mexico and then Marlene Dietrich, 'whose voice, he said, came straight from Tutankhamen's tomb'. His face, normally grey in the morning, had gone vivid red and when Ebie Blume disappeared to the pantry, she understood why – Hart had found the bottle opened the previous evening and hidden it for personal consumption. The rest of the day passed according to what were now recognized as the predictable phases of his intoxication. Enthusiasm and affection for everything and everybody gave way to elaborate and inventive discourse. 'Everything reminded him of something else: landscapes, of musical compositions; poems, of skyrockets or waterfalls; persons, of birds, animals, or piles of grimy snow; he could abstract the smile from a woman's face and make us see it in the design of the mantelpiece.' The third phase was one of suspicious silence, in which he 'glared into the shadows as if in search of enemies' and while he was still in this mood lunch ended, the afternoon ebbed and it was time to return to New York. During the twenty-mile journey to the station the car's lights illuminated the white fences and farmhouses of the route and Hart moaned from the back seat, 'Oh, the white fences, oh, the interminable white Connecticut fences.' He slept in the train and at Grand Central Station, with Cowley still looking on, he entered his fourth phase, with its nocturnal waterfront quest: 'As I watched him almost running with his two bags toward the taxi stand, I thought that he was obeying the iron laws of another country than ours, and I felt that his weekend had been a sort of furlough from the dead.'[2]

Back in New York, Hart discussed Cowley's suggestion with Frank, who had spent much of the last two years lecturing in Central and South America. His recent *America Hispana* had traced the cultural history of the Latin republics and he smiled when he learned that Hart had revived the idea of dramatizing that first moment of fusion, when Hernando Cortés met and then overthrew Montezuma II and his Aztec Empire. Despite his approval, however, Frank had reservations about his friend's plan to live in Mexico: 'I warned him it was going to threaten his stability.'[3] He understood what happened to alcohol-starved Americans once they started to drink in the thin air of the country's mountainous altitudes. More than that, 'I knew how strong the death wish was in Mexico.'[4] As it was hard to translate these misgivings into a specific warning, Waldo contented himself with making Hart promise he would avoid alcohol for the first month and the latter resolved to see if his new destination was acceptable to the Guggenheim.

He met Moe on 27 March and to his relief the adjustment was quickly made: a cheque for $300 and a letter of credit for the residual $1,700 were handed over and he was assured that henceforth it would be easy to group him with the Latin American exchange fellows. In return, noting that Hart was 'a bit tight', Moe decided to broach the delicate matter of his drinking, which had been the subject of some debate when the Guggenheim Foundation's Advisory Committee met to deliberate. It had been feared that Hart's 'liquorish tendencies', as Moe described them, might bring disgrace upon the Foundation and the final decision to make the award was something of an act of faith. Seeing his condition now Moe wondered if that confidence had been misplaced and gave Hart what he later called 'a pretty stiff talk'.[5]

Pledges were made once more and the poet left to contact his old Village acquaintance Katherine Anne Porter, now a resident of Mexico City and apparently happy to have Hart to stay until he found accommodation of his own. Favourable omens persisted when he arranged his passage: he would sail for Vera Cruz on 4 April on the SS *Orizaba*, the vessel which had carried him to Cuba at the start of his prodigious summer. Once his itinerary was established he wrote to confirm his arrival with Katherine Anne, also a newly appointed Guggenheim fellow, and asked her – with an innocence made ironic by later events – 'What happens when Guggenheimer meet Guggenheimer?'[6] He gave interviews to newspapers, spent an afternoon buying dungarees with Walker Evans and established that he could open an account at Anglo-South American Bank, the agent in Mexico City for Guaranty Trust – although by then, having paid for his ticket and discharged all his debts, he had already spent the $300 advanced by Moe.

On 28 March he attended a party given by the editors of the *New Republic* in a Fifth Avenue penthouse: among those assembled were Lincoln Kirstein, Edmund Wilson, Paul Rosenfeld, Walker Evans and the author, critic and essayist Dwight Macdonald but not, happily, any senior officials from the Guggenheim Foundation. Kirstein registered a fracas in one corner of the otherwise sedate gathering: 'two men traded punches' and there were calls to 'chuck the son of a bitch out'. Then 'Crane, slight, with rumpled shock of hair, helped by hands other than his own, was chucked out'. A while later the poet reappeared, 'pursued by a small, furious taxi driver' who had been enlisted to drive him to a Sands Street bar, only to discover on arrival that he had no money for the fare. A scuffle ensued but Hart had somehow persuaded the driver that if he took him back to the party he would be able to collect money there. The cabbie was soon mollified with alcohol while Hart, 'filthy, sodden, desperate', roamed the party 'remorseful but morose' looking for money, after which he and his reluctant chauffeur left once more. To Kirstein's astonishment nobody seemed surprised or dismayed by the poet's behaviour apart from Hart himself when he began to sober up: then came 'his patient penitence, muffled apologies, his small boy's pathetic, instinctive good manners'.[7]

At another party on 3 April, this time to bid the poet farewell, Hart's actor friend Charlie Walker introduced him to a distinguished, if improbable, guest, Dr Hans Zinsser, Professor of Bacteriology and Immunology at Harvard Medical School. Zinsser was also bound for Vera Cruz, but it was only during the course of his second day at sea, when he met the doctor aboard the *Orizaba*, that Hart established the coincidence and found that he and the professor were to be fellow travellers as far as Mexico City. If not quite a citizen of the world, Zinsser was far from being a mundane tourist: as a poet, wit, philosopher and polymath, he promised entertaining companionship during the voyage, which had been undertaken, like so many of his travels, in the name of health and science. In 1915 he had worked in Serbia for the American Red Cross Sanitary Commission and in 1923 he served in the Soviet Union as Sanitary Commissioner for the League of Nations. A member of numerous distinguished bodies and the recipient of many awards, he was to become a national figure in 1935 with the publication of *Rats, Lice and History*, a book in which he found political and destructive mankind to be less honourable than the rodents and insects it despised. His career was cut short by leukaemia but before his death he completed an autobiography, *As I Remember Him: The Biography of R.S.*, a best-seller about his own Romantic Self which was written in the third person and told the story of a life devoted to the eradication of typhus. In 1940 his devotion was crowned with success when, with only months ahead of him, he announced that a method for mass vaccination had been developed.

In 1931, when he and Hart became friends, he was determined to establish whether rats were inter-epidemic carriers of the disease and having received a rudimentary inoculation he embarked for Mexico, accompanied by Dr Maximiliano Ruiz Castaneda, with letters of accreditation supplied by the State and War departments and a sinister cargo smuggled aboard with the complicity of a well-bribed steward: six typhus-infected rats in cages. For Hart, already intrigued by stories of the decimation white men had unleashed when they brought European diseases to virgin Mexico, Zinsser's experiment was symbolically as well as scientifically fascinating and its details occupied many hours of talk during the voyage, as did the professor's plans to combat hookworm in Abyssinia the following year. Their conversations roamed far beyond science, as Loveman was soon informed: Zinsser 'has more interesting ideas about literature than almost anyone I have ever met' and 'in carelessness and largesse is a thoroughbred if ever I saw one'. An enthusiastic and bow-legged equestrian, he looked a decade younger than his years and produced impressive poetry. Hart felt he could write numerous books in praise of his accomplishments and the best of it was, 'I've made a friend who will be a perennial stimulus to the best that I can do'.[8] Zinsser was equally enthusiastic: he noted the way the poet walked along the deck, 'with a glass in one hand, a bottle of beer in the other', and saw how, although 'obviously drunk', he smiled at the other passengers and charmed them. Despite intoxication Hart's literary discrimination seemed unimpaired; his conversation was 'impressively intelligent' and his 'breadth of literary information was extraordinary'.[9] There were disquieting depths beneath, however, and Zinsser soon began to feel a degree of responsibility 'because of [Hart's] mental and physical condition'. He considered him 'a very sick boy' and concluded that his life had become miserable 'in regard to mental suffering and his apparently hopeless struggles against his inclinations and his alcoholism'.[10]

The long talks and the drinking still left plenty of time for correspondence. On 5 April Hart wrote to Caresse, anxious about the plight of Peter Christiansen, the 'sweet tall boy friend' he had known in Paris who was now 'starving' in the Hotel Richmond in Nice. Could she do nothing to help, considering 'his sterling qualities and desire to work'?[11] The next day, confusing the *Orizaba*'s Captain Blackadder with First Officer Jensen, Hart sent a letter to Bill Brown saying there was rum on board and that 'the Captain is very much a Dane!'[12] On 7 April the *Orizaba* made its scheduled stop in Havana and Hart took Zinsser and Castaneda to La Diana, where five years before he had eaten with Alfredo. Some weeks later, recalling the dinner in his prose-poem 'Havana Rose', he quoted the professor's analysis of his character: 'You cannot heed the negative –, so might go on to undeserved doom ... must therefore loose yourself within a pattern's mastery that you can conceive, that you can yield to – by which also you win and gain that mastery and happiness which is your own from birth.'[13] The wine flowed, and Hart decided while on shore that he should also replenish his cabin supplies and bought two quarts of Bacardi with $10 borrowed from Zinsser.

Back on board he was unfit for much beyond retreating to his cabin and there the scientists left him, to inspect their rats, two of which they discovered to be dying. Hoping to save the remaining four, they cleaned the cages, wrapped the stricken rodents in paper and furtively made for the top deck, whence they proposed to jettison them. Freight was still being loaded on to the ship and strong searchlights illuminated the wharf, the adjacent lighters and the surrounding water: the scientists threw the rats overboard nevertheless, only to see them revive on contact with the water and begin swimming for another vessel anchored nearby. Nightmarish possibilities of plague flickered before them and their relief when the current prevailed and the animals were borne out to sea was great – or would have been, had they not suddenly discovered the extremely drunk and horrified poet standing beside them. As Zinsser later described events, Hart now 'saw rats in every silvery wave' and as though declaiming *The Bridge* he began loudly to orate that the doctor had thrown rats, had thrown typhus, into the waters of Havana.[14] The more they attempted to reassure him the noisier he became and then steps approached: darting behind a lifeboat, Zinsser and Castaneda listened as First Officer Jensen arrived to investigate, followed soon afterwards by a Cuban port officer. In view of Hart's condition his claims were quickly dismissed but it was a relief all the same for the scientists to overhear his protests as he was locked in his cabin for the night. Jensen submitted a report of the disturbance and the next morning, when Hart was roaming the deck, a bottle of beer in his hand, Zinsser and Castaneda were amused to note the appearance of Captain Blackadder, come in person to meet his imaginative passenger. A conversation ensued before Blackadder asked, 'And what are you in private life, sir?' Drawing himself up proudly, Hart replied: 'A poet, sir!' Shaking his head, Blackadder walked away prepared henceforth – or so he thought – for any poetical extravagance.[15]

The *Orizaba* reached Vera Cruz on 10 April but once the friends had gone to their respective hotels Hart spent a restless night, his imagination stirred by the proximity of the decrepit palace built by Cortés in this town of the True Cross from which the Spanish conquest was begun. It was a windy spring evening, and 'Havana Rose' records 'the clamour of incessant shutters, trundle doors – and the cheroot watchman – tiptoeing the successive patio balconies with a typical pistol – trying to muffle doors'. From nearby, as though beckoning from the sea, a lighthouse repeatedly flooded his room with light, 'the mid-wind midnight stroke of it, its milk-light regularity above my bath partition through the lofty, dusty glass – *Cortez* – *Cortez* – his crumbled palace in the square'.[16] The next day Hart joined Zinsser and Castaneda for the final leg of their journey: the train's one and a half mile climb to Mexico City took five hours but the distractions of the journey, as relayed to Sam Loveman, were vivid and seductive. Hart marvelled at 'the country people all along the way who swarmed around the train selling fruits, cakes, tortillas, serapies, canes, flowers, pulque, beer', and at the dramatic scenery, with 'incredible ledges over valleys filled with tropical vegetation' and then the vast and austere plateau which began at volcanic Mount Orizaba: mountains commanded three horizons, while in the foreground were 'burros and brown natives jogging along dry roads'.[17]

A little more than four centuries previously the conquistadores had surmounted the same steep heights to the Aztec capital of Tenochtitlán and Montezuma, believing Cortés to be the god Quetzalcoatl, had greeted the fair-skinned invader prior to being imprisoned by the Spaniards and then stoned by his own people. The train reached Mexico City: beneath these streets lay the rubble of treasure houses and pagan temples looted and then razed when Tenochtitlán was rebuilt as the first city of New Spain. Here surely was the place to write a historical epic, where archaeology confirmed the inherence of the past in the present – and here surely his imagination would flourish, when all around there was vibrant evidence of the fusion of Catholic imperialism with the ancient religions and tribal cultures of the conquered. It was this aspect of Mexico as a vast cultural palimpsest that had fascinated D.H. Lawrence, whose novel *The Plumed Serpent*, published only five years before Hart's arrival, had galvanized the Anglo-American literary world and made the country, long synonymous with danger and unrest, a fashionable destination. A few intrepid souls, among them Jack London and Ambrose Bierce, literary mentor of Sam Loveman, had arrived during the bloody years preceding 1920 but it was only when the country's protracted revolution ended that a new stability took hold, bringing with it a renaissance of cultural activity: exploration of Aztec and Mayan ruins was resumed and Rivera and Orozco made contemporary Mexican art internationally famous. British and American investment returned and with it – between 1931 and the Second World War – came a whole school of writers in search of distraction or inspiration, among them Langston Hughes, John Dos Passos, Somerset Maugham, Aldous Huxley, Evelyn Waugh, Graham Greene and Malcolm Lowry. Most of them arrived without knowing what to expect and many left even more uncertain. Graham Greene was uneasy here and Lawrence himself was profoundly unsettled by what he saw: the cruelty, the hard light and the dagger-edged cacti seemed all of a piece and he left Mexico behind as 'a land of death'. But for some writers this shadow of mortality was integral to the country's enchantment. Hart Crane arrived without expectations but, if only through Loveman, he must have known of the fate of Ambrose Bierce, whose disappearance and presumed death in Mexico in 1914 compounded the country's notoriety in American eyes. Surviving evidence suggests, however, that Bierce's journey was an act of deliberate self-destruction. Old and arthritic, he was tired of life when he crossed the Río Grande and apparently convinced he would never return. But as he wrote before departure, there was much to be said for sudden death abroad: 'It beats old age, disease or falling down the cellar stairs. To be a Gringo in Mexico – ah, that is euthanasia!'[18]

Hart and the two scientists arrived in Mexico City on a Saturday evening and although the poet was saddened to think that Zinsser would leave again in only three weeks Castaneda planned to remain for at least three months and promised companionship and useful introductions. Hart registered at the Hotel Panuco and devoted the following day to relaxation and writing letters – to Eyler Simpson, senior associate for the Institute of Current World Affairs, authority on Mexican politics and Guggenheim representative in Mexico City; and to Sam Loveman, to state that he felt 'at home here already, despite my complete ignorance of the language'.[19] On 13 April he went to Anglo-South American Bank to collect mail and investigate finances and although, as usual, he was poorer than he thought, he withdrew $75 in order to repay Zinsser and settle his bill at the Panuco. Waldo had supplied him with several letters of introduction, including one to the poet León Felipe Camino, but Hart misdirected the letter, so it was days before Camino paid his courtesy call. Meanwhile he renewed attempts to contact Eyler Simpson and decided, on 14 April, to cable Moe in New York asking if he would send Simpson's address in Mexico City. Then, a nervous and isolated monoglot, he turned to the one dependable friend at hand, the bottle, and by the time Simpson called to welcome him to Mexico in the name of the Guggenheim Foundation Hart Crane, the hope of American poetry, was incapable with drink. On behalf of the Guggenheim, Simpson nevertheless contacted a journalist named Rafael Heliodoro Valle the following day to suggest an interview, but as Camino discovered, the visiting poet was not easily accessible. Having finally received Waldo's letter he went to the Panuco several times, only to be frustrated: 'At the hotel they told me that he did not leave his room ... I think that he did not eat, that he only drank. He didn't open to anyone.'[20] Hart did manage one outing, however, despite the drinking – to Katherine Anne Porter, to investigate her promised hospitality. 'He burst in upon me one evening,' she informed Caroline Tate a few days later, 'screamed with joy over the garden, saw the big front room standing empty, declared that he could live no where else in Mexico, and could he move out the next day?' In view of his condition she assumed his request was merely 'a drunken whim' and agreed without thinking. The following day, however, he turned up 'cold sober with trunks and bags and in two days he was dug into that room with the victrola going, which was never stopped'.[21]

If Katherine Anne scarcely knew the poet she had taken in, she was certainly no stranger to Mexico. Born in 1890 near San Antonio, Texas, she considered it her 'familiar country' from the time of her first visit and returned frequently before she was twenty. In 1920, in anticipation of the cultural renaissance, she moved there and met an international crowd of sensation-seekers, among them Shelley's great-great-nephew, who briefly persuaded her of the glories of bullfighting. She befriended Rivera and his fellow-artist David Siqueiros, wrote about Mexican art for American magazines and in 1922 involved herself in the organization of the Los Angeles exhibition which introduced that art to the American public. She also began work on a story set in the Mexican Revolution which she carried with her as she moved backwards and forwards to New York: 'Flowering Judas', finally published in 1929, formed the title story of her first collection of short fictions which appeared in 1930.

The following year, on the strength of that book, she won her Guggenheim fellowship and decided to spend it in Germany. The journal she kept during her voyage to Bremerhaven formed the inspiration for her only novel, *Ship of Fools*, an account of an oceanic crossing on the eve of the Second World War which was published in 1962. In the intervening years she continued to evoke Mexico in her short stories, one of which, 'Hacienda', took its inspiration from an expedition undertaken shortly before Hart's arrival, when she travelled to Hidalgo to watch the Russian director Sergei Eisenstein at work on his ill-fated documentary about Mexican society, *Que Viva México*. Porter herself looked like a platinum starlet from Hollywood, since her hair had turned white when she nearly died in the great flu epidemic of 1918. Her manners, outdated and over-feminine, were the product of a genteel education received in Texas and Louisiana; her impulse to embroider the facts of her long life with enthusiasm appears to have been innate. The account she left behind of her time with Hart appears somewhat lurid – but there is every reason to believe he stimulated her romancer's imagination.

At any event she offered handsome accommodation and in his earliest surviving report from Mexico to CA and Bess, Hart described his 'splendid work room with a ceiling 15 feet high, beautiful Mexican wainscoting, a grand piano'. The room's white plaster walls were embellished 'with the raised decoration of Louis XIV' and he vowed not to 'clutter it up with more than the absolutely essential items of furniture'. The house was surrounded with a garden profuse with roses where an orchard containing 'several gigantic avocado trees' also produced apricots, figs and apples, all of which were gathered and prepared by Porter's cook, Theodora. They ate 'the most enormous amounts of lettuce, tomatoes (the tiny delicious variety) and cucumbers, besides tortillas – a kind of native pancake that the girls throw up in the air and pat into shape with their hands while singing'. There was no point in expecting Mexican servants to obey orders which contradicted their natural impulses but there was a stoicism about the ordinary people which commanded admiration: 'A blow is *fate*! I respect that. And the rest of the time – well, they just suffer and smile back into the sun.'[22]

At first Hart was 'wild with delight and enthusiasm' in his new home, Porter informed Caroline Tate, and lent the eager assistance of a child in various domestic routines: often up early, whatever the excesses of the previous night, he put a record on the Victrola and fed the turkeys and chickens or watered the garden before sunning himself on the ledge of the water tank.[23] If he pounded the piano a little too incessantly he atoned with the generosity of gifts and trinkets bought at the market or with the willingness with which he went to buy beer for the household, clad in a red sweater, white sailor pants and a blue silk handkerchief donated by Zinsser which complemented the blue glass pitcher used for the beer. Most of all, however, he liked to talk on the rooftop with Katherine Anne and during these morning-long conversations they strayed well beyond gossip about friends or discussion of their literary projects. He knew he was destroying himself and would describe, in what Porter later called 'a slow ordinary voice', the routine of that self-destruction, whereby 'the life he lived was blunting his sensibilities, [so] that he was no longer capable of feeling anything except under the most violent and brutal shocks'. Often he invoked the names of idols, whether Marlowe, Rimbaud or Baudelaire, who had lived – and died – by excess and 'almost every day' he spoke of suicide. 'Whenever he read of a suicide in the newspapers, he approved and praised the act' – Harry Crosby's was 'imaginative; the act of a poet'.[24] With nowhere else to turn, Hart also told Katherine Anne about his emotional expectations, but these too she found disquieting and unanswerable. 'He told me he wished to let himself go,' she later informed their mutual friend Mary Doherty, 'he had come to Mexico for that, he was sick of living in two worlds.' Inquiry revealed that Cowley and others 'had told him that all Indians were openly homosexual and incestuous, that their society was founded on this, he would encounter no difficulties whatever'. She explained that with discretion he would find sexual morality more forgiving than in America but his next admission was scarcely reassuring:

> He said he feared he had gone as far as he could in the road he had taken, and there was no way back. He confessed that his sexual feelings were now largely a matter of imagination, which drove and harried him continually, creating images of erotic frenzy and satisfactions for which he could find no counterpart in reality.... He said, he now found himself imagining that if he could see blood, or cause it to be shed, he might be satisfied.[25]

Zinsser was equally concerned. Sensitive and fastidious as Hart was, he could also be crude, yet in a manner seemingly desperate and bewildered. He sneered when the biologist suggested one day that it would be safer to buy bottled water or beer rather than lemonade from a street vendor and gratuitously catalogued all the things he had done without contracting syphilis. Zinsser concluded there was a 'pathetic' aspect to his nature – an aspect which became particularly apparent when the professor mentioned his departure. Hart admitted how lonely he would be, but announced his intention of finding a young man and settling down. Foreseeing practical difficulties, Zinsser suggested he involve himself with a girl instead but the poet insisted that the most beautiful women in the world were incapable of giving him what he termed 'a quarter inch erection'.[26]

Mexico, like France two years before, confronted Hart with his loneliness: profound because lifelong. An only child, an unofficial orphan, an idealistic misfit, he was lonely in America without really knowing it – but when life around him suddenly spoke an alien tongue there was no escaping his isolation and with it he was desperate. Once he had expressed, and so exorcized, this condition in poetry which evoked his solitary visions, but now that he wrote so little he was unable to pacify himself – and now that he wrote so little he began to suspect he was spent poetically, which compounded his distress. With no friends nearby to alleviate his fears he drank, and the more he drank the more he was alone, since relentless consumption can only end with ostracism. To make it all more poignant, the intellectuals of Mexico City were eager to befriend their New York brethren and Hart's arrival had been heralded as an event of significance. On 18 April *El Universal* had included a large article, complete with photograph, 'Señor Hart Crane, distinguido literato norteamericano, que se encuentra en México en viaje de estudio', and Rafael Valle published a high-flown profile, 'El camarada Crane a la intemperie', which was syndicated as far afield as Honduras and Guatemala. In a country where the arts were accorded unquestioned significance, and where poets sometimes doubled as government officials, Hart commanded a respect which could only be enhanced by his known friendship with Waldo Frank, great prophet of pan-American prosperity and a familiar figure in Latin American intellectual circles, and within two weeks he had met a variety of newspaper editors and painters, several notable poets, including Genaro Estrada, who was also Minister of Foreign Relations, and Moisés Sáenz, a promising young government official. But it was not enough. If Hart knew the worth of his poetry, he lacked self-confidence socially, with the result that he was over-sensitive: even among English-speaking people he was apt to take offence where none was intended, but among pupils of the language the scope for misunderstanding was endless and in no time he was complaining to Cowley that 'Latin American manners' could be 'rather baffling' and that people promised hospitality that never ensued.[27] To make matters worse, he confided to Waldo, all the poets he met seemed provincial and outdated, obsessed with Baudelaire and orchids, and not one of them 'really interested one iota in expressing anything indigenous'.[28]

Sailors, he had once intimated to Underwood, were a refuge from the society of his peers because they levied no expectations and broke no promises. Here, far from the sea yet more than ever in need of rough comfort, he took to the streets, but this operation also involved alcohol, since it required courage to make dangerous overtures he lacked the language to deliver with subtlety. Thus a sex life once conducted with discretion entered into its final phase of open and degrading squalor, with Katherine Anne forced into spectation along with her lover and eventual husband Eugene Pressly, a minor official at the American Embassy. The dramas seem to have begun on Hart's first night at her house, when a drunken squabble over a cab fare extended to the local police station. A few evenings later,

Porter reported to Caroline Tate, 'he was raging about in the streets quite drunk, and a police man came home with him'; it was left to Eugene Pressly to resolve the matter and thereafter he and Hart appear to have cordially disliked each other. By contrast, Katherine Anne applied a saintly patience – at least at first – even though Hart took to lecturing her during the course of supper about her attitude towards Mexico and the Indians until Pressly took it upon himself to order: 'Stop talking rot'.[29] Hart began to bring men home late at night: money disappeared, she heard prowling in the small hours or would go to the bathroom only to encounter strange men, 'drunk and buttoning up their trousers, as they stumbled out'.[30] He even attempted to seduce the fourteen-year-old apprentice employed by the carpenter she had commissioned to build bookcases. Writing to Caroline Tate on 24 April, Katherine Anne wondered how she could have allowed her home to be invaded to such a degree and was now 'remembering darkly all the things that happened in the country when YOU had Hart Crane in the same house'. Determined on restoring order, she gave her guest a lecture 'in my most motherly Dutch Aunt style' and he promised reform. 'From this out I should see a changed man.'[31]

Meanwhile, the changed man himself was writing to Otto Kahn and in the optimistic tone which characterized his correspondence, but which was increasingly at variance with deteriorating reality, he assured his patron of life's newest satisfactions. His mind was 'literally teeming with work and projects' – the Cortés drama, critical essays, short stories – and now it was only 'a matter of getting it down'.[32] That evening, already fairly drunk, he climbed to the roof of Katherine Anne's one-storey house and threatened to throw himself off. When she pointed out that he would do no more than hurt himself he began to laugh – 'a curiously fresh sober humor in the laughter', she later recalled – before climbing down an adjacent apricot tree and disappearing to pound her piano.[33] An hour or so later he left to go the round of the bars and at some stage in the night, when he was unable to pay a drinks bill of 1.80 pesos and a cab fare of 50 centavos, he was arrested and thrown into gaol. At 9 a.m. on 25 April he telephoned the American Embassy to say he was being held at La Demarcácion; an hour later he was visited there by an embassy official, Nathaniel Lancaster Junior, who established that he could not be released prior to midday, when the judge would levy a fine. Whatever the penalty, he would not be able to pay, so Hart directed the Embassy to notify Eyler Simpson, who duly appeared and discharged the fine of 12 pesos, whereupon Hart was released. He went to Zinsser's hotel, the Mancera, where his credit was still good, and fortified himself with rum before setting out to find a house of his own: eventually he signed a lease beginning 1 May on a ten-room property belonging to a Señor Lepine which was round the corner from Katherine Anne at 15 Michoacán Norte and cost approximately $35 a month.

He returned to Porter's, as he thought for the remainder of April, only to face another unexpected problem: a mysterious rash, which broke out all over his body and itched so unbearably that he could find no repose. He had had many skin inflammations in the course of his life but none with similarities to his present condition, and now he began to wonder if his affliction was something picked up in La Demarcácion. It was all too easy to imagine what Porter and Pressly would speculate, however, so rather than disturb them with his restless condition or endure their knowing looks, he disappeared in the night to the Mancera, reassuring his hostess by note that 'Lysol isn't necessary in the bathtub' and that whatever other conditions itched, syphilis did not.[34] At the Mancera he drank and drank, his worries aggravated by financial anxiety. He had withdrawn a further $75 to pay Señor Lepine and to buy certain domestic necessities but weeks remained before the Guggenheim were to release the next instalment of his scholarship. He applied to CA for help and on 29 April cabled Tommy Smith at Liveright asking for $50 to be sent urgently to the hotel. On 30 April he sent another note of apology to Pressly and Porter, and Eyler Simpson wrote a brief letter asking Hart to come and see him 'during the next two or three days' to discuss 'a matter of mutual interest'.[35] The summons had an ominous ring and he was pleased to be able to avoid it with a truthful excuse, written hastily from his new house on 1 May: he was leaving imminently to spend the weekend in Taxco with Moisés Sáenz but hoped he and Simpson would be able to meet on Monday afternoon. As he waited for Sáenz in his empty property he apologized yet again to Katherine Anne, 'too jittery to write a straight sentence' but confident that now he could settle down. Her recent notes of love and consolation had meant a lot to him, he liked his new home, he was glad she and Gene were nearby and eager to visit, and although his bill at the Mancera had been enormous he knew he would pay it somehow. Above all, however, 'The recent cyclone is my last – at least for a year.'[36]

Sáenz had suggested the visit to Taxco when he learned of Hart's desire to explore historic Mexico – what better way to evoke the cupidity of the conquistadores than with a visit to the old silver capital, perched like a fastness five hours away among the mountains? Sáenz had a house in the town and so was already familiar with the spectacular scenery of the journey and the charms of their destination, but for Hart Taxco was a revelation: ten cathedrals were crammed into serpentine and vertiginous streets which the fiesta then in progress had scattered with confetti, candles and flowers. Here once again was the ancient fusion of pagan and Christian, but there was little sign of contemporary life: only two silversmiths still worked here and most of the silver mines which honeycombed the surrounding mountains had long ago been exhausted. Taxco's fortunes were about to be changed, however, by William Spratling, an American resident Sáenz was eager to introduce to the visiting poet. A year younger than Hart and himself an accomplished painter and writer, Spratling had arrived in Mexico in 1927 and lectured on art at the National University for two years before moving to Taxco, along the way beginning what became one of the most important collections of pre-

Columbian artefacts in the country. He was not a man to overlook the present in the interests of the past, however, and his faith in the traditions of Mexican artistry led him to found the silver craft school which restored Taxco's fame and made him its most venerated citizen. Beguiled by Spratling's expertise and more eager for American company than he realized, Hart was delighted by the introduction and when, a few weeks later, Spratling was obliged to travel to New York he left Hart in charge of his collection. As for Sáenz, the poet was soon praising his courage, generosity and 'innate Aztec refinement' to Cowley and boasting of the 'ancient silver pony bridle (bells and all!)' that he had helped him acquire.[37]

Back in Mexico City, his confidence ebbed again. He saw Eyler Simpson, who bluntly explained that although he had 'neither the desire nor the right to assume any responsibility for his actions' he was not prepared to allow Hart 'to muddy the water down here for other Guggenheim Fellows' – the drinking and the lawlessness must stop.[38] Temporarily chastened, Hart turned to domestic details for the illusion of activity: his new home was without furniture and servants, to say nothing of electricity; indeed would remain without power until 5 June, when he was connected to the supply as 'Señor Hard Crane'. Daniel Hernandez and his wife and two children moved in to clean, cook and garden for $8 a month and Hart furnished his house with a combination of furniture bought from the market and 'the main "standard American" essentials', which, he told Cowley, 'in Mexico cost like hell'.[39] By the end of the first week in May he was once again critically short of money and wrote to Simpson advising him of the necessity of recent expenditure and wondering if the Foundation could advance $100 of the $400 due to him on 1 July. Lending his support to the request, Simpson relayed it to Moe in New York and the payment was authorized one week later, by which time CA had replied to his son's urgent plea for assistance with the wisdom of Polonius. Sending money by wire for the first time, he cautioned that 'more friends are lost by the intrusion of financial obligations than by anything else' and advised his son to be prudent when it came to borrowing from friends. He wondered 'who this Miss Porter is that you are living with' and thanked Hart for his recent description of Mexican life, which struck a false note only once, 'when you said that poverty was respected. There isn't any place in the World that I have ever heard of where we get along without paying our way, but there are sections of the World where it costs less to do that.'[40]

On 9 May Hart sent a note to Mony Grunberg declaring that 'I've never been so nearly happy' and delighted to be in 'my own *home* at last'.[41] Two days later he wrote to Tommy Smith at Liveright asking for news of anthology earnings from his poems and indicating that he needed more copies of *White Buildings* and *The Bridge* for the repayment of various recent courtesies. Also on 11 May he reassured Henry Allen Moe that he was 'far from having any regrets about Mexico as my choice of a residence' and promised that if his enthusiasm had been 'a little *too* intense thus far' he was now 'starting to work with vast enthusiasm'.[42] About now he began writing 'Havana Rose' and on a sheet of Hotel Panuco stationery, enclosed with a note begging for letters and promising he felt 'as near Paradise as necessary', he typed fourteen words for Peter Blume: ' "Cortez: The Enactment." "And he put the Cross upon that People." By Hart Crane.'[43]

Indicating how little thought he had really given to the proposed venture, he variously described it as an epic and a drama. It would be 'rather Elizabethan, but actable, I hope', he assured the poet Selden Rodman – but if Shakespeare had his Hall and Holinshed, there was no source material Hart could easily plunder and he lacked the language to read primary sources.[44] In any case it was dull to think of sitting in a library, especially when he could carouse around Mexico City with a newly befriended drunk: redheaded Ernest O'Malley claimed friendship with the novelist Liam O'Flaherty as well as veteran status as an Irish revolutionary. He was 'the most quietly sincere and appreciative person', Cowley was informed, and together he and Hart drank and looked at frescos until O'Malley revealed that after three years of travel he wanted to return to Dublin.[45] At last the poet Léon Felipe Camino tracked Hart down in Mixcoac but was disconcerted to find him lying 'on a soiled bed, unmade, surrounded with empty beer bottles, a keg of I don't know what kind of liquor in a corner and an old phonograph which was playing harshly, endlessly repeating a song then in style, popularized in a movie by Marlene Dietrich'. When Camino identified himself Hart got up and his visitor saw the celebrated poet for the first time. 'He was tall and had an angelic face, with eyes large and blue, filled with *asombro*: fright, astonishment, amazement.' His manner betrayed 'bewilderment, somber darkness and fear' and he struck his guest as 'a little lost boy'. Since 'it was impossible to talk with him', it was agreed that Hart should visit Camino in the near future, 'but he never came'.[46]

Somewhat gratuitously, Camino reported to Waldo that he had been rebuffed by 'an unruly drunk person' and the latter was furious: Hart had broken his promise not to drink until fully accustomed to the altitude of Mexico City, and Waldo punished him by withholding future correspondence.[47] Though guiltily half aware that something was wrong, Hart at first ignored the silence and relayed enthusiastic details of his house and garden and of Mexico itself, which continued to provide him with 'the illusion that there is a soil, a mythology, a people and a spirit here that are capable of unique and magnificent utterance'.[48] Yet attempts to discuss that ambition with neighbouring Katherine Anne proved frustrating to them both, not least because she knew enough about the vexed subject of *indigenismo* to resent his easy division of Mexican society into two groups, the middle-class and fraudulent *mestizos*, and the *indios*, inscrutable and magnificent in their remote villages. How could he be so specious? What did he know about the complex relations four centuries old that existed between conqueror and conquered, European and native, when he was unable to write or speak Spanish, let alone Nuahatl or any of the other Indian tongues? As she soon learned, however, Hart was now far too uncertain to withstand plain speech: 'He would simply twist his lips into a hurt smile and wander back to his house with both hands stuck in the front pockets of the baggy white sailor pants he usually wore.' Often he would accompany his exit with one of Marlene Dietrich's songs, 'something he always tried to sing whenever he felt uncomfortable or rejected, though he never got it quite right, the lyrics somehow lumping over each other'.[49]

Despite the Guggenheim's recent flexibility in advancing a quarter of Hart's next allocation of funds, he was in dire straits by the end of May. Rather than approach his father once again, however, he decided to contact one of CA's former employees, Hazel Hasham, who was now living in Avenida Insurgentes with her husband Arthur Cazes and running a Mexican confectionery business. Having been given vague instructions by CA to keep an eye on Hart, she was happy to cook dinner for him and to supply $50 for his immediate needs but decided to let Clarence Crane know of the transaction anyway. CA wrote to her on 2 June, 'glad to see that even though God did not bless you with a family, you evidence strong motherly tendencies'. He reimbursed her but indicated that when Hart next asked for money she should resist, and blame him if need be. 'Of course when I tell you this you understand that it applies only when things are running smoothly and no emergency exists.' The fact was that Hart had got to manage his Guggenheim money more satisfactorily. 'I know there is a time coming after the lapse of a year when they won't send him a ticket home or do a lot of things that Harold will want to do. He has got to learn to live within his income the same as I am trying to do – unsuccessfully – during these trying times.'[50] To avoid embarrassment, CA informed Hart of his position that same day and pointed out that since he was in Mexico 'to work and study and not to entertain' it should be easy for him to survive without further assistance.[51] As he never tired of stressing, nobody could be financially frivolous, especially now, when Wall Street was so uncertain and US Steel was at its lowest level for years. 'I don't see much of American papers here,' Hart replied on 5 June, 'so anything about the stock market would surprise me.' Enclosing a photograph of himself wearing the recently acquired silver pony bridle, he promised that from now on he would be self-sufficient and insisted that although he spent some time listening to records on his portable Orthophonic, or else to radio programmes from Los Angeles and San Diego audible from behind his neighbour's wall, he was 'getting well into the language study and my work'.[52]

Hart tinkered with 'Havana Rose' and continued to wonder what form his work on Cortés should assume – and then received an honourable distraction from these labours when Morton Dauwen Zabel, associate editor of *Poetry*, wrote on 11 June to suggest that Hart assemble his lyrics written on the Isle of Pines for publication in the magazine, indicating that he would happily 'publish as much prose as you will let us have during the coming months'.[53] To begin, he wondered if Hart would care to review James Whaler's *Green River* and Roy Helton's *Lonesome Water*.

Zabel's overture showed more enthusiasm for his work than Harriet Monroe herself had ever betrayed and for a while Hart was elated. Replying on 20 June he accepted the challenge and thanked Zabel for the issue of *Poetry* he had sent. He hoped soon to have new material to submit to the magazine, but composition in a foreign land had proved more difficult than he had ever supposed. Things might have been easier 'if the entire world didn't positively hate us Americans so much' but that was only half the story, as he well knew. 'I'm too attached to the consciousness of my own land to write "tourist sketches" elsewhere.' He liked Mexico, 'but I'd rather be in my favourite corner of Connecticut'.[54]

And so it was when inspiration did finally stir: 'Purgatorio', the twenty-one-line poem he began between one implacable tequila hangover and another, was not about Mexico but about himself, his nostalgia for the North, with its 'too-keen cider – the too-soft snow', and his realization that 'Exile is thus a purgatory'. Memories of his reading of Dante are implicit in this brief and anguished cry – 'I am unraveled, umbilical anew' – and although the lines tail away, as though mumbled in distraction, they are among the most moving he ever wrote:

> My country, O my land, my friends –
> Am I apart, – here from you in a land
> Where all your gas lights – faces, – sputum gleam
> Like something left, forsaken, – here am I –
> And are these stars – the high plateau – the scents
> Of Eden – and the dangerous tree – are these
> The landscape of confession – and if confession
> So absolution?[55]

He was disintegrating, 'unraveling', and at a pace at once painfully apparent to himself and spectacularly obvious to onlookers. He began drinking heavily again in the third week of June – Katherine Anne passed his house on 20 June on her way out for the evening and seeing him 'reading Blake by the light of a single candle' she stopped briefly to talk. She had advised him about planting his garden – nasturtiums, roses, violets, dahlias, lilies, cosmos, mignonette – and seeing how advanced it already looked she praised its beauty through the iron gate. He came to greet her and they exchanged amenities: she could see he had been drinking but was unprepared for what followed: 'Holding to the grill he suddenly began to cry and said, "You don't know what my life has been. This is the only place I ever felt was my own. This is the only place I ever loved." '[56] At some stage Hart invited Porter and Pressly for lunch the next day and made elaborate preparations that morning for the feast in their honour, 'nipping at a bottle of tequila meanwhile', as he subsequently admitted to Lorna Dietz. Katherine Anne was already in the process of arranging her visit to Germany, however, and delays at the Consulate left her unable to return to Mixcoac in time. Hart angrily gave the food to his servants and, in no state for rejections, real or imagined, left for a reception at the American Embassy, only to be escorted unceremoniously from its precincts. Deciding to get even drunker, he made the round of various cantinas before returning to Mixcoac some time after midnight. In the course of the inevitable squabble over the cab fare he challenged the driver to arbitration at the local police station and on the way to that arbitration he found himself outside Katherine Anne's gate. Seeing her and Pressly in the garden, Hart broke out, by his own admission, 'Katherine Anne, I have my opinion of you.'[57] In the account he later sent to Lorna he did not record what that opinion was. Katherine Anne, more sober, did. He shouted at her in terms of 'the monotonous dull obscenity which was the only language he knew after a certain point of drunkenness', for the first time cursing the inanimate as well as the animate:

> His voice at these times was intolerable; a steady harsh inhuman bellow which stunned the ears and shocked the nerves and caused the heart to contract. In this voice and with words so foul there is no question of repeating them, he cursed separately and by name the moon, and its light: the heliotrope, the heaven-tree, the sweet-by-night, the star jessamine, and their perfumes. He cursed the air we breathed together, the pool of water with its two small ducks huddled at the edge, and the vines on the wall and the house. But those were not the things he hated. He did not even hate us, for we were nothing to him. He hated and feared himself.[58]

She was used to hearing him weeping and shaking his fist and shouting in drunken frustration, 'I am Baudelaire, I am Whitman, I am Christopher Marlowe, I am Christ', but these all-encompassing, almost Shakespearean imprecations were new and she realized future friendship was untenable. The cab driver and his passenger proceeded to the police station and Hart duly spent his second night in a Mexican gaol, emerging later the next day to write Katherine Anne yet another apology. He blamed 'the malfeasance of an overdose of tequila' for his excesses but acknowledged that forgiveness was 'probably past hope'.[59]

She confirmed his fears in a long and forcefully worded letter written the same day. He had insulted her 'ancestry, upbringing, and habits of life' many times, and many times had been forgiven or ignored, simply because she shared 'the superstition of our time about the somewhat romantic irresponsibility of drunkenness, holding it a social offense to take seriously things said and done by a drunken person'. She had finally begun to believe, however, that 'you bear a fixed dislike of me, of a very nasty kind' and had begun to feel 'that a sanitarium for the mentally defective is the proper place for you'. Short of that destination, he should grow up or else reconcile himself to being treated as a fool. 'Your emotional hysteria is not impressive, except possibly to those little hangers-on of literature who feel your tantrums are a mark of genius. To me they do not add the least value to your poetry, and take away my last shadow of a wish to ever see you again.'[60]

Following his ejection from the American Embassy, an anonymous letter of complaint about Hart's behaviour was sent to Señor Jiménez, secretary to the Mexican Minister of Education, and representations were made to American diplomats and to Mexican officials of the Guggenheim Foundation. On 26 June, having hoped 'I would not have to write you this letter', Eyler Simpson contacted Henry Allen Moe, himself typing a catalogue of Hart's misdemeanours which he wanted no one else to see.[61] Individually the trespasses were minor: poets were different from other men, for better or worse, and in any case scarcely a day went by without some drunken American being thrown into a Mexican gaol. Cumulatively, however, Hart Crane's transgressions now defied connivance and Simpson feared that unless the Foundation took action soon Hart would either be knifed by some gringo-hating Mexican or shot by a general. On 27 June, and with faultless timing, the *New Yorker* published a Carl Rose cartoon in which one drunk seated at the Dôme confided to another: 'The Guggenheims will be awfully sore at me if I don't get down to writing pretty soon.'[62] Otto Myers, treasurer to the Guggenheim Foundation, was already aware of events in Mexico City when he saw the magazine and sent a copy to Moe, who agreed the cartoon was 'almost prophetic'.[63] Even in Paris this was not the sort of publicity the Guggenheim Foundation welcomed but in Mexico, where anti-Americanism continued in the wake of recent border skirmishes, Hart's antics could have far-reaching consequences. Straight after writing to Myers, Moe sent Hart a blunt letter, with a duplicate to Simpson, pointing out that his fellowship could be terminated for a variety of reasons, one of which was deportation, a penalty to which his behaviour was making him increasingly liable. He had never before had to write a letter telling a Guggenheim fellow to get down to work – but then no fellow had ever been thrown in gaol before. With the Fourth of July approaching, Hart had one more opportunity for excess and irresponsibility, after which he must honour the Foundation and the faith it reposed in him or else face the consequences.

Even as he wrote, however, Moe and his colleagues knew threats to terminate Hart's fellowship could not be executed immediately: his next letter of credit became valid on 1 July and without involving the Foundation's entire apparatus of support, including Guaranty Trust and all the banks in Mexico, there was nothing that could be done to annul it. So Hart had received his next instalment of money by the time Frank Aydelotte, president of Swarthmore College and chairman of the Guggenheim Foundation's Advisory Board for Latin American Exchange Fellows, wrote to Moe on 6 July to advocate firm action. Doubtful 'about any promises toward reform', he was convinced the poet's fellowship should be terminated at once and that he should be asked to return the letter of credit. At some future stage it might be possible to consider awarding him support once again but 'what he needs at the moment is a hard jolt'.[64] The thunderbolt came only hours later, when Bess Crane sent her stepson a telegram advising his immediate return: CA was seriously ill. A second telegram soon followed: Clarence Arthur Crane was dead.

For the only time in his life Hart flew – across Chihuahua, the Sierra Madre and the Río Grande – to New Mexico, at Albuquerque boarding the Santa Fe Railroad's Grand Canyon Limited for the 1,500-mile journey to Cleveland. *En route* he wrote to Morton Dauwen Zabel, explaining that his reviews for *Poetry* would be delayed, and to Henry Allen Moe, acknowledging his letter of rebuke and suggesting that they might meet in New York on his way back to Mexico. He reached Chagrin Falls late on Friday 11 July and the following day he joined company employees, his stepmother and his father's father for the funeral of Clarence Crane, killed by a stroke at fifty-six and interred in the family plot at Garrettsville.

Letters of condolence arrived for widow and son, with Hart himself devoting much of 15 July to replies. To Bill Brown and Lorna Dietz he admitted how glad he was in retrospect to have spent Christmas, his father's last, in Ohio. CA had enjoyed their time together and Hart himself had come to realize 'his qualities and affection for me more fully than ever before'.[1] The elder Crane's last weeks had been cheerful and his death swift and unwitting, and as Hart indicated to William Wright, the only one of his close friends to have known CA, 'I can say that his character and the impress of it that I lately received will be a real inspiration to me.'[2] In the end, however, Hart Crane's reaction to his father's death is inscrutable: if he gave the matter much thought, either privately or with friends, his opinions have not survived. But it is conceivable that the subject was too large and distressing for analysis: without CA there was no bulwark against Grace and without CA there was no one whose approbation poetry could still win. His mother had read genius in the lame lines of his juvenilia but his father had failed to concede even the amplitude of his maturity – and now never would. The day Clarence Crane died saw also the death of one of the deepest impulses of his son's ambition.

Together Hart and Bess addressed the fortunes of Crane's embattled empire, driving daily to the factory in Cleveland to read the large volume of mail and going over the books of the various businesses, realizing as they did so the extent of the anxiety that must have been CA's daily condition. The enterprises which had once generated a seven-figure fortune for their owner were in a sorry state as a result of misjudgement and a decline in confectionery revenues which had continued since the end of the war. The Depression had rendered much of CA's stock worthless and many of the candy stores, as well as the wholesale confectionery business, were now running at a loss. The picture reproduction venture was still struggling in its infancy. Canary Cottage, which Crane had borrowed heavily to establish, continued to enjoy brisk business, but since he had recently reduced prices there in a bid to sustain patronage in hard times there was no knowing what profit, if any, it would show. Bess was left with direction of all the companies and decided that the Cottage should stay open but it was clear that many of the other concerns should be closed as soon as their leases expired or could be discontinued. It was also clear that Hart would have to remain in Ohio for at least a month to assist with terminal administration of an estate which CA's will divided between widow and son. Nominating his brother-in-law Byron Madden as executor, CA provided an immediate bequest of $1,000 for Hart as well as an annual payment from company profits of $2,000 for the next four years, after which time he and his stepmother were designated joint-legatees. Perhaps Hart once had expected to inherit great wealth – but then once he had also expected to light the firmament with his poetry. Life trimmed all expectations, but if his inheritance was modest, it was, as he indicated to Lorna, 'as good as an annual Guggenheim anyway, and that is all I really require'.[3]

Having pined for home beneath Mexico's cerulean skies, he now occupied himself as best he could in a place where he no longer belonged. Moe sent a letter of sympathy: he was eager for the New York meeting Hart had suggested and in his reply Hart promised he would be back in Mexico 'within six weeks at the latest'.[4] Long before then, Peggy Cowley would arrive in Mexico City to begin divorce proceedings and when he wrote to her to give practical advice prior to her departure he suggested that she live in his house while he was in America 'and possibly continue to remain with me following my return'. Once back he would buy another bed but the one he already owned was 'more comfortable than any I've experienced while in Mexico'. All he asked was that she pay the electricity bill and the servants' wages, which totalled 25 pesos a month. There was a kerosene stove in the kitchen if she wanted to cook but Katherine Anne could always guide her round the corner to Tiziano's, whence 'a whopping big dinner' could be delivered 'for the modest price of 50 centavos'. There was one last thing – 'Take my advice and "lay off" tequila, mescal and other agents of fatality to northerners in Mexico.'[5] Whether or not Peggy accepted his offer, she would inevitably contact Katherine Anne and Hart squirmed and raged to think how the latter would describe him. Letters from friends had already made it clear that Greenwich Village was alive with versions of the feud and when he wrote to Margaret Robson on 29

July he indicated how tired he was 'of so much "concern" about my soul, waggling heads and tongues'. If Katherine Anne had nothing better to do in Mexico than tittle-tattle by letter to New York it was just as well she was leaving for Germany. She would no doubt attempt to turn Cowley's wife against him but what really did he care? 'I'm not counting much on much future intimacy with Peggy – probably no more than she premeditates right now with me.' Indeed indifference seemed to characterize his response to everything: 'I feel as though a sort of "full stop" had occurred. I've never been less emotional – and yet never less satisfied, with myself or anything else in general. But really not depressed; and maybe that's the worst of it.'[6]

In August he spent several days in Warren as the guest of his cousin Helen, still happily married to naval officer Griswold Hurlbert, and although she enjoyed 'flashes of Hart's marvelous wit and humor' she found him 'more philosophical, less exuberant' than usual.[7] 'Gooz' Hurlbert's best friend was married to a Hungarian countess who played a czymbalin and one Sunday afternoon the countess gave an impromptu recital in one of the practice rooms at Hiram College. Nobody enjoyed it – and Hart's glum mood still prevailed when his cousin found him playing with a stray kitten in her garden and took one of the last photographs of the poet on American soil. He was happy to see the Rychtariks and Laukhuff and to have a reconciliation with Sommer but the only friend he met almost daily was Sam Loveman, who was in Cleveland at the same time. The latter was bewildered by his friend's moods and surprised to find that 'he was not in the slightest degree emotional about his father's death'.[8] At the same time he was clearly 'terribly lonely' and Loveman found himself haunted by a confession Hart had once made – 'Unless I can find someone that I can live with and attach myself to, I face spiritual annihilation.' They went to the cinema regularly and the poet revealed that he was still in correspondence with Peter Christiansen and was thinking of sending him the money to come to America or Mexico. What did Sam think? Despite never having met him, Loveman had reservations about Christiansen – 'really a male gigolo, a very handsome boy who used to send Hart provocative photographs of himself' – but for whatever reason decided the scheme should be encouraged and replied: 'Excellent. By all means.'[9] By 14 August, when Hart referred to his plan in a letter, he and Christiansen had exchanged further correspondence and the money for a transatlantic ticket had been sent: 'It looks as though we'd meet in Havana,' Loveman was informed, 'though I haven't heard absolutely regarding his sailing date. I'm full of anticipation anyway.'[10] He was getting restless: before returning to New York, however, there was one more visit Hart wanted to make; so it was duly arranged that he should spend a weekend at William and Margaret Wright's in Pennsylvania. The poet struck his oldest friend as being 'very cheerful and self-contained' but when Wright, ignorant of the true finality of the occasion, produced his camera to mark a special event it recorded a greying and wistful face. On Sunday morning, to the accompaniment of distant church bells, they sat on the porch and Hart admitted, 'not with panic, but with the sense that such a hiatus was wholly in the nature of things', that he might not write again 'for several years'. Then suddenly the two men found themselves discussing suicide and the poet, perhaps thinking of his inheritance, promised: 'At least I should never commit suicide because of money.'[11]

A few days later Hart returned to New York and decided to lie low at the Hotel Albert until his return to Mexico: as the Ward Line was now offering favourable rates to Guggenheim fellows he made a reservation with that company – on the faithful *Orizaba* – for 29 August. He made his peace with Henry Allen Moe and paid his respects to the littoral in an evening of carousing in Hoboken with Carl Carlsen but Manhattan itself had nothing now to offer him. Central Park was full of the homeless; Greenwich Village, where the aesthetes and misfits of a continent had once sought asylum, now earnestly anticipated the doctrinal struggles of the 1930s; and the pinnacles of the newly constructed Empire State and Chrysler Buildings soared intimidatingly above the careless city of his and America's twenties. From Mexico he would admit to Underwood, 'I find myself more and more out of touch with that metropolitan world.'[12] Still embarrassed about the quarrel with Katherine Anne, he saw none of his old friends and would probably have passed through his former home undetected had not Bill Brown once again run into him in Washington Square. Brown was astonished, given how alien secrecy was to Hart's nature, but found himself as usual disarmed by the warmth of the latter's greeting, which was 'cheerful and open-hearted'. They made for a nearby speakeasy, the poet conspicuous in 'a bright red scarf and Spanish beret' all too congruous with his vivid face, 'blotched and discolored as it always became when he had been drinking'. Ordering the customary 'corrosive Italian wine', they gossiped about anything other than writing, which Brown sensed was a subject best avoided. Abruptly, with an expression 'almost of despair', Hart asked if Brown thought he had written so much as one line that would endure. Bill was amazed: 'It was totally unlike him to ask the question.' But the more he attempted reassurance, the more he felt as though he were 'talking in epitaphs'.[13] Walker Evans, who saw the poet on 28 August, also marked the steep decline – after spending most of the last few days drinking in his hotel room Hart was scarcely capable of organizing himself for embarkation and so the photographer took it upon himself to get the voyager and his luggage on board the *Orizaba*. Evans never saw Hart again, nor did Brown, and nor did Sam Loveman, to whom the poet confided just before departure, 'I've become so lonely I could die.'[14]

The rainy season made Mexico City cool after the terrible heat of the journey but there was no sign of Peggy to alleviate the isolation he dreaded. A few days after Hart's return, however, companionship emerged in the unforeseen shape of Milton Rourke, a young archaeologist from Wisconsin who was studying at the University of Mexico and who was convinced of the existence in Mixcoac of a buried Aztec pyramid. Eager for English-speaking friendship as much as for Aztec experience, Hart quickly volunteered assistance with excavation and on 10 September the two men spent a day of arduous labour on the grass-scented slopes above the valley of Anahuac: the prospect – of volcanoes, Lake Texcoco and distantly shimmering Mexico City – was sublime, but the rewards of their digging – an obsidian blade and a few shards of Aztec pottery – were less spectacular. Nevertheless when Rourke revealed that he was planning an expedition to the Aztec town of Tepoztlan Hart declared himself keen to go along. They left Mexico City on 12 September, travelling four hours by train to El Porque, whence they began a wearying three-hour descent by foot, with Hart in his oldest clothes, a bag of blankets slung over his shoulder, to begin what he described to cousin Helen as 'five of the most absorbing days of my life'.[15]

Though only about ten miles east of Cuernavaca, the town was situated in a ravine and isolated by surrounding cliffs 800 feet high which were dense with tropical vegetation and coursed by countless waterfalls. For four pesos the explorers lived on tortillas and beans as the guest of a baker who doubled as town barber and they shared a bamboo-cane bed in the room that was occupied by their host and his family. Sleep came sweetly after days spent bathing in streams with Indian youths or ascending the precipitous cliffs or searching for Aztec fragments in the nearby cornfields. In the evening the visitors returned to the town with their spoils and usually went to a coffee stall where the young men congregated to play their guitars and sing. 'And what music!' Bess was informed. 'I'll never forget the strange melancholy tonality and the plangent accompaniment of their instruments. You can't imagine how picturesque they are with their dark eyes and faces set in almost complete abstraction below the great white hats tilted on the backs of their heads.'[16]

To Hart's delight, the population of Tepoztlan was entirely Indian; more excitingly still, he and Rourke discovered that the town was poised for the annual festival of Tepoztecatl, the Aztec god of *pulque* whose temple, though ravaged by the Spaniards, still clung to the slopes above. Some townsfolk kept a nocturnal vigil at the temple itself while others congregated on the roof of the cathedral or the monastery to listen to the votive music of flute and drum which alternated, at tenminute intervals, with carillons of church bells. 'Two voices, still in conflict here in Mexico,' Hart told Wright in wonder, 'the idol's and the Cross.'[17] Fireworks from churchtop were answered by fireworks from the temple as the spectating poet reflected that most of the officiating Aztec elders attended Mass without hesitation or ambivalence. And as though to confirm the contradictions of the pageant, stars glittered in a sky simultaneously bright with lightning and the declining moon. At about nine o'clock the music stopped. 'It was like being in the land of Oz,' Hart informed his stepmother, as he and Rourke invited various town elders to tequila at a market stall before promising to rejoin the festivities six hours later.[18] The potent liquor scarcely made for an easy rising: nevertheless at five o'clock in the morning the explorers woke and rushed to the monastery once more, to the further accompaniment of fife and drum, to be offered coffee spiked with *pulque* as the ceremony reached its climactic intensity. An Aztec drum, 'pre-Conquest and guarded year after year from the destruction of the priests and conquerors', was produced to serenade the rising sun: Hart marvelled at its embellishment, 'exquisitely carved and showing a figure with animal head, upright, and walking through thick woods', but his joy and disbelief were complete when the Indians passed the drumsticks to him and signalled that he should continue the tattoo as the rising sun illuminated the ancient rite.

Hart had returned to Mexico with a determination divulged to William Wright, 'to get out more into the smaller cities and pueblos, to get as thoroughly acquainted with the native indian population as possible', and shortly after his return from Tepoztlan, as though in answer to the inspiration of ancient Mexico, he began 'The Circumstance', a poem addressed to Xochipilli, sun god of the Aztecs and patron of youth, joy, poetry and masculine fecundity.[19] Inspiring as these attributes should have been, Hart was unable to make significant progress with this lyric bid to outpace Time and after only a week he left for Taxco and the hospitality of William Spratling. The old uncompromising gods were forgotten again, on this occasion after Hart's introduction to the painter David Siqueiros, who was living under house arrest in the town after spending most of 1930 in gaol following his involvement in a communist demonstration. Shades of the prison house lay long over a life of protest and dissent – but as Hart soon discovered, persecution had little effect on the determination of this volatile and flamboyant man, who went into exile in 1932, fought against Franco in the Spanish Civil War and was later rumoured to have been involved in an attempt to assassinate Trotsky.

Born in 1896, Siqueiros began his turbulent career during the Mexican upheavals of 1913, but after attaining the rank of captain in the forces of General Obregon he was sent as military attaché to the Mexican legations in Madrid and Paris. Wandering the great museums, he saw how European art both inspired and constricted the painting of the Americas and, ever determined to help the oppressed, he wrote 'A Manifesto to the Painters of America' calling for an art of the New World in which painters would exploit indigenous cultures and traditions. Returning to Mexico in 1922, he founded the National Union of Revolutionary Painters, Sculptors and Engravers, organized a union for miners in the state of Jalisco, and edited a communist newspaper. He also began to paint – and the work which made him internationally famous spoke with gaudy palette of the passions of the man: tirelessly experimenting with new media and techniques, Siqueiros produced canvases and murals which exalted the suffering poor and the downcast Indian and constituted a body of New World proletarian art unrivalled by any other painter. As an individual he was far from oppressed: moody, histrionic and invincibly egotistical, he galvanized crowds with his tantrums yet was said to exude charm the way a papaya exudes juice.[20]

With his New World ardour and pedigree artistic temperament, he certainly delighted Hart – 'the very soil of Mexico seems spread on his canvases', the Rychtariks were assured – and in no time, despite his parlous finances, the poet had bought a watercolour of a Mexican boy and commissioned his own portrait, which Siqueiros conceived in characteristic fashion as a monumental close-up with massive head tightly cropped by the frame.[21] Although he was working on various projects at the time, including *La Madre Campesina* and *La Madre Proletaria*, he began the undertaking at once: he and Hart soon became 'very good friends' but there was something in the poet's gaze that was unsettling and Siqueiros rendered him in almost devotional pose – with his eyes looking down at a book.[22] The sitter was delighted with the finished work: for a mere $80 he had acquired a likeness of himself which he told the Rychtariks was 'astounding'.[23] Furthermore, he reassured his stepmother, if he ever wanted or needed to sell it, the painting would command $500 in New York.

Between sittings, Hart renewed his acquaintance with Lesley Byrd Simpson, a Guggenheim fellow eight years his senior whose study of Mexican cultural history would eventually be published as *Many Mexicos*. A professor of history at the University of California, Simpson had taken at once to 'the gray-haired, boyish man with the sensitive face' he had first met in Eyler Simpson's office but now, listening in Doña Berta's bar in Taxco to Hart's plan to turn the Spanish Conquest into poetry, he felt misgivings. The poet's ideas seemed 'completely naïve' and as a historian Simpson had to ask how anyone could write 'a decent poem on the conquest without knowing all there was to know about it'. Not entirely sober himself, he began compiling a bibliography for Hart's benefit but the latter, growing 'restless and disputatious' in the face of this friendly scepticism, finally said 'to hell with all that' and left the bar 'in something of a huff'. As ever impressed by intellectual authority, however, Hart could not let the matter go and a few hours later, in the course of a dramatic storm, he sought the professor out to justify himself and his plan. Simpson and his sociologist colleague Paul Taylor were startled when the poet 'burst into the room' they were sharing: 'words and rain water were pouring from him', Simpson recalled, but he sat on Taylor's bed and began an incoherent argument about 'soaking in the traditions of the country and writing from the spirit'. Taylor was outraged by such imprecision and an argument ensued until two in the morning, with Hart damning the sociologist as 'a middle class pedant' and Simpson suspecting the best thing to do with a drunk was 'to give him his head'. Some time later he escorted the poet, now considerably mollified, back to Spratling's but was once again taken by surprise when Hart's mood shifted and he put his arm around Simpson's neck and declared, 'Lesley, I love you!' He had heard, 'of course, that Hart was a homo', but soon decided that this was not a proposal. 'It was more like the cry of a youngster who had been making a nuisance of himself and felt badly about it.'[24]

Despite its turbulent beginning, the acquaintance blossomed into affection in Mexico City, where Simpson had already befriended another lonely American, Peggy Cowley, and introduced her, as she later remembered, 'to a Mexico of gaiety and fiestas I would never have discovered'.[25] Homesick, and depressed about her divorce, Peggy decided on arrival that she wanted companionship rather than solitude and so decided to stay with Katherine Anne until her departure for Germany rather than accepting Hart's invitation to stay in his empty house. But there were other reasons for avoiding him, as she confessed by letter to Cowley: having 'fallen into the habit of reviling his friends in public', the poet was an increasingly dangerous social proposition and she anticipated the reunion with some apprehension.[26] Hart had his own reasons for shyness following the feud with Katherine Anne but since Cowley had asked him to keep an eye on Peggy in Mexico City he could not avoid her indefinitely and when they did finally meet there was delight on both sides. As Peggy reflected, 'We were "home" to each other and both of us needed "home".'[27] She mentioned how upset Malcolm had been when Hart failed to look him up in New York and then gave her husband the poet's excuse: 'he said he wasn't sure you would want to see him'. Hart seemed 'rather pathetic and subdued' but a few nights later he went all the way to Peggy's apartment in Mexico City to take her to dinner in Mixcoac and when Cowley received Peggy's next letter he learned that 'we do enjoy each other so much. I am on the water wagon and Hart says I am taking it like some religious enthusiast.'[28]

Gregarious and convivial as she was, Peggy had already started to form her own social circle among Mexico City's expatriate colony and soon, through her, Hart met the group of friends – reassuring if also distracting – that he had yearned for since arrival, among them Pierre Durieux, head of General Motors in Mexico, and his wife Caroline; and Betty Beals and her husband Carleton, a writer and journalist from California whose Guggenheim fellowship was devoted to researching a biography of Mexican President Porfirio Díaz. Spratling was integral to this group, as was Anita Brenner, the Mexican-born daughter of an American ranch owner who had published the first history of Mexican art, *Idols behind Altars*, in 1929. Concluding that beneath their Hispanic veneer all Mexicans were really Aztec, Brenner continued to explore the ambiguities of her adopted country as a Guggenheim fellow. She translated Mexican literature, wrote several children's books set in the country, edited a magazine for its tourists, wrote intermittently about it for the *New York Times*, and in 1943 published *The Wind That Swept Mexico: The History of the Mexican Revolution 1910–1942*.[29] But it was Lesley Simpson, single until the arrival of his wife a few months later, who spent most time with Hart and Peggy as they settled into companionship and who accompanied them as they explored the city's parks and museums or combed its markets for trinkets. Since Peggy's apartment was centrally situated, they met and returned there, usually laden with flowers, fruit and vegetables, hats for Peggy from the Palacio de Hierro, statues of saints or blown glass ornaments, and in no time every corner was piled with the easy extravagance with which two lonely people filled the hours between cocktails. For Hart himself the pleasure of it all lay not in acquisition but in companionship, especially with Peggy, who offered a link to distant days in Patterson and Greenwich Village, and in her company he regained an imaginative buoyancy which enabled him to reinvent the lives of their fellow shoppers and pedestrians. 'Passing ordinary people,' she later recalled, 'he promptly clothed them in his own fantasy; they were pimps, cutthroats, prostitutes, femmes fatales, or princes in disguise.'[30]

But what was Peggy herself, the last – and in some ways the most improbable – player to enter Hart Crane's life? Regarding her age, at least, she was more than she claimed: generally she registered 1890 as her year of birth and 'Marguerite Frances' as her given names but several variations existed, including 'Marjory Francis', whose birth as the daughter of Frank and Cecilia Baird at Babylon, Long Island, was recorded as 18 November 1887. But the small print of life was never Peggy's specialism: a born bohemian, insouciant, inventive, easygoing and vain, she lived in the moment and took people as they came. Nobody expected her to earn her living and she seldom indicated a contrary ambition. Her father was an impoverished jeweller whose authority she quickly escaped, not because she longed for fame and wealth – Peggy never showed signs of material greed – but because there was nothing for her in suburban New York. After attendance at the Art Students League she married Orrick Johns, a one-legged poet from Missouri, and once settled in Greenwich Village she established herself as drinking companion to its editors, artists, poets and journalists.

Life around Washington Square was not all cakes and ale, however. Quickly abandoning watercolourist ambitions, Peggy involved herself in Village politics and since she was already emancipated in spirit it was inevitable that the causes of the New Woman would attract her. In 1917, along with various members of the National Women's Party, she was sentenced to thirty days in prison for picketing outside the White House; she survived sixteen days, the first ten of them on hunger strike, before President Wilson's pardon intervened. Despite being one of the first Villagers to bob her hair, however, she never became a strident suffragette – she scorned conventional femininity but her reasons for doing so were cheerfully practical rather than doctrinal: 'A woman in these days can't afford to be feminine unless some nice kind of man has an income of ten thousand to spend on her. A good majority of the present day women have got to be ready to face any emergency and to stand on their own feet at any moment.'[31] At the end of 1918, following the failure of her first marriage, she was struggling to do exactly that – but when Malcolm Cowley began his courtship he had little to offer in the way of security beyond cold-water tenement living in Bedford Street and an ambition grounded in Pennsylvania Dutch determination. Far from flinching, Peggy introduced him to every writer in the Village and by putting him in touch with editors, including her former boyfriend Clarence Britten, literary editor at the *Dial*, she began his career. They were married in August 1919, twelve days before Cowley's majority: although his mother politely detested Peggy as an irreligious slattern, and although the latter's promiscuity brought syphilis into their marriage, the Malcolm Cowleys lived happily for some years, until her easy interpretation of good housekeeping and marital fidelity made Cowley realize he was less bohemian than he thought.

Somewhere in her forties when she arrived in Mexico City, Peggy retained a diminutive, almost elfin, shape; her dark yellow eyes were much remarked, as was her extremely dark hair. Hart Crane's first biographer met her a few years later and found her 'very bawdy', 'a very inventive woman' who never told the same story twice. 'She was very vain, like Crane's mother; she was neurotic, like Crane's mother.'[32] In later life Peggy married twice more and finally came to rest at a home for the destitute at Tivoli, New York, where she was cared for by her lifelong friend, the writer Dorothy Day, and where she died in 1970. She survives on film as a bibulous but endearing chain-smoker with a drawl; men found her attractive but to women she was a variable commodity. Sue Brown thought her 'an undemanding dependent, rather like a well-disposed child'[33] but to Anita Brenner there was a restlessness that made her appear 'sexually pathological'.[34] By contrast Caroline Tate considered her 'almost sexless'. She was at once 'cold, masculine and irresponsible' – 'full of vitality' but 'attractive because not feminine'.[35]

Whatever her allure, Peggy was soon joking in letters to Malcolm about the ease with which she conquered the unconquerable. On 1 October, noting that Hart was once again 'drinking all too heavily' and 'talking very erratically', she declared him 'more than a little in love with me and almost fiendishly jealous' of Cowley. So acute was his possessiveness that he even resented their correspondence. 'By being in love with me,' she explained, 'I don't mean he wants my body, but he does want to marry me, all of course because he is more than a bit lonely and desires a close companionship that he has never found in sex.'[36] On 5 October Hart dropped in to see whether she had recuperated from a fever and once back at home he wrote to Malcolm to report her recovery. Emotionally and psychologically, Peggy seemed 'pretty fragile' but he was convinced she was as happy in Mexico as she could be anywhere else in the circumstances. As for himself, he was delighted by her proximity: 'Old friends are a God-send anywhere!'[37]

Whatever she liked to think, however, Peggy was not the only contender in Hart's romantic life: his sexual activities, he told Mony Grunberg, would now 'take a book' to describe and to Wilbur Underwood he sent almost lyrical reports detailing his extensive fieldwork among the locals.[38] As D.H. Lawrence had said, the nature of the Mexican Indian was far from being sunny, 'but he is more stirred by the moon, if you get what I mean, than any other type I've ever known'. The pure Indian was 'decidedly the most beautiful animal imaginable' and the combination of skin which was 'rich coffee brown [and] always so clear and silken smooth' and 'voices whose particular pitch will make the welkin ring' was seductive indeed. Fortunately, one could do more than just admire: 'The fluttering gait and the powder puff are unheard of here, but that doesn't matter in the least. Ambidexterity is all in the fullest masculine tradition.' Reading this account, Underwood may have wondered if his friend was doing any work at all and Hart's quick reference to his Conquest drama was hardly reassuring. With every passing day he realized 'how intricate the subject is' and how much longer than antici-pated it was going to take.[39] To Grunberg he gave other excuses for not writing. His recent time in New York had left him 'much discouraged' and convinced that 'our civilization is on the lurch'. It would survive, no doubt, 'but with consider-able pain and a number of economic modifications'. Whatever course the future took, it was almost impossible at the moment 'to write a line of sincere lyricism'. So depressing did prospects seem, and so annoying were the comments made about him by journalists, that he was altogether glad to be in Mexico, 'where I never even read the papers, and have developed a great incuriosity regarding most world doings'.[40]

In the middle of October this easy indifference was jolted by a bank statement from Guaranty Trust: he was $350 overdrawn. He knew the deficit resulted from the cheques written to pay for his own and Peter Christiansen's steamship tickets but was at a loss to understand why his account had not since been replenished by payments from CA's estate. He had returned to Mexico with half of the $1,000 left him outright by his father's will and an understanding that the residual $500 would be deposited in his account. Byron Madden had warned that prevailing economic conditions would make the will's annual provision of $2,000 harder to guarantee but had promised the estate would give thirty days' notice if it found itself unable to make the payments. Having received neither warning nor money, Hart wrote to Bess with some anxiety on 20 October, wondering how the companies' balance sheets stood and asking her to authorize payment of the out-standing $500 to his Guaranty Trust account 'as soon as possible' if the other moneys were not going to be paid.[41] A few days later a letter from Byron explained that it would be impossible to consider releasing any of the first pay-ment of $2,000 before the beginning of 1932, since there was no knowing until then whether the various companies had made any profits out of which dividends could be declared. 'For this reason I say again to you ... that it will not be advis-able for you to place any dependence on such payments until you know that they have actually been made.'[42] On 26 October Bess asked Hart to let her know 'how you are financially' and promised that the $150 that remained of the $500 after payment of his bank overdraft would be sent immediately. 'But that is as far as we can go until we know more about things and how they are going to show up.'[43] A few days later she felt more optimistic – matters were bound to look better in

January as a result of Christmas sales and in the long term she was convinced her late husband's probity would continue to operate posthumously: 'I suppose we should feel grateful, and I do Harold, that CA left things in a marvellously clear condition, far more so than one should expect these days, you know it was his boast that he never owed anything at any time that he couldn't take care of.'[44]

It turned unusually chilly at the end of October and Hart caught a cold which he told Lorna he attributed to excessive consumption of habanero at a party 'and then motoring in a large open Lincoln up to Toluca with a couple of Harvard boys', one of whom knew Bill Brown.[45] Unfortunately they were unable to stay in Mexico owing to the imminence of the Game against Yale but Hart saw them off with a tequila-sodden party which even he found 'a little too lively' after one of the young men climbed on to his roof, drew up the ladder behind him and started throwing tiles into his neighbour's courtyard.[46] But any amount of chaos was better than an empty house and a reproachful typewriter, so he permitted Daniel Hernandez and his wife to entertain friends and relations in the kitchen every day. Through his two brothers in the force Hernandez knew about twenty policemen and they seemed happy to divide their time between mounting unofficial guard at Hart's gate and in the evening playing the guitar and singing at his house, 'in a strange, artificial tone, something like Hawaiians, but considerably better,' Bess was informed, 'that is, with more decided rhythm and accent'.[47]

Between these distractions Milton Rourke came and went at will, the beneficiary of Hart's lonely generosity despite Lesley Simpson's warning that he was 'a student of anthropology, a queer, a fuzzy Marxian, and a tremendous sponger, all in one'.[48] At the beginning of November the Day of the Dead arrived and once again Hart marvelled at the pagan permutations of Christian culture, as Mexico City and the country beyond re-enacted the ancestral superstitions: firecrackers in the image of Judas crackled and exploded, stalls selling clay skulls and skeletons appeared in the parks and whole families maintained candlelit vigils on the tombs of their forebears. He succumbed to the grippe a few days later: his home-made medicine, a cocktail of port and brandy, might have felled less seasoned drinkers, but he was soon on his feet again and roaming Mexico City in clothes that Peggy felt came perilously close to travesty – white flannel trousers, a brown and white serape, the silver bridle around his neck and on his head 'one of the largest straw sombreros ever woven, tied under his chin by a multi-colored cord'.[49]

No wonder that anecdotes about Hart were 'snow-balling', to use Lesley Simpson's term.[50] The clowning excess of a vulnerable and insecure character who attracted attention because attention might lead to love provided as much entertainment in Mexico City as it had done in the Village or among the Patterson hills: but as winter approached the expatriates' cynical gaze shifted from the predictability of his drinking and love life to an aspect of the comedy that was wholly unforeseen – the bizarre intimacy that appeared to be developing between the poet and Peggy Cowley. The lurching manoeuvres of this strange dance are hard to establish with accuracy, since heavy drinkers seldom make allowances for the scruples of historians: the letters are undated and their contents often shy or indirect. Yet one bulletin Peggy sent to Malcolm in November informed him of rumours 'that Hart was my lover and that it was a shame that a nice girl like myself was being led astray by a degenerate'. Perhaps the fiction pleased her – for some reason she declined to issue a denial and contented herself with relaying the story to Hart, who replied: 'You'd better marry me and make me a decent woman.'[51]

There could be no question of orthodox courtship, since both parties were disqualified from such procedure by temperament and experience; as it was, they found themselves moving by stormy stages towards a closeness based on mutual dependency for which nothing else in the poet's life had prepared him. Peggy quickly learned to reckon with his delicate pride: following yet another scene with a cab driver she left instructions that he was not to be admitted to her apartment building until further notice, thus prompting one petulant line of retaliation: 'Dear Peggy, I don't think you need bother to consider me a friend any more.'[52] There was a reconciliation and then another severance recorded in another undated letter, this one written by Hart after Peggy had made a drunken and belligerent exit from his house at 4 a.m., apparently with more than her thirst for alcohol left unsatisfied. Again it is impossible to say how closeness began to turn to carnality but it was clear that Hart's initiation into the heterosexual mysteries would have to be undertaken in easier circumstances, as he begged her to understand: 'If you wanted to go further, as you claimed, last night – how could you expect me to, with Maria sick on the bed, and the floor covered with vomit!'[53] By 15 November Peggy and Hart were friends – but only friends – once more and whatever personal regrets she had about him she disguised behind the now-conventional lament: 'God, I hate to see that boy simply making a wreck of himself, how pitiful with his really great power.'[54]

The expatriates' cocktail hour debated the extent to which Peggy was a catalyst in Hart's clear decline but she herself seems never to have pondered the question and she was right to ignore it: his slide towards perdition had begun long ago and would sustain itself regardless of accomplices. Indeed it began to seem as though events were conspiring to hinder him from all achievement. When David Siqueiros succumbed to malaria and had to be moved to Mexico City for medical supervision his wife asked if Hart's house was available as a refuge, 'and of course', Bess Crane was informed, 'there was nothing to do but consent'.[55] The painter's condition was so extreme that he had to be carried across the threshold and for a few days Hart found some excitement in the crisis and the thought that he was assisting in the salvation of Mexican art. More exciting still were the reports that emerged of the place where Siqueiros had contracted the fever in the tropical jungles of the Pacific coast near Acapulco. Here, Loveman was told, were 'native villages where a tax collector has never dared venture, and where the people wear the same Aztec costume that Cortez found them in'. Once again Mexico's 'layer on layer of various races and cultures scattered in the million gorges and valleys' excited his poetic fancy, only to be forgotten a few minutes later amidst the mayhem Siqueiros had imported.[56] Doctors, visitors and assorted courtiers invaded the house, the bills for food and more particularly drink escalated, and Milton Rourke returned to promote the tenets of Marxism in what should have been a home of earnest literary endeavour. But when Hart no longer had any control over his own life he was scarcely in a position to regulate his guests and rather than restoring order he fled – to the Hotel Mancera for one night and then to Tepoztlàn, where he bathed in mountain streams, saw natives who recognized him from his previous visit and wandered lost for thirty-five miles one day when he decided to walk from Tepoztlàn to Cuernavaca.

He felt better on his return, especially after seeing Siqueiros up and about, and learning that in another week he would be fully recovered. But the disappearance of one problem threw another into relief: until the next instalment of Guggenheim funds fell due on 1 January, money was once again a pressing anxiety, not least because Hart had been compelled to pay for his Siqueiros paintings out of his fellowship as a result of the complications surrounding his father's estate. He knew he could always turn to Bess in extremity but as the Depression deepened and banks in the North continued to fail it proved increasingly difficult to cash cheques drawn on overseas accounts. And if money was running out, so too was time: half his Guggenheim year had gone and the Foundation was already recruiting its next generation of fellows, with Eda Lou Walton among the contenders for support. She had given Hart as one of her referees and when he wrote on 27 November it was to assure her that 'my response to Mr Moe will be very warm in your favor'. He warned her that competition for the awards was fierce but was sure her application was being considered seriously. Regarding his own aspirations, he was far from confident. 'These are dull times for poetry,' he told her, and 'with all my present salutary circumstances my impulses in that direction are surprisingly low. A beautiful environment and economic security are far from compensating for a world of chaotic values and frightful spiritual depression.'[57] Yet where could one escape such conditions? Mexico seemed as good a place as any, and he was thinking of staying, he told her, perhaps as a teacher of English literature in some private educational establishment. Having completed his review of James Whaler's *Green River*, which *Poetry* would publish the following April, he continued in dilatory fashion to work on his remaining commission for the magazine, at the same time sustaining a correspondence with Morton Dauwen Zabel regarding other possible articles – a critical study of Wallace Stevens; an essay about William Spratling's forthcoming *Little Mexico*; reviews of James Feibleman's *Death of the God in Mexico* and Phelps Putnam's *Five Seasons*; a consideration of the writer's lot in Mexico or else that country's appeal to the American exile. Nothing came of any of these ideas, despite Zabel's encouragement, but by the beginning of December Hart had come up with a much easier way of making money: he decided to sublet his house, move into more modest quarters and on the financial surplus explore more of the diverse country that was to remain his home for five months more.

Peggy was also thinking of moving: Mexico City's mountain air gave her one cold after another and when William Spratling mentioned that Natalie Scott's house in the lower, warmer zones of Taxco was available for rent she packed her bags, promising before her departure to invite Hart and Lesley Simpson for Christmas. Traditional Mexican festivity began long before then: on 12 December Hart was among the vast throng that processed to Guadalupe Hidalgo, a town on the periphery of Mexico City where four centuries previously the Virgin of Guadalupe, patroness of Mexico, had first appeared to a peon named Juan Diego. As many as 200,000 pilgrims had come from all over the country to attend a festival which as usual combined Christian and pre-Christian rituals in the gaudily ambiguous and now familiar frenzy: fireworks and pealing bells maintained a jubilant cacophony as groups of Indians dressed as Death, the Devil, and Old Man of the Mountain danced in ancient measure before the Cathedral. Determined to see as much of the pomp as possible, Hart had gone to the Cathedral by cab at four in the morning, luckily taking along Daniel Hernandez, who was there to extricate him when his attempts to photograph the rituals provoked grave offence. The huge crowds eliminated all possibility of entering the church itself but Hart was satisfied with watching the dances and glimpsing effigies of the Virgin, 'a typical Mexican product', he informed Bess that evening, 'a strange blend of Christian and pagan strains. What a country and people! The most illogical and baffling on earth; but how appealing!'[58] His stepmother sent seasonal provisions, as did Aunt Bess Madden and the Bill Wrights, but Hart's Christmas really began on 20 December when he arrived at Peggy's house in Taxco. He was two days early but it had been obvious from the moment she left Mexico City how much he missed her: heedless of cost, and of the steep ascent the delivery boy had to make to her door, he serenaded her with telegrams, sometimes two in as many hours, until she decided to telegram him to plead that he send her no more. Returning home from the telegraph office via a cocktail at the cantina she found his reply: 'Why not?'[59] Maria Louisa and Jesus, the servants inherited with her tenancy, took this correspondence as the devotion of a suitor and now his premature presence strengthened their suspicions. Peggy reserved her opinions, merely observing to Malcolm the next day that in view of his early arrival Hart had clearly decided 'that either I needed to be taken care of or he did'.[60]

He found her installed in what she described as 'a tiny white spot on the top of an inaccessible mountain, with steps cut into the ascent' and the moment he arrived he was entranced with the views her house commanded: 'At one moment it was a perfect Breughel and in the next it was painted by Grandma Moses.' It was a hot day: they drank rum sharpened with limes picked from the garden and later Bill Spratling arrived bearing Peggy's Christmas gift – a pair of silver flower basket earrings. Since he and Hart insisted she wear them at once Peggy went to her room to change and on emerging recalled that Hart 'whirled me around' for admiration before jokingly threatening to fall in love. Then, 'in a different tone', he added: 'Of course I really am already.' On arrival Hart had promised Peggy and himself that he would settle the next day to completing the Phelps Putnam review still awaited by Zabel but when the next day dawned and the breathtaking view over the deep *barranca* shimmered and Peggy complained that Christmas was not Christmas unless trimmed with scarlet and green he forgot his good intentions in order to mollify the only figure life seemed to have left him close at hand. She watched as he conspired with the servants – 'Hart's Spanish was a hodge-podge of words strung together with gestures – an animated picture with sound' – and then he descended into the town, to return later with twenty-five unidentified yellow blossoms and 200 scarlet and green poinsettias.[61] Christmas was not Christmas without a lot to drink either: 'I can't say we had a very "dry" time of it,' Hart confessed to Bess. 'We were invited to dances in the houses of the Mayor and other city officials – and more brandy poured out to us in various toasts to one thing and another than would be needed to sink a battleship.' It was a Mexican custom that the nine nights preceding Christmas should be marked by dances or *posadas*: after enjoying the culminating party in the sequence Hart attended midnight Mass and, 'pretty well lit' as he was, he admitted to his stepmother that he almost wept at the singing and the decorations in the Cathedral 'as well as the touching beauty of the indian people kneeling'.[62]

A dozen friends arrived to celebrate Christmas Day amidst Hart's poinsettia meadows, and as Peggy related to Malcolm, he 'carved chickens for dinner, moved tables, ordered servants, made guests feel at home, squeezed lemons for the rum punch, stayed sober and filled other glasses before his own'.[63] Hours later Peggy and the poet saw the last of her guests into the bus departing from the town and adjourned to the cantina as a prelude to a quiet night and what they hoped would be several days of peace in which he could do some writing. Back at the house, however, the cathedral bells which had sounded agreeably in the plaza below now proved deafening and put an end to all hopes of conversation, let alone sleep. Retracing their steps, they watched the town fireworks and joined the dancing in the plaza. 'We danced until we could dance no longer,' Peggy remembered years later, in a memoir which sometimes reads like cheap fiction but which nevertheless survives as the only account of Hart Crane's foray into heterosexuality. 'Everything appeared to be spinning off into an infinity of color and music. "It's all a poem and I shall write it, with us right in the middle of it, darling." '

They became lovers that night, 'the clamor of the bells our wedding music', and in observance of their new involvement Maria Louisa departed from precedent the following morning by knocking before she entered Peggy's room with coffee and orange juice. They were 'ludicrously happy', Peggy felt, with Hart 'drunk in the excitement of the moment, a bit awed, but still unafraid'.[64] At last he was no longer an outsider: at last he could hold his head high among the married couples back home or the hard-drinking expatriates who gathered at Doña Berta's bar. When he made his way there later on 26 December William Spratling detected a swagger in his manner as he walked up to the crowd of familiar drinkers and declared: 'Boys, I did it!'[65] Lady Duff Twysden – Hemingway's 'Brett' in *The Sun Also Rises* – her future husband, the American painter Clinton King, and the poet Witter Bynner were in Taxco for the holiday and in no time they were familiar with the details of Hart's conversion and happy to join him in shouting lewd limericks from rooftops, 'your collection being more than ever in demand', Hart assured Cowley a few days later.[66] For now, however, Malcolm would not be told what had happened: his best friend and his wife had decided to keep news of their involvement a strictly Mexican affair; there would be plenty of time later for gossip in New York.

Back at Peggy's, Hart began work on the poem he had mentioned in another lifetime less than twenty-four hours before: the pealing of the cathedral bells continued, to be joined now by the rhythms from the phonograph, the mechanical muse he played at full volume as he adjusted himself to the half-forgotten struggles of poetry. He had always included any friends who happened to be nearby in the labours of composition – now that he planned a variation on an epithalamium it was inevitable that Peggy, integral to the poem's inspiration, should also be involved in its execution. 'And so he began,' she recorded later, 'phrases scribbled on paper, voiced in words to test the sound, discarded completely, or held for a later trial. He was the instrument on which he played the words, changing each perhaps a hundred times before retaining one small fragment.' For three days, with little or no respite, he worked, 'keyed to the highest pitch' and possessed, she felt, of an energy that seemed 'inexhaustible'.[67] With New Year's Eve in sight he managed to produce a rough draft of three stanzas, one of which Peggy sent to Malcolm:

The bell-cord that gathers God at dawn
Dispatches me – as though I climbed the knell
Of a clear morn – I could walk the cathedral lawn
Clear to the meridian – and back from hell.[68]

Much work remained to be done but 'The Broken Tower', as the poem would come to be called, was under way. For some time, Peggy recalled, Hart had confided his fear that he would never write again but now his anxieties were dispelled. Her explanation for his renewed creativity – that now 'he felt purified of a sense of guilt which he had always had as a homosexual' – bore little scrutiny in the light of his past achievement but Peggy was nevertheless crucial to the 'The Broken Tower', because she believed, not in his sexual, but in his poetic, potency and she did so, like Grace Crane before her, unfailingly and unquestioningly.[69]

Fireworks lit the Taxco skies once more as 1932 dawned, and a few days later Hart returned to Mixcoac to address practicalities ignored for more than two weeks. Although his passport had disappeared, its loss to be reported to the Consulate, he established that his tourist permit remained valid until 4 March. Katherine Anne had given him the name of a doctor months before and now he determined to search for his address for vaccination against typhoid. The house was still not sublet but the rent had to be paid nevertheless and numerous letters from New York awaited replies. But the correspondence he pursued with most eagerness was with Peggy, his 'Twidget', just as he (and his phallus) were now her 'Old Mizzentop'. Almost his first act on returning to Mexico City on 5 January was to send her $75, which he followed the next day with a hastily written letter reminding her 'that you already know the depth of my love for you' and stating that he hoped Lesley Simpson would sublet the house, in which case they might go to Acapulco together at the end of the month.[70] When he wrote the next day it was to report that Simpson could not commit himself about the house before the arrival of his wife Marian at the end of the month and that Acapulco therefore seemed unlikely. But if his plans varied, his sentiments and his desires had not changed: 'I missed your darling hands last night. Old Mizzentop doesn't like air pockets either!'[71] On 9 January Peggy urged him to 'go on the wagon for a while especially when you're not with me as you can get into packs of trouble by yourself'. She had received 'a very depressing letter from Malcolm' which told of bank failures and suicides in the North. The world was a bleak place and she knew of only one sanctuary: 'Be a bit, just a tiny bit faithful to me . . . I do miss you so dearest and don't like this enforced purity. I want to be held in your arms the entire night and wake up melting with passion.'[72] A few hours later she wrote again, saying that it 'seems simply ages since you left' and that she missed him terribly. 'I neither trust your virginity nor my own on so long a separation, although I'll admit you're worth waiting for a long time.'[73] The following day her tone was more serious and her range more long-sighted: 'I haven't the vaguest notion that I want anyone for the pleasures of the moment. I'm frankly afraid of marriage, which is my right, *that* I feel is *out* forever.' A secret affair seemed impossible also, when they realized the morning he left Taxco that discretion was alien to both their temperaments. 'I knew then as I know now that I wanted you to come back and close me in your arms; they, thank God, are more intimate, stronger, frailer and humbler than I knew existed.'[74] Yet to Malcolm on 12 January she spoke of Hart's return to Mixcoac in clinical terms, as though she were conducting a scientific study: 'I presume he will wait until the house and the servants became an albatross around his neck, go out on a binge and then rush to me for salvation.'[75] She could scarcely be blamed for suggesting his dependence, however, when Hart's letters now verged on the abject:

> Why is it that you love me so? I'm just a careening idiot with a talent for humor at times, and for insult and desecration at others. But I can, and must say that your love is very precious to me. For one thing it has given me an assurance that

I thought long buried.... Do you remember my saying that I would not fall in love with you, or with anyone again? But I find that though I like to perpetuate that statement, I have really over-ruled it in a thousand thoughts and emotions.[76]

Peggy too had revisions of feeling to declare. Admitting that she was 'an exceedingly lusty woman', she insisted he had affected her more deeply than she had ever intended, not least because she had promised herself she was done with all fallacies of the heart: 'But perhaps love is the only illusion in the world worth having, even [if] while having it one is sensible of the fact that it has no lasting qualities.'[77]

On 16 January Peggy reported to Malcolm that Hart had returned to Taxco 'just as I expected'.[78] He had now abandoned all hope of subletting his house and had paid Señor Lepine a further $70 to perpetuate his tenancy. 'The family will just have to fork up a loan or something for me,' he announced, 'and I feel sure they will.'[79] Nevertheless he still planned to explore more of Mexico and hoped that Peggy would accompany him not only to Acapulco but also to Michoacan, Morelia, Lake Chapala and perhaps even Jalapa, near Vera Cruz. Contentedly drinking coffee on her terrace, Peggy was disinclined for adventure – Acapulco was one thing, but she felt reluctant to go anywhere else, not least because even staying at home with Hart was exhausting: 'It was hard to keep up with his fierce tempo, charging everything with tremendous energy, drinking, writing, making love, and just enjoying himself. It was like living with an erupting volcano.'[80] Festivity once again prevailed in Taxco, this time in honour of the name day of the town's saint and when Hart and Peggy descended to investigate they encountered a veritable circus of religious devotion: a crowd of people heading to church for priestly blessing – not for themselves but for the animals they accompanied, each of which had been painted and adorned with all the inventiveness Mexican piety could devise. Peggy saw a green pig on a purple ribbon and a pink cat with earrings. 'Green parrots were turned blue and blue ones green, while a white cockatoo was completely silvered. Not to be outdone, there was Maria Louisa carrying our tomorrow's meal, a turkey, with strands of tiny silvered Christmas beads wound round its neck, at which it was pecking vigorously.' Hart was unimpressed and whispered: 'Whores, dressed up for an Easter parade.'[81] He resumed work on the new poem and on 26 January an early draft was finished. The urgent and dramatic images which punctuated the writing continued to circulate in his mind, compounding the anxieties – about money, Peggy, and life after Mexico – of what looked like being a turning point in life. He and Peggy had gone into Taxco to celebrate poetic progress, and despite drinking 'a terrific amount', she told Malcolm, 'neither one of us got drunk'.[82]

That night, Hart was unable to sleep – he rose in the dark, retraced his steps to the town plaza, and as though by assignation met his friend the old Indian bell-ringer who was on his way to church to ring in the dawn. He invited the poet to assist him and the scene that ensued acquired the aspect of an epiphany: as Hart pulled down the thunderous music that would awaken the town, dawn broke over the mountains like the revelation that followed the Word or the enlightenment that was the prerogative of poets. Five years later, when the novelist Paul Bowles visited Taxco, he discovered that the town was still talking of Hart's climb to the turrets of Santa Prisca – not as a rite of illumination but the antic of a drunk – yet when Lesley Simpson saw the poet 'striding up the hill afterwards in a sort of frenzy' he knew this was no ordinary morning visit. Hart 'refused his breakfast, and paced up and down the porch impatiently waiting for me to finish my coffee. Then he seized my arm and bore me off to the plaza, where we sat in the shadow of the church, Hart the while pouring out a magnificent cascade of words.'[83] He returned home to revise the work yet again, with Peggy discreetly supervising progress. 'All prophecies to the contrary,' she told Malcolm on 27 January, 'he is by no means finished. It is a magnificent piece of lyric poetry that is built with the rhetorical splendor of a Dante in Hell.' She promised he would receive a copy as soon as the poem was complete. 'The boy can commit any fool flamboyant act he wishes, or rot in jail, if he only gets something like this out of his system once in a while.'[84]

No sooner said than done. On the evening of 28 January he went into Taxco alone and a while later an Indian boy came to the house with a note saying Hart was in gaol. Peggy conferred with William Spratling, who said there was nothing for it but to let him languish overnight and in the morning face the sort of heavy fine the town always imposed on drunken foreigners. But the next day, when he paid a visit and then conveyed Hart's message that Peggy was 'acting high hat' by declining to see him, Spratling also revealed that his houseboy was involved. Suddenly it became clear why Hart had decided that evening to go into the town alone for a drink, when the natural thing would have been to take her along. She was furious. So much for her attempts to change him: by chance or design he had met Spratling's servant and they had been caught together, and it was the disgrace of discovery that so annoyed her and made her attempts at conversion look so foolish. No wonder she was angry, so angry that she refused to visit the prisoner, refused to see him on to the bus that took him back to Mexico City on 29 January, and refused to admit to posterity what had actually happened. Hurt pride made her claim Hart's crime had been 'a too-loud voice, or solo dancing in the street'[85] but such trespasses, already so familiar, could never have provoked the banishment the poet mentioned when he cabled for her on 31 January: CAN NEVER ENTER TAXCO AGAIN BUT SO NEED YOU HERE FOR A FEW DAYS. WILL FOOT ALL EXPENSE THANKS DARLING.[86]

22

Hart returned to Mixcoac to find his house reduced to turmoil by Milton Rourke, who had come and gone during his absence in Taxco. It was bad enough that everywhere was dirty and untidy but the discovery that his typewriter had been damaged outraged him beyond words and by main force he removed the Marxist archaeologist from his property. Yet without Rourke he was once again thrown back on himself, with the increasingly morose Daniel Hernandez for companionship, and no sooner had he returned home than he began pleading by telegram for Peggy's presence. She capitulated at the beginning of February and spent most of the journey to Mexico City wondering, as she subsequently admitted to Malcolm, 'what in hell was in store for me on my arrival'.

Having proposed a rendezvous at 7.30 at her favourite restaurant, the Broadway, located on the upper side of the Alameda, she arrived to find him sober and eager for forgiveness, and without even touching the cocktail before him he proffered his peace offerings – two new records and a bouquet of violets and sweet peas. Returning to Mixcoac after dinner, Peggy found that 'the servants had spent the whole day fixing wreaths all over the place for my reception and the whole thing', she told Malcolm, 'was very touching and sweet'.[1] Hernandez and his wife greeted her with 'graceful cordiality' and if their manner also suggested 'a great relief at my presence', Peggy could find no other sign of the domestic disarray Hart had described. Daniel's extended kin now seemed to be an unquestioned presence in a household which also comprised Hart's flea-infested spitz, Paloma, and a tiny white kid eventually destined for the table but intended in the interim as a pet for Peggy. 'If it found itself alone,' she remembered, 'it would run around bleating for attention, its tiny hoofs clicking like a woman's high heels on the tiled floors.' And hanging from a wall, serene yet disturbing above the *ménage*, was the portrait the poet had commissioned from Siqueiros: 'It showed him reading, the luminous light focussed on his silver hair.'[2]

Hart developed a fever following his return to Mexico City's unforgiving altitude but he was up and about again by 5 February, when he wrote to Bess wondering 'whether or not I can plan on having at least part of the annual payment from the estate to draw on beginning the first of April'. By then his fellowship would have ended, and although for the time being he wanted to prolong his stay in Mexico he remained 'very much worried' about the future.[3] 'You must tell me more about Peggy, sounds interesting,' his stepmother replied, promising to help financially whenever she could.[4] Whatever details he supplied, they would be less revealing than the admissions Hart began to send to friends in New York. To Sam Loveman he insisted that 'conjugal life, however unofficial, [is] a great consolation to a loneliness that had about eaten me up',[5] and to Mony Grunberg, revealing that he had indeed 'broken ranks with my much advertised "brotherhood" ', Hart said his involvement with Peggy had 'given me new perspectives, and after many tears and groans – something of a reason for living'.[6] He bought her an onyx ring as an earnest of his love yet wherever they went they were stared at as strange and incongruous: when he took her to see one of Charlie Chaplin's films, briefly playing far across Mexico City in a shanty-town cinema for which they were absurdly over-dressed, she decided she had never felt 'more conspicuous than when I walked down that aisle, conscious of the orchids on my shoulder'. To make matters worse, 'there was Hart in an immaculate white linen suit, a gardenia in his button-hole and carrying a box of Huyler's candy he had bought for me. Everyone in the audience turned to stare at us silently, as if their heads moved on well-oiled pivots.'[7] Peggy stayed at Mixcoac for slightly more than a week and during that time she and Hart saw a lot of Lesley Simpson, now joined by his wife Marian, but withdrew to Hart's rooftop when in reclusive mood to sit in peaceful contemplation of distant Popocatepetl as it shimmered against the blue sky and the bluer blossoms that covered his parapet. He even managed while she was there to contribute to a pamphlet published by the Salon Espagnol to mark its exhibition in honour of Siqueiros, thus joining Elie Faure and Sergei Eisenstein, among others, in praise of an art which seemed 'classic in its grounding in those persistent earth-problems that both challenge and nourish the man who is strong enough to invite them and incorporate them as major elements in his own cosmos of design'.[8]

Despite Hart's entreaties, Peggy returned to Taxco, only to discover that her landlady had sold the house and that she was obliged to move almost immediately. As an interim measure she could stay with friends but before long she would have to decide whether or not to accept the suggestion that she move in permanently with Hart. Writing on 10 February she ignored the dilemma in favour of pledges of adoration: 'I do so love you and wish intensely for your happiness. By getting the best out of yourself you will give the best to me. I've been a person very disappointed with life, but you have given me a new strength and a new will.'[9] At other times, however, she felt overwhelmed by the challenges of the involvement. 'True, I knew by now I loved Hart', she remembered, but she also knew that living with him meant 'accepting his tremendous vitality'. He lived by a 'high tension' which was exhausting for all around him – however, 'to think of changing him would be as absurd as trying to change the course of a hurricane'.[10] But the fact remained that she *had* tried to change him, which is why she was so angry when he let her down by getting caught with a boy in Taxco. She was not alone in her misgivings, as Hart suggested when he wrote to her on 11 February. Emphasizing his gratitude for the way she had transformed his life – 'I am bound to you more than I ever dreamed of being' – he once again invited her to move in with him. However, 'I don't think that either one of us ought to urge the other into anything but the most spontaneous and mutually liberal arrangements.'[11] These were hardly the words of blind love and when on St Valentine's Day he wrote to Wilbur Underwood to break the news of his sexual defection he insisted that nothing had really changed. His liaison with 'gorgeous Jorge' was over, because the latter had stolen one of his suits, but when it came to matters with Peggy, Hart was hesitant, even doubtful. The affair had done him 'considerable good' but he had no way of knowing how long it would last and had certainly 'engaged in no promises of any sort'. Women were all very well but, 'The old beauty still claims me and my eyes roam as much as ever.'[12]

In the midst of these uncertainties, Daniel Hernandez suddenly became an impossible presence: for some time his manner had been sulkily unsatisfactory, but now – like the mimicking servant of theatrical farce – he often returned home incapably drunk. This was not behaviour Hart could easily condemn and any kind of confrontation had become doubly difficult now that Hernandez had taken to walking around with a knife and pistol. He declined to work and was often scarcely polite but firing him might prove both difficult and dangerous: he knew the details of Hart's love life and the communist loyalties of Lisa, a member of the Siqueiros entourage who had stayed behind to work in the kitchen and who was 'scared to death of him'.[13] In the end Hart prevailed on his landlord to find him another servant and by the time he wrote to Peggy on 16 February Hernandez was working for a neighbouring general.

But by now Hart was openly sceptical of the possibility of any constancy between Peggy and himself. With her friend Luz in Taxco, he doubted her evenings were either sober or chaste and moreover he seemed not to care: 'Just as long as you don't let your right hand know what your left hand doeth, as they say, I'll keep the same code, at least with my index finger.' He was going out for the evening and his parting words – 'Ahoy and ahoy and AHOY!' – gave an indication of his intentions if not his exact destination.[14] Sexual fidelity aside, however, there was a mutual need or sympathy that reunited them again and again and the following day, in a letter he could never have written to his mother, Hart struggled to define the significance of Peggy's friendship to Bess. 'We probably won't ever marry,' he told his stepmother, but Peggy's 'devotion and companionship' were invaluable to him, not least because they helped assuage 'that terrible virus of criticism that all the Cranes are born with'. There had been times, as Bess knew, when that virus had threatened to destroy his very reasons for living but now, and in part due to Peggy, he had regained an intermittent love for existence: 'I may care now, at times, and I suspect that *unconsciously* I'm very much on the side of Life.'[15] Bess's reply was in every way encouraging: in view of economic conditions in America she agreed he might as well remain in Mexico if he felt happier there and by now she was confident that CA's estate would soon yield sufficient funds for Hart's inheritance payments. As for Peggy, 'I am so glad you have found someone of whom you are fond, there is nothing like the companionship of the one who understands us, I know, that is what I miss now more than I can say.' So few people could ever comprehend one's moods or prove conducive to personal peace, 'so don't you be the one to spoil it, with SELF'.[16] Then in the middle of February Peggy agreed – she would move in: Hart had one of his rooms contrived as a studio and study for her and promised, 'I'll make you a good husband yet. Nothing ostentatious. It will be a paltry thing but my own.'[17] He wanted her first dinner in the house to be a festive affair and opened 'good white Spanish wine', Malcolm was told, 'which we sat over after dinner until all hours of the night, our tongues going at both ends and scarcely listening to each other'.[18] They posed in the garden for photographs – an incongruous yet tentatively happy couple beneath a tree – and once the pictures had been made into postcards Hart scrawled further declarations of his love and at the beginning of March sent them to friends in America. Subject to her divorce, they were living together in the spirit of matrimony: vows and resolutions were exchanged – less drink, more work – and since an engagement had effectively been declared with postcards, it was clearly time for a honeymoon.

Withdrawing his remaining $150 of Guggenheim funds, Hart deposited $100 in a newly opened Mexican bank account and with the balance he took Peggy to the ancient city of Puebla. The few days they spent there seemed a vindication of his desire to stay in Mexico: with its vivid bazaars, wide streets, tree-shaded plazas and pastel-painted houses, it struck him, he told Bess, as 'one of the most beautiful places I have ever seen'. There were 365 churches in the city, among them the second-largest cathedral in the Americas, the interior of which blazed with sufficient gold 'to pay off Germany's reparation debts'.[19] He and Peggy were more acquisitive than devout, however, and after visiting precisely two of the sacred buildings they headed for the markets and with easy prodigality bought flowers, blown glass trinkets and textiles. After all, with Bess's assurance that his inheritance would materialize, Hart could afford to be extravagant and his generosity towards Peggy was in part an expression of 'a sort of 18th century chivalry', to use Anita Brenner's term, 'a gentlemanliness that involved a feeling of protection and responsibility for a fragile American lady in a somewhat difficult, apparently very dangerous foreign land'.[20]

Back in Mixcoac, Hart reminded Bess that he was depending on his inheritance for survival: once his lease expired he would move into a smaller and less expensive house but he stressed that he would still need $125 every month, to be paid into his new bank account. Otherwise, everything was satisfactory: Peggy was doing him 'a great deal of good' and he was working on 'one of the strongest pieces of poetry I've ever written'.[21] The gradual arrival in mid-March of the new school of Guggenheim fellows reminded him of the timeliness of his financial calculations but in apparent harmony he and Peggy attended expatriate cocktail parties as a couple, and as a couple they reciprocated the hospitality. Hart continued to revise and expand 'The Broken Tower' and when not writing he would often join Peggy on the porch of the house, 'a large glass pitcher of beer at hand,' she recalled, 'comfortable in pillows and serapes, books, my cigarettes, Hart's cigars'.[22] He read *Idols behind Altars*, W.C. Redfield's account of shipping and storm systems off Mexico, Madame Calderon de la Barca's *Life in Mexico, during a Residence of Two Years in that Country* and Charles Malcolm Flandreau's *Viva Mexico!* He decided to send for Eugene O'Neill's plays and in a reversion to old passions he acquired a volume of Donne, edited by Hugh L'Anson Fausset and published in 1931, and found, in the career of the great Metaphysical, a pattern of self-discovery that was more resonant to him now than it could ever have been a decade before. Poetic experimentation, physical gratification, self-disgust and a mystical apprehension of the spirituality that lay beyond carnal ecstasy – if Hart's career had not followed the same course he could nevertheless trace a significance in Donne's life pattern and he underlined numerous lines and titles as the force of parallel experience struck him. Most of the books Hart owned in Mexico were subsequently lost, but this *Donne*, complete with bookplate, survives, its marked passages assuming a disturbing significance in the light of subsequent events:

> I joy, that in these straits, I see my West;
>   For, though their currents yield return to none,
> What shall my West hurt me? As West and East
>   In all flat Maps (and I am one) are one,
>   So death doth touch the Resurrection.[23]

The tranquillity was short-lived: within two weeks of Peggy's arrival she and Hart were drinking and quarrelling in spectacular fashion – about money, mutual accountability, his Indian boys, her expectations – with corresponding theories of blame and exoneration circulating among the expatriates. Natalie Scott condemned Peggy squarely for the increasing turbulence of Hart's life and Anita Brenner, suspecting that he confronted 'sexual exhaustion, alcoholic depression, and a seeming impossibility of escape', was inclined to agree. She remembered how he 'spoke bitterly about the relationship … and spoke of attempting to escape, while at the same reiterating his affection for her, and repeating that she was "a lovely person"'.[24] Lesley Simpson was sure 'Hart was squirming to get off the hook' of engagement but lacked the resolve. 'Peggy knew what she wanted. Hart didn't. My guess is that Hart was fed up with their relationship, because Peggy worried and irritated him continually.'[25] Marian Simpson used to hear him complaining about Peggy's domestic untidiness and remembered that 'he was almost inarticulate with disgust when she longed for them to go back to New England to see the first arbutus'. Since her arrival weeks before, Marian had seen much of the poet through her husband but the attraction to his personality had been immediate – 'he seemed to me good and childlike, no matter what mad obsessions drove him' – and soon she and Hart developed an independent friendship based on outings to the cinema or afternoons of café gossip. She found something endearing in the 'jovial grey-haired youth, gulping chocolate ice-cream soda at Sanborn's' but was too realistic to absolve him of blame for all his domestic problems: the more she heard of their life together, the more she was convinced Peggy was no more than 'a jolly companion on the way to hell'. She formed the impression that Hart 'rather liked women to be nuisances – until they cramped *his* style' and was intrigued one afternoon to witness his reactions to Greta Garbo's performance in a film she misremembered as 'The Green Hat'. 'After a few wise-cracks he fell silent and insisted on sitting through the whole of it, absorbed and fascinated by the hysterical lost lady. He said she reminded him of his mother.'[26] The Simpsons suspected that 'Peggy had some foggy notion of rescuing Hart from his Indian boys' and their suspicions were confirmed one evening when their servant announced the arrival of a visitor. 'A wild man?' Simpson wondered. Yes, the servant conceded, he did seem 'a little *raro*'. Simpson went to investigate, 'and there was Hart, all rigged up in a French sailor's outfit, very merry and noisy'. Clearly the worse for wear, he loudly declared his intention of moving to San Francisco but proved placid when Simpson decided he should be fed. Between mouthfuls, 'he entertained me and the whole café relating his adventures with Peggy. "She thinks she can reform me, does she? I'll show her! Why, God damn her, I'd rather sleep with a man any time than with her!"'[27]

The apparent regularity of these dramas places Peggy's simultaneous accounts to Malcolm – 'frankly it's a real joy to see Hart so happy, contented, and really in love for the first time' – in a near-comic light besides lending justification to the Simpsons' anxiety that their friend was unable to do any writing.[28] Yet somehow 'The Broken Tower' was completed and on 27 March, as the Easter bells rang across Mexico, Hart dispatched copies to Loveman, to Morton Dauwen Zabel at *Poetry* and to Malcolm Cowley, to whom he explained that he had become almost 'too damned self-critical to write at all' and whose opinion he invited 'of this verse, prose or nonsense – whatever it may seem'.[29] Thanks to Peggy, Cowley had received fragments of the work as it progressed, but seeing it now in perfected form he might well have concluded that Hart Crane's last poem – and the only significant achievement of his Guggenheim fellowship – was also his most allegorical. Begun and completed to the bell-music of Christmas and Easter, it is a poem concerned with death and resurrection. Yet it is not a Christian poem, any more than Mexico's religious festivals were strictly Christian: its death and possible redemption are Crane's, rather than Christ's. It appears ambiguous in intent and success but the fact remains that it was a poem that mattered profoundly to its author: many lyrics were begun between the publication of *The Bridge* and Crane's death, but the only one he considered it worthwhile to complete was 'The Broken Tower', a poem of retrospection written by a man who suspected the time had come to summarize life and its achievements. It was a life of poetry begun in a tower – the 'Sanctum de la Tour' where he had first endeavoured to map his quest and first struggled with the force of love as an inspiration, not only for poetry, but for existence itself. It was a search that had taken him to the skyscrapers of commercial Manhattan and the massive pylons of Brooklyn Bridge before bringing him now to this land of older towers – at Tepoztlàn, Taxco, Guadalupe and Puebla – where the ceremonial of faith was ubiquitous and where his belief, in his own poetic greatness and in the very value of poetry, had forsaken him. The bells of the opening stanza, which call the devout to prayer, proclaim this loss of conviction – 'The bell-rope that gathers God at dawn/Dispatches me' – and the ghostly poet, dead because he can no longer write, wanders 'the cathedral lawn', his 'feet chill on steps from hell'. Skirting the edifice of belief, his eye is caught by disturbing shades within:

Have you not heard, have you not seen that corps
Of shadows in the tower, whose shoulders sway
Antiphonal carillons . . .

These dead men, who swing as though hanged on the gallows, sang in antiphons to the common chorus of humanity, much as Crane himself did – some as sexual outlaws and others as romantic or visionary poets who proposed an ecstatic alternative to daily existence. Although they remain unnamed, all Crane's literary heroes are imagined here – Blake, Marlowe, Rimbaud, Baudelaire and Melville – destroyed not only by society but by the inspiring force that blazed within them. 'The bells, I say, the bells break down their tower;/And swing I know not where.' Poetry is now imagined as a form of possession which can 'engrave/Membrane through marrow' but which in the end will inevitably destroy those from whom it rings. Yet it too will die, or fade away, as 'Banked voices slain' or 'terraced echoes prostrate on the plain'. Mankind is forever eager for belief and wisdom, and Crane considers how poet after poet has tried to offer enlightenment, only to find himself spent and his achievement forgotten. The catalogue of literary oblivion is so long and dispiriting that he now looks to his own achievement and wonders how valid it has been:

And so it was I entered the broken world
To trace the visionary company of love, its voice

An instant in the wind (I know not whither hurled)
But not for long to hold each desperate choice.

My word I poured. But was it cognate, scored
Of that tribunal monarch of the air
Whose thigh embronzes earth, strikes crystal Word
In wounds pledged once to hope, – cleft to despair?

His thraldom to his calling has been complete – but was his poetry 'cognate'? Did it have the validity, the universality, that expectant mankind wanted, and for which it turned repeatedly to religion? The poet cannot answer his own question – and with the seventh stanza 'The Broken Tower' changes course. Having argued in general terms the human need for faith and the visionary company's doomed attempt to meet that need, the poem veers towards autobiography. With his customary love of word-play, Crane also conceived 'The Broken Tower' as a lyric of phallic disappointment and thus of homosexual disenchantment: each 'broken interval', 'each desperate choice', that it mentions acknowledges another painful all-male love affair. 'The steep encroachments of my blood left me/No answer.' For all the sexual and emotional intensities he has experienced with other men, he is as bewildered about the nature of love – the poet's ultimate authority – as ever and now wonders 'could blood hold such a lofty tower/As flings the question true?' In view of his sexuality could he ever hope to determine love's true mysteries? But suddenly his life appears to have changed: 'is it she/Whose sweet mortality stirs latent power?'

With Peggy's advent he seems to have regained poetic conviction and to have been purged of childhood memories of heterosexual strife: 'My veins recall and add, revived and sure/The angelus of wars my chest evokes:/What I hold healed, original now, and pure.' All well and good – except that Crane himself knew it was not true. All his life he had longed to heal with affirmation and all his life he had suffered anxieties that because of his sexuality he was not 'pure'. Inevitably he yearned more than anything to be 'original', to reach back to an existence that predated the anguish of sexual guilt and the misery of parental discord. The corollary to this longing involved union with Peggy and participation in the cycles of 'sweet mortality' which might lead to the conception of children. As he well knew, however, the reality was that those unborn innocents would be exposed to turbulence quite as great as any he had experienced during his own childhood. And if sexual conversion was in certain respects a happy idea it was also paradoxically an emasculating one, because it would involve a kind of negation of all the coded intensities of his finest, and pre-heterosexual, love lyrics – a contingency which would have made him an even greater failure than he now felt himself to be. But of course it could never happen: he knew, however much he told himself Peggy had redirected his erotic urges, that he still turned his head at every 'gorgeous

Jorge' who came his way. The poem ends with two stanzas promising contentment and reconciliation: instead of attempting to scale the firmament, the poet will look within himself for peace, and will do so assisted by this woman's love:

And builds, within, a tower that is not stone
(Not stone can jacket heaven) – but slip
Of pebbles, – visible wings of silence sown
In azure circles, widening as they dip

The matrix of the heart, lift down the eye
That shrines the quiet lake and swells a tower . . .

The metaphorical landscape – with the tranquil waters of her adoration and the majestic edifice of male desire – is idyllic but also surreal, not unlike the devoutly willed conclusion of 'Atlantis'. It is also confused, in light of the earlier claim that contentment will come from sublimation, from 'towers' built 'within'. Hart Crane had never known any kind of love which brought serenity and the events of recent weeks scarcely justified claims that Peggy had changed that pattern; but then the last couplet moves away from personal relations between man and woman to the union of earth and heaven and envisages a final peace which has about it the aspect of an assumption, realized against 'The commodious, tall decorum of that sky'.[30]

On 31 March Hart's Guggenheim fellowship officially ended: as he told Lorna, somewhat forlornly, 'I'm just plain Hart Crane again.'[31] With the affiliation expired, numerous practicalities had to be addressed, among them the subject of accommodation and country of abode, but since he was in no state to make any significant decisions Hart's plans varied from day to day. San Francisco still appealed, and an undated memo urges consultation with Lesley Simpson, a native of the city, about finding somewhere to store possessions ('in case I land in Frisco without funds') and somewhere else to live – 'possible place of residence, – cheap, windy and perspective'.[32] A change of mood could see him equally determined to remain where he was, however, and to Caresse Crosby he was persuasive and evocative in his conviction that Mexico would remain a haven and a source of inspiration: 'There is never an end to dancing, singing, rockets and the rather lurking and suave dangers that give the same edge to life here that the mountains give to the horizon.'[33] His epic, he confessed, was not even begun and if she thought his French had been embarrassing after months in France he had to confess that his Spanish was equally lame – and after a whole year in which to acquire proficiency. Had his Mexican time gone quickly or slowly? He never said – but by a predictable coincidence he suddenly ran into one of the earliest acquaintances he had made in Mexico City, Léon Felipe Camino, who was startled to hear Hart declare, 'very joyfully and in a loud voice as if he wished all the world should know, "I'm very happy because I have discovered that I am not a homosexual".'³⁴

The news must have come as a revelation to Marsden Hartley, a recent arrival in Mexico who had secured the poet's address from Mary Doherty, secretary to the Guggenheim Foundation in Mexico City. Invited to tea in Mixcoac, Hartley arrived to find Hart flamboyantly clad in his idea of Mexican costume and 'in a gay mood, with Mrs Cowley, an old friend of his, receiving. They had already imbibed their "tea", of which I never saw a sign.' Poet and painter had last seen each other in Marseilles, but when Hartley, presuming considerable intervening achievement, politely inquired about Hart's writing in Mexico, he was surprised to learn that only one poem had been completed, 'which I thought rather meagre product for any one's poetical year'. Whether expressed or not, his surprise must have been apparent, because Hart began explaining and apologizing, 'but when he added – I do not think I have anything more to say I returned with something like vehemence, nonsense, you have only just begun' – an assertion to which Hart made no reply. They went for a walk through the agave fields to the Molinas de las Rosas and for a while surveyed the country 'in its brown volcanic splendour' before returning to Hart's house, where at 8.30 Hartley asked for a cab to return him to the Hotel Regis. 'I will go with you,' said Hart, 'I have had enough of this.' Without making his boredom and claustrophobia obvious to Peggy, however, he was in no position to insist, and Hartley was able to extricate himself. Some time later, as he was getting ready for bed, the telephone rang. It was Hart: 'I followed you into town, I just couldn't stand another moment of that.' He was desperate to drink and talk but Hartley was firm. 'Well then,' the poet pleaded, 'may I look you up tomorrow?'³⁵

With practically nothing remaining of his Guggenheim funds, Hart was now completely dependent on money from Ohio and when at the beginning of April it failed to arrive he turned frantic. Without pausing to wonder what difficulties could have made his stalwart stepmother fail him (and the least of them included a car accident at Canary Cottage in which one of her best friends was seriously injured), he adopted the time-honoured expedient of borrowing where he could, but lacking the self-confidence which had once enabled him to live from day to day he found buying time to be an excruciatingly nerve-racking business, and drank accordingly. The resulting scenes varied from high farce to low drama: early one morning he called on Caroline Durieux with a bloody hand after his palm had been slashed with a razor in a drunken skirmish and one evening he was imprisoned in Mixcoac for his own safety after he and Daniel almost came to blows (and butchers' knives) over a missing serape Hart accused his servant of stealing. The loyal Simpsons were on hand to defuse that situation and they were also present at another evening early in April when Hart, 'uplifted by many rum punches and talk of San Francisco', had an altercation in Bach's bar with Witter Bynner. Marian Simpson remembered how he called him 'Mr Bitter Winter, a writer of nice verses', and listened as Hart proceeded to discuss the work of Robinson Jeffers, whose 'negation of humanity' he deplored. He admitted that he had often wanted to introduce satire and burlesque into his own poetry but was afraid of what his literary friends in New York would think. 'He said he feared their reaction to every word he wrote.' In the background someone was singing sad songs to a guitar and under the onslaught of drink Hart's mood turned from regret – and the claim that he could better have used his Guggenheim fellowship to travel the Mississippi – to bitter fury. 'The full mouth began to turn down, the ardent eyes to bulge with an accusing glare, the skin of the face to coarsen and look less elastic.' Remorselessly he catalogued his grievances against Mexico and left Marian with the impression that he considered the country 'a living, unjust goddess'.[36]

Marian in particular found the spectacle of Hart's disintegration unbearably distressing and she and her husband decided on a respite in Cuernavaca. Peggy was also beginning to look around for exits, not only for Hart but for herself. 'Moroseness and anger against the world possessed him,' she recalled. 'He became an ugly, sick man in mind and body. Constant tirades against the servants, Mexico, his friends in the States.'[37] Inveterate bohemian as she was, even she began to find Hart's turbulence unendurable and on 7 April she confided to Malcolm:

> To keep me here he has promised to give up tequila. I didn't ask him to, but am frankly admitting to you that should he start drinking heavily again I shall wire immediately for money home. I don't want you to let him know I wrote this, and as you knew it already, it doesn't seem very disloyal.... Drinking only beer, the poor child is steadily losing his waist-line and gaining the healthy color of a Burgundian friar.[38]

Meanwhile, having borrowed enough to eat (and drink), the beleaguered couple faced other deprivations: 'The light has been turned off and it has all been most embarrassing,' Hart informed Bess on 7 April. The money he expected from her had still not arrived and because 'borrowing money and the incidentals to getting it of course always cost something', he explained that this month he would have to ask her for 'the entire $166'. He would check to see if the payment had arrived at the bank the next morning but warned that unless he could find the money for his passport renewal he might be liable to deportation.[39] Amidst these dramas, two guests – Katie Seabrook and Claire Spencer Smith – suddenly appeared one morning in a taxi. To say the least, they were unexpected: Katie and Peggy were old friends but Claire and Hart, mutually distrustful and resentful ever since her marriage, had seen almost nothing of each other for years. Such hostility belonged to a time when the poet seemed to have a surplus of friends, however, and now he was almost as pleased to see her as Peggy was to see Seabrook. 'We both let out a call of welcome and ran to the gate to meet them,' Peggy recalled, and soon everyone was supplied with tequila, 'which, all agreed, was no worse than bootleg liquor in the States'.[40] Claire had just completed a second novel, having published *Gallows Orchard* in 1930, and Hart concluded, as he later informed Sam Loveman, that 'I'm not the only one who has improved since our ancient misunderstandings'.[41] Nor was he the only one to make comparisons with the past: Claire was astonished by Hart's heterosexual arrangements but not altogether convinced by them, and her doubts seemed justified when she also heard his frantic admission, 'If you had not come I don't know how I should have stood it any longer – I was desperate.' Knowing that he was 'very ambitious, not in a vulgar way, but to justify himself', she suspected that 'it weighed on him terribly that he had done no work to speak of in Mexico'. Moreover she questioned his solution to anxiety and feared his 'attempt with Peggy was a torture to him, purely because he was betraying his affection for his mother by touching another woman'.[42] Agreeing to a lunch or dinner on their return, the two women continued to Cuernavaca, leaving behind a copy of John Dos Passos's new novel, *1919*, which Hart read enthusiastically. Never one to resent the triumphs of his contemporaries, he was impressed with the achievement and happy for its author, and informed Lorna Dietz on 12 April that 'it's the best book Dos has ever written – the same technique as the *42nd Parallel*, but developed and perfected finally into an almost perfect instrument'.[43] He reminded Lorna that whenever she chose to visit she would be warmly received: and he reiterated the loveliness of Mexico in sentences that spoke tacitly of loneliness. Letters had continued to arrive from Aunt Sally, Bob Thompson and Bob Stewart, but Stewart's well-being had become a matter for concern following the widespread devastation unleashed by cyclones in Alabama. Having written for news as soon as he knew of the disaster, Hart continued to await reassurance, his worries acting to emphasize the loyalty and goodness of one sailor who had not gone away. 'I can never forget that sweet boy,' he confided to Loveman, 'and his letters to me for the last two years have been so consistently affectionate and nostalgic that they sometimes bring tears to my eyes.'[44]

If only other correspondents had proved so loyal. It was an abiding grievance, and one voiced with increasing bitterness, that the closest friends failed to write: he never heard any longer from Bill and Sue, the Tates, Waldo and Malcolm. Neglect was bad enough – but why had Cowley failed to send any word about Hart's new poem, dispatched two weeks before? Perhaps he disliked it or judged it a falling off? Perhaps Morton Dauwen Zabel, similarly taciturn, felt the same way? In fact, far from disliking the poem, Zabel had never received it, but with abysmal morale Hart never stopped to consider the possibility of postal failure and construed the silence as disapproval. Cowley thought the lyric 'splendid', but life at the *New Republic* was hectic and many of his free hours were now dedicated to *Exile's Return*, the book that would chronicle his literary generation's struggle to reconcile Francophile aestheticism with American life in the Twenties.[45] How remote that struggle seemed; now writers had political, as opposed to artistic, consciences and searched for social solutions rather than the *mot juste*. Cowley himself was involved with the National Committee for the Defense of Political Prisoners and its attempts to assist the starving, striking miners of Kentucky. In a widely publicized visit to the colliery towns in February he had joined Waldo Frank and Edmund Wilson at the labour barricades, distributed food parcels, addressed meetings and confronted the county attorney before being arrested and escorted to the Tennessee border, where Frank, a Jew as well as a socialist, was badly beaten. There were meetings in Washington and rallies in New York and day after day Cowley delayed writing to Hart, unaware that 'The Broken Tower' was not just a poem but a potential justification for existence. Hart knew of the Kentucky expedition and mouthed approval, but concluded privately that 'Waldo and Malcolm are just cutting paper dollies'.[46] Indeed the more he heard of life in America, now preparing itself for the election that would establish FDR in the White House and his New Deal in the Capitol, the more reluctant he felt to return North. It was one thing to receive an invitation from a complete stranger such as Oakley Johnson, executive secretary of the John Reed Society, asking him to address a symposium entitled 'Poetry and Revolution'. But it was quite another to reflect that his close literary friends, the joint-tenants of his youth – whether Frank and Cowley, or Matty Josephson, now writing the manifesto for the communist ticket of William Z. Foster and James W. Ford – were lost to political sectarianism. During the course of his Mexican sabbatical Hart had become an anomaly, an irreligious exile – and, if only by the terms of Scott Fitzgerald's dictum, that the Jazz Age had absolutely no interest in politics, the lone survivor of a vanished age. Far better to remain in his flower-filled garden than return as a freak to a country where even among artists he would feel incongruous.

Now it was obvious that Mexican residence was of paramount importance, Hart explored various ways of trying to secure it: at first it seemed it could be done through contacts with the son-in-law of the President, but when that avenue failed he consigned the matter to a lawyer who turned out to be crooked. By then, however, Peggy had unleashed a greater worry – the possibility that she was pregnant – and then a letter written by Bess on 12 April eclipsed even that anxiety: CA's estate was not, after all, unencumbered. Three weeks earlier Bess had learned that when divesting himself of his operations in Kansas City Crane had personally guaranteed an eight-year lease on a factory building which the new occupants were no longer able to sustain – with the result that CA's legatees were now accountable for the $600 that had to be paid each month. Explaining that the news had come to her 'like a bolt from the blue', Bess detailed the implications:

> You can see, Harold, what that does to the estate. Nothing can be paid from the estate account to you in the way of your bequest, as the executors are liable, and there isn't any income from stocks to speak of. We are not making any money

from our different businesses. The only thing we can do is to give you an allowance from my salary each month, and that I have made arrangements to do. You will have to economize, as there isn't any money we can just get for the asking.

She promised he would have $125 each month but beyond that could offer nothing but bromides: 'We do have a place to live and eat. I guess that's more than many have to-day.'[47] True enough: there were thirteen million unemployed in America and the thought of joining their desperate ranks was appalling. Yet perhaps that is what he might now have to do, since even in Mexico $125 would not stretch indefinitely and at least in Chagrin Falls, as Bess had already suggested, he could count on free accommodation. But why live for nothing in a country that held him to be valueless? In recent months he had been the subject of attacks by H.L. Mencken in the *American Mercury* and Max Eastman in *Harper's* and now, it seemed, his friends had forgotten him in the course of their political conversion. 'What good are poets today!' Peggy often heard him exclaim in the last days in which he could sustain coherent utterance.[48] The poet Vachel Lindsay, associate of *Seven Arts* and the *Little Review*, had clearly asked himself the same question in December – only to commit suicide.

At some stage in April the idea emerged into coherence in Hart's mind: perhaps it was the solution of a moment, perhaps the inevitability of a tendency implicit in his emotional disposition, as it might have been in uncle Frank Hart's. Peggy's pregnancy turned out to be a false alarm but even without the added burden of a child born to financial problems and the certainty of two parents who fought interminably, as CA and Grace had fought, the balance between life's pleasures and its pains had tipped irreversibly. Self-destruction now appeared to be the answer and it was an answer he candidly advertised. He was in the habit of meeting Howard Phillips, editor of *Mexican Life*, at a German restaurant near the latter's office and when they ate together for the last time in April Phillips found him in a bad way – incoherent and frankly fearful of returning to New York but at the same time so obviously saturated with alcohol from weeks of excess that it was hard to credit some of his gloomier claims, including 'his calm assurance that he would take his life'. Later Phillips discovered that Hart had, 'in most casual manner, confided his intention to a number of other people'.[49] Among them were Anita Brenner, who described him in his last weeks as being 'obsessed by the idea of death',[50] and Lesley Simpson, who recalled that Hart 'frequently mentioned suicide as the only way out'.[51] But he was ignored in his despair, as he had often been ignored when visionary and optimistic, and there is no surviving evidence to suggest that anyone took his claims seriously enough to attempt dissuasion or restraint. In a bid to dispel his misery, Peggy invited Mary Doherty and another friend, Louise Howard, for lunch on Sunday and Hart was all enthusiasm. 'Company is just what we need,' she remembered him agreeing. But when she woke that morning it was to discover that Hart had been awake – and drinking – for hours already: far from being slothful or sedentary, however, he was 'wild, talking to himself incoherently', and determined to pursue her all over the house, thus making it impossible for her to cancel her guests by telephone. The women duly arrived but horrified as they were by Hart's condition they decided not to leave for fear of abandoning Peggy. She herself found Hart 'worse than I had ever seen him', his speech so confused 'that we couldn't understand him most of the time'. But his actions were clear enough: suddenly he was before them, raving in fury at the portrait by Siqueiros, the surface of which had begun to flake, and before anyone could stop him he slashed the canvas repeatedly with a razor. This was self-destruction by iconoclasm but worse was to come: announcing his desire to make a will, which would divide trinkets between Bess and Zell but make Peggy the principal legatee because of her abiding faith in his genius, he nominated the women as witnesses. After completing the document he handed it to Mary and asked her to keep it safe and then remarked, in a voice Peggy remembered as 'even [and] steady', 'There, I wanted to get that out of the way because this afternoon I am going to kill myself.'[52]

There were five witnesses to what ensued – Peggy, Mary, Louise, Daniel Hernandez and a doctor – but since only the first two left behind accounts, and since Mary's is undetailed and Peggy's contained in two characteristically inconsistent versions, the events of the remainder of the afternoon are confused. Mary has Hart dictating several wills but Peggy mentions only one; and while in her later account Peggy mentions that Hart swallowed a few drops of iodine from a bottle she dashed from his mouth, in her earlier version, imparted to Hart Crane's first biographer, she has him drinking a whole bottle of iodine and then, a few hours later, a bottle of mercurochrome. She was emphatic, however, in stating that the suicide attempts were 'absolutely staged' and seems never to have considered – to extend the theatrical metaphor – that they might have been dress rehearsals.[53] None of the various wills ever came to light, while one other document written that afternoon has subsequently disappeared. Forgetting his earlier decision to leave almost everything to Peggy, Hart decided instead that Bob Stewart should inherit what ought to have come to him from CA's estate and committed his instructions to a letter to Stewart to be posted after his death. Explaining that he had 'very wilfully killed' himself, he hoped the sailor would 'happily marry and realize some of the conversations we have had together' and concluded, 'Dear Bob, I remember so many things, and I have loved you always, and this is my only end.'[54]

The doctor who had been summoned after Hart's ingestion of iodine reappeared to administer a sedative injection and, leaving nothing to chance, he also supplied Peggy with some sleeping pills which he said Hart should be given if he stirred during the night. He did wake once to complain that he was 'burning up' but the next morning, though looking like 'a whipped pup', he seemed equable. Peggy was unable to tell what, if anything, he remembered of the day before but was happy to find that he was hungry, and happier still when he agreed with her that it was time they returned to the United States.[55] In view of Mary Doherty's warning, that the doctor would be legally obliged to report Hart's attempted suicide, which under Mexico's Catholic jurisdiction constituted a serious offence, the case for departure seemed unanswerable: Hart agreed to go into Mexico City to investigate options for their return, apparently destroying the various wills and a copy of the letter to Stewart and forgetting about the duplicate he had entrusted to Mary. He ran into Lesley Simpson in the course of his errands and regaled him uproariously with details of the recent suicidal dramas. The latter was appalled – and would no doubt have endorsed the argument now advanced by both Mary Doherty and Marsden Hartley, that a return journey by train seemed altogether less traumatic and risky than any undertaken by ship. But Hart loved ships and the sea and there was something appropriate in the discovery that the *Orizaba* which had brought him to his Mexican adventure was sailing from Vera Cruz for New York City on 24 April.

He made reservations, wired Bess for the money and returned to Mixcoac to the home he would soon relinquish. A few days later he and Peggy had lunch with Claire Spencer Smith and Katie Seabrook and when the women revealed they were planning their own return to America Hart urged them to book passage on the same ship: the four friends could then make a merry voyage together. The women were uncertain – only later, when back at their hotel, did they act with conviction, cancelling the reservations they had made on the *Orizaba* but left unmentioned. They could return a day or two later: delay seemed a small price to pay for smooth seas. On 17 April Peggy wrote to Bess with confirmation of their plan to sail six days later. 'Dysentery, temperature and nerves have made [Hart] really sick,' she explained, but there seemed every reason to hope that the voyage would speed his recovery. Besides, 'I am going up on the same boat, so can see that he is well taken care of and completely rests.'[56] On 20 April the passage money had still not arrived and Hart wired his stepmother the frantic reminder, TWO HUNDRED DOLLARS NEEDED NOW.[57] He wrote to Eyler Simpson wondering if the Guggenheim would advance funds to pay for the journey if no money came from Cleveland and that same day he asked Mony Grunberg to leave some cash for him at the Hotel Lafayette: hoping they could meet in New York, he would repay the loan before he began his 'middle western exile'.[58] He sent a mailing address to Mary Doherty – Box 604, Chagrin Falls, Ohio – should the Guggenheim Foundation need the information on file and also a letter to *Poetry* wondering if Morton Dauwen Zabel had had any thoughts yet about 'The Broken Tower'? Unaware, as Cowley was unaware, of the immense significance these ten stanzas carried, Zabel replied on 24 April 'alarmed to hear that you sent a poem to the *Poetry* office, for none has reached me or H[arriet] M[onroe] there'. Perhaps it had been lost in the mail? Nor had Hart's review of Phelps Putnam's *Five Seasons* ever arrived. 'Was this sent, and lost, too?'[59]

The passage money was telegraphed on 21 April and converted at the telegraph office into hundreds of silver *tostones* which Hart and Peggy took in canvas bags to the Ward Line office. There, learning that currency restrictions prevented the shipping line from changing more than a minimal sum each day, they were referred to the Bank of Mexico, which in turn closed for the long local lunch soon after their arrival. Knowing the stubbornness of Mexican bureaucracy and the volatility of Hart's prevailing temper, Peggy suggested he eat alone and then go back to Mixcoac; she would secure the tickets and meet friends in Mexico City before returning home later. The bank reopened and as she watched the clerk summon the excruciating deliberation required to count the 600-odd small coins involved she despaired of returning to the Ward Line office ahead of the deadline for securing reserved tickets. When she threatened to call the American Embassy the cashier informed her that only the president of the bank had the authority to circumvent bank procedure – and the next thing she knew she was proceeding under military escort to the long and thickly carpeted room which was the institution's inner sanctum. 'It was only then that I realized the man facing me behind the desk, with hard obsidian eyes, was none other than Plutarco Calles, once the President of all Mexico and still the power behind the throne.'[60] Retired to private life, however, the dictator proved tractable and as soon as he had authorized the currency conversion Peggy rushed to the Ward Line to buy the tickets home before meeting Carleton and Betty Beals for cocktails. Later in the evening, having driven to Mixcoac to collect Hart for dinner, they were greeted with high drama: according to Daniel the poet had returned to write letters and begin packing but a drink or two later, with Peggy still not back, he fell prey to lurid imaginings that she had been robbed, raped and left for dead and duly reported the atrocity to the police. At last he reappeared, somewhat annoyed to find Peggy unscathed, especially in view of the fact that he had applied to the American Embassy for assistance and demanded that an attaché accompany him to the official radio station to broadcast her description.

Most of 22 April was devoted to last-minute correspondence and packing. The Simpsons dropped in and Marian recorded a scene of poignant disarray, 'the little house dismantled, Hart striding up and down, packing his treasures into *chiquihuites*, going out to the kitchen to demolish the carcase of a turkey with all the gusto of Henry the Eighth, while his little white Spitz, Paloma, laid her head on her master's knee, looking unutterably melancholy and resigned'. Peggy appeared equable in the face of departure but Hart was as usual in a turmoil of moods and 'worked himself into a rage at Mexico, whom he had loved, and who had betrayed him'.[61] It was a familiar refrain to Simpson himself, who knew the poet 'gave himself without reserve to anyone who showed sympathy and understanding' and was therefore 'continually being "betrayed", as he put it, because most of his friends refused to put up with his madness'. It often seemed that 'what Hart needed was a silent and understanding friend to shield him from life as far as it could possibly be done. For Hart was totally unfitted to cope with life. He lacked the weapons that make it possible for the rest of us to survive.'[62] The next day, once their trunks had gone and a tearful Daniel had presented his floral tributes, they were off. After depositing their luggage at the train station they went to the Broadway, where a cocktail party had been convened in their honour: Marsden Hartley found Hart 'completely sober, in excellent mood and very cheerful' and the Simpsons, the Bealses, Eyler Simpson, Mary Doherty and the rest of the expatriate circle cheered and raised their glasses when the poet announced he and Peggy were to be married and would return within two years.[63] They drove quickly round Mexico City in valediction and called at the Guggenheim Foundation offices one last time for Hart to collect a $60 loan extended against travelling costs. Since the Foundation kept a limited fund of petty cash, Eyler Simpson himself had been obliged to supply the money but as far as he was concerned the irregularity was well worth it and as soon as the most notorious fellow in the Guggenheim's annals walked from his office he wrote to Henry Allen Moe to ask for reimbursement and to indicate his future policy regarding fellows sent to Mexico City: 'All I've got to say is that I'm going to take a good look at the new poet you are sending down here and if he doesn't present all the earmarks of what we sociologists would call a completely adjusted individual, I'm going to send him back to you on the next boat.'[64] Meanwhile the couple's friends had reunited at the station to see them off. They arrived, 'drunk and apparently in high spirits', the Simpsons noted, with only minutes to spare before the train left. Hart made a date to meet Lesley in Cleveland in June and then turned to Marian, who had extended her hand. 'He took it,' she recalled, 'then impulsively kissed me instead (for the first and last time). His lips were trembling and his face felt as plastic as a child's when it is about to cry.'[65]

After Mexico City's mountainous cool, Vera Cruz seemed intolerably hot and it was with relief that they felt sea breezes on board the *Orizaba*. As a regular passenger, Hart was familiar with the ship and its company, which included fifty-one-year-old Captain James Blackadder, First Officer Oswald Martinson and the ship's surgeon, Richard Newman. He introduced Peggy to the officers he had befriended and she noted 'raised eyebrows among the uniformed men when [he] informed them of our marriage in the near future'.[66] This was not the moment to consider the poet's revelation, however: preparations for the *Orizaba's* 279th voyage were under way, its crew of 117 men were at their stations and twenty-eight passengers, eighteen of them American citizens, were expected for embarkation.[67] By remarkable coincidence one of the Americans who boarded the vessel, a thirty-three-year-old artist named Stefan Hirsch, lived at Hart's old address, 100 Columbia Heights, and was a friend of Gorham Munson. Also on board was a twenty-nine-year-old woman from New York called Gertrude Berg whose sharp eyes provide history with its final glimpse of Hart Crane. As usual the *Orizaba* was scheduled to stop in Havana and the night before arrival Peggy and Hart made plans for the six hours they would have on shore. Since she wanted to shop in the morning it was agreed they would separate, to meet again at a café Hart knew – the Diana? – prior to sightseeing and then boarding the ship once more. So far, at least according to the record subsequently written by Peggy, their time on the *Orizaba* had been uneventful; in fact, without knowing it, the couple were notorious, with a reputation which Gertrude Berg stated 'had spread quickly through the ship'. They were known to be 'drunk and boisterous' and although Berg's acquaintance with them extended no further than sightings on the dance floor they were nevertheless a memorable pair: 'To me Peggy Cowley looked like someone who had been picked up on the street.' The couple spent the night in Peggy's cabin and awoke, as she related, 'to see Morro Castle slide past the porthole in the early morning'. They breakfasted on board before making their way into Havana and after Hart had pointed out the café where they were to meet, he went his own way. Peggy shopped, her purchases including 'a few records as a surprise for Hart'. But we know nothing whatever of the poet's activities: he slipped down a street in the white, gold and azure Cuban capital and for one of the few times in his life disappeared entirely from view. He wrote postcards, admittedly, to Aunt Sally and Lesley Simpson, but the forty-nine words of amenities noted on the cards can scarcely have occupied more than a moment. Perhaps he drank. Perhaps, as rumour later reported, he had an assignation with a sailor. But nothing about his activities is clear beyond the certainty, bizarre in a man who now spoke of honeymoons, that he wanted to perform them alone.

Peggy arrived at what she thought was the right restaurant, selected by Hart because the waiters spoke English, and had a drink and a sandwich while she waited for him to arrive. When she tried to establish whether or not a man corresponding to her description of him had appeared, however, it turned out that the staff spoke only Spanish. The *Orizaba* was due to weigh anchor at 4.30 and when an English-speaking stranger finally confirmed that no one resembling Hart had been in the restaurant she knew her anxieties about the missed rendezvous were justified. She caught a cab to the pier and was met at the gangplank by the ship's purser, Alfred Mason, who seemed somewhat nervous. Although a further seventy-four passengers had embarked at Havana, including a group of thirty-eight Cantonese Chinese merchants, Hart had continued to commandeer the attention of the crew and although Mason's message was straightforward – 'Mr Crane is worried about you: he has been on the ship for over an hour' – there was something in his tone that dismayed her.[68] She herself was angry and the fact that several other people stopped her to repeat the purser's message only irritated her more. Hart must have been in the ship's bar all along, which is why he had failed to meet her, and she made her way there after changing for dinner. She took one of the new records to play at the bar: there was no sign of Hart, but the bartender confirmed that he had been looking for her and that he had had a few drinks. She ordered a cocktail, put on the record and struck a match to light her cigarette. The box of Cuban matches exploded and flame had circled her wrist and arm before she passed out with the pain.

She was carried to the surgery and it was there, as Newman, twenty-five years a ship's surgeon, was treating her arm with a solution of tannic acid, that Hart finally appeared. He was emotional and intractable and Newman ordered him from the surgery, only to see him return at intervals increasingly intoxicated and belligerent and full of threats to sue the match company and the Ward Line itself. The doctor dosed Peggy with neat whiskey and a sleeping pill and told her to go to bed but, sedated and in pain as she was, she resisted Hart's attempts to carry her to her cabin and instead groped her way along the wall. She could never remember when – or how often – he entered her room that night full of imperative questions and recriminations and clumsy comfort but she did register relief when a member of the crew spoke through her drugged stupor and told her Hart had at last been confined to his cabin. Somehow he broke free and in circumstances that remain enigmatic he was badly beaten in a fight before being incarcerated in his cabin once more at 4 a.m.

It was broad daylight on 27 April when Peggy, stultified with pain and narcotics, finally woke and rang for a stewardess. She ordered coffee, then went to the surgery to have her arm dressed again and was relieved when Newman made no mention of Hart's condition the night before. Meanwhile, according to the report subsequently made by Captain Blackadder the details of which were extended to Henry Allen Moe by the Ward Line's passenger traffic manager, M. Seckendorf, Hart had woken at 10 a.m. and immediately begun drinking. By the time Newman and a steward called on him an hour later he was 'drinking copiously from a bottle of whisky'.[69] Nevertheless, when he appeared in Peggy's cabin after she had seen the doctor he struck her as being 'sober' if also 'nervous and, I thought, frightened'. He complained that his ring and wallet were missing but when she tried to find out what had happened he claimed he could remember nothing of the previous evening. They went to his cabin to look for them and Hart said he needed a drink at once. Peggy agreed, but insisted that he should also eat and was pleased to see him order a large breakfast when the steward appeared. They tried to retrace the previous day's misadventure in Havana but then breakfast appeared and Hart proceeded to 'devour' grapefruit, cereal, eggs and bacon and toast. She told him to dress and come to her cabin but when he appeared a few minutes later, 'he was still in his pajamas, wearing a light topcoat for a robe'. In front of the stewardess who was helping her to dress, Peggy asked him again to put on some clothes and to shave. This time he could not assent and even if only accidentally he invoked his mother's name as a measure of his exile and incapacity: 'I'm not going to make it, dear. I'm utterly disgraced.' She persisted: he was neat and fastidious by nature and would feel better in clean clothes. 'All right, dear. Good-bye.'[70]

Peggy failed to record the time this exchange occurred but it must have been shortly before noon, when by tradition the results of the ship's pool were announced. The *Orizaba* was now carrying over ninety passengers and quite a number of them were then on deck, including Stefan Hirsch. Some yards away Gertrude Berg was also present among a small crowd of people eagerly awaiting the pool news. Suddenly, incongruous and arresting to the last, Hart appeared, his condition infamous and his own game of fortune concluded. Berg recalled that 'one of the ship's officers told us that Crane had been in the sailors' quarters the previous night, trying to make one of the men, and had been badly beaten' and although Hirsch was too far away to detail the poet's appearance Berg could see clearly that 'he had a black eye and looked generally battered'. It was hard to imagine he cared about the pool results, and it soon became apparent that he was not on deck for a casual stroll either. 'He walked to the railing,' she remembered, 'took off his coat, folded it neatly over the railing (not dropping it on deck), placed both hands on the railing, raised himself on his toes, and then dropped back again.' Time stops with her description, its details sufficiently precise to disqualify for ever all suspicions that what followed might have been an accident. Where were the crew in these moments that lasted for ever? Why did no one intercede? After all, the eyes of the ship were upon him: 'We all fell silent and watched him,' she continued, 'wondering what in the world he was up to. Then, suddenly, he vaulted over the railing and jumped into the sea.' From his remoter vantage point Hirsch had witnessed the manoeuvre less clearly and later would only say that he had seen the poet 'drop – not dive or leap – overboard'.[71] He ran to the stern of the ship but there was no sign of his fellow-passenger in the churning water below. Berg herself was temporarily paralysed with disbelief: 'For what seemed like five minutes, but was more like five seconds, no one was able to move; then cries of "man overboard" went up.' Her eyes went automatically to the blue circumambient sea: 'Just once I saw Crane, swimming strongly, but never again. It was a scene I am unable to forget.'[72]

The Ward Line's passenger traffic manager stated later that Hart went overboard at two minutes before noon while the ship's manifests position the act precisely four minutes later. In any event, the *Orizaba* was riding the elusive Tropic of Cancer at the time in the same Caribbean waters where Columbus had once searched for signs of terrestrial proximity. Conditions seem to have been almost ideal – the vessel was 275 miles out of Havana and may well have been heading for temperate seas at something approaching her maximum speed of 17 knots an hour. Even if she was not running at capacity, her tonnage – almost 7,000 at gross – and her four-turbine engines would have generated a wake thunderous and unrelenting beyond the poetic imagination. In that endless moment of death Peggy, still below, heard the ship's shrill whistle and felt its shuddering halt and knew it was Hart. With the assistance of the stewardess she ran to the lower deck, aware as she moved of the woman's starched white sleeve in her hand. Almost immediately she saw Richard Newman descending in one of the four lifeboats that were lowered for rescue. A while later she was summoned to the bridge and at her arrival Captain Blackadder, who in twenty-six years had never experienced a sea suicide, delivered himself of what she remembered as 'a stream of furious profanity'. Apart from that initial sighting there had been no further sign of the poet and after two hours of fruitless search the lifeboats were recalled. The sea, as Peggy surveyed it, was 'like a mirror that could be walked on', its serenity giving no sign of the grimness of Hart Crane's self-execution, as summarized by the desperate captain: 'If the propellers didn't grind him to mincemeat, then the sharks got him immediately.'[73]

ULTRAMARINE: A CODA

Both Peggy and Blackadder sent telegrams, the Captain to the Ward Line announcing the presumed death and the fact that the body had not been recovered, and Peggy to her former husband: HART COMMITTED SUICIDE MEET ME PEGGY.[74] On the following day, 28 April, brief notices appeared in the *New York Evening Post*, the *New York Times* and the *New York World Telegram*, which embellished the bare summaries supplied by the other newspapers with an opinion volunteered by Sam Loveman, that 'because of [Crane's] aloofness, his mysterious travels, legends would form from the manner of his disappearance'.[75] On 29 April the *New York Times* confirmed the news and revealed that the *Orizaba* was due in quarantine in New York at 6 p.m. that evening. In the interim, in accordance with Peggy's plea, Malcolm had obtained a reporter's pass for the Coast Guard cutter permitted to meet incoming ships at quarantine. On boarding the press vessel, however, Cowley was appalled to find sixty journalists already aboard: was it conceivable that the death of a poet could stir such curiosity? He should have known better: the reporters stopped at the *Berengaria* to welcome seventy-nine-year-old Alice Hargreaves, who as a young girl had inspired Lewis Carroll to write *Alice's Adventures in Wonderland* and who had come to New York as the guest of honour at Columbia University's celebration of Lewis Carroll's centenary. Dead only a matter of hours, the late, great poet could not rival this degree of fame. There was a newspaper conference under way in New York at the time and Zell Deming was given much prominence as one of America's few women editors and newspaper proprietors but no enterprising journalist connected her with the deceased or his uncle, Frank Hart, whose untimely death had left Zell a young widow. Hart Crane's death was not news any more: indeed he was not even accorded an obituary in the *New York Times*.

Grace Crane learned of her son's death from the newspapers and on 28 April she sent a telegram to Carol Dexter, a friend in New York, asking her to represent her at quarantine formalities and to retrieve Hart's possessions on her behalf from the *Orizaba*. Dexter went to the Ward Line offices the following evening and met the manager, who was confused by the fact that another Mrs Crane – Bess – had also cabled to say that she would be in New York on Friday and would come to the company offices. In the event Carol Dexter, Zell Deming and Bess Crane all met in the manager's office where they were joined by Captain Blackadder, who said 'he knew very little about Hart's death and did not know him personally'. He had completed his official report and asserted that all Hart's chattels were secured in his state room. Since it was his understanding that the deceased and Peggy Cowley, despite occupying separate rooms and travelling under separate names, were always together and had intended to marry after her divorce, he had arranged for Peggy to come to the office to meet them. 'She is a small, thin, wiry, dark woman, probably in her late forties, always dowdy in appearance and utterly lacking in charm,' Dexter informed Grace. 'She is a writer and poet and doubtless she and Hart had a wonderful mental companionship, but one couldn't conceive of anyone building a romance around her.' Peggy gave her understanding of events, in which Hart 'didn't pause at the last railing except to take off his coat ... and then he dove headlong'. Blackadder repeated the details of the attempted rescue – lifebelts, four lifeboats, the two-hour search – and Dexter continued her terrible paraphrase: 'The captain said that in such cases, bodies were never recovered, owing to the great depth and pressure of the water. Mrs Cowley of course was prostrated over the matter for she feels she might have averted the tragedy.' The matter of the poet's estate was introduced and Peggy announced that Hart had often said he wanted her to oversee publication of his complete canon in the event of his death. Carol Dexter pointed out that in the absence of any letter or will Grace was her son's automatic legatee and the others at once conceded her prior rights. She told her friend, 'I know it is not much comfort Grace darling but other people took Hart from you, and he left them, and now you really have him back.'[76]

Repossession was both abstract and physical – Hart Crane's literary rights were now hers, as were the possessions he scattered in a life spent searching for something he never found. The items he had left behind in Patterson remained there, to pass quietly into the ownership of Browns and Cowleys, but everything he had with him in Mexico, including all the correspondence saved throughout his life, now went to Grace Crane's modest apartment at Oak Park, Illinois. It was there that Peggy wrote on 4 May offering sympathy to the mother-in-law she never had and reconciliation in the face of a distrust that had not yet become official. She and Hart had been 'very much in love with each other' and as a sign of his love the poet 'for years intended me being his literary executor'.[77] But Grace was unmoved and told Peggy four days later that literary executorship constituted 'a privilege I could not relinquish to anyone – it was the last loving service I could render & a loving duty for me to perform'.[78] As for Peggy's other claims, 'If he was so calm & greatly in love with her', Grace asked Sam Loveman, 'why did he commit suicide in the face of a happy marriage?'[79]

She was not alone in asking why her son had killed himself. Indeed it is one of the contradictions of suicide that rather than ending life it somehow extends it, since the deceased lives on in the speculations and soul-searching of those who survive. Hart's death came as a profound shock to his closest friends, for all the warnings, explicit and otherwise, that he gave in his last months – and when they attempted to interpret his end they found themselves inextricably involved in his struggle to wrest meaning from life's pain and ecstasy. 'It's as if he asked a question which all of us tried to answer in our own terms,' Cowley ventured to Tate.[80] 'When all is said Hart's career is mysterious and impenetrable,' Tate wrote to Slater Brown. 'I think he felt that most of us had deserted him; but it wasn't true. He deserted us, when he demanded too much of us; and he wouldn't face out the implications of that situation.'[81] The inquiry continued into print: the suicide formed the subject of essays in many of the literary periodicals, with Cowley's unsigned 'Death of a Poet', which appeared in the *New Republic* on 11 May, voicing the consensus, that Crane's death could, and should, be read symbolically, since it was the last act of a man who felt there was no longer any room in the world for poets.

The editorial annoyed Tate, who considered it ludicrous to apply political significance to Crane's life, and it annoyed Grace by citing the relationship with Peggy, whom she now considered largely responsible for her son's death. She had begun to read the correspondence Hart had saved and told Loveman that Peggy's letters contained 'some of the most obscene filthy indecent language' she had ever encountered and that 'they beat anything I have ever heard or ever read in French novels'. The more she read, the more she convinced herself the letters betrayed 'a nature so far from one that ever brought any abiding happiness to Hart that it is inconceivable how he could have any great affection for her. The question arises, Did he, or did he feel himself in a trap from which there seemed no hope of extricating himself, & had not the courage to tell her so, having accepted her love & professed such to her.'[82] Not the least of Peggy's crimes was her involvement with what Grace took to calling 'that Cowley clique', various members of which now approached her offering to collect and edit the final version of Crane's poems which they felt posterity deserved.[83] Grace agreed with the principle but detected ulterior aims in the offers and within two weeks of her son's death she had sent letters to Horace Liveright, the *Nation* and the *New Republic* which reasserted her control of the literary rights and the choice of editor best equipped to give the canon permanent form.

With Sam Loveman's guidance she eventually nominated Waldo Frank, and Crane's *Collected Poems* appeared in 1933, by which time Grace had also decided a biography should be written 'in collaboration with me in revealing some of [Hart's] life that is known only to me'.[84] A young graduate from Princeton named Philip Horton was appointed to this daunting task, but not before Grace's determination to shape her son's reputation and personality for ever had run its damaging course. The more she explored the contents of the trunks, the more distressed she became. Peggy's vivid letters were the least of it. There were pornographic pictures, 'the dirtiest I've ever seen', she told Lorna Dietz.[85] Should history gaze on these, and so think less of the lyric genius she had helped nurture? There was nothing for it but destruction, and once the decision was taken it seemed legitimate to eliminate all the cycles of correspondence which had any bearing on her son's sexual temper. Besides many of Peggy's letters she appears to have destroyed all the correspondence sent by Harry Candee, Wilbur Underwood, Emil Opffer, Jack Fitzin and any unlettered sailor who had struggled to express feelings and desires for which he never knew a name. More loyal than any of these was Bob Stewart. 'There are more letters from him than from any other person,' Grace told Loveman, 'all of which seem to be trying to convince Hart, that he still loves him ... and evidently in reply to some expression on Hart's part'. She concluded that Stewart was 'a very simple-minded, naïve person, totally incapable of any intellectual companionship, or understanding of Hart's mentality' and in no time his declarations, which had meant so much to their recipient, were ashes in the fire.[86] As the last of them was consumed, however, her conscience stirred: the sheer volume of the letters attested to great constancy and she knew from Loveman that the sailor had tried to limit her son's drinking. So even as she deleted him from Hart Crane's life, Grace sent Stewart a letter of acknowledgement in July 1932:

Sam Loveman says that Hart loved me very deeply, always, so I am at a loss to understand his actions. If I had been in communication with him at the last, I am sure he would never have taken his life. He always relied upon me to comfort and encourage him, treated me with the devotion of a sweetheart rather than a mother.[87]

Grace moved to New York and by the time Philip Horton first met her she was living in what he termed 'a little fleabag hotel on upper Broadway' in a room just large enough to accommodate a bed and chair.[88] The writer's first impressions were equivocal: she seemed 'a dominating, shrewd and somewhat vulgar person in a worldly way' and although he conceded that 'she did understand the extreme sensuousness of [Hart's] temperament' he doubted she grasped 'the complementary problems that went with it'. Nevertheless, 'when she told of some especially intimate experience of herself and Hart, the hard surfaces would crack for a moment and in her laughter usually so meaningless there could be heard a fresh unspoiled naïvete and charm of humour that redeemed many of her more unpleasant characteristics.'[89] A year later, when he saw her again, she was installed as chief housekeeper at an expensive new hotel on East 38th Street called the Towne House. 'She had a lovely suite of rooms and obviously a very good job and was out buying her black lace underwear again [and] French perfumes.' There was no doubt about it, 'she was quite a character', and although 'very flighty [and] very vain' she had 'a lot of energy and courage'. Yet there was also something dubious about her resilience and Horton was shocked when she suggested they collaborate on a play about Hart's homosexuality.[90]

His biography, *Hart Crane: The Life of an American Poet*, was published in 1937 but its appearance did nothing to halt Grace's distressing slide into penury. Having lost her job at the hotel, she survived for a while on the sale of heirlooms, including the four-poster bed her forebears had carried across the continent in a cart in 1832, but by 1942 she was living in one room in the Henry Hudson Hotel on West 57th Street. It was a threadbare reality and one she escaped whenever she could – by renewing her faith in Christian Science, by resorting frequently to the Psychic Book Store on East 39th Street, by attending regular audiences with a spiritualist through whom she claimed communion with her son; above all, by the simple expedient of living in the past. When William and Margaret Wright visited her they were unprepared for the shrine that lay beyond her hotel door: a tiny room crowded with the dead poet's treasures, 'the shining tin, and silver and paintings, modern, vivid, gorgeous', which Grace had arranged around her bed.[91] She liked 'gossiping to our Hart's content' with such friends of Hart's as she saw and she cherished the condolences extended by those who were no more than a name. 'As you probably know,' Yvor Winters wrote to her, 'I disagreed with most of Hart's central ideas, and disapproved of the general direction in which his poetry was working, but in spite of those facts he seemed to me one of the most powerful and at times one of the most perfect poets of the last two centuries. His greatness, and the certitude of his high place in the history of English poetry, should in time afford a kind of consolation for his loss.'[92] It certainly provided motivation for the protectiveness of executorship: in 1945 his mother prohibited the release of a volume of Hart Crane's correspondence – it was not until the publication of the *Letters* in 1952 that the world was able to read the poet's own account of his parental problems.

Grace Crane ended her working life as a maid in New Jersey, earning $15 a month and dreaming of future royalties from the poems. She was sustained into her seventieth year by the loyalty and friendship of Sam Loveman, who visited her in a Catholic hospital in Teaneck, New Jersey, the day before she died on 30 July 1947 from cirrhosis of the liver. Her condition was acute but when one of the orderlies asked who she was and Loveman replied, 'the mother of a very brilliant and wonderful American poet', she revived and demanded to know what had been said. Almost immediately, however, she relapsed into coma, murmuring as she did so her final verdict on her son, herself and her relations with him, 'Poor Boy'.[93]

Abbreviations

Complete Poems	*Complete Poems of Hart Crane*, ed. Marc Simon. Liveright, New York, 1986
Complete Poems & *Selected Letters &* *Prose*	*Hart Crane. The Complete Poems & Selected Letters & Prose*, ed. Brom Weber. Liveright, New York, 1966
Hart Crane Collection, Beinecke, Yale University	Hart Crane Collection, Beinecke RareBook and Manuscript Library, Yale University Library
Baker Papers	Baker Papers, Hart Crane Collection, Beinecke Rare Book and Manuscript Library, Yale University Library
Horton Papers	Horton Papers, Hart Crane Collection, Beinecke Rare Book and Manuscript Library, Yale University Library
Hart Crane Papers, Columbia University	Hart Crane Papers, Rare Book and Manuscript Library, Columbia University, New York
Hart Crane Papers, Kent State University	Hart Crane Papers, Special Collections, University Library, Kent State University, Ohio
Horton	Philip Horton, *Hart Crane: The Life of an American Poet.* W.W. Norton, New York, 1937
John Unterecker Papers	John Unterecker Papers, Rare Book and Manuscript Library, Columbia University, New York
Letters	*The Letters of Hart Crane 1916–1932*, ed. Brom Weber. University of California Press, Berkeley and Los Angeles, 1965 (first published in New York, 1952)
Lewis	*Letters of Hart Crane and His Family*, ed. Thomas S.W. Lewis. Columbia University Press, New York and London, 1974
Maxfield Parrish Papers	Maxfield Parrish Papers, Dartmouth College Library, Hanover, New Hampshire
Parkinson	*Hart Crane & Yvor Winters: Their Literary Correspondence*, ed. Thomas Parkinson. University of California Press, Berkeley, Los Angeles and London, 1978
Selected Letters	*O My Land, My Friends: The Selected Letters of Hart Crane*, ed. Langdon Hammer and Brom Weber. Four Walls Eight Windows, New York and London, 1997
Unterecker	John Unterecker, *Voyager: A Life of Hart Crane.* Farrar, Strauss & Giroux, New York, 1969; Anthony Blond, London, 1969, 1970

All his life Hart Crane was a poor speller but since the mistakes which litter his correspondence seem neither entertaining nor revealing they have been silently corrected.

Chapter 1

1. 'Recollection of Hart Crane's grandfather, Arthur E. Crane, on his father's side.' Undated typescript, John Unterecker Papers.
2. Letter from N.B. Madden to Jethro Robinson, 26 November 1956. John Unterecker Papers.
3. Quoted in Unterecker, p. 16.
4. *Atlas and Directory of Trumbull County, Ohio, Including a Directory of Freeholders and Official Register of the County.* The American Atlas Company, Cleveland, Ohio, 1899.
5. Harriet Taylor Upton, *A Twentieth Century History of Trumbull County, Ohio. A Narrative Account of Its Historical Progress, Its People, And Its Principal Interests,* Chicago, 1909.
6. N.B. Madden to Jethro Robinson, 26 November 1956. John Unterecker Papers.
7. 'An Interview with Philip C. Horton', *Hart Crane Newsletter,* volume II, number II, Spring 1979.
8. Transcript of an interview between John Unterecker and Sam Loveman, 4 August 1962. John Unterecker Papers.
9. Vivian H. Pemberton, '"Broken Intervals" – The Continuing Biography of Hart Crane', *The Visionary Company, A Magazine of the Twenties,* Spring 1982.
10. Grace Crane to Hart Crane [1 November 1917?]. Lewis, p. 91.
11. N.B. Madden to Jethro Robinson, 26 November 1956. John Unterecker Papers.
12. Quoted in Unterecker, p. 9.
13. N.B. Madden to Jethro Robinson, 26 November 1956. John Unterecker Papers.
14. Pemberton, '"Broken Intervals"'.
15. Quoted in Unterecker, p. 10.
16. Quoted ibid., p. 8.
17. Quoted ibid., p. 20.
18. Hart Crane to Grace Crane, 19 March 1927. Lewis, p. 532.
19. 'Van Winkle', *Complete Poems,* pp. 55–6.
20. 'The Dance', ibid., pp. 62–5.
21. 'The River', ibid., pp. 57–61.
22. 'Van Winkle', ibid., p. 55.
23. 'Porphyro in Akron', ibid., pp. 150–2.
24. 'Van Winkle', ibid., p. 56.
25. Grace Crane to Hart Crane [late April or early May, 1918?]. Lewis, p. 98.
26. 'Passage', *Complete Poems,* pp. 21–2.
27. Quoted in Unterecker, p. 25.
28. Undated letter from Mrs Griswold Hurlbert (Helen Hart) to John Unterecker. John Unterecker Papers.
29. Ona Kraft to William Wright, 15 January 1936. Hart Crane Collection, Beinecke, Yale University.
30. Eleanor Clarage, 'Class Prophet and Class Poet Might Be Introduced, If Things Went Right', *Cleveland Plain Dealer,* 20 June 1937.
31. Elbert Hubbard, 'A Little Journey to Crane's Chocolate Studio', 1914. Hart Crane Collection, Beinecke, Yale University. I have been unable to verify the exact title and date of the Munch painting referred to here.

Chapter 2

1. Clarence Crane to Hart Crane, 7 July 1926. Lewis, p. 499.
2. Clarence Crane to Grace Crane, 15 February 1915. Quoted in Unterecker, p. 35.
3. Clarence Crane to Grace Crane, 6 February 1915. Quoted ibid., p. 37.

4. Clarence Crane to Grace Crane [24 January 1915]. Quoted ibid., p. 36.
5. Quoted in Unterecker, p. 37.
6. Ibid., p. 37.
7. Clarence Crane to Grace Crane, 6 February 1915. Quoted ibid., p. 37.
8. Quoted in Horton, p. 27.
9. Quoted in Unterecker, p. 38.
10. William Wright to Philip Horton, 4 January 1936. Horton Papers.
11. William Wright to Grace Crane, 9 January 1933. Hart Crane Papers, Columbia University.
12. William Wright to Grace Crane, 11 April 1933. Hart Crane Papers, Columbia University.
13. Quoted in Unterecker, p. 31.
14. William Wright to Grace Crane, 9 January 1933. Hart Crane Papers, Columbia University.
15. From undated photocopies. John Unterecker Papers.
16. Quoted in a letter from Clarence Crane to Hart Crane, 25 November 1925. Lewis, p. 443.
17. From the Pemberton Collection. Reproduced in Vivian Pemberton, ' "Broken Intervals" – The Continuing Biography of Hart Crane', *The Visionary Company, A Magazine of the Twenties.* Spring 1982.
18. Quoted in Unterecker, pp. 33 and 34.
19. 'The Moth That God Made Blind', *Complete Poems*, pp. 167–9.
20. Hart Crane to Elizabeth Belden Hart, 7 January 1916. Lewis, p. 8.
21. Hart Crane to Elizabeth Belden Hart, 26 January 1916. Ibid., p. 9.
22. Hart Crane to Elizabeth Belden Hart, 10 February 1916. Ibid., p. 10.
23. Quoted in Unterecker, p. 48.
24. Copy of a letter in the John Unterecker Papers.
25. Copy of a letter in the John Unterecker Papers.
26. Clarence Crane to Maxfield Parrish, 4 April 1916. Maxfield Parrish Papers.
27. George Bryan to John Unterecker, 28 June 1962. Quoted in Unterecker, p. 44.
28. *Pagan*, volume I, number 6, October 1916.
29. 'C 33', *Complete Poems*, p. 135.
30. 'An Interview with Philip C. Horton', *Hart Crane Newsletter*, volume II, number II, Spring 1979.
31. Mrs Fred Nev (Vivian Brown) to John Unterecker, 25 July [1961?]. John Unterecker Papers.
32. Clarence Crane to Maxfield Parrish, 12 June 1916. Maxfield Parrish Papers.
33. 'Society', *Warren Daily Tribune*, 18 September 1916.
34. Ibid., 14 October 1916.
35. Quoted in Unterecker, p. 49.
36. Quoted in Horton, p. 35.
37. 'October–November', *Complete Poems*, p. 136.
38. Quoted in Unterecker, p. 72.
39. This letter was quoted in Horton (p. 36), who did not supply any date. The original was subsequently lost. There is therefore no possibility of dating the letter.

Chapter 3

1. Malcolm Bradbury, 'The American Risorgimento', in Marcus Cunliffe (ed.), *The Penguin History of Literature: American Literature since 1900*, Sphere Books, 1975, revised edn, Penguin Books, London, 1993, p. 9.
2. Gordon B. Munson, *The Awakening Twenties: A Memoir-History of a Literary Period*, Louisiana State University Press, Baton Rouge and London, 1985, p. 9.
3. Richard Rulard and Malcolm Bradbury, *From Puritanism to Postmodernism*, Viking Penguin, New York, 1991, p. 125.
4. Ibid., p. xi.

5. Ibid., p. 220.
6. Gertrude Stein, *The Autobiography of Alice B. Toklas*, Vintage Books, New York, 1961, p. 260.
7. Munson, *The Awakening Twenties*, p. 22.
8. Rulard and Bradbury, *From Puritanism to Postmodernism*, p. xiv.
9. Munson, *The Awakening Twenties*, p. 55.
10. Hart Crane to Clarence Crane, 31 December 1916. Lewis, p. 17.
11. Grace Crane to Hart Crane, 3 January 1917. Ibid., p. 19.
12. Grace Crane to Hart Crane, 19 January 1917. Ibid., p. 26.
13. Hart Crane to Clarence Crane, 5 January 1917. Ibid., p. 21.
14. Clarence Crane to Hart Crane, 18 January 1917. Hart Crane Papers, Kent State University.
15. Clarence Crane to Hart Crane, 20 January 1917. Lewis, p. 27.
16. Hart Crane to Clarence Crane, 20 January 1917. Hart Crane Papers, Kent State University.
17. Hart Crane to Clarence Crane, 27 January 1917. Hart Crane Papers, Kent State University.
18. Hart Crane to Clarence Crane, 2 February 1917. Hart Crane Papers, Kent State University.
19. Clarence Crane to Hart Crane, 10 February 1917. Hart Crane Papers, Kent State University.
20. Grace Crane to Hart Crane, 4 February 1917. Lewis, p. 39.
21. Hart Crane to Elizabeth Belden Hart, 7 January 1917. Lewis, p. 23.
22. Hart Crane to Grace Crane and Elizabeth Belden Hart, 2 January 1917. Lewis, p. 17.
23. Hart Crane to Grace Crane and Elizabeth Belden Hart, 26 January 1917. Lewis, p. 31.
24. Hart Crane to Elizabeth Belden Hart, 7 January 1917. Lewis, p. 23.
25. Quoted from Mary Colum, *Life and the Dream*, Dufour Editions, New York, 1958, 1966.
26. Joseph Kling in interview with John Unterecker, 1960. Quoted in Unterecker, p. 53.
27. Carl Schmitt in interview with John Unterecker, 1960. Quoted in ibid., p. 68.
28. Hart Crane to Grace Crane, 19 February 1917. Lewis, p. 42.
29. 'The Hive', *Complete Poems*, p. 137.
30. Hart Crane to Grace Crane, 22 February 1917. *Selected Letters*, p. 10.
31. Grace Crane to Hart Crane, 26 February 1917. Lewis, p. 46.
32. Hart Crane to Clarence Crane, 23 March 1917. Lewis, p. 48.
33. Grace Crane to Hart Crane, 29 March 1917. Lewis, p. 53.
34. Grace Crane to Hart Crane [26 March 1917?]. Lewis, p. 50.
35. Clarence Crane to Hart Crane, 29 March 1917. Lewis, p. 52.
36. Grace Crane to Hart Crane, 29 March 1917. Lewis, p. 53.
37. Clarence Crane to Hart Crane, 4 April 1917. Hart Crane Papers, Kent State University.
38. Hart Crane to Clarence Crane, 7 April 1917. Hart Crane Papers, Kent State University.
39. William Carlos Williams to Hart Crane, 17 April 1917. Hart Crane Papers, Columbia University.
40. Quoted in Unterecker, p. 16.
41. Clarence Crane to Hart Crane, 14 April 1917. Hart Crane Papers, Kent State University.
42. Hart Crane to Clarence Crane, 13 April 1917. Hart Crane Papers, Kent State University.
43. Hart Crane to Clarence Crane, 17 April 1917. Hart Crane Papers, Kent State University.
44. Clarence Crane to Hart Crane, 28 April 1917. Hart Crane Papers, Kent State University.
45. Hart Crane to Clarence Crane, 15 May 1917. Lewis, p. 59.
46. Hart Crane to Clarence Crane, 5 May 1917. Ibid.
47. Clarence Crane to Hart Crane, 7 May 1917. Hart Crane Papers, Kent State University.
48. Telegram, Grace Crane to Clarence Crane, 15 May 1917. Hart Crane Papers, Kent State University.
49. Clarence Crane to Hart Crane, 16 May 1917. Lewis, p. 60.
50. Hart Crane to Clarence Crane, 19 May 1917. Hart Crane Papers, Kent State University.

51. Hart Crane to Clarence Crane, 27 June 1917. Hart Crane Papers, Kent State University.

52. Undated letter from Hart Crane to Clarence Crane. Hart Crane Papers, Kent State University.

53. Hart Crane to Clarence Crane, 14 July 1917. Hart Crane Papers, Kent State University.

54. Claire Spencer to John Unterecker, 11 July 1962. Quoted in Unterecker, p. 106.

55. Claire Spencer to Philip Horton, May 1936. Horton Papers.

56. Clarence Crane to Grace Crane, 10 July 1917. Hart Crane Papers, Columbia University.

57. Grace Crane to Clarence Crane, 17 July [1917]. Hart Crane Papers, Columbia University.

58. Clarence Crane to Hart Crane, 20 July 1917. Hart Crane Papers, Kent State University.

Chapter 4

1. Hart Crane to Clarence Crane, 18 September 1917. Lewis, p. 67.

2. Grace Crane to Clarence Crane, 23 September [191]7. Quoted in Unterecker, p. 84.

3. Grace's suicide attempt was first disclosed in an interview on 27 August 1971 between Alma Crane's daughter Helen Crane Sherwood and Vivian H. Pemberton, Emeritus Professor of English at Kent State University. Professor Pemberton subsequently documented the attempted suicide in her essay ' "Broken Intervals" – The Continuing Biography of Hart Crane', published in *The Visionary Company, a Magazine of the Twenties* (Spring 1982) and kindly elaborated further on 3 May 2000 in a letter to the author.

4. Clarence Crane to Hart Crane, 1 August 1917. Lewis, p. 65.

5. Clarence Crane to Hart Crane, 4 August 1917. Hart Crane Papers, Kent State University.

6. Hart Crane to Clarence Crane, 8 August 1917. Lewis, p. 66.

7. Clarence Crane to Hart Crane, 8 August 1917. Hart Crane Papers, Kent State University.

8. Clarence Crane to Hart Crane, 10 August 1917. Hart Crane Papers, Kent State University.

9. Clarence Crane to Hart Crane, 11 August 1917. Hart Crane Papers, Kent State University.

10. Telegram from Hart Crane to Clarence Crane, 15 August 1917. Hart Crane Papers, Kent State University.

11. Clarence Crane to Hart Crane, 20 August 1917. Hart Crane Papers, Kent State University.

12. Clarence Crane to Grace Crane [21 August 1917]. Quoted in Unterecker, p. 82.

13. Clarence Crane to Hart Crane, 19 September 1917. Hart Crane Papers, Kent State University.

14. 'Quaker Hill', *Complete Poems*, pp. 92–4.

15. Hart Crane to Clarence Crane, 18 September 1917. Lewis, p. 67.

16. Clarence Crane to Hart Crane, 19 September 1917. Hart Crane Papers, Kent State University.

17. Hart Crane to Grace Crane, 28 September 1917. Lewis, p. 69.

18. Grace Crane to Hart Crane [28 September 1917?]. Ibid., p. 71.

19. Hart Crane to Grace Crane [1 October 1917]. Ibid., p. 73.

20. 'Modern Craft', *Complete Poems*, p. 142.

21. 'The Bathers', ibid., p. 141.

22. Quoted in Horton, p. 56.

23. Hart Crane to Clarence Crane, 14 July 1917. Hart Crane Papers, Kent State University.

24. Margaret Anderson, *My Thirty Years' War: An Autobiography*, Alfred A. Knopf, London, 1930, pp. 4, 58.

25. Quoted in Hans Bak, *Malcolm Cowley: The Formative Years*, University of Georgia Press, Athens and London, 1993, p. 136.

26. Joseph Kling in interview with John Unterecker, 1960. Quoted in Unterecker, p. 88.

27. Anderson, *My Thirty Years' War*, p. 153.
28. Hart Crane to Clarence Crane, 23 November 1917. Hart Crane Papers, Kent State University.
29. Hart Crane to Clarence Crane, 14 November 1917. Hart Crane Papers, Kent State University.
30. Clarence Crane to Hart Crane, 20 November 1917. Hart Crane Papers, Kent State University.
31. Margaret Anderson to John Unterecker, 14 September 1961. John Unterecker Papers.
32. Margaret Anderson in interview with John Unterecker, 14 September 1961. Quoted in Unterecker, p. 89.
33. Undated letter from Margaret Anderson to Hart Crane. Hart Crane Papers, Columbia University.
34. Hart Crane to Grace Crane, 28 September 1917. Lewis, p. 69.
35. Ezra Pound to Margaret Anderson, 2 February 1918. The *Little Review* Papers, Special Collections of the University of Wisconsin-Milwaukee Library.
36. Undated letter from Ezra Pound to Hart Crane. Undated pencil copy in the John Unterecker Papers.
37. Hart Crane to Grace Crane [1 October 1917]. Lewis, p. 73.
38. Grace Crane to Hart Crane, 3 October 1917. Ibid., p. 75.
39. Clarence Crane to Hart Crane, 10 October 1917. Ibid., p. 82.
40. Hart Crane to Clarence Crane, 14 October 1917. Hart Crane Papers, Kent State University.
41. Mary Colum, *Life and the Dream*, Dufour Editions, New York, 1966, p. 257.
42. Clarence Crane to Hart Crane, 5 November 1917. Hart Crane Papers, Kent State University.
43. Quoted in Horton, pp. 53–4.
44. Quoted in Horton, pp. 54–5.
45. Quoted in Horton, p. 58.
46. 'To Portapovitch', *Complete Poems*, p. 147.
47. 'The Case against Nietzsche', *Complete Poems & Selected Letters & Prose*, p. 197.
48. Quoted in Unterecker, p. 108.
49. 'Exile' (aka 'Carrier Letter') and 'Postscript', *Complete Poems*, pp. 144–5.
50. Hart Crane to George Bryan, 23 April 1918. *Selected Letters*, p. 13.
51. Grace Crane to Hart Crane [early May 1918?]. Lewis, p. 99.
52. William Wright to Grace Crane, 11 April 1933. Quoted in Unterecker, p. 30.
53. Hart Crane to William Wright, 14 December 1919. Quoted ibid., p. 162.
54. Quoted in Brom Weber, *Hart Crane: A Biographical and Critical Study*, The Bodley Press, New York, 1948, p. 144.
55. 'Joyce and Ethics', *Complete Poems & Selected Letters & Prose*, p. 199.
56. Hart Crane to William Wright, 12 August 1918. *Letters*, p. 11.
57. 'To Brooklyn Bridge', *Complete Poems*, pp. 43–4.
58. Quoted in Horton, p. 61.

Chapter 5
1. Hart Crane to Carol Zigrosser [late February 1919]. *Selected Letters*, p. 18.
2. Hart Crane to the Reverend Charles C. Bubb, 13 November 1918. Ibid., p. 15.
3. Quoted in Unterecker, p. 120.
4. Hart Crane to George Bryan, 8 January 1919. *Selected Letters*, p. 17.
5. 'Review of *The Ghetto and Other Poems*', *Complete Poems & Selected Letters & Prose*, p. 201.
6. Quoted in Unterecker, p. 121.
7. Quoted ibid., p. 123.

8. Alexander Baltzly quoted in interview with John Unterecker, October 1962, ibid., p. 127.
9. Hart Crane to Grace Crane, 21 March 1919. Lewis, p. 119.
10. From the transcript of an undated interview between John Unterecker and Charmion von Wiegand. John Unterecker Papers.
11. Hart Crane to Grace Crane [22 February 1919]. Lewis, p. 110.
12. Hart Crane to Grace Crane and Elizabeth Belden Hart [27 February 1919]. Ibid., p. 114.
13. Hart Crane to Grace Crane, 7 March 1919. Ibid., p. 115.
14. Hart Crane to Grace Crane, 2 April 1919. Ibid., p. 125.
15. Hart Crane to William Wright, 2 May 1919. *Selected Letters*, p, 21.
16. 'Review of *Minna and Myself*', *Complete Poems & Selected Letters & Prose*, p. 203.
17. Hart Crane to George Bryan, 17 March 1919. *Selected Letters*, p. 20.
18. Joseph Kling in interview with John Unterecker, 1961. Quoted in Unterecker, p. 135.
19. Gorham B. Munson, *The Awakening Twenties: A Memoir-History of a Literary Period*, Louisiana State University Press, Baton Rouge and London, 1985, p. 189.
20. Ibid., p. 190.
21. Ibid., p. 160.
22. Ibid., pp. 190–1.
23. Hart Crane to Grace Crane, 2 April 1919. Lewis, p. 125.
24. Hart Crane to Grace Crane [20 April 1919?]. Ibid., p. 131.
25. Hart Crane to Grace Crane, 'Decoration Day, [19]19'. Ibid., p. 135.
26. Quoted in John Baker, 'Hart Crane Tries Advertising', undated typescript monograph, p. 3, Hart Crane Collection, Beinecke, Yale University.
27. Hart Crane to Grace Crane, 10 July 1919. Lewis, p. 137.
28. Claire Spencer to Philip Horton, undated letter, May 1936. Horton Papers.
29. Quoted from 'A Visit to a Poet', in Charles S. Brooks, *Hints To Pilgrims* (a collection of essays), Yale University Press, New Haven, 1921.
30. Undated notes from interviews conducted by Philip Horton. Horton Papers.
31. Munson, *The Awakening Twenties*, p. 160.
32. Hart Crane to William Wright, 17 June 1919. *Letters*, p. 19.
33. Hart Crane to William Wright, 14 May 1919. Ibid., p. 17.
34. Hart Crane to William Wright, 17 June 1919. Ibid., p. 19.
35. Hart Crane to Grace Crane, 'Decoration Day, [19]19.' Lewis, p. 135.
36. Hart Crane to William Wright, 17 June 1919. *Letters*, p. 19.
37. Claire Spencer to Philip Horton, undated letter 1936. Horton Papers.
38. Hart Crane to Grace Crane, 10 July 1919. Lewis, p. 137.
39. Claire Spencer to John Unterecker, 1962. Quoted in Unterecker, p. 140.
40. Harrison Smith to Philip Horton, 21 January 1936. Horton Papers.
41. Claire Spencer to Philip Horton, undated letter May 1936. Horton Papers.
42. Hart Crane to Grace Crane, 30 July 1919. Lewis, p. 141.
43. Margaret Anderson to Hart Crane, 24 August [19]19. Hart Crane Papers, Columbia University.
44. 'Sherwood Anderson', *Complete Poems & Selected Letters & Prose*, p. 208.
45. 'Review of *Winesburg, Ohio*', ibid., p. 205.
46. Sherwood Anderson to Hart Crane [1 November 1919]. Quoted in Unterecker, p. 144.
47. Quoted in Sherwood Anderson's obituary, *New York Times*, 9 March 1941.
48. Hart Crane to Grace Crane, 22 September 1919. Lewis, p. 143.
49. Hart Crane to Grace Crane, 31 October 1919. Ibid., p. 145.
50. Hart Crane to Grace Crane, 22 September 1919. Lewis, p. 143.
51. Hart Crane to Charmion Wiegand, 5 November 1919. *Letters*, p. 22.

Chapter 6

1. Hart Crane to Gorham Munson, 13 November 1919. *Selected Letters*, p. 24.
2. *Beacon Journal* (Akron), 17 December 1919.
3. Hart Crane to Gorham Munson, 27 December 1919. *Selected Letters*, p. 29.
4. Undated letter from Wilbur Underwood to Philip Horton. Horton Papers.
5. Hart Crane to Wilbur Underwood, 3 January [1927]. *Selected Letters*, p. 304.
6. Herbert Fletcher to Samuel Loveman, 30 December 1947. Hart Crane Papers, Columbia University.
7. Hart Crane to Gorham Munson, 9 January 1920. *Selected Letters*, p. 31.
8. Herbert Fletcher to Samuel Loveman, 30 December 1947. Hart Crane Papers, Columbia University.
9. Hart Crane to Gorham Munson, 27 December 1919. *Selected Letters*, p. 29.
10. 'Porphyro in Akron', *Complete Poems*, pp. 150–2.
11. 'A Note on Minns', *Complete Poems & Selected Letters & Prose*, p. 207.
12. Hart Crane to Gorham Munson, 28 January 1921. *Selected Letters*, p. 58.
13. Waldo Frank quoted in Brom Weber, *Hart Crane: A Biographical and Critical Study*, The Bodley Press, New York, 1948, p. 164.
14. Quoted in Gorham B. Munson, *The Awakening Twenties: A Memoir-History of a Literary Period*, Louisiana State University Press, Baton Rouge and London, 1985, p. 69.
15. Hart Crane to Gorham Munson, 13 December 1919. *Selected Letters*, p. 28.
16. The Akron *Sunday Times*, 21 December 1919.
17. Hart Crane to Gorham Munson, 27 December 1919. *Selected Letters*, p. 29.
18. Hart Crane to Gorham Munson, 22 November [1919]. *Letters*, p. 24.
19. Ibid.
20. 'My Grandmother's Love Letters', *Complete Poems*, p. 6.
21. Hart Crane to Gorham Munson [28 November 1919?]. *Selected Letters*, p. 27.
22. Sherwood Anderson to Hart Crane, 3 December 1919. Hart Crane Papers, Columbia University.
23. Hart Crane to Gorham Munson, 13 December 1919. *Selected Letters*, p. 28.
24. Sherwood Anderson to Hart Crane [17 December 1919]. Hart Crane Papers, Columbia University.
25. Hart Crane to Gorham Munson, 27 December 1919. *Selected Letters*, p. 29.
26. Hart Crane to Gorham Munson [mid-February 1920]. Ibid., p. 33.
27. Hart Crane to Gorham Munson, 26 April 1920. Ibid., p. 40.
28. Hart Crane to William Wright, 5 February 1920. Quoted in Unterecker, p. 175.
29. Hart Crane to William Wright, 24 February 1920. Quoted ibid., p. 170.
30. Louise Howard to John Unterecker, 4 February 1962. John Unterecker Papers.
31. Hart Crane to Gorham Munson, 6 March 1920. *Selected Letters*, p. 34.
32. Ibid.
33. Hart Crane to Gorham Munson, 14 April 1920. Ibid., p. 38.
34. 'Episode of Hands', *Complete Poems*, p. 173.
35. Hart Crane to Gorham Munson, 14 April 1920. *Selected Letters*, p. 38.
36. Mrs John White McCaslin to John Unterecker, 26 June 1963. John Unterecker Papers.
37. Hart Crane to Gorham Munson [mid-February 1920]. *Selected Letters*, p. 33.
38. Hart Crane to Matthew Josephson, 15 March 1920. *Letters*, p. 35.
39. 'Garden Abstract', *Complete Poems*, p. 9.
40. Hart Crane to Gorham Munson, 8 June 1920. *Letters*, p. 40.
41. Hart Crane to Gorham Munson, 18 August 1920. Ibid., p. 41.
42. 'Porphyro in Akron', *Complete Poems*, pp. 150–2.

43. Hart Crane to Gorham Munson, 1 September 1920. Hart Crane Collection, Beinecke, Yale University.
44. Hart Crane to Gorham Munson, 30 July 1920. *Letters*, p. 40.
45. Hart Crane to Gorham Munson, 18 August 1920. Hart Crane Collection, Beinecke, Yale University.
46. Hart Crane to Gorham Munson, 13 September 1920. *Letters*, p. 42.
47. Hart Crane to Gorham Munson, 24 September 1920. *Selected Letters*, p. 41.
48. Hart Crane to Gorham Munson, 20 October 1920. Ibid., p. 42.
49. Undated letter from Wilbur Underwood to Philip Horton. Horton Papers.
50. Hart Crane to Wilbur Underwood, 3 January [1927]. *Selected Letters*, p. 304.
51. Hart Crane to Gorham Munson, 20 November 1922. Ibid., p. 108.
52. Samuel Loveman to Alfred Galpin, undated typescript May–Dec. 1972. John Unterecker Papers.
53. Allen Tate to Hart Crane, 15 September [1924?]. Hart Crane Papers, Columbia University.
54. Hart Crane to Gorham Munson, 20 October 1920. *Selected Letters*, p. 42.
55. Hart Crane to Wilbur Underwood, 31 January 1921. Ibid., p. 59.

Chapter 7
1. Hart Crane to Gorham Munson, 23 November 1920. *Letters*, p. 46.
2. Hart Crane to Gorham Munson, 9 November 1920. Ibid., p. 45.
3. Hart Crane to Gorham Munson, 23 November 1920. Ibid., p. 46.
4. Hart Crane to Gorham Munson, 9 November 1920. Ibid., p. 45.
5. Hart Crane to Gorham Munson, 5 December 1920. Ibid., p. 48.
6. Hart Crane to Wilbur Underwood [22 December 1920?]. *Selected Letters*, p. 55.
7. Hart Crane to Gorham Munson, 14 January 1921. *Letters*, p. 50.
8. Hart Crane to Gorham Munson, 19 September 1921. Ibid., p. 64.
9. Hart Crane to Gorham Munson, 11 February 1921. Ibid., p. 53.
10. Bert Ginther to John Unterecker, 8 August 1963. John Unterecker Papers.
11. Quoted in Unterecker, p. 185.
12. Undated interview between Sam Loveman and John Unterecker. John Unterecker Papers.
13. Sam Loveman interviewed by John Unterecker, 4 August 1962. Transcript in John Unterecker Papers.
14. Sam Loveman to Alfred Galpin, undated typescript May–Dec. 1972. John Unterecker Papers.
15. Hart Crane to Gorham Munson, 13 October 1920. *Letters*, p. 43.
16. Hart Crane to Matthew Josephson, 14 January 1921. *Selected Letters*, p. 57.
17. Quoted in Brom Weber, *Hart Crane: A Biographical and Critical Study*, The Bodley Press, New York, 1948, p. 122.
18. Hart Crane to Gorham Munson [early July 1921?]. *Selected Letters*, p. 64.
19. 'Black Tambourine', *Complete Poems*, p. 4.
20. Hart Crane to Gorham Munson, 12 March 1921. Quoted in Unterecker, p. 189.
21. Hart Crane to Sherwood Anderson, 10 January 1922. *Letters*, p. 76.
22. Hart Crane to Gorham Munson [early July 1921?]. *Selected Letters*, p. 64.
23. Allen Tate, 'Hart Crane and the American Mind', *Poetry*, volume XL (July 1932). Quoted in R.W. Butterfield, *The Broken Arc: A Study of Hart Crane*, Oliver & Boyd, Edinburgh, 1969, p. 33.
24. Hart Crane to Gorham Munson, 14 January 1921. *Letters*, p. 50.
25. Hart Crane to Gorham Munson, 12 March 1921. Quoted in Unterecker, p. 189.
26. Hart Crane to Gorham Munson, 20 April [1921]. *Selected Letters*, p. 61.

27.   Hart Crane to Gorham Munson, 3 May 1921. Hart Crane Papers, Columbia University.
28.   Hart Crane to Gorham Munson, 16 May 1921. *Letters*, p. 56.
29.   Hart Crane to Gorham Munson, 12 June 1921. Hart Crane Papers, Columbia University.
30.   Hart Crane to Gorham Munson, 22 July 1921. *Letters*, p. 62.
31.   Hart Crane to Gorham Munson, 10 April [1921]. Ibid., p. 54.
32.   Quoted in 'A Cleveland Old Master on Exhibit', Cleveland *Plain Dealer* Sunday magazine, 28 January 1962.
33.   Undated letter, Hart Crane to Gorham Munson. Quoted in Unterecker, p. 207.
34.   Hart Crane to Gorham Munson, 12 June 1921. *Letters*, p. 58.
35.   Undated letter, Hart Crane to Gorham Munson. Ibid., p. 60.
36.   Quoted in 'A Drawing of Crane by William Sommer', *Hart Crane Newsletter*, volume I, number I, Winter 1977.
37.   Hart Crane to Gorham Munson 19 September 1921. Quoted in Unterecker, p. 207.
38.   Hart Crane to Gorham Munson, 16 May 1921. *Letters*, p. 56.
39.   Sam Loveman to Alfred Galpin, undated typescript May–Dec. 1972. John Unterecker Papers.
40.   Undated transcript of an interview between John Unterecker and Richard Rychtarik. John Unterecker Papers.
41.   Hart Crane to Gorham Munson, 3 November 1921. *Letters*, p. 69.
42.   Undated transcript of an interview between John Unterecker and William Lescaze. John Unterecker Papers.
43.   'Voyages', Part I, *Complete Poems*, p. 34.
44.   Hart Crane to Gorham Munson, 1 October 1921. *Selected Letters*, p. 65.
45.   Undated letter, Hart Crane to Gorham Munson. *Letters*, p. 99.
46.   Hart Crane to Gorham Munson, 1 October 1921. Ibid., p. 65.
47.   Hart Crane to Gorham Munson, 16 May 1921. Ibid., p. 56.
48.   Hart Crane to Gorham Munson, 1 October 1921. *Selected Letters*, p. 65.
49.   Hart Crane to Gorham Munson, 6 October 1921. Ibid., p. 67.
50.   Hart Crane to William Wright, 17 October 1921. *Letters*, p. 67.
51.   'Chaplinesque', *Complete Poems*, p. 11.
52.   Hart Crane to Gorham Munson, 3 November 1921. *Letters*, p. 69.
53.   Hart Crane to Gorham Munson, 6 October 1921. *Selected Letters*, p. 67.
54.   Hart Crane to Gorham Munson, 21 November [1921]. *Letters*, p. 70.
55.   Hart Crane to Gorham Munson, 1 November 1921. Ibid., p. 68.
56.   Hart Crane to Gorham Munson, 3 November 1921. Hart Crane Collection, Beinecke, Yale University.
57.   Hart Crane to William Wright, 17 October 1921. *Selected Letters*, p. 69.
58.   Hart Crane to Gorham Munson, 26 November 1921. Ibid., p. 71.
59.   Quoted in John Baker, 'Hart Crane Tries Advertising', p. 12. Undated typescript, Hart Crane Collection, Beinecke, Yale University.
60.   Hart Crane to Gorham Munson, 10 December [1921]. *Selected Letters*, p. 73.
61.   Hart Crane to Gorham Munson, 25 December 1921. Ibid., p. 75.

Chapter 8

1.   Quoted in John Baker, 'Hart Crane Tries Advertising', p. 14. Hart Crane Collection, Beinecke, Yale University.
2.   Hart Crane to Gorham Munson, 2 January 1922. Hart Crane Collection, Beinecke, Yale University.
3.   G.W. Freeman to John Baker [January 1963?]. Baker Papers.
4.   Undated advertising copy. Baker Papers.

5. Undated letter from G.W. Freeman to John Baker. Baker Papers.
6. Hart Crane to Gorham Munson, 23 January 1922. *Selected Letters*, p. 80.
7. G.W. Freeman to John Baker [January 1963?]. Baker Papers.
8. Hart Crane to Gorham Munson, 23 January 1922. *Selected Letters*, p. 80.
9. Hart Crane to Wilbur Underwood, 31 January 1921. Ibid., p. 59.
10. Hart Crane to Gorham Munson, 2 March 1922. *Letters*, p. 81.
11. Hart Crane to William Wright, 11 February 1922. *Selected Letters*, p. 82.
12. Hart Crane to William Wright, 13 February 1922. Quoted in Unterecker, p. 231.
13. Hart Crane to Gorham Munson, 25 December 1921. *Letters*, p. 74.
14. Hart Crane to Wilbur Underwood, 4 July [1922]. Ibid., p. 93.
15. 'Praise for an Urn', *Complete Poems*, p. 8.
16. Hart Crane to Gorham Munson, 2 March 1922. *Letters*, p. 81.
17. Hart Crane to Gorham Munson, 23 January 1922. *Selected Letters*, p. 80.
18. Hart Crane to Gorham Munson, 25 February 1922. *Letters*, p. 79.
19. Hart Crane to Gorham Munson, 24 March [1922]. Ibid., p. 82.
20. Hart Crane to Gorham Munson, 19 April 1922. Ibid., p. 84.
21. Hart Crane to Gorham Munson, 16 May 1922. *Selected Letters*, p. 83.
22. Hart Crane to Gorham Munson, 24 March [1922]. *Letters*, p. 82.
23. Hart Crane to Charmion Wiegand, 6 May 1922. Ibid., p. 84.
24. Hart Crane to Wilbur Underwood, 15 June [1922]. *Selected Letters*, p. 90.
25. Hart Crane to Gorham Munson, 25 May [1922]. Ibid., p. 86.
26. Hart Crane to Gorham Munson, 4 June 1922. Ibid., p. 88.
27. Transcript of an interview between Allen Tate and John Unterecker, 11 September 1962. John Unterecker Papers.
28. Hart Crane to Allen Tate, 16 May 1922. *Selected Letters*, p. 85.
29. Hart Crane to Allen Tate, 12 June [1922]. Ibid., p. 89.
30. Allen Tate in interview with John Unterecker, 11 September 1962. Quoted in Unterecker, p. 240.
31. Hart Crane to Gorham Munson [18 June 1922]. *Selected Letters*, p. 91.
32. Hart Crane to Wilbur Underwood, 15 June [1922]. Ibid., p. 90.
33. Hart Crane to Gorham Munson [18 June 1922]. Ibid., p. 91.
34. 'For the Marriage of Faustus and Helen', Part II. *Complete Poems*, pp. 29–30.
35. Hart Crane to Wilbur Underwood, 4 July [1922]. *Selected Letters*, p. 94.
36. Gorham Munson in interview with John Unterecker, 1963. Quoted in Unterecker, p. 246.
37. Undated transcript of an interview between Gorham Munson and John Unterecker. John Unterecker Papers,
38. From undated interview notes by Philip Horton. Horton Papers.
39. Allen Tate to Hart Crane, 13 July 1922. Hart Crane Collection Papers, Columbia University.
40. Hart Crane to Allen Tate, 19 July 1922. *Selected Letters*, p. 95.
41. Gorham B. Munson, *The Awakening Twenties*, Louisiana State University Press, Baton Rouge and London, 1985, p. 194.
42. Hart Crane to Wilbur Underwood, 27 July 1922. *Selected Letters*, p. 96.
43. Quoted in Munson, *The Awakening Twenties*, pp. 196–9.
44. Sherwood Anderson to Philip Horton, 2 January 1936. Horton Papers.
45. Sherwood Anderson to Hart Crane [late August 1922]. Quoted in Unterecker, p. 252.
46. Hart Crane to Gorham Munson [late August 1922]. *Letters*, p. 97.
47. Hart Crane to Wilbur Underwood, 27 July 1922. *Selected Letters*, p. 96.
48. 'General Aims and Theories', *Complete Poems & Selected Letters & Prose*, p. 217.

49. Hart Crane to Waldo Frank, 7 February 1923. *Selected Letters*, p. 125.
50. 'For the Marriage of Faustus and Helen', Part I. *Complete Poems*, pp. 26–8.
51. Hart Crane to Gorham Munson, 7 August 1922. *Letters*, p. 95.
52. 'Sunday Morning Apples', *Complete Poems*, p. 7.
53. Baker, 'Hart Crane Tries Advertising', pp. 26–32. Baker Papers,.
54. Stanley Patno in interview with John Unterecker, 1961. Quoted in Unterecker, p. 254.
55. Hart Crane to Gorham Munson [late August 1922]. *Letters*, p. 97.
56. G.W. Freeman to John Baker [January 1963?]. Baker Papers.
57. Hart Crane to Gorham Munson [late August 1922]. *Letters*, p. 97.
58. Hart Crane to William Wright, 25 August 1922. Quoted in Unterecker, p. 257.
59. Hart Crane to Gorham Munson [late August 1922]. *Selected Letters*, p. 98.
60. Stanley Patno to John Baker, 14 September 1962. Baker Papers.
61. Stanley Patno in interview with John Unterecker, 1961. Quoted in Unterecker, p. 254.
62. Stanley Patno to John Baker, 3 September 1962. Baker Papers.
63. Ibid.
64. Stanley Patno to John Baker, 23 April 1963. Baker Papers.
65. Hart Crane to Wilbur Underwood, 2 September [1922]. *Selected Letters*, p. 102.
66. Hart Crane to Wilbur Underwood [19 September 1922]. Ibid., p. 105.
67. Hart Crane to Gorham Munson [September 1922]. *Letters*, p. 99.
68. Hart Crane to Charmion von Wiegand, 9 October 1922. Quoted in Unterecker, p. 263.
69. Hart Crane to Gorham Munson, 12 October 1922. *Letters*, p. 102.
70. 'The Great Western Plains', *Complete Poems*, p. 156.
71. Hart Crane to Gorham Munson, 29 September 1922. *Letters*, p. 100.
72. Hart Crane to Gorham Munson, 7 November 1922. Ibid., p. 103.
73. Hart Crane to Gorham Munson, 20 November 1922. *Selected Letters*, p. 108.
74. Waldo Frank to Hart Crane, 6 December 1922. Hart Crane Papers, Columbia University.
75. Hart Crane to Wilbur Underwood, 10 December 1922. *Selected Letters*, p. 112.
76. Hart Crane to William Wright, 4 December 1922. Ibid., p. 111.
77. Hart Crane to Wilbur Underwood, 10 December 1922. Ibid., p. 112.
78. Hart Crane to Gorham Munson, 12 December [1922]. Ibid., p. 114.
79. Hart Crane to Gorham Munson [late August 1922]. *Letters*, p. 97.
80. Hart Crane to Gorham Munson, 5 January 1923. *Selected Letters*, p. 115.
81. 'For the Marriage of Faustus and Helen', Part III. *Complete Poems*, pp. 31–2.
82. Hart Crane to Gorham Munson, 14 January 1923. *Selected Letters*, p. 118.
83. Hart Crane to Louis Untermeyer, 19 January 1923. Ibid., p. 119.
84. 'Review of *Eight More Harvard Poets*', *Complete Poems & Selected Letters & Prose*, p. 214.
85. Hart Crane to Gorham Munson, 24 January 1923. *Letters*, p. 117.
86. 'Stark Major', *Complete Poems*, p. 10.
87. Hart Crane to Allen Tate, 6 February 1923. *Selected Letters*, p. 124.
88. Hart Crane to Gorham Munson, 9 February 1923. Ibid., p. 126.
89. Hart Crane to Wilbur Underwood, 20 February 1923. Ibid., p. 133.
90. Joseph Frease to John Unterecker, 15 November 1963. Quoted in Unterecker, p. 273.
91. Hart Crane to Wilbur Underwood, 20 February 1923. *Selected Letters*, p. 133.
92. Waldo Frank to Hart Crane [1 February 1923]. Hart Crane Papers, Columbia University.
93. Hart Crane to the *Little Review*, 12 February 1923. The *Little Review* Papers, Special Collections of the University of Wisconsin-Milwaukee Library.
94. Hart Crane to Allen Tate, 12 February 1923. *Selected Letters*, p. 128.
95. Hart Crane to Gorham Munson, 18 February 1923. Ibid., p. 130.
96. Waldo Frank to Hart Crane, 21 February [1923]. Hart Crane Papers, Columbia University.

97. Hart Crane to Waldo Frank, 27 February 1923. *Selected Letters*, p. 135.
98. Hart Crane to Gorham Munson, 2 March 1923. *Selected Letters*, p. 136.
99. Stanley Patno, in interview with John Unterecker, 1962. Quoted in Unterecker, p. 285.

Chapter 9

1. F. Scott Fitzgerald, 'My Lost City', *The Crack-Up, With Other Pieces and Stories*, Penguin, London, 1965, p. 22.
2. Ibid., p. 27.
3. Undated transcript of an interview between Gorham Munson and John Unterecker. John Unterecker Papers.
4. Hart Crane to Waldo Frank, 'Easter' [1923]. *Selected Letters*, p. 147.
5. Undated transcript of an interview between Waldo Frank and John Unterecker. John Unterecker Papers.
6. Van Wyck Brooks to Waldo Frank, May 1919. Quoted in Paul Johnson, *A History of the American People*, Weidenfeld and Nicolson, London, 1997, p. 670.
7. Jay Paul (ed.), *The Selected Correspondence of Kenneth Burke and Malcolm Cowley 1915–1981*, Viking, New York, 1988, p. 353.
8. Hart Crane to Gorham Munson, 6 March 1920. *Selected Letters*, p. 34.
9. Hart Crane to William Sommer, 9 May 1923. Ibid., p. 149.
10. Undated transcript of an interview between Gorham Munson and John Unterecker. John Unterecker Papers.
11. Hart Crane to William Wright. Quoted in Horton, p. 25.
12. Hart Crane to Richard Rychtarik, 4 April 1923. Quoted in Unterecker, p. 296.
13. Hart Crane to Charlotte Rychtarik, 13 April 1923. *Letters*, p. 131.
14. Alfred Stieglitz exhibition catalogue. Hart Crane Papers, Columbia University.
15. Undated transcript of an interview between Waldo Frank and John Unterecker. John Unterecker Papers.
16. Hart Crane to Alfred Stieglitz, 15 April 1923. *Letters*, p. 131.
17. Alfred Stieglitz to Hart Crane, 16 April 1923. Hart Crane Papers, Columbia University.
18. Georgia O'Keeffe to John Unterecker, 29 June 1963. John Unterecker Papers.
19. Hart Crane to Alfred Stieglitz, 15 April 1923. *Selected Letters*, p. 148.
20. 'To Brooklyn Bridge', *Complete Poems*, p. 44.
21. Quoted in Unterecker, p. 290.
22. Hart Crane to Grace Crane and Elizabeth Hart [25 May 1923?] Lewis, p. 166.
23. Allen Tate to Hart Crane, 14 May 1923. Hart Crane Papers, Columbia University.
24. Undated transcript of an interview between William Slater Brown and John Unterecker. John Unterecker Papers.
25. Undated letter 1964 from Slater Brown to John Unterecker. John Unterecker Papers.
26. Hart Crane to William Sommer, 9 May 1923. *Selected Letters*, p. 149.
27. Hart Crane to Wilbur Underwood [9 May 1923]. Ibid., p. 151.
28. Slater Brown to Philip Horton, 8 July 1936. Horton Papers.
29. Hart Crane to Charlotte Rychtarik, 13 April 1923. Quoted in Unterecker, p. 297.
30. Hart Crane to Charles Harris, 11 May 1923. Photocopied letter in the John Unterecker Papers.
31. Hart Crane to Grace Crane, 10 June 1923. *Selected Letters*, p. 152.
32. Hart Crane to Grace Crane and Elizabeth Hart [25 May 1923]. Lewis, p. 166.
33. Hart Crane to Grace Crane, 10 June 1923. *Selected Letters*, p. 152.
34. Hart Crane to Grace Crane and Elizabeth Hart, 1 June 1923. Lewis, p. 172.
35. Undated notes from Jean Toomer's journals 1924–1925. Beinecke, Yale University.

36. Hart Crane to Grace Crane and Elizabeth Hart, 1 June 1923. Lewis, p. 172.

37. Hart Crane to Charlotte and Richard Rychtarik, 30 May 1923. Quoted in Unterecker, p. 297.

38. Hart Crane to Grace Crane, 10 June 1923. Lewis, p. 174.

39. Hart Crane to Charles Harris, 8 July 1923. Photocopied letter in the John Unterecker Papers.

40. Hart Crane to Grace Crane, 10 June 1923. Lewis, p. 174.

41. Hart Crane to Charles Harris, 8 July 1923. Photocopied letter in the John Unterecker Papers.

42. Allen Tate to Hart Crane, 14 June 1923. Hart Crane Papers, Columbia University.

43. Allen Tate to Hart Crane, 28 June 1923. Hart Crane Papers, Columbia University.

44. Hart Crane to Grace Crane, 2 July 1923. Lewis, p. 183.

45. Hart Crane to Alfred Stieglitz, 4 July [1923]. *Selected Letters*, p. 154.

46. 'Lines sent to Alfred Stieglitz, July 4, 1923.' Brom Weber, *Hart Crane: A Biographical and Critical Study*, The Bodley Press, New York, 1948, p. 427.

47. Hart Crane to Grace Crane, 22 July 1923. Lewis, p. 191.

48. Hart Crane to Charlotte Rychtarik, 21 July 1923. *Selected Letters*, p. 157.

49. Hart Crane to Alfred Stieglitz, 4 July 1923. Ibid., p. 154.

50. Malcolm Cowley to Hart Crane, 20 May 1923. Quoted in Susan Jenkins Brown, *Robber Rocks: Letters and Memories of Hart Crane, 1923–1932*, Wesleyan University Press, Middletown, Connecticut, 1969, p. 10.

51. Malcolm Cowley, 'Hart Crane: A Memoir', *A Second Flowering: Works and Days of the Lost Generation*, André Deutsch, London, 1973, p. 191.

52. Hart Crane to Jean Toomer, 19 August [1923]. *Selected Letters*, p. 161.

53. Quoted in George Chauncey, *Gay New York*, Flamingo, London, 1995, p. 136.

54. Ernest Hemingway quoted in a letter from Charles W. Mann to John Unterecker, 3 July 1972. John Unterecker Papers.

55. Hart Crane to Grace Crane and Elizabeth Hart [August 1923]. Lewis, p. 193.

56. 'Possessions', *Complete Poems*, p. 18.

57. Jean Toomer to Hart Crane, 30 September 1923, quoted in 'Bright Stones: An Exchange of Letters', *The Yale Review*, April 1996.

58. Quoted in a letter from Hart Crane to Allen Tate, 1 March 1924. *Letters*, p. 175.

59. 'General Aims and Theories', *Complete Poems & Selected Letters & Prose*, p. 222.

60. Hart Crane to Grace Crane and Elizabeth Hart, 8 September 1923. Lewis, p. 199.

61. Hart Crane to Charlotte Rychtarik, 23 September 1923. *Letters*, p. 147.

62. Quoted in Gorham B. Munson, *The Awakening Twenties*, Louisiana State University Press, Baton Rouge and London, 1985, p. 69.

63. Hart Crane to Grace Crane, 5 October 1923. *Selected Letters*, p. 165.

64. Undated transcript of an interview between Waldo Frank and John Unterecker. John Unterecker Papers.

65. Hart Crane to Grace Crane, 5 October 1923. *Selected Letters*, p. 165.

66. Quoted in a letter from Hart Crane to Grace Crane, 12 October 1923. *Letters*, p. 150.

67. Hart Crane to Gorham Munson [October 1923]. Quoted in Unterecker, p. 313.

68. Quoted in Hans Bak, *Malcolm Cowley: The Formative Years*, University of Georgia Press, Athens and London, 1993, p. 284.

69. Hart Crane to Gorham Munson [October 1923]. Quoted in Unterecker, p. 314.

70. Malcolm Cowley, *Exile's Return*, Penguin, New York, 1976, pp. 181–2.

71. Quoted in Bak, *Malcolm Cowley*, p. 287.

72. Gorham Munson to Alfred Stieglitz, 24 November 1923. Quoted in Munson, *The Awakening Twenties*, p. 175.

73. Hart Crane to Grace Crane and Elizabeth Hart, 20 October 1923. Lewis, p. 218.

74. Hart Crane to Grace Crane, 26 October 1923. Ibid., p. 221.

75. Undated transcript of an interview between Gorham Munson and John Unterecker, John Unterecker Papers.

76. Clarence Crane to Hart Crane, 27 October 1923. Lewis, p. 222.

77. Hart Crane to Grace Crane and Elizabeth Hart, 1 November 1923. Ibid., p. 224.

78. Hart Crane to Gorham Munson, 2 March 1923. *Selected Letters*, p. 136.

79. Hart Crane to Wilbur Underwood, 3 November 1923. Ibid., p. 168.

80. Hart Crane to Jean Toomer, 4 November 1923. Ibid., p. 168.

81. Hart Crane to Jean Toomer, 23 November [1923]. Ibid., p. 169.

82. 'This Way Where November' ('White Buildings'), *Complete Poems*, p. 192.

83. Eugene O'Neill to Philip Horton, 14 February 1936. Horton Papers.

84. Hart Crane to Jean Toomer, 4 November 1923. *Selected Letters*, p. 168.

85. Hart Crane to Richard and Charlotte Rychtarik [16 November 1923]. Quoted in Unterecker, p. 327.

86. Undated letter from Slater Brown to John Unterecker [1964]. John Unterecker Papers.

87. Hart Crane to Jean Toomer, 23 November 1923. *Selected Letters*, p. 169.

88. Undated transcript of an interview between William Slater Brown and John Unterecker. John Unterecker Papers.

89. Hart Crane to Jean Toomer, 14 December 1923. 'Bright Stones: An Exchange of Letters'.

90. Undated letter from Slater Brown to John Unterecker [1964]. John Unterecker Papers.

91. Hilton Kramer, *The Sculpture of Gaston Lachaise*, The Eakins Press, New York, 1967, pp. 27 and 29.

92. Quoted in Munson, *The Awakening Twenties*, p. 295.

93. Hart Crane to Alfred Stieglitz, 5 December 1923. *Letters*, p. 157.

94. Hart Crane to Gilbert Seldes, 21 November 1923. Hart Crane Collection, Beinecke, Yale University.

95. Hart Crane to Gorham Munson, 10 December 1923. *Letters*, p. 160.

96. Hart Crane to Allen Tate, 1 March 1924. *Selected Letters*, p. 182.

97. Undated letter from Hart Crane to Gorham Munson [1923]. Hart Crane Papers, Columbia University.

98. Hart Crane to Allen Tate, 1 March 1924. *Selected Letters*, p. 182.

99. 'Recitative', *Complete Poems*, p. 25.

100. Hart Crane to Grace Crane and Elizabeth Hart, 21 November 1923. Lewis, p. 230.

101. Hart Crane to Grace Crane, 14 December 1923. Ibid., p. 239.

102. Hart Crane to Jean Toomer, 14 December 1923. 'Bright Stones: An Exchange of Letters'.

103. Hart Crane to Gorham Munson, 10 December 1923. *Letters*, p. 160.

104. Waldo Frank to Hart Crane, 10 December 1923. Hart Crane Papers, Columbia University.

105. Alfred Stieglitz to Hart Crane, 10 December 1923. Hart Crane Papers, Columbia University.

106. Clarence Crane to Hart Crane, 10 December 1923. Lewis, p. 238.

107. Hart Crane to Grace Crane, 14 December 1923. Ibid., p. 239.

108. Hart Crane to Gorham Munson, 20 December 1923. *Letters*, p. 161.

109. Quoted in Marc Simon, *Samuel Greenberg, Hart Crane and the Lost Manuscripts*, Humanities Press, Atlantic Highlands, New Jersey, 1978, p. 44.

110. Hart Crane to Gorham Munson, 20 December 1923. *Letters*, p. 161.

111. Quoted in Marc Simon, *Samuel Greenberg, Hart Crane and the Lost Manuscripts*, Humanities Press, Atlantic Highlands, New Jersey, 1978, p. 45.

112. Hart Crane to Gorham Munson, 20 December 1923. *Letters*, p. 161.

113. Hart Crane to Grace Crane, 21 December 1923. Lewis, p. 241.

114. Hart Crane to Gorham Munson, 9 January 1924. *Selected Letters*, p. 175.
115. Clarence Crane to Hart Crane, 7 January 1924. Lewis, p. 248.
116. Hart Crane to Grace Crane, 9 January 1924. Ibid., p. 251.
117. Hart Crane to Clarence Crane, 12 January 1924. Ibid., p. 258.
118. Hart Crane to Grace Crane and Elizabeth Hart, 24 January 1924. Ibid., p. 268.
119. Hart Crane to Grace Crane, 3 February 1924. Ibid., p. 273.
120. Hart Crane to Grace Crane, 12 February 1924. Ibid., p. 280.
121. Quoted in Munson, *The Awakening Twenties*, p. 208.
122. Quoted in Jenkins Brown, *Robber Rocks*, p. 25.
123. Hart Crane to Grace Crane, 3 February 1924. Lewis, p. 273.
124. Quoted in Munson, *The Awakening Twenties*, pp. 210–11.
125. William Slater Brown to Philip Horton, 4 November 1936. Horton Papers.
126. Hart Crane to Allen Tate, 1 March 1924. *Letters*, p. 175.
127. Hart Crane to Grace Crane, 13 February 1924. Lewis, p. 280.
128. Clarence Crane to Hart Crane, 21 February 1924. Ibid., p. 282.
129. Hart Crane to Grace Crane, 15 March 1924. Ibid., p. 290.
130. Hart Crane to Jean Toomer, 16 June 1924. *Selected Letters*, p. 192.
131. Hart Crane to Grace Crane, 23 March 1924. *Letters*, p. 179.
132. 'Lachrymae Christi', *Complete Poems*, pp. 19–20.
133. Quoted in Dennis Read, 'Hart Crane's Letters to the *Little Review*'. Undated photocopy, John Unterecker Papers.
134. Waldo Frank to Hart Crane, 24 February 1924. Hart Crane Papers, Columbia University.
135. Waldo Frank to Hart Crane, 28 March 1924. Hart Crane Papers, Columbia University.
136. Malcolm Cowley to Kenneth Burke, 19 February 1924. Quoted in Paul Jay (ed.), *Selected Correspondence*, p. 159.
137. Quoted in Bak, *Malcolm Cowley*, p. 311.
138. Hart Crane to Gorham Munson, 28 October 1923. *Letters*, p. 154.
139. Quoted in Cowley, *A Second Flowering*, p. 192.
140. Quoted in Bak, *Malcolm Cowley*, p. 16.
141. Munson, *The Awakening Twenties*, p. 180.
142. Quoted in Bak, *Malcolm Cowley*, p. 64.
143. Quoted ibid., p. 89.
144. Bak, *Malcolm Cowley*, p. 122.
145. Quoted in Cowley, *Exile's Return*, p. 114.

Chapter 10

1. 'A Note on Emil Opffer, Jr. and the Opffer Family', Susan Jenkins Brown to Norman Holmes Pearson, 21 March 1966. John Unterecker Papers.
2. Susan Jenkins Brown, *Robber Rocks: Letters and Memories of Hart Crane, 1923–1932*, Wesleyan University Press, Middletown, Connecticut, 1969, p. 44.
3. 'A Note on Emil Opffer, Jr. and the Opffer Family'.
4. Jenkins Brown, *Robber Rocks*, p. 44.
5. F. Scott Fitzgerald, *The Crack-Up, With Other Pieces and Stories*, Penguin, London, 1965, p. 43.
6. Quoted from 'Hart Crane: Conversation with Samuel Loveman, New York, 1964', introduced by Ray C. Longtin. New York Public Library.
7. 'A Note on Emil Opffer, Jr. and the Opffer Family'.
8. Helge Normann Nilsen, 'Memories of Hart Crane: A Talk with Emil Opffer', *Hart Crane Newsletter*, volume II, number I (Summer 1978).

9. Alex Gildzen, 'A Walk in the Starlight: Emil Opffer and James Broughton', *The Visionary Company*, double issue, volume I, number II and volume II, number I (Spring 1982).

10. Notes dated 21 January 1962 from an interview between Susan Jenkins Brown and John Unterecker. John Unterecker Papers.

11. 'A Note on Emil Opffer, Jr. and the Opffer Family.'

12. Quoted in Jenkins Brown, *Robber Rocks*, p. 46.

13. Hart Crane to Grace Crane [20 April 1924?]. Lewis, p. 305.

14. 'Hart Crane: Conversation with Samuel Loveman, New York, 1964'.

15. Hart Crane to Grace Crane [20 April 1924?]. Lewis, p. 305.

16. Hart Crane to Waldo Frank, 21 April 1924. *Selected Letters*, p. 186.

17. Nilsen, 'Memories of Hart Crane'.

18. Undated notes from an interview between John Dos Passos and John Unterecker. John Unterecker Papers.

19. Gildzen, 'A Walk in the Starlight'.

20. Undated notes from an interview between John Dos Passos and John Unterecker. John Unterecker Papers.

21. 'An Interview with Philip C. Horton', *Hart Crane Newsletter*, volume II, number II (Spring 1979).

22. James Broughton quoted in Gildzen, 'A Walk in the Starlight'.

23. William Slater Brown to Philip Horton, 4 November 1936. Horton Papers.

24. Malcolm Cowley, *A Second Flowering*, André Deutsch, London, 1973, p. 196.

25. Transcript of an interview between Allen Tate and John Unterecker, 11 September 1962. John Unterecker Papers.

26. Jenkins Brown, *Robber Rocks*, p. 15.

27. Quoted from an undated typescript by Nathan Asch. John Unterecker Papers.

28. Malcolm Cowley to Philip Horton, 12 April 1937. Horton Papers.

29. Hart Crane to Gorham Munson, 9 July 1924. *Letters*, p. 184.

30. 'To Brooklyn Bridge', *Complete Poems*, pp. 43–4.

31. Hart Crane to Grace Crane and Elizabeth Hart, 11 May 1924. Lewis, p. 312.

32. Hart Crane to Grace Crane, 4 May 1924. Ibid., p. 309.

33. Hart Crane to Grace Crane [13 May 1924?] Ibid., p. 314.

34. Hart Crane to Jean Toomer, 28 May 1924. *Selected Letters*, p. 191.

35. Hart Crane to Jean Toomer, 16 June 1924. Ibid., p. 192.

36. Clarence Crane to Hart Crane, 23 June 1924. Lewis, p. 324.

37. Jenkins Brown, *Robber Rocks*, p. 102.

38. Lorna Dietz to Philip Horton, 30 October 1936. Horton Papers.

39. Radcliffe Squires, *Allen Tate: A Literary Biography*, Pegasus, New York, 1971, p. 52.

40. Cowley, *A Second Flowering*, p. 194.

41. Squires, *Allen Tate*, p. 52.

42. Cowley, *A Second Flowering*, p. 194.

43. Quoted in Langdon Hammer, *Hart Crane & Allen Tate: Janus-Faced Modernism*, Princeton University Press, Princeton, 1993, p. 73.

44. Cowley, *A Second Flowering*, p. 194.

45. Hart Crane to Gorham Munson, 9 July 1924. *Selected Letters*, p. 194.

46. Undated letter from Allen Tate to Hart Crane [Summer 1924]. Hart Crane Papers, Columbia University.

47. Allen Tate to Hart Crane, 15 September [1924] Hart Crane Papers, Columbia University.

48. Hart Crane to Grace Crane and Elizabeth Hart, 22 July 1924. Lewis, p. 331.

49. Hart Crane to Gorham Munson, 9 July 1924. *Letters*, p. 184.

50. Hart Crane to Grace Crane [28 July 1924]. Lewis, p. 333.
51. Malcolm Cowley, *Exile's Return*, Penguin, New York, 1976, p. 230.
52. 'Notes for VOYAGES, NO II', typescript dated 27 September 1924. Hart Crane Papers, Columbia University.
53. Obverse of typescript, 'Frondage of dark islands, breathing/the crocus lustres of the stars'. Hart Crane Papers, Columbia University.
54. 'General Aims and Theories', *Complete Poems & Selected Letters & Prose*, p. 221.
55. 'Voyages' II, *Complete Poems*, p. 35.
56. Hart Crane to Grace Crane, 16 November 1924. *Letters*, p. 192.
57. 'Notes for VOYAGES No II [and III]', 27 September 1924. Hart Crane Papers, Columbia University.
58. 'Voyages' III, *Complete Poems*, p. 36.
59. Hart Crane to Waldo Frank, 6 September 1924. *Letters*, p. 187.
60. 'Voyages' IV, *Complete Poems*, p. 37.
61. Cowley, *Exile's Return*, p. 230.
62. Hart Crane to Grace Crane, 23 September 1924. Lewis, p. 347.
63. Grace Crane to Hart Crane [18 November 1924?]. Ibid., p. 373.
64. 'Voyages' V, *Complete Poems*, p. 38.
65. 'Voyages' VI, ibid., pp. 39–40.
66. Hart Crane to Grace Crane, 23 September 1924. Lewis, p. 347.
67. 'Paraphrase', *Complete Poems*, p. 17.
68. Hart Crane to Grace Crane and Elizabeth Hart, 21 October 1924. Lewis, p. 359.
69. 'Legend', *Complete Poems*, p. 3.
70. Hart Crane to Grace Crane and Elizabeth Hart, 9 November 1924. Lewis, p. 367.
71. Hart Crane to Grace Crane, 16 November 1924. Ibid., p. 371.
72. 'The Harbor Dawn', in *The Bridge, Complete Poems*, pp. 53–4..
73. Hart Crane to Grace Crane and Elizabeth Hart, 26 November 1924. Lewis, p. 376.
74. Hart Crane to Grace Crane, 30 November 1924. Ibid., p. 377.
75. Hart Crane to Gorham Munson, 5 December 1924. *Selected Letters*, p. 200.
76. Hart Crane to Gorham Munson, 8 December 1924. Ibid., p. 202.

Chapter 11

1. Hart Crane to Grace Crane and Elizabeth Hart, 21 October 1924. Lewis, p. 359.
2. Elizabeth Hart to Hart Crane, 6 October 1924. Ibid., p. 350.
3. Hart Crane to Grace Crane and Elizabeth Hart, 14 September 1924. Ibid., p. 342.
4. Grace Crane to Hart Crane, 15 October [1924]. Ibid., p. 356.
5. Hart Crane to Grace Crane, 23 September 1924. Ibid., p. 347.
6. Grace Crane to Hart Crane, 31 October 1924. Ibid., p. 363.
7. Susan Jenkins Brown, *Robber Rock: Letters and Memories of Hart Crane, 1923–1932*, Wesleyan University Press, Middletown, Connecticut, 1969, p. 41.
8. Quoted in Jeffrey Meyers, *Edmund Wilson: A Biography*, Houghton Mifflin, Boston and New York, 1995, p. 117.
9. Jenkins Brown, *Robber Rocks*, p. 26.
10. Quoted in Hans Bak, *Malcolm Cowley: The Formative Years*, University of Georgia Press, Athens and London, 1993, p. 329.
11. Quoted in Malcolm Cowley, *A Second Flowering: Works and Days of the Lost Generation*, André Deutsch, London, 1973, p. 296.
12. Quoted in Unterecker, p. 371.
13. Hart Crane to Grace Crane, 10 February 1925. Lewis, p. 389.

14. Hart Crane to Grace Crane, 29 January 1925. Ibid., p. 386.
15. Hart Crane to Charlotte and Richard Rychtarik, 28 February 1925. *Selected Letters*, p. 202.
16. Hart Crane to Grace Crane and Elizabeth Hart [23 February 1925?]. Lewis, p. 391.
17. Hart Crane to Grace Crane and Elizabeth Hart, 13 April 1925. Ibid., p. 399.
18. Grace Crane to Hart Crane, 21 March 1925. Ibid., p. 395.
19. Hart Crane to Grace Crane and Elizabeth Hart, 7 May 1925. Ibid., p. 405.
20. Cowley, *A Second Flowering*, p. 198.
21. Hart Crane to Grace Crane and Elizabeth Hart, 2 May 1925. Lewis, p. 402.
22. Hart Crane to Grace Crane and Elizabeth Hart, 7 May 1925. Ibid., p. 405.
23. Cowley, *A Second Flowering*, p. 198.
24. Hart Crane to Grace Crane, 28 May 1925. Lewis, p. 408.
25. Cowley, *A Second Flowering*, p. 198.
26. Quoted from the undated transcript of an interview between Susan Jenkins Brown and John Unterecker. John Unterecker Papers.
27. Quoted in Malcolm Cowley, *Exile's Return*, Penguin, New York, 1976, p. 228.
28. Cowley, *A Second Flowering*, p. 204.
29. Quoted from the undated transcript of an interview between Susan Jenkins Brown and John Unterecker. John Unterecker Papers.
30. Hart Crane to Elizabeth Hart, 17 June 1925. Lewis, p. 417.
31. Hart Crane to Grace Crane and Elizabeth Hart, 10 July 1925. Ibid., p. 423.
32. Cowley, *A Second Flowering*, p. 198.
33. Hart Crane to Grace Crane and Elizabeth Hart, 10 July 1925. Lewis, p. 423.
34. Cowley, *A Second Flowering*, p. 199.
35. Hart Crane to Grace Crane and Elizabeth Hart, 10 July 1925. Lewis, p. 423.
36. Allen Tate to Hart Crane, 7 July [1925]. Hart Crane Papers, Columbia University.
37. Quoted in Cowley, *A Second Flowering*, p. 199.
38. Quoted in Unterecker, p. 406.
39. Hart Crane to Waldo Frank, 19 August 1925. *Letters*, p. 214.
40. 'Passage', *Complete Poems*, pp. 21–2.
41. Harrison Smith (Harcourt Brace) to Hart Crane, 10 July 1925. Hart Crane Papers, Columbia University.
42. Undated letter from Hart Crane to Waldo Frank [Summer 1925]. *Letters*, p. 212.
43. Hart Crane to Wilbur Underwood, 3 January [1927]. *Selected Letters*, p. 304.
44. Hart Crane to Grace Crane [19 July 1925?]. Lewis, p. 429.
45. Hart Crane to Grace Crane and Elizabeth Hart, 10 July 1925. Ibid., p. 423.
46. Hart Crane to William Slater Brown and Susan Jenkins Brown [mid-August 1925]. Jenkins Brown, *Robber Rocks*, p. 31.
47. Hart Crane to Grace Crane and Elizabeth Hart, 10 July 1925. Lewis, p. 423.
48. Hart Crane to William Slater Brown and Susan Jenkins Brown, 3 August 1925. Jenkins Brown, *Robber Rocks*, p. 29.
49. Hart Crane to Waldo Frank, 19 August [1925]. *Letters*, p. 214.
50. Hart Crane to William Slater Brown and Susan Jenkins Brown [mid-August 1925]. Jenkins Brown, *Robber Rocks*, p. 31.
51. Hart Crane to Slater Brown, 27 August [1925]. Quoted in Unterecker, p. 396.
52. 1709 East 115th Street had been demolished by 1961 and its site was subsequently acquired by Western Reserve University, then in the course of expansion. In 1967 the place where Hart Crane measured his first lyrical lines was designated a 'Western Reserve University Athletic Area Parking Lot'. (Anonymous and undated typescript among the Baker Papers.)

53. Susan Jenkins Brown to Hart Crane, 4 September 1925. Hart Crane Papers, Columbia University.

54. Zell Hart Deming to Hart Crane, 12 September 1925. Hart Crane Collection, Beinecke, Yale University.

55. Hart Crane to Charlotte and Richard Rychtarik, 15 September 1925. Quoted in Unterecker, p. 398.

56. Undated letter from Hart Crane to Zell Hart Deming. Hart Crane Collection, Beinecke, Yale University.

57. Hart Crane to Charlotte and Richard Rychtarik, 15 September 1925. *Letters*, p. 215.

58. Hart Crane to Charlotte and Richard Rychtarik [4 October 1925?]. Quoted in Unterecker, p. 399.

59. Hart Crane to Charlotte and Richard Rychtarik [October 1925?]. *Letters*, p. 216.

60. Quoted in Jenkins Brown, *Robber Rocks*, p. 34.

61. Hart Crane to Slater Brown, 11 October [1925]. Quoted in Unterecker, p. 401.

62. Quoted ibid., p. 402.

63. Quoted ibid., p. 404.

64. 'The Wine Menagerie', *Complete Poems*, p. 23.

65. Hart Crane to William Slater Brown and Susan Jenkins Brown, 21 October 1925. Jenkins Brown, *Robber Rocks*, p. 36.

66. Hart Crane to William Slater Brown, 27 August 1925. Hart Crane Papers, Columbia University.

67. Quoted in Deborah Baker, *In Extremis: The Life of Laura Riding,* Hamish Hamilton, London, 1993, p. 72.

68. Hart Crane to William Slater Brown and Susan Jenkins Brown, 21 October 1925. Jenkins Brown, *Robber Rocks*, p. 36.

69. Ibid., p. 40.

70. Quoted in Baker, *In Extremis*, p. 77.

71. Undated notes by John Unterecker. John Unterecker Papers.

72. Hart Crane to Susan Jenkins Brown and William Slater Brown, 21 October 1925. Jenkins Brown, *Robber Rocks*, p. 36.

73. Agnes O'Neill to Hart Crane, 31 October 1925. Hart Crane Papers, Columbia University.

74. Hart Crane to William Sommer, 27 October 1925. *Letters*, p. 218.

75. 'General Aims and Theories', *Complete Poems & Selected Letters & Prose*, p. 217.

76. 'At Melville's Tomb', *Complete Poems*, p. 33. I am indebted for my interpretation of this poem to Langdon Hammer's *Hart Crane & Allen Tate: Janus-Faced Modernism*, Part III, Chapter 6.

77. Hart Crane to Charlotte and Richard Rychtarik, 15 September 1925. *Letters*, p. 215.

78. Harriet Monroe to Hart Crane, open letter published in *Poetry*, volume 29 (October 1926).

79. Hart Crane to Harriet Monroe, editor of *Poetry*. Ibid.

80. Grace Crane to Elizabeth Hart, 16 October 1925. Lewis, p. 433.

81. Hart Crane to Grace Crane, 24 October 1925. Ibid., p. 438.

82. Hart Crane to Clarence Crane, 4 November 1925. Hart Crane Papers, Kent State University.

83. Clarence Crane to Hart Crane, 17 November 1925. Lewis, p. 440.

84. Hart Crane to Clarence Crane [21 November 1925?]. Ibid., p. 442.

85. Clarence Crane to Hart Crane, 25 November 1925. Ibid., p. 443.

86. Hart Crane to Waldo Frank, 19 August [1925]. *Selected Letters*, p. 204.

87. Marianne Moore to Hart Crane, 10 November 1925. Hart Crane Collection, Beinecke, Yale University.

88. Hart Crane to Marianne Moore, 10 November 1925. Hart Crane Collection, Beinecke, Yale University.

89. Hart Crane to Charlotte and Richard Rychtarik, 1 December 1925. *Selected Letters*, p. 209.
90. Matthew Josephson to Philip Horton, 19 August 1937. Horton Papers.
91. Hart Crane to Marianne Moore, 30 November 1925. Hart Crane Collection, Beinecke, Yale University.
92. Hart Crane to Otto Kahn, 3 December 1925. *Selected Letters*, p. 212.
93. E. Mutke to Hart Crane, 5 December 1925. Hart Crane Papers, Columbia University.
94. Hart Crane to Clarence Crane, 3 December 1925. Lewis, p. 445.
95. Quoted from the undated transcript of an interview between Waldo Frank and John Unterecker. John Unterecker Papers.
96. 'In Tune with the Finite', by 'Search-Light' (Waldo Frank), *New Yorker*, 20 February 1926, p. 23.
97. Hart Crane to Wilbur Underwood, 25 December 1925. Copy in John Unterecker Papers.
98. Laura Riding to Philip Horton, 1 January 1937. Horton Papers.
99. Marianne Moore to Hart Crane, 10 December 1925. Hart Crane Collection, Beinecke, Yale University.
100. Hart Crane to Jane Heap, 16 December [1925]. The *Little Review* Papers, Special Collections of the University of Wisconsin-Milwaukee Library.
101. Hart Crane to Grace Crane, 9 December 1925. Lewis, p. 447.
102. Allen Tate to Hart Crane, 9 December [1925]. Quoted in Unterecker, p. 418.

Chapter 12

1. Quoted in Susan Jenkins Brown, *Robber Rocks: Letters and Memories of Hart Crane, 1923–1932*, Wesleyan University Press, Middletown, Connecticut, 1969, p. 31.
2. Malcolm Cowley, *A Second Flowering: Works and Days of the Lost Generation*, André Deutsch, London, 1973, p. 200.
3. Ibid. p. 204.
4. Quoted from the transcript of an interview between Allen Tate and John Unterecker, 11 September 1962. John Unterecker Papers.
5. Quoted from an undated transcript of a recording by Nathan Asch. Ibid.
6. Jenkins Brown, *Robber Rocks*, p. 48.
7. Hart Crane to Charlotte and Richard Rychtarik [31 December 1925]. *Letters*, p. 225.
8. Hart Crane to Clarence Crane, 3 December 1925. Lewis, p. 445.
9. Clarence Crane to Hart Crane, 16 December 1925. Ibid., p. 449.
10. Hart Crane to Clarence Crane, 25 December 1925. Ibid., p. 451.
11. Hart Crane to Wilbur Underwood, 25 December 1925. Warren Herendeen and Donald G. Parker (eds), 'Wind-Blown Flames: Letters of Hart Crane to Wilbur Underwood', *Southern Review*, volume XVI, number I (April 1980), pp. 360–2.
12. Quoted from the undated transcript of an interview between Susan Jenkins Brown and John Unterecker. John Unterecker Papers.
13. Hart Crane to Malcolm Cowley, 3 January 1926. Jenkins Brown, *Robber Rocks*, p. 47.
14. William Slater Brown to Philip Horton, 8 July 1936. Horton Papers.
15. 'Repose of Rivers', *Complete Poems*, p. 16.
16. Hart Crane to Charlotte and Richard Rychtarik [31 December 1925]. *Letters*, p. 225.
17. Reported by Allen Tate to John Unterecker. Undated interview notes in the John Unterecker Papers.
18. Quoted in Unterecker, p. 420.
19. Hart Crane to Waldo Frank, 21 April 1924. *Selected Letters*, p. 186.
20. Hart Crane to Elizabeth Hart, 5 January 1926. Lewis, p. 458.
21. Hart Crane to Waldo Frank, 18 January 1926. *Selected Letters*, p. 226.
22. 'Atlantis', *Complete Poems*, pp. 105–8.

23. Hart Crane to Grace Crane and Elizabeth Hart, 7 January [1926?]. Lewis, p. 459.

24. Hart Crane to Elizabeth Hart, 27 January [1926?]. Ibid., p. 470.

25. 'Ave Maria', *Complete Poems*, pp. 47–50.

26. Hart Crane to Grace Crane, 26 January [1926?]. Lewis, p. 467.

27. Hart Crane to Gaston Lachaise, 10 February 1926. *Selected Letters*, p. 227.

28. Cowley, *A Second Flowering*, p. 202.

29. Hart Crane to Charles Harris, 20 February 1926. *Selected Letters*, p. 228.

30. Hart Crane to Charlotte and Richard Rychtarik, 2 March [1926]. Ibid.

31. Hart Crane to Gorham Munson, 5 March [1926]. Ibid. p. 229.

32. Hart Crane to Malcolm Cowley, 28 March [1926]. Ibid. p. 238.

33. Gorham B. Munson, 'Hart Crane: Young Titan in the Sacred Wood', *Destinations: A Canvas of American Literature since 1900*. J.H. Sears, New York, 1928.

34. Hart Crane to Gorham Munson, 17 March 1926. *Selected Letters*, p. 231.

35. Otto Kahn to Hart Crane, 6 January 1926. Hart Crane Papers, Columbia University.

36. Hart Crane to Otto Kahn, 18 March 1926. *Selected Letters*, p. 235.

37. Otto Kahn to Hart Crane, 22 March 1926. Hart Crane Papers, Columbia University.

38. Hart Crane to Waldo Frank, 20 March 1926. *Selected Letters*, p. 237.

39. Hart Crane to Grace Crane [28 March 1926?]. Lewis, p. 475.

40. Hart Crane to Malcolm Cowley, 28 March [1926]. *Selected Letters*, p. 238.

41. Hart Crane to Gorham Munson, 5 March [1926]. Ibid., p. 229.

42. Quoted in Langdon Hammer, *Hart Crane & Allen Tate: Janus-Faced Modernism*, Princeton University Press, Princeton, 1993, p. 34.

43. Quoted from the transcript of an interview between Allen Tate and John Unterecker, 11 September 1962. John Unterecker Papers.

44. Cowley, *A Second Flowering*, p. 201.

45. Ibid., p. 204.

46. Hart Crane to Gorham Munson, 5 April [1926]. *Selected Letters*, p. 239.

47. Quoted in Ashley Brown, 'Caroline Gordon [Tate] and Hart Crane: A Literary Relationship', *The Visionary Company*, double issue, volume I, number II and volume II, number I (Spring 1982).

48. Quoted in Unterecker, p. 431.

49. Hart Crane to Charlotte and Richard Rychtarik, 11 April 1926. Quoted ibid., p. 432.

50. Quoted by Hart Crane in a letter to Grace Crane, 18 April [1926]. *Selected Letters*, p. 241.

51. Undated letter from Allen Tate to Hart Crane. Ibid., p. 246.

52. Hart Crane to Grace Crane, 18 April [1926]. Ibid., p. 241.

53. Unsigned and undated letter from Hart Crane to Allen Tate and Caroline Gordon [Tate] [April 1926?]. Ibid., p. 247.

54. Fragment of an undated letter from Hart Crane to Allen Tate [April 1926?]. Ibid., p. 249.

55. Hart Crane to Charlotte and Richard Rychtarik, 25 April 1926. *Letters*, p. 249.

56. Hart Crane to Grace Crane, 18 April [1926]. *Selected Letters*, p. 241.

57. Hart Crane to Grace Crane, 24 April [1926?]. Lewis, p. 484.

58. Jenkins Brown, *Robber Rocks*, p. 58.

59. Quoted from the undated transcript of an interview between Waldo Frank and John Unterecker. John Unterecker Papers.

60. Hart Crane to Grace Crane, 8 May [1926?]. Lewis, p. 487.

Chapter 13

1. Hart Crane to Grace Crane, 3 May [1926?]. Lewis, p. 486.

2. Hart Crane to William Slater Brown and Susan Jenkins Brown, 7 May 1926. Susan Jenkins

Brown, *Robber Rocks: Letters and Memories of Hart Crane, 1923–1932*, Wesleyan University Press, Middletown, Connecticut, 1969, p. 53.

3. Hart Crane to Grace Crane, 8 May [1926?]. Lewis, p. 487.
4. Hart Crane to Grace Crane and Elizabeth Hart, 14 May [1926?]. Ibid., p. 491.
5. Hart Crane to Charles Harris, 30 November 1926. Photocopy of original letter in the John Unterecker Papers.
6. Frederick L. Swetland to John Unterecker, 17 August 1961. John Unterecker Papers.
7. Quoted from the undated transcript of an interview between Waldo Frank and John Unterecker. John Unterecker Papers.
8. Mrs T.W. Simpson to Grace Crane, 21 November 1935. Hart Crane Papers, Columbia University.
9. Mrs T.W. Simpson to Hart Crane, 15 September 1928. Hart Crane Papers, Columbia University.
10. Mrs T.W. Simpson to Hart Crane, 14 December 1926. Hart Crane Papers, Columbia University.
11. Hart Crane to Grace Crane, 1 June 1926. Lewis, p. 496.
12. 'Royal Palm', *Complete Poems*, p. 122.
13. Hart Crane to Susan Jenkins Brown and William Slater Brown, 7 May 1926. Jenkins Brown, *Robber Rocks*, p. 53.
14. Hart Crane to Clarence Crane, 20 May 1926. Lewis, p. 493.
15. Hart Crane to Susan Jenkins Brown, 22 May [1926]. *Selected Letters*, p. 253.
16. Hart Crane to Wilbur Underwood [1 July 1926?]. Ibid., p. 260.
17. 'Island Quarry', *Complete Poems*, p. 116.
18. Hart Crane to Susan Jenkins Brown, 22 May [1926]. *Selected Letters*, p. 253.
19. Hart Crane to Wilbur Underwood [1 July 1926?]. Ibid., p. 260.
20. Hart Crane to Grace Crane, 1 June 1926. Lewis, p. 496.
21. Hart Crane to Grace Crane, 8 July 1926. Ibid., p. 500.
22. Hart Crane to Waldo Frank, 19 June 1926. *Letters*, p. 258.
23. Hart Crane to Yvor Winters, 27 January 1927. *Selected Letters*, p. 313.
24. Hart Crane to Grace Crane, 8 July 1926. Lewis, p. 500.
25. Hart Crane to Waldo Frank, 19 June 1926. *Letters*, p. 258.
26. Hart Crane to William Slater Brown and Susan Jenkins Brown, 14 July 1926. Jenkins Brown, *Robber Rocks*, p. 61.
27. 'The Air Plant', *Complete Poems*, p. 123.
28. 'O Carib Isle!', ibid., pp. 111–12.
29. Hart Crane to Waldo Frank, 19 June 1926. *Letters*, p. 258.
30. Hart Crane to Waldo Frank, 20 June [1926]. *Selected Letters*, p. 257.
31. Hart Crane to Waldo Frank, 3 July 1926. Ibid., p. 261.
32. Hart Crane to Elizabeth Hart, 29 June [1926?]. Lewis, p. 505.
33. Hart Crane to Waldo Frank, 24 July 1926. *Selected Letters*, p. 263.
34. 'To Brooklyn Bridge', *Complete Poems*, pp. 43–4.
35. Hart Crane to Waldo Frank, 26 July 1926. *Selected Letters*, p. 265.
36. Eugene O'Neill to Hart Crane, 21 August 1926. Hart Crane Papers, Columbia University.
37. Hart Crane to Horace Liveright, 20 July 1926. Hart Crane Papers, Kent State University.
38. Hart Crane to Waldo Frank, 24 July 1926. *Selected Letters*, p. 263.
39. Hart Crane to Allen Tate, 25 July 1926. Ibid., p. 264.
40. Hart Crane to Waldo Frank, 26 July 1926. Ibid., p. 265.
41. Hart Crane to Malcolm and Peggy Cowley, 29 July [1926]. Ibid., p. 266.
42. Hart Crane to Waldo Frank, 3 August [1926]. Ibid., p. 266.

43. 'Cutty Sark', in *The Bridge, Complete Poems*, pp. 71–4.
44. Hart Crane to Otto Kahn, 12 September 1927. *Letters*, p. 304.
45. Hart Crane to Grace Crane, 30 July [1926?]. Lewis, p. 506.
46. Hart Crane to Wilbur Underwood, 3 August 1926. Copy of the original letter in the John Unterecker Papers.
47. Hart Crane to Waldo Frank, 3 August [1926]. *Selected Letters*, p. 266.
48. Hart Crane to Waldo Frank, 12 August [1926]. Ibid., p. 267.
49. Hart Crane to Waldo Frank, 19 August 1926. Ibid., p. 269.
50. Hart Crane to Waldo Frank, 23 August [1926]. Ibid., p. 272.
51. 'The Tunnel', in *The Bridge, Complete Poems*, pp. 95–101.
52. Hart Crane to Grace Crane [28 August 1926]. Lewis, p. 509.
53. Hart Crane to Waldo Frank, 3 July 1926. *Selected Letters*, p. 261.
54. Hart Crane to Yvor Winters, 27 January 1927. Ibid., p. 313.
55. Hart Crane to Waldo Frank, 3 September 1926. Ibid., p. 274.
56. Hart Crane to Waldo Frank, 5 September [1926]. Ibid., p. 275.
57. Hart Crane to Grace Crane, 6 September 1926. Lewis, p. 511.
58. Hart Crane to Grace Crane, 19 September [1926?]. Ibid., p. 513.
59. Hart Crane to Otto Kahn, 19 September 1926. *Selected Letters*, p. 275.
60. Hart Crane to Mrs T.W. Simpson, 4 July 1927. Ibid., p. 341.
61. Hart Crane to Waldo Frank, 19 August 1926. Ibid., p. 269.
62. 'The River', in *The Bridge, Complete Poems*, pp. 57–61.
63. Hart Crane to Kenneth Burke, 28 September [1926]. *Selected Letters*, p. 276.
64. Yvor Winters to Harriet Monroe, reproduced in *Poetry* (October 1926) and quoted in Thomas Parkinson (ed.), *Hart Crane & Yvor Winters: Their Literary Correspondence*, University of California Press, Berkeley, Los Angeles and London, 1978, p. 8.
65. Hart Crane to Yvor Winters, 5 October 1926. *Selected Letters*, p. 283.
66. *New York Times*, 21 October 1926.
67. Mrs T.W. Simpson to Hart Crane, 19 November 1926. Hart Crane Papers, Columbia University.
68. Mrs T.W. Simpson to Hart Crane, 9 November 1926. Hart Crane Papers, Columbia University.
69. Information from reports in the *New York Times*, Thursday, 21 October to Wednesday, 27 October 1926.
70. Information from the *Dictionary of American Naval Fighting Ships*, Naval History Division, Washington D.C., 1969, Volume IV.
71. 'Eternity', *Complete Poems*, pp. 186–7.
72. Hart Crane to Mrs T.W. Simpson, 5 December 1926. *Selected Letters*, p. 292.
73. William Wright to Hart Crane, 23 October [1926]. Hart Crane Papers, Columbia University.

Chapter 14
1. Telegram from Grace Crane to Hart Crane, 30 October 1926. Lewis, p. 515.
2. Waldo Frank to Hart Crane, 27 October 1926. Hart Crane Papers, Columbia University.
3. Hart Crane to Yvor Winters, 1 November 1926. Parkinson, p. 15.
4. Hart Crane to Harriet Monroe, 1 November 1926. Hart Crane Collection, Beinecke, Yale University.
5. Hart Crane to Charlotte Rychtarik, 1 November [1926]. *Letters*, p. 276.
6. Clarence Crane to Hart Crane, 2 November 1926. Lewis, p. 516.
7. Mrs T.W. Simpson to Hart Crane, 29 October 1926. Hart Crane Papers, Columbia University.

8. Mrs T.W. Simpson to Hart Crane, 19 November 1926. Hart Crane Papers, Columbia University.

9. Charles Curtis to Hart Crane, 10 November 1926. Hart Crane Collection, Beinecke, Yale University.

10. Hart Crane to Wilbur Underwood, 10 November 1926. Copy of original letter in the John Unterecker Papers.

11. Hart Crane to Yvor Winters, 12 November [1926]. *Selected Letters*, p. 285.

12. Hart Crane to Yvor Winters, 15 November 1926. Ibid., p. 287.

13. Hart Crane to Waldo Frank, 21 November [1926]. Ibid., p. 289.

14. 'To Emily Dickinson', *Complete Poems*, p. 128.

15. Hart Crane to Mrs T.W. Simpson, 5 December 1926. *Selected Letters*, p. 292.

16. Hart Crane to Wilbur Underwood, 16 December [1926]. Ibid., p. 293.

17. Hart Crane to Grace Crane, 22 December 1926. Lewis, p. 518.

18. Hart Crane to Wilbur Underwood, 3 January [1927]. *Selected Letters*, p. 304.

19. Hart Crane to Grace Crane, 22 December 1926. Lewis, p. 518.

20. Hart Crane to Allen Tate [7 January 1927?]. *Selected Letters*, p. 306.

21. Hart Crane to Horace Liveright, 6 January 1927. Hart Crane Papers, Columbia University.

22. Hart Crane to Edgell Rickword, 7 January 1927. *Letters*, p. 283.

23. Hart Crane to Grace Crane, 23 January 1927. *Selected Letters*, p. 311.

24. Hart Crane to Yvor Winters, 19 January 1927. Ibid., p. 309.

25. Hart Crane to Wilbur Underwood, 11 January [1927]. Ibid., p. 308.

26. Hart Crane to Yvor Winters, 27 January 1927. Ibid., p. 313.

27. Hart Crane to Grace Crane, 19 March 1927. Lewis, p. 532.

28. Gorham B. Munson, *The Awakening Twenties: A Memoir-History of a Literary Period*, Louisiana State University Press, Baton Rouge and London, 1985, p. 137.

29. Quoted from the undated transcript of an interview between Waldo Frank and John Unterecker. John Unterecker Papers.

30. Quoted in Tom Dardis, *Firebrand: The Life of Horace Liveright*, Random House, New York, 1995, p. 149.

31. Quoted ibid., p. 86.

32. Hart Crane to William Slater Brown and Susan Jenkins Brown, 16 February 1927. Susan Jenkins Brown, *Robber Rocks: Letters and Memories of Hart Crane*, Wesleyan University Press, Middletown, Connecticut, 1969, p. 67.

33. Eugene Jolas to Hart Crane, 24 February 1927. Hart Crane Papers, Columbia University.

34. Hart Crane to Yvor Winters, 23 February 1927. Parkinson, p. 55.

35. Hart Crane to Yvor Winters, 26 February 1927. Ibid., p. 56.

36. Mrs T.W. Simpson to Hart Crane, 1 January 1927. Hart Crane Papers, Columbia University.

37. Hart Crane to Waldo Frank, 28 January [1927]. *Selected Letters*, p. 316. The typescript of Philip Horton's *Hart Crane* contains the following note to his publishers, W.W. Norton & Co.: 'Do you think it advisable/interesting to go into details about the technical arrangements made by Kahn? He seems to have taken out a "policy" (some kind of insurance) on Crane for $2500, the premiums for which ... were to be assumed by Crane although he seems not to have learned of this til [*sic*] later. In the Kahn files I found this: "Total of loans to Crane $2500 less proceeds of insurance policy surrendered $107.58. Written off as worthless, 1928, makes a total of $2,392.42." This is all Sanskrit to me, of course, and I don't know whether or not it would make amusing or interesting sense to readers. What is your opinion?' Malcolm Cowley, who read the typescript, wrote in the margin: 'Leave out I'd say.' From the Philip Horton *Hart Crane* typescript, New York Public Library.

38. Hart Crane to Elizabeth Hart, 28 February 1927. Lewis, p. 527.
39. Hart Crane to Grace Crane, 19 March 1927. Ibid., p. 532.
40. Hart Crane to William Slater Brown and Susan Jenkins Brown, 9 March 1927. Jenkins Brown, *Robber Rocks*, p. 70.
41. Hart Crane to Mrs T.W. Simpson, 6 March 1927. Hart Crane Papers, Columbia University.
42. Hart Crane to Allen Tate, 24 February [1927]. *Selected Letters*, p. 318.
43. Hart Crane to Allen Tate, 10 March [1927]. Ibid., p. 324.
44. Marianne Moore to James Sibley Watson, 9 March 1927. *Selected Letters of Marianne Moore*, Bonnie Costello (general ed.), Celeste Goodridge and Cristanne Miller (assoc. eds), Knopf, New York, 1997), p. 213.
45. Hart Crane to Allen Tate, 14 March 1927. *Selected Letters*, p. 325.
46. Quoted by Hart Crane in a letter to Grace Crane, 23 January 1927. Lewis, p. 520.
47. Hart Crane to Grace Crane, 19 March 1927. Ibid., p. 532.
48. Hart Crane to Yvor Winters, 19 March 1927. *Selected Letters*, p. 326.
49. Jenkins Brown, *Robber Rocks*, p. 72.
50. Hart Crane to Allen Tate, 21 March 1927. *Selected Letters*, p. 329.
51. Hart Crane to Yvor Winters, 27 March [1927]. Parkinson, p. 75.
52. Hart Crane to Wilbur Underwood, 21 March 1927. Copy of an original letter in the John Unterecker Papers.
53. Hart Crane to Harriet Monroe, 4 April 1927. Hart Crane Collection, Beinecke, Yale University.
54. Hart Crane to Allen Tate, 26 March [1927]. *Letters*, p. 293.
55. Hart Crane to Allen Tate, 30 March [1927]. Ibid., p. 294.
56. Waldo Frank to Philip Horton, 18 June 1937. Horton Papers.
57. Mrs T.W. Simpson to Hart Crane, 9 January 1927. Lewis, p. 531.
58. Grace Crane to Hart Crane, 20 March 1927. Ibid., p. 538.
59. Hart Crane to Grace Crane, 19 March 1927. Ibid., p. 532.
60. *Cleveland Press*, 4 June 1927.
61. Hart Crane to Grace Crane, 23 January 1927. Lewis, p. 520.
62. *New York Sun*, 22 January 1927.
63. Hart Crane to Waldo Frank, 28 January [1927]. *Selected Letters*, p. 316.
64. Waldo Frank, 'The Poetry of Hart Crane', *New Republic*, 16 March 1927.
65. *Saturday Review of Literature*, 2 April 1927.
66. Quoted in Horton, p. 222.
67. Hart Crane to Grace Crane, 28 March [1927?]. Lewis, p. 540.
68. Omnibus review by Herbert S. Gorman, *New York Times Book Review*, 27 March 1927.
69. *Boston (Massachusetts) Transcript*, 16 April 1927.
70. Anonymous, 'Briefer Mention', *Dial*, May 1927.
71. Hart Crane to Allen Tate, 27 March [1927]. *Selected Letters*, p. 330.
72. Hart Crane to Allen Tate, 30 March [1927]. Ibid., p. 331.
73. *Times Literary Supplement*, 24 February 1927.
74. Quoted in Parkinson, p. 41. Winters's review of *White Buildings* and Harriet Monroe's note both appeared in *Poetry* (April 1927).
75. Hart Crane to Yvor Winters, 2 April 1927. Parkinson, p. 76.

Chapter 15

1. Hart Crane to Clarence Crane [23 April 1927?]. Quoted in Unterecker, p. 489.
2. Hart Crane to Yvor Winters, 18 April [1927]. Parkinson, p. 77.
3. Hart Crane to Grace Crane [28 April 1927]. Lewis, p. 549.

4. Hart Crane to Yvor Winters, 29 April 1927. *Selected Letters*, p. 333.
5. Hart Crane to Wilbur Underwood, 4 May 1927. Ibid., p. 334.
6. Undated notebook entry. Hart Crane Papers, Columbia University.
7. Hart Crane to Wilbur Underwood, 4 May 1927. *Selected Letters*, p. 334.
8. Hart Crane to Wilbur Underwood, 12 May [1927]. Ibid., p. 335.
9. Hart Crane to Wilbur Underwood, 23 May [1927]. Copy of an original letter in the John Unterecker Papers.
10. Hart Crane to Wilbur Underwood, 6 June [1927]. *Selected Letters*, p. 335.
11. Hart Crane to Yvor Winters, 21 May 1927. Parkinson, p. 81.
12. Lorna Dietz to Philip Horton, 30 October 1936. Horton Papers.
13. Quoted in Susan Jenkins Brown, *Robber Rocks*, Wesleyan University Press, Middletown, Connecticut, 1969, p. 85.
14. Susan Jenkins Brown to John Unterecker, 27 September 1966. John Unterecker Papers.
15. William Slater Brown to Philip Horton, 8 July 1936. Horton Papers.
16. 'Thou Canst Read Nothing . . .', *Complete Poems*, p. 193.
17. Hart Crane to Clarence Crane, 21 June 1927. Lewis, p. 588.
18. Hart Crane to Wilbur Underwood, 23 May [1927]. Copy of an original letter in the John Unterecker Papers.
19. Edmund Wilson, 'The Muses out of Work', *New Republic*, 11 May 1927.
20. Hart Crane to Yvor Winters, 29 May 1927. *Selected Letters*, p. 335.
21. Hart Crane to Mrs T.W. Simpson, 4 July 1927. Ibid., p. 341.
22. Hart Crane to Yvor Winters, 1 July 1927. Parkinson, p. 94.
23. Hart Crane to Mrs T.W. Simpson, 4 July 1927. *Selected Letters*, p. 341.
24. 'The River', in *The Bridge, Complete Poems*, p. 57.
25. Hart Crane to Mrs T.W. Simpson, 4 July 1927. *Selected Letters*, p. 341.
26. Hart Crane to Otto Kahn, 12 September 1927. Ibid., p. 344.
27. 'The Dance', in *The Bridge, Complete Poems*, p. 62.
28. Mrs T.W. Simpson to Hart Crane, 24 July 1927. Hart Crane Papers, Columbia University.
29. Hart Crane to Yvor Winters, 5 July 1927. Parkinson, p. 95.
30. Clarence Crane to Hart Crane, 31 May 1927. Lewis, p. 574.
31. Clarence Crane to Hart Crane, 17 August 1927. Ibid., p. 605.
32. Clarence Crane to Hart Crane, 3 May 1927. Ibid., p. 552.
33. Clarence Crane to Hart Crane, 15 June 1927. Ibid., p. 581.
34. Clarence Crane to Hart Crane, 12 July 1927. Ibid., p. 595.
35. Hart Crane to Wilbur Underwood, 17 August 1927. *Selected Letters*, p. 344.
36. Hart Crane to Otto Kahn, 12 September 1927. Ibid., p. 344.
37. Otto Kahn to Hart Crane, 19 September 1927. Hart Crane Papers, Columbia University.
38. Paul Rosenfeld to Hart Crane, 18 September 1927. Hart Crane Papers, Columbia University.
39. Hart Crane to Clarence Crane, 11 October 1927. Lewis, p. 610.
40. Hart Crane to William Slater Brown and Susan Jenkins Brown, 11 October 1927. Jenkins Brown, *Robber Rocks*, p. 74.
41. Clarence Crane to Hart Crane, 13 October 1927. Lewis, p. 611.
42. Hart Crane to Wilbur Underwood [late October 1927]. *Selected Letters*, p. 350.
43. Quoted from the transcript of an interview between Sam Loveman and John Unterecker, 4 August 1962. John Unterecker Papers.
44. Hart Crane to Wilbur Underwood, 11 November 1927. Copy of an original letter in the John Unterecker Papers.

45. Jenkins Brown, *Robber Rocks*, p. 77.

46. Hart Crane to Grace Crane, 3 November 1927. Lewis, p. 612.

47. Jenkins Brown, *Robber Rocks*, p. 77.

48. Harriet Monroe to Philip Horton, 17 May 1935. Horton Papers.

49. Hart Crane to Wilbur Underwood, 11 November 1927. Copy of an original letter in the John Unterecker Papers.

50. Hart Crane to William Slater Brown and Susan Jenkins Brown, 16 November 1927. Jenkins Brown, *Robber Rocks*, p. 76.

51. William Slater Brown to Philip Horton, 4 November 1936. Horton Papers.

52. Hart Crane to Grace Crane, 3 November 1927. Lewis, p. 612.

53. Mrs T.W. Simpson to Hart Crane, 10 December 1927. Hart Crane Papers, Columbia University.

Chapter 16

1. Hart Crane to Yvor Winters, 23 November 1927. *Selected Letters*, p. 352.

2. Details taken from Herbert Wise's obituary in the *New York Times*, 4 October 1961.

3. Quoted from Bennett Cerf, *At Random: The Reminiscences of Bennett Cerf*. Random House, New York, 1977, p. 7.

4. Hart Crane to Wilbur Underwood, 7 November 1927. *Selected Letters*, p. 351.

5. Hart Crane to Charlotte and Richard Rychtarik, 29 November 1927. *Letters*, p. 311.

6. Hart Crane to Yvor Winters, 23 November 1927. *Selected Letters*, p. 352.

7. Hart Crane to Isidor Schneider, 15 December 1927. Hart Crane Papers, Columbia University.

8. Hart Crane to William Slater Brown, 19 December 1927. Susan Jenkins Brown, *Robber Rocks: Letters and Memories of Hart Crane, 1923–1932*, Wesleyan University Press, Middletown, Connecticut, 1969, p. 78.

9. Hart Crane to Yvor Winters, 23 November 1927. *Selected Letters*, p. 352.

10. Hart Crane to Wilbur Underwood, 27 April 1928. Ibid., p. 372.

11. Hart Crane to Sam Loveman, 1 December 1927. Hart Crane Papers, Columbia University.

12. Hart Crane to Malcolm and Peggy Cowley, 31 January 1928. Jenkins Brown, *Robber Rocks*, p. 82.

13. Hart Crane to Wilbur Underwood, 27 April 1928. *Selected Letters*, p. 372.

14. Hart Crane to Yvor Winters, 8 December [1927]. Ibid., p. 353.

15. Hart Crane to Isidor and Helen Schneider, 15 December 1927. Hart Crane Papers, Columbia University.

16. Hart Crane to Waldo Frank, 12 June 1928. *Letters*, p. 325.

17. Undated typescript by Nathan Asch, John Unterecker Papers.

18. Hart Crane to William Slater Brown, 19 December 1927. *Selected Letters*, p. 354.

19. Hart Crane to Isidor and Helen Schneider, 15 December 1927. Hart Crane Papers, Columbia University.

20. Yvor Winters, *In Defense of Reason*, The Swallow Press, New York, 1947. Quoted in Parkinson, p. 107.

21. 'The Hurricane', *Complete Poems*, p. 124.

22. Winters, *In Defense of Reason*. Quoted in Parkinson, p. 109.

23. Hart Crane to Yvor Winters, 10 January 1928. Parkinson, p. 110.

24. Hart Crane to Yvor Winters, 27 January 1928. *Selected Letters*, p. 359.

25. Hart Crane to Sam Loveman, 5 February 1928. *Letters*, p. 316.

26. Hart Crane to Isidor and Helen Schneider, 16 July 1928. Quoted in Unterecker, p. 529.

27. 'Fugitives', in Francis Murphy (ed.), *The Uncollected Essays and Reviews of Yvor Winters*, Chicago 1973. Quoted in Parkinson, p. 119.

28. Hart Crane to Yvor Winters, 20 January 1928. *Selected Letters*, p. 357.

29. William Rose Benét, 'The Phoenix Nest', *Saturday Review of Literature,* 10 December 1927.

30. Hart Crane to William Slater Brown, 22 February 1928. *Selected Letters*, p. 362.

31. Hart Crane to William Slater Brown and Susan Jenkins Brown, 27 March 1928. Ibid., p. 364.

32. Hart Crane to Sam Loveman, 5 February 1928. *Letters*, p. 316.

33. Hart Crane to William Slater Brown, 22 February 1928. *Selected Letters*, p. 362.

34. Hart Crane to Malcolm and Peggy Cowley, 31 January 1928. Jenkins Brown, *Robber Rocks*, p. 82.

35. Hart Crane to Wilbur Underwood, 27 April 1928. *Selected Letters*, p. 372.

36. Hart Crane to William Slater Brown and Susan Jenkins Brown, 27 March 1928. Ibid., p. 364.

37. Hart Crane to William Slater Brown, 22 February 1928. Ibid., p. 362.

38. Undated letter to Hart Crane, misattributed to Emil Opffer. Hart Crane Papers, Columbia University.

39. Hart Crane to William Slater Brown and Susan Jenkins Brown, 27 March 1928. *Selected Letters*, p. 364.

40. Hart Crane to Isidor Schneider, 28 March 1928. Quoted in Unterecker, p. 535.

41. Hart Crane to William Slater Brown and Susan Jenkins Brown, 27 March 1928. *Selected Letters*, p. 364.

42. Hart Crane to Yvor Winters, 29 March 1928. Parkinson, p. 118.

43. Grace Crane to Sam Loveman, 23 June 1932. Hart Crane Papers, Columbia University.

44. Hart Crane to William Slater Brown and Susan Jenkins Brown, 27 March 1928. *Selected Letters*, p. 364.

45. Hart Crane to William Slater Brown, 27 April [1928]. *Letters*, p. 324.

46. Hart Crane to Isidor Schneider, 28 March 1928. Ibid., p. 322.

47. Hart Crane to Waldo Frank [4 April 1928?]. *Selected Letters*, p. 368.

48. Hart Crane to Gorham Munson, 17 April 1928. Ibid., p. 370.

49. Hart Crane to William Slater Brown, 27 April 1928. Jenkins Brown, *Robber Rocks*, p. 91.

50. Hart Crane to Wilbur Underwood, 27 April 1928. *Selected Letters*, p. 372.

51. Ralph Crane to John Unterecker, 23 September 1963. John Unterecker Papers.

52. Clarence Crane to Hart Crane, 28 March 1928. Lewis, p. 617.

53. Hart Crane to Clarence Crane, 14 April 1928. Hart Crane Papers, Kent State University.

54. Grace Crane to Sam Loveman, 13 May 1932. Hart Crane Papers, Columbia University.

55. Jenkins Brown, *Robber Rocks*, p. 94.

56. Hart Crane to Isidor and Helen Schneider, 16 July 1928. *Letters*, p. 326.

57. Hart Crane to Zell Hart Deming [late October 1928?]. Hart Crane Collection, Beinecke, Yale University.

58. Grace Crane to Sam Loveman, 13 May 1932. Quoted in Unterecker, p. 763.

59. Hart Crane to Charlotte and Richard Rychtarik, 26 February 1929. *Selected Letters*, p. 398.

60. Hart Crane to Zell Hart Deming [late October 1928?]. Hart Crane Collection, Beinecke, Yale University.

Chapter 17

1. Quoted in Horton, p. 243.

2. Grace Crane to Sam Loveman, 13 May 1932. Quoted in Unterecker, p. 763.

3. 'A Postscript', *Complete Poems*, p. 196.

4. Hart Crane to Yvor Winters, 27 June 1928. *Selected Letters*, p. 374.

5. Hart Crane to Clarence Crane, 14 June 1928. Lewis, p. 619.

6. Clarence Crane to Hart Crane, 18 June 1928. Ibid., p. 621.

7. Quoted in Hans Bak, *Malcolm Cowley: The Formative Years*, University of Georgia Press, Athens and London, 1993, p. 412.

8. William Slater Brown to Philip Horton, 4 November 1936. Horton Papers.

9. From an undated typescript by Nathan Asch in the John Unterecker Papers.

10. Clarence Crane to Hart Crane, 18 July 1928. Hart Crane Papers, Kent State University.

11. From an undated typescript by Nathan Asch in the John Unterecker Papers.

12. Hart Crane to Clarence Crane, 25 July 1928. Lewis, p. 626.

13. Clarence Crane to Hart Crane, 27 July 1928. Ibid., p. 627.

14. Donald W. Faulkner (ed.), *The Portable Malcolm Cowley*, Penguin Viking, New York, 1990, p. 38.

15. Malcolm Cowley, *A Second Flowering: Works and Days of the Lost Generation*, André Deutsch, London, 1973, p. 204.

16. Quoted from the undated transcript of an interview between Charmion von Wiegand and John Unterecker. John Unterecker Papers.

17. Hart Crane to Clarence Crane, 2 August 1928. Lewis, p. 629.

18. Hart Crane to Clarence Crane, 14 August 1928. Ibid., p. 630.

19. Hart Crane to Clarence Crane, 19 August 1928. Ibid., p. 632.

20. Hart Crane to Yvor Winters, 17 August 1928. Parkinson, p. 125.

21. Undated letter from Hart Crane to Malcolm Cowley [August 1928]. Hart Crane Collection, Beinecke, Yale University.

22. Hart Crane to Yvor Winters, 9 September 1928. Parkinson, p. 125.

23. Telegram from Grace Crane to Hart Crane, 6 September 1928. Hart Crane Papers, Columbia University.

24. Clarence Crane to Hart Crane, 12 September 1928. Lewis, p. 635.

25. Hart Crane to Charlotte and Richard Rychtarik, 16 September 1928. *Selected Letters*, p. 377.

26. Hart Crane to William Carlos Williams, 16 September [1928]. Ibid., p. 378.

27. William Carlos Williams to Philip Horton. Quoted in *Selected Letters*, p. 379.

28. William Carlos Williams to Ezra Pound, 12 July [1928] and 11 August 1928. See Hugh Witemeyer (ed.), *Selected Letters of Ezra Pound and William Carlos Williams*, New Directions, New York, 1996, pp. 86 and 91. See also Paul Mariani, *The Broken Tower: The Life of Hart Crane*, W.W. Norton, New York, 1999, p. 311.

29. Yvor Winters, 'In Vindication of Poetry', *New Republic*, 17 October 1928.

30. Hart Crane to Yvor Winters, 23 October 1928. *Selected Letters*, p. 379.

31. Hart Crane to Wilbur Underwood, 5 October [1928]. Ibid., p. 379.

32. Lorna Dietz to Philip Horton, 30 October 1936. Horton Papers.

33. Telegram from Grace Crane to Hart Crane, 15 October 1928. Hart Crane Papers, Columbia University.

34. Quoted in a letter from Hart Crane to Zell Hart Deming [late October 1928?]. Hart Crane Collection, Beinecke, Yale University.

35. Hart Crane to Yvor Winters, 23 October 1928. *Selected Letters*, p. 379.

36. Hart Crane to Charlotte Rychtarik, 23 October 1928. Ibid., p. 381.

37. Quoted in Belinda Rathbone, *Walker Evans: A Biography*, Houghton Mifflin, Boston and New York, 1995, pp. 41–3.

38. Hart Crane to Malcolm Cowley [20 November 1928]. *Selected Letters*, p. 382.

39. Quoted from Susan Jenkins Brown, *Robber Rocks: Letters and Memories of Hart Crane, 1923–1932*, Wesleyan University Press, Middletown Connecticut, 1969, pp. 108–9.

40. E.A. Stockwell (Guardian Trust Co.) to Hart Crane, 16 November 1928. Hart Crane Papers, Columbia University.

41. Hart Crane to Charlotte and Richard Rychtarik, 26 February 1929. *Selected Letters*, p. 398.

42. E.A. Stockwell (Guardian Trust Co.) to Hart Crane, 22 November 1928. Hart Crane Papers, Columbia University.

43. Hart Crane to Zell Hart Deming, 29 November 1928. Hart Crane Collection, Beinecke, Yale University.

44. Hart Crane to Malcolm Cowley [20 November 1928]. *Selected Letters*, p. 382.

45. Walker Evans interviewed by John Unterecker. Quoted in Unterecker, p. 563.

46. Hart Crane to Malcolm Cowley, 1 December 1928. *Selected Letters*, p. 383.

47. Quoted in Unterecker, p. 569.

48. Hart Crane to Sam Loveman, 9 December 1928. *Letters*, p. 331.

49. Hart Crane to Charmion von Wiegand [December 1928]. Ibid., p. 332.

50. Hart Crane to William Slater Brown [December 1928]. Jenkins Brown, *Robber Rocks*, p. 112.

51. Hart Crane to Wilbur Underwood, 12 December 1928. Warren Herendeen and Donald G. Parker (eds), 'Wind-Blown Flames', *Southern Review*, volume XVI, number I (April 1980), p. 371.

52. Hart Crane to Waldo Frank, 28 December 1928. *Selected Letters*, p. 394.

53. Hart Crane to Isidor Schneider, 1 May 1929. Ibid., p. 405.

54. Hart Crane to Charlotte and Richard Rychtarik, 26 February 1929. Ibid., p. 398.

55. Hart Crane to Sam Loveman, 25 December 1928. Quoted in Unterecker, p. 576.

56. Hart Crane to Waldo Frank, 28 December 1928. *Selected Letters*, p. 394.

57. Hart Crane to Isidor Schneider, 1 May 1929. Ibid., p. 405.

58. Laura Riding to Philip Horton, 11 April 1936. Horton Papers.

59. Robert Graves to Hart Crane, 25 March 1929. Hart Crane Papers, Columbia University.

60. Laura Riding to Philip Horton, 14 July 1936. Horton Papers.

61. Laura Riding to Philip Horton, 1 January 1937. Horton Papers.

Chapter 18

1. Quoted in Humphrey Carpenter, *Geniuses Together: American Writers in Paris in the 1920s*, Houghton Mifflin, Boston, 1988, p. 214.

2. Quoted in Gorham B. Munson, *The Awakening Twenties: A Memoir-History of a Literary Period*, Louisiana State University Press, Baton Rouge and London, 1985, p. 213.

3. Undated letter from Waldo Frank to André Gide. Hart Crane Papers, Columbia University.

4. Forrest Anderson, 'Remembering Hart Crane'. Undated typescript in the John Unterecker Papers.

5. Undated postcard from Hart Crane to Wilbur Underwood [February 1929]. *Selected Letters*, p. 398.

6. Quoted in Unterecker, p. 578.

7. Harry Crosby, *Shadows of the Sun*, Black Sun Press, Paris, 1930, p. 6. Quoted in Unterecker, p. 578.

8. Passages quoted are from H. Crosby, *Shadows of the Sun*, pp. 8, 10 and 12.

9. Quoted in Geoffrey Wolff, *Black Sun: The Brief Transit and Violent Eclipse of Harry Crosby*, Vintage Books, New York, 1977, p. 228.

10. H. Crosby, *Shadows of the Sun*, p. 12.

11. Hart Crane to Malcolm Cowley, 4 February 1929. *Selected Letters*, p. 396.

12. Hart Crane to Waldo Frank, 7 February 1929. *Letters*, p. 335.

13. Undated entries from one of Hart Crane's notebooks. Hart Crane Papers, Columbia University.

14. The certificate for the syphilis test, at the Laboratoire d'Analyses in the Boulevard Saint-Germain, is in the Hart Crane Papers, Columbia University.

15. H. Crosby, *Shadows of the Sun*, p. 13.

16. Hart Crane to Charlotte and Richard Rychtarik, 26 February 1929. *Selected Letters*, p. 398.

17. H. Crosby, *Shadows of the Sun*, p. 14.

18. Caresse Crosby, *The Passionate Years*, Alvin Redman, London, 1955, p. 246.

19. Harry Crosby to Hart Crane, 1 March 1929. Quoted in Unterecker, p. 586.

20. Hart Crane to Harry Crosby [3 March 1929?]. *Selected Letters*, p. 402.

21. H. Crosby, *Shadows of the Sun*, p. 15.

22. C. Crosby, *The Passionate Years*, p. 248.

23. Quoted in Susan Jenkins Brown, *Robber Rocks: Letters and Memories of Hart Crane, 1923–1932*, Wesleyan State University Press, Middletown, Connecticut, 1969, p. 116.

24. C. Crosby, *The Passionate Years*, p. 246.

25. Hart Crane to Harry and Caresse Crosby, 22 April 1929. Quoted in Unterecker, p. 591.

26. Caresse Crosby to Hart Crane, 23 April 1929. Quoted ibid., p. 589.

27. Hart Crane to Caresse Crosby, 25 April 1929. *Selected Letters*, p. 403.

28. Hart Crane to Isidor Schneider, 1 May 1929. Ibid., p. 405.

29. Hart Crane to Harry Crosby, 16 May 1929. Ibid., p. 407.

30. Undated entries from one of Hart Crane's notebooks. Hart Crane Papers, Columbia University.

31. Hart Crane to Harry Crosby, 16 May 1929. *Selected Letters*, p. 407.

32. Quoted from Marsden Hartley, 'The Spangle of Existence' (Casual Dissertations), undated typescript, John Unterecker Papers.

33. Quoted in Townsend Ludington, *Marsden Hartley: The Biography of an American Artist*, Little Brown, Boston, Toronto and London, 1992, p. 195.

34. Quoted in Jonathan Weinberg, *Speaking for Vice: Homosexuality in the Art of Charles Demuth, Marsden Hartley, and the First American Avant-Garde*, Yale University Press, New Haven and London, 1993, p. 166.

35. Quoted in Joseph Pearce, *Bloomsbury and Beyond: The Friends and Enemies of Roy Campbell*, HarperCollins, London, 2001, pp. 119, 120 and 122.

36. Roy Campbell, *Light on a Dark Horse: An Autobiography 1901–1935*, Hollis & Carter, London, 1951. Quoted ibid. p. 120.

37. Quoted in Pearce, *Bloomsbury and Beyond*, p. 120.

38. Undated letter from Roy Campbell to Wyndham Lewis [June or July 1929]. Quoted ibid., p. 121.

39. Ibid., p. 122.

40. Quoted from an untitled, undated typescript by Nathan Asch in the John Unterecker Papers.

41. Hart Crane to Allen Tate, 11 June 1929. *Selected Letters*, p. 409.

42. H. Crosby, *Shadows of the Sun*, pp. 39–40.

43. Hart Crane to Harry and Caresse Crosby, 1 July [1929]. *Selected Letters*, p. 410.

44. Quoted in Unterecker, p. 596.

45. Willard A. Whitney to John Unterecker, 8 October 1962. John Unterecker Papers.

46. From an interview between Allen Tate and John Unterecker, 11 September 1962. John Unterecker Papers.

47. Stuart Davis to John Baker, 8 April 1963. Baker Papers.

48. Quoted from the warrant for Crane's arrest. Hart Crane Papers, Columbia University.

49. Character reference written by Jean Paulhan on behalf of the *Nouvelle Revue Française*, 'Le 9 Juillet' [9 July 1929]. Hart Crane Papers, Columbia University.

50. H. Crosby, *Shadows of the Sun*, pp. 41–2.

51. *New York Times*, 11 July 1929, p. 5.

52. H. Crosby, *Shadows of the Sun*, p. 43.

53. Copy of a letter from Hart Crane to Roy Campbell, 12 July 1929, John Unterecker Papers.

54. Allen Tate to Philip Horton, 9 April 1937. Horton Papers.

55. Hart Crane to Caresse Crosby, 8 August 1929. *Selected Letters*, p. 413.

56. Hart Crane to Jane Heap, 11 July 1929. The *Little Review* Papers, Special Collections of the University of Wisconsin-Milwaukee Library.

57. Hart Crane to Harry Crosby, 16 May 1929. *Selected Letters*, p. 407.

58. Hart Crane to Charlotte and Richard Rychtarik, 26 February 1929. Ibid., p. 398.

59. Entries in a notebook entitled 'Vocabulary' in the Hart Crane Papers, Columbia University.

60. Hart Crane to Harry Crosby, 23 July 1929. *Selected Letters*, p. 412.

61. Mrs T.W. Simpson to Hart Crane, 30 September 1929. Hart Crane Papers, Columbia University.

62. William Slater Brown to Philip Horton, 21 November 1936. Horton Papers.

63. Jenkins Brown, *Robber Rocks*, p. 117.

64. Hart Crane to Caresse Crosby, 8 August 1929. *Selected Letters*, p. 413.

65. Hart Crane to Harry and Caresse Crosby, 30 August 1929. Ibid., p. 415.

66. 'Singers of the New Age: A Group of Distinguished Young Poets Who Have Found Fresh Material in the American Scene', *Vanity Fair*, September 1929, p. 89.

67. Hart Crane to Caresse Crosby, 6 September 1929. *Selected Letters*, p. 416.

68. Hart Crane to Caresse Crosby, 17 September 1929. Ibid., p. 417.

69. 'Cape Hatteras', *Complete Poems*, pp. 75–84.

70. Fairfield Porter to John Unterecker, 14 July 1961. John Unterecker Papers.

71. Paul Rosenfeld to Hart Crane, 10 September 1929. Hart Crane Papers, Columbia University.

72. Quoted in Belinda Rathbone, *Walker Evans: A Biography*, Houghton Mifflin, Boston and New York, 1995, p. 73.

73. Quoted in Gerald Wallop, *A Knot of Roots: An Autobiography*, New American Library, New York, 1965.

74. Hart Crane to Otto Kahn [25 September 1929]. *Selected Letters*, p. 417.

75. Peter Blume to John Baker, 28 December 1962. Baker Papers.

76. Quoted in Peter Blume, 'A Recollection of Hart Crane', *Yale Review*, volume LXXVI, number II (Winter 1987), p. 154.

77. Hart Crane to Sam Loveman, 22 October 1929. Quoted in Unterecker, p. 604.

78. Hart Crane to Lorna Dietz, 23 October 1929. Quoted ibid., p. 604.

79. Quoted from undated interview notes taken by Philip Horton. Horton Papers.

80. Telegram from Hart Crane to Harry and Caresse Crosby, 30 October 1929. Quoted in Unterecker, p. 605.

81. Hart Crane to Harry and Caresse Crosby, 29 October 1929. *Selected Letters*, p. 418.

82. Hart Crane to Sam Loveman, 11 November 1929. Quoted in Unterecker, p. 606.

83. Hart Crane to William Slater Brown, 11 November 1929. Quoted ibid., p. 606.

84. Clarence Crane to Hart Crane, 26 November 1929. Lewis, p. 638.

85. 'Quaker Hill', *Complete Poems*, pp. 91–4.

86. Malcolm Cowley, *A Second Flowering*, André Deutsch, London, 1973, p. 199.

87. Horace Gregory, 'Vital Contemporary Poetry', *New York Sun*, 17 August 1929.

88. Quoted in Hans Bak, *Malcolm Cowley*, University of Georgia Press, Athens and London, 1993, p. 425.

89. Quoted ibid., p. 421.

90. Malcolm Cowley, *The Dream of the Golden Mountains: Remembering the 1930s*, Viking Press, New York, 1980, p. 52.

91.   Malcolm Cowley, *Exile's Return*, Penguin, New York, 1976, p. 234.

92.   Quoted in Wolff, *Black Sun*, p. 5.

93.   C. Crosby, *The Passionate Years*, p. 257.

94.   Cowley, *Exile's Return*, p. 246.

95.   Quoted in Hugh Ford, *Published in Paris: American and British Writers, Printers and Publishers in Paris, 1920–1939*, Garnstone Press, London, 1975, p. 209.

96.   C. Crosby, *The Passionate Years*, p. 257.

97.   Quoted in Ford, *Published in Paris*, p. 208.

98.   Quoted in Unterecker, p. 610.

99.   Quoted in Wolff, *Black Sun*, p. 309.

Chapter 19

1.   Caresse Crosby to Hart Crane, 22 December [1929]. Hart Crane Papers, Columbia University.

2.   Hart Crane to Charlotte Rychtarik, 11 February 1930. *Letters*, p. 348.

3.   Hart Crane to Allen Tate, 14 December 1929. *Selected Letters*, p. 420.

4.   Otto Kahn to Hart Crane, 15 March 1930. Quoted ibid., p. 403.

5.   Hart Crane to Caresse Crosby, 26 December 1929. Ibid., p. 421.

6.   Robert Elwin Stewart is the only sailor love of Hart Crane's whose identity survived Grace Crane's posthumous editing of her son's life. He was born on 4 March 1910 at Tuscaloosa, Alabama and joined the US Navy at Birmingham, AL in July 1927. He served as a Seaman 2nd Class (service number 271–91–29) on the USS *Milwaukee* from 17 September 1927 until 6 March 1931 and was honourably discharged from the Navy in December of that year. His last known address was at 1302 12th Avenue, Tuscaloosa. John Unterecker left no stone unturned in his attempts to trace Stewart in the early 1960s, contacting, among others, his neighbours in Tuscaloosa, the Navy Veterans' Administration, the Postmaster and the Chief of Police in Tuscaloosa, the FBI and W.R. Smedberg, then Vice-Admiral of the US Navy and Chief of Naval Personnel. He also placed an advertisement in the *Navy Times*. If Stewart kept the letters Hart Crane sent him, they appear to be for ever lost to biography.

7.   Hart Crane to Caresse Crosby, 2 January 1930. *Selected Letters*, p. 422.

8.   Undated letter from Samuel Loveman to Grace Crane. Hart Crane Papers, Columbia University.

9.   Bob Stewart to Hart Crane, 16 March 1930. Hart Crane Papers, Columbia University.

10.   Lorna Dietz to Philip Horton, 30 October 1936. Horton Papers.

11.   Grace Crane to Samuel Loveman, 19 July 1932. Hart Crane Papers, Columbia University.

12.   Hart Crane to Caresse Crosby, 2 January 1930. *Selected Letters*, p. 422.

13.   Hart Crane to Horace Liveright, 4 January 1930. Hart Crane Papers, Columbia University.

14.   Hart Crane to Dr Henry Seidel Canby, 4 January 1930. The Berg Collection, New York Public Library.

15.   Telegram from Horace Liveright to Hart Crane, 11 January, 1930. Hart Crane Papers, Columbia University,

16.   Hart Crane to Yvor Winters, 14 January 1930. *Selected Letters*, p. 423.

17.   Quoted in Parkinson, p. 137.

18.   Caresse Crosby to Hart Crane, 11 February 1930. Hart Crane Papers, Columbia University.

19.   Caresse Crosby to Hart Crane, 3 April 1930. Hart Crane Papers, Columbia University.

20.   Hart Crane to Caresse Crosby, 19 April 1930. Quoted in Unterecker, p. 615.

21.   Hart Crane to Otto Kahn, 6 April 1930. *Selected Letters*, p. 425.

22.   Otto Kahn to Hart Crane, 8 April 1930. Hart Crane Papers, Columbia University.

23. *Milwaukee Journal*, 12 April 1930.
24. *New York Evening Post*, 19 April 1930.
25. *New York Herald-Tribune*, 20 April 1930.
26. 'The Rediscovery of America', *Nation*, 30 April 1930.
27. 'Hart Crane's Cubistic Poetry in "The Bridge"', *New York Times Book Review*, 27 April 1930.
28. Postcard from Demetrius Mattoi to Hart Crane, 28 May 1930. Hart Crane Papers, Columbia University.
29. Undated letter from William Slater Brown to John Unterecker [1964]. John Unterecker Papers.
30. Lincoln Kirstein, 'Crane and Carlsen, New York 1931–1932', *Mosaic*, Farrar, Strauss & Giroux, New York, 1994, pp. 192, 193, 200, 201 and 206.
31. Hart Crane to Caresse Crosby, 13 May 1930. Quoted in Unterecker, p. 627.
32. Howard P. Lovecraft to Mrs F.C. Clark, 24 May 1930. Quoted ibid., p. 626.
33. *Saturday Review of Literature*, 14 June 1930.
34. Ibid., 5 July 1930.
35. Mark Van Doren, 'The Poetry of Hart Crane', *Theatre Guild Magazine*, June 1930.
36. Isidor Schneider, 'A Noteworthy Structure', *Chicago Evening Post*, 25 July 1930.
37. *New Republic*, 23 April 1930.
38. Yvor Winters, 'The Progress of Hart Crane', *Poetry*, June 1930.
39. Hart Crane to Yvor Winters, 4 June 1930. *Selected Letters*, p. 427.
40. Hart Crane to Isidor Schneider, 8 June 1930. Ibid., p. 430.
41. Allen Tate to Hart Crane, 10 June 1930. Quoted in Unterecker, p. 621.
42. Allen Tate, 'A Distinguished Poet', *Hound and Horn*, July–September 1930.
43. Hart Crane to Allen Tate, 13 July 1930. *Selected Letters*, p. 431.
44. Allen Tate to Hart Crane, 16 July 1930. Hart Crane Papers, Columbia University.
45. Quoted in Malcolm Cowley, *A Second Flowering*, André Deutsch, London, 1973, p. 211.
46. Hart Crane to Allen Tate, 13 July 1930. *Selected Letters*, p. 431.
47. Hart Crane to Lorna Dietz [17 July 1930?]. Quoted in Unterecker, p. 631.
48. Hart Crane to Solomon Grunberg, 30 September 1930. Hart Crane Papers, Columbia University.
49. 'A Letter from Peter Blume', *Hart Crane Newsletter*, volume II, number I (Summer 1978).
50. Quoted from Susan Jenkins Brown, 'Explanatory Notes on Letters Written by Hart Crane to William Slater Brown and Susan Jenkins Brown from 1923 to 1931', 21 March 1966. John Unterecker Papers.
51. Fellowship Application Form, 1931–32, The John Simon Guggenheim Memorial Foundation. Completed by Hart Crane 29 August 1930. (All Guggenheim material is from the John Simon Guggenheim Memorial Foundation Archives.)
52. Waldo Frank to John Simon Guggenheim Memorial Foundation, 23 September 1930.
53. Paul Rosenfeld to John Simon Guggenheim Memorial Foundation, 3 October 1930.
54. Allen Tate to John Simon Guggenheim Memorial Foundation, 29 September 1930.
55. Allen Tate to Philip Horton, 9 April 1937. Horton Papers.
56. Hart Crane to Allen Tate, 7 September 1930. *Selected Letters*, p. 435.
57. Hart Crane to John A. Roebling, 18 August 1930. Ibid., p. 434.
58. Margaret Roebling to Hart Crane, 23 August 1930. Hart Crane Papers, Kent State University.
59. Hart Crane to Solomon Grunberg, 30 September 1930. *Letters*, p. 356.
60. William Slater Brown to Philip Horton, 2 July 1936. Horton Papers.
61. Hart Crane to William Wright, 21 November 1930. *Letters*, p. 357.
62. Hart Crane to Wilbur Underwood, 20 November [1930]. *Selected Letters*, p. 437.

63. Hart Crane to William Wright, 21 November 1930. *Letters*, p. 357.

64. Wright's comment quoted in Hart Crane's reply, 29 November 1930. Ibid., p. 358.

65. Hart Crane to Samuel Loveman, 29 December 1930. *Selected Letters*, p. 440.

66. *Nation*, 17 January 1931.

67. Hart Crane to Solomon Grunberg, 25 February 1931. Hart Crane Papers, Columbia University.

68. Hart Crane to Lorna Dietz, 10 February 1931. *Selected Letters,* p. 444.

69. Hart Crane to Samuel Loveman, 16 February 1931. Ibid., p. 445.

70. Hart Crane to Waldo Frank, 19 February [1931]. Ibid., p. 446.

71. Bess Crane to Philip Horton, 17 July 1935. Horton Papers.

Chapter 20

1. Hart Crane to Henry Allen Moe, 16 March 1931. John Simon Guggenheim Memorial Foundation Archives.

2. Malcolm Cowley, *A Second Flowering: Works and Days of the Lost Generation*, André Deutsch, London, 1973, pp. 212–15.

3. Waldo Frank to Philip Horton, 18 June 1937. Horton Papers.

4. Quoted in Unterecker, p. 650.

5. Henry Allen Moe to Otto Myers, 29 June 1931. (Guggenheim)

6. Hart Crane to Katherine Anne Porter [30 March 1931?]. *Selected Letters*, p. 459.

7. Lincoln Kirstein, *Mosaic: Memoirs*, Farrar, Strauss & Giroux, New York, 1994, p. 190.

8. Hart Crane to Sam Loveman, 12 April 1931. *Selected Letters*, p. 461.

9. Hans Zinsser, *As I Remember Him*, Little, Brown, Boston, 1940, p. 335.

10. Hans Zinsser to Philip Horton, 13 August 1935. Horton Papers.

11. Hart Crane to Caresse Crosby, 5 April 1931. *Selected Letters*, p. 459.

12. Hart Crane to William Slater Brown, 6 April 1931. Susan Jenkins Brown, *Robber Rocks: Letters and Memories of Hart Crane, 1923–1932*, Wesleyan University Press, Middletown, Connecticut, 1969, p. 123.

13. 'Havana Rose', *Complete Poems*, pp. 200–1.

14. Zinsser, *As I Remember Him*, p. 337.

15. Ibid., p. 339.

16. 'Havana Rose', *Complete Poems*, p. 200.

17. Hart Crane to Sam Loveman, 12 April 1931. *Selected Letters*, p. 461.

18. Quoted in Drewey Wayne Gunn, *American and British Writers in Mexico, 1556–1973*, University of Texas Press, Austin and London, 1974, pp. 58 and 128.

19. Hart Crane to Sam Loveman, 12 April 1931. *Selected Letters*, p. 461.

20. Léon Felipe Camino to John Unterecker, 3 June 1961. John Unterecker Papers.

21. Katherine Anne Porter to Caroline Gordon [Tate], 24 April 1931. Isabel Bayley (ed.), *Letters of Katherine Anne Porter*, Atlantic Monthly Press, New York, 1990, p. 37.

22. Undated fragment of a letter from Hart Crane to Clarence and Bess Crane. Hart Crane Papers, Kent State University.

23. Katherine Anne Porter to Caroline Gordon [Tate], 24 April 1931. Bayley, *Letters*, p. 37.

24. Quoted in Horton, pp. 286–7.

25. Katherine Anne Porter to Mary Doherty, 21 October 1932. Bayley, *Letters*, p. 83.

26. Undated interview notes by Philip Horton. Horton Papers.

27. Hart Crane to Malcolm Cowley, 2 June 1931. *Selected Letters*, p. 465.

28. Hart Crane to Waldo Frank, 13 June 1931. Ibid., p. 468.

29. Katherine Anne Porter to Caroline Gordon [Tate], 24 April 1931. Bayley, *Letters*, p. 37.

30. Quoted from Joan Givner, *The Life of Katherine Anne Porter*, Jonathan Cape, London, 1983, p. 235.

31. Katherine Anne Porter to Caroline Gordon [Tate], 24 April 1931. Bayley, *Letters*, p. 37.
32. Hart Crane to Otto Kahn, 24 April 1931. *Selected Letters*, p. 462.
33. Quoted in Horton, p. 287.
34. Hart Crane to Katherine Anne Porter and Eugene Pressly, 28 April 1931. *Selected Letters*, p. 464.
35. Eyler Simpson to Hart Crane, 30 April 1931. (Guggenheim)
36. Hart Crane to Katherine Anne Porter [1 May 1931]. *Selected Letters*, p. 464.
37. Hart Crane to Malcolm Cowley, 2 June 1931. Ibid., p. 465.
38. Eyler Simpson to Henry Allen Moe, 26 June 1931. (Guggenheim)
39. Hart Crane to Malcolm Cowley, 2 June 1931. *Selected Letters*, p. 465.
40. Clarence Crane to Hart Crane, 1 May 1931. Lewis, p. 642.
41. Postcard from Hart Crane to Solomon Grunberg, 9 May 1931. Hart Crane Papers, Columbia University.
42. Hart Crane to Henry Allen Moe, 11 May 1931. (Guggenheim)
43. Quoted from a note written by Peter Blume on 12 June 1981 in the Hart Crane Papers, Columbia University.
44. Hart Crane to Selden Rodman, 23 May 1931. Quoted in Unterecker, p. 666.
45. Hart Crane to Malcolm Cowley, 2 June 1931. *Selected Letters*, p. 465.
46. Léon Felipe Camino to John Unterecker, 3 June 1961. John Unterecker Papers.
47. Waldo Frank to Philip Horton, 18 June 1937. Horton Papers.
48. Hart Crane to Waldo Frank, 13 June 1931. *Selected Letters*, p. 468.
49. Quoted in Enrique Hank Lopez, *Conversations with Katherine Anne Porter: Refugee from Indian Creek*, Little, Brown, Boston, 1981, p. 157.
50. Clarence Crane to Hazel Cazes, 2 June 1931. Hart Crane Papers, Kent State University.
51. Clarence Crane to Hart Crane, 2 June 1931. Lewis, p. 643.
52. Hart Crane to Clarence Crane, 5 June 1931. *Selected Letters*, p. 467.
53. Morton Dauwen Zabel to Hart Crane, 11 June 1931. Quoted in Unterecker, p. 666.
54. Hart Crane to Morton Dauwen Zabel, 20 June 1931. *Letters*, p. 373.
55. 'Purgatorio', *Complete Poems*, p. 202.
56. Quoted in Horton, p. 285.
57. Hart Crane to Lorna Dietz, 15 July 1931. *Selected Letters*, p. 475.
58. Quoted in Horton, p. 286.
59. Hart Crane to Katherine Anne Porter, 22 June 1931. *Selected Letters*, p. 471.
60. Katherine Anne Porter to Hart Crane, 22 June 1931. Bayley, *Letters*, p. 45.
61. Eyler Simpson to Henry Allen Moe, 26 June 1931. (Guggenheim)
62. *New Yorker*, 27 June 1931.
63. Henry Allen Moe to Otto Myers, 29 June 1931. (Guggenheim)
64. Frank Aydelotte to Henry Allen Moe, 6 July 1931. (Guggenheim)

Chapter 21
1. Hart Crane to William Slater Brown, 15 July [1931]. *Selected Letters*, p. 474.
2. Hart Crane to William Wright, 15 July 1931. *Letters*, p. 376.
3. Hart Crane to Lorna Dietz, 15 July 1931. *Selected Letters*, p. 475.
4. Hart Crane to Henry Allen Moe, 22 July 1931. Quoted in Unterecker, p. 680.
5. Hart Crane to Peggy Cowley, 19 July [1931]. Hart Crane Collection, Beinecke, Yale University.
6. Hart Crane to Margaret Robson, 29 July 1931. Quoted in Unterecker, p. 681.
7. Vivian Pemberton, 'Poetry and Portraits: Reflections of Hart Crane', *Hart Crane Newsletter*, volume I, number II (Fall 1977).

8. Undated letter from Sam Loveman to Grace Crane. Hart Crane Papers, Columbia University.

9. Quoted from 'Hart Crane: Conversation with Samuel Loveman, New York 1964', introduced by Ray C. Longtin. New York Public Library.

10. Hart Crane to Sam Loveman, 14 August 1931. Hart Crane Papers, Columbia University.

11. Quoted from an untitled, undated memorandum by William Wright in the John Unterecker Papers.

12. Hart Crane to Wilbur Underwood, 30 November [1931]. *Selected Letters*, p. 493.

13. Quoted from an undated, untitled typescript in the John Unterecker Papers.

14. Quoted in Unterecker, p. 684.

15. Hart Crane to Helen and Griswold Hurlbert, 20 September 1931. Quoted in Unterecker, p. 690.

16. Undated letter from Hart Crane to Bess Crane [September 1931]. Hart Crane Papers, Columbia University.

17. Hart Crane to William Wright, 21 September 1931. *Selected Letters*, p. 479.

18. Undated letter from Hart Crane to Bess Crane [September 1931]. Hart Crane Papers, Columbia University.

19. Hart Crane to William Wright, 21 September 1931. *Selected Letters*, p. 479.

20. Information taken from the obituary of David Siqueiros in the *New York Times*, 7 January 1974.

21. Hart Crane to Charlotte and Richard Rychtarik, 4 November 1931. *Letters*, p. 384.

22. Quoted from 'Interview with David Alfaro Siqueiros', Cuernavaca, Mexico, 18 February 1967. John Unterecker Papers.

23. Hart Crane to Charlotte and Richard Rychtarik, 4 November 1931. *Letters*, p. 384.

24. Lesley Byrd Simpson to Philip Horton, 7 June 1936. Horton Papers.

25. Peggy Cowley, 'The Last Days of Hart Crane'. Susan Jenkins Brown, *Robber Rocks: Letters and Memories of Hart Crane, 1923–1932*, Wesleyan University Press, Middletown, Connecticut, 1969, p. 147.

26. Quoted in Malcolm Cowley, *The Dream of the Golden Mountains: Remembering the 1930s*, Viking Press, New York, 1980, p. 59.

27. P. Cowley 'The Last Days of Hart Crane', p. 147.

28. Peggy Cowley to Malcolm Cowley, 8 September and 12 September 1931. M. Cowley, *The Dream of the Golden Mountains*, pp. 63 and 64.

29. Details from the obituary of Anita Brenner in the *New York Times*, 3 December 1974.

30. P. Cowley, 'The Last Days of Hart Crane', p. 148.

31. Quoted in Hans Bak, *Malcolm Cowley*, University of Georgia Press, Athens and London, 1993, p. 126.

32. 'An Interview with Philip C. Horton', *Hart Crane Newsletter*, volume II, number II (Spring 1979).

33. Jenkins Brown, *Robber Rocks*, p. 140.

34. Anita Brenner to Grace Crane, 3 September 1932. Hart Crane Collection, Beinecke, Yale University.

35. Undated interview notes by John Unterecker. John Unterecker Papers.

36. Peggy Cowley to Malcolm Cowley, 1 October 1931. M. Cowley, *The Dream of the Golden Mountains*, p. 64.

37. Hart Crane to Malcolm Cowley, 5 October 1931. *Selected Letters*, p. 483.

38. Hart Crane to Solomon Grunberg, 20 October 1931. Ibid., p. 485.

39. Hart Crane to Wilbur Underwood, 30 November 1931. Ibid., p. 493.

40. Hart Crane to Solomon Grunberg, 20 October 1931. Ibid., p. 485.

41. Hart Crane to Bess Crane, 20 October 1931. Hart Crane Collection, Beinecke, Yale University.

42. Byron Madden to Hart Crane, 19 October 1931. Quoted in Unterecker, p. 704.

43. Bess Crane to Hart Crane, 26 October 1931. Hart Crane Papers, Columbia University.

44. Bess Crane to Hart Crane, 9 November 1931. Hart Crane Papers, Columbia University.

45. Hart Crane to Lorna Dietz, 4 November 1931. Hart Crane Collection, Beinecke, Yale University.

46. Hart Crane to Charlotte and Richard Rychtarik, 4 November 1931. *Letters*, p. 384.

47. Hart Crane to Bess Crane, 20 October 1931. Hart Crane Collection, Beinecke, Yale University.

48. Lesley Byrd Simpson to Philip Horton, 7 June 1936. Horton Papers.

49. P. Cowley, 'The Last Days of Hart Crane', p. 148.

50. Lesley Byrd Simpson to Philip Horton, 7 June 1936. Horton Papers.

51. Undated letter from Peggy Cowley to Malcolm Cowley [November 1931]. M. Cowley, *The Dream of the Golden Mountains*, p. 64.

52. Hart Crane to Peggy Cowley, 13 November 1931. *Letters*, p. 386.

53. Undated letter from Hart Crane to Peggy Cowley [November 1931]. *Selected Letters*, p. 489.

54. Peggy Cowley to Malcolm Cowley, 15 November 1931. M. Cowley, *The Dream of the Golden Mountains*, p. 65.

55. Hart Crane to Bess Crane, 23 November [1931]. Quoted in Unterecker, p. 702.

56. Hart Crane to Sam Loveman, 17 November [1931]. *Selected Letters*, p. 490.

57. Hart Crane to Eda Lou Walton, 27 November 1931. Ibid., p. 492.

58. Hart Crane to Bess Crane, 12 December 1931. Ibid., p. 495.

59. P. Cowley, 'The Last Days of Hart Crane', p. 150.

60. Peggy Cowley to Malcolm Cowley, 21 December 1931. M. Cowley, *The Dream of the Golden Mountains*, p. 65.

61. P. Cowley, 'The Last Days of Hart Crane', pp. 150–2.

62. Hart Crane to Bess Crane, 9 January 1932. Hart Crane Papers, Kent State University.

63. Peggy Cowley to Malcolm Cowley, 26 December 1931. M. Cowley, *The Dream of the Golden Mountains*, p. 65.

64. P. Cowley, 'The Last Days of Hart Crane', p. 153.

65. Quoted in Unterecker, p. 716.

66. Hart Crane to Malcolm Cowley, 9 January 1932. *Selected Letters*, p. 500.

67. P. Cowley, 'The Last Days of Hart Crane', p. 154.

68. Quoted in M. Cowley, *The Dream of the Golden Mountains*, p. 66.

69. P. Cowley, 'The Last Days of Hart Crane', p. 154.

70. Hart Crane to Peggy Cowley, 6 January [1932]. *Selected Letters*, p. 497.

71. Hart Crane to Peggy Cowley [7 January 1932?]. Ibid., p. 498.

72. Peggy Cowley to Hart Crane, 9 January 1932. Hart Crane Collection, Beinicke, Yale University.

73. Peggy Cowley to Hart Crane, 9 January [1932]. Hart Crane Collection, Beinecke, Yale University.

74. Peggy Cowley to Hart Crane, 10 January 1932. Hart Crane Collection, Beinecke, Yale University.

75. Peggy Cowley to Malcolm Cowley, 12 January 1932. M. Cowley, *The Dream of the Golden Mountains*, p. 66.

76. Undated letter from Hart Crane to Peggy Cowley [January 1932]. *Selected Letters*, p. 502.

77. Peggy Cowley to Hart Crane [21 January 1932?]. Hart Crane Collection, Beinecke, Yale University.

78. Peggy Cowley to Malcolm Cowley, 16 January 1932. M. Cowley, *The Dream of the Golden Mountains*, p. 66.

79. Undated letter from Hart Crane to Peggy Cowley [January 1932]. *Selected Letters*, p. 502.

80. P. Cowley, 'The Last Days of Hart Crane', p. 155.

81. Ibid., pp. 156–7.

82. Peggy Cowley to Malcolm Cowley, 27 January 1932. M. Cowley, *The Dream of the Golden Mountains*, p. 66.

83. Lesley Byrd Simpson, 'The Late Hart Crane', *New English Weekly*, 15 September 1932. Quoted in Unterecker, p. 722.

84. Peggy Cowley to Malcolm Cowley, 27 January 1932. M. Cowley, *The Dream of the Golden Mountains*, p. 66.

85. Quoted in Unterecker, p. 723.

86. Telegram from Hart Crane to Peggy Cowley, 31 January 1932. Quoted ibid.

Chapter 22

1. Peggy Cowley to Malcolm Cowley, 3 February 1932. Malcolm Cowley, *The Dream of the Golden Mountains: Remembering the 1930s*, Viking Press, New York, 1980, p. 66.

2. Peggy Cowley, 'The Last Days of Hart Crane'. Susan Jenkins Brown, *Robber Rocks: Letters and Memories of Hart Crane, 1923–1932*, Wesleyan University Press, Middletown, Connecticut, 1969, p. 159.

3. Hart Crane to Bess Crane, 5 February 1932. Hart Crane Collection, Beinecke, Yale University.

4. Bess Crane to Hart Crane, 11 February 1932. Hart Crane Papers, Columbia University.

5. Hart Crane to Sam Loveman, 10 March 1932. *Selected Letters*, p. 512.

6. Hart Crane to Solomon Grunberg, 8 February 1932. Ibid., p. 503.

7. P. Cowley, 'The Last Days of Hart Crane', p. 158.

8. Hart Crane, 'Note on the Paintings of David Siqueiros'. Hart Crane Papers, Columbia University.

9. Peggy Cowley to Hart Crane, 10 February [1932]. Hart Crane Collection, Beinecke, Yale University.

10. P. Cowley, 'The Last Days of Hart Crane', p. 160.

11. Hart Crane to Peggy Cowley, 11 February [1932]. *Selected Letters*, p. 506.

12. Hart Crane to Wilbur Underwood, 14 February 1932. Ibid., p. 507.

13. Hart Crane to Peggy Cowley, 10 February [1932]. Ibid., p. 505.

14. Hart Crane to Peggy Cowley, 16 February [1932]. Ibid., p. 507.

15. Hart Crane to Bess Crane, 17 February 1932. Ibid., p. 509.

16. Bess Crane to Hart Crane, 26 February 1932. Hart Crane Papers, Columbia University.

17. P. Cowley, 'The Last Days of Hart Crane', p. 161.

18. Peggy Cowley to Malcolm Cowley, 22 February 1932. M. Cowley, *The Dream of the Golden Mountains*, p. 77.

19. Hart Crane to Bess Crane, 8 March 1932. Lewis, p. 650.

20. Anita Brenner to Grace Crane, 3 September 1932. Hart Crane Collection, Beinecke, Yale University.

21. Hart Crane to Bess Crane, 8 March 1932. Lewis, p. 650.

22. P. Cowley, 'The Last Days of Hart Crane', p. 161.

23. John Donne, 'Hymn to God My God, In My Sickness'. I am indebted for this information to Alfred B. Cohen, 'Hart Crane's Ghost Written Suicide Notes', *Hart Crane Newsletter*, volume I, number II (Fall 1977).

24. Anita Brenner to Grace Crane, 3 September 1932. Hart Crane Collection, Beinecke, Yale University.

25. Lesley Byrd Simpson to Philip Horton, 9 July 1936. Horton Papers.

26. Marian Simpson to Philip Horton, 19 June 1936. Horton Papers.

27. Lesley Byrd Simpson to Philip Horton, 7 July 1936. Horton Papers.

28. Peggy Cowley to Malcolm Cowley, 21 March 1932. M. Cowley, *The Dream of the Golden Mountains*, p. 78.

29. Hart Crane to Malcolm Cowley [27 March 1932]. *Selected Letters*, p. 516.

30. 'The Broken Tower', *Complete Poems*, pp. 160–1.

31. Hart Crane to Lorna Dietz, 12 April 1932. *Selected Letters*, p. 519.

32. Undated typewritten notes on a typed version of 'The Circumstance'. Hart Crane Papers, Columbia University.

33. Hart Crane to Caresse Crosby, 31 March 1932. *Letters*, p. 405.

34. Léon Felipe Camino to John Unterecker, 3 June 1961. John Unterecker Papers.

35. Quoted in Marsden Hartley, 'The Spangle of Existence' (Casual Dissertations). Undated typescript in the John Unterecker Papers.

36. Marian Simpson to Philip Horton, 19 June 1936. Horton Papers.

37. P. Cowley, 'The Last Days of Hart Crane', p. 162.

38. Peggy Cowley to Malcolm Cowley, 7 April 1932. M. Cowley, *The Dream of the Golden Mountains*, p. 79.

39. Hart Crane to Bess Crane, 7 April 1932. Hart Crane Papers, Kent State University.

40. P. Cowley, 'The Last Days of Hart Crane', p. 161.

41. Hart Crane to Sam Loveman, 13 April 1932. *Letters*, p. 408.

42. Undated letter from Claire Spencer to Philip Horton [May 1936]. Horton Papers.

43. Hart Crane to Lorna Dietz, 12 April 1932. *Selected Letters*, p. 519.

44. Hart Crane to Sam Loveman, 13 April 1932. *Letters*, p. 408.

45. M. Cowley, *The Dream of the Golden Mountains*, p. 80.

46. Quoted ibid. p. 79.

47. Bess Crane to Hart Crane, 12 April 1932. Quoted in Unterecker, p. 744.

48. Quoted in M. Cowley, *The Dream of the Golden Mountains*, p. 80.

49. Howard S. Phillips to Philip Horton, 20 November 1935. Horton Papers.

50. Anita Brenner to Grace Crane, 3 September 1932. Hart Crane Collection, Beinecke, Yale University.

51. Lesley Byrd Simpson to Philip Horton, 7 June 1936. Horton Papers.

52. P. Cowley, 'The Last Days of Hart Crane', pp. 163–4.

53. Quoted from undated interview notes by John Unterecker in the John Unterecker Papers.

54. Quoted in Horton, p. 298. I have been unable to find extant copies of this letter in any of the Hart Crane archives.

55. P. Cowley, 'The Last Days of Hart Crane', pp. 165–6.

56. Peggy Cowley to Bess Crane, 17 April 1932. Hart Crane Papers, Kent State University.

57. Telegram from Hart Crane to Bess Crane, 20 April 1932. John Simon Guggenheim Memorial Foundation Archives.

58. Hart Crane to Solomon Grunberg, 20 April [1932]. *Selected Letters*, p. 522.

59. Morton Dauwen Zabel to Hart Crane, 24 April 1932. Hart Crane Papers, Columbia University.

60. P. Cowley, 'The Last Days of Hart Crane', p. 167.

61. Marian Simpson to Philip Horton, 19 June 1936. Horton Papers.

62. Lesley Byrd Simpson to Philip Horton, 7 June 1936. Horton Papers.

63. Quoted in Hartley, 'The Spangle of Existence'.

64. Eyler Simpson to Henry Allen Moe, 23 April 1932. (Guggenheim)

65. Marian Simpson to Philip Horton, 19 June 1936. Horton Papers.

66. P. Cowley, 'The Last Days of Hart Crane', p. 168.

67. All details pertaining to the *Orizaba* are taken from the ship's manifests, housed in National Archives, Northeast Region, 201 Varick Street, New York City, and from *Lloyd's Register of Shipping*, 1933–41.

68. P. Cowley, 'The Last Days of Hart Crane', pp. 169–70.

69. Henry Allen Moe, 'Memorandum', 30 April 1932. (Guggenheim)

70. P. Cowley, 'The Last Days of Hart Crane', pp. 171–2.

71. Quoted in Gorham B. Munson, *The Awakening Twenties: A Memoir-History of a Literary Period*, Louisiana State University Press, Baton Rouge and London, 1985, p. 230.

72. Gertrude E. Vogt (Gertrude Berg) to John Unterecker, 27 September 1969. John Unterecker Papers.

73. P. Cowley, 'The Last Days of Hart Crane', p. 173.

74. Telegram from Peggy Cowley to Malcolm Cowley, 27 April 1932. M. Cowley, *The Dream of the Golden Mountains*, p. 80.

75. 'Poet's Death at Sea Verified; Crane's Body Lost, Ship Says', *New York World Telegram*, 28 April 1932.

76. Carol Dexter to Grace Crane 'Friday 8.30' [29 May 1932?]. Hart Crane Papers, Columbia University.

77. Peggy Cowley to Grace Crane, 4 May 1932. Hart Crane Papers, Columbia University.

78. Grace Crane to Sam Loveman, 9 May 1932. Hart Crane Papers, Columbia University.

79. Grace Crane to Sam Loveman, 10 May 1932. Hart Crane Papers, Columbia University.

80. Malcolm Cowley to Allen Tate, 28 June 1932. Quoted in Langdon Hammer, *Hart Crane & Allen Tate*, Princeton University Press, Princeton, 1993, p. 204.

81. Allen Tate to William Slater Brown, 28 May 1932. Hart Crane Collection, Columbia University.

82. Grace Crane to Sam Loveman, 13 May 1932. Hart Crane Papers, Columbia University.

83. Grace Crane to Sam Loveman, 10 May 1932. Hart Crane Papers, Columbia University.

84. Grace Crane to Sam Loveman, 9 May 1932. Hart Crane Papers, Columbia University.

85. Quoted by Lorna Dietz in an interview with John Unterecker, 7 September 1960. John Unterecker Papers.

86. Grace Crane to Sam Loveman, 19 July 1932. Hart Crane Papers, Columbia University.

87. Grace Crane to Bob Stewart, 23 July 1932. Hart Crane Papers, Columbia University.

88. 'An Interview with Philip C. Horton', *Hart Crane Newsletter*, volume II, number II (Spring 1979).

89. Philip Horton to Sam Loveman, 5 November 1933. Hart Crane Papers, Columbia University.

90. 'An Interview with Philip C. Horton', *Hart Crane Newsletter*.

91. Margaret Wright to John Unterecker, 26 October 1960. John Unterecker Papers.

92. Yvor Winters to Grace Crane, 29 March 1933. Hart Crane Papers, Columbia University.

93. 'Hart Crane: Conversation with Samuel Loveman, New York 1964', introduced by Ray C. Longtin, New York Public Library.

SELECT BIBLIOGRAPHY

Primary Sources

Berg Collection, New York Public Library

Hart Crane Collection, Beinecke Rare Book and Manuscript Library, Yale University Library

    Baker Papers, Hart Crane Collection, Beinecke Rare Book and Manuscript Library, Yale University Library

    Horton Papers, Hart Crane Collection, Beinecke Rare Book and Manuscript Library, Yale University Library

'Hart Crane: Conversation with Samuel Loveman, New York, 1964', introduced by Ray C. Longtin. New York Public Library

Hart Crane Papers, Rare Book and Manuscript Library, Columbia University, New York

Hart Crane Papers, Special Collections, University Library, Kent State University, Ohio

Jean Toomer's Journals 1924–25, Beinecke Rare Book and Manuscript Library, Yale University Library

John Simon Guggenheim Memorial Foundation Archives, New York City

John Unterecker Papers, Rare Book and Manuscript Library, Columbia University, New York

Little Review Papers, Special Collections of the University of Wisconsin-Milwaukee Library

Maxfield Parrish Papers, Dartmouth College Library, Hanover, New Hampshire

Philip Horton, *Hart Crane: The Life of an American Poet* typescript, New York Public Library

Secondary Sources

Allen, Hugh, *Rubber's Home Town: The Real-Life Story of Akron*. Stratford House, New York, 1949.

Anderson, Margaret, *My Thirty Years' War: An Autobiography*. Alfred A. Knopf, London, 1930.

Bak, Hans. *Malcolm Cowley: The Formative Years*. University of Georgia Press, Athens and London, 1993.

Baker, Deborah, *In Extremis: The Life of Laura Riding*. Hamish Hamilton, London, 1993.

Bayley, Isabel, (ed.), *Letters of Katherine Anne Porter*. Atlantic Monthly Press, New York, 1990.

Bethell, Leslie (ed.), *Cuba: A Short History*. Cambridge University Press, Cambridge and New York, 1993.

Bittner, William, *The Novels of Waldo Frank*. University of Pennsylvania Press, Philadelphia, 1955.

Brooks, Charles S., *Hints to Pilgrims*. Yale University Press, New Haven, 1921.

Butterfield, R.W., *The Broken Arc: A Study of Hart Crane*. Oliver & Boyd, Edinburgh, 1969.

Campbell, Roy, *Light on a Dark Horse: An Autobiography 1901–1935*. Hollis & Carter, London, 1951.

Campbell, Thomas F. and Miggins, Edward M. (eds), *The Birth of Modern Cleveland, 1865–1930*. Western Reserve Historical Society, Associated University Presses, London and Toronto, 1988.

Carpenter, Humphrey, *Geniuses Together: American Writers in Paris in the 1920s*. Houghton Mifflin, Boston, 1988.

Cerf, Bennett, *At Random: The Reminiscences of Bennett Cerf*. Random House, New York, 1977.

Chauncey, George, *Gay New York: The Making of the Gay Male World, 1890–1940*. Flamingo, London, 1995.

Colum, Mary, *Life and the Dream*. Dufour Editions, New York, 1958, 1966.

Costello, Bonnie (general ed.), Goodridge, Celeste and Miller, Cristanne (assoc. eds), *Selected Letters of Marianne Moore*. Knopf, New York, 1997.

Cowley, Malcolm, *A Second Flowering: Works and Days of the Lost Generation*. André Deutsch, London, 1973.

Cowley, Malcolm, *Exile's Return*. Penguin, New York, 1976.

Cowley, Malcolm, *The Dream of the Golden Mountains: Remembering the 1930s*. Viking Press, New York, 1980.

Crosby, Caresse, *The Passionate Years*. Alvin Redman, London, 1955.

Cunliffe, Marcus (ed.), *The Penguin History of Literature: American Literature since 1900*. Sphere Books, 1975, revised edn, Penguin Books, London, 1993.

Dardis, Tom, *Firebrand: The Life of Horace Liveright*. Random House, New York, 1995.

Douglas, Ann, *Terrible Honesty: Mongrel Manhattan in the 1920s*. Farrar, Strauss & Giroux, New York, 1995.

Dupee, F.W. and Stade, George (eds), *Selected Letters of E.E. Cummings*. André Deutsch, London, 1972.

Faulkner, Donald W. (ed.), *The Portable Malcolm Cowley*. Penguin Viking, New York, 1990.

Fitzgerald F. Scott, *The Crack-Up, with Other Pieces and Stories*. Penguin, London, 1965.

Ford, Hugh, *Published in Paris: American and British Writers, Printers and Publishers in Paris, 1920–1939*. Garnstone Press, London, 1975.

Gilmer, Walker, *Horace Liveright: Publisher of the 20s*. David Lewis, New York, 1970.

Givner, Joan, *The Life of Katherine Anne Porter*. Jonathan Cape, London, 1983.

Gunn, Drewey Wayne, *American and British Writers in Mexico, 1556–1973*. University of Texas Press, Austin and London, 1969, 1974.

Hammer, Langdon, *Hart Crane & Allen Tate: Janus-Faced Modernism*. Princeton University Press, Princeton, 1993.

Hammer, Langdon and Weber, Brom, ed. *O My Land, My Friends: The Selected Letters of Hart Crane*. Four Walls Eight Windows, New York and London, 1997.

Herendeen, Warren and Parker, Donald G. (eds), *Hart Crane Newsletter* (volume I, nos I and II, volume II, nos I and II) and *The Visionary Company: A Magazine of the Twenties* (double issue, volume I, number II and volume II, number I), Mercy College, Dobbs Ferry, New York.

Herendeen, Warren and Parker, Donald G. (eds), 'Wind-Blown Flames: Letters of Hart Crane to Wilbur Underwood', *Southern Review*, volume XVI, number I (April 1980).

Holden, Harold and McManis, Jack (eds), *Poems by Samuel Greenberg*. Henry Holt, New York, 1947.

Horton, Philip, *Hart Crane: The Life of an American Poet*. W.W. Norton & Co. Inc., New York, 1937.

Howe, Irving, *Sherwood Anderson*. Methuen, London, 1951.

Ingalls, Hunter, Introduction to *William Sommer Retrospective* exhibition catalogue. Akron Art Institute, Akron, Ohio, 1970.

Jackson, Kenneth T. (ed.), *The Encyclopedia of New York City*. Yale University Press, New Haven and London, 1995.

Jay, Paul (ed.), *The Selected Correspondence of Kenneth Burke and Malcolm Cowley 1915–1981.* Viking, New York, 1988.

Jenkins Brown, Susan, *Robber Rocks: Letters and Memories of Hart Crane, 1923–1932.* Wesleyan University Press, Middletown, Connecticut, 1969.

Johnson, Paul, *A History of the American People.* Weidenfeld & Nicolson, London, 1997.

Kennedy, Richard S., *Dreams in the Mirror: A Biography of E.E. Cummings.* Liveright, New York, 1980.

Kirstein, Lincoln, *Mosaic: Memoirs.* Farrar, Strauss & Giroux, New York, 1994.

Kramer, Hilton, *The Sculpture of Gaston Lachaise.* The Eakins Press, New York, 1967.

Lewis, Thomas S.W. (ed.), *Letters of Hart Crane and His Family.* Columbia University Press, New York and London, 1974.

Loeb, Harold, *The Way It Was.* Criterion Books, New York, 1959.

Lopez, Enrique Hank, *Conversations with Katherine Anne Porter: Refugee from Indian Creek.* Little Brown, Boston, 1981.

Ludington, Townsend (ed.), *The Fourteenth Chronicle: Letters and Diaries of John Dos Passos.* André Deutsch, London, 1974.

Ludington, Townsend, *Marsden Hartley: The Biography of an American Artist.* Little Brown, Boston, Toronto and London, 1992.

Ludwig, Coy L., *Maxfield Parrish.* Watson-Guptill Publications, New York, 1973.

Mariani, Paul, *The Broken Tower: The Life of Hart Crane.* W.W. Norton, New York, 1999.

Matz, Mary Jane, *The Many Lives of Otto Kahn: A Biography.* Macmillan, New York, 1963.

McClatchy, J.D. (ed.), *The Yale Review,* volume 84, number 2 (April 1996). Cambridge, Massachusetts and Oxford, England.

Meyers, Jeffrey, *Edmund Wilson: A Biography.* Houghton Mifflin, Boston and New York, 1995.

Miller, Carol P.O.H. and Wheeler, Robert, *Cleveland: A Concise History, 1796–1990.* Indiana University Press, Bloomington and Indianapolis, 1990.

Miller, Donald L., *Lewis Mumford: A Life.* Weidenfeld & Nicolson, New York, 1989.

Morgan, Ted, *FDR: A Biography.* Simon & Schuster, New York, 1985.

Morris, Lloyd, *Incredible New York: High Life and Low Life from 1850–1950.* Random House, New York, 1951.

Munson, Gorham B., *Destinations: A Canvas of American Literature since 1900.* J.H. Sears, New York, 1928.

Munson, Gorham, B., *The Awakening Twenties: A Memoir-History of a Literary Period.* Louisiana State University Press, Baton Rouge and London, 1985.

Nicholl, Charles, *Somebody Else: Arthur Rimbaud in Africa 1880–1891.* Jonathan Cape, London, 1995.

O'Connell, Shaun, *Remarkable, Unspeakable New York: A Literary History.* Beacon Press, Boston, Massachusetts, 1995.

Parkinson, Thomas (ed.), *Hart Crane & Yvor Winters: Their Literary Correspondence.* University of California Press, Berkeley, Los Angeles and London, 1978.

Pearce, Joseph, *Bloomsbury and Beyond: The Friends and Enemies of Roy Campbell.* HarperCollins, London, 2001.

Rathbone, Belinda, *Walker Evans: A Biography.* Houghton Mifflin, Boston and New York, 1995.

Ruland, Richard and Bradbury, Malcolm, *From Puritanism to Postmodernism: A History of American Literature.* Viking Penguin, New York, 1991.

Simon, Marc, *Samuel Greenberg, Hart Crane and the Lost Manuscripts.* Humanities Press, Atlantic Highlands, New Jersey, 1978.

Simon, Marc (ed.), *Complete Poems of Hart Crane.* Liveright, New York, 1986.

Squires, Radcliffe, *Allen Tate: A Literary Biography.* Pegasus, New York, 1971.

Suchlicki, Jaime, *Historical Dictionary of Cuba*. The Scarecrow Press, Metuchen, New Jersey and London, 1988.

Szarkowski, John, Introduction to *Walker Evans*, exhibition catalogue Museum of Modern Art, New York, 1971.

Tate, Allen, *Essays of Four Decades*. Oxford University Press, London, 1970.

Thirlwall, John C. (ed.), *Selected Letters of William Carlos Williams*. New Directions, New York, 1957.

Thomas, Hugh, *Cuba, or The Pursuit of Freedom*. Eyre & Spottiswoode, London, 1971.

Thomas, Richard F., *Literary Admirers of Alfred Stieglitz*. Southern Illinois University Press, Carbondale and Edwardsville, 1983.

Unterecker, John, *Voyager: A Life of Hart Crane*. Farrar, Strauss and Giroux, New York, 1969 and Anthony Blond, London, 1969, 1970.

Verrill, A. Hyatt, *Cuba of Today*. Dodd, Mead, New York, 1931.

Wallop, Gerald, *A Knot of Roots: An Autobiography*. New American Library, New York, 1965.

Weber, Brom, *Hart Crane: A Biographical and Critical Study*. The Bodley Press, New York, 1948.

Weber, Brom (ed.), *The Letters of Hart Crane 1916–1932*. University of California Press, Berkeley and Los Angeles, 1965.

Weber, Brom (ed.), *Hart Crane: The Complete Poems & Selected Letters & Prose*. Liveright, New York, 1966.

Weinberg, Jonathan, *Speaking for Vice: Homosexuality in the Art of Charles Demuth, Marsden Hartley, and the First American Avant-Garde*. Yale University Press, New Haven and London, 1993.

Wilson, Edmund, *The Shores of Light: A Literary Chronicle of the Twenties and Thirties*. W.H. Allen, London, 1952.

Witemeyer, Hugh (ed.), *Selected Letters of Ezra Pound and William Carlos Williams*. New Directions, New York, 1996.

Wolff, Geoffrey, *Black Sun: The Brief Transit and Violent Eclipse of Harry Crosby*. Vintage Books, New York, 1977.

Woon, Basil, *When it's Cocktail Time in Cuba*. Liveright, New York, 1928.

Yingling, Thomas E., *Hart Crane and the Homosexual Text: New Thresholds, New Anatomies*. University of Chicago Press, Chicago and London, 1990.

Young, Thomas Daniel (ed.), *Conversations with Malcolm Cowley*. University of Mississippi, Jackson and London, 1986.

Zaidan, Abe, *Akron: Rising toward the Twenty-First Century*. Windsor Publications, Chatsworth, California, 1990.

Zinsser, Hans, *As I Remember Him*. Little Brown, Boston, 1940.